# The American College Teacher

## National Norms for the 2007–2008 HERI Faculty Survey

by

Linda DeAngelo
Sylvia Hurtado
John H. Pryor
Kimberly R. Kelly
José Luis Santos
William S. Korn

Higher Education Research Institute
Graduate School of Education & Information Studies
University of California, Los Angeles

February, 2009

The authors wish to acknowledge Jessica Sharkness, Amy Liu, Sylvia Ruiz, and Melissa Aragon for their valuable assistance in the preparation of this report. Page layout by The Oak Co. Cover design by Escott & Associates.

Published by the Higher Education Research Institute. Suggested citation:

DeAngelo, L., Hurtado, S., Pryor, J. H., Kelly, K. R., Santos, J. L., & Korn, W. S. (2009). *The American college teacher: National norms for the 2007–2008 HERI faculty survey*. Los Angeles: Higher Education Research Institute, UCLA.

Additional copies of this report may be purchased for $25.00 (CA residents add 7.5% sales tax, Los Angeles residents add 8.25% sales tax) plus $7.00 for shipping.

Please remit to: Higher Education Research Institute
UCLA Graduate School of Education & Information Studies
3005 Moore Hall/Mailbox 951521
Los Angeles, CA 90095-1521
Website: www.heri.ucla.edu
Telephone: 310-825-1925

# The American College Teacher

## National Norms for the 2007–2008 HERI Faculty Survey

CONTENTS

TABLES

FIGURES

# The American College Teacher

National Norms for the
2007–2008 HERI Faculty Survey

Faculty carry out the main educational mission of higher education institutions. They play a vital role in determining what is taught, how it is taught, and who teaches within their particular fields of study or disciplines. Full-time faculty often remain at our institutions for many years and, therefore, have a sustained influence on students and institutional decision-making through shared governance. Given the centrality of faculty to our institutions, it continues to be important for us to monitor faculty work-life issues, their activities in terms of research productivity, teaching and learning, as well as their values and beliefs. This report summarizes the highlights of a national survey of full-time, undergraduate teaching faculty administered by the Cooperative Institutional Research Program (CIRP) at the Higher Education Research Institute (HERI) during the 2007–2008 academic year. HERI scholars initiated national faculty surveys as early as 1978, and began administering the survey through CIRP triennially in 1989–90. This is the seventh in a series of faculty surveys administered on a triennial basis.

The results reported here are based on the responses of 22,562 full-time college and university faculty members at 372 four-year colleges and universities nationwide. A "faculty member" is defined as any full-time employee of an accredited four-year college or university who spends at least part of his or her time teaching undergraduates.[1] The responses are weighted to provide a normative profile of the American faculty population for use by policy analysts, campus administrators, and educational researchers. Details of the weighting procedure, as well as other methodological considerations, can be found in Appendix A.

The data presented here are reported separately for male and female faculty in each of eight different normative groups: all institutions, public universities, private universities, public four-year colleges, and private four-year colleges (combined and broken down by three sub-groupings: nonsectarian, Roman Catholic and other religious). Community colleges have typically been included in HERI national survey reports; however, this year the number of community college participants was not sufficient to produce normative comparisons on a national level. In future reports we again expect to provide a normative comparison group for community colleges. For the first time, however, this report also offers data on each survey item by academic rank.

---

[1]Although surveys were also received from academic administrators and other types of respondents, only those who spend at least part of their time teaching undergraduates are included in the results reported here (see Appendix A).

## The Questionnaire

The 2007–2008 questionnaire was based largely on items used in previous faculty surveys, and was revised following the suggestions of researchers both inside and outside of HERI who are actively involved in studying faculty and issues related to teaching and learning. In addition to demographic information, the questionnaire focuses heavily on topics such as how faculty spend their time, how they interact with students, their preferred methods of teaching, their perceptions of institutional climate, and their primary sources of stress and satisfaction. The 2007–2008 questionnaire also includes new items related to interactions with students that foster habits of mind for life-long learning, and enhanced items on pedagogy and faculty satisfaction. For the first time, the survey also offered a specific module for part-time faculty to determine who they are and their use of institutional resources. This is a group that has significantly increased their representation at both two- and four-year institutions. A separate report will be issued on the characteristics of part-time faculty. The web-based questionnaire also includes a section that allows individual institutions to ask their faculty up to 20 locally designed questions (see Appendix B for a copy of the questions).

## An Overview of the 2007–2008 Faculty Norms

In this overview, we have abstracted highlights of the survey results as they pertain to two areas: Activities and Beliefs about Undergraduate Education and Faculty Work-Life. Within the first area we cover goals for undergraduate education, working with underprepared students, teaching and research practice and perspectives, engaged scholarship and academic citizenship, attitudes and beliefs about diversity, and institutional values and priorities as faculty perceive them. Within the second area we cover career satisfaction and perspectives, technology use, and health and wellness.

Comprehensive results of the survey, reported separately for all faculty, male faculty, female faculty, and faculty by academic rank and institutional type follow this overview. Demographic and background characteristics of respondents are also displayed in these tables.

### Goals for Undergraduate Education

Faculty demonstrate both consistent responses compared to three years ago in what goals they value for undergraduate education and increases in the value they place on particular areas of students' development. Specifically, the goals of helping students to develop critical thinking skills and discipline-specific knowledge remain at the forefront of what faculty consider essential to undergraduate education, with 99.6 percent and 95.1 percent of faculty, respectively, indicating that these goals are "very important" or "essential." Other top goals for undergraduate education include helping students to evaluate the quality and reliability of information (97.2 percent) or developing information literacy, and promoting the ability to write effectively (96.4 percent). In addition, 72.8 percent of faculty indicate that instilling an appreciation for the liberal arts among students is an important goal for undergraduate education. This percentage was just 57.9 in the 2004–05 HERI faculty survey, a 14.9 percentage point increase. Table 1 reveals the largest gains since 2004–05 faculty survey are for goals "instill in students a commitment to community service" (55.5 percent of faculty, an increase of 19.1 percentage points), and "enhance students' knowledge of and appreciation for other racial/ethnic groups" (75.2 percent of faculty, an increase of 17.6 percentage points). Many institutions are now articulating civic engagement and diversity as among their core values, and these goals are also mirrored in increases in faculty activities and beliefs in other areas of the survey (see the *Engaged Scholarship and Academic Citizenship* and *Attitudes and Views on Diversity* sections of this report).

It is important to note that increases were also evident among faculty in many goal areas of students' personal or psychosocial development, including to: "help students to develop personal values" (66.1 percent of faculty, an increase of 15.3 percentage points), "enhance students'

Table 1.
*Faculty Goals for Undergraduate Education Measured in Both 2004–05 and 2007–08*

| "Very Important" or "Essential" | All Four-Year Faculty | | |
| --- | --- | --- | --- |
| | 2004–05 | 2007–08 | Percentage Point Change |
| Instill in students a commitment to community service | 36.4 | 55.5 | 19.1 |
| Enhance students' knowledge of and appreciation for other racial/ethnic groups | 57.6 | 75.2 | 17.6 |
| Help students develop personal values | 50.8 | 66.1 | 15.3 |
| Instill basic appreciation of the liberal arts | 57.9 | 72.8 | 14.9 |
| Enhance students' self-understanding | 58.4 | 71.8 | 13.4 |
| Develop moral character | 57.1 | 70.2 | 13.1 |
| Provide for students' emotional development | 35.2 | 48.1 | 12.9 |
| Develop creative capacities | 69.0 | 81.5 | 12.5 |
| Prepare students for graduate or advanced education | 63.4 | 75.5 | 12.1 |
| Prepare students for employment after college | 70.2 | 81.5 | 11.3 |
| Develop ability to think critically | 99.0 | 99.6 | 0.6 |
| Help master knowledge in discipline | 94.6 | 95.1 | 0.5 |

self-understanding" (71.8 percent of faculty, an increase of 13.4 percentage points), "develop moral character" (70.2 percent of faculty, an increase of 13.1 percentage points) and "provide for students' emotional development" (48.1 percent of faculty, an increase of 12.9 percentage points). In the wake of recent events on our nation's campuses such as the shooting at Virginia Tech, more faculty may be attentive to their role in identifying and assisting students with psychosocial issues of development. Finally, increases in goals to "develop creative capacities" and to develop post-college career capacities (e.g. graduate school and employment) were also evident among faculty.

For the most part, across the goals for undergraduate education, there are minor differences and largely shared agreement across academic rank (full, associate, and assistant professor). The two goals for undergraduate education in which there is the greatest divergence by rank are "teach students the classic works of Western civilization" and "encourage students to become agents of social change." As shown in Figure 1, assistant professors are 10.3 percentage points *less* likely than full professors to indicate that teaching students the classics of Western civilization is at least very important and 10.8 percentage points *more* likely than full professors to indicate that encouraging students to become agents of social change is at least very important. Notably, compared with the other goals for undergraduate education, the majority of faculty (57.8 percent) indicate it is "very important" or "essential" to encourage students to become agents of social change, whereas teaching the classics is among the lowest rated goals (34.7 percent) among faculty. It is clear in these results that the emphasis is on building skills for the 21st century.

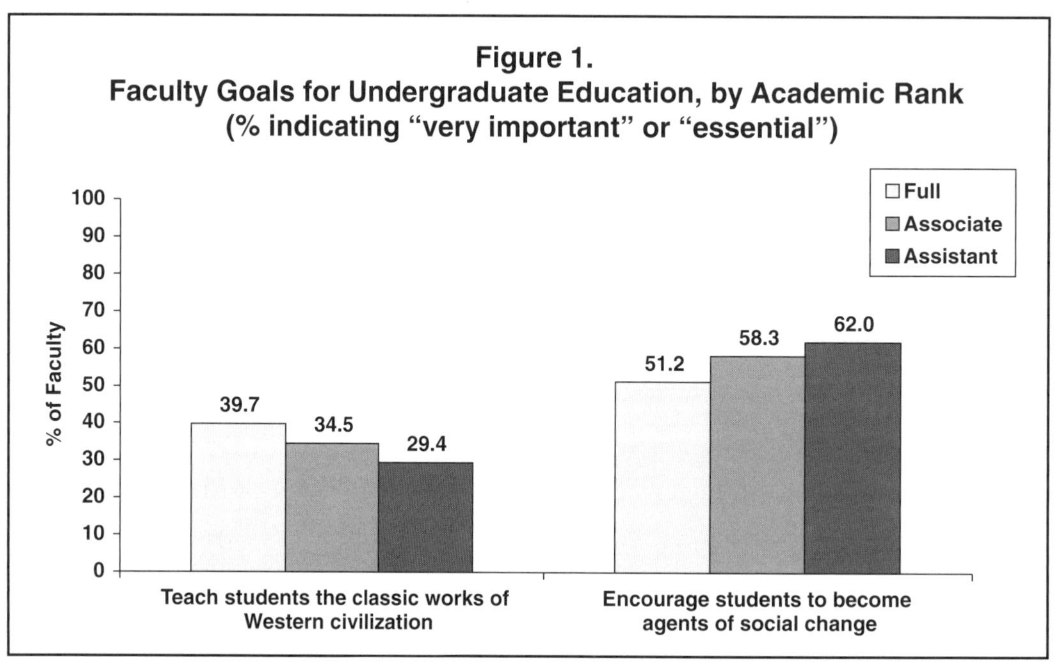

Conley (2005) has identified a number of discipline-specific and general behaviors and traits known as "habits of mind" that are important to student learning and success. The 2007–2008 faculty survey included a new set of items to capture how often faculty encourage these habits of mind for lifelong learning among undergraduates. Table 2 displays the "habits of mind" by the percentage of faculty who encourage them frequently. Faculty most frequently report that they encourage students to "ask questions in class" (94.6 percent), "support their opinions with a logical argument" (82.8 percent), "seek solutions to problems and explain them to others" (74.7 percent), "evaluate the quality and reliability of the information they receive" (73.4 percent), and "seek feedback on their academic work" (73.0 percent). Substantially fewer faculty report they frequently encourage their undergraduates to "acknowledge failure as a necessary part of the learning process" (49.5 percent) or "take risks for potential gains" (37.4 percent). These latter habits are an important part of building the dispositions for scientific reasoning and inquiry, an area where trial and error or experimentation are typical in order to make progress.

Across the various "habits of mind," a higher percentage of female than male faculty report that they encourage undergraduates frequently to engage in the learning habits (see Table 2). The most noteworthy differences relate to the percentage who frequently encourage undergraduates

Table 2.
*Faculty Encouragement of Habits of Mind, by Gender*

| "Frequently" | All | Women | Men | Percent Point Difference |
|---|---|---|---|---|
| Revise their papers to improve their writing | 58.8 | 68.9 | 52.3 | 16.6 |
| Seek feedback on their academic work | 73.0 | 82.5 | 66.9 | 15.6 |
| Evaluate the quality or reliability of the information they receive | 73.4 | 80.2 | 69.0 | 11.2 |
| Seek alternative solutions to a problem | 65.1 | 71.7 | 60.9 | 10.8 |
| Take risks for potential gains | 37.4 | 42.8 | 33.8 | 9.0 |
| Seek solutions to problems and explain them to others | 74.7 | 79.9 | 71.3 | 8.6 |
| Acknowledge failure as a necessary part of the learning process | 49.5 | 54.5 | 46.2 | 8.3 |
| Explore topics on their own, even though it is not required for a class | 52.1 | 57.1 | 48.8 | 8.3 |
| Look up scientific research articles and resources | 55.2 | 59.6 | 52.4 | 7.2 |
| Support their opinions with a logical argument | 82.8 | 86.4 | 80.4 | 6.0 |
| Ask questions in class | 94.6 | 97.1 | 92.9 | 4.2 |

to "revise their papers to improve their writing," "seek feedback on their academic work," and "evaluate the quality or reliability of information they receive." On these habits, women are 16.6 percentage points, 15.6 percentage points, and 11.2 percentage points, respectively, more likely to encourage undergraduates to frequently engage in these behaviors than are men.

**Working with Underprepared Students**

With over a third (37.5 percent) of students beginning college expecting to need special tutoring or remedial work in one or more areas (Pryor, Hurtado, Sharkness, & Korn, 2007), working with underprepared students, especially freshmen, is a reality for faculty at many institutions. From the faculty perspective, a similar percentage (36.4 percent) indicate that the majority of students they teach lack the basic skills for college-level work. The majority of faculty (63.4 percent) also indicate that their institution takes responsibility for educating underprepared students, and only 28.2 percent of faculty feel that their institution should not offer remedial/developmental education. As shown in Figure 2, however, there are differences by academic rank (full, associate, assistant professor) and gender in terms of faculty support for remedial/developmental education on campus. Assistant professors are more supportive of remedial/developmental education on their campus than associate professors, and much more supportive than full professors. Likewise, female faculty are substantially more supportive than male faculty.

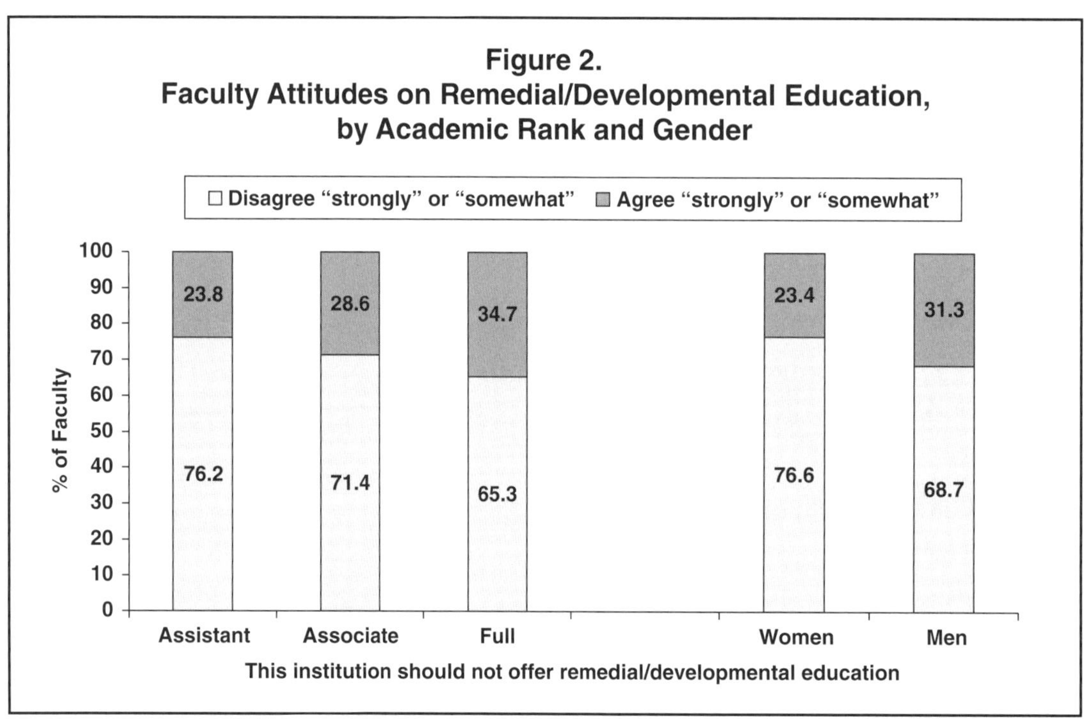

Only 5.4 percent of full-time faculty report that they have taught a remedial/developmental course in the last year. However, one in five (20.5 percent) indicate that they have taught remedial/developmental skills to students during the last year. Overall women are more likely to teach these skills than men (23.7 percent vs. 18.4 percent), except in the area of mathematics (4.3 percent of men vs. 3.8 percent of women). The fact that women are more likely than men to teach remedial/developmental skills may be one reason why more women than men report experiencing stress during the last two years associated with working with underprepared students (64.5 vs. 59.0 percent). The stress level difference between female and male faculty are most pronounced at public (60.4 vs. 52.9 percent) and private universities (49.4 vs. 42.1 percent).

The majority of undergraduate teaching faculty support the notion of achieving excellence and diversity. Similar to reports three years ago (see Lindholm, Szelenyi, Hurtado, & Korn, 2005), over three quarters of today's faculty do not agree that efforts to promote diversity lead to the admission of too many underprepared students. Specifically, only 23.7 percent of faculty agreed "strongly" or "somewhat" that "promoting diversity leads to the admission of too many underprepared students." Large differences by gender and much smaller variations by academic rank are seen here. As displayed in Figure 3, less than 20 percent of female faculty and almost 30 percent of male faculty agree that there is a connection between efforts to promote diversity and the admission of too many underprepared students.

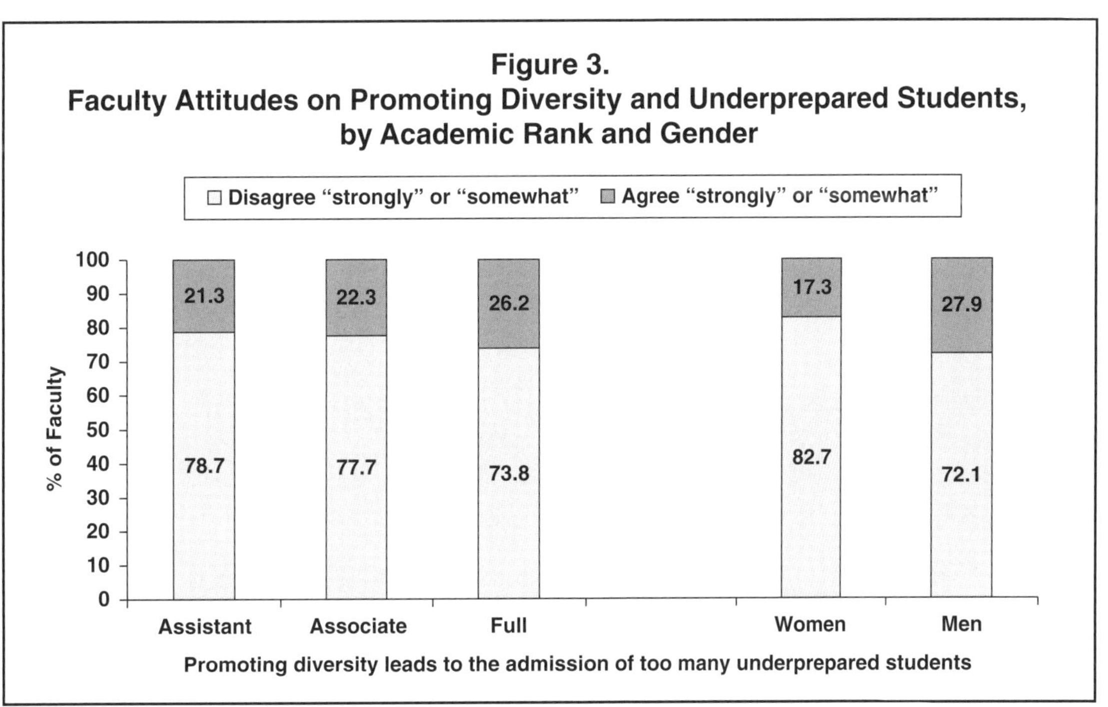

**Teaching and Research Practice and Perspectives**

Nearly all faculty (97.7 percent) rate their role as a teacher as personally "very important" or "essential" to them, a percentage that varies only slightly by gender, institutional type, and academic rank. The research and service aspects of the professoriate are rated similarly in importance by 71.4 percent and 66.1 percent of faculty, respectively. As we might expect, public and private university faculty (77.6 and 80.4 percent, respectively) are more likely to rate research as "very important" or "essential" than faculty at public and private four-year colleges (68.4 and 62.4 percent, respectively). There are few differences in how faculty at public and private universities and public and private four-year colleges rate the importance of the service aspects of their positions. Additionally, differences across gender are seen, women are less likely than men to indicate that research is important to them personally (67.5 vs. 74.0 percent) and more likely to report that service is personally important (70.3 vs. 63.3 percent).

Generally, as displayed in Table 3, the amount of time faculty dedicate to teaching, research, and service reflects the priority levels that faculty assign to these professoriate roles. Faculty spend significantly more time preparing for their teaching responsibilities and actually teaching than they spend on research or committee work, and they spend more time on research than committee work. At the higher end of the hours devoted per week category, women are *more* likely than men to

Table 3.
*Time Spent on Teaching, Research, and Service, by Gender*

| | All | Women | Men | Percent Point Difference |
|---|---|---|---|---|
| Hours per week spent on preparing for teaching | | | | |
| 8 hours or less | 34.5 | 30.1 | 37.3 | 7.2 |
| 13 hours or more | 41.1 | 46.5 | 37.4 | 9.1 |
| Hours per week spent on scheduled teaching | | | | |
| 8 hours or less | 45.2 | 42.6 | 47.1 | 4.5 |
| 13 or more | 19.6 | 22.1 | 17.9 | 4.2 |
| Hours per week spent on research and scholarly writing | | | | |
| 8 hours or less | 68.0 | 75.1 | 63.3 | 11.8 |
| 13 hours or more | 19.4 | 13.8 | 23.1 | 9.3 |
| Hours per week spent on committee work and meetings | | | | |
| 8 hours or less | 88.7 | 87.5 | 89.6 | 2.1 |
| 13 hours or more | 3.7 | 4.3 | 3.4 | 0.9 |

average 13 or more hours per week preparing for teaching (46.5 vs. 37.4 percent) and teaching (22.1 vs. 17.9 percent). Following what they value about the professoriate, women are *less* likely than men to devote 13 or more hours per week to research and scholarly writing (13.8 vs. 23.1 percent), and although they value service more than men devote basically the same amount of hours per week to meetings and working on committees.

More than half of faculty (57.3 percent) report having worked with undergraduates on a research project in the last two years. As displayed in Figure 4, this percentage remains fairly stable across institutional types, indicating that regardless of institution type roughly the same percentage of faculty are engaging students in research. Despite this fact, there are important differences by institutional type in regards to having the opportunity to work on a faculty member's own research project. Specifically, students at public and private universities (44.1 and 48.1 percent, respectively) are more likely than those at public and private four-year colleges (38.7 percent and 38.8 percent, respectively) to participate in this type of research. In addition, male faculty are more likely than female faculty to both engage students in their own research (45.2 percent vs. 36.2 percent) and to engage students generally on research projects (60.4 percent vs. 52.5 percent). Given that female faculty are much more likely than male faculty to report conducting research on women and gender issues (29.9 percent vs. 12.1 percent), and racial and ethnic minorities (25.4 percent vs.

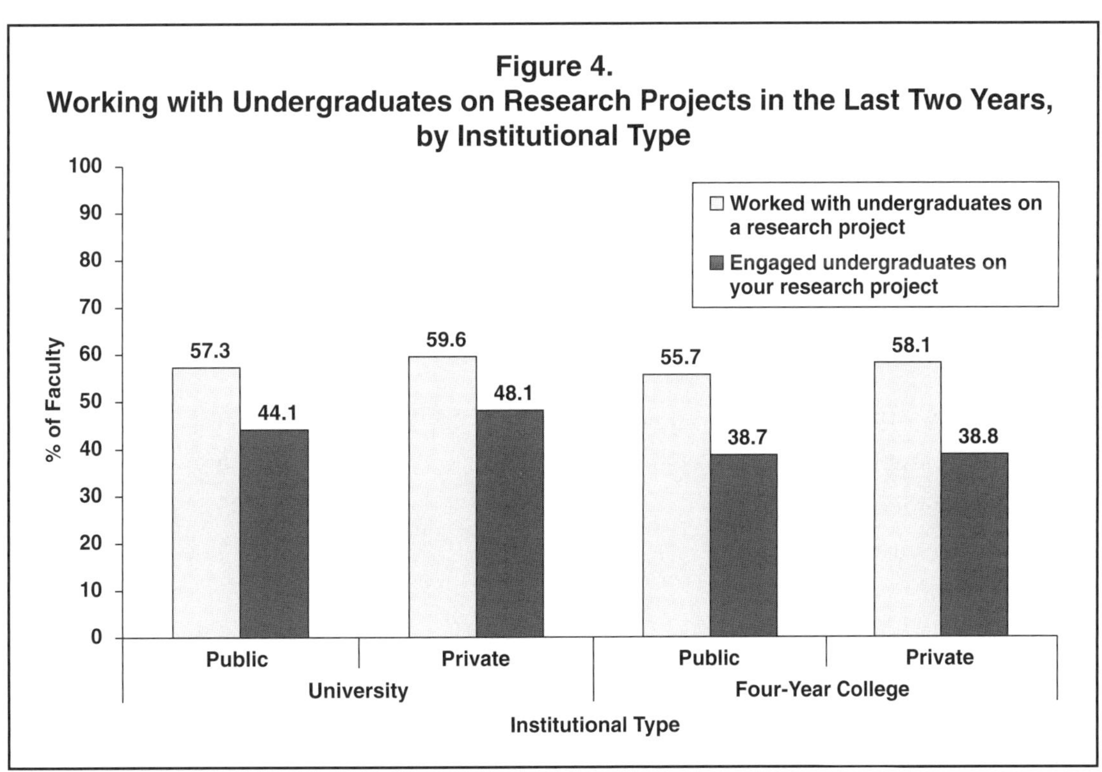

17.5 percent) as well as to report collaborating with the local community on research/teaching (51.0 percent vs. 43.1 percent), these differences between male and female faculty in research engagement with undergraduates may have implications for the types of research undergraduates engage in and have the opportunity to experience.

Student-centered or inquiry-based evaluation methods in teaching continue to gain traction among faculty (see Table 4). These methods began to get more attention starting in the 1990s when social scientists such as Seymour (1997) started discussing the relevance of these methods to learning and retention, especially in the natural sciences. Although today's faculty are just as likely as faculty in 2004–05 to use multiple-choice exams, they are 8.6 percentage points more likely to use short-answer questions and 9.6 percentage points more likely to use term/research papers to assess learning. In addition, the use of bell curves in grading coursework has diminished somewhat from three years ago to 16.8 percent overall and just 13.9 percent among faculty who are newest to the

Table 4.
*Faculty Approaches to Evaluation and Teaching, by Academic Rank and Survey Year*

| Methods Used in "All" or "Most" Courses Taught | All Faculty | | | Assistant | Associate | Full |
| --- | --- | --- | --- | --- | --- | --- |
| | 2005 | 2008 | Percent Point Change | 2008 | 2008 | 2008 |
| Selected Examination Methods | | | | | | |
| Short-answer exams** | 36.9 | 45.5 | 8.6 | 47.2 | 47.1 | 44.3 |
| Term/research papers | 34.7 | 44.3 | 9.6 | 46.4 | 45.3 | 44.2 |
| Multiple-choice exams** | 32.3 | 33.1 | 0.8 | 36.9 | 31.8 | 27.3 |
| Grading on a curve | 19.4 | 16.8 | −2.6 | 13.9 | 16.8 | 21.0 |
| Selected Pedagogy | | | | | | |
| Cooperative learning (small groups) | 47.8 | 59.1 | 11.3 | 66.3 | 58.0 | 49.6 |
| Using real-life problems* | n/a | 55.7 | n/a | 61.0 | 53.4 | 49.6 |
| Group projects | 33.3 | 35.8 | 2.5 | 40.3 | 34.6 | 31.0 |
| Multiple drafts of written work | 24.8 | 24.9 | 0.1 | 26.6 | 24.3 | 22.9 |
| Student evaluations of each other's work | 16.0 | 23.5 | 7.5 | 26.4 | 21.1 | 19.4 |
| Reflective writing/journaling | 18.1 | 21.7 | 3.6 | 25.3 | 19.4 | 16.8 |
| Electronic quizzes with immediate feedback in class* | n/a | 6.8 | n/a | 7.8 | 6.4 | 4.7 |
| Extensive lecturing (not student-centered) | 55.2 | 46.4 | −8.8 | 43.3 | 45.2 | 51.8 |

Note: *Question added to 2007–08 survey. **In 2004–05 questions were worded "methods used on mid-term and/or final exams."

professoriate (assistant professors). By rank, full professors (21.0 percent) are still much more likely to grade on a curve than assistant professors (13.9 percent), but assistant professors are much more likely to use multiple-choice exams than full professors (36.9 vs. 27.3 percent). These trends may reflect, at least in part, the type of courses these two groups of professors are teaching. For instance, in the academic year in which they completed the survey, assistant professors were more likely than full professors (15.5 vs. 9.9 percent) to teach three or more general education courses. Full, associate, and assistant professors indicate very little difference in terms of their usage of short-answer exams and term/research papers as evaluation methods.

Pedagogy in the classroom is also steadily moving in a student-centered direction. Compared with three years ago, faculty today are 8.8 percentage points *less* likely to use extensive lecturing in the classroom (46.4 vs. 55.2 percent, respectively), 11.3 percentage points *more* likely to use cooperative learning (59.1 vs. 47.8 percent, respectively), and 7.5 percentage points *more* likely to engage students in the evaluation of each other's work (23.5 vs. 16.0 percent, respectively) (see Table 4). Today's faculty are also slightly more likely than faculty three years ago to use reflective writing/journaling (21.7 vs. 18.1 percent, respectively) and group projects (35.8 vs. 33.3 percent, respectively). Assistant professors are *more* likely than associate and full professors to employ student-centered methods and *less* likely to use extensive lecturing. For instance, assistant professors are 16.7 percentage points more likely than full professors to report using cooperative learning (66.3 vs. 49.6 percent, respectively), and full professors are 8.5 percentage points more likely than assistant professors to report using extensive lecturing (51.8 vs. 43.3 percent, respectively). This suggests that the trend toward student-centered approaches in pedagogy will continue to grow, as current full professors retire and new assistant professors enter the professoriate.

This year's HERI faculty survey included new pedagogy questions that revealed that 55.7 percent of faculty use real-life problems in their classrooms and 6.8 percent of faculty use electronic quizzes with immediate feedback in class. Electronic quizzes, often called "clickers," are a reasonably new technology tool that allows professors to gain immediate feedback regarding students understanding of course material. The use of these devices is currently more common among professors in the natural sciences (29.5 percent) than other disciplines (18.5 percent), and future research will certainly be needed to understand further how the use of these tools impacts student learning.

**Engaged Scholarship and Academic Citizenship**

Generally, faculty indicate that the connection between colleges and the local community is an important part of the mission of higher education. Overall 87.9 percent of faculty report that they agree "strongly" or "somewhat" that colleges have a responsibility to work with their surrounding communities to address local issues. The same percentage indicates that colleges should encourage students to be involved in community service activities. Further, almost three-quarters of faculty (71.0 percent), agree "strongly" or "somewhat" that colleges should be involved in solving social problems, and only 18.8 percent of faculty believe that an individual can do little to bring about changes in society. This seemingly suggests that faculty believe that their actions, the actions of their students, and the actions of their institution should bring about societal change.

Faculty also think that community service should be among the factors considered in college admissions. Specifically, two-thirds of faculty (66.4 percent) agree "strongly" or "somewhat" that community service should be given weight in college admissions decisions. Faculty at private universities and four-year colleges (70.6 and 70.7 percent, respectively) are more likely than faculty at public universities and four-year colleges (63.6 and 64.1 percent, respectively) to concur that community service should play a part in admissions decisions.

In terms of their academic citizenship activities in the last two years, 46.2 percent of faculty report that they have collaborated with the local community in their research/teaching, and 42.4 percent of faculty report that they have advised student groups involved in service/volunteer work. Faculty at public and private four-year colleges (45.0 and 47.5 percent, respectively) are more likely than faculty at public and private universities (37.1 and 39.3 percent, respectively) to have advised a student group involved in service/volunteer work. The same pattern is found among faculty who have collaborated with the local community on research/teaching. At four-year colleges 51.6 and 45.7 percent of faculty at public and private institutions, respectively, have collaborated with the local community on research/teaching in the last two years, and at public and private universities the percentages are 43.7 and 40.5 percent, respectively. In addition, as shown in Figure 5, assistant and associate professors are more likely than full professors to have engaged in these activities. Lastly, just fewer than one in five faculty (19.7 percent) across institutional types indicate that they have taught a service learning course in the last two years, with more associate professors having employed this type of pedagogy than faculty at either the full or assistant professor level.

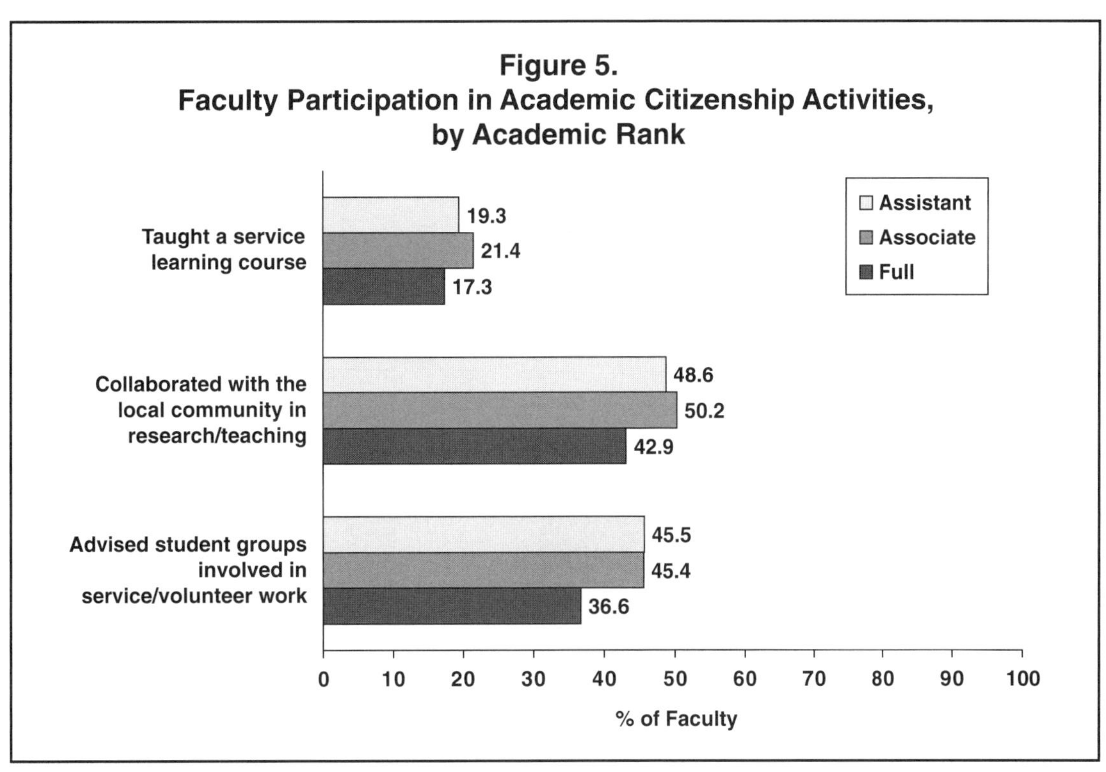



## Attitudes and Views on Diversity

The institutional climate for diversity based on race/ethnicity and gender continues to be an important topic for discussion on college campuses today. Similar to what was reported for the HERI faculty survey in 2004–05 (see Lindholm, Szelenyi, Hurtado, & Korn, 2005), the large majority (93.6 percent) of today's faculty believe that a racially/ethnically diverse student body enhances the educational experience of all students, and few faculty (10.6 percent) report that there is a lot of racial conflict on their campus. Somewhat more female than male faculty (96.8 vs. 91.6 percent) believe that student diversity enhances the educational experience for all students, and slightly more female than male faculty believe that there is racial conflict on their campus (13.6 vs. 8.6 percent). In addition, the majority of faculty (58.5 percent) support the notion that racial and ethnic diversity should be more strongly reflected in the curriculum. Here, there are substantial differences both by academic rank (full, associate, assistant professor) and by gender. As displayed in Figure 6, assistant professors are 11.6 percentage points more likely than full professors and female professors are 15.6 percentage points more likely than male professors to indicate that racial and ethnic diversity needs to be more strongly reflected in the curriculum. Another area for concern in terms of climate for diversity relates to the expression of diverse beliefs and values. Only a third (35.8 percent) of faculty indicate that "there is respect for the expression of diverse values and

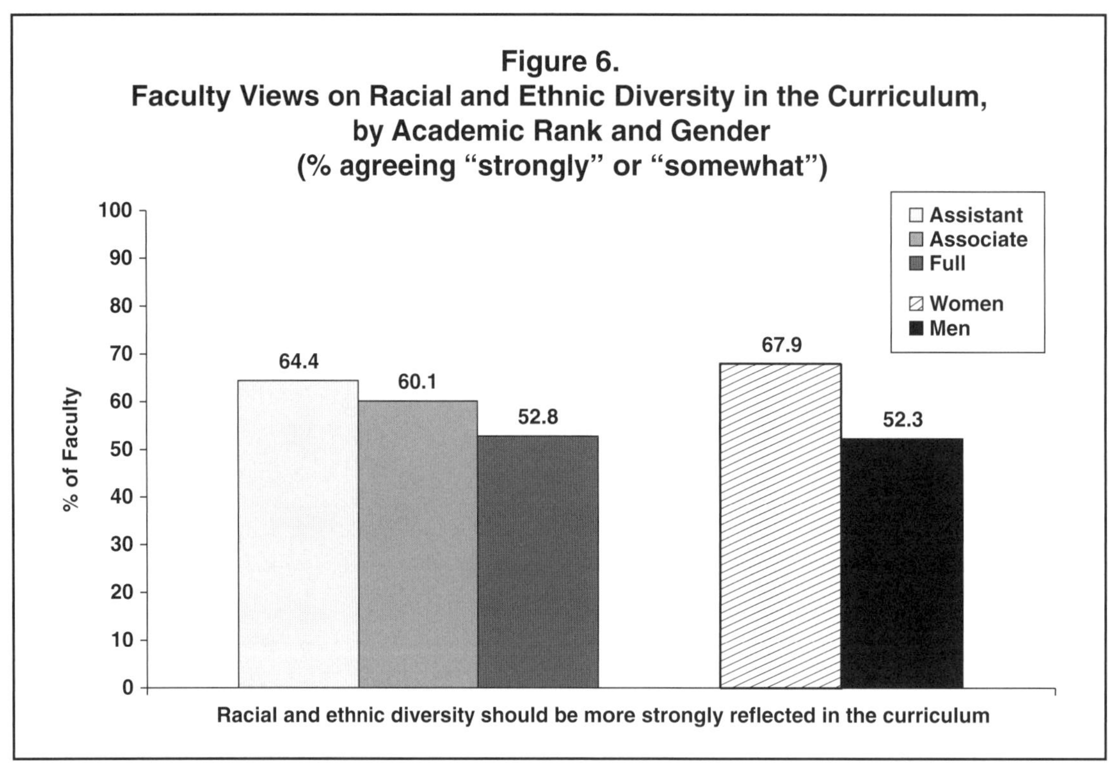


beliefs" is "very descriptive" of their institution. This percentage has moved up only slightly from 32.2 percent that was reported in the 2004–05 faculty survey.

Table 5 displays faculty attitudes toward diversity and climate in faculty work-life. What is clear in the data is that the majority of faculty believe that strides still need to be made in terms of the hiring of women and faculty of color. Almost three out of four faculty (73.2 percent) state that their institution should hire more faculty of color, and 57.1 percent think their institution needs to hire more women faculty. Differences of around 10 percentage points by gender are also apparent

Table 5.
*Faculty Views on Diversity at Their Institution, by Gender*

| Agree "Strongly" or "Somewhat" | All | Women | Men | Percent Point Difference |
|---|---|---|---|---|
| This institution should hire more faculty of color | 73.2 | 79.4 | 69.2 | 10.2 |
| This institution should hire more women faculty | 57.1 | 63.1 | 53.2 | 9.9 |
| Faculty of color are treated fairly here | 88.7 | 83.6 | 92.1 | 8.5 |
| Women faculty are treated fairly here | 85.9 | 76.4 | 92.1 | 15.7 |
| Gay and lesbian faculty are treated fairly here | 81.0 | 77.6 | 83.2 | 5.6 |

in terms of the need to hire faculty of color and female faculty. Specifically, female faculty are 10.2 percentage points and 9.9 percentage points more likely than male faculty to believe that their institution needs to hire more faculty of color and female faculty, respectively. Differences in these figures for hiring women and faculty of color are also apparent by institutional type. Faculty at public (50.9 percent) and private (50.4 percent) four-year colleges are substantially less likely than faculty at public (64.6 percent) and private (65.8 percent) universities to believe that their institution needs to hire more women, and faculty at public four-year colleges (67.6 percent) are substantially less likely than faculty at private four-year colleges (77.7 percent) to believe that their institution needs to hire more faculty of color. Some of these differences can likely be explained, at least in part, by hiring patterns at these different institutional types. For instance, at public four-year colleges there is a higher percentage of faculty of color among the professoriate than at private four-year colleges (NCES, 2003). There are no substantial differences in percentages at public (75.0 percent) and private (73.5 percent) universities in terms of the need to hire more faculty of color.

In addition, although the large majority of faculty indicate that all faculty are treated fairly on their campus, men are more likely than women to indicate that women, faculty of color, and gay and lesbian faculty are treated fairly. Specifically, 76.4 percent of women and 92.1 percent of men think that women faculty are treated fairly, 83.6 percent of women and 92.1 percent of men think that faculty of color are treated fairly, and 77.6 percent of women and 83.2 percent of men think that gay and lesbian faculty are treated fairly. There also seems to be somewhat less tolerance for gay and lesbian faculty at private universities and four-year colleges than at public institutions. At private universities 74.4 percent of faculty indicate that gay and lesbian faculty are treated fairly on their campus, whereas at public universities the figure is 82.9 percent. Likewise, at private four-year colleges the figure is 76.2 percent and at public four-year colleges the figure is 85.5 percent of faculty indicating that gay and lesbian faculty are treated fairly on their campus.

**Institutional Values and Priorities**

Faculty at all types of institutions rate "promote the intellectual development of students" as the highest priority out of the 19 possible institutional priorities on the survey. However, the second most prevalent priority that faculty indicate their institution has is to "enhance the institution's national image," with more than two out of three faculty (69.4 percent) reporting that enhancing the institution's national image is a high priority at their institution. Other priorities having to do with student development were ranked much lower.

Almost as high a perceived institutional priority is "pursuing extramural funding" (61.0 percent). In this case, however, there are great differences by institutional type. Faculty at public universities are much more likely to perceive this as a high priority for their institution (78.6 percent) compared to faculty at private universities (61.2 percent). For faculty at public universities, "pursuing extramural funding" is the third most prevalent priority; however it ranked seventh most prevalent among faculty at private universities. This may be an indication of dwindling state aid and a focus on research dollars for activities. Faculty at four-year colleges are even less likely to think this is an institutional priority, with 54.7 percent at public colleges and 45.7 percent at private colleges indicating "pursuing extramural funding" as a high priority.

As displayed in Figure 7, similar differences by institutional type are seen in faculty's ratings of the institutional priority "strengthen links with the for-profit, corporate sector." Although about half of all faculty perceive this as a high priority at their institutions, a much larger proportion of faculty at public universities than those at private universities (61.4 percent vs. 42.6 percent) report that this is the case. The difference also holds true for faculty at four year colleges (49.7 percent at public colleges and 35.6 percent at private colleges). This is despite the fact that 59.5 percent of all faculty believe that private funding sources often prevent researchers from being completely objective in conducting their work. On this issue there is general agreement amongst colleagues at different types of institutions, as well as faculty with different academic ranks or of different genders.

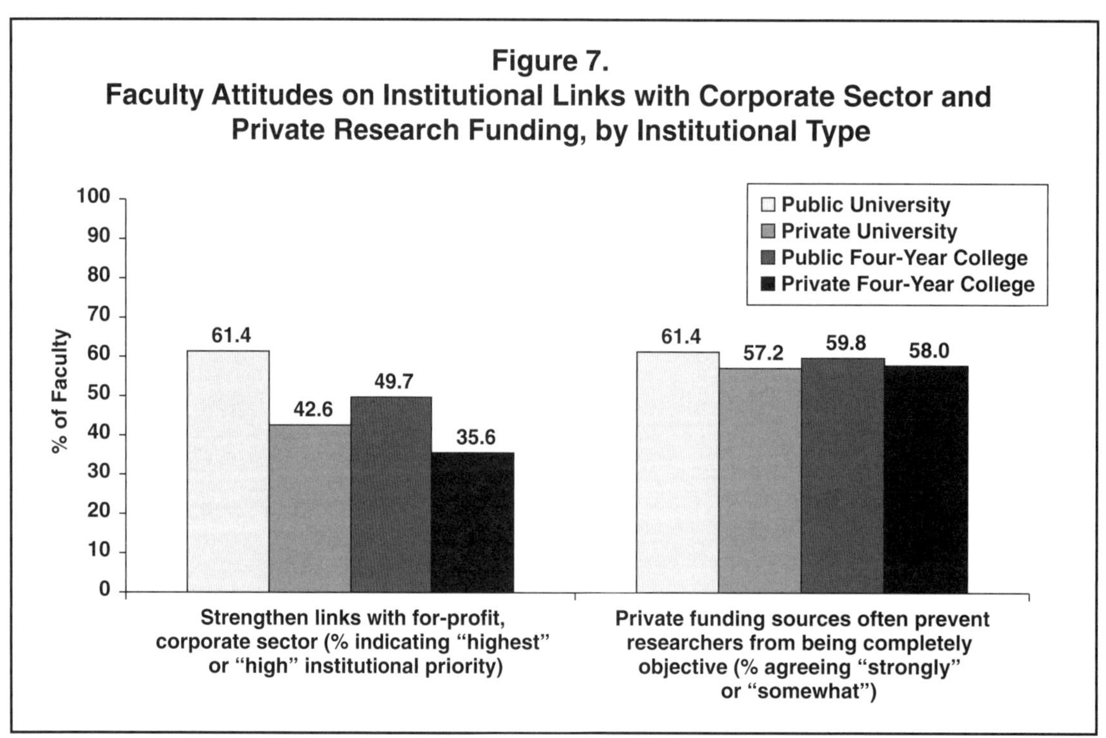

**Career Satisfaction and Perspectives**

The majority of faculty are satisfied with their careers, three out of four (74.8 percent) report overall job satisfaction. Faculty are generally most satisfied with their freedom to determine the content of the courses they teach (92.5 percent), the autonomy and independence of their positions (85.0 percent), and job security (77.7 percent). In contrast, fewer faculty express satisfaction with their teaching load (57.7 percent), their prospects for career advancement (54.6 percent), or their opportunity for scholarly pursuits (54.1 percent).

As shown in Table 6, more men are satisfied with their career than women. The largest discrepancy in satisfaction is in the area of the opportunity for scholarly pursuits (58.4 and 47.4 percent for men and women, respectively), in which male faculty are 11.0 percentage points more likely to be satisfied. Male faculty are also more likely than female faculty to be satisfied with their job security (80.8 vs. 72.8 percent, respectively) and their prospects for career advancement (57.7 vs. 49.9 percent, respectively). Women and men are almost equally satisfied with their freedom to choose the content of their courses (91.2 vs. 93.3 percent, respectively), and the autonomy and independence (83.6 vs. 85.9 percent, respectively) of their role as professors, with differences of less than 3 percentage points for both of these areas. Thus, there is greater parity by gender in terms of satisfaction in areas that generally attract individuals to the professoriate.

Differences are also apparent by academic rank (full, associate, assistant professor) for men and women. Generally, male and female professors seem to be almost equally satisfied on most measures at the assistant professor rank; however, as rank moves to full professor the central

Table 6.
*Faculty Satisfaction with Aspects of Their Career, by Academic Rank and Gender*

|  | All* | | Full | | Associate | | Assistant | |
|---|---|---|---|---|---|---|---|---|
|  | Women | Men | Women | Men | Women | Men | Women | Men |
| Freedom to determine course content | 91.2 | 93.3 | 92.2 | 95.2 | 93.4 | 93.7 | 90.4 | 91.4 |
| Autonomy and independence | 83.6 | 85.9 | 85.2 | 87.4 | 82.5 | 85.4 | 82.8 | 83.7 |
| Job security | 72.8 | 80.8 | 91.9 | 93.0 | 85.9 | 86.0 | 62.9 | 65.6 |
| Overall job satisfaction | 72.1 | 76.6 | 74.3 | 80.4 | 68.5 | 73.2 | 71.7 | 73.0 |
| Teaching load | 53.5 | 60.4 | 53.2 | 66.2 | 49.2 | 55.1 | 51.4 | 54.5 |
| Prospects for career advancement | 49.9 | 57.7 | 58.1 | 66.9 | 49.4 | 52.4 | 54.4 | 58.1 |
| Opportunity for scholarly pursuits | 47.4 | 58.4 | 50.6 | 66.0 | 42.1 | 53.9 | 46.0 | 50.2 |

*All respondents to the survey who are full-time faculty who teach undergraduates are included in the percentages

tendency is for male professors to generally be more satisfied than their female counterparts. For instance, female full professors are considerably less satisfied than their male counterparts in the areas of opportunity for scholarly pursuits (50.6 and 66.0 percent, respectively), with 15.4 percentage point gender gap in satisfaction at this rank. This gap narrows to 4.2 percentage points at the assistant professor rank. Female associate professors are also much less satisfied with their opportunity for scholarly pursuits than their male faculty counterparts (42.1 vs. 53.9 percent, respectively). Other areas where there is a large gap between female and male full professors on career satisfaction are teaching load (53.2 vs. 66.2 percent, respectively), and prospects for career advancement (58.1 vs. 66.9 percent, respectively).

For the first time faculty satisfaction with compensation was investigated using three separate items (salary, health benefits, and retirement benefits), as opposed to "salary and fringe benefits" as had been used in previous versions of the survey. Separating these different compensatory measures was instructive since results from this survey show faculty expressing greater satisfaction with health benefits (68.3 percent) and retirement benefits (68.7 percent) than with salary (46.2 percent). In the faculty survey three years ago, 47.4 percent of faculty reported satisfaction with the combined item "salary and fringe benefits" (Lindholm, Szelenyi, Hurtado, & Korn, 2005). As it turns out, faculty were largely expressing dissatisfaction with salary more than fringe benefits. Similar to the previous discussion, there are some notable differences in satisfaction with compensation by gender and academic rank (see Table 7).

Generally, men (48.9 percent) are more satisfied with their salaries than women (41.9 percent). The same trend holds for satisfaction with salary for men and women across each academic rank. In addition, both male (57.3 percent) and female (52.2 percent) full professors are much more satisfied with their salaries than are their counterparts at either the associate (44.1 and 40.6 percent for male and female, respectively) or assistant level (44.9 and 41.4 percent for male and female,

Table 7.
*Faculty Satisfaction with Salary and Benefits, by Academic Rank and Gender*

|  | Women | | | | Men | | | |
|---|---|---|---|---|---|---|---|---|
|  | All* | Full | Associate | Assistant | All* | Full | Associate | Assistant |
| Salary | 41.9 | 52.2 | 40.6 | 41.4 | 48.9 | 57.3 | 44.1 | 44.9 |
| Health benefits | 68.9 | 68.8 | 65.4 | 69.0 | 67.9 | 69.4 | 65.1 | 66.2 |
| Retirement benefits | 67.4 | 63.6 | 63.6 | 69.6 | 69.6 | 70.0 | 66.1 | 71.5 |

*All respondents to the survey who are full-time faculty who teach undergraduates are included in the percentages

respectively). Male and female faculty are much more alike when it comes to their satisfaction with health and retirement benefits, although male full professors (70.0 percent) are more satisfied with their retirement benefits than female full professors (63.6 percent).

As Figure 8 displays, trends for male faculty at both public and private institutions and female faculty at private institutions indicate a linear relationship between degree of satisfaction with salary and likelihood of considering leaving one's current institution for another in the past two years. As would be expected, for these three groups the percent of faculty that indicate they have considered leaving for another institution decreases as their satisfaction with salary increases. However, trends for female faculty at public institutions are not linear. Of those faculty at the full professor level indicating they are "very satisfied" with their salaries, women at public institutions (47.2 percent) are more likely than men at public and private institutions (20.1 and 21.0 percent, respectively) and women at private institutions (21.5 percent) to consider leaving their current institution. The same pattern is evident for women (48.8 percent) at the associate professor level at public institutions as compared to men at public and private institutions (33.8 and 30.3 percent, respectively) and women at private institutions (26.9 percent). In addition, women full professors

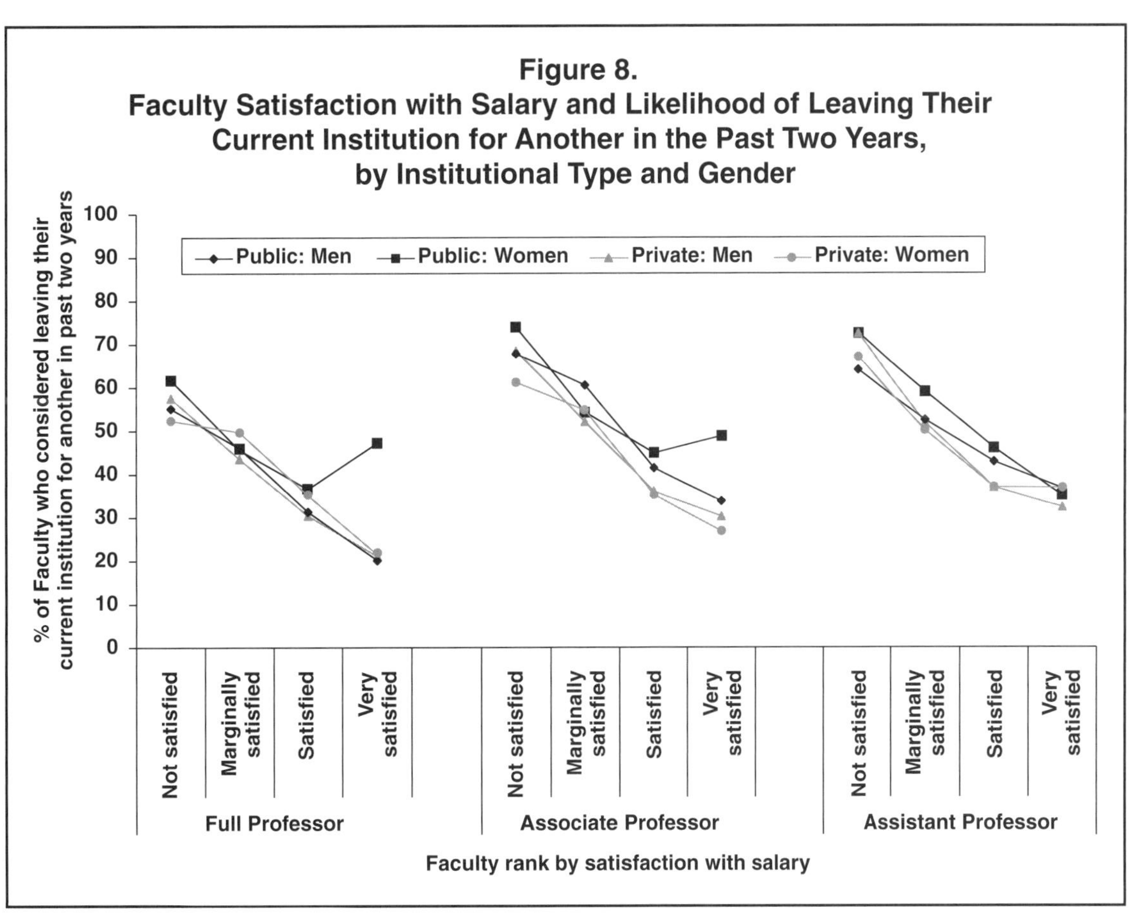

at public institutions who are very satisfied with their salaries are nearly equally as likely to have considered leaving their institution for another in the last two years (47.2 percent) as female full professors at public institutions who are only marginally satisfied with their salaries (45.6 percent). This strikingly different pattern suggests that for female faculty at public institutions there are factors other than salary that contribute to their mobility and overall job satisfaction.

**Technology Use**

It is not a question of whether faculty use email (99.6 percent do on a weekly basis), but how much time in an average week they spend doing so. In general, about one in four faculty members spend from one to four hours per week on email, and the largest category of use is five to eight hours per week (40.1 percent). In the higher use categories (i.e., those using email 13 or more hours per week), there are differences between male and female faculty, with many more women (17.2 percent) than men (9.6 percent) spending this amount of time on email.

The majority of faculty (74.4 percent) have placed or collected class assignments on the internet. The use of the internet as a tool in this way is fairly universal across institutional types, with about 72 to 77 percent of faculty from each institutional type reporting internet use with regard to class assignments. Looking at differences by rank, however, shows a slight favor towards the new faculty: 78.2 percent of assistant professors used the internet to place or collect class assignments as compared to 74.9 percent of associate professors and 70.1 percent of full professors. Women, regardless of rank, were slightly more likely than men to use the internet to collect or post assignments (78.0 percent vs. 72.0 percent, respectively).

It is a much rarer occurrence, however, for faculty to teach a class exclusively on the internet; only 13.3 percent of faculty report having done so at least once in the past two years. Teaching a course exclusively on the internet is most prominent at public institutions and especially at four-year public colleges, where one in five faculty members (19.9 percent) taught a class exclusively on the internet. Least likely to conduct online courses were faculty at private universities, where only 8.7 percent report having done so. As with using the internet to post or collect assignments, female faculty are more likely than male faculty to teach a class solely over the web (16.1 percent vs. 11.5 percent, respectively).

Although more women than men are using technology in their teaching, slightly more male faculty (85.8 percent) than female faculty (81.7 percent) believe that their institution provides adequate support for integrating technology into their teaching. Support does not equal reward, however, as only about one in five faculty (20.3 percent) indicate they believed faculty at their institution are rewarded for the use of instructional technology was "very descriptive" of their institution. Women (23.3 percent) were more likely than men (18.4 percent) to believe that faculty are rewarded for their efforts to use instructional technology.

**Health and Wellness**

Given the intensity of their teaching and research practices and engagement in scholarly activities, faculty's ability to achieve a healthy balance between their personal and professional life appears challenged at times. Only about one-third of all faculty (34.2 percent) believe they have established a healthy balance in their lives personally and professionally. When faculty's responses are examined by gender, female faculty (27.3 percent) appear to have greater difficulty than male faculty (38.7 percent) in striking a balance.

Despite the struggle to balance work and home life, faculty express strong interests in personal goals outside of academia. Most notably, the majority of faculty regard developing a meaningful philosophy of life (72.5 percent), raising a family (69.2 percent), helping others who are in difficulty (65.2 percent), and integrating spirituality into their lives (47.5 percent) as "very important" or "essential." Large gender differences are seen with regard to the importance of two of these personal goals: more women than men emphasize the importance of helping others in difficulty (71.3 percent vs. 61.2 percent) and integrating spirituality into their lives (53.1 percent vs. 43.8 percent).

College faculty appear to experience many sources of stress in both their professional and personal lives. The three most commonly cited sources of stress by faculty were self-imposed high expectations (80.1 percent), lack of personal time (74.1 percent), and managing household responsibilities (72.7 percent). Additionally, nearly two-thirds of faculty (62.8 percent) report personal finances as a stressor, and half of all respondents (49.5 percent) attribute at least moderate stress regarding the condition of their physical health.

Across virtually all stressor items, more women than men report experiencing stress; Figure 9 displays the most prominent gender differences. More women than men report at least moderate stress from lack of personal time, managing household responsibilities, self-imposed high expectations, job security, and subtle discrimination. The greatest gender differences are due to subtle discrimination, where more than twice as many women (38.7 percent) than men (18.2 percent) cite subtle discrimination in the form of prejudice, racism, and/or sexism as a source of stress.

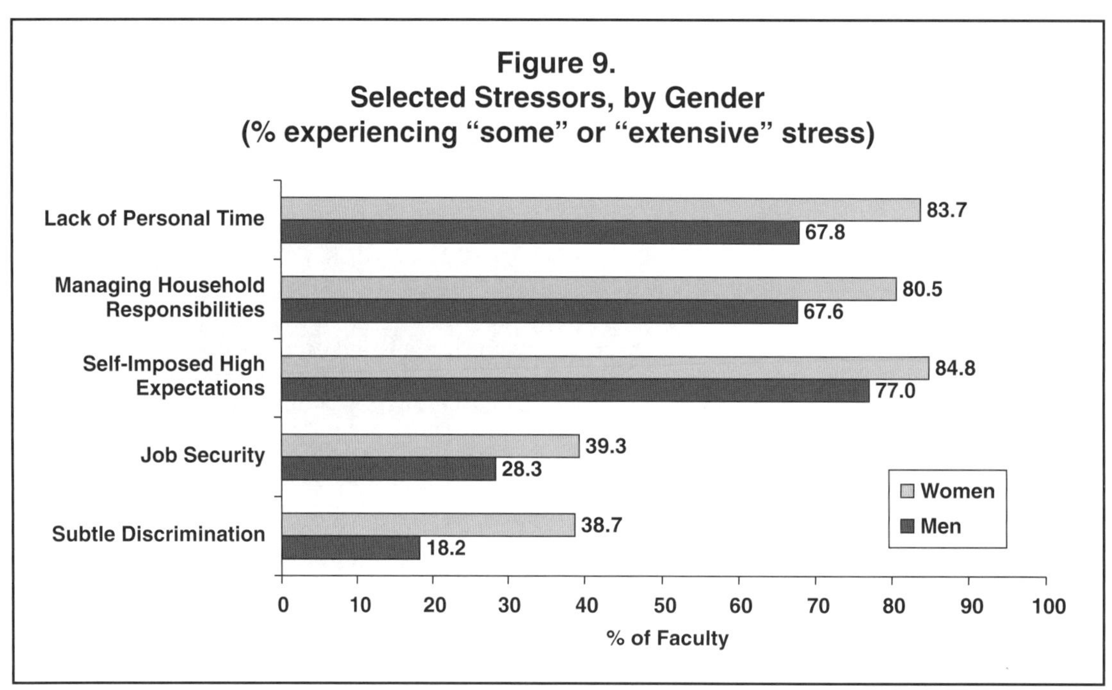


## Summary

Key findings from the 2007–2008 HERI Faculty Survey indicate that shifts are occurring in what faculty value as goals for undergraduate education and in how they interact with and teach students. Student-centered learning is becoming much more of a norm in college classrooms today than it was just three years ago, and as more senior faculty retire and new faculty are hired this pattern is likely to continue. The findings also demonstrate that men and women prioritize aspects of their roles as professors differently, and that women experience more stress and less satisfaction than men. Most troubling among these findings is the fact that female full professors who have by definition reached the pinnacle of their profession are much less satisfied than male full professors on a number of key job satisfaction areas. Highlights of the findings include the following:

*Civic Engagement and Diversity Goals Increase in Importance.* Although traditional goals for undergraduate education, such as developing students' critical thinking skills and knowledge of a specific discipline, remain at the forefront of what faculty consider important, faculty today place increased value on instilling a commitment to community service among students and enhancing students' knowledge of and appreciation for other racial/ethnic groups as important goals for undergraduate education.

*Student-Centered Pedagogy and Evaluation Methods Gain Further Traction.* Faculty today are more likely to use short-answer exams and term/research papers as evaluation methods than were faculty just three years ago, they are also slightly less likely to grade on a bell curve. In the classroom, faculty are engaging in more cooperative learning and in less lecturing. Students are also being asked to evaluate each other's work more frequently. Overall, assistant professors are more likely to use student-centered approaches than are associate and, especially, full professors.

*Female Faculty More Likely to Encourage Strong "Habits of Mind" for Life-Long Learning.* Across the various "habits of mind" a higher percentage of female than male faculty report that they encourage the habits frequently. The largest divergence is found among the habits that ask students to critically examine and reflect on their academic work products, such as encouraging students to "revise their papers to improve their writing," and to "seek feedback on their academic work."

*Male and Female Faculty Allocate Time Differently.* Male and female professors are equally committed to their role as teachers, but women spend more time preparing for their classes and actually teaching than men. Men, on average, devote more time to research and scholarly writing than women, and are more likely to indicate that the research aspects of the professoriate are personally important to them.

*Continued Need for Hiring More Women and Faculty of Color.* The majority of faculty indicate that their institution needs to hire more women and faculty of color. The majority of faculty also indicate that women and faculty of color are treated fairly at their institution. Female faculty are *more* likely than male faculty to see the need for hiring more women and faculty of color, and *less* likely than men to feel that their institution treats women and faculty of color fairly.

*Faculty Express Overall Job Satisfaction, but Women Are Less Satisfied than Men.* The large majority of faculty indicate that they have overall job satisfaction. Faculty are most satisfied with the freedom to determine the content of their courses, the autonomy and independence of their positions, and job security. These areas that draw individuals to the professoriate are places where there is gender parity in terms of satisfaction. Faculty are less satisfied with their teaching loads, prospects for career advancement, and opportunity for scholarly pursuits, and in each of these areas women are less satisfied than men. In addition, in these areas women at the assistant professor level are almost as satisfied as men, whereas women at the full professor level are much less satisfied.

*Faculty Express Dissatisfaction with Salary Compensation.* Overall in terms of compensation, the majority of faculty are satisfied with their health and retirement benefits, but dissatisfied with their salaries. Men are somewhat more satisfied with their salaries than women, and full professors are more satisfied with their salaries than associate and assistant professors.

*Very Satisfied Female Full and Associate Professors at Public Institutions at Risk for Leaving.* Female full and associate professors at public institutions who indicate that they are very satisfied with their salaries are much more likely to have recently considered leaving their institution for another institution than are female full and associate professors at private institutions who are very satisfied with their salaries and male full and associate professors at both public and private institutions who are very satisfied with their salaries. In addition, at the full professor level women at public institutions who are very satisfied with their salaries are nearly equally as likely to have considered leaving their current institution for another as are female full professors at public institutions who are only marginally satisfied.

*Striking a Personal and Professional Balance Difficult for Faculty.* Only about one-third of faculty overall indicate that they have found a healthy balance between their professional and personal lives, and male faculty are much more likely to perceive that they have balance than female faculty. In addition, the majority of faculty experience stress in both their personal and professional lives, with the biggest sources of stress stemming from self-imposed high expectations, lack of personal time, and managing household responsibilities. Women are more likely to experience stress in these areas than men, and are much more likely to report stress stemming from subtle discrimination in the form of prejudice, racism, and/or sexism.

## References


Conley, D. T. (2005). *College knowledge: What it really takes for students to succeed and what we can do to get them ready.* San Francisco: Jossey-Bass.

Lindholm, J. A., Szelenyi, K., Hurtado, S., & Korn, W. S. (2005). *The American college teacher: National norms for the 2004–2005* HERI *faculty survey.* Los Angeles: Higher Education Research Institute, UCLA.

National Center for Education Statistics (2003). *2003 National Study of Postsecondary Faculty (NSOPF:04).* Washington, DC: NCES.

Pryor, J. H., Hurtado, S., Sharkness, J., & Korn, W. S. (2007). *The American freshman: National norms for fall 2007.* Los Angeles: Higher Education Research Institute, UCLA.

Seymour, E. (1997). *Talking about leaving: Why undergraduates leave the sciences.* Boulder, CO: Westview Press.

# Full-time Undergraduate Faculty, Type of Institution and Control for

# All Faculty

**2007–2008 FACULTY SURVEY WEIGHTED NATIONAL NORMS**
**Full-time Undergraduate Faculty**

| All Respondents | All 4+ yr | Universities Pub | Priv | Four-year Colleges Pub | All Priv | Nons | Cath | Oth Relig |
|---|---|---|---|---|---|---|---|---|
| **Number of Respondents** | 22,562 | 2,967 | 3,002 | 5,629 | 10,964 | 5,005 | 1,929 | 4,030 |
| **Gender** | | | | | | | | |
| Male | 60.7 | 64.3 | 66.1 | 57.5 | 57.1 | 58.1 | 51.2 | 59.2 |
| Female | 39.3 | 35.7 | 33.9 | 42.5 | 42.9 | 41.9 | 48.8 | 40.8 |
| **What is your principal activity in your current position at this institution?** | | | | | | | | |
| Administration | 7.0 | 8.8 | 7.6 | 6.6 | 4.8 | 4.6 | 4.5 | 5.2 |
| Teaching | 83.4 | 70.7 | 80.4 | 90.0 | 93.3 | 93.5 | 93.7 | 92.6 |
| Research | 8.0 | 18.7 | 10.2 | 1.9 | 0.4 | 0.7 | 0.2 | 0.2 |
| Services to clients and patients | 0.8 | 0.7 | 1.0 | 0.8 | 0.7 | 0.2 | 1.1 | 1.2 |
| Other | 0.9 | 1.1 | 0.7 | 0.7 | 0.8 | 0.9 | 0.6 | 0.7 |
| **What is your present academic rank?** | | | | | | | | |
| Professor | 31.7 | 35.3 | 38.0 | 28.2 | 28.2 | 29.8 | 23.9 | 28.6 |
| Associate Professor | 26.1 | 26.0 | 23.8 | 25.6 | 28.0 | 26.7 | 31.3 | 27.9 |
| Assistant Professor | 27.4 | 24.4 | 22.0 | 29.5 | 31.5 | 29.4 | 34.9 | 32.5 |
| Lecturer | 7.2 | 8.7 | 7.8 | 8.4 | 3.4 | 5.2 | 2.6 | 1.4 |
| Instructor | 7.6 | 5.6 | 8.4 | 8.3 | 8.9 | 8.9 | 7.4 | 9.7 |
| **What is your tenure status at this institution?** | | | | | | | | |
| Tenured | 54.4 | 59.3 | 58.8 | 54.4 | 45.8 | 45.9 | 49.8 | 43.3 |
| On tenure track, but not tenured | 22.4 | 19.0 | 18.1 | 26.1 | 24.3 | 23.0 | 25.6 | 25.5 |
| Not on tenure track, but institution has tenure system | 19.6 | 21.3 | 22.6 | 17.8 | 18.2 | 19.0 | 15.6 | 18.6 |
| Institution has no tenure system | 3.5 | 0.3 | 0.6 | 1.7 | 11.6 | 12.1 | 9.0 | 12.6 |
| **Are you currently serving in an administrative position as: [1]** | | | | | | | | |
| Department Chair | 11.3 | 7.2 | 8.8 | 10.2 | 19.1 | 19.4 | 16.4 | 20.1 |
| Dean (Associate or Assistant) | 1.6 | 1.6 | 2.1 | 1.2 | 1.7 | 1.0 | 1.9 | 2.5 |
| President | 0.0 | 0.1 | 0.0 | 0.0 | 0.0 | 0.0 | 0.0 | 0.0 |
| Vice-President | 0.1 | 0.0 | 0.0 | 0.1 | 0.4 | 0.5 | 0.1 | 0.3 |
| Provost | 0.0 | 0.0 | 0.0 | 0.0 | 0.1 | 0.2 | 0.0 | 0.0 |
| Other | 15.9 | 18.1 | 16.9 | 14.3 | 14.7 | 14.3 | 16.7 | 14.0 |
| Not Applicable | 65.2 | 66.2 | 63.7 | 69.2 | 59.5 | 59.5 | 60.4 | 59.0 |
| **My primary place of employment in the last year was: [2]** | | | | | | | | |
| In higher education: | | | | | | | | |
|   at this institution | 94.6 | 96.0 | 93.9 | 94.3 | 93.6 | 93.2 | 94.4 | 93.8 |
|   at a different institution | 2.6 | 1.9 | 2.8 | 3.0 | 3.0 | 2.9 | 2.6 | 3.2 |
|   at more than one institution | 1.4 | 1.3 | 1.8 | 1.4 | 1.5 | 1.7 | 1.3 | 1.4 |
| Not in higher education | 1.0 | 0.6 | 0.9 | 1.0 | 1.5 | 1.8 | 1.5 | 1.2 |
| Not employed | 0.3 | 0.2 | 0.6 | 0.3 | 0.4 | 0.5 | 0.2 | 0.4 |
| **Noted as being personally "very important" or "essential": [2]** | | | | | | | | |
| Research | 71.4 | 77.6 | 80.4 | 68.4 | 62.4 | 66.5 | 65.3 | 54.7 |
| Teaching | 97.7 | 96.4 | 97.3 | 98.2 | 98.9 | 98.7 | 99.1 | 99.1 |
| Service | 66.1 | 64.2 | 67.5 | 64.7 | 69.4 | 67.8 | 74.1 | 69.0 |

[1] Response options changed from earlier Faculty Surveys.
[2] This question asked for the first time in the 2007–2008 Faculty Survey.

27

| | | | | | Four-year Colleges | | | |
|---|---|---|---|---|---|---|---|---|
| | All | Universities | | | All | | | Oth |
| **All Respondents** | 4+ yr | Pub | Priv | Pub | Priv | Nons | Cath | Relig |
| **Highest degree earned** | | | | | | | | |
| Bachelor's (B.A., B.S., etc.) | 1.0 | 1.5 | 1.4 | 0.6 | 0.7 | 1.0 | 0.3 | 0.6 |
| Master's (M.A., M.S., M.F.A., M.B.A., etc.) | 19.7 | 15.3 | 15.5 | 22.2 | 24.4 | 23.3 | 22.2 | 27.3 |
| LL.B., J.D. | 1.0 | 0.9 | 1.1 | 1.0 | 1.0 | 1.0 | 1.0 | 1.1 |
| M.D., D.D.S. (or equivalent) | 0.6 | 1.0 | 0.7 | 0.2 | 0.7 | 1.0 | 0.7 | 0.3 |
| Other first professional degree beyond B.A. (e.g., D.D., D.V.M.) | 0.7 | 0.6 | 0.3 | 0.3 | 1.4 | 2.3 | 0.2 | 0.8 |
| Ed.D. | 3.2 | 1.9 | 1.9 | 4.2 | 4.4 | 3.8 | 5.3 | 4.6 |
| Ph.D. | 71.5 | 77.0 | 77.2 | 68.9 | 64.7 | 65.4 | 67.9 | 61.8 |
| Other degree | 1.9 | 1.5 | 1.5 | 1.9 | 2.4 | 2.0 | 2.4 | 3.1 |
| None | 0.4 | 0.2 | 0.2 | 0.7 | 0.2 | 0.2 | 0.1 | 0.4 |
| **Degree currently working on** | | | | | | | | |
| Bachelor's (B.A., B.S., etc.) | 0.1 | 0.0 | 0.1 | 0.1 | 0.1 | 0.0 | 0.1 | 0.1 |
| Master's (M.A., M.S., M.F.A., M.B.A., etc.) | 0.9 | 1.0 | 1.1 | 0.6 | 0.8 | 0.7 | 0.8 | 1.1 |
| LL.B., J.D. | 0.1 | 0.1 | 0.1 | 0.1 | 0.2 | 0.3 | 0.1 | 0.0 |
| M.D., D.D.S. (or equivalent) | 0.0 | 0.1 | 0.0 | 0.0 | 0.0 | 0.0 | 0.1 | 0.0 |
| Other first professional degree beyond B.A. (e.g., D.D., D.V.M.) | 0.0 | 0.0 | 0.0 | 0.0 | 0.0 | 0.0 | 0.0 | 0.1 |
| Ed.D. | 1.0 | 0.9 | 0.6 | 0.7 | 1.6 | 1.9 | 1.3 | 1.4 |
| Ph.D. | 4.6 | 2.4 | 4.1 | 5.5 | 6.8 | 5.7 | 6.8 | 8.3 |
| Other degree | 0.6 | 0.3 | 0.6 | 0.5 | 1.0 | 0.6 | 1.3 | 1.5 |
| None | 92.7 | 95.3 | 93.3 | 92.4 | 89.5 | 90.7 | 89.6 | 87.6 |
| **During the past two years, have you engaged in any of the following activities?** | | | | | | | | |
| Taught an honors course | 19.9 | 21.4 | 23.0 | 17.1 | 19.7 | 19.9 | 21.3 | 18.6 |
| Taught an interdisciplinary course | 41.0 | 42.0 | 40.5 | 35.8 | 46.3 | 51.2 | 37.1 | 44.8 |
| Taught an ethnic studies course | 10.4 | 9.5 | 7.9 | 10.6 | 12.7 | 12.9 | 13.0 | 12.2 |
| Taught a women's studies course | 7.3 | 5.6 | 7.9 | 7.2 | 9.3 | 9.7 | 10.3 | 8.1 |
| Team-taught a course | 32.7 | 36.9 | 33.2 | 27.8 | 32.9 | 32.4 | 29.8 | 35.4 |
| Taught a service learning course | 19.7 | 19.1 | 16.3 | 20.9 | 20.7 | 20.2 | 22.2 | 20.7 |
| Placed or collected assignments on the Internet | 74.4 | 75.1 | 76.9 | 73.3 | 73.4 | 73.7 | 74.8 | 72.1 |
| Taught a course exclusively on the Internet | 13.3 | 11.9 | 8.7 | 19.9 | 9.3 | 7.7 | 12.9 | 9.5 |
| Participated in a teaching enhancement workshop | 56.5 | 50.2 | 50.3 | 60.8 | 62.7 | 60.0 | 68.5 | 63.3 |
| Advised student groups involved in service/volunteer work | 42.4 | 37.1 | 39.3 | 45.0 | 47.5 | 46.2 | 47.8 | 49.2 |
| Collaborated with the local community in research/teaching | 46.2 | 43.7 | 40.5 | 51.6 | 45.7 | 43.0 | 47.2 | 48.8 |
| Developed a new course | 66.5 | 64.9 | 66.1 | 64.6 | 71.2 | 73.6 | 68.4 | 69.4 |
| Conducted research/writing focused on: | | | | | | | | |
| International/global issues | 28.4 | 28.0 | 35.1 | 26.5 | 27.8 | 30.7 | 26.4 | 24.5 |
| Racial or ethnic minorities | 20.6 | 19.7 | 21.6 | 21.1 | 20.7 | 23.2 | 19.9 | 17.7 |
| Women and gender issues | 19.1 | 18.7 | 21.4 | 18.6 | 19.0 | 21.1 | 18.2 | 16.4 |
| Taught a seminar for first-year students | 23.6 | 19.8 | 26.4 | 21.1 | 30.1 | 31.6 | 24.7 | 31.2 |
| Engaged undergraduates on <u>your</u> research project [2] | 41.6 | 44.1 | 48.1 | 38.7 | 38.8 | 44.1 | 33.2 | 34.5 |
| Worked with undergraduates on a research project | 57.3 | 57.3 | 59.6 | 55.7 | 58.1 | 62.9 | 52.0 | 54.7 |

[2] This question asked for the first time in the 2007–2008 Faculty Survey.

## 2007–2008 FACULTY SURVEY WEIGHTED NATIONAL NORMS
### Full-time Undergraduate Faculty

| All Respondents | All 4+ yr | Universities Pub | Universities Priv | Four-year Colleges Pub | Four-year Colleges All Priv | Four-year Colleges Nons | Four-year Colleges Cath | Four-year Colleges Oth Relig |
|---|---|---|---|---|---|---|---|---|
| **DURING THE PRESENT TERM, HOW MANY HOURS PER WEEK ON AVERAGE DO YOU ACTUALLY SPEND ON:** | | | | | | | | |
| **Scheduled teaching (actual, not credit hours)** | | | | | | | | |
| None | 0.6 | 0.9 | 0.7 | 0.5 | 0.4 | 0.4 | 0.3 | 0.4 |
| 1 to 4 | 13.4 | 20.8 | 18.3 | 8.4 | 7.5 | 8.6 | 5.9 | 7.0 |
| 5 to 8 | 31.2 | 41.0 | 43.5 | 22.6 | 22.9 | 26.4 | 22.9 | 17.8 |
| 9 to 12 | 35.1 | 24.7 | 27.2 | 43.9 | 42.0 | 40.1 | 44.1 | 43.4 |
| 13 to 16 | 12.1 | 6.3 | 5.8 | 15.6 | 18.5 | 16.9 | 17.9 | 21.1 |
| 17 to 20 | 4.7 | 3.5 | 3.1 | 5.8 | 5.9 | 5.2 | 6.2 | 6.6 |
| 21 to 34 | 2.3 | 2.2 | 1.1 | 2.7 | 2.4 | 2.0 | 2.2 | 3.2 |
| 35 to 44 | 0.3 | 0.4 | 0.3 | 0.3 | 0.2 | 0.1 | 0.1 | 0.5 |
| 45 + | 0.2 | 0.2 | 0.1 | 0.2 | 0.3 | 0.3 | 0.3 | 0.1 |
| **Preparing for teaching (including reading student papers and grading)** | | | | | | | | |
| None | 0.3 | 0.4 | 0.4 | 0.1 | 0.3 | 0.4 | 0.2 | 0.1 |
| 1 to 4 | 10.3 | 13.7 | 13.5 | 8.3 | 6.7 | 7.2 | 6.1 | 6.3 |
| 5 to 8 | 23.9 | 26.3 | 27.1 | 23.0 | 20.0 | 20.8 | 20.4 | 18.5 |
| 9 to 12 | 24.5 | 25.3 | 25.3 | 24.0 | 23.8 | 22.4 | 23.5 | 26.0 |
| 13 to 16 | 15.8 | 15.1 | 14.8 | 15.6 | 17.4 | 16.7 | 18.1 | 18.1 |
| 17 to 20 | 13.8 | 11.8 | 9.8 | 15.3 | 16.4 | 16.4 | 17.8 | 15.7 |
| 21 to 34 | 8.7 | 5.8 | 7.1 | 10.1 | 11.6 | 12.4 | 9.7 | 11.4 |
| 35 to 44 | 2.1 | 1.1 | 1.6 | 2.6 | 2.8 | 2.7 | 2.7 | 2.9 |
| 45 + | 0.7 | 0.4 | 0.5 | 0.8 | 1.1 | 1.0 | 1.4 | 1.0 |
| **Advising and counseling of students** | | | | | | | | |
| None | 3.9 | 4.6 | 2.9 | 4.1 | 3.1 | 3.5 | 3.0 | 2.7 |
| 1 to 4 | 55.8 | 57.5 | 59.0 | 53.5 | 54.6 | 54.6 | 52.1 | 56.2 |
| 5 to 8 | 28.4 | 26.8 | 27.3 | 29.2 | 29.9 | 29.9 | 31.4 | 28.9 |
| 9 to 12 | 8.0 | 7.5 | 7.4 | 8.5 | 8.2 | 7.8 | 8.6 | 8.6 |
| 13 to 16 | 2.3 | 2.0 | 2.1 | 2.6 | 2.4 | 2.9 | 1.7 | 2.0 |
| 17 to 20 | 1.1 | 1.2 | 0.9 | 1.0 | 1.2 | 0.8 | 2.2 | 1.1 |
| 21 to 34 | 0.4 | 0.3 | 0.2 | 0.7 | 0.3 | 0.1 | 0.5 | 0.3 |
| 35 to 44 | 0.2 | 0.0 | 0.2 | 0.2 | 0.3 | 0.4 | 0.3 | 0.1 |
| 45 + | 0.1 | 0.1 | 0.1 | 0.2 | 0.0 | 0.0 | 0.0 | 0.1 |
| **Committee work and meetings** | | | | | | | | |
| None | 5.0 | 6.0 | 6.4 | 3.7 | 4.9 | 5.4 | 4.2 | 4.5 |
| 1 to 4 | 57.2 | 55.0 | 59.1 | 54.8 | 62.0 | 63.3 | 55.9 | 63.8 |
| 5 to 8 | 26.5 | 27.0 | 23.5 | 28.6 | 24.6 | 23.1 | 29.9 | 23.7 |
| 9 to 12 | 7.5 | 8.1 | 7.3 | 8.5 | 5.6 | 5.3 | 6.3 | 5.7 |
| 13 to 16 | 2.3 | 2.6 | 2.2 | 2.6 | 1.6 | 1.4 | 2.7 | 1.3 |
| 17 to 20 | 1.0 | 0.9 | 0.9 | 1.3 | 0.9 | 1.2 | 0.5 | 0.6 |
| 21 to 34 | 0.3 | 0.3 | 0.5 | 0.4 | 0.3 | 0.1 | 0.4 | 0.3 |
| 35 to 44 | 0.1 | 0.1 | 0.1 | 0.1 | 0.0 | 0.1 | 0.0 | 0.0 |
| 45 + | 0.0 | 0.0 | 0.0 | 0.0 | 0.1 | 0.0 | 0.1 | 0.1 |
| **Other administration** | | | | | | | | |
| None | 30.0 | 29.6 | 30.9 | 32.0 | 27.5 | 27.8 | 29.8 | 25.6 |
| 1 to 4 | 39.0 | 38.0 | 39.9 | 37.2 | 42.0 | 43.0 | 39.3 | 42.2 |
| 5 to 8 | 14.6 | 15.1 | 13.1 | 14.4 | 14.8 | 14.4 | 15.1 | 15.3 |
| 9 to 12 | 7.2 | 7.7 | 7.2 | 6.9 | 7.1 | 6.4 | 8.3 | 7.5 |
| 13 to 16 | 3.3 | 3.2 | 2.6 | 3.5 | 3.6 | 3.8 | 3.0 | 3.6 |
| 17 to 20 | 3.1 | 3.2 | 3.4 | 3.3 | 2.5 | 2.0 | 2.2 | 3.3 |
| 21 to 34 | 2.1 | 2.3 | 2.2 | 2.0 | 1.7 | 1.7 | 2.0 | 1.5 |
| 35 to 44 | 0.6 | 0.7 | 0.4 | 0.6 | 0.6 | 0.7 | 0.2 | 0.8 |
| 45 + | 0.2 | 0.2 | 0.3 | 0.2 | 0.2 | 0.2 | 0.2 | 0.2 |

29

**2007–2008 FACULTY SURVEY WEIGHTED NATIONAL NORMS**
**Full-time Undergraduate Faculty**

| All Respondents | All 4+ yr | Universities Pub | Priv | Four-year Colleges Pub | All Priv | Nons | Cath | Oth Relig |
|---|---|---|---|---|---|---|---|---|
| **DURING THE PRESENT TERM, HOW MANY HOURS PER WEEK ON AVERAGE DO YOU ACTUALLY SPEND ON:** | | | | | | | | |
| **Research and scholarly writing** | | | | | | | | |
| None | 15.5 | 13.0 | 11.3 | 15.4 | 21.1 | 20.6 | 17.9 | 23.8 |
| 1 to 4 | 32.3 | 23.9 | 24.2 | 37.6 | 40.9 | 37.4 | 42.1 | 45.3 |
| 5 to 8 | 20.2 | 17.2 | 19.8 | 22.9 | 20.8 | 23.0 | 21.5 | 17.3 |
| 9 to 12 | 12.5 | 14.7 | 16.1 | 11.5 | 9.2 | 10.5 | 9.3 | 7.2 |
| 13 to 16 | 6.6 | 9.9 | 8.4 | 5.0 | 3.4 | 3.6 | 3.6 | 2.9 |
| 17 to 20 | 6.2 | 9.8 | 9.0 | 4.2 | 2.6 | 2.6 | 3.4 | 1.9 |
| 21 to 34 | 4.2 | 7.4 | 7.0 | 2.1 | 1.3 | 1.7 | 0.9 | 1.0 |
| 35 to 44 | 1.6 | 2.7 | 2.8 | 0.8 | 0.4 | 0.4 | 0.8 | 0.3 |
| 45 + | 0.8 | 1.4 | 1.5 | 0.4 | 0.3 | 0.3 | 0.5 | 0.1 |
| **Other creative products/performances** | | | | | | | | |
| None | 50.8 | 51.9 | 53.0 | 48.8 | 50.7 | 52.0 | 48.5 | 50.1 |
| 1 to 4 | 29.5 | 28.7 | 27.1 | 30.4 | 30.4 | 28.9 | 32.9 | 31.1 |
| 5 to 8 | 11.0 | 11.2 | 9.8 | 11.7 | 10.3 | 10.3 | 10.7 | 10.2 |
| 9 to 12 | 4.4 | 4.4 | 4.3 | 4.4 | 4.6 | 5.1 | 4.0 | 4.2 |
| 13 to 16 | 1.8 | 1.7 | 1.7 | 2.0 | 1.7 | 1.4 | 1.6 | 2.2 |
| 17 to 20 | 1.4 | 0.9 | 2.1 | 1.9 | 1.2 | 1.1 | 1.5 | 1.3 |
| 21 to 34 | 0.7 | 0.7 | 0.9 | 0.5 | 0.7 | 1.0 | 0.6 | 0.4 |
| 35 to 44 | 0.2 | 0.2 | 0.5 | 0.1 | 0.1 | 0.0 | 0.1 | 0.3 |
| 45 + | 0.2 | 0.2 | 0.4 | 0.2 | 0.2 | 0.2 | 0.2 | 0.2 |
| **Consultation with clients/patients** | | | | | | | | |
| None | 80.8 | 80.8 | 82.5 | 79.4 | 81.5 | 83.1 | 79.5 | 80.4 |
| 1 to 4 | 12.2 | 13.2 | 10.6 | 12.7 | 11.3 | 10.5 | 11.4 | 12.3 |
| 5 to 8 | 3.9 | 3.5 | 3.6 | 4.4 | 3.9 | 3.2 | 4.9 | 4.4 |
| 9 to 12 | 1.3 | 0.8 | 1.6 | 1.5 | 1.6 | 1.8 | 1.6 | 1.4 |
| 13 to 16 | 0.7 | 0.7 | 0.4 | 0.8 | 0.6 | 0.4 | 0.6 | 0.9 |
| 17 to 20 | 0.6 | 0.7 | 0.6 | 0.4 | 0.6 | 0.4 | 1.3 | 0.4 |
| 21 to 34 | 0.4 | 0.1 | 0.5 | 0.7 | 0.3 | 0.4 | 0.4 | 0.2 |
| 35 to 44 | 0.1 | 0.1 | 0.0 | 0.0 | 0.1 | 0.1 | 0.1 | 0.1 |
| 45 + | 0.1 | 0.1 | 0.1 | 0.2 | 0.1 | 0.0 | 0.1 | 0.0 |
| **Community or public service** | | | | | | | | |
| None | 37.3 | 39.9 | 40.8 | 34.4 | 35.5 | 41.5 | 31.8 | 29.2 |
| 1 to 4 | 49.1 | 47.1 | 41.9 | 51.9 | 51.9 | 47.1 | 55.0 | 56.9 |
| 5 to 8 | 10.1 | 9.9 | 11.8 | 10.2 | 9.5 | 8.2 | 10.1 | 10.8 |
| 9 to 12 | 2.5 | 2.4 | 3.2 | 2.4 | 2.4 | 2.4 | 2.2 | 2.3 |
| 13 to 16 | 0.6 | 0.5 | 1.3 | 0.6 | 0.5 | 0.4 | 0.5 | 0.5 |
| 17 to 20 | 0.3 | 0.1 | 0.7 | 0.3 | 0.2 | 0.2 | 0.2 | 0.1 |
| 21 to 34 | 0.1 | 0.0 | 0.2 | 0.1 | 0.1 | 0.0 | 0.1 | 0.1 |
| 35 to 44 | 0.1 | 0.2 | 0.0 | 0.0 | 0.0 | 0.0 | 0.0 | 0.0 |
| 45 + | 0.0 | 0.0 | 0.0 | 0.0 | 0.0 | 0.0 | 0.0 | 0.0 |
| **Outside consulting/freelance work** | | | | | | | | |
| None | 67.7 | 65.4 | 66.2 | 68.3 | 70.8 | 71.6 | 71.1 | 69.5 |
| 1 to 4 | 23.9 | 25.8 | 24.6 | 23.5 | 21.8 | 21.1 | 22.1 | 22.5 |
| 5 to 8 | 5.7 | 6.2 | 5.9 | 5.6 | 5.0 | 4.7 | 4.9 | 5.5 |
| 9 to 12 | 1.7 | 1.8 | 1.4 | 1.7 | 1.6 | 1.8 | 1.1 | 1.6 |
| 13 to 16 | 0.4 | 0.4 | 0.8 | 0.4 | 0.3 | 0.3 | 0.4 | 0.4 |
| 17 to 20 | 0.3 | 0.3 | 0.7 | 0.2 | 0.2 | 0.2 | 0.2 | 0.3 |
| 21 to 34 | 0.1 | 0.0 | 0.1 | 0.1 | 0.2 | 0.3 | 0.2 | 0.0 |
| 35 to 44 | 0.1 | 0.0 | 0.3 | 0.0 | 0.0 | 0.0 | 0.0 | 0.0 |
| 45 + | 0.1 | 0.1 | 0.0 | 0.1 | 0.0 | 0.0 | 0.1 | 0.0 |

30

## 2007–2008 FACULTY SURVEY WEIGHTED NATIONAL NORMS
### Full-time Undergraduate Faculty

| All Respondents | All 4+ yr | Universities Pub | Universities Priv | Four-year Colleges Pub | Four-year Colleges All Priv | Four-year Colleges Nons | Four-year Colleges Cath | Oth Relig |
|---|---|---|---|---|---|---|---|---|
| **DURING THE PRESENT TERM, HOW MANY HOURS PER WEEK ON AVERAGE DO YOU ACTUALLY SPEND ON:** | | | | | | | | |
| **Household/childcare duties** | | | | | | | | |
| None | 12.2 | 14.1 | 12.7 | 12.3 | 9.3 | 8.0 | 11.5 | 9.8 |
| 1 to 4 | 18.0 | 17.1 | 18.1 | 17.9 | 19.4 | 20.6 | 17.8 | 18.6 |
| 5 to 8 | 25.3 | 25.0 | 24.1 | 25.4 | 26.1 | 25.9 | 24.7 | 27.4 |
| 9 to 12 | 16.3 | 16.0 | 16.6 | 16.7 | 15.9 | 16.1 | 14.9 | 16.2 |
| 13 to 16 | 8.3 | 8.8 | 8.3 | 7.7 | 8.6 | 8.7 | 10.0 | 7.5 |
| 17 to 20 | 7.8 | 8.0 | 8.2 | 7.8 | 7.5 | 7.6 | 7.2 | 7.6 |
| 21 to 34 | 5.7 | 5.9 | 5.3 | 5.5 | 5.9 | 6.1 | 5.5 | 5.9 |
| 35 to 44 | 2.9 | 2.7 | 3.0 | 2.9 | 3.1 | 3.3 | 3.2 | 2.8 |
| 45 + | 3.5 | 2.4 | 3.9 | 3.8 | 4.2 | 3.8 | 5.1 | 4.2 |
| **Communicating via email** | | | | | | | | |
| None | 0.4 | 0.3 | 0.4 | 0.3 | 0.6 | 0.9 | 0.4 | 0.4 |
| 1 to 4 | 28.8 | 25.6 | 28.7 | 29.2 | 32.5 | 31.3 | 30.8 | 35.5 |
| 5 to 8 | 40.1 | 40.4 | 39.8 | 39.7 | 40.3 | 40.8 | 40.5 | 39.5 |
| 9 to 12 | 18.2 | 20.2 | 18.0 | 18.0 | 15.9 | 15.5 | 17.3 | 15.6 |
| 13 to 16 | 7.2 | 7.9 | 7.2 | 7.4 | 6.2 | 7.2 | 5.4 | 5.3 |
| 17 to 20 | 3.4 | 3.8 | 4.2 | 3.1 | 2.8 | 2.8 | 3.5 | 2.6 |
| 21 to 34 | 1.3 | 1.3 | 1.3 | 1.7 | 1.0 | 1.1 | 1.3 | 0.8 |
| 35 to 44 | 0.3 | 0.3 | 0.2 | 0.4 | 0.2 | 0.2 | 0.3 | 0.2 |
| 45 + | 0.3 | 0.2 | 0.3 | 0.3 | 0.3 | 0.4 | 0.4 | 0.2 |
| **Commuting to campus [2]** | | | | | | | | |
| None | 6.0 | 5.9 | 4.0 | 5.6 | 7.8 | 9.1 | 4.0 | 8.0 |
| 1 to 4 | 61.5 | 66.1 | 56.1 | 61.7 | 57.9 | 58.1 | 52.9 | 60.7 |
| 5 to 8 | 23.0 | 21.0 | 26.8 | 23.3 | 23.1 | 21.9 | 27.7 | 22.1 |
| 9 to 12 | 8.0 | 6.1 | 10.7 | 7.9 | 9.3 | 9.1 | 12.2 | 7.9 |
| 13 to 16 | 1.0 | 0.7 | 1.6 | 0.9 | 1.4 | 1.5 | 2.4 | 0.6 |
| 17 to 20 | 0.3 | 0.2 | 0.6 | 0.3 | 0.3 | 0.2 | 0.5 | 0.4 |
| 21 to 34 | 0.1 | 0.1 | 0.2 | 0.1 | 0.1 | 0.1 | 0.2 | 0.2 |
| 35 to 44 | 0.0 | 0.0 | 0.0 | 0.0 | 0.0 | 0.0 | 0.0 | 0.0 |
| 45 + | 0.1 | 0.0 | 0.0 | 0.2 | 0.1 | 0.1 | 0.1 | 0.1 |
| **Other employment, outside of academia [2]** | | | | | | | | |
| None | 87.0 | 89.3 | 87.7 | 86.2 | 84.8 | 84.7 | 85.2 | 84.7 |
| 1 to 4 | 6.8 | 6.0 | 6.3 | 6.9 | 8.0 | 8.6 | 6.6 | 7.9 |
| 5 to 8 | 3.1 | 2.5 | 2.4 | 3.7 | 3.4 | 2.6 | 4.8 | 3.7 |
| 9 to 12 | 1.5 | 1.1 | 1.3 | 1.7 | 1.8 | 2.2 | 1.3 | 1.5 |
| 13 to 16 | 0.7 | 0.6 | 0.8 | 0.5 | 0.9 | 0.9 | 0.6 | 0.9 |
| 17 to 20 | 0.4 | 0.3 | 0.6 | 0.4 | 0.5 | 0.3 | 1.1 | 0.4 |
| 21 to 34 | 0.3 | 0.2 | 0.3 | 0.3 | 0.2 | 0.3 | 0.3 | 0.2 |
| 35 to 44 | 0.2 | 0.0 | 0.3 | 0.1 | 0.3 | 0.3 | 0.1 | 0.4 |
| 45 + | 0.1 | 0.0 | 0.1 | 0.1 | 0.1 | 0.0 | 0.0 | 0.2 |

[2]  This question asked for the first time in the 2007–2008 Faculty Survey.

31

**2007–2008 FACULTY SURVEY WEIGHTED NATIONAL NORMS**
**Full-time Undergraduate Faculty**

| All Respondents | All 4+ yr | Universities Pub | Priv | Four-year Colleges Pub | All Priv | Nons | Cath | Oth Relig |
|---|---|---|---|---|---|---|---|---|
| **Including all institutions at which you teach, how many undergraduate courses are you teaching this term? [2]** | | | | | | | | |
| None | 0.0 | 0.0 | 0.0 | 0.0 | 0.0 | 0.0 | 0.0 | 0.0 |
| One | 21.7 | 35.2 | 29.4 | 12.8 | 10.9 | 11.9 | 12.0 | 9.0 |
| Two | 28.8 | 35.6 | 34.5 | 24.4 | 22.2 | 26.8 | 19.9 | 17.0 |
| Three | 25.8 | 17.6 | 25.2 | 29.8 | 31.6 | 31.9 | 30.5 | 31.9 |
| Four | 15.4 | 7.9 | 7.6 | 21.5 | 21.6 | 17.7 | 23.4 | 26.3 |
| Five | 5.2 | 1.9 | 1.7 | 7.0 | 9.1 | 7.6 | 9.2 | 11.1 |
| Six or more | 3.2 | 1.7 | 1.5 | 4.5 | 4.5 | 4.1 | 5.1 | 4.8 |
| **FOR UP TO FOUR OF THE UNDERGRADUATE COURSES MENTIONED ABOVE, HOW MANY STUDENTS ARE ENROLLED IN: [2]** | | | | | | | | |
| **Course #1** | | | | | | | | |
| 10 or fewer | 12.0 | 11.2 | 10.3 | 9.6 | 16.8 | 18.2 | 13.0 | 17.2 |
| 11 to 20 | 27.1 | 24.4 | 28.4 | 22.8 | 35.6 | 37.7 | 35.6 | 32.5 |
| 21 to 30 | 26.2 | 22.1 | 24.3 | 30.1 | 27.8 | 25.7 | 30.9 | 28.8 |
| 31 to 50 | 20.8 | 20.3 | 21.7 | 25.8 | 14.7 | 12.8 | 16.4 | 16.6 |
| 51 to 100 | 9.1 | 13.1 | 9.4 | 9.2 | 3.7 | 3.5 | 3.4 | 4.0 |
| More than 100 | 4.8 | 9.0 | 6.0 | 2.6 | 1.4 | 2.0 | 0.7 | 0.8 |
| **Course #2** | | | | | | | | |
| 10 or fewer | 16.9 | 17.9 | 15.9 | 13.4 | 20.6 | 21.0 | 17.9 | 21.6 |
| 11 to 20 | 31.5 | 26.5 | 31.9 | 27.8 | 40.5 | 43.5 | 37.1 | 38.3 |
| 21 to 30 | 26.7 | 24.5 | 23.2 | 30.2 | 26.1 | 23.6 | 30.7 | 27.0 |
| 31 to 50 | 17.9 | 18.8 | 20.2 | 22.5 | 10.4 | 9.1 | 12.5 | 11.1 |
| 51 to 100 | 5.0 | 7.8 | 6.5 | 5.0 | 1.7 | 1.8 | 1.4 | 1.9 |
| More than 100 | 2.1 | 4.6 | 2.3 | 1.1 | 0.6 | 1.0 | 0.3 | 0.2 |
| **Course #3** | | | | | | | | |
| 10 or fewer | 24.9 | 28.9 | 22.0 | 19.5 | 29.7 | 28.8 | 27.7 | 31.9 |
| 11 to 20 | 32.8 | 27.1 | 31.7 | 30.9 | 38.5 | 38.1 | 38.1 | 39.2 |
| 21 to 30 | 24.9 | 21.9 | 23.5 | 28.4 | 22.8 | 23.4 | 25.1 | 20.9 |
| 31 to 50 | 13.8 | 14.6 | 16.6 | 18.1 | 7.4 | 6.9 | 8.5 | 7.4 |
| 51 to 100 | 2.7 | 4.9 | 4.9 | 2.7 | 0.9 | 1.5 | 0.5 | 0.4 |
| More than 100 | 1.0 | 2.6 | 1.5 | 0.5 | 0.6 | 1.3 | 0.1 | 0.2 |
| **Course #4** | | | | | | | | |
| 10 or fewer | 31.7 | 30.7 | 27.6 | 27.4 | 38.0 | 32.7 | 39.5 | 42.4 |
| 11 to 20 | 31.6 | 31.2 | 28.0 | 28.6 | 35.9 | 38.0 | 32.5 | 35.6 |
| 21 to 30 | 23.2 | 22.2 | 21.0 | 27.8 | 18.5 | 18.2 | 23.8 | 16.2 |
| 31 to 50 | 11.1 | 10.8 | 14.3 | 14.6 | 6.6 | 10.0 | 3.9 | 4.7 |
| 51 to 100 | 1.8 | 3.6 | 7.2 | 1.5 | 0.6 | 0.2 | 0.4 | 1.0 |
| More than 100 | 0.6 | 1.6 | 2.0 | 0.2 | 0.4 | 0.9 | 0.0 | 0.2 |

[2] This question asked for the first time in the 2007–2008 Faculty Survey.

32

**2007–2008 FACULTY SURVEY WEIGHTED NATIONAL NORMS**
**Full-time Undergraduate Faculty**

| All Respondents | All 4+ yr | Universities Pub | Priv | Four-year Colleges Pub | All Priv | Nons | Cath | Oth Relig |
|---|---|---|---|---|---|---|---|---|
| **HOW MANY OF THE FOLLOWING COURSES ARE YOU TEACHING THIS ACADEMIC YEAR?** | | | | | | | | |
| **General education courses** | | | | | | | | |
| None | 56.0 | 66.1 | 60.7 | 50.7 | 47.1 | 49.0 | 51.1 | 42.0 |
| One | 17.5 | 16.1 | 15.6 | 18.2 | 19.7 | 20.3 | 15.2 | 21.3 |
| Two | 12.2 | 8.9 | 11.3 | 14.3 | 14.1 | 13.0 | 13.4 | 16.2 |
| Three | 6.1 | 3.8 | 5.4 | 6.7 | 8.7 | 8.1 | 8.5 | 9.7 |
| Four | 3.9 | 2.6 | 2.7 | 4.9 | 4.8 | 4.3 | 6.1 | 4.8 |
| Five or more | 4.2 | 2.4 | 4.3 | 5.1 | 5.6 | 5.3 | 5.5 | 6.0 |
| **Developmental/remedial courses** | | | | | | | | |
| None | 94.6 | 95.9 | 96.3 | 94.3 | 92.6 | 91.5 | 94.3 | 93.0 |
| One | 3.0 | 2.5 | 2.2 | 3.0 | 4.0 | 4.3 | 3.4 | 3.9 |
| Two | 1.2 | 0.8 | 0.7 | 1.4 | 1.5 | 2.3 | 0.8 | 0.9 |
| Three | 0.5 | 0.3 | 0.5 | 0.6 | 0.8 | 1.0 | 0.3 | 0.8 |
| Four | 0.4 | 0.3 | 0.1 | 0.4 | 0.5 | 0.5 | 0.4 | 0.7 |
| Five or more | 0.3 | 0.3 | 0.2 | 0.3 | 0.6 | 0.4 | 0.7 | 0.7 |
| **Other undergraduate credit courses** | | | | | | | | |
| None | 18.0 | 20.1 | 22.1 | 15.6 | 16.1 | 16.5 | 17.3 | 14.8 |
| One | 20.4 | 25.6 | 24.7 | 17.8 | 14.6 | 15.0 | 16.6 | 12.9 |
| Two | 23.1 | 25.8 | 22.8 | 22.7 | 20.3 | 21.8 | 20.5 | 18.1 |
| Three | 16.0 | 13.9 | 14.3 | 16.9 | 18.4 | 18.3 | 18.5 | 18.6 |
| Four | 9.9 | 6.4 | 8.3 | 12.1 | 12.8 | 11.2 | 12.6 | 15.2 |
| Five or more | 12.5 | 8.2 | 7.9 | 14.9 | 17.7 | 17.2 | 14.6 | 20.4 |
| **Graduate courses** | | | | | | | | |
| None | 63.4 | 47.0 | 58.9 | 66.9 | 82.9 | 85.9 | 70.9 | 85.8 |
| One | 22.4 | 33.7 | 26.5 | 19.7 | 8.9 | 7.4 | 15.3 | 7.3 |
| Two | 8.7 | 12.2 | 8.9 | 8.5 | 4.1 | 3.9 | 6.4 | 3.0 |
| Three | 2.9 | 4.2 | 3.4 | 2.3 | 1.7 | 1.2 | 3.5 | 1.5 |
| Four | 1.5 | 1.7 | 1.3 | 1.6 | 1.1 | 0.8 | 1.9 | 0.9 |
| Five or more | 1.1 | 1.2 | 0.9 | 1.0 | 1.2 | 0.8 | 1.9 | 1.4 |
| **Vocational or technical courses** | | | | | | | | |
| None | 97.4 | 97.4 | 97.6 | 97.2 | 97.6 | 97.4 | 97.4 | 97.9 |
| One | 1.0 | 1.0 | 1.1 | 1.0 | 1.0 | 1.2 | 0.9 | 0.9 |
| Two | 0.6 | 0.6 | 0.6 | 0.7 | 0.6 | 0.7 | 0.9 | 0.3 |
| Three | 0.4 | 0.3 | 0.3 | 0.5 | 0.5 | 0.5 | 0.3 | 0.4 |
| Four | 0.3 | 0.5 | 0.1 | 0.1 | 0.1 | 0.1 | 0.2 | 0.2 |
| Five or more | 0.3 | 0.2 | 0.2 | 0.4 | 0.2 | 0.1 | 0.3 | 0.3 |
| **Non-credit courses (other than above)** | | | | | | | | |
| None | 95.0 | 94.5 | 94.9 | 95.6 | 94.7 | 94.7 | 94.8 | 94.7 |
| One | 3.5 | 3.8 | 3.9 | 2.8 | 3.8 | 3.6 | 4.2 | 3.8 |
| Two | 1.0 | 1.1 | 0.6 | 1.0 | 1.0 | 1.1 | 0.8 | 1.1 |
| Three | 0.2 | 0.3 | 0.4 | 0.3 | 0.1 | 0.2 | 0.1 | 0.1 |
| Four | 0.1 | 0.1 | 0.1 | 0.1 | 0.1 | 0.1 | 0.1 | 0.1 |
| Five or more | 0.2 | 0.2 | 0.2 | 0.1 | 0.2 | 0.3 | 0.1 | 0.2 |
| **Do you teach remedial/developmental skills in any of the following areas?** | | | | | | | | |
| Reading | 4.2 | 3.6 | 3.8 | 4.3 | 5.1 | 5.4 | 5.4 | 4.5 |
| Writing | 10.3 | 9.3 | 9.5 | 10.4 | 12.0 | 13.6 | 10.6 | 10.4 |
| Mathematics | 4.1 | 4.0 | 2.7 | 4.6 | 4.4 | 4.7 | 5.2 | 3.5 |
| ESL | 1.0 | 0.8 | 0.7 | 1.0 | 1.3 | 1.3 | 1.0 | 1.4 |
| General academic skills | 8.5 | 8.1 | 6.8 | 8.6 | 9.8 | 11.3 | 8.3 | 8.7 |
| Other subject areas | 5.6 | 5.3 | 5.0 | 5.4 | 6.5 | 7.5 | 5.4 | 5.9 |

33

**2007–2008 FACULTY SURVEY WEIGHTED NATIONAL NORMS**
**Full-time Undergraduate Faculty**

| All Respondents | All 4+ yr | Universities Pub | Priv | Four-year Colleges Pub | All Priv | Nons | Cath | Oth Relig |
|---|---|---|---|---|---|---|---|---|
| **HAVE YOU ENGAGED IN ANY OF THE FOLLOWING PROFESSIONAL DEVELOPMENT OPPORTUNITIES AT YOUR INSTITUTION? [2]** | | | | | | | | |
| **Workshops focused on teaching in the classroom** | | | | | | | | |
| Yes | 70.1 | 67.4 | 67.8 | 70.7 | 74.0 | 73.2 | 76.0 | 73.9 |
| No | 27.5 | 31.7 | 30.7 | 26.5 | 21.7 | 22.8 | 20.7 | 20.5 |
| Not eligible | 0.2 | 0.1 | 0.2 | 0.2 | 0.2 | 0.2 | 0.2 | 0.2 |
| Not available | 2.2 | 0.7 | 1.3 | 2.6 | 4.2 | 3.8 | 3.1 | 5.4 |
| **Paid workshops outside the institution focused on teaching** | | | | | | | | |
| Yes | 24.6 | 18.7 | 17.5 | 27.5 | 32.4 | 29.6 | 35.0 | 35.1 |
| No | 70.6 | 77.4 | 77.2 | 67.1 | 62.8 | 65.6 | 61.3 | 59.5 |
| Not eligible | 0.8 | 0.8 | 1.3 | 1.0 | 0.4 | 0.4 | 0.1 | 0.6 |
| Not available | 3.9 | 3.1 | 4.0 | 4.4 | 4.4 | 4.4 | 3.6 | 4.8 |
| **Paid sabbatical leave** | | | | | | | | |
| Yes | 28.7 | 29.7 | 38.6 | 22.0 | 30.6 | 36.0 | 26.6 | 25.2 |
| No | 54.6 | 55.2 | 46.4 | 59.6 | 52.0 | 46.8 | 59.4 | 55.0 |
| Not eligible | 13.4 | 11.1 | 13.3 | 14.5 | 15.2 | 15.3 | 13.3 | 16.2 |
| Not available | 3.2 | 4.0 | 1.6 | 3.9 | 2.2 | 1.9 | 0.7 | 3.6 |
| **Travel funds paid by the institution** | | | | | | | | |
| Yes | 78.9 | 76.7 | 78.3 | 80.3 | 80.4 | 80.4 | 79.0 | 81.3 |
| No | 18.1 | 20.0 | 18.6 | 17.0 | 16.7 | 15.8 | 19.8 | 16.2 |
| Not eligible | 1.4 | 1.0 | 2.2 | 1.4 | 1.4 | 2.1 | 0.5 | 0.8 |
| Not available | 1.6 | 2.3 | 0.9 | 1.3 | 1.5 | 1.8 | 0.8 | 1.6 |
| **Association membership/dues paid by the institution** | | | | | | | | |
| Yes | 28.9 | 22.6 | 30.7 | 21.3 | 45.7 | 42.1 | 44.3 | 51.8 |
| No | 55.0 | 61.9 | 54.5 | 59.1 | 41.1 | 43.7 | 43.8 | 35.7 |
| Not eligible | 2.6 | 2.4 | 4.0 | 2.7 | 2.2 | 3.2 | 1.3 | 1.4 |
| Not available | 13.4 | 13.1 | 10.7 | 16.9 | 11.0 | 11.1 | 10.6 | 11.0 |
| **Tuition remission** | | | | | | | | |
| Yes | 14.4 | 10.2 | 21.3 | 11.9 | 19.5 | 19.2 | 16.7 | 21.7 |
| No | 77.5 | 81.5 | 73.4 | 79.0 | 72.6 | 71.8 | 76.9 | 71.0 |
| Not eligible | 3.5 | 3.0 | 3.9 | 3.1 | 4.4 | 4.8 | 3.5 | 4.3 |
| Not available | 4.6 | 5.3 | 1.4 | 6.0 | 3.5 | 4.1 | 2.8 | 3.1 |
| **Internal grants for research** | | | | | | | | |
| Yes | 46.8 | 51.0 | 52.1 | 44.8 | 41.0 | 45.6 | 37.6 | 36.3 |
| No | 49.2 | 45.9 | 43.7 | 51.7 | 53.4 | 48.3 | 58.4 | 57.9 |
| Not eligible | 2.1 | 2.2 | 3.0 | 1.8 | 1.8 | 2.1 | 1.3 | 1.6 |
| Not available | 1.9 | 1.0 | 1.2 | 1.6 | 3.8 | 4.0 | 2.7 | 4.2 |
| **Training for administrative leadership** | | | | | | | | |
| Yes | 13.2 | 13.6 | 13.6 | 13.4 | 12.3 | 12.7 | 13.1 | 11.4 |
| No | 76.4 | 78.5 | 76.9 | 76.2 | 73.8 | 72.5 | 75.8 | 74.5 |
| Not eligible | 2.7 | 2.1 | 3.7 | 2.8 | 2.8 | 3.2 | 2.0 | 2.6 |
| Not available | 7.6 | 5.8 | 5.9 | 7.6 | 11.1 | 11.6 | 9.1 | 11.5 |

[2] This question asked for the first time in the 2007–2008 Faculty Survey.

34

## 2007–2008 FACULTY SURVEY WEIGHTED NATIONAL NORMS
### Full-time Undergraduate Faculty

| All Respondents | All 4+ yr | Universities Pub | Universities Priv | Four-year Colleges Pub | Four-year Colleges All Priv | Four-year Colleges Nons | Four-year Colleges Cath | Four-year Colleges Oth Relig |
|---|---|---|---|---|---|---|---|---|
| **Goals for undergraduates noted as "very important" or "essential"** | | | | | | | | |
| Develop ability to think critically | 99.6 | 99.6 | 99.4 | 99.6 | 99.6 | 99.4 | 99.8 | 99.7 |
| Prepare students for employment after college | 81.5 | 80.4 | 76.9 | 84.8 | 81.1 | 78.9 | 83.3 | 83.1 |
| Prepare students for graduate or advanced education | 75.5 | 72.8 | 77.8 | 74.7 | 78.7 | 77.5 | 78.9 | 80.4 |
| Develop moral character | 70.2 | 64.4 | 75.7 | 68.1 | 77.6 | 72.5 | 83.7 | 81.2 |
| Provide for students' emotional development | 48.1 | 42.3 | 50.5 | 46.8 | 55.9 | 52.0 | 60.2 | 58.9 |
| Prepare students for family living | 21.2 | 16.1 | 25.5 | 20.9 | 26.1 | 21.9 | 29.4 | 30.3 |
| Teach students the classic works of Western civilization [2] | 34.7 | 30.2 | 40.4 | 33.8 | 38.6 | 34.6 | 43.6 | 41.4 |
| Help students develop personal values | 66.1 | 59.3 | 69.9 | 64.6 | 74.9 | 71.0 | 77.5 | 78.9 |
| Enhance students' self-understanding | 71.8 | 67.1 | 71.4 | 71.8 | 78.1 | 75.7 | 82.3 | 79.0 |
| Instill in students a commitment to community service | 55.5 | 48.4 | 56.8 | 57.3 | 61.7 | 57.1 | 66.6 | 65.5 |
| Enhance students' knowledge of and appreciation for other racial/ethnic groups | 75.2 | 71.6 | 74.6 | 75.6 | 79.5 | 78.3 | 82.6 | 79.2 |
| Study a foreign language [2] | 54.2 | 52.1 | 58.9 | 51.1 | 58.3 | 57.8 | 58.4 | 59.1 |
| Help master knowledge in a discipline | 95.1 | 94.2 | 93.6 | 96.0 | 95.9 | 95.3 | 96.4 | 96.4 |
| Develop creative capacities | 81.5 | 82.0 | 82.6 | 80.3 | 81.8 | 84.0 | 80.0 | 79.6 |
| Instill a basic appreciation of the liberal arts | 72.8 | 66.8 | 73.3 | 71.8 | 81.5 | 81.7 | 81.2 | 81.4 |
| Promote ability to write effectively | 96.4 | 95.8 | 95.8 | 96.2 | 97.8 | 97.9 | 98.0 | 97.4 |
| Help students evaluate the quality and reliability of information [2] | 97.2 | 96.9 | 97.5 | 97.0 | 97.8 | 98.0 | 98.4 | 97.1 |
| Engage students in civil discourse around controversial issues [2] | 72.4 | 67.7 | 71.6 | 72.6 | 78.7 | 79.0 | 79.9 | 77.7 |
| Teach students tolerance and respect for different beliefs [2] | 82.5 | 79.7 | 83.2 | 82.7 | 85.5 | 84.9 | 89.3 | 84.2 |
| Encourage students to become agents of social change [2] | 57.8 | 50.8 | 59.0 | 59.3 | 64.6 | 63.2 | 69.5 | 63.9 |

[2] This question asked for the first time in the 2007–2008 Faculty Survey.

| All Respondents | All 4+ yr | Universities Pub | Universities Priv | Four-year Colleges Pub | Four-year Colleges All Priv | Four-year Colleges Nons | Four-year Colleges Cath | Four-year Colleges Oth Relig |
|---|---|---|---|---|---|---|---|---|
| **HOW MANY OF THE FOLLOWING HAVE YOU PUBLISHED?** | | | | | | | | |
| **Articles in academic or professional journals** | | | | | | | | |
| None | 18.8 | 12.3 | 13.7 | 20.1 | 28.2 | 26.6 | 25.6 | 31.9 |
| 1 to 2 | 17.6 | 10.9 | 13.5 | 21.7 | 23.2 | 20.7 | 24.0 | 26.4 |
| 3 to 4 | 14.5 | 12.4 | 11.5 | 16.6 | 15.9 | 15.5 | 17.2 | 15.8 |
| 5 to 10 | 18.4 | 18.6 | 16.8 | 19.9 | 17.0 | 18.5 | 17.0 | 14.8 |
| 11 to 20 | 12.7 | 15.7 | 16.4 | 11.2 | 8.8 | 10.3 | 8.7 | 6.6 |
| 21 to 50 | 11.4 | 17.5 | 15.8 | 7.8 | 5.5 | 6.7 | 5.4 | 3.8 |
| 51+ | 6.7 | 12.5 | 12.3 | 2.6 | 1.4 | 1.7 | 2.1 | 0.7 |
| **Chapters in edited volumes** | | | | | | | | |
| None | 49.5 | 39.1 | 36.9 | 56.8 | 60.7 | 56.3 | 60.1 | 67.6 |
| 1 to 2 | 25.5 | 24.8 | 25.8 | 26.9 | 24.5 | 25.9 | 25.5 | 21.9 |
| 3 to 4 | 11.8 | 15.2 | 15.2 | 9.3 | 8.7 | 10.3 | 8.7 | 6.4 |
| 5 to 10 | 8.8 | 13.2 | 13.5 | 5.6 | 4.4 | 5.4 | 4.1 | 3.2 |
| 11 to 20 | 3.0 | 5.0 | 6.4 | 1.0 | 1.2 | 1.6 | 1.2 | 0.7 |
| 21 to 50 | 1.1 | 2.2 | 1.6 | 0.3 | 0.4 | 0.5 | 0.4 | 0.2 |
| 51+ | 0.3 | 0.6 | 0.5 | 0.1 | 0.0 | 0.1 | 0.0 | 0.0 |
| **Books, manuals, or monographs** | | | | | | | | |
| None | 61.1 | 52.2 | 52.0 | 66.7 | 70.4 | 67.8 | 69.5 | 74.7 |
| 1 to 2 | 25.7 | 30.2 | 26.7 | 24.0 | 21.2 | 22.9 | 22.4 | 18.0 |
| 3 to 4 | 7.3 | 9.3 | 11.0 | 5.8 | 4.6 | 4.6 | 4.5 | 4.6 |
| 5 to 10 | 4.4 | 6.0 | 7.0 | 2.6 | 3.0 | 3.9 | 3.0 | 1.8 |
| 11 to 20 | 1.1 | 1.5 | 2.3 | 0.6 | 0.7 | 0.6 | 0.5 | 0.9 |
| 21 to 50 | 0.4 | 0.7 | 0.7 | 0.2 | 0.1 | 0.1 | 0.1 | 0.1 |
| 51+ | 0.1 | 0.1 | 0.2 | 0.1 | 0.0 | 0.0 | 0.0 | 0.0 |
| **Other, such as patents or computer software products** | | | | | | | | |
| None | 85.1 | 80.3 | 82.2 | 88.1 | 89.2 | 89.1 | 88.0 | 90.0 |
| 1 to 2 | 8.6 | 10.9 | 10.2 | 7.2 | 6.4 | 6.6 | 7.5 | 5.6 |
| 3 to 4 | 3.2 | 4.5 | 3.3 | 2.4 | 2.3 | 2.0 | 2.7 | 2.4 |
| 5 to 10 | 1.9 | 2.9 | 2.6 | 1.2 | 1.1 | 1.2 | 1.0 | 0.9 |
| 11 to 20 | 0.6 | 0.8 | 0.8 | 0.5 | 0.5 | 0.5 | 0.6 | 0.6 |
| 21 to 50 | 0.3 | 0.3 | 0.3 | 0.4 | 0.2 | 0.3 | 0.0 | 0.2 |
| 51+ | 0.3 | 0.3 | 0.5 | 0.2 | 0.3 | 0.3 | 0.2 | 0.3 |
| **IN THE LAST TWO YEARS, HOW MANY:** | | | | | | | | |
| **Exhibitions or performances in the fine or applied arts have you presented?** | | | | | | | | |
| None | 81.8 | 86.3 | 82.3 | 80.3 | 77.4 | 75.2 | 81.8 | 78.1 |
| 1 to 2 | 5.8 | 3.7 | 6.0 | 6.0 | 8.0 | 9.6 | 7.1 | 6.1 |
| 3 to 4 | 4.4 | 3.5 | 4.4 | 5.0 | 4.8 | 4.9 | 4.1 | 5.0 |
| 5 to 10 | 4.1 | 3.1 | 3.6 | 4.3 | 5.4 | 6.1 | 4.2 | 5.0 |
| 11 to 20 | 1.9 | 1.4 | 1.6 | 2.3 | 2.1 | 2.1 | 1.2 | 2.8 |
| 21 to 50 | 1.1 | 0.9 | 1.2 | 1.4 | 1.1 | 0.8 | 0.9 | 1.5 |
| 51+ | 1.0 | 1.1 | 0.9 | 0.7 | 1.3 | 1.3 | 0.6 | 1.6 |
| **Of your professional writings have been published or accepted for publication?** | | | | | | | | |
| None | 30.0 | 20.7 | 20.4 | 33.3 | 43.0 | 40.0 | 40.8 | 48.5 |
| 1 to 2 | 32.2 | 27.6 | 28.6 | 36.7 | 34.4 | 35.0 | 35.4 | 32.8 |
| 3 to 4 | 20.9 | 24.3 | 25.0 | 20.0 | 15.3 | 16.8 | 15.7 | 13.1 |
| 5 to 10 | 13.3 | 21.0 | 20.5 | 8.2 | 6.0 | 6.8 | 6.4 | 4.5 |
| 11 to 20 | 2.7 | 4.9 | 4.1 | 1.3 | 0.9 | 1.2 | 0.7 | 0.7 |
| 21 to 50 | 0.7 | 1.1 | 1.0 | 0.5 | 0.3 | 0.2 | 0.8 | 0.2 |
| 51+ | 0.2 | 0.3 | 0.4 | 0.1 | 0.1 | 0.0 | 0.3 | 0.2 |

## 2007–2008 FACULTY SURVEY WEIGHTED NATIONAL NORMS
### Full-time Undergraduate Faculty

| All Respondents | All 4+ yr | Universities Pub | Universities Priv | Four-year Colleges Pub | Four-year Colleges All Priv | Four-year Colleges Nons | Four-year Colleges Cath | Four-year Colleges Oth Relig |
|---|---|---|---|---|---|---|---|---|
| **General activities** | | | | | | | | |
| Are you a member of a faculty union? | 21.5 | 17.8 | 8.7 | 40.2 | 9.5 | 8.6 | 17.9 | 5.9 |
| Are you a U.S. citizen? | 93.6 | 91.9 | 93.4 | 94.3 | 95.0 | 94.6 | 95.5 | 95.5 |
| Were you born in the U.S.A.? | 85.3 | 82.9 | 83.1 | 86.7 | 87.7 | 85.8 | 88.6 | 90.0 |
| Do you plan to retire within the next three years? | 13.1 | 16.4 | 10.3 | 13.3 | 9.8 | 10.1 | 10.7 | 8.7 |
| Do you use your scholarship to address local community needs? | 47.1 | 45.5 | 41.5 | 53.2 | 44.5 | 38.9 | 49.0 | 49.9 |
| Have you been sexually harassed at this institution? | 5.4 | 5.8 | 3.9 | 6.1 | 4.6 | 4.6 | 5.1 | 4.3 |
| Have you ever interrupted your professional career for more than one year for family reasons? [2] | 11.7 | 11.4 | 7.9 | 13.2 | 12.3 | 10.7 | 15.8 | 12.6 |
| Have you ever received an award for outstanding teaching? | 42.5 | 48.0 | 42.6 | 39.9 | 38.6 | 37.4 | 38.3 | 40.4 |
| Have you published op-ed pieces or editorials? | 24.0 | 25.2 | 26.4 | 22.9 | 22.3 | 22.4 | 23.3 | 21.7 |
| Is (or was) your: | | | | | | | | |
| Father an academic? | 13.6 | 13.8 | 15.2 | 12.4 | 14.0 | 14.2 | 11.8 | 15.1 |
| Mother an academic? | 9.3 | 9.0 | 8.6 | 9.1 | 10.2 | 9.7 | 9.4 | 11.5 |
| Spouse/partner an academic? | 32.9 | 35.3 | 29.4 | 31.4 | 33.6 | 34.6 | 30.9 | 33.7 |
| Are you currently teaching courses at more than one institution? | 4.7 | 3.7 | 3.8 | 4.6 | 6.6 | 7.2 | 6.3 | 5.9 |
| **During the <u>past two</u> years, have you:** | | | | | | | | |
| Considered early retirement? | 21.2 | 22.6 | 18.5 | 23.6 | 17.8 | 17.2 | 18.3 | 18.3 |
| Considered leaving academe for another job? | 32.7 | 31.2 | 29.1 | 35.6 | 32.9 | 33.2 | 29.5 | 34.7 |
| Considered leaving this institution for another? | 46.5 | 47.9 | 43.6 | 48.0 | 44.4 | 44.8 | 41.2 | 45.6 |
| Changed academic institutions? | 11.4 | 9.9 | 12.1 | 12.2 | 12.0 | 12.0 | 11.3 | 12.5 |
| Engaged in paid consulting outside of your institution? | 37.6 | 42.6 | 38.6 | 36.5 | 32.0 | 32.4 | 30.5 | 32.2 |
| Engaged in public service/professional consulting without pay? | 59.4 | 61.5 | 56.6 | 61.6 | 55.3 | 54.1 | 52.6 | 58.6 |
| Received at least one firm job offer? | 23.9 | 22.1 | 24.6 | 24.6 | 25.2 | 24.9 | 25.4 | 25.6 |
| Received funding for your work from: | | | | | | | | |
| Foundations? | 19.7 | 23.2 | 22.1 | 17.5 | 16.5 | 18.1 | 16.4 | 14.2 |
| State or federal government? | 27.1 | 39.2 | 24.9 | 26.0 | 13.5 | 16.7 | 12.8 | 9.4 |
| Business or industry? | 13.5 | 18.1 | 14.3 | 11.5 | 9.3 | 10.0 | 8.8 | 8.6 |
| Requested/sought an early promotion? | 7.3 | 7.7 | 5.4 | 8.4 | 6.2 | 7.1 | 5.3 | 5.5 |
| **IF YOU WERE TO BEGIN YOUR CAREER AGAIN, WOULD YOU STILL WANT TO:** | | | | | | | | |
| **Come to this institution? [2]** | | | | | | | | |
| Definitely yes | 35.0 | 32.2 | 42.4 | 31.6 | 39.1 | 39.4 | 37.6 | 39.5 |
| Probably yes | 33.9 | 34.9 | 32.5 | 33.6 | 33.9 | 34.4 | 33.2 | 33.6 |
| Not sure | 16.7 | 16.8 | 14.6 | 18.0 | 15.9 | 16.0 | 16.4 | 15.4 |
| Probably no | 9.4 | 10.6 | 6.3 | 10.8 | 7.5 | 6.7 | 8.4 | 8.2 |
| Definitely no | 5.0 | 5.5 | 4.2 | 6.0 | 3.6 | 3.4 | 4.4 | 3.4 |
| **Be a college professor?** | | | | | | | | |
| Definitely yes | 63.3 | 61.0 | 67.0 | 62.9 | 64.7 | 63.2 | 67.1 | 65.4 |
| Probably yes | 25.1 | 25.8 | 22.4 | 24.8 | 25.8 | 27.0 | 23.2 | 25.5 |
| Not sure | 8.4 | 9.2 | 7.5 | 8.7 | 7.6 | 7.8 | 7.4 | 7.3 |
| Probably no | 2.5 | 2.9 | 2.3 | 2.8 | 1.7 | 1.8 | 1.6 | 1.5 |
| Definitely no | 0.8 | 1.1 | 0.8 | 0.8 | 0.3 | 0.2 | 0.6 | 0.3 |

[2] This question asked for the first time in the 2007–2008 Faculty Survey.

<h1 style="text-align:center">2007–2008 FACULTY SURVEY WEIGHTED NATIONAL NORMS</h1>
<h2 style="text-align:center">Full-time Undergraduate Faculty</h2>

| All Respondents | All 4+ yr | Universities Pub | Universities Priv | Four-year Colleges Pub | Four-year Colleges All Priv | Four-year Colleges Nons | Four-year Colleges Cath | Four-year Colleges Oth Relig |
|---|---|---|---|---|---|---|---|---|
| **Attributes noted as being "very descriptive" of your institution** | | | | | | | | |
| It is easy for students to see faculty outside of regular office hours | 60.6 | 48.7 | 61.6 | 58.9 | 77.6 | 76.7 | 75.6 | 80.0 |
| There is a great deal of conformity among the students | 29.4 | 29.8 | 35.6 | 24.1 | 32.3 | 27.0 | 37.2 | 37.1 |
| The faculty are typically at odds with campus administration | 19.4 | 17.1 | 14.5 | 25.1 | 17.7 | 17.3 | 20.8 | 16.4 |
| Faculty here respect each other | 47.6 | 45.0 | 53.7 | 42.8 | 53.9 | 51.0 | 53.8 | 58.0 |
| Most students are treated like "numbers in a book" | 3.8 | 6.0 | 2.9 | 3.7 | 1.6 | 2.0 | 1.3 | 1.3 |
| Social activities are overemphasized | 8.3 | 9.4 | 8.6 | 5.8 | 9.9 | 10.1 | 6.0 | 12.0 |
| Faculty are rewarded for being good teachers | 16.0 | 12.7 | 17.5 | 14.9 | 20.9 | 24.7 | 15.5 | 18.6 |
| There is respect for the expression of diverse values and beliefs | 35.8 | 33.4 | 38.9 | 35.5 | 37.7 | 41.9 | 38.6 | 31.2 |
| Faculty are rewarded for their efforts to use instructional technology | 20.3 | 20.9 | 23.7 | 21.8 | 16.1 | 17.6 | 14.4 | 14.8 |
| Faculty are rewarded for their efforts to work with underprepared students | 5.7 | 3.9 | 5.1 | 6.3 | 7.4 | 8.5 | 5.8 | 6.6 |
| Administrators consider faculty concerns when making policy [2] | 13.0 | 10.2 | 13.6 | 11.7 | 18.2 | 19.2 | 13.4 | 19.6 |
| The administration is open about its policies | 16.5 | 14.0 | 16.5 | 15.9 | 20.6 | 21.6 | 16.6 | 21.6 |
| **Do you, "to a great extent":** | | | | | | | | |
| Engage in academic work that spans multiple disciplines | 38.7 | 41.0 | 43.2 | 35.2 | 37.8 | 41.5 | 34.8 | 34.3 |
| Feel that the training you received in graduate school prepared you well for your role as a faculty mentor | 39.1 | 39.0 | 39.8 | 41.1 | 36.4 | 34.6 | 38.9 | 37.5 |
| Achieve a healthy balance between your personal life and your professional life | 34.2 | 35.5 | 37.6 | 33.3 | 32.0 | 31.7 | 34.7 | 30.8 |
| Experience close alignment between your work and your personal values | 65.3 | 62.0 | 70.4 | 63.7 | 68.9 | 66.8 | 70.2 | 71.3 |
| Feel that you have to work harder than your colleagues to be perceived as a legitimate scholar | 26.7 | 27.1 | 27.5 | 27.6 | 24.8 | 26.1 | 23.0 | 23.9 |
| Mentor new faculty [2] | 22.3 | 22.4 | 22.5 | 23.1 | 21.1 | 22.0 | 24.2 | 18.1 |

[2] This question asked for the first time in the 2007–2008 Faculty Survey.

**2007–2008 FACULTY SURVEY WEIGHTED NATIONAL NORMS**
**Full-time Undergraduate Faculty**

| All Respondents | All 4+ yr | Universities | | Four-year Colleges | | | | |
|---|---|---|---|---|---|---|---|---|
| | | Pub | Priv | Pub | All Priv | Nons | Cath | Oth Relig |
| **Aspects of your job with which you are "very satisfied" or "satisfied": [3]** | | | | | | | | |
| Salary [2] | 46.2 | 47.2 | 53.0 | 42.0 | 46.4 | 48.2 | 45.7 | 44.3 |
| Health benefits [2] | 68.3 | 71.2 | 72.8 | 70.6 | 59.0 | 60.6 | 66.2 | 52.4 |
| Retirement benefits [2] | 68.7 | 72.9 | 68.2 | 68.9 | 63.3 | 64.0 | 61.6 | 63.3 |
| Opportunity for scholarly pursuits | 54.1 | 63.5 | 65.0 | 44.0 | 48.7 | 51.2 | 44.6 | 47.5 |
| Teaching load | 57.7 | 66.7 | 64.7 | 47.3 | 55.4 | 57.9 | 52.5 | 53.5 |
| Quality of students | 57.1 | 59.7 | 73.5 | 46.8 | 58.2 | 60.8 | 53.7 | 57.1 |
| Office/lab space | 67.3 | 69.8 | 68.3 | 61.9 | 70.3 | 71.2 | 68.0 | 70.3 |
| Autonomy and independence | 85.0 | 87.0 | 86.2 | 81.7 | 85.7 | 87.0 | 83.3 | 85.3 |
| Professional relationships with other faculty | 77.6 | 74.8 | 78.0 | 76.4 | 82.5 | 81.6 | 82.0 | 84.0 |
| Social relationships with other faculty | 67.4 | 64.1 | 67.4 | 66.1 | 73.2 | 71.8 | 75.7 | 73.6 |
| Competency of colleagues | 78.2 | 78.3 | 81.0 | 73.9 | 82.0 | 82.4 | 79.2 | 83.0 |
| Visibility for jobs at other institutions/organizations | 53.8 | 60.4 | 61.2 | 47.6 | 48.3 | 47.6 | 47.5 | 49.8 |
| Job security | 77.7 | 79.3 | 78.3 | 77.1 | 75.9 | 75.0 | 78.7 | 75.6 |
| Relationship with administration | 58.3 | 57.5 | 59.8 | 54.6 | 63.0 | 64.0 | 61.2 | 62.6 |
| Departmental leadership [2] | 69.1 | 64.8 | 72.5 | 67.8 | 74.8 | 75.3 | 70.8 | 76.4 |
| Course assignments [2] | 84.0 | 83.6 | 84.7 | 81.8 | 87.0 | 88.6 | 83.6 | 86.5 |
| Freedom to determine course content [2] | 92.5 | 93.1 | 92.4 | 91.4 | 93.1 | 94.1 | 89.9 | 93.7 |
| Availability of child care at this institution | 30.9 | 32.5 | 33.9 | 34.6 | 22.5 | 23.7 | 18.0 | 23.5 |
| Prospects for career advancement | 54.6 | 54.1 | 58.9 | 52.4 | 55.7 | 55.3 | 56.3 | 56.0 |
| Clerical/administrative support | 60.8 | 58.9 | 65.5 | 60.9 | 60.7 | 61.9 | 60.6 | 59.0 |
| Overall job satisfaction | 74.8 | 74.0 | 78.9 | 72.2 | 77.2 | 78.8 | 75.8 | 75.6 |

[2]  This question asked for the first time in the 2007–2008 Faculty Survey.
[3]  Respondents marking "Not Applicable" were not included in the computation of these results.

39

## 2007–2008 FACULTY SURVEY WEIGHTED NATIONAL NORMS
### Full-time Undergraduate Faculty

| All Respondents | All 4+ yr | Universities Pub | Universities Priv | Four-year Colleges Pub | Four-year Colleges All Priv | Four-year Colleges Nons | Four-year Colleges Cath | Oth Relig |
|---|---|---|---|---|---|---|---|---|
| **Do you agree "strongly" or "somewhat"?** | | | | | | | | |
| Faculty are interested in students' personal problems | 83.2 | 73.5 | 84.6 | 84.2 | 93.9 | 92.0 | 94.6 | 96.3 |
| Racial and ethnic diversity should be more strongly reflected in the curriculum | 58.5 | 56.2 | 55.2 | 57.8 | 64.0 | 62.8 | 65.6 | 64.8 |
| Faculty feel that most students are well-prepared academically | 44.2 | 45.3 | 67.2 | 30.6 | 48.1 | 49.5 | 43.0 | 49.1 |
| This institution should hire more faculty of color | 73.2 | 75.0 | 73.5 | 67.6 | 77.7 | 76.2 | 77.3 | 80.2 |
| Student Affairs staff have the support and respect of faculty | 77.1 | 75.2 | 78.4 | 75.7 | 80.6 | 79.6 | 81.2 | 81.5 |
| Faculty are committed to the welfare of this institution | 90.7 | 87.7 | 92.3 | 89.5 | 95.2 | 94.8 | 95.4 | 95.7 |
| Faculty here are strongly interested in the academic problems of undergraduates | 87.8 | 81.3 | 89.6 | 87.8 | 95.2 | 95.2 | 94.7 | 95.5 |
| There is a lot of campus racial conflict here | 10.6 | 12.3 | 9.1 | 8.8 | 11.4 | 12.3 | 10.2 | 10.8 |
| Most students are strongly committed to community service | 51.0 | 43.4 | 76.4 | 38.0 | 63.8 | 57.6 | 68.3 | 70.1 |
| My research is valued by faculty in my department | 73.7 | 72.6 | 77.0 | 71.6 | 75.9 | 75.8 | 74.1 | 77.3 |
| My teaching is valued by faculty in my department | 89.6 | 86.7 | 89.8 | 89.5 | 93.2 | 92.8 | 92.7 | 94.2 |
| Many courses include feminist perspectives | 43.1 | 39.2 | 41.4 | 43.0 | 49.1 | 54.3 | 47.5 | 42.3 |
| Faculty of color are treated fairly here | 88.7 | 86.9 | 89.9 | 88.8 | 90.4 | 91.3 | 89.1 | 90.0 |
| Women faculty are treated fairly here | 85.9 | 83.2 | 86.9 | 86.4 | 88.3 | 89.7 | 87.4 | 86.9 |
| Many courses involve students in community service | 48.6 | 36.9 | 59.4 | 47.3 | 59.6 | 54.0 | 67.3 | 63.1 |
| This institution should hire more women faculty | 57.1 | 64.6 | 65.8 | 50.9 | 50.4 | 49.4 | 48.0 | 53.3 |
| Gay and lesbian faculty are treated fairly here | 81.0 | 82.9 | 74.4 | 85.5 | 76.2 | 85.6 | 69.9 | 66.0 |
| My department does a good job of mentoring new faculty | 69.2 | 65.6 | 72.2 | 67.6 | 74.6 | 73.9 | 75.5 | 75.0 |
| Faculty are sufficiently involved in campus decision making | 52.9 | 50.2 | 48.3 | 51.8 | 60.1 | 63.0 | 55.8 | 58.4 |
| My values are congruent with the dominant institutional values | 72.6 | 66.2 | 77.1 | 70.3 | 81.4 | 79.7 | 81.6 | 83.6 |
| There is adequate support for integrating technology in my teaching | 84.2 | 86.3 | 89.6 | 82.0 | 81.3 | 83.1 | 82.2 | 78.3 |
| This institution takes responsibility for educating underprepared students | 63.4 | 60.0 | 63.6 | 63.5 | 67.5 | 67.5 | 68.7 | 66.7 |
| The criteria for advancement and promotion decisions are clear | 72.1 | 73.1 | 74.6 | 70.1 | 71.8 | 71.2 | 72.7 | 72.1 |
| Most of the students I teach lack the basic skills for college level work | 36.4 | 31.8 | 17.9 | 49.7 | 35.5 | 33.7 | 41.3 | 34.8 |
| There is adequate support for faculty development | 67.6 | 69.4 | 73.5 | 62.1 | 69.0 | 70.5 | 70.6 | 65.8 |
| This institution should not offer remedial/developmental education | 28.2 | 28.9 | 35.3 | 26.0 | 26.3 | 28.0 | 20.7 | 27.3 |

40

**2007–2008 FACULTY SURVEY WEIGHTED NATIONAL NORMS**
**Full-time Undergraduate Faculty**

| All Respondents | All 4+ yr | Universities Pub | Priv | Four-year Colleges Pub | All Priv | Nons | Cath | Oth Relig |
|---|---|---|---|---|---|---|---|---|
| **Issues you believe to be of "high" or "highest" priority at your institution:** | | | | | | | | |
| To promote the intellectual development of students | 85.8 | 85.0 | 89.4 | 82.6 | 89.0 | 89.4 | 88.2 | 88.8 |
| To help students examine and understand their personal values | 56.0 | 42.8 | 71.4 | 48.9 | 74.1 | 67.1 | 81.4 | 80.1 |
| To develop a sense of community among students and faculty | 54.1 | 43.7 | 59.9 | 50.9 | 68.6 | 66.0 | 69.8 | 71.7 |
| To facilitate student involvement in community service | 46.0 | 32.9 | 62.6 | 42.2 | 59.1 | 51.2 | 69.7 | 64.4 |
| To help students learn how to bring about change in American society | 35.1 | 25.9 | 44.6 | 33.7 | 43.9 | 42.3 | 48.1 | 43.7 |
| To increase or maintain institutional prestige | 64.0 | 72.0 | 72.3 | 55.3 | 60.0 | 64.0 | 59.4 | 54.6 |
| To hire faculty "stars" | 29.2 | 47.0 | 35.4 | 18.7 | 16.2 | 17.5 | 15.4 | 14.8 |
| To recruit more minority students | 50.3 | 53.8 | 46.8 | 49.0 | 49.1 | 53.1 | 46.9 | 44.5 |
| To enhance the institution's national image | 69.4 | 80.9 | 79.1 | 59.7 | 61.6 | 68.1 | 58.6 | 54.2 |
| To create a diverse multi-cultural campus environment | 53.7 | 53.6 | 51.8 | 54.7 | 53.7 | 58.4 | 52.1 | 47.8 |
| To promote gender equity among faculty | 52.1 | 55.0 | 53.9 | 49.9 | 50.0 | 54.3 | 47.7 | 45.0 |
| To provide resources for faculty to engage in community-based teaching or research | 35.3 | 31.7 | 36.8 | 39.1 | 34.3 | 34.5 | 37.8 | 31.9 |
| To create and sustain partnerships with surrounding communities | 47.5 | 44.8 | 40.9 | 54.8 | 45.4 | 43.4 | 50.6 | 45.1 |
| To pursue extramural funding | 61.0 | 78.6 | 61.2 | 54.7 | 45.7 | 46.7 | 48.8 | 42.3 |
| To increase the representation of minorities in the faculty and administration | 44.9 | 48.5 | 43.8 | 44.6 | 41.3 | 45.6 | 38.2 | 36.8 |
| To strengthen links with the for-profit, corporate sector [2] | 49.1 | 61.4 | 42.6 | 49.7 | 35.6 | 34.8 | 41.8 | 33.0 |
| To develop leadership ability among students | 59.0 | 52.4 | 69.7 | 53.4 | 68.9 | 68.8 | 67.6 | 69.8 |
| To increase the representation of women in the faculty and administration | 38.4 | 45.0 | 40.6 | 34.6 | 33.5 | 36.7 | 31.5 | 30.1 |
| To develop an appreciation for multiculturalism [2] | 54.5 | 52.0 | 53.5 | 54.1 | 58.9 | 62.3 | 58.1 | 54.6 |

[2]  This question asked for the first time in the 2007–2008 Faculty Survey.

41

**2007–2008 FACULTY SURVEY WEIGHTED NATIONAL NORMS**
**Full-time Undergraduate Faculty**

| All Respondents | All 4+ yr | Universities Pub | Priv | Four-year Colleges Pub | All Priv | Nons | Cath | Oth Relig |
|---|---|---|---|---|---|---|---|---|
| **Do you agree "strongly" or "somewhat"?** | | | | | | | | |
| Western civilization and culture should be the foundation for the undergraduate curriculum | 57.5 | 55.8 | 60.5 | 55.6 | 60.4 | 56.2 | 63.5 | 64.7 |
| College officials have the right to ban persons with extreme views from speaking on campus | 27.6 | 22.3 | 39.0 | 22.4 | 35.1 | 30.3 | 32.7 | 43.6 |
| The chief benefit of a college education is that it increases one's earning power | 28.9 | 31.0 | 23.6 | 32.7 | 24.2 | 24.1 | 26.1 | 23.2 |
| Promoting diversity leads to the admission of too many underprepared students | 23.7 | 24.7 | 24.0 | 24.7 | 21.1 | 19.8 | 21.5 | 22.8 |
| Colleges should be actively involved in solving social problems | 71.0 | 70.4 | 71.7 | 71.0 | 71.6 | 69.8 | 74.4 | 72.5 |
| Tenure is an outmoded concept | 32.0 | 31.4 | 32.1 | 32.0 | 32.9 | 31.2 | 33.4 | 35.1 |
| Colleges should encourage students to be involved in community service activities | 87.9 | 84.7 | 88.5 | 87.8 | 91.8 | 90.0 | 92.6 | 94.0 |
| Community service should be given weight in college admissions decisions | 66.4 | 63.6 | 70.6 | 64.1 | 70.7 | 70.1 | 72.1 | 70.8 |
| A racially/ethnically diverse student body enhances the educational experience of all students | 93.6 | 93.7 | 93.2 | 93.4 | 94.1 | 93.7 | 93.4 | 95.0 |
| Realistically, an individual can do little to bring about changes in society | 18.8 | 19.9 | 20.5 | 18.8 | 16.7 | 17.3 | 16.9 | 15.7 |
| Colleges should be concerned with facilitating undergraduate students' spiritual development | 36.6 | 23.1 | 56.0 | 26.0 | 57.2 | 40.5 | 73.3 | 71.7 |
| Colleges have a responsibility to work with their surrounding communities to address local issues | 87.9 | 86.4 | 86.3 | 89.0 | 89.2 | 87.2 | 90.5 | 91.4 |
| Private funding sources often prevent researchers from being completely objective in the conduct of their work | 59.5 | 61.4 | 57.2 | 59.8 | 58.0 | 58.5 | 57.4 | 57.7 |

42

## 2007–2008 FACULTY SURVEY WEIGHTED NATIONAL NORMS
### Full-time Undergraduate Faculty

| All Respondents | All 4+ yr | Universities Pub | Universities Priv | Four-year Colleges Pub | Four-year Colleges All Priv | Four-year Colleges Nons | Four-year Colleges Cath | Four-year Colleges Oth Relig |
|---|---|---|---|---|---|---|---|---|
| **Factors noted as a source of stress for you during the <u>last two</u> years** | | | | | | | | |
| Managing household responsibilities | 72.7 | 70.9 | 70.7 | 73.0 | 75.5 | 75.8 | 73.2 | 76.5 |
| Child care | 30.9 | 29.3 | 30.9 | 30.4 | 33.6 | 34.0 | 30.9 | 34.7 |
| Care of elderly parent | 33.5 | 31.5 | 35.2 | 34.2 | 34.4 | 34.5 | 33.7 | 34.8 |
| My physical health | 49.5 | 48.8 | 49.2 | 51.1 | 48.6 | 47.3 | 50.9 | 49.2 |
| Health of spouse/partner | 35.9 | 35.8 | 36.5 | 36.4 | 35.3 | 37.0 | 32.9 | 34.3 |
| Review/promotion process | 51.1 | 50.7 | 45.6 | 54.7 | 49.7 | 50.4 | 50.7 | 48.2 |
| Subtle discrimination (e.g., prejudice, racism, sexism) | 26.3 | 26.8 | 23.9 | 28.5 | 24.0 | 24.1 | 26.0 | 22.8 |
| Personal finances | 62.8 | 58.4 | 61.4 | 65.6 | 65.8 | 66.2 | 63.7 | 66.6 |
| Committee work | 61.5 | 58.6 | 55.8 | 66.8 | 61.6 | 61.2 | 65.0 | 60.2 |
| Faculty meetings | 53.0 | 51.4 | 48.0 | 56.5 | 53.4 | 52.4 | 58.2 | 52.1 |
| Colleagues | 64.2 | 63.4 | 60.0 | 68.0 | 62.6 | 64.0 | 62.3 | 60.9 |
| Students | 64.4 | 62.0 | 57.7 | 67.4 | 67.0 | 65.2 | 64.6 | 71.1 |
| Research or publishing demands | 62.7 | 67.7 | 68.0 | 62.4 | 53.6 | 54.9 | 57.4 | 49.6 |
| Institutional procedures and "red tape" | 71.8 | 74.5 | 66.8 | 76.3 | 65.4 | 63.2 | 69.5 | 66.3 |
| Teaching load | 63.3 | 57.1 | 58.9 | 68.9 | 66.7 | 65.6 | 66.7 | 68.5 |
| Children's problems | 31.4 | 30.1 | 34.5 | 31.4 | 31.4 | 31.2 | 29.7 | 32.7 |
| Friction with spouse/partner | 26.3 | 27.1 | 25.2 | 25.9 | 26.4 | 27.2 | 25.8 | 25.5 |
| Lack of personal time | 74.1 | 72.7 | 73.1 | 74.3 | 76.1 | 75.7 | 75.5 | 77.0 |
| Keeping up with information technology | 52.7 | 52.0 | 48.2 | 55.2 | 52.7 | 50.5 | 55.9 | 54.0 |
| Job security | 32.6 | 29.6 | 31.6 | 34.1 | 35.1 | 36.1 | 34.7 | 34.0 |
| Being part of a dual career couple | 43.4 | 41.9 | 40.3 | 43.2 | 47.1 | 48.2 | 43.0 | 48.0 |
| Working with underprepared students | 61.1 | 55.6 | 44.6 | 70.4 | 65.5 | 61.0 | 70.0 | 69.3 |
| Classroom conflict | 19.4 | 17.2 | 13.7 | 23.3 | 20.4 | 19.0 | 24.1 | 20.2 |
| Self-imposed high expectations | 80.1 | 80.0 | 78.6 | 79.9 | 81.1 | 80.8 | 78.5 | 83.0 |
| Change in work responsibilities | 46.4 | 43.9 | 43.4 | 48.6 | 48.5 | 48.3 | 49.7 | 48.2 |
| **Personal goals noted as "very important" or "essential":** | | | | | | | | |
| Becoming an authority in my field | 60.0 | 67.7 | 66.1 | 55.4 | 52.4 | 52.9 | 53.2 | 51.3 |
| Influencing the political structure | 19.0 | 20.3 | 19.4 | 19.2 | 17.0 | 16.0 | 20.6 | 16.4 |
| Influencing social values | 39.8 | 36.6 | 42.9 | 39.0 | 43.5 | 41.5 | 46.1 | 44.7 |
| Raising a family | 69.2 | 69.6 | 72.6 | 65.9 | 71.1 | 71.4 | 66.7 | 73.4 |
| Becoming very well off financially | 32.6 | 36.9 | 29.8 | 34.0 | 26.7 | 28.2 | 27.8 | 24.0 |
| Helping others who are in difficulty | 65.2 | 61.7 | 68.3 | 65.3 | 68.1 | 65.9 | 70.4 | 70.0 |
| Becoming involved in programs to clean up the environment | 35.1 | 34.6 | 33.1 | 36.1 | 35.5 | 36.2 | 36.5 | 33.9 |
| Developing a meaningful philosophy of life | 72.5 | 69.6 | 74.4 | 71.6 | 76.4 | 75.6 | 78.3 | 76.4 |
| Helping to promote racial understanding | 53.8 | 52.0 | 52.7 | 53.3 | 57.4 | 57.6 | 60.5 | 55.2 |
| Obtaining recognition from my colleagues for contributions to my special field | 47.5 | 56.1 | 52.2 | 42.7 | 39.6 | 41.4 | 43.1 | 35.0 |
| Integrating spirituality into my life | 47.5 | 39.9 | 54.2 | 45.5 | 56.3 | 46.0 | 62.0 | 67.8 |

| All Respondents | All 4+ yr | Universities Pub | Priv | Four-year Colleges Pub | All Priv | Nons | Cath | Oth Relig |
|---|---|---|---|---|---|---|---|---|
| **IN YOUR INTERACTIONS WITH UNDERGRADUATES, HOW OFTEN DO YOU ENCOURAGE THEM TO: [2]** | | | | | | | | |
| **Ask questions in class** | | | | | | | | |
| Frequently | 94.6 | 93.9 | 94.2 | 95.1 | 95.0 | 95.2 | 94.7 | 94.8 |
| Occasionally | 5.3 | 5.7 | 5.7 | 4.8 | 5.0 | 4.8 | 5.2 | 5.1 |
| Not at all | 0.2 | 0.4 | 0.1 | 0.1 | 0.1 | 0.0 | 0.1 | 0.1 |
| **Support their opinions with a logical argument** | | | | | | | | |
| Frequently | 82.8 | 81.2 | 82.0 | 83.8 | 84.0 | 84.9 | 85.2 | 82.0 |
| Occasionally | 16.4 | 17.7 | 17.2 | 15.5 | 15.3 | 14.6 | 14.0 | 17.2 |
| Not at all | 0.9 | 1.1 | 0.9 | 0.7 | 0.7 | 0.6 | 0.8 | 0.8 |
| **Seek solutions to problems and explain them to others** | | | | | | | | |
| Frequently | 74.7 | 74.1 | 71.0 | 76.6 | 75.1 | 76.5 | 77.5 | 71.5 |
| Occasionally | 23.6 | 23.9 | 27.2 | 21.9 | 23.5 | 21.9 | 21.1 | 27.2 |
| Not at all | 1.7 | 1.9 | 1.8 | 1.5 | 1.5 | 1.6 | 1.5 | 1.3 |
| **Revise their papers to improve their writing** | | | | | | | | |
| Frequently | 58.8 | 56.0 | 55.7 | 60.0 | 62.6 | 66.1 | 61.0 | 58.7 |
| Occasionally | 32.7 | 32.9 | 34.5 | 33.2 | 30.9 | 28.0 | 32.8 | 34.1 |
| Not at all | 8.5 | 11.1 | 9.8 | 6.8 | 6.4 | 5.9 | 6.2 | 7.2 |
| **Evaluate the quality or reliability of information they receive** | | | | | | | | |
| Frequently | 73.4 | 72.7 | 70.7 | 75.1 | 73.6 | 75.2 | 74.5 | 70.9 |
| Occasionally | 24.6 | 25.1 | 27.0 | 23.3 | 24.4 | 23.2 | 23.1 | 27.0 |
| Not at all | 2.0 | 2.2 | 2.3 | 1.7 | 1.9 | 1.6 | 2.4 | 2.1 |
| **Take risks for potential gains** | | | | | | | | |
| Frequently | 37.4 | 37.0 | 35.3 | 37.6 | 38.6 | 40.7 | 37.7 | 36.0 |
| Occasionally | 48.4 | 48.0 | 48.4 | 48.1 | 49.4 | 48.0 | 50.0 | 51.2 |
| Not at all | 14.2 | 15.0 | 16.3 | 14.3 | 12.0 | 11.3 | 12.3 | 12.8 |
| **Seek alternative solutions to a problem** | | | | | | | | |
| Frequently | 65.1 | 63.7 | 62.8 | 68.0 | 64.7 | 66.6 | 64.4 | 62.0 |
| Occasionally | 32.6 | 34.0 | 34.5 | 30.0 | 33.2 | 31.4 | 33.0 | 35.8 |
| Not at all | 2.2 | 2.3 | 2.7 | 2.0 | 2.2 | 1.9 | 2.6 | 2.2 |
| **Look up scientific research articles and resources** | | | | | | | | |
| Frequently | 55.2 | 57.5 | 54.9 | 56.7 | 50.4 | 52.7 | 51.4 | 46.7 |
| Occasionally | 33.5 | 32.9 | 32.6 | 33.3 | 35.0 | 32.8 | 34.7 | 38.3 |
| Not at all | 11.3 | 9.6 | 12.5 | 9.9 | 14.6 | 14.5 | 13.9 | 15.1 |
| **Explore topics on their own, even though it was not required for a class** | | | | | | | | |
| Frequently | 52.1 | 52.4 | 52.4 | 53.3 | 49.9 | 52.5 | 49.3 | 46.3 |
| Occasionally | 44.1 | 44.0 | 43.8 | 42.8 | 46.1 | 43.6 | 47.6 | 48.7 |
| Not at all | 3.8 | 3.6 | 3.8 | 3.9 | 4.1 | 3.9 | 3.1 | 5.0 |
| **Acknowledge failure as a necessary part of the learning process** | | | | | | | | |
| Frequently | 49.5 | 47.6 | 46.4 | 52.4 | 49.8 | 52.2 | 49.4 | 46.7 |
| Occasionally | 43.7 | 44.7 | 45.8 | 41.4 | 44.3 | 42.0 | 45.2 | 47.1 |
| Not at all | 6.8 | 7.7 | 7.9 | 6.2 | 5.8 | 5.8 | 5.4 | 6.1 |
| **Seek feedback on their academic work** | | | | | | | | |
| Frequently | 73.0 | 70.0 | 70.2 | 75.4 | 75.4 | 76.7 | 75.7 | 73.4 |
| Occasionally | 25.3 | 28.0 | 27.5 | 23.1 | 23.3 | 22.1 | 23.1 | 25.2 |
| Not at all | 1.7 | 2.0 | 2.3 | 1.5 | 1.2 | 1.1 | 1.2 | 1.4 |

[2]  This question asked for the first time in the 2007–2008 Faculty Survey.

| All Respondents | All 4+ yr | Universities | | Four-year Colleges | | | | |
| --- | --- | --- | --- | --- | --- | --- | --- | --- |
| | | Pub | Priv | Pub | All Priv | Nons | Cath | Oth Relig |
| **Methods you use in "all" or "most" of the courses you teach:** | | | | | | | | |
| Multiple-choice exams [2] | 33.1 | 30.5 | 27.3 | 39.0 | 32.1 | 25.4 | 39.2 | 37.6 |
| Essay exams [2] | 44.3 | 41.1 | 46.8 | 42.5 | 49.3 | 48.4 | 50.2 | 50.1 |
| Short-answer exams [2] | 45.5 | 42.9 | 44.5 | 46.3 | 48.3 | 46.1 | 49.4 | 50.7 |
| Quizzes | 39.8 | 37.5 | 37.2 | 42.8 | 40.5 | 36.6 | 42.8 | 44.7 |
| Weekly essay assignments | 21.7 | 21.7 | 20.8 | 20.2 | 24.0 | 26.2 | 22.6 | 21.5 |
| Student presentations | 46.7 | 45.1 | 42.0 | 45.8 | 52.6 | 55.0 | 50.1 | 50.6 |
| Term/research papers | 44.3 | 42.8 | 47.4 | 43.2 | 46.2 | 48.7 | 43.3 | 44.4 |
| Student evaluations of each others' work | 23.5 | 23.2 | 20.6 | 23.8 | 25.3 | 27.0 | 22.8 | 24.3 |
| Grading on a curve | 16.8 | 20.2 | 19.6 | 15.1 | 13.2 | 14.0 | 14.7 | 11.0 |
| Competency-based grading | 53.0 | 52.3 | 52.6 | 54.7 | 51.9 | 52.5 | 50.3 | 52.0 |
| Class discussions | 82.2 | 79.3 | 83.1 | 83.0 | 84.3 | 84.5 | 84.4 | 84.1 |
| Cooperative learning (small groups) | 59.1 | 56.8 | 52.8 | 60.8 | 63.4 | 62.3 | 63.2 | 65.2 |
| Experiential learning/Field studies | 30.0 | 28.7 | 25.4 | 31.7 | 32.0 | 31.7 | 30.1 | 33.6 |
| Teaching assistants | 11.8 | 18.0 | 19.7 | 6.1 | 6.6 | 8.2 | 3.8 | 6.0 |
| Recitals/Demonstrations | 21.9 | 22.4 | 21.8 | 22.1 | 21.0 | 21.3 | 20.2 | 20.9 |
| Group projects | 35.8 | 37.0 | 29.7 | 36.3 | 36.7 | 35.6 | 37.1 | 38.1 |
| Extensive lecturing | 46.4 | 47.9 | 50.3 | 47.9 | 40.5 | 38.8 | 43.1 | 41.4 |
| Multiple drafts of written work | 24.9 | 23.4 | 25.3 | 24.6 | 27.1 | 31.2 | 22.7 | 23.6 |
| Readings on racial and ethnic issues | 23.9 | 22.5 | 22.1 | 24.7 | 25.5 | 28.0 | 24.7 | 22.4 |
| Readings on women and gender issues | 21.1 | 20.7 | 20.5 | 21.6 | 21.4 | 22.6 | 21.8 | 19.5 |
| Student-developed activities (assignments, exams, etc.) | 26.7 | 26.0 | 27.5 | 28.0 | 25.6 | 26.1 | 27.5 | 23.9 |
| Student-selected topics for course content | 17.0 | 16.3 | 15.6 | 18.2 | 17.1 | 17.4 | 17.9 | 16.3 |
| Reflective writing/journaling | 21.7 | 18.2 | 20.8 | 23.2 | 24.6 | 24.0 | 26.0 | 24.5 |
| Community service as part of coursework | 8.1 | 7.2 | 7.2 | 8.9 | 8.8 | 7.9 | 10.0 | 9.4 |
| Electronic quizzes with immediate feedback in class [2] | 6.8 | 6.3 | 6.8 | 8.5 | 5.2 | 4.2 | 6.4 | 5.8 |
| Using real-life problems [2] | 55.7 | 54.4 | 53.6 | 58.5 | 55.1 | 53.4 | 58.3 | 55.5 |
| Using student inquiry to drive learning | 47.1 | 43.9 | 46.3 | 48.9 | 49.3 | 51.3 | 50.8 | 45.6 |

[2] This question asked for the first time in the 2007–2008 Faculty Survey.

| All Respondents | All 4+ yr | Universities Pub | Universities Priv | Four-year Colleges Pub | All Priv | Nons | Cath | Oth Relig |
|---|---|---|---|---|---|---|---|---|
| **YOUR BASE INSTITUTIONAL SALARY** | | | | | | | | |
| **9/10 month contract** | | | | | | | | |
| Less than $20,000 | 2.0 | 1.8 | 2.1 | 2.0 | 2.1 | 2.4 | 2.0 | 1.8 |
| $20,000 to 29,999 | 0.7 | 0.7 | 0.2 | 1.0 | 0.3 | 0.1 | 0.2 | 0.8 |
| $30,000 to 39,999 | 4.8 | 4.6 | 3.3 | 5.3 | 5.0 | 4.7 | 2.5 | 6.9 |
| $40,000 to 49,999 | 14.5 | 9.1 | 7.7 | 17.6 | 21.5 | 16.6 | 24.1 | 26.4 |
| $50,000 to 59,999 | 22.1 | 20.0 | 11.2 | 24.9 | 26.8 | 24.3 | 27.6 | 29.6 |
| $60,000 to 69,999 | 16.8 | 15.9 | 13.0 | 18.7 | 17.2 | 17.5 | 17.0 | 16.9 |
| $70,000 to 79,999 | 12.5 | 13.7 | 13.0 | 12.2 | 10.8 | 11.4 | 12.7 | 9.0 |
| $80,000 to 89,999 | 8.9 | 10.1 | 10.9 | 8.4 | 6.8 | 8.4 | 6.9 | 4.8 |
| $90,000 to 99,999 | 6.8 | 7.7 | 11.7 | 6.1 | 4.2 | 5.4 | 4.5 | 2.5 |
| $100,000 to 124,999 | 8.1 | 11.5 | 19.1 | 3.6 | 4.0 | 6.9 | 2.3 | 1.2 |
| $125,000 to 149,999 | 1.7 | 2.8 | 4.8 | 0.1 | 0.7 | 1.4 | 0.3 | 0.1 |
| $150,000 or more | 1.2 | 2.1 | 2.9 | 0.1 | 0.5 | 1.0 | 0.0 | 0.2 |
| **11/12 month contract** | | | | | | | | |
| Less than $20,000 | 2.6 | 2.6 | 3.1 | 2.7 | 2.3 | 2.3 | 4.5 | 1.2 |
| $20,000 to 29,999 | 0.6 | 0.5 | 0.6 | 0.5 | 0.7 | 0.1 | 0.2 | 2.0 |
| $30,000 to 39,999 | 4.3 | 3.2 | 2.3 | 7.0 | 4.1 | 3.4 | 1.6 | 6.6 |
| $40,000 to 49,999 | 14.1 | 8.1 | 9.1 | 14.7 | 22.1 | 18.1 | 21.9 | 29.0 |
| $50,000 to 59,999 | 18.3 | 12.8 | 16.3 | 21.3 | 22.0 | 19.7 | 25.6 | 24.0 |
| $60,000 to 69,999 | 15.3 | 11.1 | 13.6 | 18.6 | 17.0 | 17.3 | 14.9 | 17.4 |
| $70,000 to 79,999 | 10.0 | 8.3 | 11.4 | 9.8 | 11.1 | 12.3 | 10.5 | 9.3 |
| $80,000 to 89,999 | 10.6 | 14.0 | 10.7 | 9.4 | 8.6 | 9.9 | 10.6 | 5.3 |
| $90,000 to 99,999 | 7.1 | 8.7 | 9.4 | 6.2 | 5.2 | 7.2 | 3.7 | 2.4 |
| $100,000 to 124,999 | 10.9 | 17.4 | 14.6 | 7.9 | 5.5 | 7.7 | 5.1 | 1.9 |
| $125,000 to 149,999 | 3.2 | 5.9 | 5.9 | 1.4 | 0.9 | 1.3 | 0.0 | 0.5 |
| $150,000 or more | 2.9 | 7.5 | 3.1 | 0.6 | 0.7 | 0.7 | 1.4 | 0.4 |
| **Your base institutional salary is based on:** | | | | | | | | |
| 9/10 months | 74.2 | 77.7 | 67.8 | 77.6 | 68.7 | 65.2 | 73.1 | 71.2 |
| 11/12 months | 25.8 | 22.3 | 32.2 | 22.4 | 31.3 | 34.8 | 26.9 | 28.8 |
| **WHAT PERCENTAGE OF YOUR CURRENT YEAR'S SALARY COMES FROM: [2]** | | | | | | | | |
| **Income from this institution** | | | | | | | | |
| All | 63.6 | 62.7 | 59.7 | 65.6 | 64.2 | 63.8 | 67.0 | 63.1 |
| 75 to 99 | 29.4 | 29.5 | 34.2 | 28.4 | 28.1 | 28.1 | 25.5 | 29.7 |
| 50 to 74 | 5.0 | 5.8 | 4.4 | 4.5 | 5.1 | 5.1 | 5.6 | 4.9 |
| 25 to 49 | 1.4 | 1.3 | 1.2 | 1.1 | 2.1 | 2.5 | 1.5 | 1.8 |
| 1 to 24 | 0.3 | 0.4 | 0.4 | 0.2 | 0.4 | 0.5 | 0.2 | 0.4 |
| None | 0.2 | 0.3 | 0.1 | 0.2 | 0.1 | 0.1 | 0.1 | 0.1 |
| **Other academic income** | | | | | | | | |
| All | 0.1 | 0.1 | 0.0 | 0.1 | 0.0 | 0.0 | 0.1 | 0.0 |
| 75 to 99 | 0.1 | 0.2 | 0.0 | 0.0 | 0.1 | 0.1 | 0.1 | 0.1 |
| 50 to 74 | 0.5 | 0.7 | 0.2 | 0.5 | 0.3 | 0.3 | 0.2 | 0.2 |
| 25 to 49 | 1.9 | 2.7 | 1.7 | 1.4 | 1.7 | 2.3 | 1.5 | 1.1 |
| 1 to 24 | 16.0 | 15.7 | 19.4 | 14.6 | 16.2 | 16.5 | 16.2 | 15.8 |
| None | 81.5 | 80.6 | 78.7 | 83.4 | 81.6 | 80.8 | 81.9 | 82.7 |
| **Non-academic income** | | | | | | | | |
| All | 0.2 | 0.3 | 0.1 | 0.1 | 0.1 | 0.1 | 0.1 | 0.1 |
| 75 to 99 | 0.4 | 0.3 | 0.6 | 0.3 | 0.5 | 0.6 | 0.3 | 0.5 |
| 50 to 74 | 1.8 | 1.8 | 1.6 | 1.3 | 2.4 | 2.8 | 1.6 | 2.3 |
| 25 to 49 | 4.4 | 4.2 | 3.6 | 4.5 | 5.1 | 5.0 | 5.5 | 5.0 |
| 1 to 24 | 20.6 | 20.9 | 24.0 | 19.8 | 19.4 | 18.8 | 17.9 | 21.1 |
| None | 72.7 | 72.5 | 70.0 | 74.1 | 72.5 | 72.7 | 74.6 | 71.0 |

[2] This question asked for the first time in the 2007–2008 Faculty Survey.

**2007–2008 FACULTY SURVEY WEIGHTED NATIONAL NORMS**
**Full-time Undergraduate Faculty**

| All Respondents | All 4+ yr | Universities Pub | Universities Priv | Four-year Colleges Pub | Four-year Colleges All Priv | Four-year Colleges Nons | Four-year Colleges Cath | Four-year Colleges Oth Relig |
|---|---|---|---|---|---|---|---|---|
| **What is your age as of 12/31/2007?** | | | | | | | | |
| Less than 30 | 1.6 | 1.1 | 1.6 | 1.7 | 2.2 | 2.3 | 1.1 | 2.5 |
| 30 to 34 | 6.6 | 5.8 | 7.2 | 6.2 | 8.0 | 8.1 | 6.9 | 8.5 |
| 35 to 39 | 12.1 | 11.3 | 11.8 | 12.1 | 13.4 | 14.3 | 10.9 | 13.6 |
| 40 to 44 | 12.3 | 11.3 | 11.3 | 13.0 | 13.3 | 14.0 | 11.5 | 13.2 |
| 45 to 49 | 13.1 | 12.1 | 12.1 | 13.9 | 14.0 | 13.5 | 13.2 | 15.2 |
| 50 to 54 | 15.1 | 14.1 | 14.7 | 16.3 | 15.1 | 14.7 | 15.8 | 15.4 |
| 55 to 59 | 17.2 | 18.8 | 15.9 | 17.9 | 14.7 | 13.8 | 16.0 | 15.2 |
| 60 to 64 | 12.8 | 13.8 | 13.8 | 12.2 | 11.8 | 11.6 | 13.6 | 10.9 |
| 65 to 69 | 6.9 | 8.8 | 8.5 | 5.2 | 5.6 | 5.7 | 8.2 | 3.8 |
| 70 or more | 2.3 | 2.9 | 3.0 | 1.6 | 2.0 | 2.0 | 2.7 | 1.6 |
| **Year of highest degree now held** | | | | | | | | |
| Before 1970 | 5.7 | 9.1 | 7.5 | 3.0 | 3.7 | 4.4 | 4.1 | 2.4 |
| 1971 to 1975 | 7.3 | 8.3 | 10.8 | 6.0 | 5.7 | 5.6 | 6.7 | 5.3 |
| 1976 to 1980 | 9.8 | 11.6 | 10.7 | 9.0 | 8.1 | 8.5 | 8.0 | 7.5 |
| 1981 to 1985 | 10.7 | 11.3 | 12.1 | 9.9 | 10.0 | 10.4 | 11.2 | 8.7 |
| 1986 to 1990 | 12.5 | 12.3 | 12.1 | 12.6 | 12.7 | 12.1 | 13.7 | 12.9 |
| 1991 to 1995 | 13.9 | 12.5 | 12.4 | 15.0 | 14.9 | 14.7 | 13.2 | 16.4 |
| 1996 to 2000 | 16.6 | 15.5 | 13.5 | 18.3 | 17.5 | 17.4 | 17.0 | 17.9 |
| 2001 to 2005 | 18.0 | 15.3 | 15.4 | 19.8 | 20.6 | 20.8 | 19.0 | 21.2 |
| 2006 to 2007 | 5.7 | 4.2 | 5.6 | 6.3 | 6.8 | 6.1 | 7.0 | 7.7 |
| **Year of appointment at current position** | | | | | | | | |
| Before 1970 | 3.3 | 4.5 | 4.7 | 2.0 | 2.5 | 2.6 | 3.1 | 2.0 |
| 1971 to 1975 | 3.6 | 4.4 | 4.9 | 3.1 | 2.6 | 2.6 | 3.5 | 2.1 |
| 1976 to 1980 | 6.0 | 7.7 | 7.6 | 4.6 | 4.7 | 5.1 | 4.4 | 4.2 |
| 1981 to 1985 | 7.6 | 8.8 | 8.2 | 6.4 | 7.1 | 7.7 | 7.5 | 5.9 |
| 1986 to 1990 | 11.1 | 11.4 | 12.3 | 10.9 | 10.5 | 10.8 | 11.4 | 9.6 |
| 1991 to 1995 | 11.4 | 11.6 | 10.5 | 11.8 | 11.1 | 11.1 | 9.9 | 11.7 |
| 1996 to 2000 | 16.8 | 15.7 | 14.8 | 18.1 | 17.6 | 18.1 | 15.9 | 17.7 |
| 2001 to 2005 | 27.5 | 25.5 | 23.1 | 29.6 | 29.8 | 28.9 | 30.8 | 30.4 |
| 2006 to 2007 | 12.7 | 10.4 | 13.7 | 13.5 | 14.2 | 13.0 | 13.3 | 16.4 |
| **If tenured, year tenure was awarded** | | | | | | | | |
| Before 1970 | 1.2 | 1.3 | 1.9 | 0.6 | 1.2 | 1.3 | 1.6 | 0.8 |
| 1971 to 1975 | 4.0 | 5.8 | 5.1 | 2.5 | 2.3 | 2.4 | 2.8 | 1.7 |
| 1976 to 1980 | 6.2 | 7.2 | 8.4 | 5.0 | 5.0 | 5.4 | 6.1 | 3.6 |
| 1981 to 1985 | 9.5 | 12.5 | 11.0 | 7.0 | 7.1 | 7.5 | 6.7 | 6.7 |
| 1986 to 1990 | 12.1 | 12.7 | 15.0 | 10.6 | 11.5 | 13.1 | 9.8 | 10.2 |
| 1991 to 1995 | 16.0 | 16.0 | 17.9 | 15.3 | 15.9 | 16.0 | 16.6 | 15.4 |
| 1996 to 2000 | 17.0 | 16.4 | 16.5 | 17.9 | 17.2 | 17.3 | 18.3 | 16.3 |
| 2001 to 2005 | 20.0 | 16.6 | 16.6 | 24.0 | 22.1 | 20.7 | 20.2 | 25.5 |
| 2006 to 2007 | 13.9 | 11.3 | 7.6 | 17.2 | 17.7 | 16.3 | 17.8 | 19.8 |

47

**2007–2008 FACULTY SURVEY WEIGHTED NATIONAL NORMS**
**Full-time Undergraduate Faculty**

| All Respondents | All 4+ yr | Universities Pub | Priv | Four-year Colleges Pub | All Priv | Nons | Cath | Oth Relig |
|---|---|---|---|---|---|---|---|---|
| **WHAT IS THE MAJOR OF THE HIGHEST DEGREE YOU HOLD?** | | | | | | | | |
| **Biological Science** | | | | | | | | |
| Agriculture | 0.9 | 1.9 | 0.4 | 0.6 | 0.2 | 0.1 | 0.1 | 0.3 |
| Forestry | 0.2 | 0.5 | 0.0 | 0.1 | 0.1 | 0.1 | 0.1 | 0.0 |
| Bacteriology, Molecular Biology | 0.9 | 0.9 | 1.0 | 0.9 | 0.9 | 0.8 | 0.7 | 1.0 |
| Biochemistry | 0.8 | 1.0 | 1.3 | 0.5 | 0.8 | 0.8 | 0.9 | 0.8 |
| Biophysics | 0.1 | 0.0 | 0.1 | 0.1 | 0.1 | 0.1 | 0.2 | 0.0 |
| Botany | 0.6 | 0.6 | 0.6 | 0.8 | 0.5 | 0.5 | 0.4 | 0.5 |
| Environmental Science | 0.5 | 0.5 | 0.4 | 0.5 | 0.4 | 0.4 | 0.5 | 0.4 |
| Marine (life) Sciences | 0.2 | 0.1 | 0.1 | 0.3 | 0.2 | 0.3 | 0.3 | 0.0 |
| Physiology, Anatomy | 0.7 | 0.6 | 1.0 | 0.5 | 0.9 | 1.1 | 0.5 | 0.9 |
| Zoology | 1.1 | 1.1 | 0.8 | 1.1 | 1.1 | 1.0 | 1.1 | 1.3 |
| General, Other Biological Sciences | 1.9 | 2.0 | 2.1 | 1.4 | 2.1 | 2.5 | 1.4 | 1.8 |
| **Business** | | | | | | | | |
| Accounting | 1.0 | 0.9 | 1.1 | 1.3 | 0.8 | 0.6 | 1.4 | 0.9 |
| Finance | 0.7 | 0.8 | 0.7 | 0.7 | 0.5 | 0.4 | 0.5 | 0.6 |
| International Business | 0.1 | 0.0 | 0.2 | 0.1 | 0.1 | 0.0 | 0.3 | 0.2 |
| Management | 2.2 | 2.1 | 1.4 | 2.6 | 2.3 | 2.1 | 2.6 | 2.6 |
| Marketing | 0.8 | 0.8 | 0.7 | 0.9 | 0.8 | 0.5 | 1.6 | 0.9 |
| Secretarial Studies | 0.0 | 0.0 | 0.0 | 0.0 | 0.0 | 0.0 | 0.0 | 0.0 |
| General, Other Business | 1.2 | 1.3 | 0.8 | 1.0 | 1.3 | 1.2 | 1.8 | 1.3 |
| **Education** | | | | | | | | |
| Business Education | 0.2 | 0.3 | 0.1 | 0.3 | 0.1 | 0.1 | 0.1 | 0.1 |
| Educational Administration | 1.2 | 0.9 | 0.9 | 1.3 | 1.8 | 0.8 | 2.8 | 2.6 |
| Educational Psychology/Counseling | 1.0 | 0.8 | 0.9 | 1.3 | 0.8 | 0.6 | 1.1 | 0.8 |
| Elementary Education | 0.9 | 0.8 | 0.3 | 1.3 | 0.7 | 0.4 | 1.1 | 0.8 |
| Higher Education | 1.5 | 1.4 | 0.8 | 1.5 | 1.9 | 2.1 | 2.0 | 1.5 |
| Music or Art Education | 0.3 | 0.1 | 0.2 | 0.4 | 0.3 | 0.3 | 0.2 | 0.5 |
| Physical or Health Education | 1.5 | 0.8 | 0.5 | 2.4 | 1.6 | 1.3 | 0.9 | 2.6 |
| Secondary Education | 0.8 | 0.9 | 0.3 | 1.3 | 0.5 | 0.5 | 0.4 | 0.7 |
| Special Education | 0.9 | 0.9 | 0.2 | 1.1 | 1.1 | 1.0 | 1.1 | 1.1 |
| General, Other Education Fields | 2.9 | 2.2 | 1.9 | 3.9 | 3.0 | 2.4 | 3.6 | 3.5 |
| **Engineering** | | | | | | | | |
| Aero-/Astronautical Engineering | 0.2 | 0.5 | 0.2 | 0.0 | 0.1 | 0.0 | 0.0 | 0.2 |
| Chemical Engineering | 0.3 | 0.6 | 0.7 | 0.0 | 0.1 | 0.1 | 0.1 | 0.1 |
| Civil Engineering | 0.7 | 1.4 | 1.2 | 0.3 | 0.2 | 0.2 | 0.2 | 0.1 |
| Electrical Engineering | 0.9 | 1.4 | 1.3 | 0.6 | 0.3 | 0.3 | 0.4 | 0.3 |
| Industrial Engineering | 0.2 | 0.3 | 0.1 | 0.3 | 0.1 | 0.1 | 0.1 | 0.1 |
| Mechanical Engineering | 1.0 | 1.6 | 1.3 | 0.8 | 0.3 | 0.3 | 0.4 | 0.2 |
| General, Other Engineering Fields | 1.0 | 1.9 | 0.9 | 0.6 | 0.3 | 0.5 | 0.1 | 0.2 |
| **Health** | | | | | | | | |
| Dentistry | 0.3 | 0.7 | 0.2 | 0.1 | 0.1 | 0.0 | 0.5 | 0.0 |
| Health Technology | 0.0 | 0.0 | 0.0 | 0.1 | 0.0 | 0.0 | 0.0 | 0.0 |
| Medicine or Surgery | 0.2 | 0.4 | 0.3 | 0.0 | 0.1 | 0.1 | 0.1 | 0.1 |
| Nursing | 3.1 | 2.6 | 2.5 | 3.6 | 3.3 | 1.8 | 6.7 | 3.4 |
| Pharmacy, Pharmacology | 0.8 | 1.0 | 1.0 | 0.2 | 1.0 | 1.9 | 0.2 | 0.4 |
| Therapy (speech, physical, occup.) | 0.6 | 0.7 | 0.5 | 0.7 | 0.3 | 0.2 | 0.9 | 0.3 |
| Veterinary Medicine | 0.1 | 0.2 | 0.0 | 0.0 | 0.1 | 0.2 | 0.0 | 0.0 |
| General, Other Health Fields | 0.9 | 0.9 | 0.7 | 1.0 | 0.8 | 0.8 | 1.0 | 0.8 |

48

**2007–2008 FACULTY SURVEY WEIGHTED NATIONAL NORMS**
**Full-time Undergraduate Faculty**

| All Respondents | All 4+ yr | Universities Pub | Priv | Four-year Colleges Pub | All Priv | Nons | Cath | Oth Relig |
|---|---|---|---|---|---|---|---|---|
| **WHAT IS THE MAJOR OF THE HIGHEST DEGREE YOU HOLD?** | | | | | | | | |
| **Humanities** | | | | | | | | |
| History | 4.1 | 3.8 | 4.6 | 4.0 | 4.4 | 4.6 | 4.2 | 4.1 |
| Political Science, Government | 2.4 | 2.1 | 3.4 | 2.4 | 2.4 | 2.8 | 2.0 | 2.0 |
| English Language & Literature | 6.8 | 6.2 | 6.0 | 7.0 | 7.8 | 8.8 | 6.9 | 6.9 |
| Foreign Languages & Literature | 1.2 | 1.1 | 2.0 | 0.7 | 1.7 | 2.0 | 0.9 | 1.6 |
| French | 0.7 | 0.9 | 0.6 | 0.5 | 0.6 | 0.8 | 0.3 | 0.6 |
| German | 0.4 | 0.5 | 0.6 | 0.3 | 0.4 | 0.6 | 0.1 | 0.3 |
| Spanish | 1.1 | 1.0 | 1.1 | 1.0 | 1.4 | 1.2 | 1.0 | 1.8 |
| Other Foreign Languages | 0.4 | 0.6 | 0.7 | 0.2 | 0.4 | 0.5 | 0.2 | 0.2 |
| Linguistics | 0.8 | 1.0 | 0.7 | 0.6 | 0.7 | 1.2 | 0.1 | 0.4 |
| Philosophy | 2.0 | 1.5 | 3.2 | 1.6 | 2.3 | 1.7 | 4.2 | 1.9 |
| Religion or Theology | 1.9 | 0.4 | 4.1 | 0.5 | 4.6 | 3.5 | 5.1 | 5.7 |
| General, Other Humanities Fields | 1.3 | 1.4 | 1.6 | 1.0 | 1.2 | 1.3 | 1.0 | 1.1 |
| **Fine Arts** | | | | | | | | |
| Architecture/Urban Planning | 0.6 | 1.2 | 0.5 | 0.3 | 0.1 | 0.2 | 0.2 | 0.1 |
| Art | 1.9 | 1.2 | 1.9 | 2.0 | 2.5 | 3.3 | 1.2 | 2.1 |
| Dramatics or Speech | 1.6 | 1.1 | 1.4 | 2.0 | 2.0 | 2.2 | 1.8 | 1.9 |
| Music | 3.1 | 2.7 | 2.3 | 3.1 | 3.9 | 3.4 | 2.4 | 5.6 |
| Television or Film | 0.4 | 0.3 | 0.4 | 0.4 | 0.4 | 0.6 | 0.2 | 0.2 |
| Other Fine Arts | 1.1 | 1.0 | 1.9 | 1.1 | 1.0 | 1.3 | 0.6 | 0.8 |
| **Physical Science** | | | | | | | | |
| Mathematics and/or Statistics | 4.8 | 4.7 | 4.5 | 5.2 | 4.5 | 4.6 | 5.1 | 4.0 |
| Astronomy | 0.2 | 0.3 | 0.3 | 0.1 | 0.2 | 0.3 | 0.1 | 0.2 |
| Atmospheric Sciences | 0.2 | 0.3 | 0.0 | 0.2 | 0.0 | 0.0 | 0.0 | 0.1 |
| Chemistry | 3.3 | 3.6 | 3.1 | 3.2 | 3.3 | 3.1 | 4.1 | 3.3 |
| Earth Sciences | 1.0 | 1.4 | 0.6 | 1.1 | 0.6 | 1.0 | 0.4 | 0.3 |
| Geography | 0.7 | 1.0 | 0.3 | 1.0 | 0.2 | 0.2 | 0.2 | 0.2 |
| Marine Sciences (incl. Oceanography) | 0.1 | 0.1 | 0.1 | 0.1 | 0.0 | 0.1 | 0.0 | 0.0 |
| Physics | 2.1 | 2.2 | 2.8 | 1.8 | 1.9 | 2.4 | 1.6 | 1.4 |
| General, Other Physical Sciences | 0.1 | 0.1 | 0.0 | 0.1 | 0.1 | 0.1 | 0.2 | 0.0 |
| **Social Science** | | | | | | | | |
| Anthropology | 1.1 | 1.6 | 1.1 | 0.9 | 0.7 | 1.1 | 0.2 | 0.5 |
| Archaeology | 0.1 | 0.1 | 0.1 | 0.1 | 0.1 | 0.1 | 0.0 | 0.1 |
| Clinical Psychology | 1.1 | 1.1 | 1.3 | 1.0 | 1.1 | 0.9 | 1.6 | 1.3 |
| Counseling and Guidance | 0.3 | 0.0 | 0.2 | 0.6 | 0.5 | 0.2 | 0.8 | 0.5 |
| Experimental Psychology | 1.3 | 1.0 | 1.8 | 1.4 | 1.2 | 1.3 | 1.2 | 1.1 |
| Social Psychology | 0.9 | 0.7 | 0.8 | 1.2 | 0.8 | 0.8 | 0.8 | 0.8 |
| General, Other Psychology | 1.3 | 1.1 | 1.0 | 1.4 | 1.7 | 2.1 | 1.4 | 1.3 |
| Economics | 2.4 | 2.3 | 3.6 | 2.0 | 2.3 | 2.6 | 2.1 | 2.0 |
| Sociology | 2.4 | 2.6 | 3.1 | 2.5 | 1.8 | 1.6 | 1.8 | 1.9 |
| Social Work, Social Welfare | 0.7 | 0.5 | 0.4 | 1.0 | 0.9 | 1.0 | 0.6 | 1.0 |
| General, Other Social Sciences | 1.4 | 1.7 | 1.4 | 1.3 | 1.0 | 1.5 | 0.5 | 0.8 |

49

## 2007–2008 FACULTY SURVEY WEIGHTED NATIONAL NORMS
### Full-time Undergraduate Faculty

| All Respondents | All 4+ yr | Universities Pub | Priv | Four-year Colleges Pub | All Priv | Nons | Cath | Oth Relig |
|---|---|---|---|---|---|---|---|---|
| **WHAT IS THE MAJOR OF THE HIGHEST DEGREE YOU HOLD?** | | | | | | | | |
| **Technical** | | | | | | | | |
| Computer Science | 1.7 | 1.8 | 1.6 | 1.6 | 1.7 | 1.8 | 1.9 | 1.5 |
| Data Processing, Computer Prog. | 0.0 | 0.0 | 0.0 | 0.1 | 0.1 | 0.0 | 0.0 | 0.1 |
| Drafting/Design | 0.0 | 0.0 | 0.1 | 0.0 | 0.0 | 0.0 | 0.0 | 0.0 |
| Electronics | 0.0 | 0.1 | 0.0 | 0.0 | 0.0 | 0.0 | 0.0 | 0.0 |
| Industrial Arts | 0.1 | 0.1 | 0.0 | 0.2 | 0.0 | 0.0 | 0.0 | 0.0 |
| Mechanics | 0.0 | 0.0 | 0.0 | 0.0 | 0.0 | 0.0 | 0.0 | 0.0 |
| Other Technical | 0.2 | 0.2 | 0.4 | 0.3 | 0.1 | 0.1 | 0.3 | 0.0 |
| **Other Fields** | | | | | | | | |
| Building Trades | 0.0 | 0.0 | 0.0 | 0.0 | 0.0 | 0.0 | 0.0 | 0.0 |
| Communications | 2.1 | 1.8 | 1.7 | 2.3 | 2.3 | 2.1 | 2.0 | 2.7 |
| Ethnic Studies | 0.0 | 0.0 | 0.0 | 0.0 | 0.0 | 0.0 | 0.0 | 0.0 |
| Human Ecology/Family Science | 0.4 | 0.7 | 0.2 | 0.4 | 0.2 | 0.2 | 0.2 | 0.2 |
| Journalism | 0.5 | 0.7 | 0.5 | 0.5 | 0.3 | 0.2 | 0.1 | 0.6 |
| Law | 0.8 | 0.5 | 1.1 | 1.0 | 0.8 | 0.7 | 1.1 | 0.8 |
| Law Enforcement | 0.1 | 0.0 | 0.1 | 0.3 | 0.0 | 0.1 | 0.1 | 0.0 |
| Library Science | 0.5 | 0.2 | 0.5 | 0.6 | 0.7 | 0.6 | 0.3 | 1.1 |
| Women's Studies | 0.0 | 0.0 | 0.0 | 0.0 | 0.0 | 0.0 | 0.0 | 0.1 |
| Other Vocational | 0.0 | 0.1 | 0.0 | 0.0 | 0.0 | 0.0 | 0.0 | 0.0 |
| All Other Fields | 0.8 | 0.7 | 0.5 | 1.0 | 0.7 | 0.7 | 0.8 | 0.6 |

50

## 2007–2008 FACULTY SURVEY WEIGHTED NATIONAL NORMS
### Full-time Undergraduate Faculty

| All Respondents | All 4+ yr | Universities Pub | Priv | Four-year Colleges Pub | All Priv | Nons | Cath | Oth Relig |
|---|---|---|---|---|---|---|---|---|
| **WHAT IS THE DEPARTMENT OF YOUR CURRENT FACULTY APPOINTMENT?** | | | | | | | | |
| **Biological Science** | | | | | | | | |
| Agriculture | 1.0 | 2.3 | 0.1 | 0.6 | 0.1 | 0.1 | 0.0 | 0.1 |
| Forestry | 0.1 | 0.2 | 0.0 | 0.0 | 0.0 | 0.0 | 0.0 | 0.0 |
| Bacteriology, Molecular Biology | 0.3 | 0.4 | 0.5 | 0.2 | 0.1 | 0.2 | 0.1 | 0.0 |
| Biochemistry | 0.2 | 0.4 | 0.2 | 0.1 | 0.1 | 0.2 | 0.1 | 0.1 |
| Biophysics | 0.0 | 0.1 | 0.0 | 0.0 | 0.0 | 0.0 | 0.0 | 0.0 |
| Botany | 0.2 | 0.5 | 0.2 | 0.1 | 0.0 | 0.0 | 0.0 | 0.0 |
| Environmental Science | 0.6 | 0.6 | 0.3 | 0.6 | 0.6 | 0.8 | 0.1 | 0.4 |
| Marine (life) Sciences | 0.1 | 0.0 | 0.0 | 0.2 | 0.0 | 0.0 | 0.0 | 0.0 |
| Physiology, Anatomy | 0.3 | 0.3 | 0.5 | 0.2 | 0.3 | 0.2 | 0.3 | 0.3 |
| Zoology | 0.4 | 1.0 | 0.2 | 0.1 | 0.1 | 0.1 | 0.1 | 0.0 |
| General, Other Biological Sciences | 4.5 | 3.3 | 4.9 | 4.7 | 5.5 | 6.0 | 4.7 | 5.4 |
| **Business** | | | | | | | | |
| Accounting | 1.3 | 0.9 | 1.3 | 1.8 | 1.3 | 0.9 | 2.0 | 1.5 |
| Finance | 0.7 | 0.9 | 0.9 | 0.7 | 0.4 | 0.4 | 0.8 | 0.3 |
| International Business | 0.1 | 0.0 | 0.1 | 0.1 | 0.4 | 0.3 | 0.9 | 0.2 |
| Management | 2.4 | 2.4 | 1.8 | 2.6 | 2.3 | 1.7 | 3.1 | 2.6 |
| Marketing | 1.1 | 1.3 | 0.8 | 1.2 | 0.9 | 0.8 | 1.8 | 0.5 |
| Secretarial Studies | 0.0 | 0.0 | 0.0 | 0.0 | 0.0 | 0.0 | 0.0 | 0.0 |
| General, Other Business | 1.7 | 1.2 | 1.2 | 1.6 | 2.5 | 1.9 | 2.6 | 3.4 |
| **Education** | | | | | | | | |
| Business Education | 0.0 | 0.1 | 0.0 | 0.0 | 0.1 | 0.0 | 0.0 | 0.1 |
| Educational Administration | 0.2 | 0.1 | 0.1 | 0.2 | 0.3 | 0.1 | 0.6 | 0.3 |
| Educational Psychology/Counseling | 0.4 | 0.6 | 0.2 | 0.4 | 0.1 | 0.0 | 0.2 | 0.1 |
| Elementary Education | 1.7 | 1.2 | 0.5 | 2.2 | 2.3 | 2.4 | 2.6 | 2.0 |
| Higher Education | 0.5 | 0.6 | 0.1 | 0.3 | 0.8 | 1.0 | 0.5 | 0.6 |
| Music or Art Education | 0.1 | 0.0 | 0.1 | 0.2 | 0.1 | 0.0 | 0.0 | 0.2 |
| Physical or Health Education | 2.0 | 1.5 | 0.6 | 2.9 | 2.1 | 1.9 | 0.8 | 3.1 |
| Secondary Education | 0.8 | 0.8 | 0.3 | 1.1 | 0.6 | 0.5 | 0.8 | 0.8 |
| Special Education | 0.5 | 0.3 | 0.3 | 1.0 | 0.4 | 0.2 | 0.7 | 0.6 |
| General, Other Education Fields | 2.0 | 1.5 | 0.9 | 2.5 | 2.5 | 2.0 | 3.3 | 2.7 |
| **Engineering** | | | | | | | | |
| Aero-/Astronautical Engineering | 0.2 | 0.6 | 0.0 | 0.0 | 0.0 | 0.0 | 0.0 | 0.0 |
| Chemical Engineering | 0.3 | 0.6 | 0.6 | 0.0 | 0.1 | 0.1 | 0.1 | 0.0 |
| Civil Engineering | 0.7 | 1.4 | 1.4 | 0.2 | 0.1 | 0.1 | 0.2 | 0.1 |
| Electrical Engineering | 0.8 | 1.4 | 1.3 | 0.3 | 0.2 | 0.2 | 0.4 | 0.2 |
| Industrial Engineering | 0.1 | 0.2 | 0.0 | 0.1 | 0.0 | 0.1 | 0.0 | 0.1 |
| Mechanical Engineering | 1.0 | 1.8 | 1.5 | 0.6 | 0.2 | 0.3 | 0.4 | 0.1 |
| General, Other Engineering Fields | 1.0 | 1.7 | 1.3 | 0.8 | 0.4 | 0.5 | 0.0 | 0.6 |
| **Health** | | | | | | | | |
| Dentistry | 0.3 | 0.7 | 0.2 | 0.1 | 0.2 | 0.2 | 0.8 | 0.0 |
| Health Technology | 0.1 | 0.1 | 0.0 | 0.1 | 0.0 | 0.0 | 0.2 | 0.0 |
| Medicine or Surgery | 0.3 | 0.8 | 0.2 | 0.0 | 0.1 | 0.1 | 0.0 | 0.1 |
| Nursing | 3.7 | 3.1 | 3.1 | 4.0 | 4.3 | 3.1 | 7.6 | 4.1 |
| Pharmacy, Pharmacology | 0.8 | 1.0 | 1.1 | 0.2 | 1.0 | 1.8 | 0.0 | 0.5 |
| Therapy (speech, physical, occup.) | 0.8 | 1.0 | 0.8 | 0.8 | 0.5 | 0.2 | 0.9 | 0.6 |
| Veterinary Medicine | 0.0 | 0.1 | 0.0 | 0.0 | 0.0 | 0.0 | 0.0 | 0.0 |
| General, Other Health Fields | 1.3 | 1.4 | 0.8 | 1.9 | 0.6 | 0.4 | 0.9 | 0.8 |

51

| All Respondents | All 4+ yr | Universities Pub | Priv | Four-year Colleges Pub | All Priv | Nons | Cath | Oth Relig |
|---|---|---|---|---|---|---|---|---|
| **WHAT IS THE DEPARTMENT OF YOUR CURRENT FACULTY APPOINTMENT?** | | | | | | | | |
| **Humanities** | | | | | | | | |
| History | 3.6 | 3.3 | 4.0 | 3.5 | 3.8 | 3.6 | 4.2 | 4.0 |
| Political Science, Government | 2.3 | 2.1 | 3.3 | 2.2 | 2.2 | 2.3 | 1.8 | 2.3 |
| English Language & Literature | 7.5 | 7.1 | 7.4 | 7.4 | 8.1 | 8.3 | 7.6 | 8.1 |
| Foreign Languages & Literature | 2.6 | 2.7 | 3.7 | 2.1 | 2.6 | 2.5 | 1.8 | 3.1 |
| French | 0.2 | 0.3 | 0.2 | 0.1 | 0.3 | 0.5 | 0.1 | 0.3 |
| German | 0.2 | 0.3 | 0.4 | 0.1 | 0.2 | 0.4 | 0.0 | 0.1 |
| Spanish | 0.7 | 0.8 | 0.8 | 0.4 | 1.1 | 1.3 | 0.5 | 1.2 |
| Other Foreign Languages | 0.4 | 0.7 | 0.7 | 0.1 | 0.3 | 0.4 | 0.1 | 0.4 |
| Linguistics | 0.2 | 0.4 | 0.2 | 0.1 | 0.1 | 0.1 | 0.0 | 0.0 |
| Philosophy | 1.8 | 1.4 | 2.7 | 1.6 | 2.1 | 1.4 | 4.1 | 1.8 |
| Religion or Theology | 1.9 | 0.5 | 4.8 | 0.3 | 4.3 | 2.9 | 5.5 | 5.5 |
| General, Other Humanities Fields | 1.6 | 1.3 | 1.8 | 1.3 | 2.2 | 3.7 | 0.7 | 1.0 |
| **Fine Arts** | | | | | | | | |
| Architecture/Urban Planning | 0.7 | 1.6 | 0.4 | 0.1 | 0.2 | 0.4 | 0.3 | 0.0 |
| Art | 2.3 | 1.6 | 2.3 | 2.6 | 2.9 | 3.8 | 1.4 | 2.6 |
| Dramatics or Speech | 1.6 | 0.9 | 1.3 | 2.0 | 2.0 | 2.3 | 1.3 | 2.0 |
| Music | 3.2 | 2.8 | 2.4 | 3.3 | 4.0 | 3.5 | 2.2 | 5.8 |
| Television or Film | 0.4 | 0.3 | 0.5 | 0.5 | 0.2 | 0.4 | 0.0 | 0.1 |
| Other Fine Arts | 0.8 | 0.8 | 0.9 | 0.8 | 0.6 | 0.8 | 0.5 | 0.3 |
| **Physical Science** | | | | | | | | |
| Mathematics and/or Statistics | 4.9 | 4.4 | 4.6 | 5.7 | 4.8 | 4.5 | 5.1 | 5.0 |
| Astronomy | 0.1 | 0.2 | 0.0 | 0.0 | 0.1 | 0.1 | 0.1 | 0.1 |
| Atmospheric Sciences | 0.1 | 0.2 | 0.0 | 0.0 | 0.0 | 0.0 | 0.0 | 0.0 |
| Chemistry | 3.4 | 3.5 | 3.3 | 3.2 | 3.7 | 3.6 | 4.3 | 3.6 |
| Earth Sciences | 1.0 | 1.4 | 0.6 | 1.1 | 0.6 | 0.9 | 0.1 | 0.3 |
| Geography | 0.7 | 1.0 | 0.3 | 1.0 | 0.1 | 0.1 | 0.2 | 0.1 |
| Marine Sciences (incl. Oceanography) | 0.1 | 0.1 | 0.0 | 0.1 | 0.0 | 0.0 | 0.0 | 0.0 |
| Physics | 2.1 | 2.0 | 2.9 | 2.0 | 1.8 | 2.1 | 1.4 | 1.6 |
| General, Other Physical Sciences | 0.4 | 0.2 | 0.1 | 0.5 | 0.5 | 0.6 | 0.5 | 0.4 |
| **Social Science** | | | | | | | | |
| Anthropology | 0.8 | 1.4 | 0.8 | 0.6 | 0.5 | 0.7 | 0.1 | 0.3 |
| Archaeology | 0.0 | 0.0 | 0.0 | 0.0 | 0.0 | 0.0 | 0.0 | 0.0 |
| Clinical Psychology | 0.6 | 1.0 | 0.8 | 0.3 | 0.2 | 0.1 | 0.5 | 0.3 |
| Counseling and Guidance | 0.1 | 0.0 | 0.2 | 0.2 | 0.2 | 0.1 | 0.3 | 0.2 |
| Experimental Psychology | 0.8 | 0.5 | 1.1 | 1.1 | 0.6 | 0.8 | 0.4 | 0.5 |
| Social Psychology | 0.3 | 0.2 | 0.2 | 0.4 | 0.2 | 0.1 | 0.3 | 0.2 |
| General, Other Psychology | 2.5 | 1.1 | 2.1 | 3.1 | 3.9 | 4.2 | 3.6 | 3.6 |
| Economics | 1.9 | 2.0 | 3.0 | 1.5 | 1.8 | 2.5 | 1.5 | 1.1 |
| Sociology | 2.2 | 2.2 | 2.9 | 2.2 | 2.0 | 2.0 | 2.1 | 2.0 |
| Social Work, Social Welfare | 0.8 | 0.5 | 0.3 | 1.2 | 0.8 | 0.8 | 0.7 | 1.0 |
| General, Other Social Sciences | 2.1 | 2.1 | 1.9 | 2.3 | 1.9 | 2.8 | 1.4 | 1.0 |

## 2007–2008 FACULTY SURVEY WEIGHTED NATIONAL NORMS
### Full-time Undergraduate Faculty

| | | | | Four-year Colleges | | | | |
|---|---|---|---|---|---|---|---|---|
| | **All** | **Universities** | | | **All** | | | **Oth** |
| **All Respondents** | **4+ yr** | **Pub** | **Priv** | **Pub** | **Priv** | **Nons** | **Cath** | **Relig** |
| **WHAT IS THE DEPARTMENT OF YOUR CURRENT FACULTY APPOINTMENT?** | | | | | | | | |
| **Technical** | | | | | | | | |
| Computer Science | 1.9 | 2.0 | 1.5 | 2.0 | 1.9 | 1.9 | 2.3 | 1.7 |
| Data Processing, Computer Prog. | 0.1 | 0.1 | 0.1 | 0.1 | 0.1 | 0.1 | 0.0 | 0.1 |
| Drafting/Design | 0.1 | 0.1 | 0.1 | 0.1 | 0.0 | 0.0 | 0.0 | 0.0 |
| Electronics | 0.1 | 0.2 | 0.0 | 0.1 | 0.0 | 0.0 | 0.0 | 0.0 |
| Industrial Arts | 0.1 | 0.1 | 0.1 | 0.2 | 0.0 | 0.0 | 0.0 | 0.0 |
| Mechanics | 0.0 | 0.0 | 0.0 | 0.0 | 0.0 | 0.0 | 0.0 | 0.0 |
| Other Technical | 0.5 | 0.6 | 0.3 | 0.9 | 0.2 | 0.1 | 0.4 | 0.1 |
| **Other Fields** | | | | | | | | |
| Building Trades | 0.0 | 0.0 | 0.1 | 0.0 | 0.0 | 0.0 | 0.0 | 0.0 |
| Communications | 2.5 | 1.8 | 2.7 | 2.8 | 2.9 | 2.1 | 3.2 | 3.7 |
| Ethnic Studies | 0.2 | 0.3 | 0.0 | 0.4 | 0.1 | 0.1 | 0.0 | 0.0 |
| Human Ecology/Family Science | 0.4 | 0.8 | 0.3 | 0.3 | 0.2 | 0.1 | 0.2 | 0.3 |
| Journalism | 0.6 | 1.0 | 0.6 | 0.6 | 0.1 | 0.1 | 0.0 | 0.1 |
| Law | 0.2 | 0.1 | 0.8 | 0.1 | 0.2 | 0.1 | 0.4 | 0.0 |
| Law Enforcement | 0.2 | 0.0 | 0.1 | 0.4 | 0.1 | 0.0 | 0.2 | 0.1 |
| Library Science | 0.5 | 0.2 | 0.6 | 0.6 | 0.6 | 0.3 | 0.4 | 1.0 |
| Women's Studies | 0.1 | 0.2 | 0.1 | 0.1 | 0.1 | 0.2 | 0.0 | 0.0 |
| Other Vocational | 0.1 | 0.2 | 0.1 | 0.1 | 0.1 | 0.1 | 0.0 | 0.0 |
| All Other Fields | 1.4 | 1.3 | 1.0 | 1.7 | 1.1 | 1.5 | 0.6 | 0.7 |
| **HOW MANY CHILDREN DO YOU HAVE IN THE FOLLOWING AGE RANGES?** | | | | | | | | |
| **Under 18 years old** | | | | | | | | |
| None | 62.5 | 63.7 | 61.5 | 63.7 | 60.0 | 60.2 | 63.5 | 57.7 |
| One | 16.4 | 15.4 | 15.7 | 16.6 | 17.6 | 17.7 | 16.2 | 18.4 |
| Two | 15.1 | 15.4 | 13.9 | 14.5 | 16.2 | 16.8 | 14.1 | 16.6 |
| Three | 4.3 | 3.8 | 4.9 | 4.0 | 4.9 | 4.5 | 4.2 | 5.9 |
| Four or more | 1.7 | 1.6 | 4.0 | 1.2 | 1.2 | 0.9 | 2.0 | 1.3 |
| **18 years or older** | | | | | | | | |
| None | 55.3 | 52.2 | 55.1 | 55.7 | 58.8 | 61.3 | 57.7 | 55.8 |
| One | 12.9 | 13.6 | 12.6 | 12.5 | 12.7 | 12.8 | 13.3 | 12.1 |
| Two | 19.2 | 21.7 | 16.8 | 19.2 | 17.3 | 16.0 | 16.6 | 19.6 |
| Three | 7.8 | 8.1 | 7.2 | 8.1 | 7.3 | 6.2 | 7.9 | 8.4 |
| Four or more | 4.8 | 4.4 | 8.3 | 4.4 | 4.0 | 3.7 | 4.5 | 4.1 |
| **How would you characterize your political views?** | | | | | | | | |
| Far left | 8.8 | 8.7 | 8.7 | 8.8 | 8.9 | 10.9 | 7.6 | 6.8 |
| Liberal | 47.0 | 50.3 | 44.7 | 45.5 | 45.6 | 50.8 | 46.2 | 37.6 |
| Middle of the Road | 28.4 | 27.8 | 28.7 | 30.1 | 26.7 | 23.4 | 31.1 | 28.8 |
| Conservative | 15.2 | 12.3 | 17.2 | 15.1 | 18.1 | 14.2 | 14.5 | 25.9 |
| Far right | 0.7 | 0.9 | 0.7 | 0.5 | 0.7 | 0.7 | 0.6 | 0.8 |
| **Are you currently:** | | | | | | | | |
| Single | 10.8 | 8.3 | 12.8 | 12.0 | 11.4 | 10.4 | 15.5 | 10.4 |
| Married | 76.8 | 79.5 | 77.8 | 73.4 | 77.0 | 76.9 | 71.8 | 80.2 |
| Unmarried, living with partner | 4.5 | 4.6 | 3.3 | 5.2 | 4.0 | 5.0 | 3.8 | 2.8 |
| Divorced | 5.8 | 5.4 | 4.5 | 6.9 | 5.7 | 6.0 | 6.6 | 4.9 |
| Widowed | 1.4 | 1.9 | 1.0 | 1.4 | 1.0 | 0.8 | 1.2 | 1.2 |
| Separated | 0.7 | 0.4 | 0.5 | 1.0 | 0.8 | 1.0 | 1.0 | 0.5 |

53

**2007–2008 FACULTY SURVEY WEIGHTED NATIONAL NORMS**
**Full-time Undergraduate Faculty**

| All Respondents | All 4+ yr | Universities Pub | Universities Priv | Four-year Colleges Pub | Four-year Colleges All Priv | Four-year Colleges Nons | Four-year Colleges Cath | Oth Relig |
|---|---|---|---|---|---|---|---|---|
| **Is English your native language?** | | | | | | | | |
| Yes | 89.6 | 88.3 | 88.8 | 89.7 | 91.4 | 90.2 | 90.5 | 93.7 |
| No | 10.4 | 11.7 | 11.2 | 10.3 | 8.6 | 9.8 | 9.5 | 6.3 |
| **Are you: [4]** | | | | | | | | |
| White/Caucasian | 88.6 | 88.3 | 89.5 | 87.2 | 90.2 | 88.8 | 90.1 | 92.3 |
| African American/Black | 2.8 | 2.4 | 2.3 | 3.5 | 2.6 | 3.5 | 2.0 | 1.6 |
| American Indian/Alaska Native | 1.7 | 2.0 | 1.1 | 1.9 | 1.4 | 1.5 | 1.1 | 1.3 |
| Asian American/Asian | 4.5 | 5.0 | 5.0 | 4.8 | 3.3 | 3.8 | 3.1 | 2.7 |
| Native Hawaiian/Pacific Islander | 0.3 | 0.3 | 0.2 | 0.2 | 0.3 | 0.2 | 0.6 | 0.2 |
| Mexican American/Chicano | 1.1 | 0.9 | 0.8 | 1.7 | 0.8 | 1.1 | 0.5 | 0.6 |
| Puerto Rican | 0.3 | 0.3 | 0.3 | 0.4 | 0.4 | 0.3 | 1.0 | 0.3 |
| Other Latino | 1.8 | 1.9 | 1.7 | 1.5 | 2.0 | 2.0 | 2.6 | 1.5 |
| Other | 2.6 | 2.6 | 2.4 | 2.9 | 2.3 | 2.3 | 2.4 | 2.3 |
| **Do you give the Higher Education Research Institute (HERI) permission to retain your contact information (i.e., your email address and name) for possible follow-up research?** | | | | | | | | |
| Yes | 72.5 | 76.4 | 66.6 | 71.4 | 72.0 | 72.0 | 70.8 | 72.9 |
| No | 27.5 | 23.6 | 33.4 | 28.6 | 28.0 | 28.0 | 29.2 | 27.1 |

[4] Percentages will sum to more than 100.0 if any respondent marked more than one category.

# Full-time Undergraduate Faculty, Type of Institution and Control for

# Men

| | | Universities | | Four-year Colleges | | | | |
|---|---|---|---|---|---|---|---|---|
| | **All** | | | **All** | | | | **Oth** |
| **Male Respondents** | **4+ yr** | **Pub** | **Priv** | **Pub** | **Priv** | **Nons** | **Cath** | **Relig** |
| **Number of Respondents** | 12,683 | 1,805 | 1,884 | 2,973 | 6,021 | 2,762 | 942 | 2,317 |
| **What is your principal activity in your current position at this institution?** | | | | | | | | |
| Administration | 7.9 | 10.4 | 8.3 | 7.4 | 4.8 | 4.7 | 4.6 | 5.1 |
| Teaching | 81.4 | 67.8 | 79.0 | 88.8 | 93.6 | 93.7 | 93.4 | 93.4 |
| Research | 9.2 | 20.1 | 11.1 | 2.4 | 0.5 | 0.8 | 0.1 | 0.2 |
| Services to clients and patients | 0.7 | 0.9 | 0.8 | 0.7 | 0.6 | 0.3 | 1.8 | 0.3 |
| Other | 0.8 | 0.8 | 0.9 | 0.7 | 0.6 | 0.6 | 0.2 | 0.9 |
| **What is your present academic rank?** | | | | | | | | |
| Professor | 39.5 | 43.8 | 46.1 | 35.1 | 34.7 | 35.9 | 30.2 | 35.5 |
| Associate Professor | 25.9 | 25.4 | 23.1 | 26.2 | 28.1 | 26.4 | 32.6 | 28.1 |
| Assistant Professor | 23.7 | 21.1 | 18.8 | 26.4 | 27.0 | 25.3 | 30.1 | 28.0 |
| Lecturer | 5.7 | 6.2 | 6.3 | 6.8 | 3.4 | 5.7 | 2.0 | 0.9 |
| Instructor | 5.2 | 3.5 | 5.8 | 5.5 | 6.7 | 6.8 | 5.2 | 7.5 |
| **What is your tenure status at this institution?** | | | | | | | | |
| Tenured | 61.6 | 67.8 | 65.8 | 61.1 | 50.4 | 49.0 | 56.1 | 49.3 |
| On tenure track, but not tenured | 20.1 | 17.1 | 15.9 | 23.8 | 22.1 | 20.7 | 22.8 | 23.8 |
| Not on tenure track, but institution has tenure system | 15.0 | 14.9 | 17.7 | 13.5 | 15.6 | 17.4 | 14.3 | 13.7 |
| Institution has no tenure system | 3.4 | 0.2 | 0.6 | 1.5 | 12.0 | 13.0 | 6.8 | 13.2 |
| **Are you currently serving in an administrative position as: [1]** | | | | | | | | |
| Department Chair | 12.5 | 8.1 | 10.1 | 11.9 | 21.1 | 21.0 | 19.1 | 22.3 |
| Dean (Associate or Assistant) | 1.8 | 1.7 | 2.5 | 1.4 | 2.1 | 1.2 | 2.5 | 3.1 |
| President | 0.0 | 0.1 | 0.0 | 0.0 | 0.0 | 0.0 | 0.0 | 0.0 |
| Vice-President | 0.2 | 0.0 | 0.0 | 0.1 | 0.6 | 0.9 | 0.3 | 0.4 |
| Provost | 0.1 | 0.0 | 0.0 | 0.0 | 0.2 | 0.4 | 0.0 | 0.1 |
| Other | 15.7 | 18.6 | 16.0 | 13.8 | 13.7 | 14.2 | 14.5 | 12.5 |
| Not Applicable | 63.1 | 64.0 | 62.2 | 66.9 | 57.3 | 57.2 | 58.3 | 56.8 |
| **My primary place of employment in the last year was: [2]** | | | | | | | | |
| In higher education: | | | | | | | | |
| at this institution | 95.0 | 96.2 | 94.5 | 94.8 | 93.9 | 93.7 | 94.3 | 94.0 |
| at a different institution | 2.5 | 1.7 | 2.6 | 3.0 | 2.8 | 2.7 | 2.7 | 3.0 |
| at more than one institution | 1.4 | 1.4 | 1.5 | 1.2 | 1.3 | 1.1 | 1.6 | 1.6 |
| Not in higher education | 0.9 | 0.5 | 0.8 | 0.8 | 1.8 | 2.3 | 1.1 | 1.3 |
| Not employed | 0.2 | 0.2 | 0.5 | 0.2 | 0.2 | 0.3 | 0.3 | 0.2 |
| **Noted as being personally "very important" or "essential": [2]** | | | | | | | | |
| Research | 74.0 | 80.9 | 83.0 | 69.4 | 64.1 | 69.3 | 67.3 | 55.1 |
| Teaching | 97.6 | 96.3 | 97.2 | 98.4 | 98.9 | 98.7 | 99.0 | 99.1 |
| Service | 63.3 | 63.8 | 65.5 | 60.0 | 65.2 | 63.9 | 69.0 | 65.2 |

[1] Response options changed from earlier Faculty Surveys.
[2] This question asked for the first time in the 2007–2008 Faculty Survey.

**2007–2008 FACULTY SURVEY WEIGHTED NATIONAL NORMS**
**Full-time Undergraduate Faculty**

| Male Respondents | All 4+ yr | Universities Pub | Universities Priv | Four-year Colleges Pub | Four-year Colleges All Priv | Four-year Colleges Nons | Four-year Colleges Cath | Oth Relig |
|---|---|---|---|---|---|---|---|---|
| **Highest degree earned** | | | | | | | | |
| Bachelor's (B.A., B.S., etc.) | 1.2 | 1.9 | 1.4 | 0.6 | 0.7 | 1.1 | 0.1 | 0.5 |
| Master's (M.A., M.S., M.F.A., M.B.A., etc.) | 14.9 | 10.4 | 11.4 | 17.7 | 20.1 | 20.6 | 15.3 | 21.7 |
| LL.B., J.D. | 1.0 | 1.1 | 0.8 | 1.2 | 0.8 | 0.6 | 1.4 | 0.9 |
| M.D., D.D.S. (or equivalent) | 0.7 | 1.3 | 0.8 | 0.2 | 0.6 | 0.5 | 1.0 | 0.5 |
| Other first professional degree beyond B.A. (e.g., D.D., D.V.M.) | 0.7 | 0.6 | 0.3 | 0.3 | 1.7 | 2.9 | 0.5 | 0.8 |
| Ed.D. | 2.5 | 1.8 | 1.5 | 3.4 | 2.9 | 2.2 | 3.9 | 3.5 |
| Ph.D. | 77.0 | 81.3 | 82.3 | 74.4 | 70.6 | 70.1 | 76.0 | 68.4 |
| Other degree | 1.7 | 1.4 | 1.2 | 1.9 | 2.4 | 1.9 | 1.8 | 3.5 |
| None | 0.3 | 0.3 | 0.3 | 0.3 | 0.2 | 0.1 | 0.0 | 0.3 |
| **Degree currently working on** | | | | | | | | |
| Bachelor's (B.A., B.S., etc.) | 0.0 | 0.0 | 0.1 | 0.0 | 0.0 | 0.0 | 0.0 | 0.1 |
| Master's (M.A., M.S., M.F.A., M.B.A., etc.) | 0.8 | 1.0 | 1.1 | 0.6 | 0.7 | 0.7 | 0.5 | 0.9 |
| LL.B., J.D. | 0.1 | 0.1 | 0.1 | 0.0 | 0.0 | 0.0 | 0.1 | 0.0 |
| M.D., D.D.S. (or equivalent) | 0.0 | 0.0 | 0.0 | 0.0 | 0.0 | 0.0 | 0.0 | 0.0 |
| Other first professional degree beyond B.A. (e.g., D.D., D.V.M.) | 0.0 | 0.0 | 0.1 | 0.0 | 0.0 | 0.0 | 0.0 | 0.1 |
| Ed.D. | 0.8 | 0.8 | 0.2 | 0.5 | 1.4 | 1.9 | 1.3 | 0.8 |
| Ph.D. | 3.3 | 1.3 | 3.0 | 4.2 | 5.4 | 4.2 | 5.5 | 6.9 |
| Other degree | 0.4 | 0.2 | 0.4 | 0.2 | 0.8 | 0.5 | 0.6 | 1.4 |
| None | 94.6 | 96.5 | 95.0 | 94.4 | 91.5 | 92.6 | 92.0 | 89.8 |
| **During the past two years, have you engaged in any of the following activities?** | | | | | | | | |
| Taught an honors course | 20.9 | 21.5 | 24.1 | 18.1 | 21.8 | 21.3 | 25.8 | 20.4 |
| Taught an interdisciplinary course | 40.9 | 42.1 | 40.8 | 35.1 | 46.4 | 50.0 | 37.3 | 45.9 |
| Taught an ethnic studies course | 8.8 | 8.2 | 6.7 | 8.4 | 11.3 | 11.0 | 11.7 | 11.4 |
| Taught a women's studies course | 2.6 | 1.9 | 3.4 | 2.5 | 3.5 | 3.3 | 3.3 | 3.8 |
| Team-taught a course | 31.1 | 36.7 | 31.1 | 24.5 | 31.3 | 32.0 | 25.9 | 33.1 |
| Taught a service learning course | 16.4 | 15.8 | 14.0 | 17.5 | 17.4 | 16.3 | 17.9 | 18.5 |
| Placed or collected assignments on the Internet | 72.0 | 72.5 | 75.1 | 69.9 | 72.0 | 73.1 | 70.4 | 71.4 |
| Taught a course exclusively on the Internet | 11.5 | 9.4 | 8.5 | 17.9 | 8.5 | 7.7 | 9.6 | 8.9 |
| Participated in a teaching enhancement workshop | 50.1 | 44.5 | 44.5 | 54.7 | 55.8 | 51.7 | 61.4 | 58.8 |
| Advised student groups involved in service/volunteer work | 39.2 | 34.7 | 37.9 | 41.3 | 43.8 | 41.5 | 42.4 | 47.7 |
| Collaborated with the local community in research/teaching | 43.1 | 41.1 | 37.8 | 48.1 | 42.9 | 40.3 | 42.9 | 46.5 |
| Developed a new course | 65.4 | 63.7 | 63.7 | 63.5 | 71.3 | 74.2 | 67.9 | 69.0 |
| Conducted research/writing focused on: | | | | | | | | |
| International/global issues | 29.7 | 29.7 | 34.7 | 27.5 | 29.5 | 30.4 | 31.6 | 27.0 |
| Racial or ethnic minorities | 17.5 | 16.8 | 17.3 | 17.3 | 19.0 | 20.8 | 18.5 | 16.8 |
| Women and gender issues | 12.1 | 12.7 | 13.7 | 10.8 | 11.7 | 12.8 | 11.2 | 10.4 |
| Taught a seminar for first-year students | 22.6 | 19.9 | 26.1 | 18.8 | 29.1 | 30.3 | 22.9 | 30.7 |
| Engaged undergraduates on your research project [2] | 45.2 | 47.3 | 51.8 | 41.9 | 42.2 | 48.0 | 35.8 | 37.2 |
| Worked with undergraduates on a research project | 60.4 | 60.5 | 62.1 | 59.1 | 61.0 | 66.3 | 54.0 | 57.0 |

[2]  This question asked for the first time in the 2007–2008 Faculty Survey.

58

**2007–2008 FACULTY SURVEY WEIGHTED NATIONAL NORMS**
**Full-time Undergraduate Faculty**

| Male Respondents | All 4+ yr | Universities Pub | Priv | Four-year Colleges Pub | All Priv | Nons | Cath | Oth Relig |
|---|---|---|---|---|---|---|---|---|
| **DURING THE PRESENT TERM, HOW MANY HOURS PER WEEK ON AVERAGE DO YOU ACTUALLY SPEND ON:** | | | | | | | | |
| **Scheduled teaching (actual, not credit hours)** | | | | | | | | |
| None | 0.6 | 0.9 | 0.6 | 0.4 | 0.4 | 0.6 | 0.5 | 0.1 |
| 1 to 4 | 14.5 | 24.0 | 19.2 | 7.2 | 6.9 | 8.4 | 5.6 | 5.3 |
| 5 to 8 | 32.0 | 41.6 | 43.4 | 23.4 | 21.8 | 25.0 | 24.0 | 16.2 |
| 9 to 12 | 35.0 | 23.7 | 27.3 | 45.9 | 42.4 | 40.2 | 44.6 | 44.4 |
| 13 to 16 | 11.1 | 4.9 | 5.3 | 14.5 | 19.4 | 18.1 | 17.2 | 22.4 |
| 17 to 20 | 4.4 | 2.5 | 3.3 | 5.8 | 6.2 | 5.1 | 6.3 | 7.6 |
| 21 to 34 | 2.0 | 1.8 | 0.7 | 2.4 | 2.5 | 2.2 | 1.6 | 3.4 |
| 35 to 44 | 0.3 | 0.5 | 0.2 | 0.3 | 0.1 | 0.1 | 0.1 | 0.2 |
| 45 + | 0.1 | 0.1 | 0.1 | 0.1 | 0.2 | 0.4 | 0.0 | 0.2 |
| **Preparing for teaching (including reading student papers and grading)** | | | | | | | | |
| None | 0.3 | 0.3 | 0.3 | 0.2 | 0.3 | 0.5 | 0.4 | 0.0 |
| 1 to 4 | 11.9 | 15.8 | 15.4 | 8.8 | 7.8 | 8.9 | 6.9 | 6.6 |
| 5 to 8 | 25.1 | 27.9 | 28.6 | 23.6 | 20.9 | 21.5 | 20.7 | 20.1 |
| 9 to 12 | 25.3 | 25.7 | 25.4 | 25.7 | 24.1 | 21.2 | 26.7 | 27.0 |
| 13 to 16 | 15.6 | 14.7 | 14.5 | 15.6 | 17.8 | 17.2 | 17.7 | 18.6 |
| 17 to 20 | 12.3 | 9.9 | 8.6 | 14.4 | 15.5 | 16.1 | 15.7 | 14.4 |
| 21 to 34 | 7.3 | 4.5 | 5.9 | 8.9 | 10.3 | 10.9 | 8.9 | 10.2 |
| 35 to 44 | 1.7 | 0.8 | 0.9 | 2.4 | 2.5 | 2.8 | 2.1 | 2.3 |
| 45 + | 0.5 | 0.3 | 0.4 | 0.4 | 0.8 | 1.0 | 0.9 | 0.6 |
| **Advising and counseling of students** | | | | | | | | |
| None | 4.1 | 4.8 | 3.1 | 4.2 | 3.7 | 4.4 | 2.9 | 3.0 |
| 1 to 4 | 58.6 | 59.2 | 60.2 | 57.7 | 58.0 | 57.5 | 55.1 | 60.0 |
| 5 to 8 | 26.4 | 25.3 | 26.4 | 26.8 | 27.5 | 27.6 | 28.5 | 26.9 |
| 9 to 12 | 7.6 | 7.4 | 7.2 | 7.8 | 7.7 | 7.8 | 8.5 | 7.2 |
| 13 to 16 | 1.9 | 1.9 | 2.1 | 1.8 | 1.8 | 2.0 | 1.5 | 1.7 |
| 17 to 20 | 0.9 | 0.9 | 0.6 | 0.9 | 1.0 | 0.4 | 2.9 | 0.9 |
| 21 to 34 | 0.4 | 0.4 | 0.2 | 0.6 | 0.3 | 0.2 | 0.4 | 0.3 |
| 35 to 44 | 0.1 | 0.0 | 0.2 | 0.1 | 0.0 | 0.1 | 0.0 | 0.0 |
| 45 + | 0.0 | 0.0 | 0.1 | 0.1 | 0.0 | 0.0 | 0.1 | 0.0 |
| **Committee work and meetings** | | | | | | | | |
| None | 5.7 | 6.2 | 7.2 | 3.8 | 6.4 | 7.4 | 5.4 | 5.7 |
| 1 to 4 | 58.5 | 55.1 | 59.8 | 57.8 | 63.4 | 64.0 | 58.1 | 65.5 |
| 5 to 8 | 25.4 | 26.5 | 23.0 | 27.4 | 22.6 | 20.7 | 28.8 | 22.0 |
| 9 to 12 | 7.0 | 8.4 | 6.4 | 7.3 | 5.0 | 5.2 | 4.1 | 5.0 |
| 13 to 16 | 2.1 | 2.4 | 2.0 | 2.2 | 1.6 | 1.6 | 2.7 | 1.0 |
| 17 to 20 | 0.9 | 1.0 | 1.0 | 1.0 | 0.8 | 1.0 | 0.5 | 0.7 |
| 21 to 34 | 0.3 | 0.3 | 0.4 | 0.4 | 0.2 | 0.0 | 0.4 | 0.3 |
| 35 to 44 | 0.1 | 0.2 | 0.1 | 0.1 | 0.0 | 0.1 | 0.0 | 0.0 |
| 45 + | 0.0 | 0.0 | 0.0 | 0.1 | 0.0 | 0.0 | 0.0 | 0.0 |
| **Other administration** | | | | | | | | |
| None | 30.4 | 28.9 | 33.0 | 31.6 | 29.5 | 31.1 | 32.8 | 25.6 |
| 1 to 4 | 39.2 | 39.6 | 38.3 | 37.9 | 41.1 | 40.4 | 37.8 | 43.8 |
| 5 to 8 | 14.0 | 14.1 | 12.6 | 14.1 | 14.6 | 14.2 | 15.5 | 14.6 |
| 9 to 12 | 6.9 | 7.8 | 6.8 | 6.3 | 6.4 | 6.0 | 6.5 | 7.0 |
| 13 to 16 | 3.4 | 3.1 | 2.6 | 3.8 | 3.7 | 4.0 | 3.2 | 3.5 |
| 17 to 20 | 3.0 | 2.9 | 3.3 | 3.4 | 2.5 | 2.1 | 2.6 | 3.2 |
| 21 to 34 | 2.2 | 2.5 | 2.6 | 2.2 | 1.6 | 1.7 | 1.6 | 1.5 |
| 35 to 44 | 0.7 | 1.0 | 0.4 | 0.6 | 0.4 | 0.4 | 0.0 | 0.7 |
| 45 + | 0.2 | 0.1 | 0.4 | 0.1 | 0.2 | 0.2 | 0.1 | 0.2 |

59

**2007–2008 FACULTY SURVEY WEIGHTED NATIONAL NORMS**
**Full-time Undergraduate Faculty**

| Male Respondents | All 4+ yr | Universities Pub | Universities Priv | Four-year Colleges Pub | Four-year Colleges All Priv | Four-year Colleges Nons | Four-year Colleges Cath | Four-year Colleges Oth Relig |
|---|---|---|---|---|---|---|---|---|
| **DURING THE PRESENT TERM, HOW MANY HOURS PER WEEK ON AVERAGE DO YOU ACTUALLY SPEND ON:** | | | | | | | | |
| **Research and scholarly writing** | | | | | | | | |
| None | 13.2 | 10.9 | 8.9 | 13.3 | 19.2 | 19.7 | 13.8 | 21.1 |
| 1 to 4 | 29.3 | 21.1 | 22.4 | 34.5 | 38.9 | 34.2 | 40.0 | 44.9 |
| 5 to 8 | 20.8 | 16.9 | 19.0 | 24.8 | 22.8 | 24.4 | 26.1 | 18.7 |
| 9 to 12 | 13.5 | 15.5 | 17.0 | 12.2 | 10.0 | 11.9 | 9.2 | 7.9 |
| 13 to 16 | 7.5 | 10.9 | 9.1 | 5.8 | 3.9 | 4.1 | 4.6 | 3.3 |
| 17 to 20 | 7.4 | 11.1 | 10.1 | 5.4 | 3.0 | 3.1 | 3.9 | 2.3 |
| 21 to 34 | 5.3 | 9.1 | 8.5 | 2.6 | 1.3 | 1.6 | 0.7 | 1.2 |
| 35 to 44 | 1.9 | 3.0 | 3.4 | 0.9 | 0.6 | 0.6 | 1.3 | 0.3 |
| 45 + | 1.0 | 1.5 | 1.7 | 0.5 | 0.3 | 0.4 | 0.4 | 0.2 |
| **Other creative products/performances** | | | | | | | | |
| None | 50.4 | 51.5 | 53.0 | 48.4 | 49.9 | 51.7 | 47.2 | 48.6 |
| 1 to 4 | 29.2 | 29.0 | 26.5 | 30.2 | 30.0 | 27.4 | 34.1 | 31.5 |
| 5 to 8 | 11.0 | 10.9 | 9.7 | 12.1 | 10.4 | 9.9 | 11.4 | 10.5 |
| 9 to 12 | 4.5 | 4.3 | 4.3 | 3.8 | 5.8 | 7.4 | 4.1 | 4.4 |
| 13 to 16 | 1.9 | 1.8 | 1.6 | 2.2 | 1.7 | 1.2 | 1.7 | 2.6 |
| 17 to 20 | 1.8 | 1.2 | 2.9 | 2.2 | 1.3 | 1.3 | 0.7 | 1.6 |
| 21 to 34 | 0.7 | 0.8 | 1.0 | 0.6 | 0.7 | 0.9 | 0.6 | 0.5 |
| 35 to 44 | 0.3 | 0.4 | 0.5 | 0.2 | 0.1 | 0.1 | 0.1 | 0.2 |
| 45 + | 0.3 | 0.2 | 0.5 | 0.2 | 0.2 | 0.2 | 0.2 | 0.1 |
| **Consultation with clients/patients** | | | | | | | | |
| None | 81.7 | 81.0 | 83.9 | 80.6 | 82.7 | 83.4 | 82.3 | 81.7 |
| 1 to 4 | 12.3 | 13.1 | 10.4 | 12.8 | 11.7 | 11.6 | 10.3 | 12.6 |
| 5 to 8 | 3.5 | 3.4 | 3.3 | 3.7 | 3.5 | 3.3 | 4.1 | 3.5 |
| 9 to 12 | 1.0 | 0.6 | 1.2 | 1.1 | 1.1 | 1.1 | 1.0 | 1.2 |
| 13 to 16 | 0.6 | 0.8 | 0.2 | 0.7 | 0.2 | 0.1 | 0.0 | 0.5 |
| 17 to 20 | 0.5 | 0.7 | 0.6 | 0.3 | 0.5 | 0.3 | 1.6 | 0.4 |
| 21 to 34 | 0.3 | 0.1 | 0.4 | 0.7 | 0.1 | 0.1 | 0.5 | 0.1 |
| 35 to 44 | 0.1 | 0.1 | 0.0 | 0.1 | 0.1 | 0.1 | 0.1 | 0.0 |
| 45 + | 0.1 | 0.1 | 0.1 | 0.0 | 0.0 | 0.1 | 0.0 | 0.0 |
| **Community or public service** | | | | | | | | |
| None | 40.0 | 42.9 | 43.1 | 37.0 | 37.5 | 42.9 | 35.9 | 30.5 |
| 1 to 4 | 47.0 | 45.1 | 39.2 | 50.5 | 50.1 | 46.3 | 51.4 | 54.9 |
| 5 to 8 | 9.5 | 8.8 | 12.4 | 9.0 | 9.4 | 8.0 | 9.4 | 11.5 |
| 9 to 12 | 2.3 | 2.3 | 3.1 | 2.2 | 2.2 | 2.1 | 2.8 | 2.2 |
| 13 to 16 | 0.6 | 0.4 | 1.3 | 0.7 | 0.4 | 0.3 | 0.2 | 0.6 |
| 17 to 20 | 0.3 | 0.1 | 0.7 | 0.4 | 0.2 | 0.3 | 0.3 | 0.2 |
| 21 to 34 | 0.1 | 0.0 | 0.2 | 0.1 | 0.0 | 0.0 | 0.1 | 0.1 |
| 35 to 44 | 0.1 | 0.3 | 0.0 | 0.1 | 0.0 | 0.0 | 0.0 | 0.0 |
| 45 + | 0.0 | 0.0 | 0.0 | 0.0 | 0.0 | 0.1 | 0.0 | 0.0 |
| **Outside consulting/freelance work** | | | | | | | | |
| None | 66.1 | 63.5 | 65.7 | 67.7 | 68.0 | 68.9 | 66.6 | 67.4 |
| 1 to 4 | 24.9 | 26.6 | 24.6 | 23.5 | 24.3 | 23.7 | 25.7 | 24.4 |
| 5 to 8 | 6.3 | 7.2 | 6.3 | 5.9 | 5.4 | 5.0 | 5.9 | 5.6 |
| 9 to 12 | 1.7 | 1.9 | 1.3 | 1.8 | 1.4 | 1.5 | 1.1 | 1.5 |
| 13 to 16 | 0.5 | 0.5 | 0.9 | 0.5 | 0.4 | 0.3 | 0.5 | 0.4 |
| 17 to 20 | 0.3 | 0.2 | 0.7 | 0.3 | 0.3 | 0.2 | 0.1 | 0.4 |
| 21 to 34 | 0.1 | 0.0 | 0.2 | 0.1 | 0.3 | 0.4 | 0.2 | 0.1 |
| 35 to 44 | 0.1 | 0.0 | 0.3 | 0.1 | 0.0 | 0.0 | 0.0 | 0.0 |
| 45 + | 0.1 | 0.1 | 0.1 | 0.1 | 0.0 | 0.0 | 0.1 | 0.0 |

60

<h1 align="center">2007–2008 FACULTY SURVEY WEIGHTED NATIONAL NORMS</h1>
<h2 align="center">Full-time Undergraduate Faculty</h2>

| Male Respondents | All 4+ yr | Universities Pub | Universities Priv | Four-year Colleges Pub | Four-year Colleges All Priv | Four-year Colleges Nons | Four-year Colleges Cath | Four-year Colleges Oth Relig |
|---|---|---|---|---|---|---|---|---|
| **DURING THE PRESENT TERM, HOW MANY HOURS PER WEEK ON AVERAGE DO YOU ACTUALLY SPEND ON:** | | | | | | | | |
| **Household/childcare duties** | | | | | | | | |
| None | 16.6 | 18.3 | 16.7 | 17.3 | 13.1 | 10.9 | 18.2 | 13.7 |
| 1 to 4 | 19.3 | 19.0 | 19.3 | 18.7 | 20.6 | 21.9 | 18.8 | 19.7 |
| 5 to 8 | 25.4 | 25.4 | 25.4 | 24.9 | 25.9 | 25.5 | 24.5 | 27.1 |
| 9 to 12 | 15.6 | 15.2 | 16.8 | 15.3 | 16.0 | 16.7 | 13.7 | 16.1 |
| 13 to 16 | 8.1 | 8.7 | 7.5 | 7.6 | 8.2 | 8.6 | 8.8 | 7.3 |
| 17 to 20 | 7.1 | 6.9 | 7.2 | 7.2 | 7.4 | 7.2 | 7.0 | 7.8 |
| 21 to 34 | 4.4 | 4.1 | 3.6 | 4.9 | 4.7 | 5.1 | 4.2 | 4.4 |
| 35 to 44 | 1.7 | 1.2 | 1.7 | 2.2 | 1.8 | 1.8 | 1.8 | 1.8 |
| 45 + | 1.8 | 1.2 | 1.8 | 2.0 | 2.4 | 2.3 | 3.0 | 2.1 |
| **Communicating via email** | | | | | | | | |
| None | 0.6 | 0.5 | 0.5 | 0.4 | 1.0 | 1.5 | 0.6 | 0.5 |
| 1 to 4 | 33.3 | 29.7 | 33.5 | 34.6 | 37.0 | 35.9 | 36.6 | 38.8 |
| 5 to 8 | 40.5 | 41.2 | 40.0 | 40.5 | 39.8 | 39.2 | 40.5 | 40.2 |
| 9 to 12 | 16.1 | 18.4 | 16.2 | 14.7 | 14.2 | 14.3 | 15.0 | 13.8 |
| 13 to 16 | 5.6 | 6.0 | 5.3 | 5.6 | 5.0 | 6.4 | 3.5 | 3.9 |
| 17 to 20 | 2.5 | 2.5 | 3.3 | 2.5 | 2.1 | 1.8 | 2.9 | 2.2 |
| 21 to 34 | 1.1 | 1.3 | 0.9 | 1.4 | 0.6 | 0.7 | 0.5 | 0.5 |
| 35 to 44 | 0.2 | 0.2 | 0.1 | 0.3 | 0.2 | 0.2 | 0.2 | 0.1 |
| 45 + | 0.2 | 0.2 | 0.3 | 0.2 | 0.1 | 0.1 | 0.2 | 0.0 |
| **Commuting to campus [2]** | | | | | | | | |
| None | 6.4 | 5.7 | 4.5 | 6.6 | 8.5 | 10.1 | 4.9 | 8.0 |
| 1 to 4 | 63.8 | 69.5 | 56.6 | 64.0 | 59.7 | 58.1 | 56.1 | 63.8 |
| 5 to 8 | 21.6 | 19.0 | 26.8 | 21.6 | 22.0 | 22.0 | 24.7 | 20.7 |
| 9 to 12 | 7.0 | 5.1 | 9.8 | 6.7 | 8.4 | 8.8 | 10.7 | 6.6 |
| 13 to 16 | 0.9 | 0.6 | 1.5 | 0.7 | 1.0 | 0.8 | 2.9 | 0.4 |
| 17 to 20 | 0.2 | 0.0 | 0.5 | 0.2 | 0.2 | 0.1 | 0.3 | 0.4 |
| 21 to 34 | 0.1 | 0.0 | 0.2 | 0.0 | 0.1 | 0.0 | 0.4 | 0.1 |
| 35 to 44 | 0.0 | 0.0 | 0.0 | 0.0 | 0.0 | 0.0 | 0.0 | 0.0 |
| 45 + | 0.1 | 0.0 | 0.0 | 0.2 | 0.0 | 0.0 | 0.1 | 0.0 |
| **Other employment, outside of academia [2]** | | | | | | | | |
| None | 87.2 | 89.1 | 88.4 | 86.7 | 84.3 | 84.7 | 85.9 | 82.8 |
| 1 to 4 | 6.9 | 5.9 | 6.2 | 7.1 | 8.4 | 8.7 | 6.0 | 9.4 |
| 5 to 8 | 2.7 | 2.6 | 1.9 | 3.1 | 3.0 | 2.1 | 3.7 | 4.1 |
| 9 to 12 | 1.5 | 1.2 | 1.1 | 1.5 | 2.1 | 2.9 | 1.2 | 1.4 |
| 13 to 16 | 0.7 | 0.6 | 0.9 | 0.6 | 0.7 | 0.4 | 0.6 | 1.2 |
| 17 to 20 | 0.5 | 0.3 | 0.7 | 0.5 | 0.6 | 0.3 | 2.0 | 0.5 |
| 21 to 34 | 0.2 | 0.1 | 0.3 | 0.3 | 0.3 | 0.4 | 0.5 | 0.2 |
| 35 to 44 | 0.2 | 0.1 | 0.4 | 0.2 | 0.4 | 0.5 | 0.1 | 0.4 |
| 45 + | 0.1 | 0.1 | 0.1 | 0.1 | 0.1 | 0.1 | 0.0 | 0.1 |

[2]  This question asked for the first time in the 2007–2008 Faculty Survey.

| Male Respondents | All 4+ yr | Universities Pub | Priv | Four-year Colleges Pub | All Priv | Nons | Cath | Oth Relig |
|---|---|---|---|---|---|---|---|---|
| **Including all institutions at which you teach, how many undergraduate courses are you teaching this term? [2]** | | | | | | | | |
| None | 0.0 | 0.0 | 0.0 | 0.0 | 0.0 | 0.0 | 0.0 | 0.0 |
| One | 22.7 | 37.2 | 30.3 | 12.4 | 9.9 | 11.2 | 12.9 | 6.6 |
| Two | 29.5 | 36.6 | 34.6 | 24.6 | 22.1 | 27.5 | 19.9 | 15.6 |
| Three | 24.9 | 16.9 | 23.9 | 30.9 | 29.9 | 28.1 | 29.9 | 32.3 |
| Four | 14.5 | 6.3 | 8.2 | 20.7 | 22.5 | 19.1 | 22.9 | 27.3 |
| Five | 5.2 | 1.6 | 1.5 | 7.2 | 10.2 | 8.5 | 9.8 | 12.7 |
| Six or more | 3.2 | 1.5 | 1.6 | 4.2 | 5.4 | 5.6 | 4.6 | 5.6 |
| **FOR UP TO FOUR OF THE UNDERGRADUATE COURSES MENTIONED ABOVE, HOW MANY STUDENTS ARE ENROLLED IN: [2]** | | | | | | | | |
| **Course #1** | | | | | | | | |
| 10 or fewer | 12.2 | 11.3 | 10.5 | 10.5 | 16.9 | 19.3 | 12.1 | 15.9 |
| 11 to 20 | 25.8 | 23.6 | 26.8 | 21.5 | 33.9 | 35.4 | 35.0 | 31.2 |
| 21 to 30 | 25.5 | 22.2 | 23.1 | 28.8 | 27.9 | 25.9 | 31.1 | 29.0 |
| 31 to 50 | 21.4 | 19.8 | 23.5 | 26.5 | 16.1 | 13.5 | 17.9 | 18.8 |
| 51 to 100 | 9.4 | 13.1 | 9.3 | 9.6 | 3.8 | 3.8 | 3.3 | 4.0 |
| More than 100 | 5.6 | 10.0 | 6.9 | 3.0 | 1.5 | 2.2 | 0.6 | 0.9 |
| **Course #2** | | | | | | | | |
| 10 or fewer | 17.0 | 18.5 | 15.9 | 13.8 | 20.0 | 20.3 | 17.0 | 21.1 |
| 11 to 20 | 30.4 | 25.1 | 31.3 | 27.2 | 39.2 | 42.3 | 34.4 | 37.2 |
| 21 to 30 | 26.6 | 24.1 | 22.7 | 29.8 | 27.1 | 24.7 | 33.3 | 27.3 |
| 31 to 50 | 18.3 | 18.6 | 20.7 | 23.0 | 11.1 | 9.1 | 13.9 | 12.4 |
| 51 to 100 | 5.2 | 8.2 | 6.8 | 4.8 | 1.9 | 2.3 | 1.2 | 1.8 |
| More than 100 | 2.5 | 5.5 | 2.6 | 1.4 | 0.7 | 1.2 | 0.2 | 0.2 |
| **Course #3** | | | | | | | | |
| 10 or fewer | 24.9 | 30.8 | 22.4 | 19.4 | 28.8 | 27.9 | 23.8 | 32.1 |
| 11 to 20 | 32.4 | 27.8 | 30.9 | 30.0 | 38.5 | 38.3 | 35.9 | 39.8 |
| 21 to 30 | 24.7 | 19.3 | 22.2 | 29.1 | 23.2 | 23.5 | 30.1 | 19.9 |
| 31 to 50 | 14.0 | 13.5 | 18.2 | 18.6 | 7.5 | 6.5 | 9.7 | 7.5 |
| 51 to 100 | 2.8 | 5.4 | 4.4 | 2.4 | 1.3 | 2.4 | 0.5 | 0.4 |
| More than 100 | 1.2 | 3.2 | 1.9 | 0.6 | 0.7 | 1.5 | 0.0 | 0.2 |
| **Course #4** | | | | | | | | |
| 10 or fewer | 33.3 | 37.4 | 29.4 | 28.2 | 37.9 | 32.6 | 38.0 | 43.4 |
| 11 to 20 | 30.9 | 28.0 | 28.2 | 28.7 | 34.8 | 35.2 | 31.5 | 35.8 |
| 21 to 30 | 21.7 | 18.7 | 16.1 | 27.2 | 17.9 | 18.3 | 23.7 | 15.0 |
| 31 to 50 | 11.2 | 9.0 | 14.8 | 14.3 | 8.1 | 12.5 | 6.3 | 4.4 |
| 51 to 100 | 2.0 | 4.0 | 8.9 | 1.3 | 0.7 | 0.2 | 0.5 | 1.3 |
| More than 100 | 0.9 | 2.9 | 2.6 | 0.3 | 0.6 | 1.3 | 0.0 | 0.1 |

[2] This question asked for the first time in the 2007–2008 Faculty Survey.

| | | | | Four-year Colleges | | | | |
| Male Respondents | All | Universities | | | All | | | Oth |
| | 4+ yr | Pub | Priv | Pub | Priv | Nons | Cath | Relig |
|---|---|---|---|---|---|---|---|---|
| **HOW MANY OF THE FOLLOWING COURSES ARE YOU TEACHING THIS ACADEMIC YEAR?** | | | | | | | | |
| **General education courses** | | | | | | | | |
| None | 56.0 | 66.5 | 61.1 | 49.3 | 45.8 | 49.8 | 46.6 | 39.8 |
| One | 18.1 | 16.6 | 15.3 | 19.7 | 19.9 | 19.8 | 16.3 | 21.9 |
| Two | 12.5 | 9.3 | 11.5 | 14.4 | 15.2 | 13.4 | 14.8 | 17.9 |
| Three | 6.0 | 3.5 | 5.1 | 7.0 | 9.1 | 8.2 | 9.9 | 10.1 |
| Four | 3.5 | 2.3 | 2.8 | 4.5 | 4.5 | 3.9 | 6.3 | 4.5 |
| Five or more | 3.9 | 1.8 | 4.2 | 5.1 | 5.5 | 4.9 | 6.1 | 5.9 |
| **Developmental/remedial courses** | | | | | | | | |
| None | 95.1 | 96.3 | 96.5 | 94.5 | 93.2 | 92.4 | 94.3 | 93.6 |
| One | 2.8 | 2.4 | 1.9 | 2.8 | 3.8 | 3.9 | 3.0 | 3.9 |
| Two | 1.2 | 0.7 | 0.6 | 1.6 | 1.7 | 2.6 | 1.2 | 0.7 |
| Three | 0.4 | 0.3 | 0.5 | 0.5 | 0.5 | 0.7 | 0.2 | 0.5 |
| Four | 0.2 | 0.2 | 0.2 | 0.3 | 0.3 | 0.2 | 0.3 | 0.4 |
| Five or more | 0.3 | 0.1 | 0.3 | 0.3 | 0.6 | 0.2 | 1.0 | 0.9 |
| **Other undergraduate credit courses** | | | | | | | | |
| None | 17.5 | 20.7 | 21.1 | 13.9 | 15.1 | 15.4 | 18.9 | 12.6 |
| One | 21.2 | 27.2 | 25.8 | 17.6 | 14.0 | 14.2 | 16.6 | 12.5 |
| Two | 24.2 | 26.8 | 23.6 | 24.8 | 19.9 | 21.3 | 21.3 | 17.3 |
| Three | 16.1 | 13.6 | 14.2 | 17.7 | 18.9 | 18.7 | 17.6 | 19.9 |
| Four | 9.5 | 5.7 | 7.9 | 11.4 | 13.6 | 12.3 | 12.4 | 16.0 |
| Five or more | 11.6 | 6.1 | 7.5 | 14.6 | 18.5 | 18.1 | 13.2 | 21.7 |
| **Graduate courses** | | | | | | | | |
| None | 61.9 | 45.1 | 57.7 | 66.8 | 82.9 | 84.9 | 71.1 | 86.1 |
| One | 24.1 | 35.4 | 28.2 | 20.8 | 9.1 | 7.9 | 14.5 | 7.9 |
| Two | 9.1 | 13.6 | 8.4 | 8.0 | 4.2 | 4.3 | 6.2 | 3.1 |
| Three | 2.5 | 3.2 | 3.3 | 2.0 | 1.6 | 1.2 | 4.1 | 1.0 |
| Four | 1.3 | 1.5 | 1.3 | 1.6 | 0.9 | 0.8 | 1.8 | 0.6 |
| Five or more | 1.1 | 1.2 | 1.1 | 0.9 | 1.2 | 0.8 | 2.4 | 1.2 |
| **Vocational or technical courses** | | | | | | | | |
| None | 97.2 | 96.9 | 97.7 | 97.1 | 97.5 | 96.9 | 98.1 | 98.0 |
| One | 1.2 | 1.4 | 0.8 | 1.1 | 1.1 | 1.5 | 0.6 | 0.8 |
| Two | 0.7 | 0.8 | 0.7 | 0.6 | 0.6 | 0.7 | 0.9 | 0.4 |
| Three | 0.5 | 0.4 | 0.5 | 0.5 | 0.5 | 0.7 | 0.3 | 0.3 |
| Four | 0.2 | 0.4 | 0.2 | 0.1 | 0.1 | 0.1 | 0.1 | 0.1 |
| Five or more | 0.3 | 0.2 | 0.1 | 0.5 | 0.2 | 0.1 | 0.0 | 0.4 |
| **Non-credit courses (other than above)** | | | | | | | | |
| None | 95.5 | 95.1 | 95.3 | 96.0 | 95.5 | 95.2 | 97.5 | 94.9 |
| One | 3.2 | 3.4 | 3.5 | 2.7 | 3.2 | 3.4 | 1.8 | 3.7 |
| Two | 0.9 | 1.0 | 0.6 | 1.0 | 0.8 | 0.7 | 0.5 | 1.0 |
| Three | 0.2 | 0.2 | 0.4 | 0.2 | 0.1 | 0.0 | 0.1 | 0.2 |
| Four | 0.1 | 0.1 | 0.1 | 0.0 | 0.2 | 0.2 | 0.0 | 0.1 |
| Five or more | 0.2 | 0.2 | 0.1 | 0.1 | 0.3 | 0.6 | 0.1 | 0.2 |
| **Do you teach remedial/developmental skills in any of the following areas?** | | | | | | | | |
| Reading | 3.5 | 2.9 | 3.6 | 3.5 | 4.5 | 4.4 | 5.0 | 4.4 |
| Writing | 8.6 | 7.5 | 8.1 | 8.6 | 10.5 | 11.6 | 9.3 | 9.5 |
| Mathematics | 4.3 | 3.9 | 3.0 | 5.1 | 4.8 | 5.5 | 5.0 | 3.7 |
| ESL | 0.6 | 0.7 | 0.5 | 0.5 | 0.8 | 0.6 | 1.0 | 0.8 |
| General academic skills | 7.5 | 6.9 | 6.1 | 8.1 | 8.7 | 9.7 | 6.3 | 8.6 |
| Other subject areas | 5.1 | 4.7 | 4.2 | 5.4 | 5.8 | 7.3 | 4.8 | 4.3 |

**2007–2008 FACULTY SURVEY WEIGHTED NATIONAL NORMS**
**Full-time Undergraduate Faculty**

| Male Respondents | All 4+ yr | Universities Pub | Universities Priv | Four-year Colleges Pub | Four-year Colleges All Priv | Four-year Colleges Nons | Four-year Colleges Cath | Oth Relig |
|---|---|---|---|---|---|---|---|---|
| **HAVE YOU ENGAGED IN ANY OF THE FOLLOWING PROFESSIONAL DEVELOPMENT OPPORTUNITIES AT YOUR INSTITUTION? [2]** | | | | | | | | |
| **Workshops focused on teaching in the classroom** | | | | | | | | |
| Yes | 66.0 | 62.7 | 63.5 | 66.7 | 71.4 | 70.5 | 72.0 | 72.4 |
| No | 31.9 | 36.4 | 35.0 | 30.7 | 25.0 | 26.7 | 25.1 | 22.4 |
| Not eligible | 0.2 | 0.2 | 0.2 | 0.2 | 0.2 | 0.2 | 0.4 | 0.2 |
| Not available | 1.9 | 0.7 | 1.2 | 2.4 | 3.4 | 2.6 | 2.5 | 5.0 |
| **Paid workshops outside the institution focused on teaching** | | | | | | | | |
| Yes | 19.4 | 13.7 | 15.3 | 22.0 | 27.1 | 24.6 | 25.7 | 31.4 |
| No | 76.4 | 83.1 | 80.7 | 72.7 | 68.5 | 70.9 | 71.2 | 63.8 |
| Not eligible | 0.8 | 0.8 | 1.2 | 1.1 | 0.3 | 0.2 | 0.2 | 0.6 |
| Not available | 3.3 | 2.3 | 2.9 | 4.2 | 4.0 | 4.2 | 2.9 | 4.2 |
| **Paid sabbatical leave** | | | | | | | | |
| Yes | 32.0 | 32.5 | 41.8 | 25.2 | 34.0 | 39.1 | 29.9 | 28.8 |
| No | 55.1 | 56.8 | 47.7 | 59.8 | 51.1 | 45.8 | 60.3 | 54.0 |
| Not eligible | 9.6 | 6.6 | 9.4 | 10.8 | 12.6 | 13.3 | 9.4 | 13.4 |
| Not available | 3.3 | 4.1 | 1.2 | 4.3 | 2.2 | 1.9 | 0.4 | 3.8 |
| **Travel funds paid by the institution** | | | | | | | | |
| Yes | 78.4 | 76.1 | 78.5 | 79.7 | 80.2 | 80.3 | 77.1 | 81.6 |
| No | 18.8 | 20.6 | 19.1 | 17.7 | 17.2 | 15.9 | 22.3 | 16.3 |
| Not eligible | 1.1 | 0.8 | 1.4 | 1.4 | 1.1 | 1.9 | 0.1 | 0.3 |
| Not available | 1.7 | 2.5 | 1.0 | 1.2 | 1.6 | 1.8 | 0.4 | 1.8 |
| **Association membership/dues paid by the institution** | | | | | | | | |
| Yes | 29.1 | 22.9 | 32.0 | 21.3 | 46.1 | 41.5 | 43.9 | 53.9 |
| No | 57.6 | 64.4 | 55.9 | 61.8 | 43.4 | 47.1 | 47.2 | 36.3 |
| Not eligible | 2.1 | 1.7 | 3.0 | 2.4 | 1.7 | 2.7 | 0.9 | 0.8 |
| Not available | 11.2 | 11.0 | 9.1 | 14.5 | 8.7 | 8.7 | 7.9 | 9.0 |
| **Tuition remission** | | | | | | | | |
| Yes | 14.2 | 10.0 | 21.7 | 10.6 | 20.4 | 19.1 | 18.0 | 23.5 |
| No | 78.5 | 82.5 | 73.6 | 80.8 | 73.0 | 72.9 | 78.0 | 70.4 |
| Not eligible | 3.1 | 2.3 | 3.3 | 3.0 | 4.2 | 4.9 | 2.9 | 3.8 |
| Not available | 4.2 | 5.2 | 1.4 | 5.7 | 2.5 | 3.1 | 1.1 | 2.3 |
| **Internal grants for research** | | | | | | | | |
| Yes | 48.5 | 52.5 | 53.7 | 46.2 | 42.4 | 46.0 | 40.1 | 38.6 |
| No | 48.2 | 45.2 | 42.6 | 51.0 | 52.7 | 49.0 | 57.4 | 55.7 |
| Not eligible | 1.7 | 1.7 | 2.7 | 1.3 | 1.5 | 1.8 | 0.7 | 1.3 |
| Not available | 1.6 | 0.6 | 1.0 | 1.5 | 3.3 | 3.2 | 1.8 | 4.4 |
| **Training for administrative leadership** | | | | | | | | |
| Yes | 13.5 | 13.9 | 14.3 | 13.7 | 12.4 | 12.5 | 13.2 | 11.7 |
| No | 78.0 | 79.9 | 78.2 | 77.5 | 75.8 | 74.5 | 79.1 | 75.9 |
| Not eligible | 2.0 | 1.1 | 3.2 | 2.2 | 2.4 | 2.8 | 1.1 | 2.5 |
| Not available | 6.4 | 5.2 | 4.4 | 6.6 | 9.5 | 10.1 | 6.6 | 10.0 |

[2] This question asked for the first time in the 2007–2008 Faculty Survey.

64

## 2007–2008 FACULTY SURVEY WEIGHTED NATIONAL NORMS
### Full-time Undergraduate Faculty

| Male Respondents | All 4+ yr | Universities Pub | Priv | Four-year Colleges Pub | All Priv | Nons | Cath | Oth Relig |
|---|---|---|---|---|---|---|---|---|
| **Goals for undergraduates noted as "very important" or "essential"** | | | | | | | | |
| Develop ability to think critically | 99.4 | 99.4 | 99.3 | 99.4 | 99.3 | 99.0 | 99.7 | 99.6 |
| Prepare students for employment after college | 79.0 | 78.1 | 75.8 | 82.2 | 78.3 | 76.5 | 78.3 | 81.0 |
| Prepare students for graduate or advanced education | 74.7 | 72.6 | 77.6 | 73.8 | 77.1 | 75.6 | 77.1 | 79.1 |
| Develop moral character | 67.7 | 62.2 | 74.4 | 64.5 | 75.5 | 70.0 | 81.1 | 80.5 |
| Provide for students' emotional development | 43.3 | 38.8 | 46.9 | 40.6 | 51.3 | 47.7 | 53.5 | 55.3 |
| Prepare students for family living | 20.1 | 15.1 | 26.5 | 19.0 | 25.1 | 22.1 | 26.5 | 28.5 |
| Teach students the classic works of Western civilization [2] | 36.3 | 31.1 | 42.5 | 35.9 | 40.8 | 36.9 | 44.8 | 44.3 |
| Help students develop personal values | 63.4 | 57.1 | 68.4 | 61.1 | 72.7 | 69.0 | 73.7 | 77.4 |
| Enhance students' self-understanding | 68.5 | 64.0 | 68.6 | 67.7 | 76.1 | 74.5 | 78.3 | 77.3 |
| Instill in students a commitment to community service | 49.6 | 43.3 | 53.0 | 50.8 | 55.5 | 50.9 | 57.7 | 60.9 |
| Enhance students' knowledge of and appreciation for other racial/ethnic groups | 67.4 | 64.5 | 67.3 | 67.1 | 71.9 | 70.9 | 74.1 | 72.4 |
| Study a foreign language [2] | 50.5 | 49.3 | 55.2 | 46.5 | 54.4 | 53.2 | 55.0 | 55.9 |
| Help master knowledge in a discipline | 94.7 | 94.3 | 92.8 | 95.5 | 95.5 | 95.1 | 96.1 | 95.8 |
| Develop creative capacities | 81.7 | 82.5 | 81.9 | 80.3 | 82.1 | 84.2 | 79.0 | 80.6 |
| Instill a basic appreciation of the liberal arts | 70.2 | 64.3 | 69.9 | 69.4 | 80.2 | 80.2 | 78.7 | 80.9 |
| Promote ability to write effectively | 95.3 | 95.1 | 94.7 | 94.7 | 96.8 | 97.1 | 97.0 | 96.4 |
| Help students evaluate the quality and reliability of information [2] | 96.4 | 96.1 | 96.9 | 96.0 | 96.9 | 97.1 | 97.6 | 96.3 |
| Engage students in civil discourse around controversial issues [2] | 67.7 | 62.4 | 67.0 | 68.1 | 75.3 | 74.2 | 76.6 | 76.2 |
| Teach students tolerance and respect for different beliefs [2] | 76.6 | 73.7 | 78.3 | 76.3 | 80.1 | 79.9 | 83.2 | 78.8 |
| Encourage students to become agents of social change [2] | 49.0 | 42.8 | 50.7 | 49.3 | 56.6 | 55.5 | 57.8 | 57.5 |

[2] This question asked for the first time in the 2007–2008 Faculty Survey.

| Male Respondents | All 4+ yr | Universities Pub | Priv | Four-year Colleges Pub | All Priv | Nons | Cath | Oth Relig |
|---|---|---|---|---|---|---|---|---|
| **HOW MANY OF THE FOLLOWING HAVE YOU PUBLISHED?** | | | | | | | | |
| **Articles in academic or professional journals** | | | | | | | | |
| None | 15.0 | 8.9 | 10.9 | 16.4 | 24.9 | 24.6 | 19.8 | 27.8 |
| 1 to 2 | 14.1 | 7.0 | 10.8 | 18.3 | 21.2 | 18.9 | 21.4 | 24.3 |
| 3 to 4 | 12.9 | 10.3 | 9.6 | 15.8 | 15.1 | 13.8 | 17.2 | 15.8 |
| 5 to 10 | 18.7 | 17.8 | 15.9 | 21.0 | 18.9 | 19.6 | 20.3 | 17.2 |
| 11 to 20 | 14.9 | 17.5 | 17.8 | 13.5 | 10.8 | 12.3 | 11.1 | 8.7 |
| 21 to 50 | 14.7 | 21.4 | 19.1 | 10.9 | 7.1 | 8.6 | 6.9 | 5.1 |
| 51+ | 9.7 | 17.0 | 15.9 | 4.1 | 2.0 | 2.2 | 3.3 | 1.1 |
| **Chapters in edited volumes** | | | | | | | | |
| None | 46.4 | 35.5 | 33.9 | 55.2 | 58.8 | 55.7 | 55.9 | 64.8 |
| 1 to 2 | 24.8 | 23.8 | 24.7 | 26.4 | 24.4 | 25.2 | 26.3 | 22.4 |
| 3 to 4 | 13.0 | 16.6 | 16.3 | 9.8 | 9.7 | 11.2 | 10.1 | 7.4 |
| 5 to 10 | 10.3 | 14.8 | 15.5 | 6.7 | 5.1 | 5.5 | 5.8 | 4.1 |
| 11 to 20 | 3.7 | 5.7 | 7.0 | 1.4 | 1.6 | 2.0 | 1.6 | 1.0 |
| 21 to 50 | 1.4 | 2.8 | 1.9 | 0.3 | 0.3 | 0.3 | 0.3 | 0.3 |
| 51+ | 0.4 | 0.8 | 0.7 | 0.1 | 0.0 | 0.0 | 0.0 | 0.0 |
| **Books, manuals, or monographs** | | | | | | | | |
| None | 57.0 | 49.6 | 47.6 | 63.1 | 66.0 | 63.5 | 63.4 | 70.9 |
| 1 to 2 | 26.8 | 30.0 | 27.2 | 25.7 | 23.3 | 24.8 | 26.6 | 19.5 |
| 3 to 4 | 8.3 | 10.0 | 11.8 | 6.7 | 5.5 | 5.4 | 5.5 | 5.6 |
| 5 to 10 | 5.7 | 7.4 | 9.1 | 3.3 | 4.1 | 5.4 | 3.8 | 2.5 |
| 11 to 20 | 1.5 | 1.9 | 3.2 | 0.7 | 0.9 | 0.7 | 0.6 | 1.2 |
| 21 to 50 | 0.5 | 0.9 | 0.7 | 0.2 | 0.2 | 0.1 | 0.1 | 0.2 |
| 51+ | 0.2 | 0.2 | 0.3 | 0.2 | 0.0 | 0.0 | 0.0 | 0.0 |
| **Other, such as patents or computer software products** | | | | | | | | |
| None | 82.1 | 77.2 | 78.9 | 85.0 | 87.3 | 87.9 | 85.2 | 87.7 |
| 1 to 2 | 9.9 | 11.9 | 12.0 | 8.7 | 7.2 | 7.0 | 8.9 | 6.6 |
| 3 to 4 | 4.0 | 5.6 | 4.0 | 3.2 | 2.7 | 2.2 | 3.3 | 3.1 |
| 5 to 10 | 2.5 | 3.5 | 3.4 | 1.7 | 1.4 | 1.6 | 1.6 | 1.1 |
| 11 to 20 | 0.8 | 1.1 | 0.9 | 0.7 | 0.7 | 0.6 | 0.6 | 0.8 |
| 21 to 50 | 0.4 | 0.5 | 0.4 | 0.5 | 0.3 | 0.5 | 0.1 | 0.2 |
| 51+ | 0.3 | 0.3 | 0.5 | 0.2 | 0.3 | 0.3 | 0.4 | 0.4 |
| **IN THE LAST TWO YEARS, HOW MANY:** | | | | | | | | |
| **Exhibitions or performances in the fine or applied arts have you presented?** | | | | | | | | |
| None | 82.4 | 87.5 | 82.2 | 81.1 | 76.6 | 73.5 | 83.6 | 77.3 |
| 1 to 2 | 5.2 | 3.2 | 6.0 | 5.1 | 8.0 | 10.4 | 6.5 | 5.4 |
| 3 to 4 | 3.9 | 2.9 | 4.3 | 4.4 | 4.6 | 4.9 | 3.6 | 4.7 |
| 5 to 10 | 4.0 | 3.0 | 3.6 | 4.3 | 5.6 | 6.4 | 4.0 | 5.4 |
| 11 to 20 | 2.0 | 1.6 | 1.5 | 2.5 | 2.3 | 2.2 | 0.7 | 3.2 |
| 21 to 50 | 1.2 | 0.7 | 1.4 | 1.8 | 1.2 | 0.9 | 0.6 | 1.9 |
| 51+ | 1.2 | 1.1 | 1.1 | 0.9 | 1.7 | 1.8 | 1.0 | 2.0 |
| **Of your professional writings have been published or accepted for publication?** | | | | | | | | |
| None | 26.1 | 16.7 | 17.1 | 30.3 | 40.2 | 38.6 | 35.7 | 44.8 |
| 1 to 2 | 31.1 | 25.4 | 27.1 | 36.4 | 35.2 | 36.1 | 36.1 | 33.5 |
| 3 to 4 | 22.0 | 25.2 | 25.7 | 21.2 | 16.2 | 16.7 | 18.0 | 14.6 |
| 5 to 10 | 16.0 | 24.6 | 23.5 | 9.7 | 6.8 | 7.2 | 7.9 | 5.7 |
| 11 to 20 | 3.6 | 6.5 | 4.9 | 1.6 | 0.9 | 1.1 | 0.6 | 0.9 |
| 21 to 50 | 0.9 | 1.4 | 1.1 | 0.6 | 0.4 | 0.2 | 1.4 | 0.1 |
| 51+ | 0.3 | 0.3 | 0.5 | 0.1 | 0.2 | 0.0 | 0.4 | 0.3 |

## 2007–2008 FACULTY SURVEY WEIGHTED NATIONAL NORMS
### Full-time Undergraduate Faculty

| Male Respondents | All 4+ yr | Universities Pub | Priv | Four-year Colleges Pub | All Priv | Nons | Cath | Oth Relig |
|---|---|---|---|---|---|---|---|---|
| **General activities** | | | | | | | | |
| Are you a member of a faculty union? | 20.0 | 16.0 | 7.8 | 39.0 | 9.1 | 8.3 | 18.3 | 5.4 |
| Are you a U.S. citizen? | 92.9 | 90.8 | 93.5 | 93.5 | 94.7 | 94.4 | 94.3 | 95.4 |
| Were you born in the U.S.A.? | 84.4 | 82.2 | 82.8 | 85.3 | 87.4 | 84.5 | 88.4 | 91.0 |
| Do you plan to retire within the next three years? | 14.3 | 17.5 | 12.5 | 14.5 | 10.6 | 10.6 | 12.9 | 9.5 |
| Do you use your scholarship to address local community needs? | 43.8 | 42.6 | 39.2 | 49.4 | 41.2 | 34.4 | 46.3 | 48.2 |
| Have you been sexually harassed at this institution? | 2.3 | 1.7 | 1.4 | 3.7 | 2.2 | 2.5 | 2.3 | 1.6 |
| Have you ever interrupted your professional career for more than one year for family reasons? [2] | 5.0 | 4.2 | 3.2 | 6.3 | 5.8 | 5.2 | 6.3 | 6.5 |
| Have you ever received an award for outstanding teaching? | 44.0 | 49.6 | 44.4 | 40.7 | 39.5 | 37.3 | 40.7 | 42.1 |
| Have you published op-ed pieces or editorials? | 27.8 | 28.5 | 29.6 | 26.9 | 26.8 | 26.9 | 28.4 | 25.9 |
| Is (or was) your: | | | | | | | | |
|    Father an academic? | 13.3 | 13.1 | 15.2 | 12.7 | 13.3 | 13.1 | 11.0 | 14.8 |
|    Mother an academic? | 8.0 | 7.4 | 8.2 | 8.1 | 8.7 | 7.5 | 8.9 | 10.2 |
|    Spouse/partner an academic? | 31.9 | 32.2 | 28.4 | 31.8 | 33.8 | 33.4 | 33.3 | 34.5 |
| Are you currently teaching courses at more than one institution? | 4.8 | 3.7 | 4.2 | 4.2 | 7.6 | 7.9 | 7.3 | 7.2 |
| **During the <u>past two</u> years, have you:** | | | | | | | | |
| Considered early retirement? | 20.3 | 21.0 | 18.1 | 23.1 | 17.2 | 16.0 | 18.8 | 17.9 |
| Considered leaving academe for another job? | 29.7 | 26.5 | 25.8 | 33.9 | 31.2 | 32.6 | 24.2 | 32.8 |
| Considered leaving this institution for another? | 45.1 | 44.7 | 40.9 | 47.5 | 45.0 | 45.2 | 41.0 | 46.8 |
| Changed academic institutions? | 11.0 | 9.9 | 11.1 | 12.3 | 11.1 | 10.1 | 10.1 | 12.9 |
| Engaged in paid consulting outside of your institution? | 40.8 | 46.6 | 40.9 | 38.2 | 35.2 | 36.0 | 33.4 | 35.0 |
| Engaged in public service/professional consulting without pay? | 58.6 | 61.4 | 54.9 | 59.8 | 55.1 | 54.4 | 50.0 | 58.6 |
| Received at least one firm job offer? | 22.4 | 20.3 | 22.7 | 23.0 | 24.4 | 25.0 | 23.1 | 24.3 |
| Received funding for your work from: | | | | | | | | |
|    Foundations? | 20.8 | 24.9 | 23.1 | 17.5 | 17.3 | 19.9 | 15.3 | 14.7 |
|    State or federal government? | 30.2 | 44.6 | 26.7 | 27.9 | 14.1 | 17.7 | 13.2 | 9.5 |
|    Business or industry? | 16.7 | 22.2 | 16.2 | 14.8 | 11.3 | 12.7 | 10.3 | 9.9 |
| Requested/sought an early promotion? | 7.2 | 7.4 | 5.7 | 8.5 | 6.4 | 7.6 | 5.4 | 5.2 |
| **IF YOU WERE TO BEGIN YOUR CAREER AGAIN, WOULD YOU STILL WANT TO:** | | | | | | | | |
| **Come to this institution? [2]** | | | | | | | | |
| Definitely yes | 35.7 | 34.4 | 44.9 | 30.7 | 38.6 | 39.0 | 37.1 | 38.8 |
| Probably yes | 33.5 | 33.6 | 30.3 | 34.8 | 33.9 | 33.6 | 36.4 | 33.0 |
| Not sure | 16.1 | 16.4 | 14.6 | 17.3 | 15.3 | 15.8 | 14.3 | 15.2 |
| Probably no | 9.6 | 10.4 | 6.2 | 11.4 | 8.2 | 7.5 | 7.3 | 9.6 |
| Definitely no | 5.0 | 5.2 | 4.0 | 5.9 | 4.0 | 4.2 | 4.9 | 3.3 |
| **Be a college professor?** | | | | | | | | |
| Definitely yes | 65.9 | 64.9 | 69.6 | 64.7 | 66.5 | 64.5 | 70.6 | 67.4 |
| Probably yes | 23.8 | 23.5 | 20.5 | 24.6 | 25.2 | 26.8 | 21.4 | 25.0 |
| Not sure | 7.4 | 7.9 | 6.9 | 8.0 | 6.2 | 6.7 | 5.6 | 5.9 |
| Probably no | 2.3 | 2.7 | 2.3 | 2.1 | 1.7 | 1.8 | 1.7 | 1.4 |
| Definitely no | 0.7 | 0.9 | 0.7 | 0.6 | 0.3 | 0.2 | 0.6 | 0.3 |

[2] This question asked for the first time in the 2007–2008 Faculty Survey.

67

**2007–2008 FACULTY SURVEY WEIGHTED NATIONAL NORMS**
**Full-time Undergraduate Faculty**

| Male Respondents | All 4+ yr | Universities Pub | Priv | Four-year Colleges Pub | All Priv | Nons | Cath | Oth Relig |
|---|---|---|---|---|---|---|---|---|
| **Attributes noted as being "very descriptive" of your institution** | | | | | | | | |
| It is easy for students to see faculty outside of regular office hours | 60.1 | 47.4 | 61.6 | 60.3 | 77.7 | 75.8 | 77.7 | 80.5 |
| There is a great deal of conformity among the students | 29.9 | 30.5 | 35.8 | 24.0 | 32.9 | 27.1 | 40.2 | 37.4 |
| The faculty are typically at odds with campus administration | 19.1 | 17.5 | 12.9 | 25.5 | 17.3 | 16.9 | 20.7 | 16.0 |
| Faculty here respect each other | 47.3 | 45.1 | 54.9 | 41.1 | 53.9 | 50.8 | 53.9 | 58.2 |
| Most students are treated like "numbers in a book" | 4.4 | 7.1 | 2.6 | 3.9 | 2.0 | 2.4 | 1.4 | 1.6 |
| Social activities are overemphasized | 8.5 | 8.7 | 8.0 | 6.3 | 11.0 | 11.4 | 6.3 | 13.0 |
| Faculty are rewarded for being good teachers | 16.2 | 13.0 | 18.1 | 15.4 | 21.0 | 24.5 | 16.1 | 18.4 |
| There is respect for the expression of diverse values and beliefs | 36.1 | 34.7 | 38.2 | 34.8 | 38.6 | 43.2 | 39.6 | 31.6 |
| Faculty are rewarded for their efforts to use instructional technology | 18.4 | 19.0 | 22.1 | 19.1 | 14.4 | 16.5 | 12.3 | 12.7 |
| Faculty are rewarded for their efforts to work with underprepared students | 5.1 | 3.8 | 5.6 | 5.3 | 6.6 | 8.1 | 5.3 | 5.1 |
| Administrators consider faculty concerns when making policy [2] | 13.4 | 10.1 | 14.6 | 12.2 | 19.4 | 20.5 | 14.4 | 20.4 |
| The administration is open about its policies | 17.0 | 14.4 | 17.4 | 15.9 | 22.0 | 23.4 | 17.3 | 22.4 |
| **Do you, "to a great extent":** | | | | | | | | |
| Engage in academic work that spans multiple disciplines | 40.0 | 42.0 | 42.9 | 36.2 | 40.3 | 44.5 | 37.6 | 35.5 |
| Feel that the training you received in graduate school prepared you well for your role as a faculty mentor | 40.4 | 40.6 | 41.0 | 41.9 | 37.9 | 36.9 | 40.6 | 37.8 |
| Achieve a healthy balance between your personal life and your professional life | 38.7 | 38.7 | 42.3 | 38.4 | 37.0 | 36.7 | 40.6 | 35.7 |
| Experience close alignment between your work and your personal values | 64.7 | 62.4 | 69.4 | 62.6 | 68.1 | 64.7 | 70.3 | 71.7 |
| Feel that you have to work harder than your colleagues to be perceived as a legitimate scholar | 22.8 | 21.7 | 24.5 | 23.9 | 21.8 | 23.2 | 18.1 | 21.7 |
| Mentor new faculty [2] | 19.8 | 20.9 | 20.3 | 20.4 | 17.2 | 17.7 | 20.1 | 15.1 |

[2] This question asked for the first time in the 2007–2008 Faculty Survey.

68

## 2007–2008 FACULTY SURVEY WEIGHTED NATIONAL NORMS
### Full-time Undergraduate Faculty

| | | | | Four-year Colleges | | | | |
| | All | Universities | | | All | | | Oth |
| Male Respondents | 4+ yr | Pub | Priv | Pub | Priv | Nons | Cath | Relig |
|---|---|---|---|---|---|---|---|---|
| **Aspects of your job with which you are "very satisfied" or "satisfied": [3]** | | | | | | | | |
| Salary [2] | 48.9 | 51.4 | 55.6 | 43.7 | 47.9 | 48.5 | 53.6 | 44.1 |
| Health benefits [2] | 67.9 | 70.3 | 73.9 | 69.7 | 58.2 | 60.1 | 64.7 | 52.3 |
| Retirement benefits [2] | 69.6 | 73.6 | 69.0 | 70.1 | 63.3 | 64.2 | 63.1 | 62.2 |
| Opportunity for scholarly pursuits | 58.4 | 68.3 | 69.0 | 46.8 | 52.0 | 55.3 | 49.0 | 48.8 |
| Teaching load | 60.4 | 70.5 | 67.3 | 48.6 | 56.5 | 60.0 | 54.6 | 52.3 |
| Quality of students | 55.5 | 58.7 | 73.2 | 42.9 | 55.8 | 58.4 | 52.6 | 53.8 |
| Office/lab space | 68.0 | 70.5 | 69.6 | 62.3 | 70.4 | 70.9 | 69.5 | 70.2 |
| Autonomy and independence | 85.9 | 88.9 | 86.8 | 81.9 | 85.8 | 86.9 | 84.6 | 85.0 |
| Professional relationships with other faculty | 77.7 | 76.2 | 78.8 | 75.6 | 81.7 | 80.4 | 81.3 | 83.8 |
| Social relationships with other faculty | 65.6 | 63.3 | 66.3 | 63.8 | 70.7 | 68.8 | 75.1 | 71.3 |
| Competency of colleagues | 77.1 | 77.9 | 80.3 | 71.8 | 80.6 | 81.0 | 77.4 | 81.7 |
| Visibility for jobs at other institutions/organizations | 55.1 | 62.3 | 62.8 | 48.3 | 48.0 | 48.5 | 47.8 | 47.5 |
| Job security | 80.8 | 83.8 | 80.8 | 80.3 | 77.0 | 75.8 | 80.6 | 76.7 |
| Relationship with administration | 59.1 | 59.2 | 61.5 | 54.6 | 63.1 | 63.9 | 61.7 | 62.7 |
| Departmental leadership [2] | 71.4 | 67.8 | 75.7 | 68.9 | 77.1 | 76.0 | 75.6 | 79.3 |
| Course assignments [2] | 85.5 | 85.9 | 86.6 | 82.8 | 87.6 | 88.3 | 85.6 | 87.6 |
| Freedom to determine course content [2] | 93.3 | 94.5 | 93.1 | 91.8 | 93.8 | 94.5 | 90.5 | 94.4 |
| Availability of child care at this institution | 33.7 | 36.3 | 38.9 | 35.3 | 24.5 | 26.9 | 17.0 | 24.6 |
| Prospects for career advancement | 57.7 | 58.5 | 63.3 | 54.7 | 56.6 | 55.8 | 59.2 | 56.4 |
| Clerical/administrative support | 63.0 | 60.9 | 68.5 | 63.3 | 62.4 | 63.3 | 65.9 | 59.3 |
| Overall job satisfaction | 76.6 | 77.2 | 80.9 | 72.8 | 77.9 | 79.3 | 78.5 | 75.6 |

[2]  This question asked for the first time in the 2007–2008 Faculty Survey.
[3]  Respondents marking "Not Applicable" were not included in the computation of these results.

69

**2007–2008 FACULTY SURVEY WEIGHTED NATIONAL NORMS**
**Full-time Undergraduate Faculty**

| Male Respondents | All 4+ yr | Universities Pub | Universities Priv | Four-year Colleges Pub | Four-year Colleges All Priv | Four-year Colleges Nons | Four-year Colleges Cath | Oth Relig |
|---|---|---|---|---|---|---|---|---|
| **Do you agree "strongly" or "somewhat"?** | | | | | | | | |
| Faculty are interested in students' personal problems | 82.0 | 72.2 | 84.6 | 83.0 | 93.6 | 91.6 | 94.0 | 96.2 |
| Racial and ethnic diversity should be more strongly reflected in the curriculum | 52.3 | 50.9 | 48.6 | 51.0 | 58.2 | 56.5 | 61.8 | 58.8 |
| Faculty feel that most students are well-prepared academically | 43.7 | 44.3 | 67.0 | 28.7 | 47.7 | 49.9 | 42.5 | 47.2 |
| This institution should hire more faculty of color | 69.2 | 71.9 | 68.6 | 63.5 | 72.8 | 70.9 | 71.2 | 76.3 |
| Student Affairs staff have the support and respect of faculty | 75.6 | 74.3 | 77.8 | 73.1 | 79.4 | 78.7 | 81.3 | 79.4 |
| Faculty are committed to the welfare of this institution | 90.5 | 88.2 | 93.0 | 88.7 | 94.8 | 94.0 | 96.1 | 95.2 |
| Faculty here are strongly interested in the academic problems of undergraduates | 87.7 | 82.0 | 89.8 | 87.6 | 94.9 | 94.3 | 96.3 | 95.1 |
| There is a lot of campus racial conflict here | 8.6 | 10.9 | 5.9 | 7.1 | 8.9 | 9.8 | 8.1 | 8.0 |
| Most students are strongly committed to community service | 49.3 | 41.7 | 75.1 | 35.8 | 61.6 | 56.1 | 66.3 | 67.0 |
| My research is valued by faculty in my department | 75.9 | 74.7 | 78.8 | 74.1 | 78.3 | 78.2 | 79.2 | 78.1 |
| My teaching is valued by faculty in my department | 90.2 | 88.0 | 90.1 | 90.4 | 93.3 | 91.2 | 95.2 | 95.3 |
| Many courses include feminist perspectives | 40.8 | 37.9 | 38.2 | 40.6 | 46.7 | 51.0 | 46.5 | 40.5 |
| Faculty of color are treated fairly here | 92.1 | 91.2 | 93.1 | 92.4 | 92.4 | 93.0 | 91.3 | 92.0 |
| Women faculty are treated fairly here | 92.1 | 90.2 | 92.4 | 93.1 | 93.5 | 94.7 | 91.7 | 92.6 |
| Many courses involve students in community service | 44.8 | 34.1 | 55.8 | 42.5 | 56.7 | 51.1 | 64.5 | 60.6 |
| This institution should hire more women faculty | 53.2 | 61.3 | 61.2 | 45.1 | 46.4 | 44.5 | 47.1 | 48.8 |
| Gay and lesbian faculty are treated fairly here | 83.2 | 86.3 | 75.3 | 87.7 | 77.5 | 86.6 | 68.9 | 68.6 |
| My department does a good job of mentoring new faculty | 72.2 | 69.4 | 76.3 | 69.8 | 76.7 | 76.4 | 78.3 | 76.5 |
| Faculty are sufficiently involved in campus decision making | 52.5 | 49.9 | 49.1 | 50.8 | 60.3 | 63.7 | 54.5 | 58.4 |
| My values are congruent with the dominant institutional values | 72.1 | 66.9 | 78.8 | 68.1 | 80.8 | 79.1 | 79.8 | 83.6 |
| There is adequate support for integrating technology in my teaching | 85.8 | 87.9 | 91.3 | 83.1 | 82.8 | 84.6 | 84.8 | 79.3 |
| This institution takes responsibility for educating underprepared students | 65.0 | 62.1 | 65.2 | 64.9 | 69.1 | 68.6 | 70.8 | 68.8 |
| The criteria for advancement and promotion decisions are clear | 74.3 | 76.6 | 78.4 | 71.7 | 71.8 | 70.3 | 73.3 | 73.2 |
| Most of the students I teach lack the basic skills for college level work | 35.4 | 31.0 | 17.1 | 50.0 | 34.6 | 32.5 | 40.6 | 34.5 |
| There is adequate support for faculty development | 69.3 | 72.2 | 75.8 | 62.6 | 69.5 | 72.2 | 69.8 | 65.6 |
| This institution should not offer remedial/developmental education | 31.3 | 32.0 | 39.4 | 28.6 | 28.9 | 29.9 | 24.6 | 29.8 |

70

**2007–2008 FACULTY SURVEY WEIGHTED NATIONAL NORMS**
**Full-time Undergraduate Faculty**

| Male Respondents | All 4+ yr | Universities | | Four-year Colleges | | | | |
| --- | --- | --- | --- | --- | --- | --- | --- | --- |
| | | Pub | Priv | Pub | All Priv | Nons | Cath | Oth Relig |
| **Issues you believe to be of "high" or "highest" priority at your institution:** | | | | | | | | |
| To promote the intellectual development of students | 85.6 | 85.7 | 89.6 | 81.8 | 88.0 | 88.6 | 86.4 | 88.0 |
| To help students examine and understand their personal values | 55.1 | 42.9 | 71.8 | 46.7 | 73.2 | 67.2 | 78.8 | 78.8 |
| To develop a sense of community among students and faculty | 51.9 | 42.9 | 59.2 | 47.9 | 65.9 | 63.5 | 65.6 | 69.5 |
| To facilitate student involvement in community service | 42.5 | 31.1 | 59.0 | 37.8 | 55.3 | 47.2 | 66.2 | 61.3 |
| To help students learn how to bring about change in American society | 32.4 | 25.2 | 41.0 | 30.0 | 40.8 | 40.4 | 42.5 | 40.4 |
| To increase or maintain institutional prestige | 63.6 | 71.8 | 71.1 | 53.9 | 59.4 | 64.1 | 61.1 | 51.7 |
| To hire faculty "stars" | 29.0 | 47.6 | 32.7 | 17.1 | 14.6 | 16.9 | 11.8 | 12.7 |
| To recruit more minority students | 48.6 | 52.6 | 44.1 | 47.1 | 47.3 | 51.9 | 42.3 | 43.4 |
| To enhance the institution's national image | 70.0 | 81.4 | 78.6 | 59.0 | 62.0 | 68.9 | 60.1 | 53.1 |
| To create a diverse multi-cultural campus environment | 51.6 | 51.4 | 49.1 | 51.9 | 53.0 | 58.8 | 48.6 | 46.9 |
| To promote gender equity among faculty | 57.1 | 60.9 | 58.2 | 54.0 | 54.6 | 59.2 | 52.7 | 49.0 |
| To provide resources for faculty to engage in community-based teaching or research | 33.5 | 30.8 | 34.3 | 36.7 | 32.9 | 34.6 | 36.7 | 28.6 |
| To create and sustain partnerships with surrounding communities | 44.8 | 42.4 | 38.1 | 51.6 | 43.8 | 43.7 | 47.4 | 42.1 |
| To pursue extramural funding | 60.9 | 79.5 | 59.6 | 53.1 | 44.3 | 45.5 | 49.3 | 39.9 |
| To increase the representation of minorities in the faculty and administration | 44.7 | 49.0 | 42.8 | 44.1 | 40.2 | 45.5 | 34.9 | 35.4 |
| To strengthen links with the for-profit, corporate sector [2] | 48.4 | 62.7 | 40.6 | 46.7 | 34.4 | 33.8 | 40.6 | 32.0 |
| To develop leadership ability among students | 57.5 | 52.0 | 69.4 | 51.2 | 66.3 | 66.7 | 63.7 | 66.9 |
| To increase the representation of women in the faculty and administration | 41.9 | 49.5 | 42.2 | 37.6 | 35.9 | 41.0 | 32.1 | 30.7 |
| To develop an appreciation for multiculturalism [2] | 53.0 | 51.5 | 51.7 | 51.7 | 57.6 | 62.5 | 53.4 | 52.9 |

[2]  This question asked for the first time in the 2007–2008 Faculty Survey.

71

**2007–2008 FACULTY SURVEY WEIGHTED NATIONAL NORMS**
**Full-time Undergraduate Faculty**

| Male Respondents | All 4+ yr | Universities Pub | Priv | Four-year Colleges Pub | All Priv | Nons | Cath | Oth Relig |
|---|---|---|---|---|---|---|---|---|
| **Do you agree "strongly" or "somewhat"?** | | | | | | | | |
| Western civilization and culture should be the foundation for the undergraduate curriculum | 62.8 | 60.3 | 65.5 | 61.3 | 66.6 | 62.6 | 68.6 | 71.3 |
| College officials have the right to ban persons with extreme views from speaking on campus | 30.0 | 23.4 | 43.6 | 23.9 | 39.1 | 33.9 | 36.6 | 47.8 |
| The chief benefit of a college education is that it increases one's earning power | 29.5 | 32.5 | 25.5 | 32.4 | 24.1 | 24.7 | 27.5 | 21.4 |
| Promoting diversity leads to the admission of too many underprepared students | 27.9 | 28.3 | 28.4 | 29.7 | 24.8 | 23.0 | 26.7 | 26.3 |
| Colleges should be actively involved in solving social problems | 68.1 | 68.0 | 69.0 | 67.5 | 68.6 | 66.6 | 70.1 | 70.5 |
| Tenure is an outmoded concept | 28.7 | 27.6 | 29.0 | 27.9 | 31.3 | 31.5 | 30.9 | 31.1 |
| Colleges should encourage students to be involved in community service activities | 85.2 | 82.1 | 87.6 | 84.5 | 89.2 | 86.8 | 88.7 | 92.8 |
| Community service should be given weight in college admissions decisions | 64.4 | 61.8 | 69.5 | 61.5 | 68.7 | 68.3 | 70.0 | 68.6 |
| A racially/ethnically diverse student body enhances the educational experience of all students | 91.6 | 92.1 | 91.2 | 91.1 | 91.6 | 90.4 | 90.5 | 93.8 |
| Realistically, an individual can do little to bring about changes in society | 23.1 | 23.5 | 24.3 | 23.2 | 21.8 | 23.0 | 22.9 | 19.5 |
| Colleges should be concerned with facilitating undergraduate students' spiritual development | 37.0 | 23.1 | 58.9 | 26.0 | 58.1 | 42.3 | 72.0 | 73.4 |
| Colleges have a responsibility to work with their surrounding communities to address local issues | 86.1 | 85.3 | 84.8 | 87.1 | 86.7 | 83.9 | 87.4 | 90.4 |
| Private funding sources often prevent researchers from being completely objective in the conduct of their work | 58.3 | 59.6 | 56.1 | 58.7 | 57.3 | 56.6 | 59.7 | 56.9 |

72

## 2007–2008 FACULTY SURVEY WEIGHTED NATIONAL NORMS
### Full-time Undergraduate Faculty

| Male Respondents | All 4+ yr | Universities Pub | Priv | Four-year Colleges Pub | All Priv | Nons | Cath | Oth Relig |
|---|---|---|---|---|---|---|---|---|
| **Factors noted as a source of stress for you during the <u>last two</u> years** | | | | | | | | |
| Managing household responsibilities | 67.6 | 65.5 | 64.9 | 68.8 | 70.8 | 70.9 | 66.7 | 72.7 |
| Child care | 30.7 | 28.4 | 29.3 | 31.3 | 34.1 | 35.5 | 29.1 | 34.7 |
| Care of elderly parent | 30.9 | 27.7 | 32.9 | 31.5 | 33.4 | 35.3 | 30.7 | 32.2 |
| My physical health | 46.7 | 45.1 | 47.7 | 49.6 | 44.7 | 43.1 | 47.4 | 45.5 |
| Health of spouse/partner | 38.9 | 37.4 | 41.2 | 39.9 | 38.4 | 39.0 | 36.3 | 38.4 |
| Review/promotion process | 46.6 | 46.0 | 42.3 | 50.0 | 45.7 | 45.2 | 47.2 | 45.5 |
| Subtle discrimination (e.g., prejudice, racism, sexism) | 18.2 | 18.1 | 14.6 | 21.0 | 16.9 | 18.4 | 18.6 | 14.0 |
| Personal finances | 61.3 | 56.5 | 59.4 | 64.5 | 65.5 | 65.2 | 62.7 | 67.3 |
| Committee work | 59.3 | 56.4 | 54.7 | 64.2 | 60.3 | 59.4 | 63.6 | 60.0 |
| Faculty meetings | 51.0 | 48.8 | 45.6 | 54.9 | 52.5 | 51.6 | 55.4 | 52.4 |
| Colleagues | 61.3 | 60.1 | 57.0 | 66.1 | 59.5 | 60.0 | 58.4 | 59.5 |
| Students | 61.4 | 58.8 | 54.4 | 65.3 | 64.4 | 62.3 | 60.7 | 69.2 |
| Research or publishing demands | 61.1 | 67.8 | 66.0 | 58.9 | 51.2 | 50.9 | 56.1 | 49.2 |
| Institutional procedures and "red tape" | 72.0 | 74.6 | 66.6 | 76.2 | 66.4 | 63.9 | 70.6 | 67.9 |
| Teaching load | 59.6 | 52.9 | 55.3 | 65.7 | 64.2 | 62.6 | 62.7 | 67.2 |
| Children's problems | 31.7 | 29.6 | 36.1 | 31.6 | 32.0 | 31.8 | 27.5 | 34.5 |
| Friction with spouse/partner | 27.4 | 28.2 | 25.2 | 27.4 | 27.7 | 28.5 | 27.5 | 26.7 |
| Lack of personal time | 67.8 | 67.4 | 67.1 | 67.5 | 69.2 | 68.2 | 67.5 | 71.6 |
| Keeping up with information technology | 48.3 | 47.3 | 45.0 | 49.8 | 49.7 | 48.7 | 50.4 | 50.7 |
| Job security | 28.3 | 24.2 | 27.5 | 28.8 | 34.1 | 35.7 | 34.5 | 31.6 |
| Being part of a dual career couple | 40.5 | 38.0 | 34.8 | 42.5 | 44.9 | 45.8 | 40.5 | 45.9 |
| Working with underprepared students | 59.0 | 52.9 | 42.1 | 70.0 | 64.2 | 59.7 | 68.8 | 68.4 |
| Classroom conflict | 16.3 | 13.9 | 11.0 | 21.0 | 16.9 | 15.2 | 21.7 | 16.8 |
| Self-imposed high expectations | 77.0 | 77.5 | 75.0 | 76.9 | 77.7 | 77.1 | 74.2 | 80.4 |
| Change in work responsibilities | 40.6 | 38.4 | 37.1 | 43.1 | 43.0 | 43.4 | 41.9 | 43.0 |
| **Personal goals noted as "very important" or "essential":** | | | | | | | | |
| Becoming an authority in my field | 61.5 | 70.3 | 67.6 | 55.4 | 52.8 | 53.3 | 52.5 | 52.4 |
| Influencing the political structure | 18.0 | 19.2 | 17.9 | 17.6 | 16.5 | 15.6 | 19.7 | 16.3 |
| Influencing social values | 35.3 | 33.3 | 38.7 | 32.6 | 39.9 | 37.3 | 41.5 | 42.7 |
| Raising a family | 72.4 | 73.1 | 74.4 | 68.7 | 74.9 | 75.4 | 67.5 | 78.1 |
| Becoming very well off financially | 34.3 | 38.8 | 30.8 | 35.4 | 28.3 | 30.4 | 29.5 | 24.8 |
| Helping others who are in difficulty | 61.2 | 58.6 | 65.4 | 60.1 | 64.0 | 61.3 | 67.5 | 66.0 |
| Becoming involved in programs to clean up the environment | 33.1 | 33.5 | 30.8 | 33.8 | 33.0 | 34.0 | 33.6 | 31.2 |
| Developing a meaningful philosophy of life | 70.8 | 68.5 | 73.5 | 68.6 | 75.2 | 74.9 | 75.8 | 75.4 |
| Helping to promote racial understanding | 48.4 | 47.6 | 47.4 | 46.6 | 52.4 | 53.2 | 55.9 | 49.6 |
| Obtaining recognition from my colleagues for contributions to my special field | 47.0 | 56.3 | 51.3 | 41.1 | 38.3 | 40.6 | 42.2 | 33.2 |
| Integrating spirituality into my life | 43.8 | 35.5 | 54.0 | 40.3 | 54.5 | 45.7 | 57.1 | 65.5 |

73

| | | | | Four-year Colleges | | | | |
| Male Respondents | All 4+ yr | Universities Pub | Priv | Pub | All Priv | Nons | Cath | Oth Relig |
|---|---|---|---|---|---|---|---|---|
| **IN YOUR INTERACTIONS WITH UNDERGRAD-UATES, HOW OFTEN DO YOU ENCOURAGE THEM TO: [2]** | | | | | | | | |
| **Ask questions in class** | | | | | | | | |
| Frequently | 92.9 | 91.9 | 92.9 | 93.7 | 93.5 | 93.5 | 93.3 | 93.6 |
| Occasionally | 6.9 | 7.7 | 7.0 | 6.3 | 6.4 | 6.4 | 6.5 | 6.3 |
| Not at all | 0.2 | 0.4 | 0.1 | 0.1 | 0.1 | 0.0 | 0.2 | 0.1 |
| **Support their opinions with a logical argument** | | | | | | | | |
| Frequently | 80.4 | 78.8 | 79.7 | 81.4 | 82.0 | 82.5 | 84.6 | 80.0 |
| Occasionally | 18.5 | 19.8 | 19.3 | 17.7 | 17.2 | 17.0 | 14.4 | 18.9 |
| Not at all | 1.0 | 1.4 | 1.0 | 0.9 | 0.8 | 0.6 | 1.0 | 1.1 |
| **Seek solutions to problems and explain them to others** | | | | | | | | |
| Frequently | 71.3 | 71.2 | 67.8 | 73.2 | 71.3 | 73.2 | 71.7 | 68.4 |
| Occasionally | 26.7 | 26.6 | 30.3 | 25.0 | 26.9 | 25.0 | 26.2 | 30.2 |
| Not at all | 1.9 | 2.2 | 1.9 | 1.8 | 1.7 | 1.8 | 2.1 | 1.4 |
| **Revise their papers to improve their writing** | | | | | | | | |
| Frequently | 52.3 | 49.3 | 50.5 | 52.6 | 57.2 | 60.5 | 56.2 | 53.1 |
| Occasionally | 37.2 | 37.1 | 38.5 | 38.7 | 34.8 | 32.0 | 35.8 | 38.2 |
| Not at all | 10.5 | 13.5 | 11.0 | 8.6 | 8.0 | 7.5 | 7.9 | 8.7 |
| **Evaluate the quality or reliability of information they receive** | | | | | | | | |
| Frequently | 69.0 | 68.4 | 67.1 | 70.3 | 69.4 | 71.3 | 70.0 | 66.5 |
| Occasionally | 28.6 | 28.9 | 30.4 | 27.6 | 28.4 | 26.8 | 27.8 | 31.0 |
| Not at all | 2.4 | 2.7 | 2.4 | 2.1 | 2.2 | 2.0 | 2.2 | 2.5 |
| **Take risks for potential gains** | | | | | | | | |
| Frequently | 33.8 | 33.7 | 30.6 | 33.8 | 35.8 | 37.4 | 35.6 | 33.6 |
| Occasionally | 50.3 | 49.6 | 51.0 | 50.2 | 51.0 | 49.7 | 51.0 | 52.8 |
| Not at all | 15.9 | 16.7 | 18.4 | 16.0 | 13.2 | 12.9 | 13.4 | 13.5 |
| **Seek alternative solutions to a problem** | | | | | | | | |
| Frequently | 60.9 | 59.2 | 58.6 | 63.7 | 61.1 | 63.2 | 59.8 | 58.9 |
| Occasionally | 36.8 | 39.1 | 38.3 | 33.7 | 36.5 | 34.6 | 37.3 | 38.7 |
| Not at all | 2.3 | 1.6 | 3.1 | 2.6 | 2.4 | 2.2 | 2.9 | 2.4 |
| **Look up scientific research articles and resources** | | | | | | | | |
| Frequently | 52.4 | 56.4 | 52.5 | 52.4 | 46.4 | 49.2 | 45.6 | 42.9 |
| Occasionally | 36.4 | 34.6 | 35.1 | 37.2 | 38.9 | 37.0 | 39.0 | 41.6 |
| Not at all | 11.2 | 9.0 | 12.3 | 10.4 | 14.6 | 13.8 | 15.5 | 15.5 |
| **Explore topics on their own, even though it was not required for a class** | | | | | | | | |
| Frequently | 48.8 | 49.3 | 49.5 | 49.6 | 46.6 | 49.0 | 45.8 | 43.7 |
| Occasionally | 46.8 | 46.8 | 46.1 | 46.0 | 48.3 | 45.7 | 50.2 | 50.8 |
| Not at all | 4.4 | 3.9 | 4.3 | 4.4 | 5.1 | 5.3 | 3.9 | 5.4 |
| **Acknowledge failure as a necessary part of the learning process** | | | | | | | | |
| Frequently | 46.2 | 44.3 | 42.7 | 49.4 | 47.2 | 49.0 | 46.2 | 45.2 |
| Occasionally | 46.2 | 47.4 | 48.2 | 43.7 | 46.4 | 45.1 | 47.2 | 47.9 |
| Not at all | 7.6 | 8.2 | 9.1 | 7.0 | 6.4 | 6.0 | 6.6 | 7.0 |
| **Seek feedback on their academic work** | | | | | | | | |
| Frequently | 66.9 | 64.5 | 63.9 | 68.7 | 69.8 | 72.0 | 67.8 | 67.9 |
| Occasionally | 31.1 | 33.3 | 33.6 | 29.3 | 28.5 | 26.4 | 30.3 | 30.5 |
| Not at all | 2.1 | 2.3 | 2.5 | 2.0 | 1.7 | 1.6 | 1.9 | 1.6 |

[2] This question asked for the first time in the 2007–2008 Faculty Survey.

## 2007–2008 FACULTY SURVEY WEIGHTED NATIONAL NORMS
### Full-time Undergraduate Faculty

| Male Respondents | All 4+ yr | Universities Pub | Priv | Four-year Colleges Pub | All Priv | Nons | Cath | Oth Relig |
|---|---|---|---|---|---|---|---|---|
| **Methods you use in "all" or "most" of the courses you teach:** | | | | | | | | |
| Multiple-choice exams [2] | 32.0 | 29.5 | 27.4 | 38.0 | 31.0 | 25.9 | 34.4 | 36.4 |
| Essay exams [2] | 45.0 | 40.7 | 47.2 | 43.0 | 52.3 | 51.7 | 55.8 | 51.5 |
| Short-answer exams [2] | 46.4 | 43.1 | 44.7 | 48.4 | 49.7 | 48.0 | 51.5 | 51.3 |
| Quizzes | 38.9 | 35.2 | 37.9 | 43.2 | 39.5 | 35.6 | 42.6 | 43.6 |
| Weekly essay assignments | 19.5 | 20.5 | 17.4 | 17.9 | 21.2 | 23.4 | 20.0 | 18.6 |
| Student presentations | 40.6 | 40.6 | 35.9 | 38.7 | 46.0 | 49.4 | 40.8 | 43.8 |
| Term/research papers | 42.5 | 41.6 | 45.0 | 40.3 | 45.0 | 46.0 | 42.6 | 44.9 |
| Student evaluations of each others' work | 19.7 | 20.0 | 17.6 | 19.4 | 20.9 | 23.6 | 16.6 | 19.2 |
| Grading on a curve | 20.8 | 24.5 | 23.2 | 18.7 | 16.7 | 17.5 | 18.1 | 14.8 |
| Competency-based grading | 51.6 | 51.5 | 52.4 | 51.6 | 51.3 | 53.9 | 48.0 | 49.2 |
| Class discussions | 78.3 | 74.9 | 80.2 | 78.8 | 81.4 | 80.6 | 81.7 | 82.3 |
| Cooperative learning (small groups) | 50.0 | 48.5 | 44.8 | 50.5 | 54.6 | 53.7 | 53.8 | 56.5 |
| Experiential learning/Field studies | 25.5 | 24.6 | 21.4 | 27.3 | 27.0 | 27.9 | 23.3 | 27.7 |
| Teaching assistants | 13.3 | 20.5 | 22.3 | 5.9 | 6.5 | 8.2 | 3.4 | 5.8 |
| Recitals/Demonstrations | 20.9 | 21.6 | 21.1 | 20.7 | 20.0 | 21.5 | 16.7 | 19.6 |
| Group projects | 31.1 | 32.4 | 25.3 | 31.3 | 32.5 | 31.8 | 31.1 | 34.1 |
| Extensive lecturing | 54.8 | 56.5 | 56.8 | 56.9 | 48.5 | 47.1 | 51.5 | 48.9 |
| Multiple drafts of written work | 21.2 | 20.4 | 21.5 | 20.2 | 23.6 | 27.8 | 19.6 | 19.7 |
| Readings on racial and ethnic issues | 17.9 | 17.2 | 16.4 | 17.9 | 19.9 | 22.6 | 19.1 | 16.6 |
| Readings on women and gender issues | 15.5 | 15.8 | 14.6 | 15.5 | 15.6 | 16.2 | 16.8 | 14.1 |
| Student-developed activities (assignments, exams, etc.) | 26.2 | 26.1 | 25.9 | 27.7 | 24.5 | 26.0 | 27.1 | 21.2 |
| Student-selected topics for course content | 15.2 | 15.3 | 13.0 | 16.5 | 14.8 | 15.2 | 15.4 | 13.9 |
| Reflective writing/journaling | 16.3 | 14.1 | 16.2 | 17.3 | 18.3 | 17.3 | 20.5 | 18.6 |
| Community service as part of coursework | 5.3 | 4.4 | 4.6 | 6.1 | 6.1 | 5.2 | 6.6 | 7.3 |
| Electronic quizzes with immediate feedback in class [2] | 6.3 | 4.9 | 7.0 | 8.5 | 5.0 | 4.7 | 5.3 | 5.1 |
| Using real-life problems [2] | 53.8 | 53.7 | 52.0 | 55.4 | 53.1 | 52.1 | 55.8 | 53.3 |
| Using student inquiry to drive learning | 43.7 | 41.9 | 42.7 | 44.8 | 45.4 | 47.4 | 47.1 | 41.7 |

[2] This question asked for the first time in the 2007–2008 Faculty Survey.

75

| Male Respondents | All 4+ yr | Universities Pub | Universities Priv | Four-year Colleges Pub | Four-year Colleges All Priv | Four-year Colleges Nons | Four-year Colleges Cath | Oth Relig |
|---|---|---|---|---|---|---|---|---|
| **YOUR BASE INSTITUTIONAL SALARY** | | | | | | | | |
| **9/10 month contract** | | | | | | | | |
| Less than $20,000 | 1.9 | 1.5 | 2.5 | 1.9 | 2.2 | 2.8 | 1.5 | 1.8 |
| $20,000 to 29,999 | 0.4 | 0.4 | 0.1 | 0.5 | 0.2 | 0.0 | 0.2 | 0.4 |
| $30,000 to 39,999 | 3.5 | 2.7 | 3.0 | 4.3 | 4.2 | 3.8 | 2.3 | 5.7 |
| $40,000 to 49,999 | 11.8 | 7.0 | 5.7 | 14.1 | 20.0 | 16.5 | 21.3 | 24.0 |
| $50,000 to 59,999 | 18.4 | 15.4 | 8.0 | 22.5 | 23.8 | 21.1 | 22.5 | 28.2 |
| $60,000 to 69,999 | 15.8 | 14.3 | 11.7 | 18.7 | 16.5 | 16.3 | 16.3 | 17.0 |
| $70,000 to 79,999 | 13.8 | 14.5 | 12.8 | 14.4 | 12.6 | 11.7 | 16.8 | 11.6 |
| $80,000 to 89,999 | 10.7 | 11.9 | 11.8 | 10.7 | 8.1 | 9.6 | 8.7 | 5.9 |
| $90,000 to 99,999 | 8.4 | 9.5 | 12.2 | 7.6 | 5.5 | 6.7 | 6.7 | 3.4 |
| $100,000 to 124,999 | 11.2 | 15.9 | 23.1 | 5.2 | 5.0 | 8.2 | 3.2 | 1.8 |
| $125,000 to 149,999 | 2.3 | 3.7 | 5.7 | 0.3 | 1.0 | 1.9 | 0.5 | 0.1 |
| $150,000 or more | 1.7 | 3.2 | 3.5 | 0.0 | 0.7 | 1.3 | 0.1 | 0.3 |
| **11/12 month contract** | | | | | | | | |
| Less than $20,000 | 2.4 | 2.7 | 1.9 | 2.5 | 2.4 | 2.8 | 4.2 | 0.9 |
| $20,000 to 29,999 | 0.6 | 0.5 | 0.8 | 0.4 | 0.9 | 0.1 | 0.4 | 2.4 |
| $30,000 to 39,999 | 2.9 | 2.1 | 1.3 | 5.3 | 2.7 | 1.3 | 0.4 | 5.9 |
| $40,000 to 49,999 | 12.0 | 5.2 | 7.9 | 13.7 | 21.2 | 18.7 | 17.4 | 27.0 |
| $50,000 to 59,999 | 15.0 | 9.8 | 12.1 | 18.3 | 20.1 | 17.5 | 24.2 | 22.5 |
| $60,000 to 69,999 | 12.3 | 8.4 | 11.0 | 15.5 | 14.9 | 15.0 | 12.8 | 15.7 |
| $70,000 to 79,999 | 9.4 | 6.8 | 9.8 | 10.7 | 11.0 | 11.3 | 11.0 | 10.6 |
| $80,000 to 89,999 | 13.1 | 17.5 | 11.7 | 11.7 | 10.2 | 10.6 | 15.1 | 7.2 |
| $90,000 to 99,999 | 8.8 | 9.9 | 11.2 | 8.1 | 6.6 | 8.8 | 5.3 | 3.5 |
| $100,000 to 124,999 | 14.3 | 19.2 | 20.5 | 11.1 | 7.6 | 10.8 | 6.7 | 2.8 |
| $125,000 to 149,999 | 4.5 | 7.7 | 7.6 | 2.0 | 1.2 | 1.9 | 0.0 | 0.8 |
| $150,000 or more | 4.4 | 10.1 | 4.4 | 0.8 | 1.2 | 1.1 | 2.5 | 0.7 |
| **Your base institutional salary is based on:** | | | | | | | | |
| 9/10 months | 74.4 | 76.4 | 69.1 | 78.1 | 70.2 | 67.6 | 73.7 | 72.1 |
| 11/12 months | 25.6 | 23.6 | 30.9 | 21.9 | 29.8 | 32.4 | 26.3 | 27.9 |
| **WHAT PERCENTAGE OF YOUR CURRENT YEAR'S SALARY COMES FROM: [2]** | | | | | | | | |
| **Income from this institution** | | | | | | | | |
| All | 59.8 | 58.7 | 57.2 | 62.6 | 59.6 | 59.8 | 63.1 | 57.4 |
| 75 to 99 | 31.5 | 31.6 | 35.5 | 30.3 | 30.6 | 29.5 | 27.6 | 33.7 |
| 50 to 74 | 6.3 | 7.2 | 5.2 | 5.5 | 6.5 | 6.5 | 7.5 | 6.1 |
| 25 to 49 | 1.7 | 1.6 | 1.5 | 1.2 | 2.9 | 3.6 | 1.8 | 2.3 |
| 1 to 24 | 0.4 | 0.5 | 0.5 | 0.2 | 0.4 | 0.5 | 0.0 | 0.4 |
| None | 0.2 | 0.3 | 0.0 | 0.2 | 0.1 | 0.2 | 0.0 | 0.1 |
| **Other academic income** | | | | | | | | |
| All | 0.1 | 0.1 | 0.1 | 0.1 | 0.0 | 0.0 | 0.0 | 0.0 |
| 75 to 99 | 0.1 | 0.1 | 0.0 | 0.0 | 0.1 | 0.1 | 0.0 | 0.1 |
| 50 to 74 | 0.6 | 1.0 | 0.2 | 0.5 | 0.4 | 0.5 | 0.2 | 0.2 |
| 25 to 49 | 2.2 | 3.3 | 1.7 | 1.4 | 1.8 | 2.7 | 1.1 | 1.0 |
| 1 to 24 | 17.0 | 15.9 | 20.7 | 15.2 | 18.6 | 19.1 | 18.6 | 18.0 |
| None | 80.1 | 79.6 | 77.3 | 82.9 | 79.1 | 77.6 | 80.2 | 80.7 |
| **Non-academic income** | | | | | | | | |
| All | 0.1 | 0.3 | 0.0 | 0.0 | 0.1 | 0.2 | 0.1 | 0.0 |
| 75 to 99 | 0.5 | 0.4 | 0.8 | 0.4 | 0.6 | 0.8 | 0.1 | 0.6 |
| 50 to 74 | 2.0 | 2.0 | 2.0 | 1.4 | 3.0 | 3.7 | 1.8 | 2.7 |
| 25 to 49 | 5.4 | 4.8 | 4.2 | 5.7 | 6.6 | 5.8 | 8.0 | 6.9 |
| 1 to 24 | 22.7 | 23.8 | 25.1 | 21.6 | 20.9 | 19.7 | 19.3 | 23.4 |
| None | 69.2 | 68.7 | 67.8 | 70.9 | 68.7 | 69.8 | 70.6 | 66.4 |

[2] This question asked for the first time in the 2007–2008 Faculty Survey.

## 2007–2008 FACULTY SURVEY WEIGHTED NATIONAL NORMS
### Full-time Undergraduate Faculty

| Male Respondents | All 4+ yr | Universities Pub | Priv | Four-year Colleges Pub | All Priv | Nons | Cath | Oth Relig |
|---|---|---|---|---|---|---|---|---|
| **What is your age as of 12/31/2007?** | | | | | | | | |
| Less than 30 | 1.4 | 0.8 | 1.5 | 1.6 | 1.9 | 2.3 | 0.9 | 1.9 |
| 30 to 34 | 5.8 | 5.0 | 6.1 | 5.3 | 7.6 | 7.7 | 7.0 | 7.6 |
| 35 to 39 | 11.5 | 10.8 | 10.7 | 11.7 | 12.9 | 13.4 | 11.2 | 13.1 |
| 40 to 44 | 11.8 | 10.8 | 9.4 | 13.5 | 12.5 | 13.0 | 10.6 | 12.8 |
| 45 to 49 | 12.8 | 11.7 | 12.0 | 13.6 | 13.8 | 13.6 | 12.0 | 15.2 |
| 50 to 54 | 14.2 | 13.2 | 14.6 | 15.1 | 14.1 | 13.9 | 13.8 | 14.6 |
| 55 to 59 | 16.4 | 17.4 | 15.4 | 17.0 | 15.0 | 14.4 | 16.6 | 15.2 |
| 60 to 64 | 14.6 | 16.0 | 15.9 | 13.7 | 13.1 | 13.3 | 12.4 | 13.2 |
| 65 to 69 | 8.6 | 11.3 | 10.6 | 6.2 | 6.4 | 5.9 | 11.8 | 4.2 |
| 70 or more | 2.9 | 3.2 | 3.8 | 2.3 | 2.7 | 2.5 | 3.7 | 2.3 |
| **Year of highest degree now held** | | | | | | | | |
| Before 1970 | 8.0 | 12.1 | 9.9 | 4.4 | 5.3 | 6.2 | 5.9 | 3.6 |
| 1971 to 1975 | 9.5 | 10.1 | 13.7 | 8.1 | 7.6 | 6.8 | 9.9 | 7.5 |
| 1976 to 1980 | 11.3 | 13.4 | 11.9 | 10.2 | 9.3 | 9.3 | 9.5 | 9.0 |
| 1981 to 1985 | 11.7 | 11.7 | 12.6 | 11.9 | 11.0 | 11.6 | 13.4 | 9.1 |
| 1986 to 1990 | 12.2 | 11.8 | 12.2 | 12.8 | 11.9 | 11.3 | 11.6 | 13.0 |
| 1991 to 1995 | 12.3 | 10.7 | 10.3 | 13.4 | 14.7 | 15.1 | 11.3 | 15.9 |
| 1996 to 2000 | 15.1 | 14.9 | 11.6 | 16.7 | 15.5 | 15.2 | 14.8 | 16.2 |
| 2001 to 2005 | 15.4 | 12.0 | 12.7 | 17.8 | 18.8 | 18.7 | 17.0 | 20.0 |
| 2006 to 2007 | 4.5 | 3.3 | 5.0 | 4.6 | 5.9 | 5.8 | 6.6 | 5.6 |
| **Year of appointment at current position** | | | | | | | | |
| Before 1970 | 4.8 | 6.6 | 6.5 | 2.8 | 3.6 | 3.8 | 4.7 | 2.9 |
| 1971 to 1975 | 4.7 | 5.1 | 6.6 | 4.4 | 3.3 | 3.1 | 4.9 | 2.8 |
| 1976 to 1980 | 7.1 | 8.7 | 8.7 | 5.6 | 5.6 | 6.0 | 5.7 | 4.9 |
| 1981 to 1985 | 8.4 | 9.2 | 9.3 | 7.6 | 7.7 | 7.6 | 8.1 | 7.7 |
| 1986 to 1990 | 12.0 | 12.5 | 13.3 | 11.8 | 10.5 | 11.2 | 12.2 | 8.6 |
| 1991 to 1995 | 10.6 | 9.8 | 9.7 | 11.3 | 11.5 | 11.9 | 9.7 | 11.8 |
| 1996 to 2000 | 15.9 | 15.6 | 13.6 | 16.6 | 16.6 | 17.3 | 15.0 | 16.5 |
| 2001 to 2005 | 25.4 | 23.1 | 20.5 | 27.9 | 28.7 | 28.0 | 27.9 | 30.1 |
| 2006 to 2007 | 11.1 | 9.2 | 11.8 | 11.9 | 12.6 | 11.2 | 11.9 | 14.8 |
| **If tenured, year tenure was awarded** | | | | | | | | |
| Before 1970 | 1.6 | 1.8 | 2.6 | 0.9 | 1.6 | 1.7 | 2.6 | 0.9 |
| 1971 to 1975 | 5.2 | 7.5 | 6.0 | 3.3 | 3.2 | 3.7 | 3.9 | 2.3 |
| 1976 to 1980 | 7.5 | 8.1 | 10.0 | 6.1 | 6.5 | 6.8 | 8.9 | 4.5 |
| 1981 to 1985 | 11.1 | 14.0 | 12.4 | 8.5 | 8.3 | 8.7 | 8.0 | 7.9 |
| 1986 to 1990 | 13.1 | 13.4 | 15.1 | 12.2 | 12.2 | 13.1 | 10.6 | 11.7 |
| 1991 to 1995 | 16.7 | 16.6 | 17.8 | 16.3 | 16.5 | 17.5 | 17.0 | 14.8 |
| 1996 to 2000 | 15.3 | 13.3 | 15.2 | 17.2 | 16.3 | 16.5 | 15.8 | 16.4 |
| 2001 to 2005 | 17.9 | 15.9 | 14.5 | 21.2 | 19.5 | 17.5 | 18.6 | 22.7 |
| 2006 to 2007 | 11.6 | 9.5 | 6.5 | 14.1 | 16.0 | 14.6 | 14.7 | 18.7 |

| | | | | Four-year Colleges | | | | |
| Male Respondents | All 4+ yr | Universities Pub | Priv | Pub | All Priv | Nons | Cath | Oth Relig |
|---|---|---|---|---|---|---|---|---|
| **WHAT IS THE MAJOR OF THE HIGHEST DEGREE YOU HOLD?** | | | | | | | | |
| **Biological Science** | | | | | | | | |
| Agriculture | 1.2 | 2.5 | 0.5 | 0.8 | 0.2 | 0.1 | 0.0 | 0.4 |
| Forestry | 0.3 | 0.6 | 0.0 | 0.2 | 0.1 | 0.1 | 0.1 | 0.0 |
| Bacteriology, Molecular Biology | 0.9 | 1.0 | 1.2 | 0.9 | 0.8 | 0.7 | 0.8 | 0.9 |
| Biochemistry | 1.0 | 1.2 | 1.5 | 0.5 | 0.9 | 0.8 | 1.2 | 0.8 |
| Biophysics | 0.1 | 0.0 | 0.1 | 0.1 | 0.1 | 0.1 | 0.3 | 0.0 |
| Botany | 0.8 | 0.6 | 0.8 | 1.0 | 0.7 | 0.7 | 0.6 | 0.8 |
| Environmental Science | 0.6 | 0.6 | 0.3 | 0.7 | 0.5 | 0.5 | 0.6 | 0.6 |
| Marine (life) Sciences | 0.2 | 0.1 | 0.1 | 0.4 | 0.3 | 0.3 | 0.4 | 0.0 |
| Physiology, Anatomy | 0.9 | 0.8 | 1.3 | 0.7 | 1.0 | 1.2 | 0.4 | 0.9 |
| Zoology | 1.4 | 1.4 | 1.1 | 1.5 | 1.3 | 1.0 | 1.3 | 1.8 |
| General, Other Biological Sciences | 1.9 | 2.1 | 1.9 | 1.5 | 2.1 | 2.6 | 1.2 | 1.7 |
| **Business** | | | | | | | | |
| Accounting | 1.1 | 0.9 | 1.4 | 1.4 | 0.8 | 0.6 | 1.0 | 0.9 |
| Finance | 0.8 | 0.9 | 0.7 | 1.0 | 0.6 | 0.5 | 0.6 | 0.6 |
| International Business | 0.1 | 0.0 | 0.2 | 0.1 | 0.2 | 0.1 | 0.5 | 0.2 |
| Management | 2.4 | 2.0 | 1.4 | 3.1 | 2.7 | 2.2 | 3.1 | 3.2 |
| Marketing | 1.0 | 0.8 | 1.0 | 1.1 | 1.1 | 0.7 | 2.2 | 1.0 |
| Secretarial Studies | 0.0 | 0.0 | 0.0 | 0.0 | 0.0 | 0.0 | 0.0 | 0.0 |
| General, Other Business | 1.4 | 1.4 | 0.8 | 1.2 | 1.8 | 1.9 | 1.8 | 1.6 |
| **Education** | | | | | | | | |
| Business Education | 0.2 | 0.1 | 0.1 | 0.3 | 0.1 | 0.1 | 0.1 | 0.1 |
| Educational Administration | 1.0 | 0.6 | 0.7 | 0.9 | 1.7 | 0.8 | 3.1 | 2.4 |
| Educational Psychology/Counseling | 0.7 | 0.4 | 0.7 | 1.1 | 0.7 | 0.7 | 0.6 | 0.9 |
| Elementary Education | 0.4 | 0.6 | 0.1 | 0.6 | 0.2 | 0.3 | 0.3 | 0.1 |
| Higher Education | 0.9 | 0.7 | 0.6 | 1.0 | 1.1 | 0.8 | 1.8 | 1.1 |
| Music or Art Education | 0.2 | 0.0 | 0.1 | 0.4 | 0.3 | 0.1 | 0.1 | 0.7 |
| Physical or Health Education | 1.6 | 0.9 | 0.5 | 2.9 | 1.6 | 1.0 | 1.2 | 2.6 |
| Secondary Education | 0.8 | 0.9 | 0.2 | 1.2 | 0.5 | 0.5 | 0.2 | 0.5 |
| Special Education | 0.4 | 0.3 | 0.1 | 0.5 | 0.9 | 1.4 | 0.5 | 0.4 |
| General, Other Education Fields | 2.0 | 1.6 | 1.4 | 2.7 | 1.9 | 1.7 | 2.3 | 2.0 |
| **Engineering** | | | | | | | | |
| Aero-/Astronautical Engineering | 0.3 | 0.7 | 0.2 | 0.0 | 0.1 | 0.0 | 0.0 | 0.4 |
| Chemical Engineering | 0.5 | 0.9 | 0.9 | 0.0 | 0.1 | 0.1 | 0.1 | 0.1 |
| Civil Engineering | 1.1 | 1.9 | 1.6 | 0.5 | 0.2 | 0.2 | 0.3 | 0.2 |
| Electrical Engineering | 1.3 | 2.0 | 1.9 | 0.9 | 0.5 | 0.4 | 0.7 | 0.5 |
| Industrial Engineering | 0.3 | 0.4 | 0.1 | 0.5 | 0.2 | 0.1 | 0.1 | 0.2 |
| Mechanical Engineering | 1.5 | 2.4 | 1.8 | 1.2 | 0.5 | 0.5 | 0.6 | 0.4 |
| General, Other Engineering Fields | 1.4 | 2.6 | 1.1 | 0.8 | 0.6 | 0.8 | 0.2 | 0.4 |
| **Health** | | | | | | | | |
| Dentistry | 0.4 | 0.9 | 0.3 | 0.1 | 0.1 | 0.0 | 0.7 | 0.0 |
| Health Technology | 0.0 | 0.0 | 0.0 | 0.0 | 0.0 | 0.0 | 0.0 | 0.0 |
| Medicine or Surgery | 0.2 | 0.4 | 0.2 | 0.0 | 0.1 | 0.0 | 0.3 | 0.2 |
| Nursing | 0.3 | 0.2 | 0.3 | 0.4 | 0.2 | 0.1 | 0.2 | 0.4 |
| Pharmacy, Pharmacology | 0.7 | 0.9 | 0.9 | 0.2 | 1.0 | 1.7 | 0.3 | 0.3 |
| Therapy (speech, physical, occup.) | 0.2 | 0.1 | 0.3 | 0.4 | 0.1 | 0.0 | 0.2 | 0.1 |
| Veterinary Medicine | 0.1 | 0.2 | 0.0 | 0.0 | 0.0 | 0.0 | 0.0 | 0.0 |
| General, Other Health Fields | 0.6 | 0.4 | 0.6 | 0.8 | 0.5 | 0.3 | 0.8 | 0.5 |

| | | Universities | | Four-year Colleges | | | | |
| Male Respondents | All 4+ yr | Pub | Priv | Pub | All Priv | Nons | Cath | Oth Relig |
|---|---|---|---|---|---|---|---|---|
| **WHAT IS THE MAJOR OF THE HIGHEST DEGREE YOU HOLD?** | | | | | | | | |
| **Humanities** | | | | | | | | |
| History | 4.5 | 4.0 | 4.6 | 4.5 | 5.2 | 5.2 | 6.0 | 5.0 |
| Political Science, Government | 2.9 | 2.5 | 3.8 | 3.1 | 2.8 | 3.2 | 2.5 | 2.4 |
| English Language & Literature | 5.6 | 5.1 | 4.2 | 5.7 | 6.9 | 7.5 | 7.6 | 5.7 |
| Foreign Languages & Literature | 0.8 | 0.6 | 1.4 | 0.5 | 0.9 | 1.0 | 0.2 | 1.3 |
| French | 0.4 | 0.4 | 0.3 | 0.4 | 0.4 | 0.6 | 0.2 | 0.2 |
| German | 0.3 | 0.4 | 0.5 | 0.2 | 0.4 | 0.5 | 0.1 | 0.3 |
| Spanish | 0.8 | 0.8 | 0.5 | 0.9 | 1.0 | 0.9 | 0.9 | 1.2 |
| Other Foreign Languages | 0.4 | 0.5 | 0.8 | 0.2 | 0.4 | 0.5 | 0.4 | 0.3 |
| Linguistics | 0.5 | 0.6 | 0.7 | 0.5 | 0.3 | 0.3 | 0.2 | 0.3 |
| Philosophy | 2.5 | 1.9 | 3.7 | 2.0 | 3.1 | 2.3 | 6.1 | 2.8 |
| Religion or Theology | 2.3 | 0.3 | 4.6 | 0.8 | 6.0 | 5.1 | 6.7 | 7.0 |
| General, Other Humanities Fields | 1.0 | 1.0 | 1.6 | 0.7 | 0.9 | 0.8 | 0.8 | 0.9 |
| **Fine Arts** | | | | | | | | |
| Architecture/Urban Planning | 0.7 | 1.4 | 0.5 | 0.3 | 0.2 | 0.2 | 0.4 | 0.1 |
| Art | 1.8 | 1.2 | 2.1 | 1.8 | 2.4 | 3.2 | 0.8 | 2.2 |
| Dramatics or Speech | 1.6 | 1.2 | 1.0 | 2.0 | 2.0 | 2.0 | 1.5 | 2.2 |
| Music | 3.4 | 2.8 | 2.6 | 3.8 | 4.5 | 4.1 | 1.9 | 6.2 |
| Television or Film | 0.4 | 0.2 | 0.6 | 0.5 | 0.5 | 0.8 | 0.2 | 0.3 |
| Other Fine Arts | 0.9 | 0.6 | 1.8 | 0.9 | 0.7 | 0.9 | 0.3 | 0.5 |
| **Physical Science** | | | | | | | | |
| Mathematics and/or Statistics | 6.1 | 6.3 | 5.3 | 6.6 | 5.6 | 5.6 | 6.7 | 5.1 |
| Astronomy | 0.3 | 0.5 | 0.3 | 0.1 | 0.3 | 0.4 | 0.1 | 0.3 |
| Atmospheric Sciences | 0.2 | 0.4 | 0.0 | 0.3 | 0.0 | 0.0 | 0.0 | 0.1 |
| Chemistry | 4.1 | 4.2 | 3.6 | 4.2 | 4.0 | 3.8 | 4.0 | 4.3 |
| Earth Sciences | 1.4 | 1.9 | 0.8 | 1.5 | 0.9 | 1.4 | 0.5 | 0.4 |
| Geography | 0.9 | 1.2 | 0.4 | 1.4 | 0.2 | 0.3 | 0.4 | 0.1 |
| Marine Sciences (incl. Oceanography) | 0.1 | 0.1 | 0.2 | 0.2 | 0.1 | 0.1 | 0.0 | 0.0 |
| Physics | 3.0 | 3.0 | 3.6 | 2.8 | 2.9 | 3.5 | 2.8 | 2.1 |
| General, Other Physical Sciences | 0.1 | 0.2 | 0.1 | 0.1 | 0.1 | 0.1 | 0.1 | 0.0 |
| **Social Science** | | | | | | | | |
| Anthropology | 1.0 | 1.4 | 0.9 | 0.8 | 0.8 | 1.1 | 0.2 | 0.7 |
| Archaeology | 0.0 | 0.0 | 0.1 | 0.1 | 0.1 | 0.0 | 0.0 | 0.1 |
| Clinical Psychology | 1.1 | 1.2 | 1.2 | 0.9 | 1.0 | 0.9 | 1.1 | 1.1 |
| Counseling and Guidance | 0.4 | 0.1 | 0.2 | 0.7 | 0.4 | 0.4 | 0.5 | 0.5 |
| Experimental Psychology | 1.4 | 1.1 | 2.0 | 1.5 | 1.3 | 1.6 | 1.0 | 1.0 |
| Social Psychology | 0.8 | 0.8 | 0.8 | 0.8 | 0.7 | 0.7 | 0.6 | 0.7 |
| General, Other Psychology | 0.9 | 1.1 | 0.8 | 0.8 | 0.8 | 0.5 | 1.2 | 1.0 |
| Economics | 3.1 | 2.9 | 4.8 | 2.5 | 3.2 | 3.4 | 3.4 | 2.9 |
| Sociology | 2.2 | 2.1 | 3.3 | 2.1 | 1.7 | 1.6 | 1.9 | 1.8 |
| Social Work, Social Welfare | 0.6 | 0.4 | 0.2 | 0.6 | 0.9 | 1.1 | 0.7 | 0.7 |
| General, Other Social Sciences | 1.3 | 2.1 | 1.1 | 0.9 | 0.9 | 1.2 | 0.3 | 0.7 |

**2007–2008 FACULTY SURVEY WEIGHTED NATIONAL NORMS**
**Full-time Undergraduate Faculty**

| Male Respondents | All 4+ yr | Universities Pub | Universities Priv | Four-year Colleges Pub | Four-year Colleges All Priv | Four-year Colleges Nons | Four-year Colleges Cath | Four-year Colleges Oth Relig |
|---|---|---|---|---|---|---|---|---|
| **WHAT IS THE MAJOR OF THE HIGHEST DEGREE YOU HOLD?** | | | | | | | | |
| **Technical** | | | | | | | | |
| Computer Science | 2.2 | 2.4 | 1.8 | 2.1 | 2.0 | 2.3 | 2.1 | 1.7 |
| Data Processing, Computer Prog. | 0.0 | 0.0 | 0.0 | 0.1 | 0.1 | 0.1 | 0.0 | 0.1 |
| Drafting/Design | 0.0 | 0.0 | 0.0 | 0.0 | 0.0 | 0.0 | 0.0 | 0.0 |
| Electronics | 0.0 | 0.1 | 0.0 | 0.0 | 0.0 | 0.0 | 0.0 | 0.0 |
| Industrial Arts | 0.2 | 0.2 | 0.0 | 0.3 | 0.0 | 0.0 | 0.0 | 0.0 |
| Mechanics | 0.0 | 0.0 | 0.0 | 0.0 | 0.0 | 0.0 | 0.0 | 0.0 |
| Other Technical | 0.2 | 0.2 | 0.2 | 0.3 | 0.1 | 0.1 | 0.1 | 0.0 |
| **Other Fields** | | | | | | | | |
| Building Trades | 0.0 | 0.0 | 0.1 | 0.0 | 0.0 | 0.0 | 0.0 | 0.0 |
| Communications | 2.0 | 1.7 | 1.6 | 2.0 | 2.6 | 2.5 | 2.2 | 2.9 |
| Ethnic Studies | 0.0 | 0.0 | 0.0 | 0.0 | 0.0 | 0.0 | 0.0 | 0.0 |
| Human Ecology/Family Science | 0.2 | 0.1 | 0.3 | 0.2 | 0.2 | 0.2 | 0.1 | 0.1 |
| Journalism | 0.5 | 0.6 | 0.3 | 0.7 | 0.3 | 0.1 | 0.2 | 0.7 |
| Law | 0.9 | 0.6 | 0.7 | 1.2 | 1.0 | 0.9 | 1.5 | 0.8 |
| Law Enforcement | 0.1 | 0.0 | 0.1 | 0.4 | 0.1 | 0.0 | 0.2 | 0.0 |
| Library Science | 0.3 | 0.0 | 0.4 | 0.3 | 0.5 | 0.7 | 0.3 | 0.2 |
| Women's Studies | 0.0 | 0.0 | 0.0 | 0.0 | 0.0 | 0.0 | 0.0 | 0.0 |
| Other Vocational | 0.0 | 0.1 | 0.0 | 0.0 | 0.0 | 0.0 | 0.0 | 0.0 |
| All Other Fields | 0.6 | 0.5 | 0.3 | 0.9 | 0.6 | 0.6 | 0.4 | 0.7 |

80

## 2007–2008 FACULTY SURVEY WEIGHTED NATIONAL NORMS
### Full-time Undergraduate Faculty

| Male Respondents | All 4+ yr | Universities Pub | Priv | Four-year Colleges Pub | All Priv | Nons | Cath | Oth Relig |
|---|---|---|---|---|---|---|---|---|
| **WHAT IS THE DEPARTMENT OF YOUR CURRENT FACULTY APPOINTMENT?** | | | | | | | | |
| **Biological Science** | | | | | | | | |
| Agriculture | 1.3 | 2.9 | 0.2 | 1.0 | 0.1 | 0.1 | 0.0 | 0.2 |
| Forestry | 0.1 | 0.3 | 0.0 | 0.1 | 0.0 | 0.0 | 0.0 | 0.0 |
| Bacteriology, Molecular Biology | 0.3 | 0.3 | 0.6 | 0.2 | 0.2 | 0.2 | 0.2 | 0.0 |
| Biochemistry | 0.3 | 0.6 | 0.3 | 0.2 | 0.2 | 0.2 | 0.1 | 0.1 |
| Biophysics | 0.0 | 0.0 | 0.0 | 0.0 | 0.0 | 0.0 | 0.0 | 0.0 |
| Botany | 0.3 | 0.8 | 0.2 | 0.2 | 0.0 | 0.0 | 0.0 | 0.0 |
| Environmental Science | 0.7 | 0.7 | 0.5 | 0.8 | 0.7 | 0.9 | 0.1 | 0.6 |
| Marine (life) Sciences | 0.1 | 0.0 | 0.0 | 0.2 | 0.0 | 0.0 | 0.1 | 0.0 |
| Physiology, Anatomy | 0.3 | 0.3 | 0.7 | 0.1 | 0.2 | 0.0 | 0.6 | 0.2 |
| Zoology | 0.5 | 1.3 | 0.3 | 0.1 | 0.1 | 0.1 | 0.2 | 0.1 |
| General, Other Biological Sciences | 4.7 | 3.2 | 4.9 | 5.2 | 6.0 | 6.2 | 5.1 | 6.0 |
| **Business** | | | | | | | | |
| Accounting | 1.4 | 0.9 | 1.6 | 2.0 | 1.3 | 0.9 | 2.2 | 1.2 |
| Finance | 0.9 | 1.1 | 0.8 | 1.0 | 0.6 | 0.5 | 0.9 | 0.4 |
| International Business | 0.2 | 0.0 | 0.1 | 0.1 | 0.6 | 0.5 | 1.8 | 0.2 |
| Management | 2.6 | 2.4 | 2.1 | 2.8 | 2.9 | 2.1 | 4.0 | 3.3 |
| Marketing | 1.2 | 1.3 | 1.1 | 1.3 | 1.1 | 1.0 | 2.6 | 0.5 |
| Secretarial Studies | 0.0 | 0.0 | 0.0 | 0.0 | 0.0 | 0.0 | 0.0 | 0.0 |
| General, Other Business | 1.9 | 1.5 | 1.4 | 1.7 | 3.0 | 2.4 | 2.9 | 4.0 |
| **Education** | | | | | | | | |
| Business Education | 0.0 | 0.0 | 0.0 | 0.0 | 0.1 | 0.1 | 0.0 | 0.1 |
| Educational Administration | 0.2 | 0.1 | 0.1 | 0.2 | 0.3 | 0.2 | 0.6 | 0.2 |
| Educational Psychology/Counseling | 0.3 | 0.4 | 0.3 | 0.3 | 0.1 | 0.0 | 0.3 | 0.1 |
| Elementary Education | 0.8 | 0.6 | 0.2 | 1.0 | 1.5 | 2.3 | 0.8 | 0.7 |
| Higher Education | 0.5 | 0.8 | 0.1 | 0.2 | 0.8 | 1.3 | 0.2 | 0.4 |
| Music or Art Education | 0.1 | 0.0 | 0.1 | 0.2 | 0.1 | 0.0 | 0.0 | 0.2 |
| Physical or Health Education | 2.2 | 1.7 | 0.6 | 3.6 | 2.1 | 1.7 | 1.0 | 3.1 |
| Secondary Education | 0.8 | 0.9 | 0.3 | 1.1 | 0.5 | 0.2 | 0.8 | 0.8 |
| Special Education | 0.3 | 0.2 | 0.1 | 0.5 | 0.2 | 0.0 | 0.5 | 0.2 |
| General, Other Education Fields | 1.3 | 1.0 | 0.6 | 1.3 | 1.9 | 1.6 | 2.8 | 2.0 |
| **Engineering** | | | | | | | | |
| Aero-/Astronautical Engineering | 0.3 | 1.0 | 0.1 | 0.0 | 0.0 | 0.0 | 0.0 | 0.0 |
| Chemical Engineering | 0.5 | 0.9 | 0.9 | 0.0 | 0.1 | 0.1 | 0.1 | 0.0 |
| Civil Engineering | 1.0 | 2.0 | 1.9 | 0.2 | 0.1 | 0.1 | 0.3 | 0.1 |
| Electrical Engineering | 1.1 | 2.0 | 1.8 | 0.4 | 0.4 | 0.3 | 0.7 | 0.3 |
| Industrial Engineering | 0.2 | 0.3 | 0.0 | 0.2 | 0.1 | 0.1 | 0.0 | 0.1 |
| Mechanical Engineering | 1.6 | 2.6 | 2.0 | 1.0 | 0.4 | 0.4 | 0.6 | 0.2 |
| General, Other Engineering Fields | 1.4 | 2.4 | 1.4 | 1.0 | 0.6 | 0.7 | 0.0 | 0.9 |
| **Health** | | | | | | | | |
| Dentistry | 0.4 | 0.9 | 0.3 | 0.2 | 0.1 | 0.0 | 0.7 | 0.0 |
| Health Technology | 0.0 | 0.1 | 0.0 | 0.1 | 0.0 | 0.0 | 0.0 | 0.0 |
| Medicine or Surgery | 0.4 | 1.0 | 0.1 | 0.0 | 0.0 | 0.0 | 0.0 | 0.1 |
| Nursing | 0.3 | 0.3 | 0.5 | 0.4 | 0.2 | 0.1 | 0.2 | 0.5 |
| Pharmacy, Pharmacology | 0.8 | 1.1 | 1.1 | 0.2 | 0.9 | 1.7 | 0.0 | 0.4 |
| Therapy (speech, physical, occup.) | 0.3 | 0.3 | 0.5 | 0.4 | 0.1 | 0.1 | 0.3 | 0.1 |
| Veterinary Medicine | 0.0 | 0.1 | 0.0 | 0.0 | 0.0 | 0.0 | 0.0 | 0.0 |
| General, Other Health Fields | 1.0 | 0.9 | 0.7 | 1.7 | 0.6 | 0.4 | 0.9 | 0.8 |

81

## 2007–2008 FACULTY SURVEY WEIGHTED NATIONAL NORMS
### Full-time Undergraduate Faculty

| Male Respondents | All 4+ yr | Universities Pub | Priv | Four-year Colleges Pub | All Priv | Nons | Cath | Oth Relig |
|---|---|---|---|---|---|---|---|---|
| **WHAT IS THE DEPARTMENT OF YOUR CURRENT FACULTY APPOINTMENT?** | | | | | | | | |
| **Humanities** | | | | | | | | |
| History | 4.1 | 3.6 | 4.0 | 4.1 | 4.8 | 4.4 | 6.0 | 4.8 |
| Political Science, Government | 2.8 | 2.5 | 3.7 | 3.0 | 2.6 | 2.6 | 2.2 | 2.9 |
| English Language & Literature | 6.1 | 5.8 | 6.1 | 6.3 | 6.4 | 5.6 | 8.3 | 6.6 |
| Foreign Languages & Literature | 1.8 | 1.5 | 2.4 | 1.8 | 1.8 | 1.8 | 1.0 | 2.3 |
| French | 0.2 | 0.2 | 0.2 | 0.1 | 0.2 | 0.4 | 0.1 | 0.2 |
| German | 0.2 | 0.2 | 0.5 | 0.1 | 0.2 | 0.3 | 0.0 | 0.1 |
| Spanish | 0.5 | 0.6 | 0.5 | 0.3 | 0.7 | 0.7 | 0.3 | 1.0 |
| Other Foreign Languages | 0.3 | 0.3 | 0.7 | 0.0 | 0.3 | 0.3 | 0.2 | 0.3 |
| Linguistics | 0.2 | 0.3 | 0.3 | 0.1 | 0.1 | 0.1 | 0.0 | 0.0 |
| Philosophy | 2.3 | 1.8 | 3.0 | 2.1 | 2.9 | 1.9 | 6.0 | 2.6 |
| Religion or Theology | 2.2 | 0.3 | 5.6 | 0.3 | 5.6 | 4.1 | 6.9 | 6.9 |
| General, Other Humanities Fields | 1.3 | 0.8 | 1.5 | 1.0 | 2.3 | 3.9 | 0.5 | 0.9 |
| **Fine Arts** | | | | | | | | |
| Architecture/Urban Planning | 0.8 | 1.9 | 0.4 | 0.1 | 0.2 | 0.4 | 0.4 | 0.0 |
| Art | 2.1 | 1.3 | 2.3 | 2.3 | 2.8 | 3.6 | 1.0 | 2.5 |
| Dramatics or Speech | 1.6 | 1.0 | 1.1 | 2.0 | 2.2 | 2.4 | 1.1 | 2.4 |
| Music | 3.6 | 2.8 | 2.7 | 4.1 | 4.6 | 4.2 | 1.7 | 6.6 |
| Television or Film | 0.3 | 0.2 | 0.4 | 0.5 | 0.3 | 0.5 | 0.0 | 0.1 |
| Other Fine Arts | 0.6 | 0.5 | 0.6 | 0.6 | 0.5 | 0.8 | 0.2 | 0.3 |
| **Physical Science** | | | | | | | | |
| Mathematics and/or Statistics | 5.9 | 5.2 | 5.2 | 7.0 | 6.0 | 5.4 | 7.0 | 6.2 |
| Astronomy | 0.2 | 0.4 | 0.0 | 0.0 | 0.2 | 0.2 | 0.1 | 0.1 |
| Atmospheric Sciences | 0.1 | 0.2 | 0.0 | 0.1 | 0.0 | 0.0 | 0.0 | 0.0 |
| Chemistry | 4.1 | 3.8 | 3.9 | 4.3 | 4.3 | 4.3 | 4.1 | 4.5 |
| Earth Sciences | 1.4 | 1.8 | 0.8 | 1.6 | 0.7 | 1.2 | 0.2 | 0.4 |
| Geography | 0.9 | 1.3 | 0.4 | 1.3 | 0.1 | 0.1 | 0.3 | 0.1 |
| Marine Sciences (incl. Oceanography) | 0.1 | 0.1 | 0.0 | 0.1 | 0.0 | 0.0 | 0.0 | 0.0 |
| Physics | 2.9 | 2.8 | 3.8 | 2.9 | 2.6 | 2.9 | 2.6 | 2.3 |
| General, Other Physical Sciences | 0.4 | 0.3 | 0.1 | 0.5 | 0.6 | 0.9 | 0.3 | 0.5 |
| **Social Science** | | | | | | | | |
| Anthropology | 0.7 | 1.0 | 0.7 | 0.5 | 0.5 | 0.7 | 0.1 | 0.4 |
| Archaeology | 0.0 | 0.0 | 0.0 | 0.0 | 0.0 | 0.0 | 0.0 | 0.0 |
| Clinical Psychology | 0.6 | 1.1 | 0.8 | 0.3 | 0.2 | 0.1 | 0.5 | 0.2 |
| Counseling and Guidance | 0.1 | 0.0 | 0.2 | 0.1 | 0.2 | 0.0 | 0.4 | 0.3 |
| Experimental Psychology | 0.7 | 0.6 | 1.1 | 0.7 | 0.7 | 1.0 | 0.3 | 0.5 |
| Social Psychology | 0.3 | 0.2 | 0.2 | 0.6 | 0.1 | 0.1 | 0.0 | 0.2 |
| General, Other Psychology | 2.1 | 1.0 | 2.0 | 2.7 | 3.2 | 3.2 | 2.4 | 3.5 |
| Economics | 2.5 | 2.5 | 3.9 | 1.9 | 2.5 | 3.1 | 2.6 | 1.6 |
| Sociology | 1.9 | 1.7 | 2.9 | 1.8 | 1.8 | 1.8 | 2.1 | 1.8 |
| Social Work, Social Welfare | 0.6 | 0.3 | 0.3 | 0.8 | 0.9 | 1.0 | 0.8 | 0.7 |
| General, Other Social Sciences | 2.1 | 2.5 | 2.0 | 2.0 | 1.6 | 2.2 | 1.4 | 0.8 |

| | | | | Four-year Colleges | | | | |
| Male Respondents | All 4+ yr | Universities Pub | Priv | Pub | All Priv | Nons | Cath | Oth Relig |
|---|---|---|---|---|---|---|---|---|
| **WHAT IS THE DEPARTMENT OF YOUR CURRENT FACULTY APPOINTMENT?** | | | | | | | | |
| **Technical** | | | | | | | | |
| Computer Science | 2.5 | 2.7 | 1.9 | 2.8 | 2.3 | 2.3 | 2.4 | 2.2 |
| Data Processing, Computer Prog. | 0.1 | 0.1 | 0.2 | 0.2 | 0.1 | 0.2 | 0.0 | 0.0 |
| Drafting/Design | 0.1 | 0.1 | 0.0 | 0.1 | 0.0 | 0.0 | 0.0 | 0.0 |
| Electronics | 0.1 | 0.2 | 0.0 | 0.1 | 0.0 | 0.0 | 0.0 | 0.0 |
| Industrial Arts | 0.1 | 0.1 | 0.1 | 0.3 | 0.0 | 0.0 | 0.0 | 0.0 |
| Mechanics | 0.0 | 0.0 | 0.0 | 0.1 | 0.0 | 0.0 | 0.0 | 0.0 |
| Other Technical | 0.7 | 0.8 | 0.4 | 1.2 | 0.2 | 0.2 | 0.4 | 0.1 |
| **Other Fields** | | | | | | | | |
| Building Trades | 0.0 | 0.0 | 0.0 | 0.0 | 0.0 | 0.0 | 0.0 | 0.0 |
| Communications | 2.4 | 1.6 | 2.3 | 2.8 | 3.1 | 2.4 | 3.0 | 4.0 |
| Ethnic Studies | 0.2 | 0.3 | 0.0 | 0.3 | 0.0 | 0.1 | 0.0 | 0.0 |
| Human Ecology/Family Science | 0.1 | 0.2 | 0.4 | 0.1 | 0.0 | 0.0 | 0.0 | 0.0 |
| Journalism | 0.5 | 1.0 | 0.4 | 0.5 | 0.1 | 0.1 | 0.0 | 0.1 |
| Law | 0.1 | 0.0 | 0.5 | 0.1 | 0.1 | 0.2 | 0.2 | 0.0 |
| Law Enforcement | 0.2 | 0.0 | 0.1 | 0.6 | 0.1 | 0.0 | 0.3 | 0.1 |
| Library Science | 0.2 | 0.0 | 0.5 | 0.3 | 0.2 | 0.2 | 0.2 | 0.2 |
| Women's Studies | 0.0 | 0.0 | 0.0 | 0.0 | 0.0 | 0.0 | 0.0 | 0.0 |
| Other Vocational | 0.1 | 0.0 | 0.1 | 0.1 | 0.1 | 0.1 | 0.1 | 0.1 |
| All Other Fields | 1.2 | 1.4 | 0.6 | 1.4 | 0.9 | 1.3 | 0.6 | 0.6 |
| **HOW MANY CHILDREN DO YOU HAVE IN THE FOLLOWING AGE RANGES?** | | | | | | | | |
| **Under 18 years old** | | | | | | | | |
| None | 60.0 | 61.9 | 61.1 | 60.0 | 56.7 | 56.5 | 62.8 | 54.0 |
| One | 16.0 | 14.2 | 15.5 | 17.0 | 17.9 | 18.8 | 14.8 | 18.0 |
| Two | 16.3 | 17.2 | 12.8 | 15.9 | 17.8 | 17.7 | 15.5 | 19.1 |
| Three | 5.4 | 4.8 | 5.7 | 5.4 | 6.1 | 5.8 | 4.6 | 7.2 |
| Four or more | 2.2 | 2.0 | 4.9 | 1.7 | 1.5 | 1.2 | 2.3 | 1.6 |
| **18 years or older** | | | | | | | | |
| None | 52.5 | 49.1 | 49.9 | 54.2 | 56.9 | 58.9 | 59.3 | 52.9 |
| One | 12.9 | 13.6 | 12.1 | 13.2 | 11.9 | 12.1 | 11.8 | 11.5 |
| Two | 19.7 | 21.9 | 18.8 | 19.2 | 17.8 | 16.9 | 14.1 | 21.1 |
| Three | 9.0 | 9.8 | 8.6 | 8.8 | 8.4 | 7.6 | 8.6 | 9.4 |
| Four or more | 5.9 | 5.6 | 10.7 | 4.7 | 5.0 | 4.5 | 6.1 | 5.1 |
| **How would you characterize your political views?** | | | | | | | | |
| Far left | 8.0 | 7.7 | 7.4 | 8.5 | 8.4 | 9.8 | 7.9 | 6.7 |
| Liberal | 43.8 | 48.5 | 41.3 | 41.0 | 41.8 | 46.3 | 43.1 | 34.8 |
| Middle of the Road | 29.9 | 29.5 | 29.6 | 32.3 | 27.7 | 24.8 | 32.8 | 29.3 |
| Conservative | 17.3 | 13.1 | 20.8 | 17.6 | 21.2 | 18.1 | 15.6 | 28.4 |
| Far right | 0.9 | 1.2 | 0.9 | 0.6 | 0.9 | 1.1 | 0.6 | 0.9 |
| **Are you currently:** | | | | | | | | |
| Single | 8.2 | 5.9 | 10.6 | 9.3 | 8.5 | 7.3 | 14.1 | 7.3 |
| Married | 82.9 | 85.7 | 82.4 | 79.9 | 83.0 | 83.1 | 76.3 | 86.2 |
| Unmarried, living with partner | 3.7 | 3.9 | 2.7 | 4.2 | 3.4 | 4.4 | 3.1 | 2.0 |
| Divorced | 3.9 | 3.2 | 3.5 | 5.1 | 3.8 | 3.9 | 4.3 | 3.3 |
| Widowed | 0.8 | 1.0 | 0.5 | 0.8 | 0.6 | 0.4 | 0.7 | 0.7 |
| Separated | 0.6 | 0.4 | 0.3 | 0.7 | 0.9 | 0.9 | 1.4 | 0.5 |

**2007–2008 FACULTY SURVEY WEIGHTED NATIONAL NORMS**
**Full-time Undergraduate Faculty**

| Male Respondents | All 4+ yr | Universities Pub | Universities Priv | Four-year Colleges Pub | Four-year Colleges All Priv | Four-year Colleges Nons | Four-year Colleges Cath | Four-year Colleges Oth Relig |
|---|---|---|---|---|---|---|---|---|
| **Is English your native language?** | | | | | | | | |
| Yes | 89.0 | 87.4 | 89.7 | 88.9 | 91.1 | 88.9 | 90.3 | 94.7 |
| No | 11.0 | 12.6 | 10.3 | 11.1 | 8.9 | 11.1 | 9.7 | 5.3 |
| **Are you: [4]** | | | | | | | | |
| White/Caucasian | 88.2 | 87.3 | 90.3 | 87.0 | 89.9 | 88.1 | 89.8 | 92.6 |
| African American/Black | 2.4 | 2.2 | 1.6 | 3.0 | 2.4 | 3.1 | 2.2 | 1.6 |
| American Indian/Alaska Native | 1.9 | 2.1 | 0.9 | 2.3 | 1.6 | 1.8 | 1.5 | 1.4 |
| Asian American/Asian | 5.3 | 6.6 | 5.4 | 5.0 | 3.5 | 4.4 | 4.0 | 1.9 |
| Native Hawaiian/Pacific Islander | 0.3 | 0.3 | 0.1 | 0.2 | 0.4 | 0.3 | 1.2 | 0.2 |
| Mexican American/Chicano | 1.2 | 1.0 | 0.8 | 1.7 | 1.1 | 1.4 | 0.7 | 0.7 |
| Puerto Rican | 0.3 | 0.2 | 0.3 | 0.4 | 0.4 | 0.2 | 1.3 | 0.2 |
| Other Latino | 1.7 | 1.8 | 1.4 | 1.5 | 1.8 | 2.0 | 1.9 | 1.3 |
| Other | 2.7 | 2.4 | 2.4 | 3.3 | 2.8 | 2.6 | 2.7 | 3.1 |
| **Do you give the Higher Education Research Institute (HERI) permission to retain your contact information (i.e., your email address and name) for possible follow-up research?** | | | | | | | | |
| Yes | 71.2 | 74.9 | 66.3 | 69.4 | 71.1 | 70.4 | 70.0 | 72.8 |
| No | 28.8 | 25.1 | 33.7 | 30.6 | 28.9 | 29.6 | 30.0 | 27.2 |

[4] Percentages will sum to more than 100.0 if any respondent marked more than one category.

# Full-time Undergraduate Faculty, Type of Institution and Control for

# Women

## 2007–2008 FACULTY SURVEY WEIGHTED NATIONAL NORMS
### Full-time Undergraduate Faculty

| | | | | | Four-year Colleges | | | |
| --- | --- | --- | --- | --- | --- | --- | --- | --- |
| | **All** | **Universities** | | | **All** | | | **Oth** |
| **Female Respondents** | **4+ yr** | **Pub** | **Priv** | **Pub** | **Priv** | **Nons** | **Cath** | **Relig** |
| **Number of Respondents** | 9,879 | 1,162 | 1,118 | 2,656 | 4,943 | 2,243 | 987 | 1,713 |
| **What is your principal activity in your current position at this institution?** | | | | | | | | |
| Administration | 5.5 | 6.0 | 6.3 | 5.5 | 4.8 | 4.6 | 4.4 | 5.4 |
| Teaching | 86.4 | 75.9 | 83.3 | 91.5 | 92.9 | 93.3 | 94.1 | 91.4 |
| Research | 6.2 | 16.1 | 8.5 | 1.3 | 0.4 | 0.6 | 0.2 | 0.2 |
| Services to clients and patients | 0.9 | 0.4 | 1.5 | 1.0 | 0.9 | 0.2 | 0.3 | 2.5 |
| Other | 1.0 | 1.6 | 0.5 | 0.7 | 1.0 | 1.4 | 1.0 | 0.4 |
| **What is your present academic rank?** | | | | | | | | |
| Professor | 19.7 | 20.0 | 22.2 | 18.8 | 19.6 | 21.4 | 17.3 | 18.5 |
| Associate Professor | 26.3 | 27.0 | 25.0 | 24.8 | 27.8 | 27.0 | 29.8 | 27.7 |
| Assistant Professor | 33.2 | 30.4 | 28.4 | 33.7 | 37.4 | 35.1 | 39.9 | 39.0 |
| Lecturer | 9.5 | 13.2 | 10.8 | 10.7 | 3.5 | 4.6 | 3.2 | 2.0 |
| Instructor | 11.3 | 9.4 | 13.5 | 12.0 | 11.7 | 11.8 | 9.8 | 12.8 |
| **What is your tenure status at this institution?** | | | | | | | | |
| Tenured | 43.5 | 44.1 | 45.1 | 45.4 | 39.8 | 41.6 | 43.2 | 34.6 |
| On tenure track, but not tenured | 26.0 | 22.4 | 22.2 | 29.2 | 27.3 | 26.3 | 28.6 | 27.9 |
| Not on tenure track, but institution has tenure system | 26.7 | 32.9 | 32.1 | 23.5 | 21.7 | 21.3 | 16.9 | 25.8 |
| Institution has no tenure system | 3.8 | 0.6 | 0.6 | 1.9 | 11.2 | 10.9 | 11.3 | 11.7 |
| **Are you currently serving in an administrative position as: [1]** | | | | | | | | |
| Department Chair | 9.4 | 5.6 | 6.2 | 8.1 | 16.4 | 17.3 | 13.6 | 16.9 |
| Dean (Associate or Assistant) | 1.2 | 1.4 | 1.4 | 0.9 | 1.1 | 0.7 | 1.3 | 1.6 |
| President | 0.0 | 0.0 | 0.1 | 0.0 | 0.0 | 0.0 | 0.0 | 0.0 |
| Vice-President | 0.0 | 0.0 | 0.0 | 0.0 | 0.0 | 0.0 | 0.0 | 0.1 |
| Provost | 0.0 | 0.1 | 0.0 | 0.0 | 0.0 | 0.0 | 0.1 | 0.0 |
| Other | 16.3 | 17.2 | 18.5 | 14.9 | 16.0 | 14.5 | 19.0 | 16.1 |
| Not Applicable | 68.4 | 70.2 | 66.6 | 72.2 | 62.5 | 62.5 | 62.6 | 62.3 |
| **My primary place of employment in the last year was: [2]** | | | | | | | | |
| In higher education: | | | | | | | | |
| at this institution | 94.0 | 95.7 | 92.6 | 93.7 | 93.2 | 92.5 | 94.6 | 93.4 |
| at a different institution | 2.9 | 2.3 | 3.3 | 2.9 | 3.2 | 3.3 | 2.4 | 3.6 |
| at more than one institution | 1.5 | 1.1 | 2.3 | 1.5 | 1.7 | 2.5 | 0.9 | 1.2 |
| Not in higher education | 1.1 | 0.8 | 1.1 | 1.4 | 1.2 | 1.1 | 1.9 | 1.0 |
| Not employed | 0.4 | 0.2 | 0.7 | 0.4 | 0.6 | 0.7 | 0.2 | 0.8 |
| **Noted as being personally "very important" or "essential": [2]** | | | | | | | | |
| Research | 67.5 | 71.6 | 75.4 | 67.1 | 60.1 | 62.7 | 63.3 | 54.1 |
| Teaching | 97.7 | 96.4 | 97.4 | 97.9 | 99.0 | 98.8 | 99.2 | 99.2 |
| Service | 70.3 | 64.7 | 71.5 | 71.1 | 75.0 | 73.2 | 79.5 | 74.5 |

[1] Response options changed from earlier Faculty Surveys.
[2] This question asked for the first time in the 2007–2008 Faculty Survey.

87

**2007–2008 FACULTY SURVEY WEIGHTED NATIONAL NORMS**
**Full-time Undergraduate Faculty**

| Female Respondents | All 4+ yr | Universities Pub | Universities Priv | Four-year Colleges Pub | Four-year Colleges All Priv | Four-year Colleges Nons | Four-year Colleges Cath | Four-year Colleges Oth Relig |
|---|---|---|---|---|---|---|---|---|
| **Highest degree earned** | | | | | | | | |
| Bachelor's (B.A., B.S., etc.) | 0.8 | 0.8 | 1.2 | 0.6 | 0.7 | 0.8 | 0.4 | 0.8 |
| Master's (M.A., M.S., M.F.A., M.B.A., etc.) | 27.0 | 24.2 | 23.6 | 28.2 | 30.2 | 26.9 | 29.4 | 35.5 |
| LL.B., J.D. | 0.9 | 0.5 | 1.7 | 0.7 | 1.2 | 1.5 | 0.6 | 1.3 |
| M.D., D.D.S. (or equivalent) | 0.5 | 0.6 | 0.6 | 0.2 | 0.9 | 1.6 | 0.3 | 0.1 |
| Other first professional degree beyond B.A. (e.g., D.D., D.V.M.) | 0.6 | 0.6 | 0.5 | 0.4 | 1.0 | 1.6 | 0.0 | 0.8 |
| Ed.D. | 4.3 | 2.2 | 2.7 | 5.3 | 6.3 | 6.1 | 6.6 | 6.3 |
| Ph.D. | 63.2 | 69.2 | 67.3 | 61.6 | 57.0 | 59.0 | 59.4 | 52.3 |
| Other degree | 2.1 | 1.9 | 2.2 | 2.0 | 2.4 | 2.1 | 3.1 | 2.5 |
| None | 0.6 | 0.2 | 0.2 | 1.2 | 0.4 | 0.4 | 0.2 | 0.5 |
| **Degree currently working on** | | | | | | | | |
| Bachelor's (B.A., B.S., etc.) | 0.1 | 0.0 | 0.0 | 0.2 | 0.1 | 0.0 | 0.3 | 0.2 |
| Master's (M.A., M.S., M.F.A., M.B.A., etc.) | 0.9 | 1.0 | 1.2 | 0.7 | 1.0 | 0.7 | 1.1 | 1.3 |
| LL.B., J.D. | 0.1 | 0.0 | 0.2 | 0.1 | 0.3 | 0.6 | 0.0 | 0.1 |
| M.D., D.D.S. (or equivalent) | 0.1 | 0.2 | 0.0 | 0.0 | 0.0 | 0.0 | 0.2 | 0.0 |
| Other first professional degree beyond B.A. (e.g., D.D., D.V.M.) | 0.0 | 0.1 | 0.0 | 0.0 | 0.0 | 0.0 | 0.0 | 0.0 |
| Ed.D. | 1.3 | 0.9 | 1.5 | 1.0 | 1.9 | 1.8 | 1.3 | 2.3 |
| Ph.D. | 6.7 | 4.2 | 6.3 | 7.3 | 8.6 | 7.8 | 8.0 | 10.3 |
| Other degree | 0.9 | 0.4 | 0.9 | 1.0 | 1.4 | 0.9 | 2.0 | 1.7 |
| None | 89.9 | 93.1 | 89.9 | 89.7 | 86.7 | 88.1 | 87.2 | 84.1 |
| **During the past two years, have you engaged in any of the following activities?** | | | | | | | | |
| Taught an honors course | 18.3 | 21.3 | 20.9 | 15.8 | 17.0 | 17.9 | 16.5 | 16.1 |
| Taught an interdisciplinary course | 41.1 | 41.9 | 40.0 | 36.8 | 46.2 | 52.7 | 36.9 | 43.1 |
| Taught an ethnic studies course | 13.0 | 11.8 | 10.3 | 13.5 | 14.7 | 15.6 | 14.4 | 13.4 |
| Taught a women's studies course | 14.5 | 12.4 | 16.7 | 13.5 | 17.1 | 18.6 | 17.7 | 14.4 |
| Team-taught a course | 35.1 | 37.3 | 37.3 | 32.4 | 35.0 | 33.1 | 33.9 | 38.6 |
| Taught a service learning course | 24.8 | 25.0 | 20.8 | 25.6 | 25.3 | 25.6 | 26.7 | 23.8 |
| Placed or collected assignments on the Internet | 78.0 | 80.0 | 80.4 | 77.8 | 75.1 | 74.5 | 79.3 | 73.1 |
| Taught a course exclusively on the Internet | 16.1 | 16.5 | 8.9 | 22.6 | 10.5 | 7.7 | 16.3 | 10.4 |
| Participated in a teaching enhancement workshop | 66.5 | 60.5 | 61.4 | 68.9 | 71.9 | 71.5 | 76.0 | 69.8 |
| Advised student groups involved in service/volunteer work | 47.3 | 41.5 | 41.9 | 49.9 | 52.5 | 52.8 | 53.3 | 51.5 |
| Collaborated with the local community in research/teaching | 51.0 | 48.3 | 45.6 | 56.3 | 49.5 | 46.6 | 51.7 | 52.1 |
| Developed a new course | 68.2 | 67.1 | 70.7 | 66.1 | 71.0 | 72.6 | 69.0 | 69.9 |
| Conducted research/writing focused on: | | | | | | | | |
| International/global issues | 26.5 | 25.1 | 36.0 | 25.2 | 25.6 | 31.1 | 21.0 | 20.9 |
| Racial or ethnic minorities | 25.4 | 24.8 | 30.1 | 26.3 | 23.1 | 26.5 | 21.5 | 19.1 |
| Women and gender issues | 29.9 | 29.3 | 36.4 | 29.1 | 28.8 | 32.7 | 25.5 | 25.2 |
| Taught a seminar for first-year students | 25.1 | 19.7 | 26.9 | 24.2 | 31.5 | 33.5 | 26.6 | 32.0 |
| Engaged undergraduates on <u>your</u> research project [2] | 36.2 | 38.3 | 41.0 | 34.3 | 34.3 | 38.7 | 30.3 | 30.7 |
| Worked with undergraduates on a research project | 52.5 | 51.5 | 54.8 | 51.1 | 54.2 | 58.1 | 50.0 | 51.4 |

[2] This question asked for the first time in the 2007–2008 Faculty Survey.

88

| Female Respondents | All 4+ yr | Universities Pub | Priv | Four-year Colleges Pub | All Priv | Nons | Cath | Oth Relig |
|---|---|---|---|---|---|---|---|---|
| **DURING THE PRESENT TERM, HOW MANY HOURS PER WEEK ON AVERAGE DO YOU ACTUALLY SPEND ON:** | | | | | | | | |
| **Scheduled teaching (actual, not credit hours)** | | | | | | | | |
| None | 0.7 | 0.9 | 0.9 | 0.7 | 0.3 | 0.1 | 0.2 | 0.7 |
| 1 to 4 | 11.8 | 14.9 | 16.5 | 10.1 | 8.4 | 8.9 | 6.2 | 9.3 |
| 5 to 8 | 30.1 | 39.8 | 43.7 | 21.6 | 24.3 | 28.3 | 21.7 | 20.2 |
| 9 to 12 | 35.4 | 26.6 | 26.8 | 41.1 | 41.4 | 40.0 | 43.6 | 41.8 |
| 13 to 16 | 13.6 | 8.9 | 6.7 | 17.1 | 17.2 | 15.2 | 18.6 | 19.2 |
| 17 to 20 | 5.2 | 5.3 | 2.6 | 5.7 | 5.5 | 5.4 | 6.1 | 5.2 |
| 21 to 34 | 2.8 | 3.0 | 2.0 | 3.2 | 2.2 | 1.7 | 2.7 | 2.8 |
| 35 to 44 | 0.3 | 0.2 | 0.4 | 0.3 | 0.4 | 0.2 | 0.1 | 0.8 |
| 45 + | 0.2 | 0.3 | 0.2 | 0.2 | 0.3 | 0.2 | 0.7 | 0.0 |
| **Preparing for teaching (including reading student papers and grading)** | | | | | | | | |
| None | 0.3 | 0.5 | 0.7 | 0.1 | 0.2 | 0.4 | 0.0 | 0.2 |
| 1 to 4 | 7.9 | 10.0 | 9.7 | 7.7 | 5.3 | 4.8 | 5.4 | 5.8 |
| 5 to 8 | 21.9 | 23.4 | 24.3 | 22.3 | 18.8 | 19.8 | 20.2 | 16.2 |
| 9 to 12 | 23.4 | 24.7 | 25.0 | 21.7 | 23.4 | 24.1 | 20.2 | 24.6 |
| 13 to 16 | 16.0 | 15.8 | 15.3 | 15.6 | 16.9 | 15.9 | 18.5 | 17.3 |
| 17 to 20 | 16.0 | 15.2 | 12.0 | 16.6 | 17.7 | 16.7 | 20.0 | 17.4 |
| 21 to 34 | 10.9 | 8.2 | 9.6 | 11.7 | 13.3 | 14.6 | 10.6 | 13.2 |
| 35 to 44 | 2.6 | 1.6 | 2.9 | 3.0 | 3.1 | 2.7 | 3.2 | 3.8 |
| 45 + | 1.0 | 0.7 | 0.6 | 1.3 | 1.4 | 1.0 | 2.0 | 1.4 |
| **Advising and counseling of students** | | | | | | | | |
| None | 3.5 | 4.3 | 2.3 | 4.1 | 2.4 | 2.1 | 3.1 | 2.4 |
| 1 to 4 | 51.4 | 54.5 | 56.6 | 47.9 | 50.2 | 50.5 | 48.9 | 50.5 |
| 5 to 8 | 31.4 | 29.5 | 29.2 | 32.5 | 33.0 | 33.1 | 34.4 | 31.9 |
| 9 to 12 | 8.6 | 7.7 | 7.9 | 9.4 | 8.9 | 7.8 | 8.7 | 10.7 |
| 13 to 16 | 2.9 | 2.0 | 2.2 | 3.7 | 3.2 | 4.2 | 2.0 | 2.6 |
| 17 to 20 | 1.4 | 1.7 | 1.4 | 1.1 | 1.4 | 1.4 | 1.5 | 1.3 |
| 21 to 34 | 0.4 | 0.1 | 0.2 | 0.8 | 0.3 | 0.1 | 0.6 | 0.4 |
| 35 to 44 | 0.3 | 0.1 | 0.1 | 0.2 | 0.6 | 0.8 | 0.7 | 0.2 |
| 45 + | 0.2 | 0.1 | 0.1 | 0.4 | 0.0 | 0.0 | 0.0 | 0.1 |
| **Committee work and meetings** | | | | | | | | |
| None | 4.1 | 5.5 | 4.7 | 3.6 | 2.8 | 2.6 | 2.9 | 2.9 |
| 1 to 4 | 55.2 | 54.8 | 57.8 | 50.6 | 60.2 | 62.4 | 53.7 | 61.4 |
| 5 to 8 | 28.2 | 28.0 | 24.4 | 30.3 | 27.4 | 26.4 | 31.0 | 26.3 |
| 9 to 12 | 8.3 | 7.6 | 8.9 | 10.1 | 6.5 | 5.5 | 8.5 | 6.7 |
| 13 to 16 | 2.6 | 3.0 | 2.4 | 3.2 | 1.7 | 1.2 | 2.6 | 1.7 |
| 17 to 20 | 1.1 | 0.8 | 0.7 | 1.7 | 1.0 | 1.5 | 0.6 | 0.5 |
| 21 to 34 | 0.4 | 0.3 | 0.7 | 0.4 | 0.4 | 0.3 | 0.4 | 0.5 |
| 35 to 44 | 0.1 | 0.0 | 0.3 | 0.1 | 0.0 | 0.0 | 0.0 | 0.0 |
| 45 + | 0.1 | 0.1 | 0.0 | 0.0 | 0.1 | 0.1 | 0.3 | 0.1 |
| **Other administration** | | | | | | | | |
| None | 29.3 | 30.8 | 26.8 | 32.5 | 24.8 | 23.3 | 26.6 | 25.7 |
| 1 to 4 | 38.6 | 35.1 | 43.1 | 36.3 | 43.3 | 46.7 | 40.9 | 39.8 |
| 5 to 8 | 15.4 | 16.8 | 14.3 | 14.8 | 15.1 | 14.7 | 14.6 | 16.2 |
| 9 to 12 | 7.7 | 7.4 | 7.8 | 7.7 | 8.1 | 6.9 | 10.2 | 8.3 |
| 13 to 16 | 3.2 | 3.4 | 2.6 | 3.1 | 3.5 | 3.6 | 2.8 | 3.8 |
| 17 to 20 | 3.2 | 3.7 | 3.6 | 3.2 | 2.4 | 2.0 | 1.8 | 3.4 |
| 21 to 34 | 1.8 | 2.1 | 1.5 | 1.6 | 1.8 | 1.7 | 2.4 | 1.5 |
| 35 to 44 | 0.5 | 0.2 | 0.3 | 0.6 | 0.9 | 1.0 | 0.5 | 1.1 |
| 45 + | 0.3 | 0.5 | 0.1 | 0.3 | 0.2 | 0.1 | 0.3 | 0.2 |

**2007–2008 FACULTY SURVEY WEIGHTED NATIONAL NORMS**
**Full-time Undergraduate Faculty**

| Female Respondents | All 4+ yr | Universities Pub | Universities Priv | Four-year Colleges Pub | Four-year Colleges All Priv | Four-year Colleges Nons | Four-year Colleges Cath | Four-year Colleges Oth Relig |
|---|---|---|---|---|---|---|---|---|
| **DURING THE PRESENT TERM, HOW MANY HOURS PER WEEK ON AVERAGE DO YOU ACTUALLY SPEND ON:** | | | | | | | | |
| **Research and scholarly writing** | | | | | | | | |
| None | 19.1 | 16.9 | 15.9 | 18.3 | 23.8 | 21.8 | 22.2 | 27.8 |
| 1 to 4 | 36.9 | 28.8 | 27.7 | 41.7 | 43.5 | 41.7 | 44.3 | 45.8 |
| 5 to 8 | 19.1 | 17.8 | 21.3 | 20.3 | 18.3 | 21.1 | 16.7 | 15.3 |
| 9 to 12 | 11.1 | 13.2 | 14.3 | 10.7 | 8.1 | 8.5 | 9.5 | 6.3 |
| 13 to 16 | 5.1 | 8.0 | 7.1 | 4.0 | 2.6 | 2.9 | 2.5 | 2.2 |
| 17 to 20 | 4.4 | 7.6 | 7.0 | 2.5 | 2.0 | 2.0 | 2.9 | 1.4 |
| 21 to 34 | 2.6 | 4.4 | 3.9 | 1.6 | 1.3 | 1.8 | 1.1 | 0.7 |
| 35 to 44 | 1.1 | 2.2 | 1.6 | 0.7 | 0.2 | 0.2 | 0.3 | 0.3 |
| 45 + | 0.6 | 1.2 | 1.2 | 0.2 | 0.2 | 0.1 | 0.6 | 0.0 |
| **Other creative products/performances** | | | | | | | | |
| None | 51.3 | 52.6 | 53.1 | 49.3 | 51.7 | 52.3 | 49.8 | 52.1 |
| 1 to 4 | 29.8 | 28.3 | 28.4 | 30.7 | 31.1 | 31.1 | 31.7 | 30.7 |
| 5 to 8 | 11.0 | 11.8 | 10.0 | 11.2 | 10.3 | 10.9 | 10.0 | 9.8 |
| 9 to 12 | 4.3 | 4.6 | 4.4 | 5.2 | 3.0 | 1.9 | 3.9 | 3.9 |
| 13 to 16 | 1.6 | 1.6 | 1.9 | 1.7 | 1.6 | 1.6 | 1.5 | 1.6 |
| 17 to 20 | 1.0 | 0.4 | 0.8 | 1.4 | 1.1 | 0.8 | 2.3 | 0.9 |
| 21 to 34 | 0.6 | 0.6 | 0.8 | 0.4 | 0.8 | 1.3 | 0.7 | 0.3 |
| 35 to 44 | 0.1 | 0.0 | 0.6 | 0.0 | 0.2 | 0.0 | 0.0 | 0.5 |
| 45 + | 0.1 | 0.1 | 0.2 | 0.1 | 0.2 | 0.1 | 0.2 | 0.2 |
| **Consultation with clients/patients** | | | | | | | | |
| None | 79.4 | 80.7 | 79.8 | 77.7 | 80.0 | 82.6 | 76.6 | 78.5 |
| 1 to 4 | 12.2 | 13.3 | 11.1 | 12.6 | 10.8 | 9.0 | 12.6 | 12.0 |
| 5 to 8 | 4.5 | 3.8 | 4.3 | 5.2 | 4.5 | 3.1 | 5.8 | 5.5 |
| 9 to 12 | 1.8 | 1.1 | 2.2 | 1.9 | 2.3 | 2.8 | 2.3 | 1.7 |
| 13 to 16 | 0.8 | 0.4 | 0.9 | 0.9 | 1.1 | 0.8 | 1.1 | 1.4 |
| 17 to 20 | 0.6 | 0.5 | 0.7 | 0.6 | 0.6 | 0.6 | 1.1 | 0.4 |
| 21 to 34 | 0.4 | 0.1 | 0.6 | 0.6 | 0.6 | 0.9 | 0.2 | 0.3 |
| 35 to 44 | 0.0 | 0.1 | 0.0 | 0.0 | 0.1 | 0.1 | 0.1 | 0.1 |
| 45 + | 0.2 | 0.0 | 0.2 | 0.4 | 0.1 | 0.0 | 0.3 | 0.1 |
| **Community or public service** | | | | | | | | |
| None | 33.1 | 34.3 | 36.4 | 30.9 | 33.0 | 39.5 | 27.4 | 27.3 |
| 1 to 4 | 52.3 | 50.7 | 47.2 | 53.8 | 54.2 | 48.3 | 58.8 | 59.8 |
| 5 to 8 | 11.1 | 11.8 | 10.8 | 11.9 | 9.5 | 8.5 | 10.9 | 9.8 |
| 9 to 12 | 2.7 | 2.6 | 3.4 | 2.8 | 2.5 | 2.9 | 1.6 | 2.6 |
| 13 to 16 | 0.6 | 0.6 | 1.3 | 0.4 | 0.6 | 0.6 | 0.9 | 0.3 |
| 17 to 20 | 0.2 | 0.0 | 0.9 | 0.2 | 0.1 | 0.1 | 0.2 | 0.1 |
| 21 to 34 | 0.1 | 0.0 | 0.0 | 0.1 | 0.1 | 0.1 | 0.2 | 0.1 |
| 35 to 44 | 0.0 | 0.0 | 0.0 | 0.0 | 0.0 | 0.0 | 0.0 | 0.0 |
| 45 + | 0.0 | 0.1 | 0.0 | 0.0 | 0.0 | 0.0 | 0.0 | 0.0 |
| **Outside consulting/freelance work** | | | | | | | | |
| None | 70.3 | 68.9 | 67.2 | 69.2 | 74.7 | 75.5 | 75.9 | 72.5 |
| 1 to 4 | 22.5 | 24.3 | 24.6 | 23.5 | 18.4 | 17.5 | 18.3 | 19.8 |
| 5 to 8 | 4.8 | 4.5 | 5.2 | 5.1 | 4.5 | 4.2 | 3.8 | 5.2 |
| 9 to 12 | 1.7 | 1.7 | 1.6 | 1.5 | 1.8 | 2.1 | 1.2 | 1.8 |
| 13 to 16 | 0.3 | 0.2 | 0.5 | 0.4 | 0.3 | 0.3 | 0.2 | 0.3 |
| 17 to 20 | 0.3 | 0.4 | 0.6 | 0.2 | 0.1 | 0.0 | 0.3 | 0.2 |
| 21 to 34 | 0.1 | 0.1 | 0.0 | 0.1 | 0.1 | 0.2 | 0.1 | 0.0 |
| 35 to 44 | 0.0 | 0.0 | 0.2 | 0.0 | 0.0 | 0.0 | 0.0 | 0.1 |
| 45 + | 0.0 | 0.0 | 0.0 | 0.1 | 0.0 | 0.0 | 0.1 | 0.1 |

90

| Female Respondents | All 4+ yr | Universities Pub | Priv | Four-year Colleges Pub | All Priv | Nons | Cath | Oth Relig |
|---|---|---|---|---|---|---|---|---|
| **DURING THE PRESENT TERM, HOW MANY HOURS PER WEEK ON AVERAGE DO YOU ACTUALLY SPEND ON:** | | | | | | | | |
| **Household/childcare duties** | | | | | | | | |
| None | 5.4 | 6.7 | 4.9 | 5.4 | 4.1 | 3.9 | 4.6 | 4.2 |
| 1 to 4 | 16.1 | 13.8 | 15.9 | 16.8 | 17.8 | 18.7 | 16.8 | 17.0 |
| 5 to 8 | 25.2 | 24.3 | 21.4 | 26.0 | 26.5 | 26.5 | 24.8 | 27.8 |
| 9 to 12 | 17.2 | 17.3 | 16.0 | 18.6 | 15.8 | 15.2 | 16.2 | 16.3 |
| 13 to 16 | 8.8 | 9.1 | 9.7 | 7.9 | 9.1 | 8.9 | 11.3 | 7.8 |
| 17 to 20 | 9.0 | 10.0 | 10.1 | 8.7 | 7.7 | 8.1 | 7.4 | 7.3 |
| 21 to 34 | 7.7 | 9.0 | 8.6 | 6.4 | 7.5 | 7.4 | 6.9 | 7.9 |
| 35 to 44 | 4.7 | 5.3 | 5.4 | 3.8 | 4.9 | 5.4 | 4.7 | 4.3 |
| 45 + | 6.0 | 4.5 | 7.8 | 6.2 | 6.6 | 5.9 | 7.3 | 7.3 |
| **Communicating via email** | | | | | | | | |
| None | 0.1 | 0.1 | 0.1 | 0.1 | 0.2 | 0.1 | 0.1 | 0.3 |
| 1 to 4 | 21.9 | 18.4 | 19.4 | 22.0 | 26.6 | 24.8 | 24.8 | 30.6 |
| 5 to 8 | 39.4 | 39.0 | 39.4 | 38.6 | 41.1 | 43.0 | 40.5 | 38.6 |
| 9 to 12 | 21.4 | 23.3 | 21.5 | 22.4 | 18.1 | 17.2 | 19.8 | 18.2 |
| 13 to 16 | 9.8 | 11.2 | 10.8 | 9.8 | 7.8 | 8.2 | 7.4 | 7.3 |
| 17 to 20 | 4.7 | 6.1 | 5.9 | 3.8 | 3.8 | 4.1 | 4.2 | 3.2 |
| 21 to 34 | 1.7 | 1.3 | 2.0 | 2.1 | 1.5 | 1.5 | 2.1 | 1.2 |
| 35 to 44 | 0.5 | 0.4 | 0.4 | 0.6 | 0.3 | 0.2 | 0.5 | 0.3 |
| 45 + | 0.5 | 0.3 | 0.4 | 0.5 | 0.6 | 0.8 | 0.7 | 0.3 |
| **Commuting to campus [2]** | | | | | | | | |
| None | 5.4 | 6.2 | 3.1 | 4.2 | 6.8 | 7.8 | 3.2 | 8.0 |
| 1 to 4 | 57.9 | 60.1 | 55.1 | 58.7 | 55.5 | 58.0 | 49.5 | 56.2 |
| 5 to 8 | 25.1 | 24.5 | 26.6 | 25.6 | 24.5 | 21.8 | 30.9 | 24.1 |
| 9 to 12 | 9.6 | 8.0 | 12.3 | 9.5 | 10.5 | 9.5 | 13.7 | 9.8 |
| 13 to 16 | 1.3 | 0.7 | 1.8 | 1.3 | 1.8 | 2.4 | 1.8 | 0.9 |
| 17 to 20 | 0.5 | 0.4 | 0.9 | 0.4 | 0.5 | 0.3 | 0.7 | 0.5 |
| 21 to 34 | 0.1 | 0.1 | 0.1 | 0.2 | 0.1 | 0.1 | 0.1 | 0.2 |
| 35 to 44 | 0.0 | 0.0 | 0.1 | 0.1 | 0.0 | 0.0 | 0.1 | 0.0 |
| 45 + | 0.1 | 0.1 | 0.1 | 0.1 | 0.2 | 0.1 | 0.1 | 0.2 |
| **Other employment, outside of academia [2]** | | | | | | | | |
| None | 86.7 | 89.5 | 86.4 | 85.5 | 85.5 | 84.6 | 84.5 | 87.4 |
| 1 to 4 | 6.7 | 6.2 | 6.7 | 6.6 | 7.5 | 8.6 | 7.3 | 5.8 |
| 5 to 8 | 3.6 | 2.4 | 3.4 | 4.6 | 3.8 | 3.3 | 5.9 | 3.3 |
| 9 to 12 | 1.5 | 0.8 | 1.6 | 2.0 | 1.5 | 1.3 | 1.4 | 1.8 |
| 13 to 16 | 0.7 | 0.5 | 0.7 | 0.5 | 1.1 | 1.6 | 0.7 | 0.5 |
| 17 to 20 | 0.3 | 0.3 | 0.5 | 0.3 | 0.3 | 0.3 | 0.2 | 0.4 |
| 21 to 34 | 0.3 | 0.3 | 0.4 | 0.4 | 0.1 | 0.2 | 0.0 | 0.2 |
| 35 to 44 | 0.1 | 0.0 | 0.2 | 0.1 | 0.1 | 0.0 | 0.1 | 0.3 |
| 45 + | 0.1 | 0.0 | 0.0 | 0.1 | 0.1 | 0.0 | 0.0 | 0.4 |

[2]  This question asked for the first time in the 2007–2008 Faculty Survey.

**2007–2008 FACULTY SURVEY WEIGHTED NATIONAL NORMS**
**Full-time Undergraduate Faculty**

| Female Respondents | All 4+ yr | Universities Pub | Universities Priv | Four-year Colleges Pub | Four-year Colleges All Priv | Four-year Colleges Nons | Four-year Colleges Cath | Four-year Colleges Oth Relig |
|---|---|---|---|---|---|---|---|---|
| **Including all institutions at which you teach, how many undergraduate courses are you teaching this term? [2]** | | | | | | | | |
| None | 0.0 | 0.0 | 0.0 | 0.0 | 0.0 | 0.0 | 0.0 | 0.0 |
| One | 20.0 | 31.6 | 27.8 | 13.4 | 12.3 | 12.8 | 11.1 | 12.4 |
| Two | 27.7 | 33.9 | 34.5 | 24.2 | 22.4 | 25.9 | 19.8 | 19.0 |
| Three | 27.0 | 19.0 | 27.7 | 28.3 | 33.9 | 37.1 | 31.2 | 31.2 |
| Four | 16.7 | 10.8 | 6.5 | 22.5 | 20.4 | 15.7 | 23.8 | 24.9 |
| Five | 5.2 | 2.6 | 2.1 | 6.7 | 7.6 | 6.4 | 8.5 | 8.7 |
| Six or more | 3.3 | 2.2 | 1.5 | 4.9 | 3.4 | 2.1 | 5.6 | 3.8 |
| **FOR UP TO FOUR OF THE UNDERGRADUATE COURSES MENTIONED ABOVE, HOW MANY STUDENTS ARE ENROLLED IN: [2]** | | | | | | | | |
| **Course #1** | | | | | | | | |
| 10 or fewer | 11.5 | 11.0 | 10.1 | 8.3 | 16.8 | 16.6 | 13.9 | 19.1 |
| 11 to 20 | 29.2 | 25.7 | 31.4 | 24.5 | 37.9 | 41.1 | 36.2 | 34.5 |
| 21 to 30 | 27.2 | 21.9 | 26.5 | 31.8 | 27.6 | 25.5 | 30.7 | 28.5 |
| 31 to 50 | 19.9 | 21.1 | 18.1 | 24.9 | 13.0 | 11.9 | 14.8 | 13.2 |
| 51 to 100 | 8.6 | 12.9 | 9.5 | 8.6 | 3.5 | 3.1 | 3.5 | 4.0 |
| More than 100 | 3.6 | 7.3 | 4.4 | 1.9 | 1.2 | 1.8 | 0.8 | 0.7 |
| **Course #2** | | | | | | | | |
| 10 or fewer | 16.6 | 16.8 | 15.9 | 12.8 | 21.3 | 21.9 | 18.8 | 22.3 |
| 11 to 20 | 33.1 | 28.7 | 33.2 | 28.6 | 42.4 | 45.3 | 39.8 | 40.0 |
| 21 to 30 | 26.9 | 25.1 | 24.0 | 30.8 | 24.8 | 22.1 | 28.1 | 26.4 |
| 31 to 50 | 17.3 | 19.2 | 19.3 | 21.8 | 9.5 | 9.0 | 11.0 | 9.1 |
| 51 to 100 | 4.7 | 7.0 | 5.8 | 5.3 | 1.5 | 1.1 | 1.7 | 2.0 |
| More than 100 | 1.4 | 3.2 | 1.8 | 0.8 | 0.5 | 0.7 | 0.5 | 0.2 |
| **Course #3** | | | | | | | | |
| 10 or fewer | 24.8 | 26.3 | 21.2 | 19.6 | 31.0 | 30.2 | 31.7 | 31.7 |
| 11 to 20 | 33.3 | 26.2 | 32.9 | 32.3 | 38.6 | 37.9 | 40.4 | 38.2 |
| 21 to 30 | 25.2 | 25.5 | 25.9 | 27.3 | 22.2 | 23.2 | 20.0 | 22.5 |
| 31 to 50 | 13.4 | 16.0 | 13.7 | 17.4 | 7.3 | 7.3 | 7.4 | 7.1 |
| 51 to 100 | 2.6 | 4.1 | 5.7 | 3.1 | 0.3 | 0.4 | 0.4 | 0.3 |
| More than 100 | 0.7 | 1.9 | 0.6 | 0.3 | 0.6 | 1.0 | 0.1 | 0.2 |
| **Course #4** | | | | | | | | |
| 10 or fewer | 29.6 | 23.4 | 23.7 | 26.4 | 38.0 | 33.0 | 41.0 | 40.8 |
| 11 to 20 | 32.6 | 34.6 | 27.6 | 28.5 | 37.6 | 43.3 | 33.5 | 35.0 |
| 21 to 30 | 25.2 | 25.9 | 31.4 | 28.4 | 19.6 | 18.0 | 23.9 | 18.2 |
| 31 to 50 | 10.9 | 12.7 | 13.2 | 15.0 | 4.2 | 5.2 | 1.4 | 5.2 |
| 51 to 100 | 1.6 | 3.2 | 3.4 | 1.6 | 0.4 | 0.4 | 0.2 | 0.4 |
| More than 100 | 0.2 | 0.3 | 0.7 | 0.1 | 0.2 | 0.1 | 0.0 | 0.4 |

[2]  This question asked for the first time in the 2007–2008 Faculty Survey.

92

| | | Universities | | Four-year Colleges | | | | |
|---|---|---|---|---|---|---|---|---|
| | **All** | | | | **All** | | | **Oth** |
| **Female Respondents** | **4+ yr** | **Pub** | **Priv** | **Pub** | **Priv** | **Nons** | **Cath** | **Relig** |
| **HOW MANY OF THE FOLLOWING COURSES ARE YOU TEACHING THIS ACADEMIC YEAR?** | | | | | | | | |
| **General education courses** | | | | | | | | |
| None | 56.1 | 65.5 | 59.9 | 52.6 | 48.8 | 47.8 | 55.9 | 45.2 |
| One | 16.7 | 15.2 | 16.0 | 16.1 | 19.3 | 21.1 | 14.1 | 20.4 |
| Two | 11.7 | 8.2 | 10.8 | 14.3 | 12.8 | 12.5 | 12.0 | 13.8 |
| Three | 6.2 | 4.5 | 6.1 | 6.4 | 8.1 | 7.8 | 7.1 | 9.1 |
| Four | 4.4 | 3.2 | 2.6 | 5.4 | 5.2 | 4.9 | 5.9 | 5.2 |
| Five or more | 4.7 | 3.4 | 4.4 | 5.3 | 5.7 | 5.8 | 4.9 | 6.2 |
| **Developmental/remedial courses** | | | | | | | | |
| None | 94.0 | 95.1 | 95.9 | 94.2 | 91.8 | 90.3 | 94.4 | 92.1 |
| One | 3.3 | 2.6 | 2.6 | 3.2 | 4.4 | 4.9 | 3.9 | 4.0 |
| Two | 1.1 | 0.9 | 1.0 | 1.2 | 1.3 | 1.9 | 0.4 | 1.1 |
| Three | 0.7 | 0.3 | 0.5 | 0.6 | 1.2 | 1.4 | 0.4 | 1.3 |
| Four | 0.5 | 0.4 | 0.0 | 0.5 | 0.9 | 0.9 | 0.6 | 1.1 |
| Five or more | 0.4 | 0.7 | 0.0 | 0.2 | 0.5 | 0.6 | 0.4 | 0.4 |
| **Other undergraduate credit courses** | | | | | | | | |
| None | 18.8 | 18.9 | 24.0 | 17.9 | 17.6 | 18.1 | 15.7 | 18.1 |
| One | 19.3 | 22.9 | 22.5 | 18.1 | 15.4 | 16.1 | 16.5 | 13.6 |
| Two | 21.5 | 24.0 | 21.2 | 19.9 | 20.9 | 22.5 | 19.5 | 19.4 |
| Three | 15.8 | 14.5 | 14.5 | 15.9 | 17.8 | 17.8 | 19.5 | 16.6 |
| Four | 10.6 | 7.6 | 9.1 | 12.9 | 11.7 | 9.7 | 12.8 | 13.9 |
| Five or more | 14.0 | 12.2 | 8.7 | 15.3 | 16.7 | 15.8 | 16.1 | 18.4 |
| **Graduate courses** | | | | | | | | |
| None | 65.7 | 50.3 | 61.2 | 67.0 | 83.0 | 87.2 | 70.8 | 85.4 |
| One | 19.9 | 30.8 | 23.2 | 18.1 | 8.7 | 6.6 | 16.1 | 6.5 |
| Two | 8.0 | 9.7 | 10.0 | 9.2 | 4.0 | 3.4 | 6.7 | 2.8 |
| Three | 3.5 | 5.9 | 3.7 | 2.7 | 1.9 | 1.2 | 2.9 | 2.3 |
| Four | 1.7 | 2.2 | 1.2 | 1.7 | 1.2 | 0.7 | 2.1 | 1.4 |
| Five or more | 1.2 | 1.2 | 0.6 | 1.3 | 1.2 | 0.8 | 1.5 | 1.6 |
| **Vocational or technical courses** | | | | | | | | |
| None | 97.7 | 98.4 | 97.4 | 97.3 | 97.7 | 98.2 | 96.7 | 97.7 |
| One | 0.9 | 0.4 | 1.6 | 0.9 | 0.9 | 0.7 | 1.2 | 1.1 |
| Two | 0.5 | 0.3 | 0.2 | 0.8 | 0.6 | 0.7 | 0.8 | 0.2 |
| Three | 0.4 | 0.1 | 0.1 | 0.6 | 0.4 | 0.3 | 0.3 | 0.6 |
| Four | 0.3 | 0.7 | 0.1 | 0.1 | 0.1 | 0.0 | 0.3 | 0.2 |
| Five or more | 0.3 | 0.2 | 0.6 | 0.3 | 0.2 | 0.1 | 0.7 | 0.1 |
| **Non-credit courses (other than above)** | | | | | | | | |
| None | 94.2 | 93.5 | 94.0 | 95.2 | 93.7 | 94.0 | 91.9 | 94.5 |
| One | 4.0 | 4.4 | 4.7 | 3.0 | 4.6 | 3.9 | 6.7 | 4.0 |
| Two | 1.2 | 1.4 | 0.6 | 1.0 | 1.4 | 1.7 | 1.2 | 1.1 |
| Three | 0.3 | 0.5 | 0.3 | 0.3 | 0.2 | 0.4 | 0.1 | 0.0 |
| Four | 0.1 | 0.1 | 0.0 | 0.2 | 0.1 | 0.0 | 0.2 | 0.1 |
| Five or more | 0.1 | 0.1 | 0.3 | 0.2 | 0.1 | 0.0 | 0.0 | 0.2 |
| **Do you teach remedial/developmental skills in any of the following areas?** | | | | | | | | |
| Reading | 5.3 | 4.9 | 4.3 | 5.4 | 5.9 | 6.7 | 5.7 | 4.7 |
| Writing | 13.0 | 12.6 | 12.2 | 12.8 | 14.0 | 16.5 | 12.0 | 11.7 |
| Mathematics | 3.8 | 4.1 | 2.0 | 4.0 | 3.9 | 3.6 | 5.4 | 3.2 |
| ESL | 1.6 | 1.1 | 1.0 | 1.8 | 2.0 | 2.2 | 1.1 | 2.3 |
| General academic skills | 10.0 | 10.1 | 8.1 | 9.4 | 11.4 | 13.5 | 10.4 | 8.8 |
| Other subject areas | 6.4 | 6.5 | 6.5 | 5.3 | 7.5 | 7.7 | 6.0 | 8.3 |

**2007–2008 FACULTY SURVEY WEIGHTED NATIONAL NORMS**
**Full-time Undergraduate Faculty**

| Female Respondents | All 4+ yr | Universities Pub | Priv | Four-year Colleges Pub | All Priv | Nons | Cath | Oth Relig |
|---|---|---|---|---|---|---|---|---|
| **HAVE YOU ENGAGED IN ANY OF THE FOLLOWING PROFESSIONAL DEVELOPMENT OPPORTUNITIES AT YOUR INSTITUTION? [2]** | | | | | | | | |
| **Workshops focused on teaching in the classroom** | | | | | | | | |
| Yes | 76.4 | 75.9 | 76.1 | 76.1 | 77.4 | 77.0 | 80.2 | 76.1 |
| No | 20.8 | 23.4 | 22.1 | 20.9 | 17.2 | 17.4 | 16.2 | 17.7 |
| Not eligible | 0.2 | 0.0 | 0.3 | 0.2 | 0.1 | 0.2 | 0.0 | 0.2 |
| Not available | 2.7 | 0.6 | 1.5 | 2.8 | 5.2 | 5.4 | 3.6 | 6.1 |
| **Paid workshops outside the institution focused on teaching** | | | | | | | | |
| Yes | 32.6 | 27.6 | 21.8 | 35.0 | 39.5 | 36.4 | 44.8 | 40.4 |
| No | 61.7 | 67.1 | 70.3 | 59.5 | 55.1 | 58.4 | 50.8 | 53.1 |
| Not eligible | 0.8 | 0.8 | 1.7 | 0.9 | 0.5 | 0.6 | 0.1 | 0.7 |
| Not available | 4.9 | 4.5 | 6.2 | 4.7 | 4.9 | 4.7 | 4.3 | 5.7 |
| **Paid sabbatical leave** | | | | | | | | |
| Yes | 23.6 | 24.7 | 32.4 | 17.6 | 26.1 | 31.6 | 23.2 | 19.9 |
| No | 54.0 | 52.3 | 44.0 | 59.4 | 53.1 | 48.3 | 58.4 | 56.4 |
| Not eligible | 19.3 | 19.1 | 21.1 | 19.5 | 18.6 | 18.1 | 17.3 | 20.3 |
| Not available | 3.1 | 3.9 | 2.5 | 3.4 | 2.2 | 1.9 | 1.1 | 3.4 |
| **Travel funds paid by the institution** | | | | | | | | |
| Yes | 79.7 | 77.8 | 77.9 | 81.1 | 80.7 | 80.5 | 80.9 | 80.8 |
| No | 17.0 | 18.9 | 17.8 | 16.0 | 16.1 | 15.5 | 17.1 | 16.2 |
| Not eligible | 1.8 | 1.4 | 3.7 | 1.4 | 1.8 | 2.3 | 0.8 | 1.6 |
| Not available | 1.5 | 1.9 | 0.7 | 1.5 | 1.5 | 1.7 | 1.2 | 1.4 |
| **Association membership/dues paid by the institution** | | | | | | | | |
| Yes | 28.6 | 22.1 | 28.3 | 21.2 | 45.2 | 42.9 | 44.8 | 48.9 |
| No | 51.0 | 57.5 | 51.9 | 55.4 | 38.0 | 38.9 | 40.2 | 34.9 |
| Not eligible | 3.5 | 3.5 | 6.0 | 3.1 | 2.9 | 3.9 | 1.6 | 2.2 |
| Not available | 16.9 | 16.9 | 13.9 | 20.3 | 14.0 | 14.3 | 13.4 | 14.0 |
| **Tuition remission** | | | | | | | | |
| Yes | 14.8 | 10.6 | 20.5 | 13.7 | 18.4 | 19.4 | 15.4 | 19.1 |
| No | 75.9 | 79.7 | 73.1 | 76.6 | 72.0 | 70.4 | 75.8 | 71.8 |
| Not eligible | 4.1 | 4.2 | 4.9 | 3.2 | 4.7 | 4.7 | 4.2 | 5.0 |
| Not available | 5.2 | 5.5 | 1.5 | 6.5 | 4.9 | 5.6 | 4.6 | 4.1 |
| **Internal grants for research** | | | | | | | | |
| Yes | 44.1 | 48.3 | 48.9 | 42.9 | 39.0 | 45.0 | 35.0 | 33.1 |
| No | 50.7 | 47.0 | 45.9 | 52.7 | 54.3 | 47.4 | 59.5 | 61.0 |
| Not eligible | 2.7 | 3.0 | 3.7 | 2.6 | 2.2 | 2.5 | 1.8 | 2.0 |
| Not available | 2.4 | 1.7 | 1.4 | 1.8 | 4.4 | 5.1 | 3.8 | 3.9 |
| **Training for administrative leadership** | | | | | | | | |
| Yes | 12.8 | 13.2 | 12.1 | 12.9 | 12.3 | 12.9 | 12.9 | 11.1 |
| No | 74.0 | 75.9 | 74.5 | 74.4 | 71.1 | 69.6 | 72.4 | 72.5 |
| Not eligible | 3.8 | 4.0 | 4.7 | 3.7 | 3.3 | 3.9 | 3.0 | 2.8 |
| Not available | 9.5 | 6.9 | 8.7 | 8.9 | 13.2 | 13.6 | 11.7 | 13.7 |

[2] This question asked for the first time in the 2007–2008 Faculty Survey.

## 2007–2008 FACULTY SURVEY WEIGHTED NATIONAL NORMS
### Full-time Undergraduate Faculty

| Female Respondents | All 4+ yr | Universities Pub | Universities Priv | Four-year Colleges Pub | Four-year Colleges All Priv | Four-year Colleges Nons | Four-year Colleges Cath | Four-year Colleges Oth Relig |
|---|---|---|---|---|---|---|---|---|
| **Goals for undergraduates noted as "very important" or "essential"** | | | | | | | | |
| Develop ability to think critically | 99.9 | 100.0 | 99.7 | 99.9 | 99.9 | 100.0 | 100.0 | 99.8 |
| Prepare students for employment after college | 85.2 | 84.5 | 78.9 | 88.2 | 84.8 | 82.3 | 88.4 | 86.1 |
| Prepare students for graduate or advanced education | 76.7 | 73.2 | 78.0 | 75.8 | 80.9 | 80.0 | 80.8 | 82.2 |
| Develop moral character | 74.1 | 68.4 | 78.2 | 72.9 | 80.3 | 76.1 | 86.5 | 82.3 |
| Provide for students' emotional development | 55.4 | 48.6 | 57.6 | 55.3 | 62.0 | 58.0 | 67.2 | 64.1 |
| Prepare students for family living | 23.0 | 18.0 | 23.7 | 23.4 | 27.6 | 21.6 | 32.4 | 33.0 |
| Teach students the classic works of Western civilization [2] | 32.1 | 28.6 | 36.1 | 31.1 | 35.7 | 31.5 | 42.4 | 37.1 |
| Help students develop personal values | 70.2 | 63.2 | 72.9 | 69.4 | 77.8 | 73.8 | 81.6 | 81.2 |
| Enhance students' self-understanding | 76.8 | 72.6 | 76.9 | 77.3 | 80.7 | 77.4 | 86.5 | 81.5 |
| Instill in students a commitment to community service | 64.5 | 57.7 | 64.2 | 66.2 | 69.9 | 65.6 | 76.0 | 72.1 |
| Enhance students' knowledge of and appreciation for other racial/ethnic groups | 87.2 | 84.5 | 88.8 | 87.2 | 89.4 | 88.7 | 91.5 | 89.1 |
| Study a foreign language [2] | 60.0 | 57.2 | 66.4 | 57.4 | 63.6 | 64.2 | 61.9 | 63.8 |
| Help master knowledge in a discipline | 95.6 | 94.1 | 95.2 | 96.6 | 96.3 | 95.5 | 96.6 | 97.3 |
| Develop creative capacities | 81.2 | 81.1 | 84.0 | 80.3 | 81.4 | 83.6 | 81.2 | 78.2 |
| Instill a basic appreciation of the liberal arts | 76.7 | 71.3 | 79.8 | 75.1 | 83.3 | 83.8 | 83.8 | 82.1 |
| Promote ability to write effectively | 98.1 | 97.1 | 98.0 | 98.3 | 99.0 | 99.1 | 98.9 | 98.9 |
| Help students evaluate the quality and reliability of information [2] | 98.6 | 98.5 | 98.6 | 98.3 | 99.0 | 99.3 | 99.3 | 98.3 |
| Engage students in civil discourse around controversial issues [2] | 79.7 | 77.2 | 80.5 | 78.8 | 83.3 | 85.6 | 83.2 | 80.0 |
| Teach students tolerance and respect for different beliefs [2] | 91.6 | 90.5 | 92.9 | 91.4 | 92.8 | 91.9 | 95.7 | 92.0 |
| Encourage students to become agents of social change [2] | 71.5 | 65.3 | 75.2 | 72.8 | 75.4 | 73.8 | 81.7 | 73.2 |

[2]  This question asked for the first time in the 2007–2008 Faculty Survey.

95

| | | | | | Four-year Colleges | | | |
| | **All** | **Universities** | | | **All** | | | **Oth** |
| **Female Respondents** | **4+ yr** | **Pub** | **Priv** | **Pub** | **Priv** | **Nons** | **Cath** | **Relig** |
|---|---|---|---|---|---|---|---|---|
| **HOW MANY OF THE FOLLOWING HAVE YOU PUBLISHED?** | | | | | | | | |
| **Articles in academic or professional journals** | | | | | | | | |
| None | 24.5 | 18.5 | 19.1 | 25.2 | 32.5 | 29.4 | 31.7 | 37.9 |
| 1 to 2 | 23.0 | 18.0 | 18.8 | 26.4 | 25.9 | 23.0 | 26.7 | 29.6 |
| 3 to 4 | 16.8 | 16.2 | 15.1 | 17.7 | 17.1 | 17.9 | 17.3 | 15.7 |
| 5 to 10 | 17.8 | 19.9 | 18.7 | 18.4 | 14.5 | 17.1 | 13.7 | 11.2 |
| 11 to 20 | 9.4 | 12.3 | 13.8 | 8.1 | 6.0 | 7.6 | 6.1 | 3.6 |
| 21 to 50 | 6.2 | 10.6 | 9.4 | 3.6 | 3.3 | 4.0 | 3.8 | 1.9 |
| 51+ | 2.3 | 4.5 | 5.2 | 0.6 | 0.7 | 1.0 | 0.8 | 0.1 |
| **Chapters in edited volumes** | | | | | | | | |
| None | 54.4 | 45.5 | 42.8 | 58.9 | 63.2 | 57.0 | 64.5 | 71.6 |
| 1 to 2 | 26.6 | 26.6 | 28.1 | 27.6 | 24.6 | 26.8 | 24.8 | 21.0 |
| 3 to 4 | 10.0 | 12.6 | 13.1 | 8.8 | 7.4 | 9.0 | 7.2 | 5.0 |
| 5 to 10 | 6.4 | 10.2 | 9.7 | 4.2 | 3.5 | 5.2 | 2.4 | 1.9 |
| 11 to 20 | 2.0 | 3.8 | 5.3 | 0.3 | 0.7 | 1.0 | 0.8 | 0.2 |
| 21 to 50 | 0.6 | 1.0 | 1.0 | 0.2 | 0.5 | 0.8 | 0.4 | 0.1 |
| 51+ | 0.1 | 0.3 | 0.1 | 0.0 | 0.1 | 0.1 | 0.0 | 0.1 |
| **Books, manuals, or monographs** | | | | | | | | |
| None | 67.3 | 56.9 | 60.7 | 71.5 | 76.3 | 73.8 | 75.9 | 80.2 |
| 1 to 2 | 23.9 | 30.6 | 25.8 | 21.9 | 18.4 | 20.4 | 18.1 | 15.7 |
| 3 to 4 | 5.7 | 8.0 | 9.4 | 4.4 | 3.3 | 3.5 | 3.4 | 3.0 |
| 5 to 10 | 2.3 | 3.4 | 2.8 | 1.7 | 1.6 | 1.9 | 2.1 | 0.7 |
| 11 to 20 | 0.6 | 0.8 | 0.6 | 0.5 | 0.4 | 0.4 | 0.4 | 0.4 |
| 21 to 50 | 0.2 | 0.4 | 0.6 | 0.1 | 0.0 | 0.0 | 0.1 | 0.0 |
| 51+ | 0.0 | 0.0 | 0.1 | 0.0 | 0.0 | 0.0 | 0.0 | 0.0 |
| **Other, such as patents or computer software products** | | | | | | | | |
| None | 89.8 | 85.8 | 88.7 | 92.2 | 91.6 | 90.8 | 90.9 | 93.3 |
| 1 to 2 | 6.6 | 9.1 | 6.9 | 5.2 | 5.4 | 5.9 | 6.0 | 4.1 |
| 3 to 4 | 1.9 | 2.6 | 2.1 | 1.4 | 1.7 | 1.9 | 2.0 | 1.4 |
| 5 to 10 | 1.0 | 1.8 | 1.2 | 0.6 | 0.6 | 0.6 | 0.5 | 0.6 |
| 11 to 20 | 0.3 | 0.4 | 0.5 | 0.2 | 0.4 | 0.3 | 0.7 | 0.2 |
| 21 to 50 | 0.1 | 0.1 | 0.2 | 0.2 | 0.1 | 0.1 | 0.0 | 0.2 |
| 51+ | 0.2 | 0.2 | 0.3 | 0.2 | 0.2 | 0.4 | 0.0 | 0.2 |
| **IN THE LAST TWO YEARS, HOW MANY:** | | | | | | | | |
| **Exhibitions or performances in the fine or applied arts have you presented?** | | | | | | | | |
| None | 80.8 | 84.0 | 82.6 | 79.2 | 78.6 | 77.6 | 79.8 | 79.3 |
| 1 to 2 | 6.6 | 4.7 | 5.9 | 7.3 | 7.9 | 8.5 | 7.8 | 7.1 |
| 3 to 4 | 5.1 | 4.7 | 4.8 | 5.9 | 4.9 | 4.8 | 4.7 | 5.3 |
| 5 to 10 | 4.1 | 3.4 | 3.8 | 4.2 | 5.0 | 5.7 | 4.5 | 4.4 |
| 11 to 20 | 1.7 | 1.0 | 1.8 | 2.0 | 2.0 | 2.1 | 1.6 | 2.0 |
| 21 to 50 | 1.0 | 1.3 | 0.6 | 0.8 | 0.9 | 0.8 | 1.2 | 0.9 |
| 51+ | 0.7 | 1.0 | 0.4 | 0.5 | 0.6 | 0.6 | 0.3 | 0.9 |
| **Of your professional writings have been published or accepted for publication?** | | | | | | | | |
| None | 35.9 | 28.1 | 26.7 | 37.3 | 46.6 | 42.1 | 46.1 | 53.9 |
| 1 to 2 | 33.9 | 31.7 | 31.4 | 37.1 | 33.3 | 33.6 | 34.6 | 31.9 |
| 3 to 4 | 19.1 | 22.6 | 23.6 | 18.4 | 14.2 | 16.8 | 13.3 | 10.8 |
| 5 to 10 | 9.2 | 14.7 | 14.5 | 6.2 | 4.8 | 6.3 | 4.8 | 2.6 |
| 11 to 20 | 1.4 | 2.1 | 2.6 | 0.8 | 0.9 | 1.2 | 0.9 | 0.6 |
| 21 to 50 | 0.4 | 0.6 | 0.9 | 0.3 | 0.1 | 0.1 | 0.2 | 0.2 |
| 51+ | 0.1 | 0.3 | 0.2 | 0.0 | 0.1 | 0.0 | 0.2 | 0.1 |

**2007–2008 FACULTY SURVEY WEIGHTED NATIONAL NORMS**
**Full-time Undergraduate Faculty**

| | | | | | Four-year Colleges | | | |
| :--- | :---: | :---: | :---: | :---: | :---: | :---: | :---: | :---: |
| | **All** | **Universities** | | | **All** | | | **Oth** |
| **Female Respondents** | **4+ yr** | **Pub** | **Priv** | **Pub** | **Priv** | **Nons** | **Cath** | **Relig** |
| **General activities** | | | | | | | | |
| Are you a member of a faculty union? | 23.8 | 21.0 | 10.4 | 41.6 | 10.2 | 9.1 | 17.4 | 6.7 |
| Are you a U.S. citizen? | 94.6 | 93.7 | 93.1 | 95.3 | 95.5 | 94.8 | 96.7 | 95.6 |
| Were you born in the U.S.A.? | 86.6 | 84.2 | 83.7 | 88.5 | 88.1 | 87.7 | 88.8 | 88.4 |
| Do you plan to retire within the next three years? | 11.1 | 14.5 | 5.9 | 11.7 | 8.6 | 9.4 | 8.4 | 7.6 |
| Do you use your scholarship to address local community needs? | 52.3 | 50.8 | 46.0 | 58.3 | 48.9 | 45.2 | 51.7 | 52.4 |
| Have you been sexually harassed at this institution? | 10.0 | 13.1 | 8.8 | 9.3 | 7.9 | 7.6 | 8.1 | 8.4 |
| Have you ever interrupted your professional career for more than one year for family reasons? [2] | 22.1 | 24.4 | 17.1 | 22.5 | 20.9 | 18.3 | 25.7 | 21.6 |
| Have you ever received an award for outstanding teaching? | 40.3 | 45.2 | 39.2 | 38.8 | 37.2 | 37.4 | 35.8 | 38.0 |
| Have you published op-ed pieces or editorials? | 18.1 | 19.4 | 20.2 | 17.6 | 16.4 | 16.2 | 18.0 | 15.5 |
| Is (or was) your: | | | | | | | | |
|    Father an academic? | 14.0 | 15.0 | 15.2 | 12.0 | 15.0 | 15.7 | 12.6 | 15.7 |
|    Mother an academic? | 11.2 | 11.8 | 9.5 | 10.4 | 12.2 | 12.6 | 9.8 | 13.4 |
|    Spouse/partner an academic? | 34.4 | 40.9 | 31.3 | 30.7 | 33.3 | 36.2 | 28.3 | 32.6 |
| Are you currently teaching courses at more than one institution? | 4.6 | 3.8 | 3.1 | 5.1 | 5.3 | 6.2 | 5.2 | 4.0 |
| **During the <u>past two</u> years, have you:** | | | | | | | | |
| Considered early retirement? | 22.6 | 25.6 | 19.3 | 24.3 | 18.6 | 18.8 | 17.8 | 18.8 |
| Considered leaving academe for another job? | 37.4 | 39.5 | 35.7 | 37.9 | 35.3 | 34.0 | 35.0 | 37.3 |
| Considered leaving this institution for another? | 48.7 | 53.6 | 48.8 | 48.6 | 43.6 | 44.4 | 41.4 | 43.9 |
| Changed academic institutions? | 12.0 | 10.0 | 14.0 | 12.1 | 13.3 | 14.7 | 12.5 | 11.9 |
| Engaged in paid consulting outside of your institution? | 32.8 | 35.4 | 34.0 | 34.3 | 27.7 | 27.5 | 27.5 | 28.0 |
| Engaged in public service/professional consulting without pay? | 60.7 | 61.7 | 60.0 | 64.0 | 55.6 | 53.6 | 55.4 | 58.5 |
| Received at least one firm job offer? | 26.3 | 25.2 | 28.4 | 26.7 | 26.3 | 24.7 | 27.9 | 27.5 |
| Received funding for your work from: | | | | | | | | |
|    Foundations? | 18.0 | 20.0 | 20.0 | 17.6 | 15.4 | 15.4 | 17.7 | 13.6 |
|    State or federal government? | 22.2 | 29.6 | 21.3 | 23.5 | 12.7 | 15.3 | 12.4 | 9.2 |
|    Business or industry? | 8.4 | 10.8 | 10.6 | 7.1 | 6.6 | 6.3 | 7.2 | 6.6 |
| Requested/sought an early promotion? | 7.4 | 8.4 | 5.0 | 8.3 | 6.0 | 6.5 | 5.2 | 5.9 |
| **IF YOU WERE TO BEGIN YOUR CAREER AGAIN, WOULD YOU STILL WANT TO:** | | | | | | | | |
| **Come to this institution? [2]** | | | | | | | | |
| Definitely yes | 33.9 | 28.3 | 37.5 | 32.9 | 39.7 | 40.1 | 38.1 | 40.4 |
| Probably yes | 34.6 | 37.3 | 36.8 | 31.9 | 34.0 | 35.6 | 30.0 | 34.4 |
| Not sure | 17.4 | 17.6 | 14.6 | 18.9 | 16.6 | 16.3 | 18.5 | 15.7 |
| Probably no | 9.0 | 10.9 | 6.4 | 10.1 | 6.7 | 5.7 | 9.5 | 6.1 |
| Definitely no | 5.1 | 5.9 | 4.6 | 6.2 | 3.0 | 2.4 | 3.9 | 3.4 |
| **Be a college professor?** | | | | | | | | |
| Definitely yes | 59.2 | 54.0 | 61.9 | 60.6 | 62.2 | 61.5 | 63.4 | 62.4 |
| Probably yes | 27.0 | 30.0 | 26.2 | 25.1 | 26.5 | 27.2 | 25.2 | 26.3 |
| Not sure | 10.0 | 11.4 | 8.6 | 9.6 | 9.4 | 9.4 | 9.3 | 9.3 |
| Probably no | 2.8 | 3.2 | 2.4 | 3.6 | 1.7 | 1.7 | 1.6 | 1.7 |
| Definitely no | 0.9 | 1.3 | 0.9 | 1.1 | 0.3 | 0.1 | 0.6 | 0.3 |

[2] This question asked for the first time in the 2007–2008 Faculty Survey.

97

**2007–2008 FACULTY SURVEY WEIGHTED NATIONAL NORMS**
**Full-time Undergraduate Faculty**

| Female Respondents | All 4+ yr | Universities Pub | Universities Priv | Four-year Colleges Pub | Four-year Colleges All Priv | Four-year Colleges Nons | Four-year Colleges Cath | Oth Relig |
|---|---|---|---|---|---|---|---|---|
| **Attributes noted as being "very descriptive" of your institution** | | | | | | | | |
| It is easy for students to see faculty outside of regular office hours | 61.2 | 51.2 | 61.8 | 57.0 | 77.3 | 77.9 | 73.5 | 79.2 |
| There is a great deal of conformity among the students | 28.6 | 28.6 | 35.1 | 24.1 | 31.6 | 26.9 | 33.9 | 36.8 |
| The faculty are typically at odds with campus administration | 19.8 | 16.5 | 17.6 | 24.6 | 18.2 | 17.8 | 20.9 | 16.9 |
| Faculty here respect each other | 48.0 | 44.9 | 51.2 | 45.0 | 53.8 | 51.3 | 53.7 | 57.7 |
| Most students are treated like "numbers in a book" | 3.0 | 4.1 | 3.4 | 3.3 | 1.2 | 1.4 | 1.2 | 1.0 |
| Social activities are overemphasized | 8.1 | 10.6 | 9.9 | 5.1 | 8.5 | 8.4 | 5.7 | 10.5 |
| Faculty are rewarded for being good teachers | 15.6 | 12.1 | 16.3 | 14.2 | 20.8 | 24.9 | 15.0 | 19.0 |
| There is respect for the expression of diverse values and beliefs | 35.3 | 31.0 | 40.1 | 36.6 | 36.5 | 40.1 | 37.5 | 30.5 |
| Faculty are rewarded for their efforts to use instructional technology | 23.3 | 24.3 | 26.7 | 25.4 | 18.2 | 19.2 | 16.6 | 17.9 |
| Faculty are rewarded for their efforts to work with underprepared students | 6.5 | 4.1 | 4.0 | 7.7 | 8.4 | 9.2 | 6.4 | 8.7 |
| Administrators consider faculty concerns when making policy [2] | 12.4 | 10.3 | 11.6 | 11.1 | 16.6 | 17.4 | 12.4 | 18.5 |
| The administration is open about its policies | 15.8 | 13.2 | 14.7 | 16.1 | 18.8 | 19.0 | 15.8 | 20.4 |
| **Do you, "to a great extent":** | | | | | | | | |
| Engage in academic work that spans multiple disciplines | 36.7 | 39.3 | 43.7 | 33.9 | 34.6 | 37.3 | 31.9 | 32.5 |
| Feel that the training you received in graduate school prepared you well for your role as a faculty mentor | 37.1 | 36.0 | 37.5 | 39.9 | 34.5 | 31.5 | 37.2 | 37.2 |
| Achieve a healthy balance between your personal life and your professional life | 27.3 | 29.7 | 28.5 | 26.6 | 25.2 | 24.7 | 28.5 | 23.7 |
| Experience close alignment between your work and your personal values | 66.2 | 61.4 | 72.5 | 65.3 | 70.1 | 69.7 | 70.1 | 70.7 |
| Feel that you have to work harder than your colleagues to be perceived as a legitimate scholar | 32.9 | 36.7 | 33.4 | 32.6 | 28.8 | 30.2 | 28.1 | 27.2 |
| Mentor new faculty [2] | 26.2 | 25.1 | 26.7 | 26.8 | 26.3 | 27.9 | 28.5 | 22.4 |

[2]  This question asked for the first time in the 2007–2008 Faculty Survey.

98

## 2007–2008 FACULTY SURVEY WEIGHTED NATIONAL NORMS
### Full-time Undergraduate Faculty

| Female Respondents | All 4+ yr | Universities Pub | Universities Priv | Four-year Colleges Pub | Four-year Colleges All Priv | Four-year Colleges Nons | Four-year Colleges Cath | Four-year Colleges Oth Relig |
|---|---|---|---|---|---|---|---|---|
| **Aspects of your job with which you are "very satisfied" or "satisfied": [3]** | | | | | | | | |
| Salary [2] | 41.9 | 39.6 | 47.9 | 39.8 | 44.5 | 47.8 | 37.4 | 44.6 |
| Health benefits [2] | 68.9 | 72.7 | 70.7 | 71.8 | 60.0 | 61.3 | 67.7 | 52.7 |
| Retirement benefits [2] | 67.4 | 71.5 | 66.6 | 67.3 | 63.2 | 63.7 | 60.0 | 64.8 |
| Opportunity for scholarly pursuits | 47.4 | 54.9 | 57.0 | 40.1 | 44.3 | 45.5 | 39.8 | 45.7 |
| Teaching load | 53.5 | 59.8 | 59.7 | 45.6 | 54.0 | 54.9 | 50.4 | 55.1 |
| Quality of students | 59.7 | 61.4 | 74.2 | 52.1 | 61.3 | 64.0 | 54.9 | 61.8 |
| Office/lab space | 66.3 | 68.5 | 65.9 | 61.4 | 70.2 | 71.6 | 66.4 | 70.6 |
| Autonomy and independence | 83.6 | 83.7 | 85.0 | 81.4 | 85.5 | 87.1 | 81.9 | 85.7 |
| Professional relationships with other faculty | 77.4 | 72.2 | 76.3 | 77.5 | 83.4 | 83.2 | 82.7 | 84.4 |
| Social relationships with other faculty | 70.1 | 65.4 | 69.7 | 69.2 | 76.4 | 76.1 | 76.4 | 76.8 |
| Competency of colleagues | 79.9 | 79.1 | 82.3 | 76.7 | 83.9 | 84.5 | 81.2 | 84.8 |
| Visibility for jobs at other institutions/organizations | 51.6 | 56.8 | 58.1 | 46.7 | 48.7 | 46.2 | 47.2 | 53.3 |
| Job security | 72.8 | 71.1 | 73.4 | 72.8 | 74.4 | 73.8 | 76.6 | 73.9 |
| Relationship with administration | 57.0 | 54.5 | 56.4 | 54.7 | 62.9 | 64.1 | 60.7 | 62.5 |
| Departmental leadership [2] | 65.7 | 59.5 | 66.1 | 66.3 | 71.8 | 74.4 | 65.9 | 72.1 |
| Course assignments [2] | 81.7 | 79.5 | 81.0 | 80.4 | 86.2 | 89.1 | 81.6 | 85.1 |
| Freedom to determine course content [2] | 91.2 | 90.6 | 91.1 | 90.9 | 92.3 | 93.4 | 89.2 | 92.8 |
| Availability of child care at this institution | 26.9 | 25.9 | 26.7 | 33.5 | 20.1 | 19.6 | 19.0 | 21.9 |
| Prospects for career advancement | 49.9 | 46.2 | 50.4 | 49.3 | 54.6 | 54.6 | 53.4 | 55.4 |
| Clerical/administrative support | 57.4 | 55.4 | 59.5 | 57.5 | 58.4 | 60.0 | 55.1 | 58.5 |
| Overall job satisfaction | 72.1 | 68.3 | 74.9 | 71.3 | 76.2 | 78.1 | 73.1 | 75.6 |

[2]  This question asked for the first time in the 2007–2008 Faculty Survey.
[3]  Respondents marking "Not Applicable" were not included in the computation of these results.

99

**2007–2008 FACULTY SURVEY WEIGHTED NATIONAL NORMS**
**Full-time Undergraduate Faculty**

| | | | | Four-year Colleges | | | | |
| | All | Universities | | | All | | | Oth |
| **Female Respondents** | 4+ yr | Pub | Priv | Pub | Priv | Nons | Cath | Relig |
|---|---|---|---|---|---|---|---|---|
| **Do you agree "strongly" or "somewhat"?** | | | | | | | | |
| Faculty are interested in students' personal problems | 85.1 | 75.9 | 84.5 | 85.8 | 94.4 | 92.6 | 95.2 | 96.6 |
| Racial and ethnic diversity should be more strongly reflected in the curriculum | 67.9 | 65.5 | 68.2 | 66.9 | 71.7 | 71.5 | 69.6 | 73.6 |
| Faculty feel that most students are well-prepared academically | 45.1 | 47.1 | 67.6 | 33.2 | 48.6 | 48.9 | 43.4 | 52.0 |
| This institution should hire more faculty of color | 79.4 | 80.7 | 83.2 | 73.1 | 84.4 | 83.6 | 83.7 | 86.0 |
| Student Affairs staff have the support and respect of faculty | 79.4 | 76.9 | 79.5 | 79.3 | 82.1 | 81.0 | 81.2 | 84.6 |
| Faculty are committed to the welfare of this institution | 90.9 | 86.7 | 91.0 | 90.6 | 95.8 | 95.9 | 94.7 | 96.4 |
| Faculty here are strongly interested in the academic problems of undergraduates | 87.8 | 80.1 | 89.1 | 87.9 | 95.5 | 96.3 | 93.1 | 96.0 |
| There is a lot of campus racial conflict here | 13.6 | 14.8 | 15.4 | 11.0 | 14.7 | 15.8 | 12.3 | 14.8 |
| Most students are strongly committed to community service | 53.6 | 46.5 | 78.7 | 40.8 | 66.6 | 59.6 | 70.4 | 74.5 |
| My research is valued by faculty in my department | 70.1 | 68.8 | 73.4 | 68.1 | 72.7 | 72.4 | 68.7 | 76.1 |
| My teaching is valued by faculty in my department | 88.6 | 84.5 | 89.1 | 88.4 | 93.2 | 95.0 | 90.1 | 92.7 |
| Many courses include feminist perspectives | 46.6 | 41.4 | 47.7 | 46.2 | 52.3 | 58.9 | 48.6 | 45.0 |
| Faculty of color are treated fairly here | 83.6 | 79.1 | 83.7 | 84.0 | 87.9 | 88.9 | 86.8 | 87.1 |
| Women faculty are treated fairly here | 76.4 | 70.8 | 76.1 | 77.4 | 81.4 | 82.6 | 82.9 | 78.6 |
| Many courses involve students in community service | 54.4 | 42.0 | 66.5 | 54.0 | 63.4 | 58.0 | 70.2 | 66.6 |
| This institution should hire more women faculty | 63.1 | 70.5 | 74.7 | 58.8 | 55.7 | 56.1 | 48.9 | 60.0 |
| Gay and lesbian faculty are treated fairly here | 77.6 | 76.7 | 72.5 | 82.5 | 74.5 | 84.1 | 71.0 | 62.2 |
| My department does a good job of mentoring new faculty | 64.7 | 58.6 | 64.1 | 64.7 | 71.7 | 70.4 | 72.6 | 72.8 |
| Faculty are sufficiently involved in campus decision making | 53.5 | 50.6 | 46.9 | 53.3 | 59.9 | 62.2 | 57.2 | 58.3 |
| My values are congruent with the dominant institutional values | 73.3 | 65.0 | 73.9 | 73.3 | 82.2 | 80.6 | 83.5 | 83.7 |
| There is adequate support for integrating technology in my teaching | 81.7 | 83.5 | 86.4 | 80.6 | 79.3 | 81.0 | 79.5 | 76.8 |
| This institution takes responsibility for educating underprepared students | 60.9 | 56.2 | 60.5 | 61.6 | 65.4 | 66.0 | 66.5 | 63.6 |
| The criteria for advancement and promotion decisions are clear | 68.6 | 66.9 | 66.9 | 68.1 | 71.7 | 72.5 | 72.0 | 70.5 |
| Most of the students I teach lack the basic skills for college level work | 37.9 | 33.2 | 19.3 | 49.1 | 36.7 | 35.3 | 42.1 | 35.1 |
| There is adequate support for faculty development | 65.0 | 64.5 | 69.0 | 61.5 | 68.2 | 68.1 | 71.5 | 66.1 |
| This institution should not offer remedial/developmental education | 23.4 | 23.4 | 27.3 | 22.5 | 22.9 | 25.2 | 16.7 | 23.7 |

100

## 2007–2008 FACULTY SURVEY WEIGHTED NATIONAL NORMS
### Full-time Undergraduate Faculty

| Female Respondents | All 4+ yr | Universities Pub | Universities Priv | Four-year Colleges Pub | Four-year Colleges All Priv | Four-year Colleges Nons | Four-year Colleges Cath | Four-year Colleges Oth Relig |
|---|---|---|---|---|---|---|---|---|
| **Issues you believe to be of "high" or "highest" priority at your institution:** | | | | | | | | |
| To promote the intellectual development of students | 86.1 | 83.7 | 89.1 | 83.8 | 90.3 | 90.5 | 90.1 | 90.0 |
| To help students examine and understand their personal values | 57.5 | 42.6 | 70.7 | 51.8 | 75.4 | 66.9 | 84.1 | 81.9 |
| To develop a sense of community among students and faculty | 57.5 | 45.2 | 61.4 | 55.1 | 72.2 | 69.3 | 74.2 | 75.0 |
| To facilitate student involvement in community service | 51.3 | 36.1 | 69.5 | 48.1 | 64.2 | 56.7 | 73.3 | 68.9 |
| To help students learn how to bring about change in American society | 39.3 | 27.3 | 51.6 | 38.6 | 48.0 | 44.8 | 53.9 | 48.5 |
| To increase or maintain institutional prestige | 64.4 | 72.4 | 74.6 | 57.1 | 60.8 | 63.7 | 57.6 | 58.7 |
| To hire faculty "stars" | 29.6 | 45.9 | 40.6 | 20.9 | 18.3 | 18.3 | 19.1 | 17.8 |
| To recruit more minority students | 52.8 | 56.0 | 52.1 | 51.5 | 51.4 | 54.7 | 51.7 | 46.1 |
| To enhance the institution's national image | 68.6 | 80.0 | 80.0 | 60.7 | 61.2 | 66.9 | 57.0 | 55.8 |
| To create a diverse multi-cultural campus environment | 57.0 | 57.5 | 57.1 | 58.4 | 54.6 | 57.8 | 55.8 | 49.1 |
| To promote gender equity among faculty | 44.3 | 44.3 | 45.5 | 44.5 | 43.8 | 47.6 | 42.4 | 39.2 |
| To provide resources for faculty to engage in community-based teaching or research | 38.1 | 33.5 | 41.8 | 42.3 | 36.2 | 34.5 | 39.1 | 36.6 |
| To create and sustain partnerships with surrounding communities | 51.8 | 49.3 | 46.4 | 59.0 | 47.5 | 43.2 | 53.9 | 49.3 |
| To pursue extramural funding | 61.1 | 76.9 | 64.3 | 56.9 | 47.6 | 48.4 | 48.2 | 45.9 |
| To increase the representation of minorities in the faculty and administration | 45.3 | 47.5 | 45.7 | 45.3 | 42.7 | 45.8 | 41.6 | 38.8 |
| To strengthen links with the for-profit, corporate sector [2] | 50.2 | 59.2 | 46.5 | 53.9 | 37.2 | 36.3 | 43.1 | 34.5 |
| To develop leadership ability among students | 61.3 | 53.1 | 70.4 | 56.3 | 72.4 | 71.8 | 71.7 | 73.8 |
| To increase the representation of women in the faculty and administration | 33.1 | 36.8 | 37.4 | 30.6 | 30.3 | 30.9 | 30.7 | 29.1 |
| To develop an appreciation for multiculturalism [2] | 56.8 | 52.8 | 57.0 | 57.2 | 60.6 | 61.9 | 63.0 | 57.1 |

[2] This question asked for the first time in the 2007–2008 Faculty Survey.

101

**2007–2008 FACULTY SURVEY WEIGHTED NATIONAL NORMS**
**Full-time Undergraduate Faculty**

| Female Respondents | All 4+ yr | Universities | | Four-year Colleges | | | | |
| --- | --- | --- | --- | --- | --- | --- | --- | --- |
| | | Pub | Priv | Pub | All Priv | Nons | Cath | Oth Relig |
| **Do you agree "strongly" or "somewhat"?** | | | | | | | | |
| Western civilization and culture should be the foundation for the undergraduate curriculum | 49.3 | 47.6 | 50.9 | 47.9 | 52.2 | 47.5 | 58.1 | 55.1 |
| College officials have the right to ban persons with extreme views from speaking on campus | 24.0 | 20.4 | 30.0 | 20.4 | 29.8 | 25.4 | 28.6 | 37.4 |
| The chief benefit of a college education is that it increases one's earning power | 28.0 | 28.4 | 20.1 | 33.1 | 24.3 | 23.2 | 24.7 | 25.7 |
| Promoting diversity leads to the admission of too many underprepared students | 17.3 | 18.2 | 15.5 | 18.0 | 16.2 | 15.3 | 16.1 | 17.8 |
| Colleges should be actively involved in solving social problems | 75.5 | 74.7 | 76.8 | 75.7 | 75.6 | 74.3 | 78.8 | 75.4 |
| Tenure is an outmoded concept | 37.2 | 38.4 | 38.4 | 37.5 | 35.1 | 30.6 | 36.0 | 41.1 |
| Colleges should encourage students to be involved in community service activities | 92.0 | 89.6 | 90.3 | 92.1 | 95.4 | 94.5 | 96.6 | 95.9 |
| Community service should be given weight in college admissions decisions | 69.5 | 66.8 | 72.7 | 67.7 | 73.4 | 72.6 | 74.3 | 74.0 |
| A racially/ethnically diverse student body enhances the educational experience of all students | 96.8 | 96.6 | 97.1 | 96.5 | 97.4 | 98.2 | 96.6 | 96.7 |
| Realistically, an individual can do little to bring about changes in society | 12.2 | 13.3 | 13.2 | 12.8 | 9.9 | 9.4 | 10.6 | 10.1 |
| Colleges should be concerned with facilitating undergraduate students' spiritual development | 35.9 | 23.2 | 50.3 | 25.9 | 56.0 | 38.2 | 74.8 | 69.2 |
| Colleges have a responsibility to work with their surrounding communities to address local issues | 90.6 | 88.3 | 89.3 | 91.5 | 92.6 | 91.8 | 93.7 | 92.9 |
| Private funding sources often prevent researchers from being completely objective in the conduct of their work | 61.4 | 64.6 | 59.5 | 61.3 | 59.0 | 61.1 | 54.8 | 58.8 |

102

**2007–2008 FACULTY SURVEY WEIGHTED NATIONAL NORMS**
**Full-time Undergraduate Faculty**

| | | | | Four-year Colleges | | | | |
| --- | --- | --- | --- | --- | --- | --- | --- | --- |
| | **All** | **Universities** | | | **All** | | | **Oth** |
| **Female Respondents** | **4+ yr** | **Pub** | **Priv** | **Pub** | **Priv** | **Nons** | **Cath** | **Relig** |
| **Factors noted as a source of stress for you during the <u>last two</u> years** | | | | | | | | |
| Managing household responsibilities | 80.5 | 80.8 | 82.1 | 78.7 | 81.9 | 82.6 | 79.9 | 82.1 |
| Child care | 31.2 | 30.9 | 34.1 | 29.1 | 33.0 | 31.9 | 32.8 | 34.7 |
| Care of elderly parent | 37.6 | 38.2 | 39.5 | 37.9 | 35.8 | 33.4 | 36.9 | 38.6 |
| My physical health | 53.9 | 55.5 | 52.0 | 53.0 | 53.9 | 53.2 | 54.5 | 54.7 |
| Health of spouse/partner | 31.4 | 32.9 | 27.2 | 31.7 | 31.2 | 34.1 | 29.3 | 28.4 |
| Review/promotion process | 57.9 | 59.2 | 52.0 | 61.1 | 55.1 | 57.5 | 54.4 | 52.0 |
| Subtle discrimination (e.g., prejudice, racism, sexism) | 38.7 | 42.4 | 42.1 | 38.7 | 33.4 | 31.8 | 33.8 | 35.5 |
| Personal finances | 65.2 | 61.9 | 65.1 | 67.1 | 66.3 | 67.5 | 64.7 | 65.5 |
| Committee work | 64.8 | 62.5 | 58.0 | 70.3 | 63.3 | 63.8 | 66.3 | 60.5 |
| Faculty meetings | 56.2 | 56.1 | 52.8 | 58.8 | 54.6 | 53.5 | 61.1 | 51.6 |
| Colleagues | 68.7 | 69.4 | 65.9 | 70.5 | 66.7 | 69.5 | 66.4 | 62.9 |
| Students | 69.0 | 67.8 | 64.3 | 70.3 | 70.5 | 69.0 | 68.7 | 74.0 |
| Research or publishing demands | 65.0 | 67.6 | 71.8 | 67.1 | 56.9 | 60.5 | 58.7 | 50.2 |
| Institutional procedures and "red tape" | 71.5 | 74.3 | 67.3 | 76.5 | 64.1 | 62.2 | 68.3 | 63.9 |
| Teaching load | 69.1 | 64.6 | 65.7 | 73.3 | 70.2 | 69.7 | 71.0 | 70.3 |
| Children's problems | 30.9 | 30.9 | 31.4 | 31.1 | 30.6 | 30.3 | 32.1 | 30.0 |
| Friction with spouse/partner | 24.6 | 25.0 | 25.4 | 23.9 | 24.6 | 25.4 | 24.1 | 23.8 |
| Lack of personal time | 83.7 | 82.4 | 84.7 | 83.4 | 85.2 | 86.0 | 83.9 | 84.8 |
| Keeping up with information technology | 59.4 | 60.5 | 54.3 | 62.4 | 56.7 | 52.9 | 61.8 | 58.7 |
| Job security | 39.3 | 39.5 | 39.7 | 41.2 | 36.5 | 36.7 | 34.8 | 37.4 |
| Being part of a dual career couple | 47.8 | 49.0 | 50.9 | 44.1 | 50.1 | 51.5 | 45.7 | 51.0 |
| Working with underprepared students | 64.5 | 60.4 | 49.4 | 70.9 | 67.1 | 62.8 | 71.2 | 70.7 |
| Classroom conflict | 24.3 | 23.2 | 19.0 | 26.4 | 25.1 | 24.2 | 26.5 | 25.2 |
| Self-imposed high expectations | 84.8 | 84.6 | 85.7 | 84.0 | 85.5 | 85.8 | 83.1 | 86.8 |
| Change in work responsibilities | 55.3 | 53.7 | 55.7 | 56.0 | 55.9 | 55.0 | 57.9 | 55.7 |
| **Personal goals noted as "very important" or "essential":** | | | | | | | | |
| Becoming an authority in my field | 57.5 | 63.0 | 63.3 | 55.4 | 51.8 | 52.3 | 53.9 | 49.6 |
| Influencing the political structure | 20.7 | 22.3 | 22.3 | 21.3 | 17.6 | 16.5 | 21.6 | 16.5 |
| Influencing social values | 46.7 | 42.6 | 51.2 | 47.7 | 48.2 | 47.3 | 51.0 | 47.6 |
| Raising a family | 64.2 | 63.2 | 69.2 | 62.1 | 66.0 | 65.8 | 65.9 | 66.5 |
| Becoming very well off financially | 30.0 | 33.5 | 27.9 | 32.0 | 24.6 | 25.1 | 26.1 | 22.8 |
| Helping others who are in difficulty | 71.3 | 67.4 | 73.7 | 72.2 | 73.6 | 72.2 | 73.5 | 75.8 |
| Becoming involved in programs to clean up the environment | 38.1 | 36.5 | 37.4 | 39.2 | 38.9 | 39.3 | 39.5 | 37.7 |
| Developing a meaningful philosophy of life | 75.2 | 71.5 | 76.3 | 75.7 | 78.0 | 76.6 | 80.9 | 78.0 |
| Helping to promote racial understanding | 62.1 | 60.0 | 63.1 | 62.2 | 64.0 | 63.7 | 65.3 | 63.5 |
| Obtaining recognition from my colleagues for contributions to my special field | 48.2 | 55.8 | 54.1 | 45.0 | 41.4 | 42.6 | 44.0 | 37.6 |
| Integrating spirituality into my life | 53.1 | 47.8 | 54.6 | 52.7 | 58.7 | 46.4 | 67.1 | 71.0 |

103

| Female Respondents | All 4+ yr | Universities Pub | Universities Priv | Four-year Colleges Pub | Four-year Colleges All Priv | Four-year Colleges Nons | Four-year Colleges Cath | Four-year Colleges Oth Relig |
|---|---|---|---|---|---|---|---|---|
| **IN YOUR INTERACTIONS WITH UNDERGRADUATES, HOW OFTEN DO YOU ENCOURAGE THEM TO: [2]** | | | | | | | | |
| **Ask questions in class** | | | | | | | | |
| Frequently | 97.1 | 97.5 | 96.8 | 97.0 | 96.9 | 97.4 | 96.2 | 96.6 |
| Occasionally | 2.7 | 2.2 | 3.2 | 2.8 | 3.1 | 2.6 | 3.8 | 3.3 |
| Not at all | 0.2 | 0.4 | 0.1 | 0.1 | 0.1 | 0.0 | 0.1 | 0.1 |
| **Support their opinions with a logical argument** | | | | | | | | |
| Frequently | 86.4 | 85.4 | 86.4 | 87.1 | 86.7 | 88.3 | 85.8 | 84.9 |
| Occasionally | 13.0 | 13.8 | 13.0 | 12.4 | 12.8 | 11.2 | 13.7 | 14.7 |
| Not at all | 0.6 | 0.8 | 0.6 | 0.5 | 0.5 | 0.5 | 0.6 | 0.4 |
| **Seek solutions to problems and explain them to others** | | | | | | | | |
| Frequently | 79.9 | 79.4 | 77.3 | 81.1 | 80.0 | 81.2 | 83.4 | 75.9 |
| Occasionally | 18.8 | 19.2 | 21.1 | 17.7 | 18.9 | 17.7 | 15.8 | 22.9 |
| Not at all | 1.3 | 1.5 | 1.6 | 1.2 | 1.1 | 1.2 | 0.8 | 1.2 |
| **Revise their papers to improve their writing** | | | | | | | | |
| Frequently | 68.9 | 67.9 | 65.9 | 69.9 | 69.8 | 73.8 | 65.9 | 66.9 |
| Occasionally | 25.8 | 25.3 | 26.6 | 25.9 | 25.8 | 22.5 | 29.7 | 28.1 |
| Not at all | 5.4 | 6.8 | 7.6 | 4.2 | 4.3 | 3.8 | 4.5 | 5.0 |
| **Evaluate the quality or reliability of information they receive** | | | | | | | | |
| Frequently | 80.2 | 80.4 | 77.8 | 81.5 | 79.3 | 80.7 | 79.1 | 77.4 |
| Occasionally | 18.4 | 18.3 | 20.2 | 17.4 | 19.1 | 18.2 | 18.2 | 21.2 |
| Not at all | 1.4 | 1.4 | 1.9 | 1.1 | 1.6 | 1.1 | 2.6 | 1.5 |
| **Take risks for potential gains** | | | | | | | | |
| Frequently | 42.8 | 43.1 | 44.6 | 42.6 | 42.3 | 45.3 | 39.9 | 39.5 |
| Occasionally | 45.6 | 45.0 | 43.4 | 45.3 | 47.3 | 45.7 | 48.9 | 48.7 |
| Not at all | 11.6 | 11.9 | 12.0 | 12.1 | 10.4 | 9.0 | 11.2 | 11.8 |
| **Seek alternative solutions to a problem** | | | | | | | | |
| Frequently | 71.7 | 71.8 | 71.2 | 73.6 | 69.4 | 71.4 | 69.2 | 66.4 |
| Occasionally | 26.2 | 24.7 | 26.9 | 25.1 | 28.8 | 27.1 | 28.5 | 31.6 |
| Not at all | 2.1 | 3.5 | 1.9 | 1.2 | 1.8 | 1.5 | 2.3 | 2.0 |
| **Look up scientific research articles and resources** | | | | | | | | |
| Frequently | 59.6 | 59.6 | 59.4 | 62.5 | 55.8 | 57.5 | 57.4 | 52.1 |
| Occasionally | 29.0 | 29.7 | 27.7 | 28.2 | 29.7 | 26.9 | 30.4 | 33.4 |
| Not at all | 11.5 | 10.7 | 12.8 | 9.3 | 14.5 | 15.6 | 12.2 | 14.4 |
| **Explore topics on their own, even though it was not required for a class** | | | | | | | | |
| Frequently | 57.1 | 58.1 | 58.0 | 58.3 | 54.2 | 57.5 | 52.9 | 50.1 |
| Occasionally | 39.9 | 38.9 | 39.3 | 38.5 | 43.1 | 40.6 | 44.8 | 45.6 |
| Not at all | 3.0 | 3.0 | 2.7 | 3.2 | 2.7 | 1.9 | 2.2 | 4.3 |
| **Acknowledge failure as a necessary part of the learning process** | | | | | | | | |
| Frequently | 54.5 | 53.6 | 53.6 | 56.5 | 53.4 | 56.7 | 52.6 | 49.0 |
| Occasionally | 39.9 | 39.8 | 40.9 | 38.3 | 41.6 | 37.8 | 43.2 | 46.1 |
| Not at all | 5.6 | 6.6 | 5.4 | 5.2 | 5.0 | 5.4 | 4.2 | 4.9 |
| **Seek feedback on their academic work** | | | | | | | | |
| Frequently | 82.5 | 80.0 | 82.6 | 84.4 | 82.8 | 83.4 | 84.0 | 81.3 |
| Occasionally | 16.5 | 18.6 | 15.7 | 14.9 | 16.5 | 16.2 | 15.6 | 17.6 |
| Not at all | 1.0 | 1.4 | 1.7 | 0.8 | 0.6 | 0.4 | 0.4 | 1.1 |

[2] This question asked for the first time in the 2007–2008 Faculty Survey.

**2007–2008 FACULTY SURVEY WEIGHTED NATIONAL NORMS**
**Full-time Undergraduate Faculty**

| Female Respondents | All 4+ yr | Universities Pub | Universities Priv | Four-year Colleges Pub | Four-year Colleges All Priv | Four-year Colleges Nons | Four-year Colleges Cath | Four-year Colleges Oth Relig |
|---|---|---|---|---|---|---|---|---|
| **Methods you use in "all" or "most" of the courses you teach:** | | | | | | | | |
| Multiple-choice exams [2] | 34.7 | 32.1 | 27.0 | 40.4 | 33.7 | 24.9 | 44.2 | 39.3 |
| Essay exams [2] | 43.1 | 41.6 | 45.9 | 41.8 | 45.3 | 43.9 | 44.4 | 48.1 |
| Short-answer exams [2] | 44.0 | 42.5 | 44.0 | 43.5 | 46.3 | 43.3 | 47.3 | 49.9 |
| Quizzes | 41.3 | 41.6 | 35.7 | 42.4 | 41.8 | 38.1 | 43.0 | 46.4 |
| Weekly essay assignments | 25.0 | 23.8 | 27.3 | 23.2 | 27.6 | 30.0 | 25.3 | 25.8 |
| Student presentations | 56.1 | 53.1 | 53.8 | 55.3 | 61.3 | 62.7 | 59.8 | 60.3 |
| Term/research papers | 47.1 | 44.8 | 52.0 | 47.0 | 47.8 | 52.4 | 44.0 | 43.7 |
| Student evaluations of each others' work | 29.5 | 28.9 | 26.5 | 29.6 | 31.2 | 31.7 | 29.2 | 31.7 |
| Grading on a curve | 10.7 | 12.6 | 12.4 | 10.3 | 8.4 | 9.0 | 11.3 | 5.6 |
| Competency-based grading | 55.1 | 53.8 | 53.0 | 58.9 | 52.7 | 50.4 | 52.8 | 56.1 |
| Class discussions | 88.2 | 87.2 | 88.7 | 88.7 | 88.3 | 89.9 | 87.2 | 86.9 |
| Cooperative learning (small groups) | 73.2 | 71.5 | 68.3 | 74.6 | 75.1 | 74.3 | 73.0 | 77.8 |
| Experiential learning/Field studies | 36.9 | 35.8 | 33.3 | 37.6 | 38.6 | 37.0 | 37.1 | 42.1 |
| Teaching assistants | 9.5 | 13.6 | 14.7 | 6.3 | 6.7 | 8.3 | 4.2 | 6.3 |
| Recitals/Demonstrations | 23.4 | 23.9 | 23.3 | 24.0 | 22.3 | 21.1 | 23.9 | 22.8 |
| Group projects | 42.9 | 45.0 | 38.3 | 43.1 | 42.4 | 40.8 | 43.4 | 44.0 |
| Extensive lecturing | 33.4 | 32.5 | 37.6 | 35.8 | 29.8 | 27.2 | 34.3 | 30.4 |
| Multiple drafts of written work | 30.6 | 28.7 | 32.9 | 30.6 | 31.7 | 36.0 | 25.9 | 29.3 |
| Readings on racial and ethnic issues | 33.0 | 32.1 | 33.4 | 33.7 | 32.8 | 35.4 | 30.5 | 30.7 |
| Readings on women and gender issues | 29.8 | 29.4 | 32.0 | 29.8 | 29.3 | 31.6 | 27.0 | 27.4 |
| Student-developed activities (assignments, exams, etc.) | 27.5 | 25.8 | 30.7 | 28.4 | 27.1 | 26.2 | 27.8 | 27.8 |
| Student-selected topics for course content | 19.7 | 18.1 | 20.7 | 20.4 | 20.2 | 20.4 | 20.5 | 19.7 |
| Reflective writing/journaling | 29.9 | 25.7 | 29.7 | 31.1 | 32.9 | 33.3 | 31.7 | 33.1 |
| Community service as part of coursework | 12.4 | 12.4 | 12.2 | 12.6 | 12.3 | 11.6 | 13.5 | 12.4 |
| Electronic quizzes with immediate feedback in class [2] | 7.6 | 8.8 | 6.4 | 8.6 | 5.5 | 3.6 | 7.5 | 6.8 |
| Using real-life problems [2] | 58.6 | 55.7 | 56.7 | 62.7 | 57.7 | 55.4 | 61.0 | 58.7 |
| Using student inquiry to drive learning | 52.3 | 47.3 | 53.4 | 54.4 | 54.5 | 56.8 | 54.6 | 51.2 |

[2]  This question asked for the first time in the 2007–2008 Faculty Survey.

105

## 2007–2008 FACULTY SURVEY WEIGHTED NATIONAL NORMS
### Full-time Undergraduate Faculty

| Female Respondents | All 4+ yr | Universities Pub | Priv | Four-year Colleges Pub | All Priv | Nons | Cath | Oth Relig |
|---|---|---|---|---|---|---|---|---|
| **YOUR BASE INSTITUTIONAL SALARY** | | | | | | | | |
| **9/10 month contract** | | | | | | | | |
| Less than $20,000 | 2.1 | 2.4 | 1.4 | 2.1 | 2.0 | 1.7 | 2.6 | 1.9 |
| $20,000 to 29,999 | 1.1 | 1.2 | 0.2 | 1.7 | 0.5 | 0.1 | 0.2 | 1.3 |
| $30,000 to 39,999 | 6.7 | 8.0 | 4.0 | 6.8 | 6.1 | 6.0 | 2.7 | 8.8 |
| $40,000 to 49,999 | 18.7 | 12.7 | 12.0 | 22.5 | 23.7 | 16.9 | 27.2 | 30.0 |
| $50,000 to 59,999 | 27.8 | 27.9 | 17.9 | 28.2 | 30.9 | 29.3 | 32.9 | 31.7 |
| $60,000 to 69,999 | 18.3 | 18.7 | 15.8 | 18.7 | 18.0 | 19.2 | 17.7 | 16.7 |
| $70,000 to 79,999 | 10.4 | 12.4 | 13.4 | 9.1 | 8.3 | 10.9 | 8.3 | 5.0 |
| $80,000 to 89,999 | 6.1 | 6.9 | 9.0 | 5.3 | 5.0 | 6.5 | 5.0 | 3.0 |
| $90,000 to 99,999 | 4.4 | 4.5 | 10.6 | 3.9 | 2.3 | 3.4 | 2.2 | 1.1 |
| $100,000 to 124,999 | 3.4 | 4.0 | 10.8 | 1.5 | 2.5 | 4.8 | 1.3 | 0.3 |
| $125,000 to 149,999 | 0.7 | 1.0 | 3.0 | 0.0 | 0.3 | 0.6 | 0.0 | 0.0 |
| $150,000 or more | 0.3 | 0.2 | 1.8 | 0.1 | 0.2 | 0.5 | 0.0 | 0.0 |
| **11/12 month contract** | | | | | | | | |
| Less than $20,000 | 2.9 | 2.2 | 5.2 | 3.1 | 2.2 | 1.7 | 4.8 | 1.6 |
| $20,000 to 29,999 | 0.5 | 0.4 | 0.4 | 0.6 | 0.5 | 0.2 | 0.0 | 1.4 |
| $30,000 to 39,999 | 6.4 | 5.3 | 4.0 | 9.2 | 5.8 | 5.8 | 2.9 | 7.5 |
| $40,000 to 49,999 | 17.3 | 14.3 | 11.2 | 15.8 | 23.1 | 17.4 | 26.5 | 31.7 |
| $50,000 to 59,999 | 23.3 | 19.2 | 23.7 | 25.1 | 24.2 | 22.2 | 27.0 | 26.1 |
| $60,000 to 69,999 | 19.6 | 17.1 | 18.3 | 22.5 | 19.4 | 20.0 | 17.1 | 19.6 |
| $70,000 to 79,999 | 10.9 | 11.7 | 14.1 | 8.6 | 11.1 | 13.4 | 10.0 | 7.5 |
| $80,000 to 89,999 | 6.9 | 6.4 | 9.0 | 6.5 | 6.7 | 9.0 | 5.9 | 2.7 |
| $90,000 to 99,999 | 4.5 | 6.0 | 6.3 | 3.7 | 3.5 | 5.4 | 1.9 | 1.1 |
| $100,000 to 124,999 | 5.8 | 13.5 | 4.3 | 3.9 | 3.0 | 4.0 | 3.6 | 0.7 |
| $125,000 to 149,999 | 1.2 | 2.0 | 2.9 | 0.6 | 0.4 | 0.7 | 0.0 | 0.1 |
| $150,000 or more | 0.7 | 2.0 | 0.7 | 0.3 | 0.1 | 0.2 | 0.2 | 0.0 |
| **Your base institutional salary is based on:** | | | | | | | | |
| 9/10 months | 73.8 | 80.1 | 65.4 | 76.8 | 66.8 | 61.9 | 72.4 | 70.1 |
| 11/12 months | 26.2 | 19.9 | 34.6 | 23.2 | 33.2 | 38.1 | 27.6 | 29.9 |
| **WHAT PERCENTAGE OF YOUR CURRENT YEAR'S SALARY COMES FROM: [2]** | | | | | | | | |
| **Income from this institution** | | | | | | | | |
| All | 69.3 | 69.9 | 64.6 | 69.6 | 70.4 | 69.4 | 71.1 | 71.3 |
| 75 to 99 | 26.1 | 25.6 | 31.5 | 25.9 | 24.8 | 26.1 | 23.4 | 23.9 |
| 50 to 74 | 3.1 | 3.1 | 2.7 | 3.3 | 3.2 | 3.1 | 3.6 | 3.2 |
| 25 to 49 | 0.9 | 0.7 | 0.7 | 1.0 | 1.1 | 1.0 | 1.2 | 1.1 |
| 1 to 24 | 0.3 | 0.4 | 0.3 | 0.1 | 0.4 | 0.4 | 0.4 | 0.3 |
| None | 0.2 | 0.4 | 0.2 | 0.2 | 0.1 | 0.0 | 0.3 | 0.2 |
| **Other academic income** | | | | | | | | |
| All | 0.1 | 0.2 | 0.0 | 0.0 | 0.1 | 0.0 | 0.1 | 0.1 |
| 75 to 99 | 0.1 | 0.3 | 0.0 | 0.0 | 0.2 | 0.1 | 0.3 | 0.2 |
| 50 to 74 | 0.3 | 0.3 | 0.1 | 0.5 | 0.2 | 0.1 | 0.3 | 0.3 |
| 25 to 49 | 1.5 | 1.6 | 1.5 | 1.4 | 1.6 | 1.7 | 1.8 | 1.1 |
| 1 to 24 | 14.4 | 15.3 | 16.9 | 13.9 | 13.0 | 12.9 | 13.8 | 12.5 |
| None | 83.6 | 82.3 | 81.5 | 84.2 | 85.0 | 85.2 | 83.6 | 85.8 |
| **Non-academic income** | | | | | | | | |
| All | 0.2 | 0.3 | 0.2 | 0.1 | 0.1 | 0.0 | 0.1 | 0.1 |
| 75 to 99 | 0.2 | 0.1 | 0.3 | 0.1 | 0.4 | 0.2 | 0.5 | 0.5 |
| 50 to 74 | 1.3 | 1.5 | 0.9 | 1.2 | 1.5 | 1.5 | 1.3 | 1.7 |
| 25 to 49 | 2.9 | 3.0 | 2.5 | 2.8 | 3.1 | 3.9 | 2.9 | 2.1 |
| 1 to 24 | 17.4 | 15.7 | 21.7 | 17.4 | 17.4 | 17.6 | 16.4 | 17.7 |
| None | 78.0 | 79.4 | 74.4 | 78.3 | 77.6 | 76.9 | 78.8 | 77.9 |

[2] This question asked for the first time in the 2007–2008 Faculty Survey.

106

## 2007–2008 FACULTY SURVEY WEIGHTED NATIONAL NORMS
### Full-time Undergraduate Faculty

| Female Respondents | All 4+ yr | Universities Pub | Universities Priv | Four-year Colleges Pub | Four-year Colleges All Priv | Four-year Colleges Nons | Four-year Colleges Cath | Four-year Colleges Oth Relig |
|---|---|---|---|---|---|---|---|---|
| **What is your age as of 12/31/2007?** | | | | | | | | |
| Less than 30 | 1.9 | 1.6 | 1.8 | 1.7 | 2.5 | 2.3 | 1.4 | 3.4 |
| 30 to 34 | 7.9 | 7.2 | 9.5 | 7.3 | 8.6 | 8.7 | 6.7 | 9.9 |
| 35 to 39 | 13.0 | 12.2 | 14.1 | 12.6 | 14.0 | 15.5 | 10.5 | 14.3 |
| 40 to 44 | 13.1 | 12.2 | 15.2 | 12.3 | 14.2 | 15.4 | 12.4 | 13.7 |
| 45 to 49 | 13.6 | 12.8 | 12.3 | 14.3 | 14.3 | 13.4 | 14.5 | 15.4 |
| 50 to 54 | 16.6 | 15.8 | 14.9 | 18.0 | 16.5 | 15.7 | 18.0 | 16.6 |
| 55 to 59 | 18.3 | 21.4 | 17.0 | 19.1 | 14.3 | 13.0 | 15.5 | 15.3 |
| 60 to 64 | 10.0 | 10.1 | 9.7 | 10.1 | 10.0 | 9.4 | 14.8 | 7.7 |
| 65 to 69 | 4.3 | 4.5 | 4.3 | 3.9 | 4.5 | 5.3 | 4.5 | 3.3 |
| 70 or more | 1.3 | 2.3 | 1.3 | 0.6 | 1.1 | 1.1 | 1.7 | 0.4 |
| **Year of highest degree now held** | | | | | | | | |
| Before 1970 | 2.2 | 3.9 | 2.6 | 1.0 | 1.7 | 2.0 | 2.3 | 0.7 |
| 1971 to 1975 | 3.9 | 4.9 | 5.2 | 3.2 | 3.2 | 4.0 | 3.3 | 2.0 |
| 1976 to 1980 | 7.5 | 8.4 | 8.2 | 7.2 | 6.5 | 7.3 | 6.4 | 5.4 |
| 1981 to 1985 | 9.0 | 10.5 | 11.1 | 7.3 | 8.6 | 8.9 | 8.9 | 8.1 |
| 1986 to 1990 | 12.9 | 13.1 | 11.8 | 12.4 | 13.7 | 13.2 | 16.0 | 12.8 |
| 1991 to 1995 | 16.2 | 15.7 | 16.5 | 17.3 | 15.2 | 14.1 | 15.2 | 17.0 |
| 1996 to 2000 | 18.9 | 16.5 | 17.3 | 20.5 | 20.1 | 20.4 | 19.3 | 20.4 |
| 2001 to 2005 | 22.0 | 21.1 | 20.6 | 22.5 | 22.9 | 23.7 | 21.1 | 22.9 |
| 2006 to 2007 | 7.5 | 5.9 | 6.8 | 8.6 | 8.1 | 6.6 | 7.5 | 10.7 |
| **Year of appointment at current position** | | | | | | | | |
| Before 1970 | 0.9 | 0.8 | 1.3 | 0.7 | 1.0 | 1.0 | 1.4 | 0.7 |
| 1971 to 1975 | 2.0 | 3.1 | 1.6 | 1.3 | 1.7 | 1.9 | 2.1 | 1.0 |
| 1976 to 1980 | 4.3 | 5.8 | 5.7 | 3.2 | 3.4 | 3.8 | 3.1 | 3.1 |
| 1981 to 1985 | 6.3 | 7.9 | 6.2 | 4.8 | 6.3 | 7.9 | 6.9 | 3.4 |
| 1986 to 1990 | 9.9 | 9.4 | 10.3 | 9.6 | 10.6 | 10.4 | 10.6 | 11.0 |
| 1991 to 1995 | 12.7 | 14.8 | 12.0 | 12.6 | 10.6 | 10.0 | 10.2 | 11.6 |
| 1996 to 2000 | 18.2 | 16.0 | 17.1 | 20.2 | 18.8 | 19.3 | 16.9 | 19.4 |
| 2001 to 2005 | 30.7 | 29.6 | 28.4 | 32.0 | 31.2 | 30.2 | 33.9 | 31.0 |
| 2006 to 2007 | 15.1 | 12.5 | 17.4 | 15.7 | 16.4 | 15.5 | 14.8 | 18.9 |
| **If tenured, year tenure was awarded** | | | | | | | | |
| Before 1970 | 0.2 | 0.0 | 0.1 | 0.0 | 0.6 | 0.8 | 0.4 | 0.5 |
| 1971 to 1975 | 1.2 | 1.4 | 2.4 | 1.0 | 0.7 | 0.4 | 1.4 | 0.5 |
| 1976 to 1980 | 3.4 | 4.7 | 3.8 | 2.8 | 2.5 | 3.1 | 2.1 | 1.7 |
| 1981 to 1985 | 5.9 | 8.4 | 6.9 | 4.1 | 5.0 | 5.4 | 4.9 | 4.1 |
| 1986 to 1990 | 10.1 | 10.9 | 14.9 | 7.6 | 10.4 | 13.1 | 8.8 | 6.9 |
| 1991 to 1995 | 14.7 | 14.5 | 18.4 | 13.5 | 15.0 | 13.6 | 16.0 | 16.9 |
| 1996 to 2000 | 20.9 | 25.0 | 20.3 | 19.1 | 18.6 | 18.5 | 21.7 | 16.1 |
| 2001 to 2005 | 24.6 | 18.7 | 22.5 | 29.0 | 26.6 | 25.9 | 22.5 | 31.4 |
| 2006 to 2007 | 19.1 | 16.5 | 10.8 | 23.0 | 20.6 | 19.2 | 22.2 | 22.0 |

**2007–2008 FACULTY SURVEY WEIGHTED NATIONAL NORMS**
**Full-time Undergraduate Faculty**

| Female Respondents | All 4+ yr | Universities Pub | Universities Priv | Four-year Colleges Pub | Four-year Colleges All Priv | Four-year Colleges Nons | Four-year Colleges Cath | Oth Relig |
|---|---|---|---|---|---|---|---|---|
| **WHAT IS THE MAJOR OF THE HIGHEST DEGREE YOU HOLD?** | | | | | | | | |
| **Biological Science** | | | | | | | | |
| Agriculture | 0.4 | 0.9 | 0.1 | 0.2 | 0.1 | 0.1 | 0.2 | 0.1 |
| Forestry | 0.1 | 0.1 | 0.0 | 0.0 | 0.0 | 0.1 | 0.0 | 0.0 |
| Bacteriology, Molecular Biology | 0.9 | 0.6 | 0.7 | 1.0 | 0.9 | 1.0 | 0.6 | 1.1 |
| Biochemistry | 0.7 | 0.7 | 0.7 | 0.5 | 0.8 | 0.8 | 0.6 | 0.8 |
| Biophysics | 0.0 | 0.1 | 0.0 | 0.0 | 0.1 | 0.1 | 0.1 | 0.0 |
| Botany | 0.4 | 0.6 | 0.2 | 0.6 | 0.2 | 0.2 | 0.2 | 0.2 |
| Environmental Science | 0.3 | 0.2 | 0.4 | 0.3 | 0.2 | 0.3 | 0.3 | 0.1 |
| Marine (life) Sciences | 0.2 | 0.0 | 0.2 | 0.3 | 0.1 | 0.2 | 0.1 | 0.0 |
| Physiology, Anatomy | 0.5 | 0.4 | 0.5 | 0.3 | 0.8 | 0.9 | 0.5 | 0.7 |
| Zoology | 0.6 | 0.6 | 0.3 | 0.6 | 0.8 | 1.0 | 0.9 | 0.5 |
| General, Other Biological Sciences | 1.9 | 2.0 | 2.5 | 1.4 | 2.1 | 2.4 | 1.5 | 2.0 |
| **Business** | | | | | | | | |
| Accounting | 0.9 | 0.9 | 0.5 | 1.1 | 0.9 | 0.6 | 1.9 | 0.8 |
| Finance | 0.4 | 0.5 | 0.6 | 0.3 | 0.4 | 0.2 | 0.4 | 0.6 |
| International Business | 0.1 | 0.0 | 0.3 | 0.1 | 0.1 | 0.0 | 0.1 | 0.1 |
| Management | 2.0 | 2.2 | 1.4 | 1.9 | 1.9 | 1.8 | 2.0 | 1.8 |
| Marketing | 0.7 | 0.8 | 0.4 | 0.7 | 0.5 | 0.3 | 1.0 | 0.6 |
| Secretarial Studies | 0.0 | 0.0 | 0.0 | 0.0 | 0.0 | 0.0 | 0.0 | 0.0 |
| General, Other Business | 0.8 | 1.1 | 0.8 | 0.7 | 0.8 | 0.3 | 1.7 | 0.8 |
| **Education** | | | | | | | | |
| Business Education | 0.3 | 0.6 | 0.1 | 0.2 | 0.2 | 0.2 | 0.1 | 0.2 |
| Educational Administration | 1.7 | 1.5 | 1.1 | 1.9 | 1.8 | 0.8 | 2.5 | 2.8 |
| Educational Psychology/Counseling | 1.4 | 1.5 | 1.5 | 1.6 | 0.8 | 0.5 | 1.6 | 0.8 |
| Elementary Education | 1.5 | 1.2 | 0.5 | 2.2 | 1.3 | 0.6 | 2.1 | 1.8 |
| Higher Education | 2.4 | 2.7 | 1.4 | 2.1 | 2.9 | 3.9 | 2.3 | 2.0 |
| Music or Art Education | 0.4 | 0.3 | 0.4 | 0.5 | 0.4 | 0.5 | 0.2 | 0.3 |
| Physical or Health Education | 1.3 | 0.7 | 0.4 | 1.7 | 1.7 | 1.7 | 0.6 | 2.6 |
| Secondary Education | 0.9 | 0.9 | 0.6 | 1.4 | 0.6 | 0.4 | 0.7 | 0.9 |
| Special Education | 1.7 | 2.1 | 0.4 | 1.9 | 1.3 | 0.5 | 1.8 | 2.2 |
| General, Other Education Fields | 4.3 | 3.2 | 3.0 | 5.6 | 4.5 | 3.5 | 4.9 | 5.6 |
| **Engineering** | | | | | | | | |
| Aero-/Astronautical Engineering | 0.1 | 0.2 | 0.1 | 0.0 | 0.0 | 0.0 | 0.0 | 0.0 |
| Chemical Engineering | 0.1 | 0.0 | 0.4 | 0.0 | 0.1 | 0.0 | 0.0 | 0.2 |
| Civil Engineering | 0.2 | 0.5 | 0.3 | 0.1 | 0.0 | 0.1 | 0.0 | 0.0 |
| Electrical Engineering | 0.2 | 0.3 | 0.2 | 0.2 | 0.1 | 0.2 | 0.1 | 0.1 |
| Industrial Engineering | 0.1 | 0.1 | 0.1 | 0.2 | 0.1 | 0.1 | 0.1 | 0.1 |
| Mechanical Engineering | 0.2 | 0.3 | 0.4 | 0.2 | 0.1 | 0.1 | 0.2 | 0.0 |
| General, Other Engineering Fields | 0.3 | 0.5 | 0.4 | 0.3 | 0.1 | 0.1 | 0.0 | 0.0 |
| **Health** | | | | | | | | |
| Dentistry | 0.1 | 0.2 | 0.0 | 0.1 | 0.1 | 0.0 | 0.3 | 0.0 |
| Health Technology | 0.1 | 0.1 | 0.0 | 0.2 | 0.0 | 0.0 | 0.0 | 0.0 |
| Medicine or Surgery | 0.2 | 0.3 | 0.5 | 0.0 | 0.1 | 0.2 | 0.0 | 0.0 |
| Nursing | 7.4 | 6.9 | 6.8 | 7.9 | 7.4 | 4.2 | 13.5 | 7.8 |
| Pharmacy, Pharmacology | 0.8 | 1.2 | 1.0 | 0.2 | 1.1 | 2.1 | 0.1 | 0.5 |
| Therapy (speech, physical, occup.) | 1.2 | 1.6 | 0.8 | 1.2 | 0.7 | 0.3 | 1.5 | 0.6 |
| Veterinary Medicine | 0.1 | 0.1 | 0.0 | 0.0 | 0.1 | 0.3 | 0.0 | 0.0 |
| General, Other Health Fields | 1.5 | 1.9 | 1.0 | 1.3 | 1.3 | 1.5 | 1.2 | 1.1 |

108

## 2007–2008 FACULTY SURVEY WEIGHTED NATIONAL NORMS
### Full-time Undergraduate Faculty

| Female Respondents | All 4+ yr | Universities Pub | Priv | Four-year Colleges Pub | All Priv | Nons | Cath | Oth Relig |
|---|---|---|---|---|---|---|---|---|
| **WHAT IS THE MAJOR OF THE HIGHEST DEGREE YOU HOLD?** | | | | | | | | |
| **Humanities** | | | | | | | | |
| History | 3.5 | 3.5 | 4.7 | 3.2 | 3.2 | 3.8 | 2.4 | 2.9 |
| Political Science, Government | 1.7 | 1.5 | 2.5 | 1.4 | 1.8 | 2.2 | 1.5 | 1.3 |
| English Language & Literature | 8.7 | 8.1 | 9.5 | 8.7 | 9.0 | 10.6 | 6.2 | 8.7 |
| Foreign Languages & Literature | 1.9 | 1.9 | 3.1 | 0.9 | 2.6 | 3.5 | 1.7 | 2.0 |
| French | 1.2 | 1.9 | 1.4 | 0.7 | 1.0 | 1.1 | 0.5 | 1.2 |
| German | 0.5 | 0.6 | 0.6 | 0.4 | 0.5 | 0.8 | 0.2 | 0.4 |
| Spanish | 1.6 | 1.4 | 2.2 | 1.2 | 1.9 | 1.7 | 1.1 | 2.7 |
| Other Foreign Languages | 0.5 | 0.9 | 0.6 | 0.2 | 0.3 | 0.6 | 0.1 | 0.1 |
| Linguistics | 1.2 | 1.7 | 0.6 | 0.8 | 1.3 | 2.6 | 0.1 | 0.4 |
| Philosophy | 1.2 | 0.9 | 2.3 | 1.0 | 1.1 | 0.9 | 2.3 | 0.6 |
| Religion or Theology | 1.3 | 0.7 | 3.3 | 0.1 | 2.6 | 1.4 | 3.5 | 3.9 |
| General, Other Humanities Fields | 1.7 | 2.2 | 1.8 | 1.3 | 1.6 | 2.0 | 1.2 | 1.4 |
| **Fine Arts** | | | | | | | | |
| Architecture/Urban Planning | 0.4 | 0.8 | 0.4 | 0.3 | 0.1 | 0.1 | 0.0 | 0.1 |
| Art | 2.0 | 1.2 | 1.5 | 2.4 | 2.6 | 3.5 | 1.6 | 1.9 |
| Dramatics or Speech | 1.7 | 1.0 | 2.0 | 2.0 | 2.0 | 2.4 | 2.0 | 1.5 |
| Music | 2.5 | 2.6 | 1.9 | 2.1 | 3.2 | 2.4 | 2.8 | 4.6 |
| Television or Film | 0.4 | 0.6 | 0.2 | 0.3 | 0.3 | 0.3 | 0.2 | 0.2 |
| Other Fine Arts | 1.5 | 1.6 | 2.1 | 1.3 | 1.4 | 1.8 | 0.8 | 1.2 |
| **Physical Science** | | | | | | | | |
| Mathematics and/or Statistics | 2.7 | 1.8 | 2.9 | 3.3 | 3.0 | 3.1 | 3.4 | 2.4 |
| Astronomy | 0.1 | 0.1 | 0.1 | 0.1 | 0.1 | 0.2 | 0.1 | 0.0 |
| Atmospheric Sciences | 0.1 | 0.1 | 0.0 | 0.1 | 0.0 | 0.0 | 0.0 | 0.1 |
| Chemistry | 2.2 | 2.5 | 2.2 | 1.8 | 2.5 | 2.0 | 4.2 | 1.9 |
| Earth Sciences | 0.5 | 0.6 | 0.2 | 0.6 | 0.3 | 0.5 | 0.2 | 0.2 |
| Geography | 0.4 | 0.5 | 0.0 | 0.5 | 0.2 | 0.2 | 0.1 | 0.2 |
| Marine Sciences (incl. Oceanography) | 0.1 | 0.2 | 0.0 | 0.1 | 0.0 | 0.1 | 0.0 | 0.0 |
| Physics | 0.6 | 0.7 | 1.2 | 0.4 | 0.6 | 0.8 | 0.3 | 0.5 |
| General, Other Physical Sciences | 0.1 | 0.0 | 0.0 | 0.0 | 0.1 | 0.1 | 0.3 | 0.0 |
| **Social Science** | | | | | | | | |
| Anthropology | 1.3 | 2.0 | 1.6 | 1.1 | 0.5 | 1.0 | 0.1 | 0.2 |
| Archaeology | 0.2 | 0.2 | 0.1 | 0.1 | 0.1 | 0.1 | 0.0 | 0.1 |
| Clinical Psychology | 1.1 | 0.9 | 1.4 | 1.1 | 1.3 | 0.8 | 2.0 | 1.5 |
| Counseling and Guidance | 0.3 | 0.0 | 0.2 | 0.4 | 0.5 | 0.0 | 1.2 | 0.6 |
| Experimental Psychology | 1.1 | 0.8 | 1.5 | 1.3 | 1.2 | 1.0 | 1.4 | 1.2 |
| Social Psychology | 1.0 | 0.5 | 0.7 | 1.7 | 1.0 | 1.0 | 1.1 | 0.8 |
| General, Other Psychology | 2.0 | 1.2 | 1.5 | 2.1 | 2.9 | 4.3 | 1.6 | 1.6 |
| Economics | 1.2 | 1.3 | 1.3 | 1.3 | 1.0 | 1.4 | 0.7 | 0.6 |
| Sociology | 2.8 | 3.4 | 2.7 | 3.0 | 1.8 | 1.7 | 1.8 | 2.1 |
| Social Work, Social Welfare | 1.0 | 0.7 | 0.6 | 1.5 | 1.0 | 0.9 | 0.5 | 1.4 |
| General, Other Social Sciences | 1.5 | 1.1 | 1.8 | 1.9 | 1.3 | 1.8 | 0.7 | 1.0 |

109

| | | | | Four-year Colleges | | | | |
| | **All** | **Universities** | | | **All** | | | **Oth** |
| **Female Respondents** | **4+ yr** | **Pub** | **Priv** | **Pub** | **Priv** | **Nons** | **Cath** | **Relig** |
|---|---|---|---|---|---|---|---|---|
| **WHAT IS THE MAJOR OF THE HIGHEST DEGREE YOU HOLD?** | | | | | | | | |
| **Technical** | | | | | | | | |
| Computer Science | 0.9 | 0.7 | 1.2 | 0.8 | 1.2 | 1.0 | 1.6 | 1.2 |
| Data Processing, Computer Prog. | 0.0 | 0.0 | 0.0 | 0.0 | 0.1 | 0.0 | 0.0 | 0.2 |
| Drafting/Design | 0.1 | 0.1 | 0.1 | 0.0 | 0.0 | 0.0 | 0.1 | 0.1 |
| Electronics | 0.0 | 0.0 | 0.0 | 0.0 | 0.0 | 0.0 | 0.0 | 0.0 |
| Industrial Arts | 0.0 | 0.0 | 0.0 | 0.0 | 0.0 | 0.0 | 0.0 | 0.0 |
| Mechanics | 0.0 | 0.0 | 0.0 | 0.0 | 0.0 | 0.0 | 0.0 | 0.0 |
| Other Technical | 0.3 | 0.2 | 0.6 | 0.4 | 0.1 | 0.0 | 0.5 | 0.1 |
| **Other Fields** | | | | | | | | |
| Building Trades | 0.0 | 0.0 | 0.0 | 0.0 | 0.0 | 0.0 | 0.0 | 0.0 |
| Communications | 2.2 | 2.1 | 2.0 | 2.6 | 2.0 | 1.7 | 1.9 | 2.5 |
| Ethnic Studies | 0.0 | 0.0 | 0.1 | 0.0 | 0.0 | 0.0 | 0.0 | 0.0 |
| Human Ecology/Family Science | 0.8 | 1.7 | 0.1 | 0.6 | 0.3 | 0.2 | 0.3 | 0.3 |
| Journalism | 0.6 | 0.9 | 1.0 | 0.4 | 0.3 | 0.3 | 0.0 | 0.3 |
| Law | 0.7 | 0.4 | 1.8 | 0.6 | 0.6 | 0.5 | 0.7 | 0.7 |
| Law Enforcement | 0.1 | 0.0 | 0.0 | 0.2 | 0.0 | 0.1 | 0.0 | 0.0 |
| Library Science | 0.8 | 0.4 | 0.7 | 1.0 | 1.0 | 0.4 | 0.4 | 2.3 |
| Women's Studies | 0.0 | 0.0 | 0.1 | 0.0 | 0.1 | 0.0 | 0.0 | 0.3 |
| Other Vocational | 0.0 | 0.0 | 0.0 | 0.0 | 0.0 | 0.0 | 0.0 | 0.0 |
| All Other Fields | 1.0 | 1.0 | 0.9 | 1.2 | 0.8 | 0.8 | 1.1 | 0.5 |

| Female Respondents | All 4+ yr | Universities Pub | Priv | Four-year Colleges Pub | All Priv | Nons | Cath | Oth Relig |
|---|---|---|---|---|---|---|---|---|
| **WHAT IS THE DEPARTMENT OF YOUR CURRENT FACULTY APPOINTMENT?** | | | | | | | | |
| **Biological Science** | | | | | | | | |
| Agriculture | 0.5 | 1.3 | 0.0 | 0.2 | 0.1 | 0.1 | 0.0 | 0.0 |
| Forestry | 0.0 | 0.1 | 0.0 | 0.0 | 0.0 | 0.0 | 0.0 | 0.0 |
| Bacteriology, Molecular Biology | 0.3 | 0.6 | 0.3 | 0.1 | 0.1 | 0.1 | 0.1 | 0.1 |
| Biochemistry | 0.1 | 0.2 | 0.1 | 0.0 | 0.1 | 0.1 | 0.0 | 0.1 |
| Biophysics | 0.0 | 0.1 | 0.0 | 0.0 | 0.0 | 0.0 | 0.0 | 0.0 |
| Botany | 0.1 | 0.1 | 0.0 | 0.0 | 0.0 | 0.0 | 0.0 | 0.0 |
| Environmental Science | 0.4 | 0.5 | 0.1 | 0.3 | 0.4 | 0.7 | 0.1 | 0.2 |
| Marine (life) Sciences | 0.0 | 0.0 | 0.0 | 0.1 | 0.0 | 0.0 | 0.0 | 0.0 |
| Physiology, Anatomy | 0.2 | 0.2 | 0.0 | 0.2 | 0.3 | 0.4 | 0.0 | 0.5 |
| Zoology | 0.1 | 0.4 | 0.0 | 0.0 | 0.0 | 0.0 | 0.1 | 0.0 |
| General, Other Biological Sciences | 4.2 | 3.3 | 4.8 | 4.0 | 5.0 | 5.6 | 4.4 | 4.5 |
| **Business** | | | | | | | | |
| Accounting | 1.2 | 1.0 | 0.7 | 1.5 | 1.3 | 0.8 | 1.8 | 1.8 |
| Finance | 0.5 | 0.5 | 1.1 | 0.5 | 0.2 | 0.1 | 0.6 | 0.1 |
| International Business | 0.1 | 0.1 | 0.3 | 0.0 | 0.1 | 0.1 | 0.1 | 0.1 |
| Management | 2.0 | 2.5 | 1.3 | 2.4 | 1.5 | 1.2 | 2.0 | 1.6 |
| Marketing | 0.9 | 1.4 | 0.4 | 1.0 | 0.5 | 0.4 | 0.9 | 0.5 |
| Secretarial Studies | 0.0 | 0.0 | 0.0 | 0.0 | 0.0 | 0.0 | 0.0 | 0.0 |
| General, Other Business | 1.3 | 0.7 | 0.9 | 1.5 | 1.9 | 1.3 | 2.3 | 2.4 |
| **Education** | | | | | | | | |
| Business Education | 0.0 | 0.1 | 0.0 | 0.0 | 0.0 | 0.0 | 0.0 | 0.0 |
| Educational Administration | 0.2 | 0.1 | 0.2 | 0.3 | 0.3 | 0.0 | 0.6 | 0.4 |
| Educational Psychology/Counseling | 0.5 | 0.9 | 0.1 | 0.4 | 0.1 | 0.0 | 0.2 | 0.2 |
| Elementary Education | 3.0 | 2.3 | 1.3 | 3.9 | 3.4 | 2.4 | 4.6 | 3.9 |
| Higher Education | 0.4 | 0.3 | 0.2 | 0.5 | 0.7 | 0.5 | 0.8 | 0.9 |
| Music or Art Education | 0.1 | 0.1 | 0.1 | 0.1 | 0.1 | 0.1 | 0.0 | 0.2 |
| Physical or Health Education | 1.6 | 1.1 | 0.5 | 2.0 | 2.2 | 2.3 | 0.6 | 3.2 |
| Secondary Education | 0.8 | 0.5 | 0.5 | 1.0 | 0.8 | 0.9 | 0.7 | 0.8 |
| Special Education | 1.0 | 0.4 | 0.8 | 1.7 | 0.8 | 0.4 | 0.9 | 1.2 |
| General, Other Education Fields | 3.1 | 2.4 | 1.7 | 4.0 | 3.2 | 2.7 | 3.7 | 3.8 |
| **Engineering** | | | | | | | | |
| Aero-/Astronautical Engineering | 0.0 | 0.0 | 0.0 | 0.0 | 0.0 | 0.0 | 0.0 | 0.0 |
| Chemical Engineering | 0.0 | 0.0 | 0.2 | 0.0 | 0.0 | 0.0 | 0.0 | 0th |
| Civil Engineering | 0.2 | 0.4 | 0.5 | 0.1 | 0.0 | 0.1 | 0.0 | 0.0 |
| Electrical Engineering | 0.2 | 0.3 | 0.2 | 0.2 | 0.0 | 0.0 | 0.1 | 0.1 |
| Industrial Engineering | 0.0 | 0.1 | 0.0 | 0.0 | 0.0 | 0.0 | 0.0 | 0.0 |
| Mechanical Engineering | 0.2 | 0.2 | 0.5 | 0.1 | 0.1 | 0.0 | 0.2 | 0.0 |
| General, Other Engineering Fields | 0.5 | 0.4 | 1.0 | 0.6 | 0.1 | 0.1 | 0.0 | 0.1 |
| **Health** | | | | | | | | |
| Dentistry | 0.2 | 0.2 | 0.0 | 0.1 | 0.4 | 0.4 | 0.9 | 0.0 |
| Health Technology | 0.2 | 0.2 | 0.1 | 0.2 | 0.1 | 0.0 | 0.3 | 0.1 |
| Medicine or Surgery | 0.2 | 0.4 | 0.5 | 0.0 | 0.1 | 0.1 | 0.0 | 0.0 |
| Nursing | 8.7 | 8.0 | 8.2 | 8.8 | 9.7 | 7.2 | 15.5 | 9.3 |
| Pharmacy, Pharmacology | 0.8 | 1.0 | 1.2 | 0.2 | 1.1 | 2.0 | 0.0 | 0.6 |
| Therapy (speech, physical, occup.) | 1.5 | 2.3 | 1.2 | 1.4 | 0.9 | 0.3 | 1.5 | 1.3 |
| Veterinary Medicine | 0.0 | 0.1 | 0.0 | 0.0 | 0.0 | 0.0 | 0.0 | 0.0 |
| General, Other Health Fields | 1.7 | 2.3 | 1.0 | 2.2 | 0.7 | 0.4 | 1.0 | 0.8 |

## 2007–2008 FACULTY SURVEY WEIGHTED NATIONAL NORMS
### Full-time Undergraduate Faculty

| Female Respondents | All 4+ yr | Universities Pub | Universities Priv | Four-year Colleges Pub | Four-year Colleges All Priv | Four-year Colleges Nons | Four-year Colleges Cath | Four-year Colleges Oth Relig |
|---|---|---|---|---|---|---|---|---|
| **WHAT IS THE DEPARTMENT OF YOUR CURRENT FACULTY APPOINTMENT?** | | | | | | | | |
| **Humanities** | | | | | | | | |
| History | 2.8 | 2.6 | 4.0 | 2.6 | 2.5 | 2.4 | 2.2 | 2.7 |
| Political Science, Government | 1.5 | 1.2 | 2.5 | 1.2 | 1.7 | 2.0 | 1.4 | 1.4 |
| English Language & Literature | 9.5 | 9.4 | 9.8 | 8.9 | 10.3 | 12.0 | 6.8 | 10.2 |
| Foreign Languages & Literature | 3.8 | 4.9 | 6.1 | 2.4 | 3.5 | 3.4 | 2.8 | 4.2 |
| French | 0.3 | 0.5 | 0.2 | 0.1 | 0.5 | 0.7 | 0.1 | 0.5 |
| German | 0.3 | 0.5 | 0.3 | 0.1 | 0.2 | 0.4 | 0.0 | 0.1 |
| Spanish | 1.1 | 1.1 | 1.5 | 0.5 | 1.6 | 2.0 | 0.7 | 1.6 |
| Other Foreign Languages | 0.7 | 1.3 | 0.7 | 0.3 | 0.4 | 0.5 | 0.0 | 0.4 |
| Linguistics | 0.2 | 0.5 | 0.1 | 0.1 | 0.1 | 0.1 | 0.0 | 0.0 |
| Philosophy | 1.0 | 0.6 | 2.0 | 0.9 | 1.0 | 0.7 | 2.2 | 0.7 |
| Religion or Theology | 1.4 | 0.9 | 3.1 | 0.3 | 2.6 | 1.3 | 3.9 | 3.5 |
| General, Other Humanities Fields | 2.0 | 2.1 | 2.3 | 1.7 | 2.2 | 3.5 | 1.0 | 1.1 |
| **Fine Arts** | | | | | | | | |
| Architecture/Urban Planning | 0.5 | 1.2 | 0.4 | 0.1 | 0.2 | 0.4 | 0.1 | 0.0 |
| Art | 2.7 | 2.0 | 2.2 | 3.1 | 3.1 | 4.1 | 1.8 | 2.7 |
| Dramatics or Speech | 1.6 | 0.9 | 1.5 | 2.0 | 1.8 | 2.3 | 1.5 | 1.4 |
| Music | 2.5 | 2.6 | 1.9 | 2.1 | 3.2 | 2.5 | 2.7 | 4.6 |
| Television or Film | 0.4 | 0.4 | 0.6 | 0.5 | 0.2 | 0.3 | 0.0 | 0.1 |
| Other Fine Arts | 1.1 | 1.4 | 1.5 | 1.0 | 0.7 | 0.8 | 0.9 | 0.4 |
| **Physical Science** | | | | | | | | |
| Mathematics and/or Statistics | 3.4 | 3.0 | 3.3 | 4.0 | 3.1 | 3.1 | 3.2 | 3.2 |
| Astronomy | 0.0 | 0.0 | 0.0 | 0.0 | 0.0 | 0.0 | 0.0 | 0.0 |
| Atmospheric Sciences | 0.0 | 0.1 | 0.0 | 0.0 | 0.0 | 0.0 | 0.0 | 0.0 |
| Chemistry | 2.5 | 3.0 | 2.1 | 1.8 | 2.9 | 2.6 | 4.6 | 2.2 |
| Earth Sciences | 0.5 | 0.6 | 0.2 | 0.5 | 0.3 | 0.5 | 0.1 | 0.2 |
| Geography | 0.4 | 0.6 | 0.0 | 0.5 | 0.0 | 0.1 | 0.0 | 0.0 |
| Marine Sciences (incl. Oceanography) | 0.1 | 0.2 | 0.0 | 0.0 | 0.0 | 0.0 | 0.0 | 0.0 |
| Physics | 0.7 | 0.6 | 1.1 | 0.7 | 0.7 | 1.0 | 0.2 | 0.6 |
| General, Other Physical Sciences | 0.2 | 0.0 | 0.0 | 0.4 | 0.4 | 0.3 | 0.7 | 0.2 |
| **Social Science** | | | | | | | | |
| Anthropology | 1.1 | 2.1 | 1.2 | 0.7 | 0.4 | 0.8 | 0.0 | 0.2 |
| Archaeology | 0.0 | 0.1 | 0.0 | 0.0 | 0.0 | 0.0 | 0.0 | 0.0 |
| Clinical Psychology | 0.5 | 0.7 | 0.8 | 0.3 | 0.3 | 0.1 | 0.4 | 0.5 |
| Counseling and Guidance | 0.2 | 0.0 | 0.2 | 0.2 | 0.2 | 0.3 | 0.2 | 0.1 |
| Experimental Psychology | 0.9 | 0.4 | 1.2 | 1.6 | 0.6 | 0.7 | 0.4 | 0.5 |
| Social Psychology | 0.2 | 0.1 | 0.3 | 0.2 | 0.2 | 0.1 | 0.5 | 0.1 |
| General, Other Psychology | 3.1 | 1.4 | 2.2 | 3.6 | 4.8 | 5.5 | 4.7 | 3.8 |
| Economics | 1.0 | 1.0 | 1.2 | 0.9 | 0.9 | 1.6 | 0.3 | 0.3 |
| Sociology | 2.7 | 3.2 | 3.0 | 2.7 | 2.2 | 2.2 | 2.1 | 2.3 |
| Social Work, Social Welfare | 1.1 | 0.8 | 0.5 | 1.7 | 0.8 | 0.5 | 0.5 | 1.4 |
| General, Other Social Sciences | 2.0 | 1.3 | 1.6 | 2.6 | 2.4 | 3.5 | 1.5 | 1.3 |

112

| | | Universities | | Four-year Colleges | | | | |
|---|---|---|---|---|---|---|---|---|
| **Female Respondents** | **All 4+ yr** | **Pub** | **Priv** | **Pub** | **All Priv** | **Nons** | **Cath** | **Oth Relig** |
| **WHAT IS THE DEPARTMENT OF YOUR CURRENT FACULTY APPOINTMENT?** | | | | | | | | |
| **Technical** | | | | | | | | |
| Computer Science | 1.0 | 0.8 | 0.8 | 0.8 | 1.4 | 1.3 | 2.3 | 1.0 |
| Data Processing, Computer Prog. | 0.0 | 0.0 | 0.0 | 0.1 | 0.1 | 0.0 | 0.1 | 0.1 |
| Drafting/Design | 0.1 | 0.0 | 0.3 | 0.1 | 0.0 | 0.0 | 0.0 | 0.0 |
| Electronics | 0.0 | 0.0 | 0.0 | 0.1 | 0.0 | 0.0 | 0.0 | 0.0 |
| Industrial Arts | 0.0 | 0.0 | 0.0 | 0.1 | 0.0 | 0.0 | 0.0 | 0.0 |
| Mechanics | 0.0 | 0.0 | 0.0 | 0.0 | 0.0 | 0.0 | 0.0 | 0.0 |
| Other Technical | 0.3 | 0.3 | 0.1 | 0.5 | 0.1 | 0.0 | 0.4 | 0.0 |
| **Other Fields** | | | | | | | | |
| Building Trades | 0.0 | 0.0 | 0.2 | 0.0 | 0.0 | 0.0 | 0.0 | 0.0 |
| Communications | 2.6 | 2.2 | 3.3 | 2.7 | 2.6 | 1.8 | 3.4 | 3.2 |
| Ethnic Studies | 0.2 | 0.2 | 0.0 | 0.5 | 0.1 | 0.2 | 0.0 | 0.0 |
| Human Ecology/Family Science | 0.9 | 1.9 | 0.1 | 0.6 | 0.4 | 0.2 | 0.4 | 0.7 |
| Journalism | 0.7 | 1.0 | 0.9 | 0.7 | 0.1 | 0.2 | 0.0 | 0.1 |
| Law | 0.3 | 0.1 | 1.4 | 0.1 | 0.2 | 0.1 | 0.6 | 0.1 |
| Law Enforcement | 0.1 | 0.1 | 0.0 | 0.1 | 0.0 | 0.0 | 0.1 | 0.1 |
| Library Science | 0.8 | 0.4 | 0.9 | 1.0 | 1.0 | 0.4 | 0.6 | 2.1 |
| Women's Studies | 0.3 | 0.5 | 0.3 | 0.3 | 0.2 | 0.4 | 0.1 | 0.0 |
| Other Vocational | 0.2 | 0.5 | 0.1 | 0.1 | 0.1 | 0.1 | 0.0 | 0.0 |
| All Other Fields | 1.6 | 1.3 | 1.9 | 2.2 | 1.2 | 1.7 | 0.6 | 1.0 |
| **HOW MANY CHILDREN DO YOU HAVE IN THE FOLLOWING AGE RANGES?** | | | | | | | | |
| **Under 18 years old** | | | | | | | | |
| None | 66.3 | 67.1 | 62.4 | 68.6 | 64.4 | 65.2 | 64.3 | 63.2 |
| One | 16.9 | 17.7 | 15.9 | 16.0 | 17.3 | 16.2 | 17.6 | 18.9 |
| Two | 13.3 | 12.3 | 16.1 | 12.6 | 14.2 | 15.6 | 12.8 | 13.0 |
| Three | 2.6 | 2.1 | 3.5 | 2.2 | 3.3 | 2.6 | 3.7 | 4.1 |
| Four or more | 0.9 | 0.8 | 2.1 | 0.6 | 0.8 | 0.4 | 1.6 | 0.9 |
| **18 years or older** | | | | | | | | |
| None | 59.6 | 57.9 | 65.1 | 57.8 | 61.3 | 64.6 | 56.1 | 60.1 |
| One | 13.0 | 13.6 | 13.8 | 11.6 | 13.8 | 13.8 | 14.8 | 13.0 |
| Two | 18.4 | 21.2 | 12.8 | 19.3 | 16.6 | 14.7 | 19.2 | 17.5 |
| Three | 5.9 | 5.1 | 4.6 | 7.3 | 5.8 | 4.3 | 7.2 | 6.9 |
| Four or more | 3.1 | 2.2 | 3.7 | 4.0 | 2.6 | 2.6 | 2.7 | 2.5 |
| **How would you characterize your political views?** | | | | | | | | |
| Far left | 9.9 | 10.5 | 11.4 | 9.2 | 9.6 | 12.4 | 7.3 | 7.1 |
| Liberal | 51.9 | 53.5 | 51.2 | 51.6 | 50.6 | 57.2 | 49.4 | 41.8 |
| Middle of the Road | 26.0 | 24.8 | 26.8 | 27.3 | 25.3 | 21.5 | 29.2 | 28.2 |
| Conservative | 11.9 | 10.9 | 10.4 | 11.6 | 14.0 | 8.7 | 13.4 | 22.3 |
| Far right | 0.3 | 0.2 | 0.2 | 0.2 | 0.5 | 0.2 | 0.7 | 0.6 |
| **Are you currently:** | | | | | | | | |
| Single | 14.8 | 12.6 | 17.0 | 15.7 | 15.3 | 14.7 | 17.0 | 14.9 |
| Married | 67.4 | 68.5 | 69.0 | 64.7 | 69.0 | 68.3 | 67.1 | 71.5 |
| Unmarried, living with partner | 5.7 | 5.8 | 4.5 | 6.6 | 5.0 | 5.8 | 4.5 | 3.9 |
| Divorced | 8.8 | 9.2 | 6.6 | 9.4 | 8.4 | 8.9 | 9.1 | 7.1 |
| Widowed | 2.4 | 3.5 | 2.0 | 2.3 | 1.6 | 1.2 | 1.7 | 2.0 |
| Separated | 0.8 | 0.3 | 0.9 | 1.3 | 0.8 | 1.0 | 0.6 | 0.6 |

## 2007–2008 FACULTY SURVEY WEIGHTED NATIONAL NORMS
### Full-time Undergraduate Faculty

| Female Respondents | All 4+ yr | Universities Pub | Priv | Four-year Colleges Pub | All Priv | Nons | Cath | Oth Relig |
|---|---|---|---|---|---|---|---|---|
| **Is English your native language?** | | | | | | | | |
| Yes | 90.4 | 90.0 | 86.9 | 90.7 | 91.8 | 92.1 | 90.8 | 92.1 |
| No | 9.6 | 10.0 | 13.1 | 9.3 | 8.2 | 7.9 | 9.2 | 7.9 |
| **Are you: [4]** | | | | | | | | |
| White/Caucasian | 89.2 | 90.2 | 88.0 | 87.5 | 90.6 | 89.9 | 90.5 | 91.9 |
| African American/Black | 3.4 | 2.8 | 3.8 | 4.2 | 2.8 | 4.0 | 1.9 | 1.6 |
| American Indian/Alaska Native | 1.5 | 1.8 | 1.3 | 1.5 | 1.1 | 1.2 | 0.7 | 1.1 |
| Asian American/Asian | 3.4 | 2.2 | 4.3 | 4.4 | 3.1 | 3.1 | 2.3 | 3.8 |
| Native Hawaiian/Pacific Islander | 0.2 | 0.3 | 0.2 | 0.2 | 0.1 | 0.1 | 0.0 | 0.1 |
| Mexican American/Chicano | 1.0 | 0.7 | 0.9 | 1.7 | 0.5 | 0.7 | 0.3 | 0.4 |
| Puerto Rican | 0.4 | 0.3 | 0.5 | 0.3 | 0.5 | 0.5 | 0.6 | 0.4 |
| Other Latino | 1.9 | 2.0 | 2.3 | 1.5 | 2.3 | 2.0 | 3.4 | 1.8 |
| Other | 2.4 | 2.9 | 2.3 | 2.5 | 1.7 | 1.9 | 2.2 | 1.2 |
| **Do you give the Higher Education Research Institute (HERI) permission to retain your contact information (i.e., your email address and name) for possible follow-up research?** | | | | | | | | |
| Yes | 74.6 | 79.0 | 67.2 | 74.2 | 73.3 | 74.2 | 71.7 | 73.0 |
| No | 25.4 | 21.0 | 32.8 | 25.8 | 26.7 | 25.8 | 28.3 | 27.0 |

[4] Percentages will sum to more than 100.0 if any respondent marked more than one category.

114

# Full-Time Undergraduate Faculty, Rank and Control for

# All Faculty

## 2007–2008 FACULTY SURVEY WEIGHTED NATIONAL NORMS
### Full-time Undergraduate Faculty at Baccalaureate Institutions

| All Respondents | All Resp | Full Prof | Assoc Prof | Asst Prof | Lect | Inst | No Resp |
|---|---|---|---|---|---|---|---|
| **Number of Respondents** | 22,562 | 7,123 | 6,842 | 6,430 | 900 | 1,238 | 29 |
| **Gender** | | | | | | | |
| Male | 60.7 | 75.5 | 60.3 | 52.4 | 48.1 | 41.3 | 57.0 |
| Female | 39.3 | 24.5 | 39.7 | 47.6 | 51.9 | 58.7 | 43.0 |
| **What is your principal activity in your current position at this institution?** | | | | | | | |
| Administration | 7.0 | 12.0 | 6.4 | 2.1 | 7.2 | 5.2 | 37.7 |
| Teaching | 83.4 | 77.8 | 84.7 | 85.9 | 88.2 | 89.2 | 54.0 |
| Research | 8.0 | 9.2 | 7.7 | 10.8 | 1.4 | 0.3 | 0.0 |
| Services to clients and patients | 0.8 | 0.4 | 0.8 | 0.5 | 1.2 | 2.8 | 0.0 |
| Other | 0.9 | 0.6 | 0.5 | 0.7 | 2.0 | 2.5 | 8.3 |
| **What is your present academic rank?** | | | | | | | |
| Professor | 31.7 | 100.0 | 0.0 | 0.0 | 0.0 | 0.0 | 0.0 |
| Associate Professor | 26.1 | 0.0 | 100.0 | 0.0 | 0.0 | 0.0 | 0.0 |
| Assistant Professor | 27.4 | 0.0 | 0.0 | 100.0 | 0.0 | 0.0 | 0.0 |
| Lecturer | 7.2 | 0.0 | 0.0 | 0.0 | 100.0 | 0.0 | 0.0 |
| Instructor | 7.6 | 0.0 | 0.0 | 0.0 | 0.0 | 100.0 | 0.0 |
| **What is your tenure status at this institution?** | | | | | | | |
| Tenured | 54.4 | 94.6 | 85.1 | 7.7 | 0.9 | 1.4 | 8.3 |
| On tenure track, but not tenured | 22.4 | 0.6 | 6.3 | 71.8 | 1.1 | 10.4 | 1.3 |
| Not on tenure track, but institution has tenure system | 19.6 | 1.8 | 5.1 | 16.4 | 96.3 | 82.0 | 90.3 |
| Institution has no tenure system | 3.5 | 3.0 | 3.4 | 4.1 | 1.8 | 6.2 | 0.0 |
| **Are you currently serving in an administrative position as: [1]** | | | | | | | |
| Department Chair | 11.3 | 19.3 | 14.5 | 3.9 | 2.0 | 2.2 | 2.9 |
| Dean (Associate or Assistant) | 1.6 | 3.0 | 1.7 | 0.3 | 0.3 | 0.4 | 1.8 |
| President | 0.0 | 0.1 | 0.0 | 0.0 | 0.0 | 0.0 | 1.7 |
| Vice-President | 0.1 | 0.1 | 0.2 | 0.0 | 0.1 | 0.1 | 0.0 |
| Provost | 0.0 | 0.1 | 0.0 | 0.0 | 0.0 | 0.0 | 0.0 |
| Other | 15.9 | 17.0 | 17.8 | 11.2 | 22.8 | 14.9 | 34.9 |
| Not Applicable | 65.2 | 55.6 | 60.7 | 75.5 | 70.7 | 78.7 | 30.9 |
| **My primary place of employment in the last year was: [2]** | | | | | | | |
| In higher education: | | | | | | | |
| at this institution | 94.6 | 98.5 | 98.0 | 88.7 | 91.3 | 91.3 | 90.1 |
| at a different institution | 2.6 | 0.7 | 1.0 | 6.5 | 2.9 | 2.2 | 0.0 |
| at more than one institution | 1.4 | 0.6 | 0.5 | 2.6 | 2.7 | 2.4 | 0.0 |
| Not in higher education | 1.0 | 0.1 | 0.4 | 1.4 | 2.6 | 3.6 | 9.9 |
| Not employed | 0.3 | 0.1 | 0.0 | 0.7 | 0.6 | 0.5 | 0.0 |
| **Noted as being personally "very important" or "essential": [2]** | | | | | | | |
| Research | 71.4 | 78.0 | 74.2 | 76.5 | 42.0 | 43.8 | 62.2 |
| Teaching | 97.7 | 97.7 | 97.5 | 97.2 | 99.0 | 98.4 | 95.7 |
| Service | 66.1 | 66.3 | 67.0 | 61.6 | 70.7 | 73.5 | 80.4 |

[1] Response options changed from earlier Faculty Surveys.
[2] This question asked for the first time in the 2007–2008 Faculty Survey.

117

**2007–2008 FACULTY SURVEY WEIGHTED NATIONAL NORMS**
**Full-time Undergraduate Faculty at Baccalaureate Institutions**

| All Respondents | All Resp | Full Prof | Assoc Prof | Asst Prof | Lect | Inst | No Resp |
|---|---|---|---|---|---|---|---|
| **Highest degree earned** | | | | | | | |
| Bachelor's (B.A., B.S., etc.) | 1.0 | 0.5 | 0.3 | 0.4 | 4.3 | 4.8 | 1.3 |
| Master's (M.A., M.S., M.F.A., M.B.A., etc.) | 19.7 | 6.4 | 11.1 | 18.5 | 52.5 | 77.5 | 32.8 |
| LL.B., J.D. | 1.0 | 0.7 | 0.8 | 0.9 | 2.4 | 1.9 | 0.0 |
| M.D., D.D.S. (or equivalent) | 0.6 | 0.5 | 1.1 | 0.5 | 0.1 | 0.8 | 0.0 |
| Other first professional degree beyond B.A. (e.g., D.D., D.V.M.) | 0.7 | 0.4 | 0.8 | 1.1 | 0.2 | 0.3 | 0.0 |
| Ed.D. | 3.2 | 3.4 | 4.4 | 3.3 | 1.1 | 0.2 | 10.7 |
| Ph.D. | 71.5 | 85.6 | 79.2 | 73.4 | 38.1 | 11.7 | 50.8 |
| Other degree | 1.9 | 2.1 | 2.0 | 1.8 | 1.1 | 1.3 | 4.5 |
| None | 0.4 | 0.4 | 0.4 | 0.1 | 0.3 | 1.6 | 0.0 |
| **Degree currently working on** | | | | | | | |
| Bachelor's (B.A., B.S., etc.) | 0.1 | 0.0 | 0.1 | 0.1 | 0.0 | 0.0 | 0.0 |
| Master's (M.A., M.S., M.F.A., M.B.A., etc.) | 0.9 | 0.4 | 0.4 | 0.8 | 1.6 | 3.8 | 7.5 |
| LL.B., J.D. | 0.1 | 0.0 | 0.1 | 0.2 | 0.3 | 0.0 | 0.0 |
| M.D., D.D.S. (or equivalent) | 0.0 | 0.0 | 0.0 | 0.1 | 0.0 | 0.1 | 0.0 |
| Other first professional degree beyond B.A. (e.g., D.D., D.V.M.) | 0.0 | 0.0 | 0.0 | 0.0 | 0.0 | 0.0 | 0.0 |
| Ed.D. | 1.0 | 0.1 | 0.3 | 1.1 | 2.3 | 5.4 | 0.0 |
| Ph.D. | 4.6 | 0.6 | 1.6 | 6.1 | 8.5 | 23.0 | 25.0 |
| Other degree | 0.6 | 0.2 | 0.4 | 0.7 | 0.2 | 2.5 | 0.0 |
| None | 92.7 | 98.6 | 97.0 | 90.9 | 87.1 | 65.2 | 67.5 |
| **During the past two years, have you engaged in any of the following activities?** | | | | | | | |
| Taught an honors course | 19.9 | 24.2 | 21.8 | 16.6 | 17.8 | 9.5 | 19.0 |
| Taught an interdisciplinary course | 41.0 | 43.2 | 44.3 | 41.0 | 33.5 | 27.5 | 35.9 |
| Taught an ethnic studies course | 10.4 | 9.1 | 11.1 | 12.6 | 10.3 | 5.6 | 3.3 |
| Taught a women's studies course | 7.3 | 6.9 | 9.2 | 7.5 | 5.6 | 3.3 | 1.2 |
| Team-taught a course | 32.7 | 34.0 | 35.2 | 31.2 | 28.1 | 28.3 | 26.6 |
| Taught a service learning course | 19.7 | 17.3 | 21.4 | 19.3 | 24.6 | 20.8 | 11.8 |
| Placed or collected assignments on the Internet | 74.4 | 70.1 | 74.9 | 78.2 | 75.3 | 75.5 | 75.6 |
| Taught a course exclusively on the Internet | 13.3 | 10.8 | 14.6 | 13.8 | 14.8 | 16.3 | 3.9 |
| Participated in a teaching enhancement workshop | 56.5 | 46.0 | 57.7 | 65.8 | 59.8 | 59.5 | 69.6 |
| Advised student groups involved in service/volunteer work | 42.4 | 36.6 | 45.4 | 45.5 | 42.0 | 44.6 | 51.8 |
| Collaborated with the local community in research/teaching | 46.2 | 42.9 | 50.2 | 48.6 | 41.3 | 42.5 | 35.1 |
| Developed a new course | 66.5 | 62.3 | 70.6 | 73.2 | 60.9 | 50.9 | 72.8 |
| Conducted research/writing focused on: | | | | | | | |
| International/global issues | 28.4 | 33.0 | 30.4 | 27.9 | 16.8 | 15.9 | 11.3 |
| Racial or ethnic minorities | 20.6 | 18.6 | 22.6 | 24.7 | 16.2 | 11.9 | 20.1 |
| Women and gender issues | 19.1 | 16.8 | 20.8 | 23.5 | 12.6 | 13.1 | 9.4 |
| Taught a seminar for first-year students | 23.6 | 23.3 | 23.5 | 23.7 | 21.6 | 26.2 | 45.5 |
| Engaged undergraduates on <u>your</u> research project [2] | 41.6 | 45.8 | 46.3 | 45.0 | 19.5 | 17.3 | 35.2 |
| Worked with undergraduates on a research project | 57.3 | 62.3 | 62.3 | 57.1 | 40.8 | 35.1 | 49.7 |

[2] This question asked for the first time in the 2007–2008 Faculty Survey.

118

| All Respondents | All Resp | Full Prof | Assoc Prof | Asst Prof | Lect | Inst | No Resp |
|---|---|---|---|---|---|---|---|
| **DURING THE PRESENT TERM, HOW MANY HOURS PER WEEK ON AVERAGE DO YOU ACTUALLY SPEND ON:** | | | | | | | |
| **Scheduled teaching (actual, not credit hours)** | | | | | | | |
| None | 0.6 | 0.6 | 0.5 | 0.6 | 0.3 | 1.9 | 1.1 |
| 1 to 4 | 13.4 | 17.4 | 11.9 | 10.9 | 12.1 | 12.4 | 23.4 |
| 5 to 8 | 31.2 | 35.4 | 32.3 | 31.2 | 22.0 | 19.2 | 43.5 |
| 9 to 12 | 35.1 | 31.4 | 36.1 | 37.0 | 41.4 | 34.7 | 27.3 |
| 13 to 16 | 12.1 | 9.2 | 11.8 | 12.5 | 16.5 | 19.5 | 3.9 |
| 17 to 20 | 4.7 | 3.8 | 4.9 | 5.0 | 4.2 | 7.4 | 0.8 |
| 21 to 34 | 2.3 | 1.8 | 2.1 | 2.3 | 2.5 | 4.5 | 0.0 |
| 35 to 44 | 0.3 | 0.2 | 0.2 | 0.5 | 0.8 | 0.2 | 0.0 |
| 45 + | 0.2 | 0.2 | 0.2 | 0.2 | 0.2 | 0.1 | 0.0 |
| **Preparing for teaching (including reading student papers and grading)** | | | | | | | |
| None | 0.3 | 0.5 | 0.2 | 0.3 | 0.0 | 0.4 | 1.1 |
| 1 to 4 | 10.3 | 13.9 | 9.5 | 7.7 | 10.0 | 7.7 | 16.5 |
| 5 to 8 | 23.9 | 27.4 | 23.9 | 20.9 | 22.0 | 21.6 | 24.7 |
| 9 to 12 | 24.5 | 25.1 | 25.8 | 24.7 | 19.0 | 23.0 | 15.0 |
| 13 to 16 | 15.8 | 14.2 | 16.6 | 17.2 | 16.1 | 13.8 | 22.9 |
| 17 to 20 | 13.8 | 10.8 | 14.0 | 15.1 | 18.2 | 16.0 | 18.8 |
| 21 to 34 | 8.7 | 6.4 | 8.0 | 10.1 | 11.7 | 13.2 | 0.9 |
| 35 to 44 | 2.1 | 1.3 | 1.7 | 2.8 | 2.5 | 3.1 | 0.0 |
| 45 + | 0.7 | 0.5 | 0.3 | 1.2 | 0.6 | 1.2 | 0.0 |
| **Advising and counseling of students** | | | | | | | |
| None | 3.9 | 2.8 | 2.3 | 4.1 | 9.7 | 7.7 | 0.0 |
| 1 to 4 | 55.8 | 56.7 | 55.9 | 56.8 | 50.6 | 53.3 | 35.0 |
| 5 to 8 | 28.4 | 29.4 | 29.7 | 27.9 | 24.5 | 24.6 | 44.2 |
| 9 to 12 | 8.0 | 7.9 | 8.4 | 7.3 | 8.8 | 8.7 | 2.5 |
| 13 to 16 | 2.3 | 2.0 | 2.2 | 2.2 | 3.2 | 3.1 | 8.8 |
| 17 to 20 | 1.1 | 0.9 | 1.0 | 1.1 | 2.5 | 0.8 | 0.0 |
| 21 to 34 | 0.4 | 0.3 | 0.5 | 0.3 | 0.4 | 0.7 | 7.7 |
| 35 to 44 | 0.2 | 0.1 | 0.0 | 0.3 | 0.3 | 0.3 | 1.7 |
| 45 + | 0.1 | 0.0 | 0.1 | 0.0 | 0.1 | 0.7 | 0.0 |
| **Committee work and meetings** | | | | | | | |
| None | 5.0 | 2.4 | 2.0 | 4.3 | 19.5 | 15.8 | 4.1 |
| 1 to 4 | 57.2 | 52.6 | 53.0 | 63.7 | 61.4 | 62.6 | 74.5 |
| 5 to 8 | 26.5 | 30.2 | 31.4 | 23.6 | 14.5 | 16.1 | 10.0 |
| 9 to 12 | 7.5 | 9.6 | 9.4 | 5.6 | 3.2 | 3.6 | 2.5 |
| 13 to 16 | 2.3 | 3.1 | 2.7 | 1.9 | 0.7 | 0.8 | 3.3 |
| 17 to 20 | 1.0 | 1.6 | 1.0 | 0.6 | 0.5 | 0.5 | 3.8 |
| 21 to 34 | 0.3 | 0.5 | 0.4 | 0.3 | 0.2 | 0.2 | 0.0 |
| 35 to 44 | 0.1 | 0.1 | 0.0 | 0.1 | 0.0 | 0.3 | 1.7 |
| 45 + | 0.0 | 0.0 | 0.1 | 0.0 | 0.0 | 0.0 | 0.0 |
| **Other administration** | | | | | | | |
| None | 30.0 | 26.5 | 24.7 | 33.9 | 38.3 | 40.6 | 28.3 |
| 1 to 4 | 39.0 | 34.9 | 41.4 | 44.4 | 31.6 | 35.2 | 24.6 |
| 5 to 8 | 14.6 | 16.3 | 15.9 | 12.4 | 14.6 | 10.6 | 3.3 |
| 9 to 12 | 7.2 | 8.9 | 8.7 | 4.5 | 6.3 | 5.9 | 12.7 |
| 13 to 16 | 3.3 | 4.5 | 3.7 | 2.0 | 3.2 | 1.8 | 8.0 |
| 17 to 20 | 3.1 | 4.6 | 2.9 | 1.4 | 3.6 | 2.5 | 5.7 |
| 21 to 34 | 2.1 | 3.1 | 2.2 | 0.8 | 1.7 | 2.1 | 13.4 |
| 35 to 44 | 0.6 | 0.8 | 0.4 | 0.5 | 0.6 | 0.6 | 2.2 |
| 45 + | 0.2 | 0.3 | 0.1 | 0.1 | 0.1 | 0.7 | 1.8 |

| All Respondents | All Resp | Full Prof | Assoc Prof | Asst Prof | Lect | Inst | No Resp |
|---|---|---|---|---|---|---|---|
| **DURING THE PRESENT TERM, HOW MANY HOURS PER WEEK ON AVERAGE DO YOU ACTUALLY SPEND ON:** | | | | | | | |
| **Research and scholarly writing** | | | | | | | |
| None | 15.5 | 9.7 | 11.6 | 11.1 | 41.2 | 44.6 | 26.5 |
| 1 to 4 | 32.3 | 30.2 | 35.6 | 31.7 | 33.1 | 30.6 | 40.9 |
| 5 to 8 | 20.2 | 21.4 | 22.5 | 21.4 | 11.5 | 11.1 | 28.4 |
| 9 to 12 | 12.5 | 14.1 | 13.4 | 12.6 | 8.6 | 6.9 | 4.1 |
| 13 to 16 | 6.6 | 7.4 | 6.2 | 8.2 | 2.7 | 2.9 | 0.0 |
| 17 to 20 | 6.2 | 8.2 | 5.6 | 6.9 | 2.0 | 1.3 | 0.0 |
| 21 to 34 | 4.2 | 5.7 | 3.7 | 4.8 | 0.7 | 1.5 | 0.0 |
| 35 to 44 | 1.6 | 2.1 | 1.1 | 2.1 | 0.0 | 0.6 | 0.0 |
| 45 + | 0.8 | 1.2 | 0.3 | 1.2 | 0.2 | 0.6 | 0.0 |
| **Other creative products/performances** | | | | | | | |
| None | 50.8 | 53.6 | 53.7 | 49.4 | 45.8 | 39.2 | 25.2 |
| 1 to 4 | 29.5 | 26.1 | 28.9 | 32.1 | 28.1 | 36.7 | 37.8 |
| 5 to 8 | 11.0 | 11.3 | 10.1 | 10.2 | 14.2 | 12.4 | 17.4 |
| 9 to 12 | 4.4 | 4.4 | 3.8 | 4.4 | 5.5 | 5.8 | 0.0 |
| 13 to 16 | 1.8 | 2.0 | 1.4 | 1.7 | 2.4 | 1.8 | 0.0 |
| 17 to 20 | 1.4 | 1.5 | 1.2 | 1.2 | 1.4 | 3.2 | 4.1 |
| 21 to 34 | 0.7 | 0.6 | 0.7 | 0.7 | 0.8 | 0.8 | 13.9 |
| 35 to 44 | 0.2 | 0.2 | 0.1 | 0.1 | 1.7 | 0.1 | 0.0 |
| 45 + | 0.2 | 0.3 | 0.2 | 0.2 | 0.1 | 0.0 | 1.7 |
| **Consultation with clients/patients** | | | | | | | |
| None | 80.8 | 82.5 | 82.3 | 81.5 | 74.5 | 71.8 | 79.8 |
| 1 to 4 | 12.2 | 11.8 | 11.1 | 12.0 | 15.3 | 16.0 | 12.5 |
| 5 to 8 | 3.9 | 3.6 | 4.2 | 3.4 | 4.5 | 5.2 | 7.3 |
| 9 to 12 | 1.3 | 1.0 | 1.1 | 1.6 | 0.5 | 3.1 | 0.4 |
| 13 to 16 | 0.7 | 0.6 | 0.4 | 0.8 | 1.2 | 0.6 | 0.0 |
| 17 to 20 | 0.6 | 0.2 | 0.5 | 0.3 | 2.7 | 1.3 | 0.0 |
| 21 to 34 | 0.4 | 0.2 | 0.2 | 0.2 | 1.3 | 1.3 | 0.0 |
| 35 to 44 | 0.1 | 0.0 | 0.1 | 0.1 | 0.0 | 0.0 | 0.0 |
| 45 + | 0.1 | 0.1 | 0.0 | 0.1 | 0.1 | 0.7 | 0.0 |
| **Community or public service** | | | | | | | |
| None | 37.3 | 36.9 | 34.6 | 41.7 | 37.4 | 30.9 | 59.8 |
| 1 to 4 | 49.1 | 48.5 | 51.0 | 46.4 | 48.8 | 55.7 | 27.1 |
| 5 to 8 | 10.1 | 10.5 | 10.7 | 9.1 | 9.3 | 11.0 | 11.3 |
| 9 to 12 | 2.5 | 2.8 | 2.9 | 2.1 | 2.4 | 1.6 | 1.7 |
| 13 to 16 | 0.6 | 0.8 | 0.5 | 0.5 | 0.9 | 0.6 | 0.0 |
| 17 to 20 | 0.3 | 0.4 | 0.2 | 0.1 | 0.1 | 0.2 | 0.0 |
| 21 to 34 | 0.1 | 0.1 | 0.1 | 0.0 | 0.1 | 0.0 | 0.2 |
| 35 to 44 | 0.1 | 0.0 | 0.0 | 0.0 | 0.9 | 0.0 | 0.0 |
| 45 + | 0.0 | 0.0 | 0.0 | 0.0 | 0.1 | 0.0 | 0.0 |
| **Outside consulting/freelance work** | | | | | | | |
| None | 67.7 | 64.6 | 68.5 | 72.2 | 60.7 | 68.7 | 73.2 |
| 1 to 4 | 23.9 | 26.0 | 24.2 | 21.1 | 26.9 | 22.4 | 7.6 |
| 5 to 8 | 5.7 | 7.0 | 5.1 | 4.4 | 7.7 | 5.2 | 9.0 |
| 9 to 12 | 1.7 | 1.6 | 1.5 | 1.5 | 3.1 | 2.0 | 0.0 |
| 13 to 16 | 0.4 | 0.5 | 0.4 | 0.5 | 0.6 | 0.3 | 0.0 |
| 17 to 20 | 0.3 | 0.2 | 0.2 | 0.3 | 0.3 | 0.9 | 8.4 |
| 21 to 34 | 0.1 | 0.1 | 0.0 | 0.0 | 0.3 | 0.4 | 0.0 |
| 35 to 44 | 0.1 | 0.0 | 0.0 | 0.0 | 0.4 | 0.0 | 0.0 |
| 45 + | 0.1 | 0.1 | 0.0 | 0.0 | 0.1 | 0.0 | 1.7 |

| All Respondents | All Resp | Full Prof | Assoc Prof | Asst Prof | Lect | Inst | No Resp |
|---|---|---|---|---|---|---|---|
| **DURING THE PRESENT TERM, HOW MANY HOURS PER WEEK ON AVERAGE DO YOU ACTUALLY SPEND ON:** | | | | | | | |
| **Household/childcare duties** | | | | | | | |
| None | 12.2 | 16.5 | 10.4 | 9.5 | 12.6 | 9.9 | 4.4 |
| 1 to 4 | 18.0 | 20.7 | 16.2 | 17.6 | 17.5 | 15.8 | 12.2 |
| 5 to 8 | 25.3 | 28.1 | 23.3 | 23.8 | 24.7 | 25.8 | 42.2 |
| 9 to 12 | 16.3 | 15.2 | 17.5 | 15.8 | 19.0 | 15.7 | 12.2 |
| 13 to 16 | 8.3 | 7.5 | 9.9 | 8.3 | 7.1 | 7.7 | 16.9 |
| 17 to 20 | 7.8 | 6.0 | 9.2 | 8.5 | 6.5 | 9.6 | 10.4 |
| 21 to 34 | 5.7 | 3.3 | 6.4 | 7.7 | 5.8 | 5.8 | 0.0 |
| 35 to 44 | 2.9 | 1.3 | 3.4 | 3.7 | 3.1 | 4.5 | 0.0 |
| 45 + | 3.5 | 1.3 | 3.7 | 5.1 | 3.6 | 5.3 | 1.7 |
| **Communicating via email** | | | | | | | |
| None | 0.4 | 0.2 | 0.5 | 0.3 | 1.2 | 0.3 | 0.0 |
| 1 to 4 | 28.8 | 26.9 | 26.9 | 30.5 | 29.4 | 37.1 | 30.9 |
| 5 to 8 | 40.1 | 41.4 | 40.6 | 39.9 | 39.1 | 34.6 | 26.7 |
| 9 to 12 | 18.2 | 18.6 | 19.5 | 17.1 | 17.3 | 16.1 | 25.8 |
| 13 to 16 | 7.2 | 7.7 | 7.1 | 6.7 | 8.6 | 5.9 | 13.7 |
| 17 to 20 | 3.4 | 3.5 | 3.6 | 3.1 | 2.3 | 3.9 | 1.1 |
| 21 to 34 | 1.3 | 1.3 | 1.3 | 1.5 | 1.1 | 1.4 | 0.0 |
| 35 to 44 | 0.3 | 0.2 | 0.3 | 0.4 | 0.5 | 0.2 | 0.0 |
| 45 + | 0.3 | 0.2 | 0.3 | 0.4 | 0.4 | 0.5 | 1.7 |
| **Commuting to campus [2]** | | | | | | | |
| None | 6.0 | 6.0 | 5.4 | 6.9 | 5.8 | 5.2 | 0.0 |
| 1 to 4 | 61.5 | 66.3 | 60.6 | 59.4 | 58.4 | 55.0 | 44.6 |
| 5 to 8 | 23.0 | 20.5 | 24.0 | 23.1 | 26.4 | 25.5 | 32.7 |
| 9 to 12 | 8.0 | 6.0 | 8.3 | 8.7 | 8.4 | 12.3 | 22.7 |
| 13 to 16 | 1.0 | 0.9 | 1.2 | 1.1 | 0.6 | 1.1 | 0.0 |
| 17 to 20 | 0.3 | 0.2 | 0.3 | 0.3 | 0.2 | 0.9 | 0.0 |
| 21 to 34 | 0.1 | 0.1 | 0.1 | 0.2 | 0.0 | 0.0 | 0.0 |
| 35 to 44 | 0.0 | 0.0 | 0.0 | 0.0 | 0.0 | 0.0 | 0.0 |
| 45 + | 0.1 | 0.0 | 0.0 | 0.2 | 0.1 | 0.1 | 0.0 |
| **Other employment, outside of academia [2]** | | | | | | | |
| None | 87.0 | 88.6 | 89.7 | 87.9 | 77.9 | 76.8 | 81.4 |
| 1 to 4 | 6.8 | 6.4 | 6.1 | 6.3 | 8.7 | 10.8 | 0.0 |
| 5 to 8 | 3.1 | 2.9 | 2.4 | 2.5 | 6.8 | 4.9 | 5.6 |
| 9 to 12 | 1.5 | 1.1 | 0.9 | 1.9 | 2.2 | 3.3 | 0.0 |
| 13 to 16 | 0.7 | 0.4 | 0.5 | 0.8 | 1.8 | 0.7 | 0.0 |
| 17 to 20 | 0.4 | 0.4 | 0.2 | 0.2 | 0.8 | 1.6 | 13.0 |
| 21 to 34 | 0.3 | 0.1 | 0.2 | 0.1 | 0.9 | 1.2 | 0.0 |
| 35 to 44 | 0.2 | 0.0 | 0.2 | 0.1 | 0.8 | 0.4 | 0.0 |
| 45 + | 0.1 | 0.0 | 0.0 | 0.1 | 0.0 | 0.4 | 0.0 |

[2] This question asked for the first time in the 2007–2008 Faculty Survey.

## 2007–2008 FACULTY SURVEY WEIGHTED NATIONAL NORMS
### Full-time Undergraduate Faculty at Baccalaureate Institutions

| All Respondents | All Resp | Full Prof | Assoc Prof | Asst Prof | Lect | Inst | No Resp |
|---|---|---|---|---|---|---|---|
| **Including all institutions at which you teach, how many undergraduate courses are you teaching this term? [2]** | | | | | | | |
| None | 0.0 | 0.0 | 0.0 | 0.0 | 0.0 | 0.0 | 0.0 |
| One | 21.7 | 29.4 | 20.7 | 17.2 | 18.4 | 12.0 | 15.9 |
| Two | 28.8 | 31.1 | 31.5 | 27.5 | 22.5 | 19.5 | 47.6 |
| Three | 25.8 | 23.4 | 25.0 | 29.4 | 23.8 | 27.3 | 28.3 |
| Four | 15.4 | 10.5 | 15.5 | 16.4 | 22.5 | 25.0 | 8.2 |
| Five | 5.2 | 3.4 | 4.4 | 5.8 | 8.7 | 9.5 | 0.0 |
| Six or more | 3.2 | 2.1 | 2.9 | 3.7 | 4.0 | 6.8 | 0.0 |
| **FOR UP TO FOUR OF THE UNDERGRADUATE COURSES MENTIONED ABOVE, HOW MANY STUDENTS ARE ENROLLED IN: [2]** | | | | | | | |
| **Course #1** | | | | | | | |
| 10 or fewer | 12.0 | 11.7 | 12.6 | 12.0 | 7.7 | 14.7 | 25.5 |
| 11 to 20 | 27.1 | 27.1 | 26.3 | 27.7 | 26.9 | 28.1 | 36.6 |
| 21 to 30 | 26.2 | 25.3 | 27.5 | 26.2 | 24.8 | 26.8 | 17.6 |
| 31 to 50 | 20.8 | 20.6 | 19.1 | 21.9 | 24.3 | 20.2 | 20.4 |
| 51 to 100 | 9.1 | 9.9 | 9.3 | 8.6 | 9.3 | 7.1 | 0.0 |
| More than 100 | 4.8 | 5.5 | 5.2 | 3.6 | 7.0 | 3.0 | 0.0 |
| **Course #2** | | | | | | | |
| 10 or fewer | 16.9 | 19.3 | 18.0 | 15.7 | 11.4 | 13.5 | 39.2 |
| 11 to 20 | 31.5 | 31.8 | 32.2 | 31.9 | 22.4 | 34.6 | 39.2 |
| 21 to 30 | 26.7 | 23.5 | 27.2 | 28.7 | 29.5 | 27.4 | 6.5 |
| 31 to 50 | 17.9 | 18.3 | 16.4 | 17.6 | 23.3 | 17.4 | 15.1 |
| 51 to 100 | 5.0 | 4.7 | 4.6 | 4.6 | 8.6 | 5.5 | 0.0 |
| More than 100 | 2.1 | 2.4 | 1.6 | 1.6 | 4.8 | 1.5 | 0.0 |
| **Course #3** | | | | | | | |
| 10 or fewer | 24.9 | 29.6 | 27.8 | 24.4 | 13.6 | 16.9 | 28.5 |
| 11 to 20 | 32.8 | 33.6 | 32.4 | 34.2 | 32.0 | 28.0 | 45.7 |
| 21 to 30 | 24.9 | 21.1 | 25.1 | 24.1 | 26.3 | 34.5 | 9.2 |
| 31 to 50 | 13.8 | 11.5 | 11.8 | 13.7 | 22.1 | 17.0 | 16.6 |
| 51 to 100 | 2.7 | 2.4 | 2.0 | 2.7 | 4.8 | 3.3 | 0.0 |
| More than 100 | 1.0 | 1.6 | 0.9 | 0.8 | 1.2 | 0.3 | 0.0 |
| **Course #4** | | | | | | | |
| 10 or fewer | 31.7 | 37.1 | 38.9 | 31.5 | 16.7 | 22.4 | 58.8 |
| 11 to 20 | 31.6 | 35.0 | 28.8 | 34.3 | 24.2 | 31.5 | 25.9 |
| 21 to 30 | 23.2 | 17.3 | 21.4 | 22.9 | 30.2 | 30.7 | 15.3 |
| 31 to 50 | 11.1 | 8.3 | 8.6 | 9.7 | 22.9 | 13.7 | 0.0 |
| 51 to 100 | 1.8 | 0.8 | 1.5 | 1.5 | 5.4 | 1.7 | 0.0 |
| More than 100 | 0.6 | 1.5 | 0.7 | 0.2 | 0.5 | 0.0 | 0.0 |

[2] This question asked for the first time in the 2007–2008 Faculty Survey.

122

| All Respondents | All Resp | Full Prof | Assoc Prof | Asst Prof | Lect | Inst | No Resp |
|---|---|---|---|---|---|---|---|
| **HOW MANY OF THE FOLLOWING COURSES ARE YOU TEACHING THIS ACADEMIC YEAR?** | | | | | | | |
| **General education courses** | | | | | | | |
| None | 56.0 | 59.6 | 56.2 | 54.9 | 49.0 | 50.9 | 73.9 |
| One | 17.5 | 18.9 | 18.3 | 17.2 | 13.5 | 14.3 | 14.9 |
| Two | 12.2 | 11.5 | 13.2 | 12.4 | 10.2 | 12.4 | 7.0 |
| Three | 6.1 | 4.8 | 5.6 | 6.4 | 10.8 | 7.6 | 4.2 |
| Four | 3.9 | 2.9 | 3.5 | 4.2 | 6.9 | 5.5 | 0.0 |
| Five or more | 4.2 | 2.2 | 3.2 | 4.9 | 9.5 | 9.2 | 0.0 |
| **Developmental/remedial courses** | | | | | | | |
| None | 94.6 | 96.6 | 96.1 | 93.8 | 91.7 | 87.7 | 72.3 |
| One | 3.0 | 1.9 | 2.2 | 3.9 | 3.9 | 5.6 | 13.5 |
| Two | 1.2 | 0.7 | 0.8 | 1.1 | 2.5 | 3.3 | 0.0 |
| Three | 0.5 | 0.3 | 0.4 | 0.6 | 0.9 | 1.4 | 14.3 |
| Four | 0.4 | 0.3 | 0.3 | 0.3 | 0.6 | 0.7 | 0.0 |
| Five or more | 0.3 | 0.2 | 0.2 | 0.4 | 0.4 | 1.3 | 0.0 |
| **Other undergraduate credit courses** | | | | | | | |
| None | 18.0 | 16.0 | 15.0 | 17.2 | 28.8 | 29.6 | 11.9 |
| One | 20.4 | 23.8 | 20.6 | 19.0 | 15.9 | 15.2 | 15.3 |
| Two | 23.1 | 27.0 | 23.7 | 21.4 | 20.7 | 13.5 | 27.1 |
| Three | 16.0 | 14.4 | 18.2 | 17.6 | 11.5 | 12.9 | 33.8 |
| Four | 9.9 | 8.8 | 10.0 | 10.7 | 10.0 | 11.7 | 2.2 |
| Five or more | 12.5 | 10.0 | 12.6 | 14.1 | 13.0 | 17.0 | 9.9 |
| **Graduate courses** | | | | | | | |
| None | 63.4 | 56.1 | 59.1 | 64.3 | 80.7 | 89.0 | 74.4 |
| One | 22.4 | 28.5 | 23.5 | 21.3 | 13.5 | 6.2 | 2.5 |
| Two | 8.7 | 9.7 | 10.9 | 8.4 | 3.3 | 2.5 | 5.7 |
| Three | 2.9 | 3.2 | 3.5 | 2.8 | 1.5 | 1.1 | 0.0 |
| Four | 1.5 | 1.6 | 1.4 | 1.8 | 0.9 | 0.5 | 3.8 |
| Five or more | 1.1 | 0.9 | 1.5 | 1.3 | 0.1 | 0.8 | 13.6 |
| **Vocational or technical courses** | | | | | | | |
| None | 97.4 | 97.9 | 97.4 | 97.3 | 96.8 | 95.8 | 100.0 |
| One | 1.0 | 1.0 | 1.1 | 1.0 | 0.8 | 1.8 | 0.0 |
| Two | 0.6 | 0.4 | 0.6 | 0.8 | 0.4 | 0.7 | 0.0 |
| Three | 0.4 | 0.4 | 0.3 | 0.4 | 0.5 | 0.6 | 0.0 |
| Four | 0.3 | 0.2 | 0.2 | 0.1 | 0.8 | 0.8 | 0.0 |
| Five or more | 0.3 | 0.1 | 0.3 | 0.3 | 0.6 | 0.3 | 0.0 |
| **Non-credit courses (other than above)** | | | | | | | |
| None | 95.0 | 94.4 | 95.4 | 95.0 | 96.4 | 94.4 | 90.8 |
| One | 3.5 | 4.2 | 3.4 | 3.2 | 2.0 | 3.6 | 5.5 |
| Two | 1.0 | 1.0 | 0.9 | 1.2 | 0.8 | 0.6 | 2.8 |
| Three | 0.2 | 0.3 | 0.1 | 0.2 | 0.3 | 0.7 | 0.9 |
| Four | 0.1 | 0.1 | 0.1 | 0.1 | 0.1 | 0.4 | 0.0 |
| Five or more | 0.2 | 0.1 | 0.1 | 0.3 | 0.4 | 0.3 | 0.0 |
| **Do you teach remedial/developmental skills in any of the following areas?** | | | | | | | |
| Reading | 4.2 | 2.9 | 3.7 | 5.2 | 6.8 | 4.7 | 24.0 |
| Writing | 10.3 | 8.6 | 9.5 | 11.7 | 12.8 | 12.8 | 27.7 |
| Mathematics | 4.1 | 3.9 | 3.7 | 3.9 | 5.7 | 5.9 | 0.0 |
| ESL | 1.0 | 0.5 | 0.6 | 1.1 | 2.7 | 2.2 | 0.8 |
| General academic skills | 8.5 | 7.2 | 7.8 | 10.2 | 8.1 | 10.7 | 18.3 |
| Other subject areas | 5.6 | 4.2 | 4.8 | 7.0 | 6.6 | 8.2 | 0.2 |

| All Respondents | All Resp | Full Prof | Assoc Prof | Asst Prof | Lect | Inst | No Resp |
|---|---|---|---|---|---|---|---|
| **HAVE YOU ENGAGED IN ANY OF THE FOLLOWING PROFESSIONAL DEVELOPMENT OPPORTUNITIES AT YOUR INSTITUTION? [2]** | | | | | | | |
| **Workshops focused on teaching in the classroom** | | | | | | | |
| Yes | 70.1 | 65.5 | 73.7 | 72.4 | 72.9 | 65.9 | 61.9 |
| No | 27.5 | 32.9 | 24.4 | 24.3 | 25.4 | 29.7 | 30.3 |
| Not eligible | 0.2 | 0.1 | 0.1 | 0.2 | 0.7 | 0.2 | 7.9 |
| Not available | 2.2 | 1.5 | 1.8 | 3.1 | 1.0 | 4.2 | 0.0 |
| **Paid workshops outside the institution focused on teaching** | | | | | | | |
| Yes | 24.6 | 21.7 | 26.4 | 24.4 | 26.1 | 29.8 | 24.3 |
| No | 70.6 | 74.9 | 69.3 | 70.0 | 65.7 | 64.0 | 73.5 |
| Not eligible | 0.8 | 0.3 | 0.3 | 0.7 | 4.1 | 2.5 | 1.8 |
| Not available | 3.9 | 3.1 | 4.0 | 4.9 | 4.1 | 3.7 | 0.4 |
| **Paid sabbatical leave** | | | | | | | |
| Yes | 28.7 | 54.0 | 35.9 | 6.7 | 5.1 | 0.9 | 6.2 |
| No | 54.6 | 42.2 | 55.9 | 65.9 | 51.9 | 64.3 | 43.8 |
| Not eligible | 13.4 | 1.8 | 5.4 | 23.7 | 36.0 | 30.7 | 50.0 |
| Not available | 3.2 | 2.0 | 2.9 | 3.8 | 7.0 | 4.1 | 0.0 |
| **Travel funds paid by the institution** | | | | | | | |
| Yes | 78.9 | 84.4 | 84.5 | 79.7 | 57.1 | 54.7 | 78.4 |
| No | 18.1 | 14.2 | 13.6 | 17.2 | 33.6 | 38.2 | 21.6 |
| Not eligible | 1.4 | 0.1 | 0.2 | 1.2 | 8.1 | 4.7 | 0.0 |
| Not available | 1.6 | 1.3 | 1.7 | 1.9 | 1.2 | 2.4 | 0.0 |
| **Association membership/dues paid by the institution** | | | | | | | |
| Yes | 28.9 | 28.3 | 29.9 | 31.1 | 22.5 | 25.8 | 30.7 |
| No | 55.0 | 60.3 | 52.7 | 50.1 | 56.0 | 57.5 | 57.6 |
| Not eligible | 2.6 | 0.7 | 1.2 | 3.0 | 10.3 | 7.2 | 1.8 |
| Not available | 13.4 | 10.7 | 16.3 | 15.7 | 11.2 | 9.5 | 9.9 |
| **Tuition remission** | | | | | | | |
| Yes | 14.4 | 17.3 | 13.9 | 10.2 | 12.2 | 22.1 | 10.0 |
| No | 77.5 | 75.5 | 79.5 | 80.2 | 77.3 | 69.4 | 80.7 |
| Not eligible | 3.5 | 2.9 | 2.3 | 4.3 | 5.8 | 4.1 | 9.3 |
| Not available | 4.6 | 4.3 | 4.4 | 5.2 | 4.7 | 4.4 | 0.0 |
| **Internal grants for research** | | | | | | | |
| Yes | 46.8 | 55.3 | 54.4 | 47.0 | 18.6 | 11.4 | 24.4 |
| No | 49.2 | 42.3 | 43.5 | 48.9 | 70.1 | 79.3 | 48.9 |
| Not eligible | 2.1 | 0.8 | 0.6 | 1.8 | 9.6 | 6.1 | 26.7 |
| Not available | 1.9 | 1.7 | 1.5 | 2.3 | 1.6 | 3.2 | 0.0 |
| **Training for administrative leadership** | | | | | | | |
| Yes | 13.2 | 20.1 | 14.6 | 7.0 | 7.3 | 8.2 | 12.1 |
| No | 76.4 | 72.8 | 74.8 | 81.4 | 76.8 | 78.8 | 68.6 |
| Not eligible | 2.7 | 0.9 | 1.4 | 3.4 | 8.5 | 6.6 | 9.9 |
| Not available | 7.6 | 6.2 | 9.2 | 8.2 | 7.3 | 6.4 | 9.4 |

[2] This question asked for the first time in the 2007–2008 Faculty Survey.

| All Respondents | All Resp | Full Prof | Assoc Prof | Asst Prof | Lect | Inst | No Resp |
|---|---|---|---|---|---|---|---|
| **Goals for undergraduates noted as "very important" or "essential"** | | | | | | | |
| Develop ability to think critically | 99.6 | 99.5 | 99.4 | 99.8 | 99.8 | 99.7 | 100.0 |
| Prepare students for employment after college | 81.5 | 78.0 | 80.6 | 83.8 | 83.1 | 89.0 | 82.5 |
| Prepare students for graduate or advanced education | 75.5 | 77.5 | 74.0 | 76.6 | 72.5 | 71.0 | 63.9 |
| Develop moral character | 70.2 | 68.4 | 67.9 | 70.1 | 76.6 | 79.8 | 66.4 |
| Provide for students' emotional development | 48.1 | 44.6 | 45.7 | 49.6 | 52.7 | 60.9 | 41.8 |
| Prepare students for family living | 21.2 | 19.6 | 19.9 | 20.5 | 24.7 | 31.8 | 7.9 |
| Teach students the classic works of Western civilization [2] | 34.7 | 39.7 | 34.5 | 29.4 | 38.4 | 29.6 | 42.5 |
| Help students develop personal values | 66.1 | 64.3 | 64.5 | 66.3 | 68.0 | 76.2 | 79.3 |
| Enhance students' self-understanding | 71.8 | 67.8 | 70.9 | 74.2 | 76.6 | 77.8 | 76.1 |
| Instill in students a commitment to community service | 55.5 | 51.8 | 54.1 | 56.5 | 62.6 | 65.5 | 48.0 |
| Enhance students' knowledge of and appreciation for other racial/ethnic groups | 75.2 | 72.1 | 74.4 | 78.0 | 78.4 | 77.0 | 74.0 |
| Study a foreign language [2] | 54.2 | 56.4 | 54.8 | 52.3 | 55.0 | 49.4 | 56.3 |
| Help master knowledge in a discipline | 95.1 | 95.8 | 95.7 | 94.8 | 91.8 | 94.2 | 100.0 |
| Develop creative capacities | 81.5 | 81.3 | 79.6 | 82.6 | 84.4 | 81.6 | 91.4 |
| Instill a basic appreciation of the liberal arts | 72.8 | 74.7 | 74.3 | 70.7 | 73.0 | 67.1 | 66.6 |
| Promote ability to write effectively | 96.4 | 96.5 | 96.9 | 96.0 | 97.5 | 95.1 | 100.0 |
| Help students evaluate the quality and reliability of information [2] | 97.2 | 97.1 | 97.7 | 96.8 | 98.1 | 96.9 | 91.6 |
| Engage students in civil discourse around controversial issues [2] | 72.4 | 70.6 | 74.0 | 73.9 | 74.6 | 67.0 | 89.6 |
| Teach students tolerance and respect for different beliefs [2] | 82.5 | 79.5 | 83.3 | 84.3 | 87.6 | 80.4 | 87.9 |
| Encourage students to become agents of social change [2] | 57.8 | 51.2 | 58.3 | 62.0 | 62.1 | 65.3 | 51.7 |

[2] This question asked for the first time in the 2007–2008 Faculty Survey.

| All Respondents | All Resp | Full Prof | Assoc Prof | Asst Prof | Lect | Inst | No Resp |
|---|---|---|---|---|---|---|---|
| **HOW MANY OF THE FOLLOWING HAVE YOU PUBLISHED?** | | | | | | | |
| **Articles in academic or professional journals** | | | | | | | |
| None | 18.8 | 7.4 | 10.7 | 20.5 | 46.5 | 61.0 | 41.6 |
| 1 to 2 | 17.6 | 8.5 | 14.9 | 28.1 | 22.3 | 22.2 | 15.7 |
| 3 to 4 | 14.5 | 9.2 | 16.8 | 19.3 | 15.4 | 9.6 | 22.2 |
| 5 to 10 | 18.4 | 16.9 | 25.4 | 19.6 | 8.9 | 4.9 | 12.3 |
| 11 to 20 | 12.7 | 17.0 | 17.7 | 8.3 | 5.0 | 0.8 | 4.6 |
| 21 to 50 | 11.4 | 22.3 | 12.2 | 3.5 | 1.5 | 0.9 | 3.6 |
| 51+ | 6.7 | 18.6 | 2.3 | 0.6 | 0.5 | 0.6 | 0.0 |
| **Chapters in edited volumes** | | | | | | | |
| None | 49.5 | 31.3 | 44.1 | 59.5 | 71.6 | 87.2 | 63.5 |
| 1 to 2 | 25.5 | 24.0 | 28.9 | 29.3 | 20.4 | 11.5 | 24.4 |
| 3 to 4 | 11.8 | 16.8 | 15.1 | 7.5 | 5.7 | 1.0 | 9.9 |
| 5 to 10 | 8.8 | 16.8 | 9.3 | 3.1 | 1.9 | 0.2 | 2.2 |
| 11 to 20 | 3.0 | 7.5 | 1.8 | 0.5 | 0.5 | 0.1 | 0.0 |
| 21 to 50 | 1.1 | 2.8 | 0.7 | 0.0 | 0.1 | 0.0 | 0.0 |
| 51+ | 0.3 | 0.9 | 0.0 | 0.0 | 0.0 | 0.0 | 0.0 |
| **Books, manuals, or monographs** | | | | | | | |
| None | 61.1 | 40.1 | 58.2 | 77.3 | 73.3 | 88.3 | 67.6 |
| 1 to 2 | 25.7 | 30.1 | 33.1 | 19.2 | 20.3 | 9.9 | 30.3 |
| 3 to 4 | 7.3 | 14.8 | 6.0 | 2.4 | 4.1 | 0.9 | 0.0 |
| 5 to 10 | 4.4 | 10.8 | 2.1 | 0.7 | 1.7 | 0.6 | 2.1 |
| 11 to 20 | 1.1 | 2.8 | 0.5 | 0.2 | 0.5 | 0.1 | 0.0 |
| 21 to 50 | 0.4 | 1.1 | 0.1 | 0.1 | 0.0 | 0.1 | 0.0 |
| 51+ | 0.1 | 0.3 | 0.0 | 0.1 | 0.1 | 0.0 | 0.0 |
| **Other, such as patents or computer software products** | | | | | | | |
| None | 85.1 | 80.4 | 85.1 | 87.8 | 88.5 | 91.6 | 91.4 |
| 1 to 2 | 8.6 | 10.6 | 8.1 | 8.2 | 8.1 | 4.1 | 0.0 |
| 3 to 4 | 3.2 | 4.3 | 3.5 | 2.2 | 1.6 | 2.4 | 8.6 |
| 5 to 10 | 1.9 | 3.1 | 2.1 | 1.0 | 1.0 | 0.6 | 0.0 |
| 11 to 20 | 0.6 | 0.8 | 0.6 | 0.5 | 0.4 | 0.8 | 0.0 |
| 21 to 50 | 0.3 | 0.5 | 0.4 | 0.1 | 0.1 | 0.0 | 0.0 |
| 51+ | 0.3 | 0.4 | 0.2 | 0.2 | 0.3 | 0.4 | 0.0 |
| **IN THE LAST TWO YEARS, HOW MANY:** | | | | | | | |
| **Exhibitions or performances in the fine or applied arts have you presented?** | | | | | | | |
| None | 81.8 | 82.9 | 83.3 | 80.9 | 78.5 | 78.2 | 63.4 |
| 1 to 2 | 5.8 | 4.7 | 4.7 | 5.7 | 9.4 | 10.5 | 18.0 |
| 3 to 4 | 4.4 | 4.4 | 3.9 | 4.7 | 5.1 | 4.3 | 8.7 |
| 5 to 10 | 4.1 | 4.2 | 3.8 | 4.7 | 3.1 | 3.6 | 0.0 |
| 11 to 20 | 1.9 | 1.8 | 2.0 | 2.0 | 1.8 | 1.2 | 5.6 |
| 21 to 50 | 1.1 | 1.2 | 1.0 | 1.4 | 1.1 | 0.4 | 4.2 |
| 51+ | 1.0 | 0.9 | 1.2 | 0.7 | 1.0 | 1.9 | 0.0 |
| **Of your professional writings have been published or accepted for publication?** | | | | | | | |
| None | 30.0 | 20.7 | 25.3 | 26.4 | 57.9 | 70.6 | 51.8 |
| 1 to 2 | 32.2 | 30.1 | 35.2 | 35.9 | 27.8 | 21.4 | 32.3 |
| 3 to 4 | 20.9 | 22.4 | 23.6 | 23.3 | 11.3 | 5.7 | 7.8 |
| 5 to 10 | 13.3 | 19.9 | 13.2 | 12.2 | 2.3 | 1.3 | 4.4 |
| 11 to 20 | 2.7 | 5.0 | 2.2 | 1.8 | 0.2 | 0.7 | 3.6 |
| 21 to 50 | 0.7 | 1.5 | 0.6 | 0.2 | 0.2 | 0.3 | 0.0 |
| 51+ | 0.2 | 0.4 | 0.1 | 0.2 | 0.2 | 0.0 | 0.0 |

## 2007–2008 FACULTY SURVEY WEIGHTED NATIONAL NORMS
### Full-time Undergraduate Faculty at Baccalaureate Institutions

| All Respondents | All Resp | Full Prof | Assoc Prof | Asst Prof | Lect | Inst | No Resp |
|---|---|---|---|---|---|---|---|
| **General activities** | | | | | | | |
| Are you a member of a faculty union? | 21.5 | 21.6 | 23.4 | 22.3 | 21.5 | 11.6 | 10.1 |
| Are you a U.S. citizen? | 93.6 | 97.2 | 93.8 | 87.3 | 96.4 | 97.1 | 100.0 |
| Were you born in the U.S.A.? | 85.3 | 86.5 | 85.5 | 81.8 | 85.0 | 92.1 | 96.2 |
| Do you plan to retire within the next three years? | 13.1 | 23.5 | 10.1 | 3.7 | 16.3 | 10.2 | 16.3 |
| Do you use your scholarship to address local community needs? | 47.1 | 47.4 | 48.4 | 45.0 | 47.6 | 49.1 | 34.9 |
| Have you been sexually harassed at this institution? | 5.4 | 5.9 | 6.2 | 4.0 | 5.7 | 4.5 | 9.2 |
| Have you ever interrupted your professional career for more than one year for family reasons? [2] | 11.7 | 5.4 | 10.3 | 13.6 | 23.6 | 24.8 | 23.0 |
| Have you ever received an award for outstanding teaching? | 42.5 | 54.4 | 44.7 | 31.3 | 39.8 | 28.7 | 28.0 |
| Have you published op-ed pieces or editorials? | 24.0 | 34.1 | 23.1 | 16.5 | 22.6 | 13.0 | 26.5 |
| Is (or was) your: | | | | | | | |
|     Father an academic? | 13.6 | 12.0 | 14.3 | 15.6 | 12.1 | 12.0 | 5.2 |
|     Mother an academic? | 9.3 | 8.0 | 8.6 | 10.2 | 11.2 | 11.5 | 0.0 |
|     Spouse/partner an academic? | 32.9 | 36.4 | 34.0 | 28.0 | 37.8 | 27.8 | 46.0 |
| Are you currently teaching courses at more than one institution? | 4.7 | 4.4 | 3.6 | 4.3 | 8.9 | 7.5 | 4.3 |
| **During the <u>past two</u> years, have you:** | | | | | | | |
| Considered early retirement? | 21.2 | 31.1 | 22.5 | 10.0 | 18.3 | 18.3 | 33.2 |
| Considered leaving academe for another job? | 32.7 | 21.7 | 35.8 | 38.0 | 40.4 | 41.7 | 34.5 |
| Considered leaving this institution for another? | 46.5 | 39.0 | 52.2 | 52.0 | 41.8 | 43.3 | 42.3 |
| Changed academic institutions? | 11.4 | 6.5 | 7.4 | 20.2 | 12.8 | 13.0 | 0.9 |
| Engaged in paid consulting outside of your institution? | 37.6 | 44.0 | 38.9 | 30.9 | 41.9 | 26.8 | 42.5 |
| Engaged in public service/professional consulting without pay? | 59.4 | 64.3 | 62.0 | 54.5 | 55.5 | 51.2 | 71.4 |
| Received at least one firm job offer? | 23.9 | 16.7 | 19.0 | 34.7 | 26.1 | 30.7 | 4.9 |
| Received funding for your work from: | | | | | | | |
|     Foundations? | 19.7 | 23.7 | 20.6 | 19.4 | 12.6 | 7.5 | 11.8 |
|     State or federal government? | 27.1 | 36.1 | 29.1 | 22.6 | 15.3 | 10.1 | 9.8 |
|     Business or industry? | 13.5 | 18.4 | 14.0 | 10.1 | 9.7 | 6.5 | 15.2 |
| Requested/sought an early promotion? | 7.3 | 5.7 | 10.1 | 6.8 | 8.2 | 4.8 | 2.0 |
| **IF YOU WERE TO BEGIN YOUR CAREER AGAIN, WOULD YOU STILL WANT TO:** | | | | | | | |
| **Come to this institution? [2]** | | | | | | | |
| Definitely yes | 35.0 | 34.7 | 31.7 | 34.4 | 42.9 | 42.7 | 33.9 |
| Probably yes | 33.9 | 33.7 | 32.8 | 35.0 | 31.5 | 37.4 | 21.2 |
| Not sure | 16.7 | 16.7 | 18.5 | 18.1 | 9.7 | 11.8 | 14.9 |
| Probably no | 9.4 | 9.7 | 10.6 | 8.1 | 13.3 | 4.3 | 24.7 |
| Definitely no | 5.0 | 5.2 | 6.4 | 4.4 | 2.7 | 3.9 | 5.4 |
| **Be a college professor?** | | | | | | | |
| Definitely yes | 63.3 | 70.4 | 61.0 | 60.6 | 57.9 | 56.3 | 38.4 |
| Probably yes | 25.1 | 21.1 | 26.7 | 26.1 | 28.8 | 28.1 | 42.0 |
| Not sure | 8.4 | 5.9 | 8.6 | 10.0 | 9.6 | 11.1 | 15.9 |
| Probably no | 2.5 | 1.9 | 3.1 | 2.7 | 2.2 | 2.4 | 3.7 |
| Definitely no | 0.8 | 0.6 | 0.6 | 0.7 | 1.4 | 2.0 | 0.0 |

[2]  This question asked for the first time in the 2007–2008 Faculty Survey.

127

**2007–2008 FACULTY SURVEY WEIGHTED NATIONAL NORMS**
**Full-time Undergraduate Faculty at Baccalaureate Institutions**

| All Respondents | All Resp | Full Prof | Assoc Prof | Asst Prof | Lect | Inst | No Resp |
|---|---|---|---|---|---|---|---|
| **Attributes noted as being "very descriptive" of your institution** | | | | | | | |
| It is easy for students to see faculty outside of regular office hours | 60.6 | 60.5 | 61.1 | 63.4 | 51.3 | 57.8 | 52.0 |
| There is a great deal of conformity among the students | 29.4 | 28.3 | 30.1 | 32.6 | 23.3 | 25.1 | 51.4 |
| The faculty are typically at odds with campus administration | 19.4 | 20.3 | 21.7 | 19.3 | 11.7 | 15.3 | 21.4 |
| Faculty here respect each other | 47.6 | 47.7 | 44.9 | 51.7 | 41.7 | 47.7 | 25.7 |
| Most students are treated like "numbers in a book" | 3.8 | 3.9 | 3.8 | 3.6 | 5.1 | 3.0 | 14.7 |
| Social activities are overemphasized | 8.3 | 9.2 | 9.0 | 7.4 | 7.4 | 6.8 | 14.6 |
| Faculty are rewarded for being good teachers | 16.0 | 17.2 | 14.4 | 17.2 | 13.9 | 14.0 | 9.4 |
| There is respect for the expression of diverse values and beliefs | 35.8 | 36.4 | 32.1 | 35.0 | 44.4 | 40.9 | 30.8 |
| Faculty are rewarded for their efforts to use instructional technology | 20.3 | 19.7 | 18.9 | 21.8 | 22.5 | 20.7 | 7.1 |
| Faculty are rewarded for their efforts to work with underprepared students | 5.7 | 5.1 | 4.3 | 6.1 | 8.3 | 8.6 | 1.3 |
| Administrators consider faculty concerns when making policy [2] | 13.0 | 13.3 | 11.2 | 12.9 | 16.2 | 15.8 | 13.3 |
| The administration is open about its policies | 16.5 | 16.2 | 13.4 | 17.1 | 20.4 | 22.8 | 13.9 |
| **Do you, "to a great extent":** | | | | | | | |
| Engage in academic work that spans multiple disciplines | 38.7 | 40.0 | 40.7 | 40.7 | 33.6 | 24.6 | 26.6 |
| Feel that the training you received in graduate school prepared you well for your role as a faculty mentor | 39.1 | 41.3 | 36.9 | 42.2 | 31.1 | 33.9 | 35.4 |
| Achieve a healthy balance between your personal life and your professional life | 34.2 | 42.7 | 31.1 | 26.1 | 37.6 | 35.9 | 33.1 |
| Experience close alignment between your work and your personal values | 65.3 | 69.9 | 62.4 | 61.5 | 68.1 | 67.4 | 63.7 |
| Feel that you have to work harder than your colleagues to be perceived as a legitimate scholar | 26.7 | 20.0 | 26.5 | 29.9 | 37.9 | 33.5 | 37.7 |
| Mentor new faculty [2] | 22.3 | 33.4 | 26.1 | 11.4 | 12.7 | 12.0 | 2.1 |

[2]  This question asked for the first time in the 2007–2008 Faculty Survey.

128

**2007–2008 FACULTY SURVEY WEIGHTED NATIONAL NORMS**
**Full-time Undergraduate Faculty at Baccalaureate Institutions**

| All Respondents | All Resp | Full Prof | Assoc Prof | Asst Prof | Lect | Inst | No Resp |
|---|---|---|---|---|---|---|---|
| **Aspects of your job with which you are "very satisfied" or "satisfied": [3]** | | | | | | | |
| Salary [2] | 46.2 | 56.1 | 42.7 | 43.3 | 35.7 | 36.6 | 48.4 |
| Health benefits [2] | 68.3 | 69.4 | 65.2 | 67.6 | 77.8 | 67.8 | 72.4 |
| Retirement benefits [2] | 68.7 | 68.6 | 65.1 | 70.7 | 74.8 | 68.9 | 64.8 |
| Opportunity for scholarly pursuits | 54.1 | 62.3 | 49.3 | 48.3 | 56.6 | 55.1 | 53.5 |
| Teaching load | 57.7 | 63.1 | 52.8 | 53.1 | 62.4 | 64.4 | 56.2 |
| Quality of students | 57.1 | 59.1 | 54.0 | 55.1 | 64.5 | 60.1 | 61.6 |
| Office/lab space | 67.3 | 71.8 | 66.5 | 64.5 | 65.3 | 63.2 | 60.1 |
| Autonomy and independence | 85.0 | 87.0 | 84.2 | 83.4 | 85.3 | 84.5 | 62.4 |
| Professional relationships with other faculty | 77.6 | 79.8 | 75.1 | 78.9 | 74.9 | 75.3 | 52.7 |
| Social relationships with other faculty | 67.4 | 66.7 | 65.9 | 70.1 | 64.2 | 68.7 | 52.4 |
| Competency of colleagues | 78.2 | 79.1 | 75.6 | 78.0 | 80.2 | 82.4 | 81.1 |
| Visibility for jobs at other institutions/organizations | 53.8 | 60.8 | 47.7 | 52.6 | 53.6 | 50.8 | 49.7 |
| Job security | 77.7 | 93.1 | 86.2 | 64.5 | 54.0 | 53.1 | 53.4 |
| Relationship with administration | 58.3 | 58.3 | 56.4 | 57.9 | 61.9 | 62.5 | 42.5 |
| Departmental leadership [2] | 69.1 | 70.2 | 66.6 | 68.8 | 70.1 | 73.7 | 64.2 |
| Course assignments [2] | 84.0 | 87.3 | 83.2 | 81.0 | 83.6 | 84.0 | 79.8 |
| Freedom to determine course content [2] | 92.5 | 94.4 | 93.5 | 91.1 | 92.5 | 86.0 | 74.0 |
| Availability of child care at this institution | 30.9 | 36.3 | 27.4 | 29.0 | 28.8 | 34.3 | 64.3 |
| Prospects for career advancement | 54.6 | 65.0 | 51.3 | 56.5 | 33.9 | 37.3 | 27.1 |
| Clerical/administrative support | 60.8 | 59.4 | 56.2 | 61.3 | 71.3 | 71.4 | 51.2 |
| Overall job satisfaction | 74.8 | 79.1 | 71.4 | 72.5 | 76.2 | 76.7 | 66.1 |

[2] This question asked for the first time in the 2007–2008 Faculty Survey.
[3] Respondents marking "Not Applicable" were not included in the computation of these results.

129

## 2007–2008 FACULTY SURVEY WEIGHTED NATIONAL NORMS
### Full-time Undergraduate Faculty at Baccalaureate Institutions

| All Respondents | All Resp | Full Prof | Assoc Prof | Asst Prof | Lect | Inst | No Resp |
|---|---|---|---|---|---|---|---|
| **Do you agree "strongly" or "somewhat"?** | | | | | | | |
| Faculty are interested in students' personal problems | 83.2 | 81.5 | 82.8 | 85.5 | 80.1 | 87.1 | 71.2 |
| Racial and ethnic diversity should be more strongly reflected in the curriculum | 58.5 | 52.8 | 60.1 | 64.4 | 58.3 | 55.1 | 65.1 |
| Faculty feel that most students are well-prepared academically | 44.2 | 45.6 | 41.0 | 44.3 | 46.3 | 48.1 | 32.8 |
| This institution should hire more faculty of color | 73.2 | 74.0 | 75.2 | 75.3 | 66.7 | 62.2 | 51.7 |
| Student Affairs staff have the support and respect of faculty | 77.1 | 74.2 | 74.3 | 80.9 | 78.5 | 83.7 | 78.5 |
| Faculty are committed to the welfare of this institution | 90.7 | 90.3 | 90.5 | 91.7 | 87.6 | 92.1 | 82.1 |
| Faculty here are strongly interested in the academic problems of undergraduates | 87.8 | 88.2 | 87.6 | 88.7 | 82.7 | 88.0 | 83.9 |
| There is a lot of campus racial conflict here | 10.6 | 8.8 | 11.8 | 12.9 | 10.6 | 5.8 | 5.1 |
| Most students are strongly committed to community service | 51.0 | 50.5 | 50.3 | 53.3 | 46.6 | 50.9 | 42.5 |
| My research is valued by faculty in my department | 73.7 | 78.2 | 72.1 | 75.3 | 65.1 | 62.1 | 55.7 |
| My teaching is valued by faculty in my department | 89.6 | 91.0 | 88.3 | 90.4 | 88.9 | 86.0 | 69.5 |
| Many courses include feminist perspectives | 43.1 | 42.3 | 41.8 | 43.8 | 45.6 | 45.3 | 44.0 |
| Faculty of color are treated fairly here | 88.7 | 90.6 | 85.9 | 87.0 | 90.8 | 94.8 | 87.7 |
| Women faculty are treated fairly here | 85.9 | 88.6 | 82.7 | 83.8 | 90.4 | 89.1 | 81.3 |
| Many courses involve students in community service | 48.6 | 45.5 | 47.0 | 50.5 | 48.5 | 60.3 | 45.7 |
| This institution should hire more women faculty | 57.1 | 58.4 | 57.9 | 58.5 | 54.5 | 46.0 | 38.7 |
| Gay and lesbian faculty are treated fairly here | 81.0 | 83.1 | 77.9 | 78.7 | 86.8 | 85.8 | 73.0 |
| My department does a good job of mentoring new faculty | 69.2 | 76.4 | 67.6 | 63.4 | 65.8 | 69.3 | 70.4 |
| Faculty are sufficiently involved in campus decision making | 52.9 | 49.9 | 48.1 | 56.7 | 60.5 | 60.5 | 74.3 |
| My values are congruent with the dominant institutional values | 72.6 | 72.5 | 69.1 | 74.0 | 74.2 | 78.3 | 70.2 |
| There is adequate support for integrating technology in my teaching | 84.2 | 84.5 | 82.2 | 84.6 | 87.9 | 84.8 | 82.9 |
| This institution takes responsibility for educating underprepared students | 63.4 | 64.3 | 58.3 | 64.6 | 64.4 | 71.0 | 68.9 |
| The criteria for advancement and promotion decisions are clear | 72.1 | 82.6 | 68.5 | 67.8 | 62.9 | 64.7 | 56.4 |
| Most of the students I teach lack the basic skills for college level work | 36.4 | 33.2 | 36.8 | 38.9 | 37.5 | 38.8 | 29.3 |
| There is adequate support for faculty development | 67.6 | 67.1 | 62.7 | 68.9 | 76.4 | 73.6 | 57.3 |
| This institution should not offer remedial/developmental education | 28.2 | 34.7 | 28.6 | 23.8 | 20.3 | 23.1 | 25.1 |

130

## 2007–2008 FACULTY SURVEY WEIGHTED NATIONAL NORMS
### Full-time Undergraduate Faculty at Baccalaureate Institutions

| All Respondents | All Resp | Full Prof | Assoc Prof | Asst Prof | Lect | Inst | No Resp |
|---|---|---|---|---|---|---|---|
| **Issues you believe to be of "high" or "highest" priority at your institution:** | | | | | | | |
| To promote the intellectual development of students | 85.8 | 86.9 | 84.4 | 84.8 | 89.0 | 86.6 | 86.0 |
| To help students examine and understand their personal values | 56.0 | 55.2 | 53.9 | 57.7 | 53.2 | 63.4 | 68.6 |
| To develop a sense of community among students and faculty | 54.1 | 51.1 | 51.1 | 56.7 | 57.2 | 65.3 | 61.3 |
| To facilitate student involvement in community service | 46.0 | 42.3 | 43.9 | 49.2 | 47.9 | 54.9 | 53.1 |
| To help students learn how to bring about change in American society | 35.1 | 31.2 | 32.5 | 38.1 | 40.3 | 45.4 | 19.4 |
| To increase or maintain institutional prestige | 64.0 | 63.0 | 62.3 | 64.4 | 69.0 | 67.2 | 66.1 |
| To hire faculty "stars" | 29.2 | 31.5 | 26.3 | 26.6 | 40.5 | 29.0 | 5.6 |
| To recruit more minority students | 50.3 | 52.7 | 48.2 | 47.8 | 58.0 | 48.9 | 29.7 |
| To enhance the institution's national image | 69.4 | 69.8 | 67.6 | 68.8 | 76.1 | 70.6 | 53.4 |
| To create a diverse multi-cultural campus environment | 53.7 | 54.6 | 50.1 | 52.4 | 64.5 | 57.2 | 45.5 |
| To promote gender equity among faculty | 52.1 | 58.5 | 47.4 | 48.9 | 57.0 | 48.4 | 59.9 |
| To provide resources for faculty to engage in community-based teaching or research | 35.3 | 29.1 | 31.1 | 39.3 | 46.8 | 50.1 | 43.2 |
| To create and sustain partnerships with surrounding communities | 47.5 | 38.9 | 44.5 | 53.6 | 55.5 | 64.6 | 63.0 |
| To pursue extramural funding | 61.0 | 62.8 | 59.3 | 59.3 | 64.5 | 61.8 | 60.2 |
| To increase the representation of minorities in the faculty and administration | 44.9 | 48.4 | 42.1 | 43.3 | 50.2 | 40.8 | 36.6 |
| To strengthen links with the for-profit, corporate sector [2] | 49.1 | 45.8 | 48.4 | 49.2 | 60.2 | 54.8 | 28.4 |
| To develop leadership ability among students | 59.0 | 57.4 | 53.9 | 61.1 | 64.0 | 70.4 | 64.2 |
| To increase the representation of women in the faculty and administration | 38.4 | 43.1 | 34.7 | 36.7 | 40.6 | 35.9 | 37.5 |
| To develop an appreciation for multiculturalism [2] | 54.5 | 55.5 | 51.0 | 52.5 | 63.5 | 61.3 | 51.6 |

[2] This question asked for the first time in the 2007–2008 Faculty Survey.

131

| All Respondents | All Resp | Full Prof | Assoc Prof | Asst Prof | Lect | Inst | No Resp |
|---|---|---|---|---|---|---|---|
| **Do you agree "strongly" or "somewhat"?** | | | | | | | |
| Western civilization and culture should be the foundation for the undergraduate curriculum | 57.5 | 62.8 | 55.4 | 52.4 | 61.2 | 57.1 | 66.1 |
| College officials have the right to ban persons with extreme views from speaking on campus | 27.6 | 26.9 | 26.3 | 28.0 | 28.0 | 33.3 | 34.0 |
| The chief benefit of a college education is that it increases one's earning power | 28.9 | 27.0 | 27.5 | 29.1 | 31.3 | 39.1 | 17.2 |
| Promoting diversity leads to the admission of too many underprepared students | 23.7 | 26.2 | 22.3 | 21.3 | 26.7 | 24.8 | 8.6 |
| Colleges should be actively involved in solving social problems | 71.0 | 67.2 | 72.6 | 73.7 | 71.8 | 71.2 | 65.1 |
| Tenure is an outmoded concept | 32.0 | 21.6 | 25.0 | 37.0 | 57.5 | 58.3 | 34.3 |
| Colleges should encourage students to be involved in community service activities | 87.9 | 84.9 | 88.5 | 89.1 | 92.2 | 90.1 | 95.4 |
| Community service should be given weight in college admissions decisions | 66.4 | 62.2 | 67.3 | 69.2 | 67.2 | 69.5 | 87.1 |
| A racially/ethnically diverse student body enhances the educational experience of all students | 93.6 | 93.3 | 93.9 | 94.5 | 93.3 | 91.8 | 87.5 |
| Realistically, an individual can do little to bring about changes in society | 18.8 | 22.0 | 19.0 | 16.9 | 14.5 | 16.8 | 6.2 |
| Colleges should be concerned with facilitating undergraduate students' spiritual development | 36.6 | 33.7 | 36.4 | 37.7 | 37.6 | 43.8 | 47.7 |
| Colleges have a responsibility to work with their surrounding communities to address local issues | 87.9 | 84.8 | 89.1 | 90.2 | 85.2 | 91.0 | 88.7 |
| Private funding sources often prevent researchers from being completely objective in the conduct of their work | 59.5 | 56.1 | 61.5 | 58.7 | 66.4 | 63.3 | 68.9 |

**2007–2008 FACULTY SURVEY WEIGHTED NATIONAL NORMS**
**Full-time Undergraduate Faculty at Baccalaureate Institutions**

| All Respondents | All Resp | Full Prof | Assoc Prof | Asst Prof | Lect | Inst | No Resp |
|---|---|---|---|---|---|---|---|
| **Factors noted as a source of stress for you during the <u>last two</u> years** | | | | | | | |
| Managing household responsibilities | 72.7 | 61.0 | 77.6 | 79.7 | 73.1 | 78.5 | 74.9 |
| Child care | 30.9 | 22.7 | 37.4 | 36.4 | 24.7 | 29.5 | 10.5 |
| Care of elderly parent | 33.5 | 35.9 | 35.3 | 27.8 | 35.2 | 36.2 | 38.8 |
| My physical health | 49.5 | 49.3 | 50.6 | 48.4 | 54.0 | 47.1 | 36.6 |
| Health of spouse/partner | 35.9 | 38.8 | 36.3 | 33.5 | 35.6 | 32.1 | 33.0 |
| Review/promotion process | 51.1 | 22.9 | 57.6 | 77.6 | 47.6 | 53.0 | 51.6 |
| Subtle discrimination (e.g., prejudice, racism, sexism) | 26.3 | 21.9 | 30.2 | 28.2 | 26.7 | 23.2 | 39.3 |
| Personal finances | 62.8 | 49.7 | 63.4 | 72.4 | 69.7 | 74.5 | 57.9 |
| Committee work | 61.5 | 65.2 | 71.9 | 59.0 | 38.6 | 41.0 | 65.5 |
| Faculty meetings | 53.0 | 56.3 | 60.0 | 51.4 | 36.0 | 38.0 | 25.3 |
| Colleagues | 64.2 | 67.2 | 70.1 | 59.1 | 56.4 | 57.2 | 57.8 |
| Students | 64.4 | 57.6 | 67.0 | 69.3 | 61.3 | 68.8 | 55.3 |
| Research or publishing demands | 62.7 | 55.3 | 72.5 | 77.9 | 32.6 | 34.2 | 14.9 |
| Institutional procedures and "red tape" | 71.8 | 74.3 | 75.6 | 71.2 | 63.3 | 59.1 | 62.0 |
| Teaching load | 63.3 | 53.8 | 67.1 | 72.6 | 60.5 | 59.2 | 53.4 |
| Children's problems | 31.4 | 32.7 | 35.1 | 27.1 | 28.8 | 30.8 | 29.0 |
| Friction with spouse/partner | 26.3 | 21.9 | 29.5 | 29.6 | 22.1 | 25.6 | 25.8 |
| Lack of personal time | 74.1 | 68.7 | 75.9 | 79.7 | 68.0 | 75.1 | 75.7 |
| Keeping up with information technology | 52.7 | 57.6 | 53.6 | 45.2 | 57.0 | 50.6 | 84.5 |
| Job security | 32.6 | 9.2 | 23.4 | 56.3 | 52.8 | 56.4 | 40.5 |
| Being part of a dual career couple | 43.4 | 35.6 | 47.3 | 48.7 | 44.6 | 41.5 | 60.8 |
| Working with underprepared students | 61.1 | 56.1 | 63.2 | 63.2 | 62.8 | 65.9 | 74.6 |
| Classroom conflict | 19.4 | 15.4 | 19.3 | 22.8 | 19.6 | 24.5 | 17.4 |
| Self-imposed high expectations | 80.1 | 75.8 | 82.0 | 84.0 | 75.7 | 81.0 | 72.3 |
| Change in work responsibilities | 46.4 | 38.8 | 48.9 | 49.9 | 46.5 | 56.2 | 63.3 |
| **Personal goals noted as "very important" or "essential":** | | | | | | | |
| Becoming an authority in my field | 60.0 | 62.9 | 55.9 | 65.0 | 49.5 | 53.8 | 52.0 |
| Influencing the political structure | 19.0 | 19.4 | 18.6 | 19.9 | 20.3 | 15.0 | 9.8 |
| Influencing social values | 39.8 | 35.2 | 40.3 | 43.2 | 44.1 | 41.8 | 28.7 |
| Raising a family | 69.2 | 70.5 | 68.4 | 69.2 | 65.0 | 70.9 | 59.7 |
| Becoming very well off financially | 32.6 | 33.8 | 29.7 | 32.7 | 35.8 | 34.6 | 18.1 |
| Helping others who are in difficulty | 65.2 | 60.6 | 64.5 | 67.3 | 70.8 | 74.2 | 68.5 |
| Becoming involved in programs to clean up the environment | 35.1 | 33.4 | 34.3 | 36.0 | 38.2 | 38.1 | 35.8 |
| Developing a meaningful philosophy of life | 72.5 | 70.5 | 72.5 | 73.2 | 77.9 | 73.4 | 75.6 |
| Helping to promote racial understanding | 53.8 | 51.8 | 52.6 | 56.0 | 60.1 | 52.1 | 69.0 |
| Obtaining recognition from my colleagues for contributions to my special field | 47.5 | 47.7 | 46.0 | 53.8 | 39.8 | 36.2 | 39.3 |
| Integrating spirituality into my life | 47.5 | 42.9 | 45.8 | 49.3 | 52.7 | 60.8 | 42.7 |

133

| All Respondents | All Resp | Full Prof | Assoc Prof | Asst Prof | Lect | Inst | No Resp |
|---|---|---|---|---|---|---|---|
| **IN YOUR INTERACTIONS WITH UNDERGRAD-UATES, HOW OFTEN DO YOU ENCOURAGE THEM TO: [2]** | | | | | | | |
| **Ask questions in class** | | | | | | | |
| Frequently | 94.6 | 94.1 | 94.0 | 95.7 | 94.7 | 94.1 | 93.1 |
| Occasionally | 5.3 | 5.7 | 5.8 | 4.0 | 5.3 | 5.9 | 6.9 |
| Not at all | 0.2 | 0.2 | 0.2 | 0.3 | 0.0 | 0.0 | 0.0 |
| **Support their opinions with a logical argument** | | | | | | | |
| Frequently | 82.8 | 81.5 | 82.9 | 83.7 | 86.0 | 81.5 | 78.1 |
| Occasionally | 16.4 | 17.4 | 16.2 | 15.5 | 13.8 | 17.8 | 21.9 |
| Not at all | 0.9 | 1.1 | 0.9 | 0.8 | 0.2 | 0.7 | 0.0 |
| **Seek solutions to problems and explain them to others** | | | | | | | |
| Frequently | 74.7 | 71.5 | 74.2 | 75.9 | 80.0 | 80.6 | 68.9 |
| Occasionally | 23.6 | 26.4 | 24.0 | 22.5 | 19.4 | 18.5 | 31.1 |
| Not at all | 1.7 | 2.1 | 1.8 | 1.6 | 0.6 | 0.9 | 0.0 |
| **Revise their papers to improve their writing** | | | | | | | |
| Frequently | 58.8 | 57.8 | 59.0 | 58.9 | 60.5 | 59.8 | 78.1 |
| Occasionally | 32.7 | 33.2 | 33.1 | 33.1 | 29.1 | 32.2 | 16.4 |
| Not at all | 8.5 | 9.0 | 7.9 | 8.0 | 10.4 | 8.0 | 5.5 |
| **Evaluate the quality or reliability of information they receive** | | | | | | | |
| Frequently | 73.4 | 72.2 | 74.8 | 72.5 | 78.2 | 72.3 | 72.0 |
| Occasionally | 24.6 | 25.3 | 23.8 | 25.4 | 19.5 | 26.3 | 28.0 |
| Not at all | 2.0 | 2.4 | 1.4 | 2.1 | 2.3 | 1.4 | 0.0 |
| **Take risks for potential gains** | | | | | | | |
| Frequently | 37.4 | 35.5 | 37.5 | 37.4 | 43.9 | 38.3 | 50.3 |
| Occasionally | 48.4 | 49.4 | 48.2 | 47.9 | 44.5 | 50.9 | 48.6 |
| Not at all | 14.2 | 15.2 | 14.4 | 14.7 | 11.6 | 10.8 | 1.1 |
| **Seek alternative solutions to a problem** | | | | | | | |
| Frequently | 65.1 | 62.6 | 62.7 | 66.3 | 73.5 | 71.4 | 81.4 |
| Occasionally | 32.6 | 34.9 | 34.8 | 31.7 | 24.2 | 27.3 | 18.6 |
| Not at all | 2.2 | 2.4 | 2.5 | 2.0 | 2.3 | 1.4 | 0.0 |
| **Look up scientific research articles and resources** | | | | | | | |
| Frequently | 55.2 | 55.7 | 54.4 | 56.1 | 55.0 | 52.6 | 65.4 |
| Occasionally | 33.5 | 33.1 | 33.5 | 32.7 | 37.1 | 34.8 | 10.0 |
| Not at all | 11.3 | 11.2 | 12.0 | 11.2 | 7.9 | 12.6 | 24.6 |
| **Explore topics on their own, even though it was not required for a class** | | | | | | | |
| Frequently | 52.1 | 51.9 | 50.9 | 51.4 | 54.8 | 56.2 | 68.2 |
| Occasionally | 44.1 | 44.5 | 45.3 | 44.7 | 40.8 | 39.9 | 27.7 |
| Not at all | 3.8 | 3.7 | 3.8 | 3.9 | 4.4 | 3.9 | 4.1 |
| **Acknowledge failure as a necessary part of the learning process** | | | | | | | |
| Frequently | 49.5 | 45.3 | 48.1 | 51.2 | 57.1 | 57.7 | 67.7 |
| Occasionally | 43.7 | 46.7 | 44.9 | 42.3 | 38.4 | 37.6 | 26.1 |
| Not at all | 6.8 | 7.9 | 7.0 | 6.4 | 4.5 | 4.8 | 6.3 |
| **Seek feedback on their academic work** | | | | | | | |
| Frequently | 73.0 | 69.9 | 72.9 | 73.8 | 79.8 | 77.5 | 74.8 |
| Occasionally | 25.3 | 28.2 | 25.5 | 24.5 | 19.3 | 21.3 | 25.2 |
| Not at all | 1.7 | 1.9 | 1.6 | 1.8 | 0.9 | 1.3 | 0.0 |

[2]  This question asked for the first time in the 2007–2008 Faculty Survey.

**2007–2008 FACULTY SURVEY WEIGHTED NATIONAL NORMS**
**Full-time Undergraduate Faculty at Baccalaureate Institutions**

| All Respondents | All Resp | Full Prof | Assoc Prof | Asst Prof | Lect | Inst | No Resp |
|---|---|---|---|---|---|---|---|
| **Methods you use in "all" or "most" of the courses you teach:** | | | | | | | |
| Multiple-choice exams [2] | 33.1 | 27.3 | 31.8 | 36.9 | 35.6 | 45.7 | 24.0 |
| Essay exams [2] | 44.3 | 48.2 | 46.0 | 42.6 | 37.9 | 34.0 | 35.4 |
| Short-answer exams [2] | 45.5 | 44.3 | 47.1 | 47.2 | 42.1 | 41.4 | 33.1 |
| Quizzes | 39.8 | 35.7 | 38.4 | 42.6 | 44.5 | 47.5 | 34.8 |
| Weekly essay assignments | 21.7 | 20.4 | 19.6 | 22.2 | 28.1 | 25.5 | 42.1 |
| Student presentations | 46.7 | 43.6 | 47.2 | 49.4 | 46.2 | 49.2 | 52.0 |
| Term/research papers | 44.3 | 44.2 | 45.3 | 46.4 | 41.3 | 36.7 | 43.2 |
| Student evaluations of each others' work | 23.5 | 19.4 | 21.1 | 26.4 | 31.8 | 30.2 | 53.3 |
| Grading on a curve | 16.8 | 21.0 | 16.8 | 13.9 | 17.3 | 9.8 | 8.6 |
| Competency-based grading | 53.0 | 52.4 | 52.4 | 51.2 | 60.2 | 56.6 | 77.8 |
| Class discussions | 82.2 | 79.1 | 81.5 | 84.8 | 83.3 | 86.7 | 85.3 |
| Cooperative learning (small groups) | 59.1 | 49.6 | 58.0 | 66.3 | 67.1 | 69.2 | 66.4 |
| Experiential learning/Field studies | 30.0 | 26.8 | 28.6 | 33.5 | 29.6 | 35.8 | 30.4 |
| Teaching assistants | 11.8 | 14.9 | 9.8 | 10.7 | 13.5 | 7.7 | 13.1 |
| Recitals/Demonstrations | 21.9 | 21.7 | 20.3 | 21.9 | 27.1 | 23.2 | 21.4 |
| Group projects | 35.8 | 31.0 | 34.6 | 40.3 | 39.7 | 39.0 | 61.2 |
| Extensive lecturing | 46.4 | 51.8 | 45.2 | 43.3 | 44.6 | 41.6 | 22.2 |
| Multiple drafts of written work | 24.9 | 22.9 | 24.3 | 26.6 | 29.5 | 24.5 | 47.8 |
| Readings on racial and ethnic issues | 23.9 | 19.6 | 23.8 | 27.8 | 26.7 | 24.6 | 35.9 |
| Readings on women and gender issues | 21.1 | 17.7 | 22.5 | 23.8 | 22.0 | 20.3 | 27.3 |
| Student-developed activities (assignments, exams, etc.) | 26.7 | 25.4 | 24.3 | 27.6 | 30.1 | 33.8 | 43.0 |
| Student-selected topics for course content | 17.0 | 15.3 | 15.0 | 18.4 | 21.2 | 21.4 | 36.1 |
| Reflective writing/journaling | 21.7 | 16.8 | 19.4 | 25.3 | 26.8 | 31.0 | 62.3 |
| Community service as part of coursework | 8.1 | 6.0 | 7.9 | 9.5 | 9.3 | 11.5 | 5.0 |
| Electronic quizzes with immediate feedback in class [2] | 6.8 | 4.7 | 6.4 | 7.8 | 11.7 | 8.3 | 3.9 |
| Using real-life problems [2] | 55.7 | 49.6 | 53.4 | 61.0 | 60.3 | 65.9 | 51.7 |
| Using student inquiry to drive learning | 47.1 | 42.7 | 43.8 | 51.4 | 53.2 | 54.6 | 64.7 |

[2] This question asked for the first time in the 2007–2008 Faculty Survey.

135

| All Respondents | All Resp | Full Prof | Assoc Prof | Asst Prof | Lect | Inst | No Resp |
|---|---|---|---|---|---|---|---|
| **YOUR BASE INSTITUTIONAL SALARY** | | | | | | | |
| **9/10 month contract** | | | | | | | |
| Less than $20,000 | 2.0 | 2.3 | 2.1 | 1.4 | 2.1 | 2.1 | 0.0 |
| $20,000 to 29,999 | 0.7 | 0.1 | 0.0 | 0.0 | 2.7 | 6.9 | 0.0 |
| $30,000 to 39,999 | 4.8 | 0.3 | 0.8 | 3.0 | 25.8 | 30.8 | 0.0 |
| $40,000 to 49,999 | 14.5 | 1.3 | 6.6 | 28.0 | 31.4 | 37.7 | 32.6 |
| $50,000 to 59,999 | 22.1 | 5.3 | 26.4 | 39.1 | 17.9 | 16.9 | 32.6 |
| $60,000 to 69,999 | 16.8 | 12.2 | 28.7 | 14.5 | 11.3 | 4.2 | 0.0 |
| $70,000 to 79,999 | 12.5 | 18.2 | 17.1 | 6.2 | 4.1 | 0.3 | 15.7 |
| $80,000 to 89,999 | 8.9 | 17.0 | 9.8 | 2.5 | 1.0 | 0.5 | 0.0 |
| $90,000 to 99,999 | 6.8 | 15.1 | 4.3 | 2.6 | 1.2 | 0.6 | 19.1 |
| $100,000 to 124,999 | 8.1 | 20.3 | 3.6 | 1.9 | 2.5 | 0.1 | 0.0 |
| $125,000 to 149,999 | 1.7 | 4.6 | 0.4 | 0.4 | 0.0 | 0.0 | 0.0 |
| $150,000 or more | 1.2 | 3.3 | 0.3 | 0.2 | 0.0 | 0.0 | 0.0 |
| **11/12 month contract** | | | | | | | |
| Less than $20,000 | 2.6 | 2.9 | 2.3 | 1.9 | 2.4 | 4.5 | 0.0 |
| $20,000 to 29,999 | 0.6 | 0.2 | 0.2 | 0.1 | 1.9 | 2.3 | 0.0 |
| $30,000 to 39,999 | 4.3 | 0.3 | 0.2 | 2.0 | 9.6 | 25.7 | 2.2 |
| $40,000 to 49,999 | 14.1 | 1.0 | 5.5 | 22.6 | 31.5 | 32.3 | 24.6 |
| $50,000 to 59,999 | 18.3 | 3.1 | 17.0 | 33.8 | 27.8 | 16.5 | 37.0 |
| $60,000 to 69,999 | 15.3 | 7.7 | 23.2 | 20.4 | 10.5 | 11.6 | 18.0 |
| $70,000 to 79,999 | 10.0 | 10.6 | 16.6 | 7.5 | 5.2 | 4.5 | 18.3 |
| $80,000 to 89,999 | 10.6 | 16.0 | 14.4 | 7.1 | 4.8 | 1.7 | 0.0 |
| $90,000 to 99,999 | 7.1 | 14.3 | 7.5 | 2.3 | 4.6 | 0.1 | 0.0 |
| $100,000 to 124,999 | 10.9 | 25.2 | 11.5 | 1.9 | 1.6 | 0.5 | 0.0 |
| $125,000 to 149,999 | 3.2 | 9.4 | 1.0 | 0.4 | 0.2 | 0.0 | 0.0 |
| $150,000 or more | 2.9 | 9.2 | 0.6 | 0.1 | 0.0 | 0.2 | 0.0 |
| **Your base institutional salary is based on:** | | | | | | | |
| 9/10 months | 74.2 | 75.3 | 77.4 | 75.6 | 62.5 | 65.5 | 39.4 |
| 11/12 months | 25.8 | 24.7 | 22.6 | 24.4 | 37.5 | 34.5 | 60.6 |
| **WHAT PERCENTAGE OF YOUR CURRENT YEAR'S SALARY COMES FROM: [2]** | | | | | | | |
| **Income from this institution** | | | | | | | |
| All | 63.6 | 59.9 | 65.5 | 68.1 | 55.5 | 63.3 | 52.0 |
| 75 to 99 | 29.4 | 33.5 | 29.7 | 26.2 | 27.0 | 25.6 | 34.8 |
| 50 to 74 | 5.0 | 5.3 | 3.6 | 4.2 | 10.3 | 7.2 | 4.3 |
| 25 to 49 | 1.4 | 1.0 | 0.8 | 1.0 | 6.0 | 2.5 | 8.9 |
| 1 to 24 | 0.3 | 0.2 | 0.3 | 0.3 | 1.0 | 0.6 | 0.0 |
| None | 0.2 | 0.1 | 0.1 | 0.2 | 0.1 | 0.8 | 0.0 |
| **Other academic income** | | | | | | | |
| All | 0.1 | 0.0 | 0.0 | 0.0 | 0.0 | 0.5 | 0.0 |
| 75 to 99 | 0.1 | 0.1 | 0.0 | 0.1 | 0.1 | 0.0 | 0.0 |
| 50 to 74 | 0.5 | 0.3 | 0.3 | 0.5 | 1.8 | 0.4 | 0.0 |
| 25 to 49 | 1.9 | 2.4 | 1.8 | 1.5 | 2.5 | 1.4 | 0.0 |
| 1 to 24 | 16.0 | 19.1 | 16.1 | 13.8 | 15.5 | 10.9 | 8.0 |
| None | 81.5 | 78.1 | 81.7 | 84.1 | 80.1 | 86.7 | 92.0 |
| **Non-academic income** | | | | | | | |
| All | 0.2 | 0.0 | 0.2 | 0.2 | 0.1 | 0.3 | 0.0 |
| 75 to 99 | 0.4 | 0.2 | 0.4 | 0.2 | 1.0 | 1.0 | 0.0 |
| 50 to 74 | 1.8 | 1.1 | 1.0 | 1.3 | 6.7 | 3.7 | 9.4 |
| 25 to 49 | 4.4 | 4.5 | 3.1 | 3.8 | 7.5 | 7.6 | 12.1 |
| 1 to 24 | 20.6 | 23.8 | 20.1 | 18.0 | 20.6 | 18.5 | 26.4 |
| None | 72.7 | 70.3 | 75.2 | 76.4 | 64.1 | 68.9 | 52.2 |

[2] This question asked for the first time in the 2007–2008 Faculty Survey.

## 2007–2008 FACULTY SURVEY WEIGHTED NATIONAL NORMS
### Full-time Undergraduate Faculty at Baccalaureate Institutions

| All Respondents | All Resp | Full Prof | Assoc Prof | Asst Prof | Lect | Inst | No Resp |
|---|---|---|---|---|---|---|---|
| **What is your age as of 12/31/2007?** | | | | | | | |
| Less than 30 | 1.6 | 0.0 | 0.0 | 2.8 | 1.6 | 9.1 | 1.2 |
| 30 to 34 | 6.6 | 0.0 | 1.3 | 18.2 | 7.9 | 9.4 | 0.0 |
| 35 to 39 | 12.1 | 0.8 | 11.3 | 25.3 | 12.2 | 14.5 | 6.9 |
| 40 to 44 | 12.3 | 4.1 | 18.5 | 16.5 | 9.5 | 12.5 | 3.6 |
| 45 to 49 | 13.1 | 11.3 | 18.2 | 11.3 | 11.6 | 11.8 | 3.9 |
| 50 to 54 | 15.1 | 17.5 | 17.6 | 9.7 | 13.5 | 17.4 | 36.1 |
| 55 to 59 | 17.2 | 24.8 | 16.0 | 10.1 | 20.7 | 11.3 | 8.6 |
| 60 to 64 | 12.8 | 22.5 | 11.2 | 3.9 | 13.0 | 9.8 | 16.4 |
| 65 to 69 | 6.9 | 14.6 | 4.7 | 1.7 | 4.9 | 2.3 | 16.0 |
| 70 or more | 2.3 | 4.3 | 1.1 | 0.4 | 5.2 | 2.0 | 7.3 |
| **Year of highest degree now held** | | | | | | | |
| Before 1970 | 5.7 | 12.5 | 3.0 | 0.7 | 7.6 | 2.8 | 3.1 |
| 1971 to 1975 | 7.3 | 15.6 | 4.4 | 1.1 | 7.8 | 3.8 | 18.0 |
| 1976 to 1980 | 9.8 | 18.8 | 7.8 | 2.7 | 7.3 | 7.0 | 12.7 |
| 1981 to 1985 | 10.7 | 18.2 | 8.9 | 3.4 | 13.0 | 9.0 | 16.6 |
| 1986 to 1990 | 12.5 | 18.1 | 14.2 | 5.1 | 9.8 | 12.0 | 6.1 |
| 1991 to 1995 | 13.9 | 12.2 | 22.2 | 8.5 | 12.4 | 13.0 | 4.5 |
| 1996 to 2000 | 16.6 | 3.4 | 29.7 | 18.9 | 17.1 | 17.5 | 16.5 |
| 2001 to 2005 | 18.0 | 0.9 | 8.8 | 44.1 | 20.4 | 24.7 | 8.3 |
| 2006 to 2007 | 5.7 | 0.2 | 0.9 | 15.5 | 4.7 | 10.2 | 14.1 |
| **Year of appointment at current position** | | | | | | | |
| Before 1970 | 3.3 | 8.1 | 1.8 | 0.4 | 1.3 | 0.1 | 0.0 |
| 1971 to 1975 | 3.6 | 8.8 | 1.9 | 0.4 | 2.9 | 0.2 | 2.2 |
| 1976 to 1980 | 6.0 | 13.9 | 4.1 | 0.9 | 2.5 | 0.8 | 10.7 |
| 1981 to 1985 | 7.6 | 14.5 | 6.8 | 1.5 | 7.2 | 3.3 | 0.3 |
| 1986 to 1990 | 11.1 | 21.2 | 11.1 | 2.2 | 8.4 | 4.1 | 5.8 |
| 1991 to 1995 | 11.4 | 16.2 | 14.5 | 3.4 | 10.1 | 9.9 | 10.6 |
| 1996 to 2000 | 16.8 | 10.0 | 34.4 | 6.7 | 21.3 | 16.0 | 18.7 |
| 2001 to 2005 | 27.5 | 5.7 | 22.0 | 53.9 | 32.0 | 39.6 | 37.0 |
| 2006 to 2007 | 12.7 | 1.6 | 3.4 | 30.6 | 14.3 | 26.0 | 14.6 |
| **If tenured, year tenure was awarded** | | | | | | | |
| Before 1970 | 1.2 | 1.7 | 0.2 | 2.6 | 6.9 | 3.7 | 0.0 |
| 1971 to 1975 | 4.0 | 5.9 | 1.5 | 2.1 | 34.3 | 2.4 | 0.0 |
| 1976 to 1980 | 6.2 | 9.7 | 1.8 | 4.5 | 4.9 | 1.7 | 0.0 |
| 1981 to 1985 | 9.5 | 14.3 | 3.8 | 1.9 | 0.0 | 0.0 | 26.6 |
| 1986 to 1990 | 12.1 | 16.6 | 6.5 | 9.8 | 0.0 | 3.3 | 0.0 |
| 1991 to 1995 | 16.0 | 21.4 | 9.6 | 9.5 | 11.2 | 7.6 | 21.2 |
| 1996 to 2000 | 17.0 | 19.1 | 15.1 | 8.7 | 18.4 | 26.6 | 0.0 |
| 2001 to 2005 | 20.0 | 9.5 | 34.4 | 19.7 | 24.2 | 6.6 | 38.1 |
| 2006 to 2007 | 13.9 | 1.9 | 27.1 | 41.3 | 0.0 | 48.1 | 14.1 |

137

## 2007–2008 FACULTY SURVEY WEIGHTED NATIONAL NORMS
### Full-time Undergraduate Faculty at Baccalaureate Institutions

| All Respondents | All Resp | Full Prof | Assoc Prof | Asst Prof | Lect | Inst | No Resp |
|---|---|---|---|---|---|---|---|
| **WHAT IS THE MAJOR OF THE HIGHEST DEGREE YOU HOLD?** | | | | | | | |
| **Biological Science** | | | | | | | |
| Agriculture | 0.9 | 1.5 | 0.9 | 0.4 | 0.7 | 0.3 | 0.0 |
| Forestry | 0.2 | 0.1 | 0.2 | 0.4 | 0.0 | 0.1 | 0.0 |
| Bacteriology, Molecular Biology | 0.9 | 1.0 | 1.0 | 1.0 | 0.5 | 0.3 | 0.0 |
| Biochemistry | 0.8 | 0.8 | 0.9 | 1.0 | 0.7 | 0.4 | 0.0 |
| Biophysics | 0.1 | 0.0 | 0.1 | 0.1 | 0.0 | 0.0 | 0.0 |
| Botany | 0.6 | 1.1 | 0.6 | 0.4 | 0.1 | 0.4 | 0.0 |
| Environmental Science | 0.5 | 0.5 | 0.4 | 0.5 | 0.4 | 0.3 | 0.0 |
| Marine (life) Sciences | 0.2 | 0.2 | 0.2 | 0.1 | 0.1 | 0.3 | 0.0 |
| Physiology, Anatomy | 0.7 | 1.1 | 0.8 | 0.5 | 0.2 | 0.4 | 0.0 |
| Zoology | 1.1 | 1.9 | 1.0 | 0.6 | 0.3 | 0.6 | 0.0 |
| General, Other Biological Sciences | 1.9 | 2.2 | 1.9 | 1.5 | 2.4 | 1.4 | 0.0 |
| **Business** | | | | | | | |
| Accounting | 1.0 | 1.1 | 1.0 | 0.8 | 1.2 | 1.3 | 0.0 |
| Finance | 0.7 | 0.4 | 0.8 | 0.7 | 0.4 | 1.2 | 0.0 |
| International Business | 0.1 | 0.1 | 0.1 | 0.1 | 0.1 | 0.4 | 0.0 |
| Management | 2.2 | 1.3 | 2.0 | 2.9 | 3.9 | 2.9 | 0.0 |
| Marketing | 0.8 | 0.9 | 0.7 | 1.1 | 0.2 | 0.9 | 0.0 |
| Secretarial Studies | 0.0 | 0.0 | 0.0 | 0.0 | 0.0 | 0.0 | 0.0 |
| General, Other Business | 1.2 | 0.8 | 1.0 | 1.2 | 1.7 | 2.6 | 0.0 |
| **Education** | | | | | | | |
| Business Education | 0.2 | 0.2 | 0.3 | 0.1 | 0.3 | 0.5 | 0.0 |
| Educational Administration | 1.2 | 0.6 | 1.2 | 1.5 | 2.3 | 2.2 | 0.0 |
| Educational Psychology/Counseling | 1.0 | 0.6 | 0.9 | 1.3 | 1.8 | 0.6 | 12.6 |
| Elementary Education | 0.9 | 0.7 | 0.9 | 1.0 | 0.6 | 1.1 | 1.9 |
| Higher Education | 1.5 | 1.2 | 1.3 | 1.7 | 2.4 | 1.3 | 0.0 |
| Music or Art Education | 0.3 | 0.2 | 0.3 | 0.5 | 0.0 | 0.3 | 0.0 |
| Physical or Health Education | 1.5 | 1.4 | 1.2 | 1.0 | 2.1 | 3.6 | 0.0 |
| Secondary Education | 0.8 | 0.5 | 0.9 | 1.1 | 0.6 | 1.3 | 0.0 |
| Special Education | 0.9 | 0.5 | 0.9 | 1.6 | 0.0 | 1.4 | 0.0 |
| General, Other Education Fields | 2.9 | 2.0 | 3.0 | 4.0 | 2.0 | 2.9 | 10.8 |
| **Engineering** | | | | | | | |
| Aero-/Astronautical Engineering | 0.2 | 0.4 | 0.3 | 0.0 | 0.0 | 0.1 | 0.0 |
| Chemical Engineering | 0.3 | 0.5 | 0.3 | 0.3 | 0.1 | 0.0 | 0.0 |
| Civil Engineering | 0.7 | 1.0 | 0.8 | 0.6 | 0.3 | 0.1 | 0.0 |
| Electrical Engineering | 0.9 | 1.1 | 0.9 | 0.9 | 0.4 | 0.6 | 0.0 |
| Industrial Engineering | 0.2 | 0.3 | 0.3 | 0.2 | 0.0 | 0.2 | 0.0 |
| Mechanical Engineering | 1.0 | 1.1 | 1.3 | 0.9 | 0.5 | 0.4 | 0.0 |
| General, Other Engineering Fields | 1.0 | 1.4 | 0.9 | 0.8 | 0.6 | 0.6 | 0.0 |
| **Health** | | | | | | | |
| Dentistry | 0.3 | 0.1 | 0.8 | 0.2 | 0.0 | 0.1 | 0.0 |
| Health Technology | 0.0 | 0.0 | 0.0 | 0.1 | 0.0 | 0.2 | 0.0 |
| Medicine or Surgery | 0.2 | 0.3 | 0.1 | 0.2 | 0.0 | 0.1 | 0.0 |
| Nursing | 3.1 | 0.5 | 2.6 | 4.5 | 2.7 | 10.6 | 0.0 |
| Pharmacy, Pharmacology | 0.8 | 0.8 | 1.2 | 0.7 | 0.0 | 0.1 | 0.0 |
| Therapy (speech, physical, occup.) | 0.6 | 0.3 | 0.4 | 1.0 | 1.1 | 0.5 | 0.0 |
| Veterinary Medicine | 0.1 | 0.0 | 0.1 | 0.1 | 0.0 | 0.0 | 0.0 |
| General, Other Health Fields | 0.9 | 0.5 | 0.8 | 1.2 | 1.3 | 1.7 | 0.0 |

| All Respondents | All Resp | Full Prof | Assoc Prof | Asst Prof | Lect | Inst | No Resp |
|---|---|---|---|---|---|---|---|
| **WHAT IS THE MAJOR OF THE HIGHEST DEGREE YOU HOLD?** | | | | | | | |
| **Humanities** | | | | | | | |
| History | 4.1 | 4.4 | 4.9 | 3.9 | 2.6 | 2.4 | 1.9 |
| Political Science, Government | 2.4 | 2.9 | 2.7 | 2.6 | 0.9 | 0.7 | 0.0 |
| English Language & Literature | 6.8 | 6.5 | 5.9 | 6.2 | 10.0 | 10.3 | 17.4 |
| Foreign Languages & Literature | 1.2 | 1.1 | 1.2 | 1.5 | 0.9 | 1.4 | 0.0 |
| French | 0.7 | 0.7 | 0.7 | 0.4 | 2.6 | 0.2 | 0.9 |
| German | 0.4 | 0.5 | 0.6 | 0.3 | 0.2 | 0.1 | 0.0 |
| Spanish | 1.1 | 0.8 | 1.1 | 1.3 | 0.9 | 2.1 | 0.0 |
| Other Foreign Languages | 0.4 | 0.6 | 0.4 | 0.3 | 0.8 | 0.1 | 0.0 |
| Linguistics | 0.8 | 0.6 | 1.0 | 0.4 | 1.5 | 1.0 | 0.0 |
| Philosophy | 2.0 | 2.2 | 2.2 | 1.8 | 1.4 | 0.9 | 6.9 |
| Religion or Theology | 1.9 | 2.1 | 2.1 | 1.8 | 2.4 | 1.0 | 0.0 |
| General, Other Humanities Fields | 1.3 | 1.0 | 1.3 | 1.6 | 1.8 | 0.4 | 0.0 |
| **Fine Arts** | | | | | | | |
| Architecture/Urban Planning | 0.6 | 0.6 | 0.6 | 0.7 | 0.4 | 0.2 | 0.0 |
| Art | 1.9 | 2.1 | 2.0 | 1.5 | 3.0 | 1.2 | 0.0 |
| Dramatics or Speech | 1.6 | 1.9 | 1.5 | 1.4 | 1.9 | 1.4 | 5.8 |
| Music | 3.1 | 3.5 | 3.5 | 2.7 | 2.1 | 2.1 | 4.4 |
| Television or Film | 0.4 | 0.1 | 0.5 | 0.5 | 0.2 | 0.6 | 0.0 |
| Other Fine Arts | 1.1 | 0.9 | 0.9 | 1.1 | 1.8 | 2.4 | 0.0 |
| **Physical Science** | | | | | | | |
| Mathematics and/or Statistics | 4.8 | 5.7 | 4.3 | 3.7 | 5.8 | 5.4 | 0.0 |
| Astronomy | 0.2 | 0.3 | 0.3 | 0.2 | 0.2 | 0.1 | 0.0 |
| Atmospheric Sciences | 0.2 | 0.2 | 0.1 | 0.2 | 0.2 | 0.0 | 0.0 |
| Chemistry | 3.3 | 4.2 | 2.7 | 3.4 | 2.9 | 2.0 | 0.0 |
| Earth Sciences | 1.0 | 1.6 | 1.0 | 0.6 | 0.6 | 0.8 | 1.9 |
| Geography | 0.7 | 0.8 | 0.9 | 0.6 | 0.3 | 0.3 | 0.0 |
| Marine Sciences (incl. Oceanography) | 0.1 | 0.2 | 0.1 | 0.1 | 0.0 | 0.1 | 0.0 |
| Physics | 2.1 | 3.0 | 1.9 | 1.8 | 1.8 | 0.3 | 0.0 |
| General, Other Physical Sciences | 0.1 | 0.1 | 0.0 | 0.1 | 0.1 | 0.1 | 0.0 |
| **Social Science** | | | | | | | |
| Anthropology | 1.1 | 0.9 | 1.2 | 1.5 | 1.0 | 0.4 | 6.1 |
| Archaeology | 0.1 | 0.1 | 0.1 | 0.1 | 0.1 | 0.1 | 0.0 |
| Clinical Psychology | 1.1 | 0.8 | 1.1 | 1.3 | 2.2 | 0.6 | 0.0 |
| Counseling and Guidance | 0.3 | 0.3 | 0.4 | 0.1 | 1.0 | 0.4 | 0.0 |
| Experimental Psychology | 1.3 | 1.9 | 1.4 | 0.9 | 0.8 | 0.1 | 0.0 |
| Social Psychology | 0.9 | 0.9 | 1.0 | 0.7 | 0.7 | 1.4 | 0.0 |
| General, Other Psychology | 1.3 | 1.5 | 1.6 | 1.3 | 0.9 | 0.3 | 3.9 |
| Economics | 2.4 | 3.3 | 2.1 | 2.1 | 2.5 | 0.7 | 0.0 |
| Sociology | 2.4 | 2.7 | 2.3 | 2.9 | 1.5 | 0.5 | 0.0 |
| Social Work, Social Welfare | 0.7 | 0.6 | 0.7 | 1.0 | 0.4 | 0.8 | 0.0 |
| General, Other Social Sciences | 1.4 | 1.4 | 1.7 | 1.3 | 0.7 | 1.5 | 2.2 |

| All Respondents | All Resp | Full Prof | Assoc Prof | Asst Prof | Lect | Inst | No Resp |
|---|---|---|---|---|---|---|---|
| **WHAT IS THE MAJOR OF THE HIGHEST DEGREE YOU HOLD?** | | | | | | | |
| **Technical** | | | | | | | |
| Computer Science | 1.7 | 1.2 | 2.0 | 1.7 | 2.0 | 2.0 | 7.3 |
| Data Processing, Computer Prog. | 0.0 | 0.1 | 0.0 | 0.0 | 0.0 | 0.0 | 0.0 |
| Drafting/Design | 0.0 | 0.0 | 0.0 | 0.1 | 0.0 | 0.1 | 0.0 |
| Electronics | 0.0 | 0.0 | 0.0 | 0.0 | 0.0 | 0.3 | 0.0 |
| Industrial Arts | 0.1 | 0.2 | 0.1 | 0.1 | 0.0 | 0.1 | 0.0 |
| Mechanics | 0.0 | 0.0 | 0.0 | 0.0 | 0.0 | 0.0 | 0.0 |
| Other Technical | 0.2 | 0.1 | 0.2 | 0.3 | 0.5 | 0.2 | 0.0 |
| **Other Fields** | | | | | | | |
| Building Trades | 0.0 | 0.0 | 0.0 | 0.0 | 0.0 | 0.1 | 0.0 |
| Communications | 2.1 | 1.6 | 1.8 | 2.2 | 2.8 | 3.6 | 9.0 |
| Ethnic Studies | 0.0 | 0.0 | 0.0 | 0.0 | 0.0 | 0.1 | 0.0 |
| Human Ecology/Family Science | 0.4 | 0.4 | 0.8 | 0.3 | 0.0 | 0.1 | 0.0 |
| Journalism | 0.5 | 0.3 | 0.4 | 0.4 | 1.8 | 1.1 | 0.0 |
| Law | 0.8 | 0.9 | 0.8 | 0.8 | 1.0 | 0.6 | 0.0 |
| Law Enforcement | 0.1 | 0.1 | 0.0 | 0.1 | 0.3 | 0.3 | 0.0 |
| Library Science | 0.5 | 0.2 | 0.3 | 0.5 | 0.3 | 2.0 | 7.1 |
| Women's Studies | 0.0 | 0.0 | 0.0 | 0.0 | 0.0 | 0.0 | 0.0 |
| Other Vocational | 0.0 | 0.1 | 0.0 | 0.0 | 0.0 | 0.0 | 0.0 |
| All Other Fields | 0.8 | 0.7 | 0.7 | 0.9 | 0.5 | 0.8 | 0.0 |

## 2007–2008 FACULTY SURVEY WEIGHTED NATIONAL NORMS
### Full-time Undergraduate Faculty at Baccalaureate Institutions

| All Respondents | All Resp | Full Prof | Assoc Prof | Asst Prof | Lect | Inst | No Resp |
|---|---|---|---|---|---|---|---|
| **WHAT IS THE DEPARTMENT OF YOUR CURRENT FACULTY APPOINTMENT?** | | | | | | | |
| **Biological Science** | | | | | | | |
| Agriculture | 1.0 | 1.5 | 1.1 | 0.5 | 0.5 | 0.4 | 0.0 |
| Forestry | 0.1 | 0.1 | 0.1 | 0.1 | 0.0 | 0.0 | 0.0 |
| Bacteriology, Molecular Biology | 0.3 | 0.4 | 0.2 | 0.4 | 0.0 | 0.0 | 0.0 |
| Biochemistry | 0.2 | 0.3 | 0.2 | 0.1 | 0.7 | 0.0 | 0.0 |
| Biophysics | 0.0 | 0.0 | 0.1 | 0.0 | 0.0 | 0.0 | 0.0 |
| Botany | 0.2 | 0.3 | 0.2 | 0.2 | 0.0 | 0.3 | 0.0 |
| Environmental Science | 0.6 | 0.8 | 0.6 | 0.4 | 0.2 | 0.2 | 1.9 |
| Marine (life) Sciences | 0.1 | 0.1 | 0.0 | 0.1 | 0.0 | 0.0 | 0.0 |
| Physiology, Anatomy | 0.3 | 0.3 | 0.3 | 0.3 | 0.3 | 0.1 | 0.0 |
| Zoology | 0.4 | 0.8 | 0.2 | 0.3 | 0.0 | 0.0 | 0.0 |
| General, Other Biological Sciences | 4.5 | 5.8 | 4.4 | 3.6 | 3.8 | 3.1 | 0.0 |
| **Business** | | | | | | | |
| Accounting | 1.3 | 1.4 | 1.2 | 1.3 | 1.5 | 1.6 | 0.0 |
| Finance | 0.7 | 0.7 | 0.6 | 0.8 | 0.4 | 1.3 | 0.0 |
| International Business | 0.1 | 0.2 | 0.1 | 0.1 | 0.1 | 0.1 | 0.0 |
| Management | 2.4 | 1.7 | 2.3 | 2.8 | 4.0 | 2.5 | 0.0 |
| Marketing | 1.1 | 0.9 | 0.8 | 1.3 | 1.8 | 1.6 | 9.0 |
| Secretarial Studies | 0.0 | 0.0 | 0.0 | 0.0 | 0.0 | 0.0 | 0.0 |
| General, Other Business | 1.7 | 1.6 | 1.8 | 1.6 | 1.5 | 1.9 | 0.0 |
| **Education** | | | | | | | |
| Business Education | 0.0 | 0.1 | 0.0 | 0.0 | 0.0 | 0.1 | 0.0 |
| Educational Administration | 0.2 | 0.1 | 0.2 | 0.2 | 0.2 | 0.2 | 1.2 |
| Educational Psychology/Counseling | 0.4 | 0.5 | 0.3 | 0.5 | 0.0 | 0.0 | 0.0 |
| Elementary Education | 1.7 | 1.1 | 1.8 | 2.4 | 1.3 | 1.5 | 1.9 |
| Higher Education | 0.5 | 0.7 | 0.2 | 0.3 | 1.2 | 0.3 | 3.6 |
| Music or Art Education | 0.1 | 0.0 | 0.1 | 0.2 | 0.0 | 0.2 | 0.0 |
| Physical or Health Education | 2.0 | 1.7 | 1.8 | 1.6 | 2.4 | 4.5 | 0.0 |
| Secondary Education | 0.8 | 0.4 | 0.8 | 1.3 | 0.3 | 0.6 | 0.0 |
| Special Education | 0.5 | 0.2 | 0.6 | 1.0 | 0.2 | 0.5 | 0.0 |
| General, Other Education Fields | 2.0 | 1.5 | 1.8 | 2.4 | 0.6 | 4.5 | 12.6 |
| **Engineering** | | | | | | | |
| Aero-/Astronautical Engineering | 0.2 | 0.4 | 0.2 | 0.0 | 0.3 | 0.0 | 0.0 |
| Chemical Engineering | 0.3 | 0.4 | 0.3 | 0.2 | 0.0 | 0.0 | 0.0 |
| Civil Engineering | 0.7 | 1.1 | 0.8 | 0.5 | 0.3 | 0.0 | 0.0 |
| Electrical Engineering | 0.8 | 1.0 | 0.7 | 0.7 | 0.2 | 0.2 | 0.0 |
| Industrial Engineering | 0.1 | 0.2 | 0.2 | 0.0 | 0.2 | 0.0 | 0.0 |
| Mechanical Engineering | 1.0 | 1.2 | 1.4 | 0.8 | 0.5 | 0.2 | 0.0 |
| General, Other Engineering Fields | 1.0 | 1.3 | 1.0 | 1.1 | 0.9 | 0.4 | 0.0 |
| **Health** | | | | | | | |
| Dentistry | 0.3 | 0.2 | 0.9 | 0.3 | 0.0 | 0.0 | 0.0 |
| Health Technology | 0.1 | 0.0 | 0.0 | 0.2 | 0.0 | 0.3 | 0.0 |
| Medicine or Surgery | 0.3 | 0.3 | 0.1 | 0.6 | 0.0 | 0.1 | 0.0 |
| Nursing | 3.7 | 1.0 | 3.3 | 5.2 | 2.8 | 11.1 | 0.0 |
| Pharmacy, Pharmacology | 0.8 | 0.8 | 1.2 | 0.8 | 0.0 | 0.1 | 0.0 |
| Therapy (speech, physical, occup.) | 0.8 | 0.3 | 0.6 | 1.5 | 0.8 | 0.8 | 0.0 |
| Veterinary Medicine | 0.0 | 0.1 | 0.1 | 0.0 | 0.0 | 0.0 | 0.0 |
| General, Other Health Fields | 1.3 | 0.9 | 1.2 | 1.5 | 1.9 | 1.8 | 0.0 |

141

## 2007–2008 FACULTY SURVEY WEIGHTED NATIONAL NORMS
### Full-time Undergraduate Faculty at Baccalaureate Institutions

| All Respondents | All Resp | Full Prof | Assoc Prof | Asst Prof | Lect | Inst | No Resp |
|---|---|---|---|---|---|---|---|
| **WHAT IS THE DEPARTMENT OF YOUR CURRENT FACULTY APPOINTMENT?** | | | | | | | |
| **Humanities** | | | | | | | |
| History | 3.6 | 4.1 | 4.4 | 3.3 | 2.0 | 0.9 | 4.0 |
| Political Science, Government | 2.3 | 2.6 | 2.5 | 2.5 | 1.1 | 0.8 | 0.0 |
| English Language & Literature | 7.5 | 6.9 | 6.6 | 6.8 | 11.2 | 11.2 | 24.3 |
| Foreign Languages & Literature | 2.6 | 2.2 | 2.4 | 2.7 | 4.8 | 2.7 | 0.0 |
| French | 0.2 | 0.2 | 0.3 | 0.1 | 0.4 | 0.3 | 0.0 |
| German | 0.2 | 0.2 | 0.5 | 0.1 | 0.4 | 0.1 | 0.0 |
| Spanish | 0.7 | 0.5 | 0.6 | 0.8 | 1.0 | 1.3 | 0.0 |
| Other Foreign Languages | 0.4 | 0.4 | 0.3 | 0.1 | 1.9 | 0.6 | 0.0 |
| Linguistics | 0.2 | 0.1 | 0.4 | 0.2 | 0.0 | 0.2 | 0.0 |
| Philosophy | 1.8 | 2.1 | 1.9 | 1.7 | 0.9 | 0.7 | 0.0 |
| Religion or Theology | 1.9 | 2.2 | 2.3 | 1.7 | 0.9 | 0.8 | 2.7 |
| General, Other Humanities Fields | 1.6 | 1.5 | 1.6 | 1.6 | 1.5 | 2.1 | 6.9 |
| **Fine Arts** | | | | | | | |
| Architecture/Urban Planning | 0.7 | 0.7 | 0.8 | 0.8 | 0.2 | 0.2 | 0.0 |
| Art | 2.3 | 2.5 | 2.5 | 2.0 | 3.0 | 1.4 | 0.0 |
| Dramatics or Speech | 1.6 | 1.7 | 1.5 | 1.5 | 1.5 | 1.2 | 5.8 |
| Music | 3.2 | 3.7 | 3.5 | 2.8 | 2.2 | 2.0 | 4.4 |
| Television or Film | 0.4 | 0.3 | 0.4 | 0.3 | 0.3 | 0.3 | 0.0 |
| Other Fine Arts | 0.8 | 0.5 | 0.8 | 0.6 | 1.5 | 1.3 | 0.0 |
| **Physical Science** | | | | | | | |
| Mathematics and/or Statistics | 4.9 | 5.4 | 4.4 | 4.0 | 5.8 | 6.8 | 0.0 |
| Astronomy | 0.1 | 0.2 | 0.2 | 0.0 | 0.1 | 0.0 | 0.0 |
| Atmospheric Sciences | 0.1 | 0.1 | 0.0 | 0.1 | 0.0 | 0.0 | 0.0 |
| Chemistry | 3.4 | 4.3 | 2.7 | 3.6 | 3.4 | 2.2 | 0.0 |
| Earth Sciences | 1.0 | 1.5 | 1.1 | 0.6 | 0.5 | 0.7 | 0.0 |
| Geography | 0.7 | 0.9 | 0.7 | 0.7 | 0.3 | 0.2 | 0.0 |
| Marine Sciences (incl. Oceanography) | 0.1 | 0.1 | 0.0 | 0.1 | 0.0 | 0.0 | 0.0 |
| Physics | 2.1 | 2.8 | 1.7 | 2.0 | 1.6 | 1.0 | 0.0 |
| General, Other Physical Sciences | 0.4 | 0.3 | 0.5 | 0.4 | 0.2 | 0.3 | 0.0 |
| **Social Science** | | | | | | | |
| Anthropology | 0.8 | 0.7 | 1.1 | 1.0 | 0.7 | 0.2 | 0.0 |
| Archaeology | 0.0 | 0.0 | 0.0 | 0.0 | 0.0 | 0.0 | 0.0 |
| Clinical Psychology | 0.6 | 0.5 | 0.4 | 0.6 | 1.7 | 0.1 | 0.0 |
| Counseling and Guidance | 0.1 | 0.1 | 0.2 | 0.1 | 0.4 | 0.0 | 0.0 |
| Experimental Psychology | 0.8 | 1.0 | 0.7 | 0.5 | 0.3 | 1.4 | 0.0 |
| Social Psychology | 0.3 | 0.3 | 0.1 | 0.2 | 0.9 | 0.0 | 0.0 |
| General, Other Psychology | 2.5 | 2.7 | 3.0 | 2.5 | 1.9 | 0.5 | 3.9 |
| Economics | 1.9 | 2.7 | 1.6 | 1.6 | 2.2 | 0.5 | 0.0 |
| Sociology | 2.2 | 2.3 | 2.2 | 2.8 | 1.7 | 0.4 | 0.0 |
| Social Work, Social Welfare | 0.8 | 0.4 | 0.8 | 1.2 | 0.4 | 0.8 | 0.0 |
| General, Other Social Sciences | 2.1 | 2.0 | 2.2 | 2.0 | 1.5 | 2.5 | 0.0 |

142

## 2007–2008 FACULTY SURVEY WEIGHTED NATIONAL NORMS
### Full-time Undergraduate Faculty at Baccalaureate Institutions

| All Respondents | All Resp | Full Prof | Assoc Prof | Asst Prof | Lect | Inst | No Resp |
|---|---|---|---|---|---|---|---|
| **WHAT IS THE DEPARTMENT OF YOUR CURRENT FACULTY APPOINTMENT?** | | | | | | | |
| **Technical** | | | | | | | |
| Computer Science | 1.9 | 1.6 | 2.3 | 1.7 | 2.4 | 2.4 | 7.3 |
| Data Processing, Computer Prog. | 0.1 | 0.1 | 0.1 | 0.1 | 0.0 | 0.1 | 0.0 |
| Drafting/Design | 0.1 | 0.0 | 0.0 | 0.1 | 0.0 | 0.2 | 0.0 |
| Electronics | 0.1 | 0.1 | 0.1 | 0.1 | 0.0 | 0.0 | 0.0 |
| Industrial Arts | 0.1 | 0.1 | 0.1 | 0.0 | 0.2 | 0.1 | 0.0 |
| Mechanics | 0.0 | 0.0 | 0.0 | 0.0 | 0.0 | 0.0 | 0.0 |
| Other Technical | 0.5 | 0.4 | 0.6 | 0.5 | 0.8 | 0.9 | 0.0 |
| **Other Fields** | | | | | | | |
| Building Trades | 0.0 | 0.0 | 0.0 | 0.0 | 0.0 | 0.1 | 0.0 |
| Communications | 2.5 | 1.7 | 2.3 | 2.6 | 4.2 | 4.2 | 2.2 |
| Ethnic Studies | 0.2 | 0.1 | 0.1 | 0.3 | 0.9 | 0.0 | 0.0 |
| Human Ecology/Family Science | 0.4 | 0.3 | 0.7 | 0.4 | 0.3 | 0.1 | 0.0 |
| Journalism | 0.6 | 0.6 | 0.4 | 0.6 | 1.4 | 0.6 | 0.0 |
| Law | 0.2 | 0.2 | 0.1 | 0.2 | 0.2 | 0.1 | 0.0 |
| Law Enforcement | 0.2 | 0.2 | 0.0 | 0.2 | 0.1 | 0.3 | 0.0 |
| Library Science | 0.5 | 0.3 | 0.3 | 0.6 | 0.4 | 1.5 | 7.1 |
| Women's Studies | 0.1 | 0.1 | 0.2 | 0.2 | 0.2 | 0.0 | 0.0 |
| Other Vocational | 0.1 | 0.1 | 0.0 | 0.1 | 0.0 | 0.7 | 0.0 |
| All Other Fields | 1.4 | 1.1 | 1.6 | 1.2 | 1.7 | 2.1 | 1.2 |
| **HOW MANY CHILDREN DO YOU HAVE IN THE FOLLOWING AGE RANGES?** | | | | | | | |
| **Under 18 years old** | | | | | | | |
| None | 62.5 | 72.6 | 55.6 | 55.8 | 67.8 | 63.8 | 81.6 |
| One | 16.4 | 13.3 | 17.6 | 18.8 | 17.0 | 15.3 | 10.5 |
| Two | 15.1 | 10.4 | 19.1 | 18.0 | 10.1 | 15.3 | 7.9 |
| Three | 4.3 | 2.6 | 5.5 | 5.6 | 2.9 | 3.8 | 0.0 |
| Four or more | 1.7 | 1.1 | 2.2 | 1.8 | 2.1 | 1.7 | 0.0 |
| **18 years or older** | | | | | | | |
| None | 55.3 | 33.4 | 60.4 | 76.6 | 49.1 | 58.4 | 38.2 |
| One | 12.9 | 17.8 | 13.0 | 7.2 | 12.7 | 13.1 | 18.1 |
| Two | 19.2 | 28.3 | 16.0 | 10.6 | 25.6 | 16.8 | 34.1 |
| Three | 7.8 | 12.6 | 6.6 | 3.5 | 8.6 | 6.3 | 9.5 |
| Four or more | 4.8 | 7.8 | 4.0 | 2.1 | 4.0 | 5.4 | 0.0 |
| **How would you characterize your political views?** | | | | | | | |
| Far left | 8.8 | 8.0 | 10.1 | 10.0 | 7.4 | 4.6 | 10.5 |
| Liberal | 47.0 | 50.1 | 48.4 | 45.4 | 47.2 | 33.8 | 62.0 |
| Middle of the Road | 28.4 | 26.4 | 26.7 | 30.2 | 27.9 | 36.4 | 16.9 |
| Conservative | 15.2 | 14.9 | 14.0 | 13.8 | 16.4 | 24.7 | 10.5 |
| Far right | 0.7 | 0.6 | 0.8 | 0.5 | 1.0 | 0.6 | 0.0 |
| **Are you currently:** | | | | | | | |
| Single | 10.8 | 6.9 | 10.6 | 14.9 | 11.2 | 12.3 | 11.2 |
| Married | 76.8 | 82.4 | 77.2 | 72.2 | 72.0 | 73.6 | 75.1 |
| Unmarried, living with partner | 4.5 | 3.0 | 4.6 | 6.0 | 4.9 | 4.2 | 0.0 |
| Divorced | 5.8 | 5.2 | 6.2 | 5.4 | 7.0 | 7.4 | 13.7 |
| Widowed | 1.4 | 1.9 | 0.7 | 0.8 | 4.1 | 1.6 | 0.0 |
| Separated | 0.7 | 0.6 | 0.7 | 0.7 | 0.8 | 1.0 | 0.0 |

143

| All Respondents | All Resp | Full Prof | Assoc Prof | Asst Prof | Lect | Inst | No Resp |
|---|---|---|---|---|---|---|---|
| **Is English your native language?** | | | | | | | |
| Yes | 89.6 | 90.9 | 90.4 | 85.9 | 89.9 | 93.8 | 100.0 |
| No | 10.4 | 9.1 | 9.6 | 14.1 | 10.1 | 6.2 | 0.0 |
| **Are you: [5]** | | | | | | | |
| White/Caucasian | 88.6 | 91.6 | 88.0 | 85.0 | 88.3 | 91.4 | 100.0 |
| African American/Black | 2.8 | 1.6 | 3.4 | 3.6 | 2.3 | 3.0 | 0.0 |
| American Indian/Alaska Native | 1.7 | 1.6 | 1.7 | 1.7 | 1.8 | 2.4 | 0.0 |
| Asian American/Asian | 4.5 | 3.6 | 3.8 | 6.9 | 5.1 | 2.0 | 0.0 |
| Native Hawaiian/Pacific Islander | 0.3 | 0.1 | 0.3 | 0.3 | 0.5 | 0.4 | 0.0 |
| Mexican American/Chicano | 1.1 | 0.8 | 0.9 | 1.2 | 2.7 | 1.3 | 0.0 |
| Puerto Rican | 0.3 | 0.2 | 0.4 | 0.5 | 0.4 | 0.1 | 0.0 |
| Other Latino | 1.8 | 1.3 | 1.8 | 2.4 | 2.1 | 1.4 | 0.0 |
| Other | 2.6 | 2.1 | 3.0 | 2.9 | 3.3 | 1.5 | 0.0 |
| **Do you give the Higher Education Research Institute (HERI) permission to retain your contact information (i.e., your email address and name) for possible follow-up research?** | | | | | | | |
| Yes | 72.5 | 73.3 | 74.5 | 69.1 | 78.2 | 70.1 | 52.1 |
| No | 27.5 | 26.7 | 25.5 | 30.9 | 21.8 | 29.9 | 47.9 |

[4] Percentages will sum to more than 100.0 if any respondent marked more than one category.

# Full-Time Undergraduate Faculty, Rank and Control for

# Men

## 2007–2008 FACULTY SURVEY WEIGHTED NATIONAL NORMS
### Full-time Undergraduate Faculty at Baccalaureate Institutions

| Male Respondents | All Resp | Full Prof | Assoc Prof | Asst Prof | Lect | Inst | No Resp |
|---|---|---|---|---|---|---|---|
| **Number of Respondents** | 12,683 | 4,915 | 3,807 | 3,089 | 396 | 463 | 13 |
| **What is your principal activity in your current position at this institution?** | | | | | | | |
| Administration | 7.9 | 12.7 | 6.4 | 1.8 | 8.5 | 5.9 | 40.1 |
| Teaching | 81.4 | 76.4 | 84.0 | 84.7 | 86.1 | 86.8 | 59.9 |
| Research | 9.2 | 9.9 | 8.1 | 12.7 | 2.4 | 0.3 | 0.0 |
| Services to clients and patients | 0.7 | 0.4 | 1.0 | 0.2 | 1.2 | 3.5 | 0.0 |
| Other | 0.8 | 0.6 | 0.5 | 0.5 | 1.8 | 3.6 | 0.0 |
| **What is your present academic rank?** | | | | | | | |
| Professor | 39.5 | 100.0 | 0.0 | 0.0 | 0.0 | 0.0 | 0.0 |
| Associate Professor | 25.9 | 0.0 | 100.0 | 0.0 | 0.0 | 0.0 | 0.0 |
| Assistant Professor | 23.7 | 0.0 | 0.0 | 100.0 | 0.0 | 0.0 | 0.0 |
| Lecturer | 5.7 | 0.0 | 0.0 | 0.0 | 100.0 | 0.0 | 0.0 |
| Instructor | 5.2 | 0.0 | 0.0 | 0.0 | 0.0 | 100.0 | 0.0 |
| **What is your tenure status at this institution?** | | | | | | | |
| Tenured | 61.6 | 95.0 | 84.9 | 8.2 | 1.4 | 1.2 | 0.8 |
| On tenure track, but not tenured | 20.1 | 0.6 | 6.7 | 73.8 | 1.3 | 9.9 | 2.0 |
| Not on tenure track, but institution has tenure system | 15.0 | 1.6 | 5.1 | 14.2 | 94.5 | 82.7 | 97.2 |
| Institution has no tenure system | 3.4 | 2.8 | 3.3 | 3.8 | 2.8 | 6.2 | 0.0 |
| **Are you currently serving in an administrative position as: [1]** | | | | | | | |
| Department Chair | 12.5 | 19.6 | 13.8 | 3.6 | 2.1 | 4.1 | 0.0 |
| Dean (Associate or Assistant) | 1.8 | 3.3 | 1.8 | 0.2 | 0.1 | 0.1 | 3.1 |
| President | 0.0 | 0.1 | 0.0 | 0.0 | 0.0 | 0.0 | 3.0 |
| Vice-President | 0.2 | 0.2 | 0.3 | 0.0 | 0.1 | 0.2 | 0.0 |
| Provost | 0.1 | 0.2 | 0.0 | 0.0 | 0.0 | 0.0 | 0.0 |
| Other | 15.7 | 15.9 | 17.9 | 10.8 | 20.7 | 19.2 | 29.2 |
| Not Applicable | 63.1 | 55.8 | 60.4 | 73.7 | 73.6 | 72.1 | 45.4 |
| **My primary place of employment in the last year was: [2]** | | | | | | | |
| In higher education: | | | | | | | |
| at this institution | 95.0 | 98.6 | 97.9 | 88.2 | 89.7 | 90.7 | 81.7 |
| at a different institution | 2.5 | 0.6 | 1.2 | 7.0 | 2.3 | 2.4 | 0.0 |
| at more than one institution | 1.4 | 0.6 | 0.3 | 2.7 | 4.1 | 3.4 | 0.0 |
| Not in higher education | 0.9 | 0.1 | 0.5 | 1.3 | 3.8 | 3.2 | 18.3 |
| Not employed | 0.2 | 0.1 | 0.0 | 0.7 | 0.1 | 0.3 | 0.0 |
| **Noted as being personally "very important" or "essential": [2]** | | | | | | | |
| Research | 74.0 | 78.8 | 74.3 | 78.7 | 48.0 | 43.4 | 40.7 |
| Teaching | 97.6 | 97.4 | 98.1 | 96.9 | 98.4 | 98.8 | 100.0 |
| Service | 63.3 | 63.8 | 65.4 | 57.4 | 72.1 | 66.0 | 73.1 |

[1] Response options changed from earlier Faculty Surveys.
[2] This question asked for the first time in the 2007–2008 Faculty Survey.

147

| Male Respondents | All Resp | Full Prof | Assoc Prof | Asst Prof | Lect | Inst | No Resp |
|---|---|---|---|---|---|---|---|
| **Highest degree earned** | | | | | | | |
| Bachelor's (B.A., B.S., etc.) | 1.2 | 0.5 | 0.4 | 0.5 | 7.4 | 6.8 | 2.3 |
| Master's (M.A., M.S., M.F.A., M.B.A., etc.) | 14.9 | 5.2 | 10.2 | 14.6 | 49.6 | 75.7 | 3.5 |
| LL.B., J.D. | 1.0 | 0.6 | 0.9 | 1.1 | 3.8 | 1.7 | 0.0 |
| M.D., D.D.S. (or equivalent) | 0.7 | 0.6 | 1.5 | 0.3 | 0.0 | 0.1 | 0.0 |
| Other first professional degree beyond B.A. (e.g., D.D., D.V.M.) | 0.7 | 0.3 | 0.9 | 1.3 | 0.4 | 0.2 | 0.0 |
| Ed.D. | 2.5 | 2.7 | 3.1 | 2.3 | 1.0 | 0.1 | 19.4 |
| Ph.D. | 77.0 | 87.8 | 81.0 | 77.8 | 37.4 | 14.0 | 66.6 |
| Other degree | 1.7 | 1.9 | 1.7 | 2.0 | 0.0 | 1.2 | 8.2 |
| None | 0.3 | 0.4 | 0.3 | 0.0 | 0.4 | 0.2 | 0.0 |
| **Degree currently working on** | | | | | | | |
| Bachelor's (B.A., B.S., etc.) | 0.0 | 0.0 | 0.0 | 0.1 | 0.0 | 0.0 | 0.0 |
| Master's (M.A., M.S., M.F.A., M.B.A., etc.) | 0.8 | 0.4 | 0.5 | 0.7 | 1.9 | 5.3 | 4.4 |
| LL.B., J.D. | 0.1 | 0.0 | 0.1 | 0.1 | 0.7 | 0.0 | 0.0 |
| M.D., D.D.S. (or equivalent) | 0.0 | 0.0 | 0.0 | 0.0 | 0.0 | 0.0 | 0.0 |
| Other first professional degree beyond B.A. (e.g., D.D., D.V.M.) | 0.0 | 0.0 | 0.0 | 0.1 | 0.0 | 0.0 | 0.0 |
| Ed.D. | 0.8 | 0.1 | 0.3 | 0.6 | 3.1 | 6.4 | 0.0 |
| Ph.D. | 3.3 | 0.4 | 1.8 | 4.7 | 6.7 | 22.3 | 0.0 |
| Other degree | 0.4 | 0.2 | 0.2 | 0.5 | 0.4 | 2.2 | 0.0 |
| None | 94.6 | 98.9 | 97.1 | 93.3 | 87.2 | 63.9 | 95.6 |
| **During the past two years, have you engaged in any of the following activities?** | | | | | | | |
| Taught an honors course | 20.9 | 24.3 | 22.6 | 16.5 | 19.0 | 9.2 | 16.6 |
| Taught an interdisciplinary course | 40.9 | 42.0 | 42.6 | 41.0 | 37.5 | 26.7 | 39.5 |
| Taught an ethnic studies course | 8.8 | 7.7 | 9.5 | 10.1 | 10.9 | 5.0 | 0.0 |
| Taught a women's studies course | 2.6 | 2.8 | 2.6 | 2.7 | 2.7 | 0.9 | 0.0 |
| Team-taught a course | 31.1 | 32.8 | 33.9 | 27.4 | 30.1 | 22.9 | 25.1 |
| Taught a service learning course | 16.4 | 14.9 | 17.7 | 16.0 | 22.5 | 16.1 | 8.5 |
| Placed or collected assignments on the Internet | 72.0 | 69.1 | 73.1 | 76.9 | 68.9 | 69.1 | 90.5 |
| Taught a course exclusively on the Internet | 11.5 | 9.8 | 13.0 | 11.4 | 13.0 | 16.4 | 0.0 |
| Participated in a teaching enhancement workshop | 50.1 | 42.0 | 52.2 | 60.3 | 53.2 | 49.5 | 77.3 |
| Advised student groups involved in service/volunteer work | 39.2 | 35.0 | 42.0 | 41.9 | 39.2 | 43.8 | 53.3 |
| Collaborated with the local community in research/teaching | 43.1 | 40.7 | 46.5 | 44.7 | 44.2 | 36.5 | 19.7 |
| Developed a new course | 65.4 | 60.3 | 68.8 | 73.7 | 63.5 | 51.4 | 75.2 |
| Conducted research/writing focused on: | | | | | | | |
| International/global issues | 29.7 | 32.8 | 30.6 | 29.1 | 19.1 | 16.3 | 20.0 |
| Racial or ethnic minorities | 17.5 | 16.0 | 19.0 | 21.1 | 14.9 | 8.2 | 10.2 |
| Women and gender issues | 12.1 | 10.7 | 12.4 | 15.4 | 9.7 | 8.3 | 9.4 |
| Taught a seminar for first-year students | 22.6 | 22.7 | 22.4 | 21.8 | 20.7 | 27.2 | 52.0 |
| Engaged undergraduates on your research project [2] | 45.2 | 46.9 | 48.5 | 49.5 | 23.8 | 19.3 | 17.9 |
| Worked with undergraduates on a research project | 60.4 | 63.1 | 63.4 | 60.6 | 44.4 | 42.1 | 51.1 |

[2]  This question asked for the first time in the 2007–2008 Faculty Survey.

| Male Respondents | All Resp | Full Prof | Assoc Prof | Asst Prof | Lect | Inst | No Resp |
|---|---|---|---|---|---|---|---|
| **DURING THE PRESENT TERM, HOW MANY HOURS PER WEEK ON AVERAGE DO YOU ACTUALLY SPEND ON:** | | | | | | | |
| **Scheduled teaching (actual, not credit hours)** | | | | | | | |
| None | 0.6 | 0.6 | 0.4 | 0.7 | 0.0 | 1.9 | 2.0 |
| 1 to 4 | 14.5 | 18.4 | 12.8 | 11.8 | 11.2 | 9.7 | 7.5 |
| 5 to 8 | 32.0 | 36.3 | 31.8 | 31.3 | 19.2 | 17.4 | 59.0 |
| 9 to 12 | 35.0 | 30.5 | 37.0 | 36.5 | 46.7 | 39.4 | 31.5 |
| 13 to 16 | 11.1 | 9.0 | 11.2 | 12.0 | 15.4 | 17.8 | 0.0 |
| 17 to 20 | 4.4 | 3.3 | 4.6 | 5.1 | 3.6 | 9.4 | 0.0 |
| 21 to 34 | 2.0 | 1.6 | 2.0 | 2.1 | 2.2 | 4.1 | 0.0 |
| 35 to 44 | 0.3 | 0.2 | 0.2 | 0.5 | 1.3 | 0.2 | 0.0 |
| 45 + | 0.1 | 0.2 | 0.0 | 0.1 | 0.4 | 0.0 | 0.0 |
| **Preparing for teaching (including reading student papers and grading)** | | | | | | | |
| None | 0.3 | 0.4 | 0.2 | 0.4 | 0.0 | 0.1 | 2.0 |
| 1 to 4 | 11.9 | 15.1 | 11.2 | 7.9 | 11.5 | 9.6 | 0.0 |
| 5 to 8 | 25.1 | 28.1 | 25.0 | 21.9 | 22.1 | 21.2 | 27.2 |
| 9 to 12 | 25.3 | 25.5 | 25.9 | 25.7 | 19.2 | 26.1 | 10.2 |
| 13 to 16 | 15.6 | 14.1 | 15.8 | 17.4 | 17.2 | 15.9 | 36.2 |
| 17 to 20 | 12.3 | 9.8 | 13.2 | 14.3 | 14.4 | 15.2 | 22.7 |
| 21 to 34 | 7.3 | 5.6 | 7.3 | 9.0 | 10.7 | 9.1 | 1.7 |
| 35 to 44 | 1.7 | 1.0 | 1.4 | 2.6 | 4.1 | 1.6 | 0.0 |
| 45 + | 0.5 | 0.4 | 0.1 | 0.9 | 0.7 | 1.2 | 0.0 |
| **Advising and counseling of students** | | | | | | | |
| None | 4.1 | 3.2 | 3.0 | 4.5 | 11.8 | 7.0 | 0.0 |
| 1 to 4 | 58.6 | 59.0 | 58.3 | 59.6 | 58.7 | 53.3 | 34.1 |
| 5 to 8 | 26.4 | 27.4 | 27.1 | 26.5 | 16.3 | 25.7 | 42.9 |
| 9 to 12 | 7.6 | 7.7 | 8.0 | 6.7 | 7.2 | 9.5 | 4.4 |
| 13 to 16 | 1.9 | 1.8 | 2.0 | 1.4 | 3.1 | 2.4 | 15.5 |
| 17 to 20 | 0.9 | 0.6 | 1.1 | 0.7 | 2.7 | 0.5 | 0.0 |
| 21 to 34 | 0.4 | 0.3 | 0.4 | 0.5 | 0.0 | 1.2 | 0.0 |
| 35 to 44 | 0.1 | 0.0 | 0.0 | 0.2 | 0.0 | 0.1 | 3.0 |
| 45 + | 0.0 | 0.0 | 0.1 | 0.0 | 0.2 | 0.2 | 0.0 |
| **Committee work and meetings** | | | | | | | |
| None | 5.7 | 2.8 | 2.8 | 5.4 | 25.5 | 22.1 | 0.0 |
| 1 to 4 | 58.5 | 54.2 | 56.4 | 67.0 | 56.7 | 63.1 | 92.5 |
| 5 to 8 | 25.4 | 29.2 | 29.5 | 20.6 | 13.9 | 10.7 | 4.4 |
| 9 to 12 | 7.0 | 9.1 | 8.1 | 4.5 | 2.2 | 2.6 | 0.0 |
| 13 to 16 | 2.1 | 2.5 | 2.2 | 1.9 | 0.8 | 0.6 | 0.0 |
| 17 to 20 | 0.9 | 1.6 | 0.7 | 0.3 | 0.6 | 0.5 | 0.0 |
| 21 to 34 | 0.3 | 0.4 | 0.3 | 0.3 | 0.3 | 0.1 | 0.0 |
| 35 to 44 | 0.1 | 0.2 | 0.0 | 0.1 | 0.0 | 0.2 | 3.0 |
| 45 + | 0.0 | 0.0 | 0.1 | 0.0 | 0.0 | 0.0 | 0.0 |
| **Other administration** | | | | | | | |
| None | 30.4 | 28.0 | 25.9 | 34.5 | 43.3 | 37.6 | 45.4 |
| 1 to 4 | 39.2 | 34.7 | 42.4 | 44.7 | 33.7 | 39.8 | 17.6 |
| 5 to 8 | 14.0 | 15.7 | 15.0 | 12.3 | 9.8 | 9.3 | 0.0 |
| 9 to 12 | 6.9 | 8.5 | 7.9 | 4.1 | 5.7 | 4.2 | 7.5 |
| 13 to 16 | 3.4 | 4.4 | 3.6 | 1.9 | 3.4 | 1.2 | 0.0 |
| 17 to 20 | 3.0 | 4.6 | 2.5 | 1.2 | 2.1 | 3.0 | 0.0 |
| 21 to 34 | 2.2 | 3.1 | 2.2 | 0.6 | 1.5 | 3.2 | 22.7 |
| 35 to 44 | 0.7 | 0.9 | 0.3 | 0.6 | 0.3 | 1.0 | 3.7 |
| 45 + | 0.2 | 0.2 | 0.1 | 0.1 | 0.2 | 0.8 | 3.0 |

| Male Respondents | All Resp | Full Prof | Assoc Prof | Asst Prof | Lect | Inst | No Resp |
|---|---|---|---|---|---|---|---|
| **DURING THE PRESENT TERM, HOW MANY HOURS PER WEEK ON AVERAGE DO YOU ACTUALLY SPEND ON:** | | | | | | | |
| **Research and scholarly writing** | | | | | | | |
| None | 13.2 | 8.7 | 11.6 | 9.4 | 37.7 | 45.6 | 28.1 |
| 1 to 4 | 29.3 | 27.9 | 31.1 | 27.4 | 37.9 | 29.8 | 43.6 |
| 5 to 8 | 20.8 | 21.1 | 22.9 | 22.1 | 14.2 | 10.4 | 23.3 |
| 9 to 12 | 13.5 | 14.9 | 14.8 | 13.1 | 4.5 | 7.7 | 5.1 |
| 13 to 16 | 7.5 | 7.9 | 7.1 | 9.7 | 2.4 | 2.9 | 0.0 |
| 17 to 20 | 7.4 | 9.3 | 6.2 | 8.2 | 2.4 | 1.4 | 0.0 |
| 21 to 34 | 5.3 | 6.6 | 4.4 | 6.4 | 0.8 | 0.6 | 0.0 |
| 35 to 44 | 1.9 | 2.4 | 1.4 | 2.3 | 0.0 | 0.8 | 0.0 |
| 45 + | 1.0 | 1.2 | 0.4 | 1.5 | 0.2 | 0.8 | 0.0 |
| **Other creative products/performances** | | | | | | | |
| None | 50.4 | 54.0 | 52.1 | 48.5 | 42.6 | 32.7 | 18.1 |
| 1 to 4 | 29.2 | 25.8 | 29.8 | 33.2 | 27.8 | 35.3 | 34.1 |
| 5 to 8 | 11.0 | 11.5 | 10.3 | 9.5 | 14.5 | 12.6 | 22.7 |
| 9 to 12 | 4.5 | 4.2 | 3.8 | 4.6 | 5.4 | 9.2 | 0.0 |
| 13 to 16 | 1.9 | 1.8 | 1.5 | 1.8 | 3.3 | 2.6 | 0.0 |
| 17 to 20 | 1.8 | 1.6 | 1.4 | 1.5 | 2.0 | 5.8 | 7.2 |
| 21 to 34 | 0.7 | 0.5 | 0.8 | 0.7 | 1.2 | 1.8 | 14.8 |
| 35 to 44 | 0.3 | 0.2 | 0.1 | 0.0 | 3.1 | 0.0 | 0.0 |
| 45 + | 0.3 | 0.4 | 0.2 | 0.2 | 0.1 | 0.0 | 3.0 |
| **Consultation with clients/patients** | | | | | | | |
| None | 81.7 | 82.7 | 81.9 | 83.3 | 75.4 | 72.0 | 82.5 |
| 1 to 4 | 12.3 | 11.7 | 11.9 | 12.2 | 14.7 | 16.9 | 14.8 |
| 5 to 8 | 3.5 | 3.7 | 4.1 | 2.6 | 2.2 | 4.8 | 2.0 |
| 9 to 12 | 1.0 | 0.9 | 1.1 | 0.8 | 0.7 | 2.1 | 0.7 |
| 13 to 16 | 0.6 | 0.7 | 0.2 | 0.5 | 1.1 | 0.9 | 0.0 |
| 17 to 20 | 0.5 | 0.1 | 0.4 | 0.3 | 4.7 | 0.8 | 0.0 |
| 21 to 34 | 0.3 | 0.2 | 0.1 | 0.1 | 1.0 | 2.4 | 0.0 |
| 35 to 44 | 0.1 | 0.0 | 0.2 | 0.1 | 0.0 | 0.1 | 0.0 |
| 45 + | 0.1 | 0.1 | 0.0 | 0.1 | 0.2 | 0.0 | 0.0 |
| **Community or public service** | | | | | | | |
| None | 40.0 | 39.1 | 36.8 | 46.6 | 35.0 | 36.5 | 84.0 |
| 1 to 4 | 47.0 | 46.8 | 49.8 | 42.5 | 50.0 | 53.6 | 9.9 |
| 5 to 8 | 9.5 | 10.2 | 9.4 | 8.9 | 9.4 | 7.9 | 3.1 |
| 9 to 12 | 2.3 | 2.6 | 3.0 | 1.5 | 2.2 | 1.4 | 3.0 |
| 13 to 16 | 0.6 | 0.8 | 0.6 | 0.3 | 1.3 | 0.6 | 0.0 |
| 17 to 20 | 0.3 | 0.4 | 0.4 | 0.1 | 0.0 | 0.0 | 0.0 |
| 21 to 34 | 0.1 | 0.1 | 0.1 | 0.0 | 0.0 | 0.0 | 0.0 |
| 35 to 44 | 0.1 | 0.0 | 0.0 | 0.1 | 1.9 | 0.0 | 0.0 |
| 45 + | 0.0 | 0.0 | 0.0 | 0.0 | 0.2 | 0.0 | 0.0 |
| **Outside consulting/freelance work** | | | | | | | |
| None | 66.1 | 63.7 | 66.0 | 71.2 | 60.0 | 67.5 | 79.0 |
| 1 to 4 | 24.9 | 26.5 | 26.2 | 21.3 | 25.4 | 22.0 | 3.1 |
| 5 to 8 | 6.3 | 7.2 | 5.5 | 4.9 | 10.2 | 5.2 | 0.0 |
| 9 to 12 | 1.7 | 1.6 | 1.5 | 1.8 | 1.8 | 2.6 | 0.0 |
| 13 to 16 | 0.5 | 0.5 | 0.3 | 0.6 | 0.8 | 0.7 | 0.0 |
| 17 to 20 | 0.3 | 0.2 | 0.4 | 0.1 | 0.5 | 1.3 | 14.8 |
| 21 to 34 | 0.1 | 0.1 | 0.0 | 0.0 | 0.4 | 0.8 | 0.0 |
| 35 to 44 | 0.1 | 0.0 | 0.0 | 0.1 | 0.7 | 0.1 | 0.0 |
| 45 + | 0.1 | 0.1 | 0.0 | 0.0 | 0.2 | 0.0 | 3.0 |

| Male Respondents | All Resp | Full Prof | Assoc Prof | Asst Prof | Lect | Inst | No Resp |
|---|---|---|---|---|---|---|---|
| **DURING THE PRESENT TERM, HOW MANY HOURS PER WEEK ON AVERAGE DO YOU ACTUALLY SPEND ON:** | | | | | | | |
| **Household/childcare duties** | | | | | | | |
| None | 16.6 | 19.9 | 14.4 | 12.9 | 20.4 | 15.2 | 7.7 |
| 1 to 4 | 19.3 | 21.0 | 17.6 | 18.2 | 21.8 | 18.2 | 7.2 |
| 5 to 8 | 25.4 | 27.8 | 22.5 | 23.1 | 24.6 | 31.9 | 52.0 |
| 9 to 12 | 15.6 | 14.3 | 17.4 | 16.9 | 15.9 | 11.6 | 0.0 |
| 13 to 16 | 8.1 | 6.7 | 10.1 | 9.0 | 6.2 | 5.6 | 24.4 |
| 17 to 20 | 7.1 | 6.0 | 8.2 | 8.2 | 5.1 | 7.5 | 5.7 |
| 21 to 34 | 4.4 | 2.7 | 5.6 | 6.5 | 2.7 | 3.7 | 0.0 |
| 35 to 44 | 1.7 | 0.9 | 2.2 | 2.4 | 2.2 | 2.0 | 0.0 |
| 45 + | 1.8 | 0.8 | 2.1 | 2.8 | 1.1 | 4.3 | 3.0 |
| **Communicating via email** | | | | | | | |
| None | 0.6 | 0.2 | 0.7 | 0.5 | 2.3 | 0.4 | 0.0 |
| 1 to 4 | 33.3 | 29.6 | 32.3 | 37.5 | 34.8 | 46.0 | 32.1 |
| 5 to 8 | 40.5 | 41.6 | 41.2 | 39.7 | 37.9 | 34.9 | 18.1 |
| 9 to 12 | 16.1 | 17.5 | 17.2 | 13.3 | 15.6 | 11.6 | 44.7 |
| 13 to 16 | 5.6 | 6.6 | 5.1 | 4.8 | 5.3 | 3.9 | 0.0 |
| 17 to 20 | 2.5 | 3.1 | 2.2 | 2.0 | 2.9 | 1.7 | 2.0 |
| 21 to 34 | 1.1 | 1.0 | 1.0 | 1.6 | 0.8 | 0.9 | 0.0 |
| 35 to 44 | 0.2 | 0.2 | 0.2 | 0.3 | 0.0 | 0.1 | 0.0 |
| 45 + | 0.2 | 0.1 | 0.1 | 0.2 | 0.4 | 0.4 | 3.0 |
| **Commuting to campus [2]** | | | | | | | |
| None | 6.4 | 6.2 | 5.2 | 8.1 | 9.3 | 4.1 | 0.0 |
| 1 to 4 | 63.8 | 66.9 | 63.0 | 62.5 | 57.4 | 59.6 | 25.0 |
| 5 to 8 | 21.6 | 20.2 | 22.6 | 21.1 | 24.9 | 25.0 | 35.2 |
| 9 to 12 | 7.0 | 5.8 | 7.6 | 7.2 | 7.6 | 10.2 | 39.8 |
| 13 to 16 | 0.9 | 0.7 | 1.3 | 0.7 | 0.6 | 0.5 | 0.0 |
| 17 to 20 | 0.2 | 0.1 | 0.3 | 0.2 | 0.0 | 0.3 | 0.0 |
| 21 to 34 | 0.1 | 0.1 | 0.1 | 0.0 | 0.0 | 0.0 | 0.0 |
| 35 to 44 | 0.0 | 0.0 | 0.0 | 0.0 | 0.0 | 0.0 | 0.0 |
| 45 + | 0.1 | 0.0 | 0.0 | 0.1 | 0.2 | 0.2 | 0.0 |
| **Other employment, outside of academia [2]** | | | | | | | |
| None | 87.2 | 88.4 | 89.3 | 88.3 | 74.9 | 76.6 | 78.0 |
| 1 to 4 | 6.9 | 6.4 | 6.3 | 6.0 | 12.2 | 11.6 | 0.0 |
| 5 to 8 | 2.7 | 2.9 | 2.4 | 2.3 | 5.3 | 3.1 | 0.0 |
| 9 to 12 | 1.5 | 1.3 | 0.8 | 2.1 | 2.1 | 3.5 | 0.0 |
| 13 to 16 | 0.7 | 0.4 | 0.5 | 0.8 | 1.9 | 1.1 | 0.0 |
| 17 to 20 | 0.5 | 0.5 | 0.2 | 0.3 | 1.3 | 1.5 | 22.0 |
| 21 to 34 | 0.2 | 0.1 | 0.2 | 0.1 | 1.0 | 1.4 | 0.0 |
| 35 to 44 | 0.2 | 0.0 | 0.3 | 0.1 | 1.4 | 0.8 | 0.0 |
| 45 + | 0.1 | 0.0 | 0.0 | 0.1 | 0.0 | 0.5 | 0.0 |

[2] This question asked for the first time in the 2007–2008 Faculty Survey.

| Male Respondents | All Resp | Full Prof | Assoc Prof | Asst Prof | Lect | Inst | No Resp |
|---|---|---|---|---|---|---|---|
| **Including all institutions at which you teach, how many undergraduate courses are you teaching this term? [2]** | | | | | | | |
| None | 0.0 | 0.0 | 0.0 | 0.0 | 0.0 | 0.0 | 0.0 |
| One | 22.7 | 30.3 | 20.7 | 16.7 | 15.2 | 11.3 | 6.8 |
| Two | 29.5 | 31.7 | 31.5 | 27.5 | 22.3 | 18.7 | 52.3 |
| Three | 24.9 | 22.5 | 24.4 | 29.4 | 26.1 | 23.6 | 40.9 |
| Four | 14.5 | 10.1 | 15.6 | 16.2 | 22.6 | 26.0 | 0.0 |
| Five | 5.2 | 3.4 | 4.7 | 6.0 | 9.7 | 12.3 | 0.0 |
| Six or more | 3.2 | 1.9 | 3.1 | 4.2 | 4.2 | 8.1 | 0.0 |
| **FOR UP TO FOUR OF THE UNDERGRADUATE COURSES MENTIONED ABOVE, HOW MANY STUDENTS ARE ENROLLED IN: [2]** | | | | | | | |
| **Course #1** | | | | | | | |
| 10 or fewer | 12.2 | 11.0 | 12.7 | 13.1 | 9.8 | 17.3 | 36.7 |
| 11 to 20 | 25.8 | 26.0 | 25.1 | 26.1 | 26.0 | 26.6 | 32.1 |
| 21 to 30 | 25.5 | 24.8 | 26.4 | 26.1 | 22.7 | 27.9 | 15.6 |
| 31 to 50 | 21.4 | 21.4 | 19.9 | 23.3 | 21.7 | 19.4 | 15.7 |
| 51 to 100 | 9.4 | 10.6 | 9.9 | 7.6 | 11.0 | 4.8 | 0.0 |
| More than 100 | 5.6 | 6.1 | 5.9 | 3.8 | 8.9 | 4.0 | 0.0 |
| **Course #2** | | | | | | | |
| 10 or fewer | 17.0 | 19.4 | 17.6 | 15.4 | 8.8 | 15.4 | 42.9 |
| 11 to 20 | 30.4 | 30.0 | 30.1 | 32.1 | 22.7 | 34.2 | 40.3 |
| 21 to 30 | 26.6 | 23.9 | 27.6 | 28.5 | 29.6 | 27.2 | 0.0 |
| 31 to 50 | 18.3 | 18.8 | 17.0 | 17.9 | 22.4 | 18.3 | 16.8 |
| 51 to 100 | 5.2 | 5.1 | 5.8 | 4.3 | 9.7 | 3.1 | 0.0 |
| More than 100 | 2.5 | 2.7 | 1.9 | 1.8 | 6.9 | 1.9 | 0.0 |
| **Course #3** | | | | | | | |
| 10 or fewer | 24.9 | 29.0 | 26.3 | 24.7 | 13.8 | 15.5 | 0.0 |
| 11 to 20 | 32.4 | 33.8 | 32.9 | 32.7 | 29.3 | 27.0 | 73.4 |
| 21 to 30 | 24.7 | 20.5 | 26.5 | 24.9 | 21.8 | 37.8 | 0.0 |
| 31 to 50 | 14.0 | 12.2 | 11.0 | 14.5 | 26.4 | 17.4 | 26.6 |
| 51 to 100 | 2.8 | 2.7 | 2.1 | 2.7 | 7.0 | 1.8 | 0.0 |
| More than 100 | 1.2 | 1.9 | 1.3 | 0.6 | 1.7 | 0.5 | 0.0 |
| **Course #4** | | | | | | | |
| 10 or fewer | 33.3 | 37.8 | 38.7 | 31.6 | 22.1 | 22.8 | 0.0 |
| 11 to 20 | 30.9 | 34.4 | 29.5 | 34.4 | 17.5 | 28.7 | 0.0 |
| 21 to 30 | 21.7 | 15.3 | 20.8 | 22.5 | 25.5 | 34.5 | 0.0 |
| 31 to 50 | 11.2 | 9.5 | 8.0 | 9.5 | 27.7 | 13.1 | 0.0 |
| 51 to 100 | 2.0 | 1.1 | 1.9 | 1.7 | 6.6 | 0.8 | 0.0 |
| More than 100 | 0.9 | 2.0 | 1.1 | 0.2 | 0.6 | 0.0 | 0.0 |

[2]  This question asked for the first time in the 2007–2008 Faculty Survey.

| Male Respondents | All Resp | Full Prof | Assoc Prof | Asst Prof | Lect | Inst | No Resp |
|---|---|---|---|---|---|---|---|
| **HOW MANY OF THE FOLLOWING COURSES ARE YOU TEACHING THIS ACADEMIC YEAR?** | | | | | | | |
| **General education courses** | | | | | | | |
| None | 56.0 | 60.1 | 55.1 | 54.0 | 46.9 | 47.0 | 88.6 |
| One | 18.1 | 18.6 | 18.6 | 17.9 | 12.9 | 18.3 | 2.4 |
| Two | 12.5 | 11.4 | 13.6 | 12.9 | 10.6 | 15.1 | 5.8 |
| Three | 6.0 | 4.9 | 5.9 | 6.6 | 12.9 | 5.2 | 3.2 |
| Four | 3.5 | 2.7 | 3.6 | 3.6 | 7.6 | 4.2 | 0.0 |
| Five or more | 3.9 | 2.2 | 3.2 | 5.0 | 9.1 | 10.2 | 0.0 |
| **Developmental/remedial courses** | | | | | | | |
| None | 95.1 | 96.8 | 96.1 | 93.8 | 91.5 | 86.8 | 76.5 |
| One | 2.8 | 1.7 | 2.4 | 4.1 | 3.5 | 5.6 | 0.0 |
| Two | 1.2 | 0.8 | 0.8 | 0.9 | 3.6 | 4.6 | 0.0 |
| Three | 0.4 | 0.3 | 0.3 | 0.5 | 0.6 | 1.4 | 23.5 |
| Four | 0.2 | 0.3 | 0.2 | 0.3 | 0.2 | 0.0 | 0.0 |
| Five or more | 0.3 | 0.2 | 0.2 | 0.4 | 0.5 | 1.6 | 0.0 |
| **Other undergraduate credit courses** | | | | | | | |
| None | 17.5 | 16.2 | 16.0 | 16.9 | 28.9 | 25.2 | 2.1 |
| One | 21.2 | 24.5 | 20.3 | 19.5 | 15.3 | 14.4 | 5.8 |
| Two | 24.2 | 27.7 | 23.3 | 21.7 | 22.0 | 15.5 | 33.9 |
| Three | 16.1 | 14.0 | 18.4 | 17.4 | 14.4 | 15.0 | 58.2 |
| Four | 9.5 | 8.3 | 10.5 | 10.4 | 9.0 | 10.0 | 0.0 |
| Five or more | 11.6 | 9.2 | 11.6 | 14.1 | 10.5 | 19.9 | 0.0 |
| **Graduate courses** | | | | | | | |
| None | 61.9 | 55.7 | 59.5 | 63.7 | 83.8 | 88.3 | 75.8 |
| One | 24.1 | 29.7 | 23.9 | 22.0 | 10.1 | 7.9 | 0.7 |
| Two | 9.1 | 9.5 | 10.9 | 9.2 | 3.4 | 2.7 | 0.0 |
| Three | 2.5 | 2.7 | 3.1 | 2.2 | 1.6 | 0.4 | 0.0 |
| Four | 1.3 | 1.4 | 1.2 | 1.7 | 1.0 | 0.6 | 0.0 |
| Five or more | 1.1 | 0.9 | 1.6 | 1.3 | 0.1 | 0.2 | 23.5 |
| **Vocational or technical courses** | | | | | | | |
| None | 97.2 | 97.8 | 97.0 | 97.0 | 95.5 | 95.5 | 100.0 |
| One | 1.2 | 1.1 | 1.3 | 1.0 | 0.9 | 2.1 | 0.0 |
| Two | 0.7 | 0.5 | 0.7 | 0.9 | 0.6 | 1.1 | 0.0 |
| Three | 0.5 | 0.4 | 0.3 | 0.5 | 0.8 | 0.9 | 0.0 |
| Four | 0.2 | 0.1 | 0.2 | 0.1 | 1.6 | 0.0 | 0.0 |
| Five or more | 0.3 | 0.1 | 0.3 | 0.4 | 0.6 | 0.4 | 0.0 |
| **Non-credit courses (other than above)** | | | | | | | |
| None | 95.5 | 94.7 | 95.7 | 96.0 | 97.1 | 96.2 | 93.3 |
| One | 3.2 | 3.9 | 3.2 | 2.6 | 1.5 | 1.8 | 2.1 |
| Two | 0.9 | 1.0 | 0.9 | 0.8 | 0.7 | 0.3 | 4.6 |
| Three | 0.2 | 0.3 | 0.1 | 0.2 | 0.0 | 0.7 | 0.0 |
| Four | 0.1 | 0.0 | 0.1 | 0.0 | 0.0 | 0.8 | 0.0 |
| Five or more | 0.2 | 0.1 | 0.1 | 0.4 | 0.7 | 0.2 | 0.0 |
| **Do you teach remedial/developmental skills in any of the following areas?** | | | | | | | |
| Reading | 3.5 | 2.7 | 3.0 | 4.0 | 8.2 | 4.4 | 41.5 |
| Writing | 8.6 | 7.6 | 7.6 | 9.5 | 13.2 | 11.0 | 48.6 |
| Mathematics | 4.3 | 4.1 | 3.5 | 4.0 | 6.4 | 9.3 | 0.0 |
| ESL | 0.6 | 0.3 | 0.5 | 0.7 | 1.8 | 1.8 | 0.0 |
| General academic skills | 7.5 | 6.8 | 6.2 | 8.9 | 10.4 | 10.9 | 8.8 |
| Other subject areas | 5.1 | 3.7 | 4.7 | 6.4 | 7.9 | 8.3 | 0.0 |

# 2007–2008 FACULTY SURVEY WEIGHTED NATIONAL NORMS
## Full-time Undergraduate Faculty at Baccalaureate Institutions

| Male Respondents | All Resp | Full Prof | Assoc Prof | Asst Prof | Lect | Inst | No Resp |
|---|---|---|---|---|---|---|---|
| **HAVE YOU ENGAGED IN ANY OF THE FOLLOWING PROFESSIONAL DEVELOPMENT OPPORTUNITIES AT YOUR INSTITUTION? [2]** | | | | | | | |
| **Workshops focused on teaching in the classroom** | | | | | | | |
| Yes | 66.0 | 62.8 | 70.3 | 68.7 | 63.7 | 59.1 | 59.2 |
| No | 31.9 | 35.7 | 28.1 | 28.5 | 34.9 | 34.4 | 40.8 |
| Not eligible | 0.2 | 0.1 | 0.2 | 0.3 | 0.5 | 0.5 | 0.0 |
| Not available | 1.9 | 1.4 | 1.5 | 2.5 | 0.9 | 6.1 | 0.0 |
| **Paid workshops outside the institution focused on teaching** | | | | | | | |
| Yes | 19.4 | 18.8 | 22.2 | 17.7 | 18.1 | 20.2 | 12.3 |
| No | 76.4 | 78.4 | 74.1 | 77.6 | 71.7 | 72.2 | 83.8 |
| Not eligible | 0.8 | 0.3 | 0.4 | 0.6 | 6.0 | 2.5 | 3.2 |
| Not available | 3.3 | 2.5 | 3.3 | 4.1 | 4.3 | 5.1 | 0.7 |
| **Paid sabbatical leave** | | | | | | | |
| Yes | 32.0 | 53.8 | 35.2 | 5.9 | 4.8 | 0.2 | 0.7 |
| No | 55.1 | 43.1 | 57.4 | 70.2 | 54.4 | 67.3 | 42.5 |
| Not eligible | 9.6 | 1.3 | 4.3 | 19.7 | 33.5 | 25.6 | 56.8 |
| Not available | 3.3 | 1.9 | 3.1 | 4.2 | 7.3 | 6.9 | 0.0 |
| **Travel funds paid by the institution** | | | | | | | |
| Yes | 78.4 | 83.8 | 82.1 | 77.7 | 53.8 | 49.2 | 65.0 |
| No | 18.8 | 15.0 | 15.8 | 18.4 | 36.8 | 43.8 | 35.0 |
| Not eligible | 1.1 | 0.1 | 0.2 | 1.5 | 8.6 | 3.5 | 0.0 |
| Not available | 1.7 | 1.1 | 1.8 | 2.4 | 0.9 | 3.5 | 0.0 |
| **Association membership/dues paid by the institution** | | | | | | | |
| Yes | 29.1 | 28.2 | 30.1 | 31.2 | 21.2 | 29.8 | 10.7 |
| No | 57.6 | 61.9 | 55.1 | 52.6 | 59.3 | 58.3 | 85.5 |
| Not eligible | 2.1 | 0.6 | 1.0 | 3.3 | 9.9 | 5.0 | 3.1 |
| Not available | 11.2 | 9.3 | 13.8 | 12.9 | 9.6 | 6.9 | 0.7 |
| **Tuition remission** | | | | | | | |
| Yes | 14.2 | 17.4 | 13.5 | 8.4 | 11.7 | 23.4 | 3.2 |
| No | 78.5 | 76.3 | 79.9 | 82.8 | 78.5 | 68.8 | 91.0 |
| Not eligible | 3.1 | 2.2 | 2.3 | 4.3 | 6.2 | 4.2 | 5.8 |
| Not available | 4.2 | 4.1 | 4.3 | 4.4 | 3.5 | 3.7 | 0.0 |
| **Internal grants for research** | | | | | | | |
| Yes | 48.5 | 54.9 | 53.8 | 48.5 | 15.9 | 10.8 | 13.0 |
| No | 48.2 | 43.3 | 44.3 | 47.9 | 72.4 | 80.5 | 60.3 |
| Not eligible | 1.7 | 0.5 | 0.7 | 1.8 | 10.6 | 4.6 | 26.7 |
| Not available | 1.6 | 1.3 | 1.2 | 1.8 | 1.1 | 4.1 | 0.0 |
| **Training for administrative leadership** | | | | | | | |
| Yes | 13.5 | 20.1 | 13.4 | 6.1 | 6.2 | 6.4 | 4.6 |
| No | 78.0 | 74.2 | 77.3 | 83.9 | 78.4 | 83.8 | 71.3 |
| Not eligible | 2.0 | 0.5 | 1.2 | 3.1 | 8.4 | 4.2 | 17.6 |
| Not available | 6.4 | 5.1 | 8.1 | 6.8 | 7.0 | 5.6 | 6.5 |

[2] This question asked for the first time in the 2007–2008 Faculty Survey.

| Male Respondents | All Resp | Full Prof | Assoc Prof | Asst Prof | Lect | Inst | No Resp |
|---|---|---|---|---|---|---|---|
| **Goals for undergraduates noted as "very important" or "essential"** | | | | | | | |
| Develop ability to think critically | 99.4 | 99.4 | 99.0 | 99.8 | 99.7 | 99.3 | 100.0 |
| Prepare students for employment after college | 79.0 | 76.7 | 79.3 | 81.5 | 80.0 | 83.9 | 71.8 |
| Prepare students for graduate or advanced education | 74.7 | 76.9 | 72.7 | 74.8 | 74.2 | 67.9 | 54.5 |
| Develop moral character | 67.7 | 66.8 | 66.1 | 66.9 | 76.2 | 76.1 | 60.6 |
| Provide for students' emotional development | 43.3 | 42.0 | 42.1 | 43.3 | 50.6 | 51.8 | 41.3 |
| Prepare students for family living | 20.1 | 18.7 | 19.3 | 19.4 | 29.4 | 28.5 | 5.7 |
| Teach students the classic works of Western civilization [2] | 36.3 | 40.6 | 36.3 | 29.8 | 41.3 | 28.4 | 37.9 |
| Help students develop personal values | 63.4 | 62.5 | 62.3 | 62.3 | 71.7 | 71.8 | 86.9 |
| Enhance students' self-understanding | 68.5 | 65.2 | 67.8 | 71.0 | 77.4 | 75.8 | 84.9 |
| Instill in students a commitment to community service | 49.6 | 48.3 | 49.0 | 49.2 | 60.3 | 54.1 | 33.8 |
| Enhance students' knowledge of and appreciation for other racial/ethnic groups | 67.4 | 67.0 | 66.6 | 69.1 | 70.6 | 62.3 | 64.4 |
| Study a foreign language [2] | 50.5 | 53.9 | 50.0 | 46.8 | 52.6 | 42.0 | 41.7 |
| Help master knowledge in a discipline | 94.7 | 95.8 | 95.4 | 93.5 | 91.6 | 91.8 | 100.0 |
| Develop creative capacities | 81.7 | 81.3 | 79.9 | 82.8 | 87.9 | 80.9 | 94.3 |
| Instill a basic appreciation of the liberal arts | 70.2 | 72.4 | 70.9 | 66.0 | 72.1 | 67.8 | 65.3 |
| Promote ability to write effectively | 95.3 | 95.6 | 95.7 | 94.7 | 96.6 | 93.2 | 100.0 |
| Help students evaluate the quality and reliability of information [2] | 96.4 | 96.4 | 96.7 | 95.8 | 97.8 | 95.2 | 85.2 |
| Engage students in civil discourse around controversial issues [2] | 67.7 | 66.3 | 68.7 | 68.9 | 73.4 | 61.2 | 88.1 |
| Teach students tolerance and respect for different beliefs [2] | 76.6 | 75.6 | 77.2 | 77.6 | 81.7 | 70.0 | 82.4 |
| Encourage students to become agents of social change [2] | 49.0 | 44.6 | 50.4 | 52.1 | 56.0 | 53.2 | 36.0 |

[2] This question asked for the first time in the 2007–2008 Faculty Survey.

| Male Respondents | All Resp | Full Prof | Assoc Prof | Asst Prof | Lect | Inst | No Resp |
|---|---|---|---|---|---|---|---|
| **HOW MANY OF THE FOLLOWING HAVE YOU PUBLISHED?** | | | | | | | |
| **Articles in academic or professional journals** | | | | | | | |
| None | 15.0 | 6.3 | 10.0 | 17.5 | 43.7 | 63.2 | 47.0 |
| 1 to 2 | 14.1 | 7.5 | 13.1 | 23.6 | 21.6 | 18.1 | 5.7 |
| 3 to 4 | 12.9 | 8.3 | 14.6 | 18.5 | 16.0 | 10.6 | 31.9 |
| 5 to 10 | 18.7 | 15.7 | 24.1 | 23.0 | 9.8 | 5.3 | 11.0 |
| 11 to 20 | 14.9 | 16.7 | 20.1 | 11.2 | 5.5 | 1.4 | 4.4 |
| 21 to 50 | 14.7 | 24.0 | 14.8 | 5.1 | 2.9 | 1.2 | 0.0 |
| 51+ | 9.7 | 21.5 | 3.3 | 1.1 | 0.5 | 0.2 | 0.0 |
| **Chapters in edited volumes** | | | | | | | |
| None | 46.4 | 30.4 | 45.3 | 59.7 | 68.2 | 87.7 | 64.7 |
| 1 to 2 | 24.8 | 23.5 | 27.3 | 28.5 | 20.3 | 10.9 | 27.8 |
| 3 to 4 | 13.0 | 17.2 | 15.4 | 7.4 | 7.3 | 0.6 | 7.5 |
| 5 to 10 | 10.3 | 17.2 | 9.6 | 3.5 | 3.2 | 0.5 | 0.0 |
| 11 to 20 | 3.7 | 7.7 | 1.6 | 0.8 | 0.8 | 0.3 | 0.0 |
| 21 to 50 | 1.4 | 3.0 | 0.7 | 0.0 | 0.2 | 0.0 | 0.0 |
| 51+ | 0.4 | 1.0 | 0.1 | 0.1 | 0.0 | 0.0 | 0.0 |
| **Books, manuals, or monographs** | | | | | | | |
| None | 57.0 | 38.8 | 56.9 | 77.4 | 71.7 | 87.6 | 59.0 |
| 1 to 2 | 26.8 | 29.8 | 34.0 | 18.7 | 22.0 | 10.0 | 41.0 |
| 3 to 4 | 8.3 | 14.8 | 5.8 | 2.5 | 4.6 | 1.4 | 0.0 |
| 5 to 10 | 5.7 | 12.0 | 2.3 | 1.1 | 1.0 | 0.8 | 0.0 |
| 11 to 20 | 1.5 | 3.1 | 0.8 | 0.1 | 0.5 | 0.1 | 0.0 |
| 21 to 50 | 0.5 | 1.2 | 0.1 | 0.1 | 0.0 | 0.2 | 0.0 |
| 51+ | 0.2 | 0.3 | 0.1 | 0.1 | 0.2 | 0.0 | 0.0 |
| **Other, such as patents or computer software products** | | | | | | | |
| None | 82.1 | 78.6 | 82.1 | 84.9 | 87.2 | 88.8 | 84.7 |
| 1 to 2 | 9.9 | 11.6 | 9.4 | 9.6 | 7.1 | 4.7 | 0.0 |
| 3 to 4 | 4.0 | 4.6 | 4.1 | 3.1 | 2.7 | 4.0 | 15.3 |
| 5 to 10 | 2.5 | 3.2 | 2.8 | 1.3 | 1.6 | 1.0 | 0.0 |
| 11 to 20 | 0.8 | 0.9 | 0.7 | 0.8 | 0.9 | 1.0 | 0.0 |
| 21 to 50 | 0.4 | 0.6 | 0.6 | 0.2 | 0.1 | 0.1 | 0.0 |
| 51+ | 0.3 | 0.4 | 0.3 | 0.1 | 0.4 | 0.4 | 0.0 |
| **IN THE LAST TWO YEARS, HOW MANY:** | | | | | | | |
| **Exhibitions or performances in the fine or applied arts have you presented?** | | | | | | | |
| None | 82.4 | 84.4 | 83.4 | 81.1 | 77.1 | 74.5 | 58.6 |
| 1 to 2 | 5.2 | 4.4 | 4.3 | 5.2 | 11.2 | 10.0 | 18.1 |
| 3 to 4 | 3.9 | 3.9 | 3.6 | 4.2 | 3.7 | 4.6 | 15.7 |
| 5 to 10 | 4.0 | 3.7 | 4.0 | 5.0 | 2.3 | 4.3 | 0.0 |
| 11 to 20 | 2.0 | 1.8 | 2.2 | 2.0 | 2.6 | 1.8 | 0.0 |
| 21 to 50 | 1.2 | 1.0 | 1.2 | 1.4 | 2.0 | 0.9 | 7.6 |
| 51+ | 1.2 | 0.9 | 1.3 | 1.0 | 1.3 | 4.0 | 0.0 |
| **Of your professional writings have been published or accepted for publication?** | | | | | | | |
| None | 26.1 | 19.3 | 24.8 | 22.6 | 51.6 | 70.8 | 64.1 |
| 1 to 2 | 31.1 | 29.5 | 33.5 | 33.6 | 29.2 | 21.6 | 23.9 |
| 3 to 4 | 22.0 | 22.1 | 23.1 | 26.1 | 14.7 | 5.8 | 6.3 |
| 5 to 10 | 16.0 | 21.1 | 15.0 | 14.9 | 3.8 | 0.9 | 5.7 |
| 11 to 20 | 3.6 | 5.8 | 2.7 | 2.3 | 0.2 | 0.4 | 0.0 |
| 21 to 50 | 0.9 | 1.6 | 0.7 | 0.2 | 0.2 | 0.5 | 0.0 |
| 51+ | 0.3 | 0.5 | 0.1 | 0.2 | 0.2 | 0.0 | 0.0 |

## 2007–2008 FACULTY SURVEY WEIGHTED NATIONAL NORMS
### Full-time Undergraduate Faculty at Baccalaureate Institutions

| Male Respondents | All Resp | Full Prof | Assoc Prof | Asst Prof | Lect | Inst | No Resp |
|---|---|---|---|---|---|---|---|
| **General activities** | | | | | | | |
| Are you a member of a faculty union? | 20.0 | 20.0 | 21.3 | 20.2 | 21.0 | 10.7 | 0.0 |
| Are you a U.S. citizen? | 92.9 | 96.9 | 93.4 | 83.9 | 95.7 | 97.0 | 100.0 |
| Were you born in the U.S.A.? | 84.4 | 85.9 | 84.4 | 79.2 | 87.0 | 92.8 | 100.0 |
| Do you plan to retire within the next three years? | 14.3 | 24.5 | 10.5 | 3.1 | 15.0 | 6.7 | 15.1 |
| Do you use your scholarship to address local community needs? | 43.8 | 45.1 | 45.1 | 39.0 | 51.1 | 41.4 | 22.1 |
| Have you been sexually harassed at this institution? | 2.3 | 2.5 | 2.6 | 1.4 | 1.3 | 5.4 | 11.9 |
| Have you ever interrupted your professional career for more than one year for family reasons? [2] | 5.0 | 3.5 | 5.6 | 5.6 | 7.0 | 8.6 | 22.7 |
| Have you ever received an award for outstanding teaching? | 44.0 | 54.5 | 45.3 | 30.8 | 38.6 | 23.5 | 42.5 |
| Have you published op-ed pieces or editorials? | 27.8 | 36.3 | 25.5 | 18.1 | 29.6 | 16.4 | 32.6 |
| Is (or was) your: | | | | | | | |
|     Father an academic? | 13.3 | 11.5 | 14.9 | 15.4 | 11.3 | 12.1 | 8.7 |
|     Mother an academic? | 8.0 | 7.1 | 8.3 | 8.8 | 10.7 | 6.9 | 0.0 |
|     Spouse/partner an academic? | 31.9 | 34.6 | 32.6 | 26.4 | 36.4 | 27.7 | 53.3 |
| Are you currently teaching courses at more than one institution? | 4.8 | 4.2 | 4.1 | 4.1 | 10.3 | 10.4 | 7.2 |
| **During the <u>past two</u> years, have you:** | | | | | | | |
| Considered early retirement? | 20.3 | 29.2 | 20.1 | 7.5 | 15.7 | 16.6 | 30.6 |
| Considered leaving academe for another job? | 29.7 | 19.8 | 33.0 | 36.1 | 40.8 | 46.3 | 30.6 |
| Considered leaving this institution for another? | 45.1 | 37.4 | 51.5 | 50.6 | 40.7 | 50.4 | 34.7 |
| Changed academic institutions? | 11.0 | 6.6 | 8.1 | 20.8 | 14.0 | 11.8 | 1.7 |
| Engaged in paid consulting outside of your institution? | 40.8 | 45.6 | 41.9 | 32.7 | 48.0 | 27.3 | 42.7 |
| Engaged in public service/professional consulting without pay? | 58.6 | 62.8 | 59.9 | 52.6 | 57.2 | 48.8 | 62.2 |
| Received at least one firm job offer? | 22.4 | 16.0 | 19.3 | 33.9 | 27.9 | 27.8 | 2.3 |
| Received funding for your work from: | | | | | | | |
|     Foundations? | 20.8 | 23.4 | 20.5 | 20.2 | 18.9 | 6.6 | 6.1 |
|     State or federal government? | 30.2 | 37.3 | 30.8 | 25.1 | 20.3 | 8.5 | 4.4 |
|     Business or industry? | 16.7 | 19.8 | 17.4 | 13.7 | 12.5 | 7.7 | 26.8 |
| Requested/sought an early promotion? | 7.2 | 5.4 | 9.7 | 7.9 | 7.3 | 5.6 | 0.0 |
| **IF YOU WERE TO BEGIN YOUR CAREER AGAIN, WOULD YOU STILL WANT TO:** | | | | | | | |
| **Come to this institution? [2]** | | | | | | | |
|     Definitely yes | 35.7 | 36.4 | 32.6 | 35.1 | 45.9 | 38.2 | 27.9 |
|     Probably yes | 33.5 | 32.8 | 32.4 | 35.3 | 30.1 | 40.4 | 26.8 |
|     Not sure | 16.1 | 16.1 | 18.2 | 16.4 | 9.2 | 12.5 | 20.9 |
|     Probably no | 9.6 | 9.7 | 10.5 | 8.8 | 11.9 | 4.7 | 24.4 |
|     Definitely no | 5.0 | 4.9 | 6.2 | 4.4 | 2.8 | 4.2 | 0.0 |
| **Be a college professor?** | | | | | | | |
|     Definitely yes | 65.9 | 72.0 | 63.4 | 63.9 | 58.9 | 48.0 | 53.4 |
|     Probably yes | 23.8 | 19.8 | 25.5 | 24.7 | 29.6 | 34.6 | 36.1 |
|     Not sure | 7.4 | 5.7 | 7.8 | 8.5 | 8.1 | 13.1 | 10.5 |
|     Probably no | 2.3 | 2.0 | 2.8 | 2.3 | 2.2 | 2.0 | 0.0 |
|     Definitely no | 0.7 | 0.5 | 0.6 | 0.7 | 1.2 | 2.3 | 0.0 |

[2] This question asked for the first time in the 2007–2008 Faculty Survey.

157

**2007–2008 FACULTY SURVEY WEIGHTED NATIONAL NORMS**
**Full-time Undergraduate Faculty at Baccalaureate Institutions**

| Male Respondents | All Resp | Full Prof | Assoc Prof | Asst Prof | Lect | Inst | No Resp |
|---|---|---|---|---|---|---|---|
| **Attributes noted as being "very descriptive" of your institution** | | | | | | | |
| It is easy for students to see faculty outside of regular office hours | 60.1 | 60.5 | 59.7 | 63.3 | 50.0 | 56.2 | 31.5 |
| There is a great deal of conformity among the students | 29.9 | 28.3 | 30.7 | 35.0 | 23.0 | 22.0 | 57.0 |
| The faculty are typically at odds with campus administration | 19.1 | 18.9 | 21.0 | 19.5 | 11.7 | 18.3 | 19.1 |
| Faculty here respect each other | 47.3 | 47.9 | 44.6 | 51.1 | 43.4 | 43.5 | 28.4 |
| Most students are treated like "numbers in a book" | 4.4 | 4.5 | 4.2 | 3.7 | 7.8 | 2.7 | 25.9 |
| Social activities are overemphasized | 8.5 | 9.0 | 8.8 | 7.8 | 7.8 | 5.9 | 25.1 |
| Faculty are rewarded for being good teachers | 16.2 | 17.2 | 14.5 | 16.9 | 17.8 | 13.2 | 2.0 |
| There is respect for the expression of diverse values and beliefs | 36.1 | 37.4 | 32.7 | 34.4 | 47.4 | 39.1 | 16.7 |
| Faculty are rewarded for their efforts to use instructional technology | 18.4 | 18.5 | 17.5 | 18.6 | 19.6 | 20.2 | 2.0 |
| Faculty are rewarded for their efforts to work with underprepared students | 5.1 | 4.9 | 4.1 | 5.3 | 10.9 | 5.4 | 2.2 |
| Administrators consider faculty concerns when making policy [2] | 13.4 | 14.0 | 11.1 | 13.6 | 18.3 | 14.9 | 9.1 |
| The administration is open about its policies | 17.0 | 17.1 | 13.7 | 17.6 | 26.2 | 19.8 | 9.1 |
| **Do you, "to a great extent":** | | | | | | | |
| Engage in academic work that spans multiple disciplines | 40.0 | 39.1 | 41.5 | 43.5 | 38.5 | 26.2 | 38.0 |
| Feel that the training you received in graduate school prepared you well for your role as a faculty mentor | 40.4 | 43.3 | 36.4 | 44.4 | 29.4 | 32.1 | 32.6 |
| Achieve a healthy balance between your personal life and your professional life | 38.7 | 45.5 | 35.6 | 29.8 | 41.5 | 40.7 | 26.5 |
| Experience close alignment between your work and your personal values | 64.7 | 70.4 | 61.1 | 59.9 | 64.7 | 62.2 | 63.7 |
| Feel that you have to work harder than your colleagues to be perceived as a legitimate scholar | 22.8 | 17.4 | 22.7 | 27.1 | 33.1 | 32.6 | 28.4 |
| Mentor new faculty [2] | 19.8 | 29.8 | 20.3 | 7.7 | 10.1 | 8.1 | 3.0 |

[2]  This question asked for the first time in the 2007–2008 Faculty Survey.

158

# 2007–2008 FACULTY SURVEY WEIGHTED NATIONAL NORMS
## Full-time Undergraduate Faculty at Baccalaureate Institutions

| Male Respondents | All Resp | Full Prof | Assoc Prof | Asst Prof | Lect | Inst | No Resp |
|---|---|---|---|---|---|---|---|
| **Aspects of your job with which you are "very satisfied" or "satisfied": [3]** | | | | | | | |
| Salary [2] | 48.9 | 57.4 | 44.2 | 45.0 | 38.7 | 38.2 | 35.8 |
| Health benefits [2] | 67.9 | 69.5 | 65.1 | 66.3 | 76.3 | 67.3 | 81.5 |
| Retirement benefits [2] | 69.6 | 70.1 | 66.1 | 71.7 | 73.5 | 69.8 | 58.5 |
| Opportunity for scholarly pursuits | 58.4 | 66.0 | 53.9 | 50.3 | 63.3 | 54.7 | 49.1 |
| Teaching load | 60.4 | 66.3 | 55.1 | 54.6 | 62.7 | 67.0 | 50.7 |
| Quality of students | 55.5 | 58.6 | 52.1 | 52.5 | 63.3 | 53.4 | 65.5 |
| Office/lab space | 68.0 | 72.9 | 65.5 | 64.5 | 65.8 | 61.0 | 78.5 |
| Autonomy and independence | 85.9 | 87.5 | 85.4 | 83.9 | 88.2 | 82.9 | 57.1 |
| Professional relationships with other faculty | 77.7 | 80.1 | 75.2 | 78.5 | 75.7 | 70.7 | 56.5 |
| Social relationships with other faculty | 65.6 | 65.3 | 64.3 | 68.1 | 64.7 | 64.0 | 49.7 |
| Competency of colleagues | 77.1 | 78.9 | 74.4 | 75.4 | 80.6 | 79.9 | 89.6 |
| Visibility for jobs at other institutions/organizations | 55.1 | 62.8 | 47.1 | 52.6 | 52.9 | 52.4 | 59.0 |
| Job security | 80.8 | 93.4 | 86.2 | 65.8 | 56.6 | 53.3 | 35.0 |
| Relationship with administration | 59.1 | 59.6 | 56.8 | 57.7 | 67.0 | 64.2 | 45.7 |
| Departmental leadership [2] | 71.4 | 71.2 | 69.7 | 71.7 | 74.9 | 75.4 | 67.5 |
| Course assignments [2] | 85.5 | 88.2 | 83.7 | 82.9 | 86.0 | 84.8 | 74.8 |
| Freedom to determine course content [2] | 93.3 | 95.1 | 93.4 | 91.7 | 93.6 | 87.5 | 58.9 |
| Availability of child care at this institution | 33.7 | 38.2 | 29.6 | 32.5 | 30.1 | 34.3 | 82.9 |
| Prospects for career advancement | 57.7 | 67.2 | 52.5 | 58.2 | 41.3 | 32.4 | 17.2 |
| Clerical/administrative support | 63.0 | 62.0 | 59.6 | 63.4 | 77.3 | 70.5 | 58.7 |
| Overall job satisfaction | 76.6 | 80.6 | 73.2 | 73.1 | 81.7 | 74.4 | 69.3 |

[2] This question asked for the first time in the 2007–2008 Faculty Survey.
[3] Respondents marking "Not Applicable" were not included in the computation of these results.

| Male Respondents | All Resp | Full Prof | Assoc Prof | Asst Prof | Lect | Inst | No Resp |
|---|---|---|---|---|---|---|---|
| **Do you agree "strongly" or "somewhat"?** | | | | | | | |
| Faculty are interested in students' personal problems | 82.0 | 80.7 | 81.6 | 84.5 | 82.3 | 82.4 | 74.1 |
| Racial and ethnic diversity should be more strongly reflected in the curriculum | 52.3 | 47.8 | 53.1 | 58.9 | 55.9 | 49.0 | 54.5 |
| Faculty feel that most students are well-prepared academically | 43.7 | 46.0 | 39.8 | 43.5 | 45.7 | 43.9 | 34.4 |
| This institution should hire more faculty of color | 69.2 | 70.8 | 69.5 | 70.4 | 63.7 | 57.2 | 36.0 |
| Student Affairs staff have the support and respect of faculty | 75.6 | 74.2 | 73.2 | 78.4 | 79.4 | 81.9 | 89.4 |
| Faculty are committed to the welfare of this institution | 90.5 | 90.7 | 90.5 | 91.6 | 86.3 | 90.1 | 88.1 |
| Faculty here are strongly interested in the academic problems of undergraduates | 87.7 | 88.6 | 87.3 | 88.5 | 82.6 | 85.7 | 91.2 |
| There is a lot of campus racial conflict here | 8.6 | 6.5 | 9.6 | 12.0 | 8.6 | 5.0 | 1.7 |
| Most students are strongly committed to community service | 49.3 | 49.6 | 48.3 | 50.8 | 46.9 | 47.2 | 51.7 |
| My research is valued by faculty in my department | 75.9 | 79.4 | 73.8 | 77.0 | 70.4 | 61.3 | 56.0 |
| My teaching is valued by faculty in my department | 90.2 | 91.4 | 88.4 | 91.4 | 90.6 | 84.2 | 73.7 |
| Many courses include feminist perspectives | 40.8 | 40.6 | 38.2 | 41.9 | 48.1 | 41.4 | 51.4 |
| Faculty of color are treated fairly here | 92.1 | 93.3 | 90.7 | 89.9 | 95.3 | 95.6 | 94.6 |
| Women faculty are treated fairly here | 92.1 | 93.3 | 90.7 | 90.0 | 96.3 | 94.7 | 97.7 |
| Many courses involve students in community service | 44.8 | 43.0 | 43.8 | 46.6 | 46.6 | 54.1 | 49.6 |
| This institution should hire more women faculty | 53.2 | 55.3 | 52.8 | 53.9 | 50.2 | 38.7 | 29.4 |
| Gay and lesbian faculty are treated fairly here | 83.2 | 85.1 | 81.1 | 80.6 | 86.4 | 86.4 | 70.1 |
| My department does a good job of mentoring new faculty | 72.2 | 77.7 | 69.5 | 66.3 | 66.6 | 76.5 | 91.5 |
| Faculty are sufficiently involved in campus decision making | 52.5 | 50.8 | 47.6 | 56.6 | 60.1 | 61.5 | 82.3 |
| My values are congruent with the dominant institutional values | 72.1 | 73.6 | 69.1 | 72.8 | 71.6 | 74.3 | 60.8 |
| There is adequate support for integrating technology in my teaching | 85.8 | 86.0 | 84.0 | 86.3 | 91.2 | 84.9 | 92.7 |
| This institution takes responsibility for educating underprepared students | 65.0 | 65.5 | 59.7 | 67.2 | 67.4 | 74.2 | 74.8 |
| The criteria for advancement and promotion decisions are clear | 74.3 | 83.4 | 68.9 | 69.5 | 66.0 | 63.4 | 52.1 |
| Most of the students I teach lack the basic skills for college level work | 35.4 | 32.0 | 36.4 | 38.1 | 35.5 | 45.2 | 17.1 |
| There is adequate support for faculty development | 69.3 | 68.8 | 65.0 | 70.9 | 78.2 | 77.1 | 67.4 |
| This institution should not offer remedial/developmental education | 31.3 | 37.2 | 31.0 | 26.3 | 22.2 | 21.7 | 23.6 |

**2007–2008 FACULTY SURVEY WEIGHTED NATIONAL NORMS**
**Full-time Undergraduate Faculty at Baccalaureate Institutions**

| Male Respondents | All Resp | Full Prof | Assoc Prof | Asst Prof | Lect | Inst | No Resp |
|---|---|---|---|---|---|---|---|
| **Issues you believe to be of "high" or "highest" priority at your institution:** | | | | | | | |
| To promote the intellectual development of students | 85.6 | 87.2 | 83.9 | 84.2 | 91.4 | 82.8 | 97.7 |
| To help students examine and understand their personal values | 55.1 | 54.6 | 52.7 | 56.5 | 53.9 | 64.0 | 81.9 |
| To develop a sense of community among students and faculty | 51.9 | 50.6 | 48.9 | 53.7 | 58.1 | 62.4 | 72.2 |
| To facilitate student involvement in community service | 42.5 | 40.4 | 41.3 | 44.9 | 45.7 | 50.3 | 60.9 |
| To help students learn how to bring about change in American society | 32.4 | 29.6 | 30.5 | 34.8 | 41.7 | 42.2 | 13.1 |
| To increase or maintain institutional prestige | 63.6 | 63.2 | 62.8 | 63.4 | 70.3 | 64.8 | 70.5 |
| To hire faculty "stars" | 29.0 | 32.1 | 26.2 | 25.1 | 40.4 | 25.5 | 8.8 |
| To recruit more minority students | 48.6 | 52.2 | 46.7 | 44.8 | 56.4 | 39.7 | 16.8 |
| To enhance the institution's national image | 70.0 | 70.8 | 68.9 | 69.0 | 75.5 | 68.2 | 49.8 |
| To create a diverse multi-cultural campus environment | 51.6 | 53.7 | 48.3 | 49.2 | 62.6 | 50.0 | 48.2 |
| To promote gender equity among faculty | 57.1 | 62.1 | 52.6 | 53.8 | 63.2 | 49.2 | 58.4 |
| To provide resources for faculty to engage in community-based teaching or research | 33.5 | 28.3 | 31.0 | 38.1 | 48.5 | 47.5 | 44.4 |
| To create and sustain partnerships with surrounding communities | 44.8 | 37.8 | 43.0 | 51.3 | 58.6 | 61.6 | 49.3 |
| To pursue extramural funding | 60.9 | 63.5 | 59.0 | 59.0 | 63.8 | 56.7 | 68.8 |
| To increase the representation of minorities in the faculty and administration | 44.7 | 48.6 | 42.3 | 41.6 | 50.5 | 34.6 | 25.6 |
| To strengthen links with the for-profit, corporate sector [2] | 48.4 | 45.8 | 47.5 | 50.2 | 62.6 | 50.0 | 31.6 |
| To develop leadership ability among students | 57.5 | 57.5 | 53.1 | 57.7 | 66.4 | 68.0 | 79.3 |
| To increase the representation of women in the faculty and administration | 41.9 | 45.8 | 37.7 | 39.5 | 50.3 | 34.3 | 31.6 |
| To develop an appreciation for multiculturalism [2] | 53.0 | 55.5 | 49.6 | 50.0 | 59.5 | 57.3 | 43.3 |

[2]  This question asked for the first time in the 2007–2008 Faculty Survey.

161

## 2007–2008 FACULTY SURVEY WEIGHTED NATIONAL NORMS
### Full-time Undergraduate Faculty at Baccalaureate Institutions

| Male Respondents | All Resp | Full Prof | Assoc Prof | Asst Prof | Lect | Inst | No Resp |
|---|---|---|---|---|---|---|---|
| **Do you agree "strongly" or "somewhat"?** | | | | | | | |
| Western civilization and culture should be the foundation for the undergraduate curriculum | 62.8 | 66.6 | 60.3 | 57.3 | 71.5 | 61.1 | 73.0 |
| College officials have the right to ban persons with extreme views from speaking on campus | 30.0 | 28.2 | 30.1 | 31.6 | 30.0 | 34.9 | 50.8 |
| The chief benefit of a college education is that it increases one's earning power | 29.5 | 28.2 | 29.1 | 29.4 | 34.2 | 37.8 | 17.1 |
| Promoting diversity leads to the admission of too many underprepared students | 27.9 | 29.9 | 26.7 | 25.7 | 28.8 | 28.2 | 15.1 |
| Colleges should be actively involved in solving social problems | 68.1 | 65.0 | 69.2 | 71.2 | 72.9 | 67.4 | 56.5 |
| Tenure is an outmoded concept | 28.7 | 22.3 | 24.5 | 32.7 | 51.0 | 55.8 | 35.5 |
| Colleges should encourage students to be involved in community service activities | 85.2 | 82.9 | 86.9 | 86.6 | 88.2 | 84.4 | 98.3 |
| Community service should be given weight in college admissions decisions | 64.4 | 61.0 | 65.5 | 68.3 | 65.6 | 64.1 | 98.3 |
| A racially/ethnically diverse student body enhances the educational experience of all students | 91.6 | 92.3 | 91.6 | 92.0 | 89.8 | 86.1 | 88.1 |
| Realistically, an individual can do little to bring about changes in society | 23.1 | 24.8 | 23.6 | 20.9 | 18.7 | 23.6 | 7.3 |
| Colleges should be concerned with facilitating undergraduate students' spiritual development | 37.0 | 34.3 | 38.3 | 38.5 | 39.2 | 42.1 | 58.0 |
| Colleges have a responsibility to work with their surrounding communities to address local issues | 86.1 | 83.4 | 87.6 | 88.8 | 86.3 | 87.1 | 81.3 |
| Private funding sources often prevent researchers from being completely objective in the conduct of their work | 58.3 | 54.3 | 60.1 | 59.3 | 67.9 | 63.9 | 68.4 |

162

## 2007–2008 FACULTY SURVEY WEIGHTED NATIONAL NORMS
### Full-time Undergraduate Faculty at Baccalaureate Institutions

| Male Respondents | All Resp | Full Prof | Assoc Prof | Asst Prof | Lect | Inst | No Resp |
|---|---|---|---|---|---|---|---|
| **Factors noted as a source of stress for you during the <u>last two</u> years** | | | | | | | |
| Managing household responsibilities | 67.6 | 57.1 | 74.3 | 77.5 | 66.6 | 69.4 | 75.5 |
| Child care | 30.7 | 22.1 | 38.3 | 39.0 | 23.2 | 29.0 | 8.0 |
| Care of elderly parent | 30.9 | 34.6 | 31.7 | 24.5 | 29.5 | 29.1 | 29.3 |
| My physical health | 46.7 | 47.9 | 46.7 | 43.1 | 54.7 | 44.9 | 33.8 |
| Health of spouse/partner | 38.9 | 40.9 | 38.3 | 37.1 | 37.9 | 35.3 | 39.8 |
| Review/promotion process | 46.6 | 21.1 | 55.6 | 77.7 | 46.1 | 53.5 | 47.6 |
| Subtle discrimination (e.g., prejudice, racism, sexism) | 18.2 | 15.6 | 21.0 | 19.3 | 20.6 | 15.4 | 45.3 |
| Personal finances | 61.3 | 49.5 | 63.7 | 72.4 | 71.3 | 77.1 | 68.2 |
| Committee work | 59.3 | 63.0 | 67.9 | 56.0 | 31.0 | 34.3 | 73.1 |
| Faculty meetings | 51.0 | 54.1 | 56.1 | 48.7 | 30.1 | 35.8 | 15.0 |
| Colleagues | 61.3 | 64.8 | 66.5 | 53.8 | 49.2 | 56.0 | 43.3 |
| Students | 61.4 | 55.8 | 64.9 | 65.3 | 59.8 | 69.8 | 67.0 |
| Research or publishing demands | 61.1 | 54.1 | 70.4 | 76.7 | 34.0 | 28.2 | 10.4 |
| Institutional procedures and "red tape" | 72.0 | 73.7 | 75.1 | 70.5 | 62.7 | 61.9 | 49.8 |
| Teaching load | 59.6 | 50.5 | 64.6 | 70.0 | 60.1 | 54.8 | 55.3 |
| Children's problems | 31.7 | 33.6 | 35.2 | 26.8 | 28.1 | 25.4 | 17.4 |
| Friction with spouse/partner | 27.4 | 22.6 | 32.2 | 31.0 | 25.9 | 25.6 | 41.5 |
| Lack of personal time | 67.8 | 64.3 | 69.5 | 74.6 | 59.1 | 64.4 | 65.6 |
| Keeping up with information technology | 48.3 | 54.1 | 48.1 | 39.4 | 46.9 | 45.5 | 81.6 |
| Job security | 28.3 | 8.4 | 21.9 | 56.3 | 51.9 | 55.9 | 54.3 |
| Being part of a dual career couple | 40.5 | 34.3 | 46.0 | 44.6 | 44.1 | 36.4 | 62.8 |
| Working with underprepared students | 59.0 | 54.3 | 62.4 | 60.5 | 60.9 | 67.3 | 83.6 |
| Classroom conflict | 16.3 | 13.4 | 16.6 | 18.3 | 18.8 | 23.5 | 19.4 |
| Self-imposed high expectations | 77.0 | 73.8 | 79.2 | 80.5 | 72.8 | 79.3 | 82.4 |
| Change in work responsibilities | 40.6 | 34.9 | 45.5 | 42.1 | 40.6 | 53.4 | 49.6 |
| **Personal goals noted as "very important" or "essential":** | | | | | | | |
| Becoming an authority in my field | 61.5 | 63.7 | 56.9 | 67.1 | 53.0 | 53.0 | 44.2 |
| Influencing the political structure | 18.0 | 18.0 | 17.7 | 17.9 | 22.3 | 14.7 | 8.7 |
| Influencing social values | 35.3 | 31.5 | 36.6 | 38.7 | 46.3 | 30.9 | 35.9 |
| Raising a family | 72.4 | 74.0 | 72.4 | 71.2 | 69.8 | 69.1 | 70.3 |
| Becoming very well off financially | 34.3 | 35.6 | 32.3 | 33.5 | 36.8 | 35.6 | 12.1 |
| Helping others who are in difficulty | 61.2 | 57.9 | 61.8 | 62.7 | 72.9 | 63.7 | 63.0 |
| Becoming involved in programs to clean up the environment | 33.1 | 31.7 | 32.7 | 33.7 | 43.7 | 31.8 | 27.6 |
| Developing a meaningful philosophy of life | 70.8 | 69.5 | 71.4 | 70.3 | 81.5 | 67.8 | 75.2 |
| Helping to promote racial understanding | 48.4 | 48.3 | 46.3 | 49.6 | 60.4 | 40.2 | 67.5 |
| Obtaining recognition from my colleagues for contributions to my special field | 47.0 | 47.5 | 45.0 | 53.3 | 42.2 | 30.0 | 49.9 |
| Integrating spirituality into my life | 43.8 | 41.4 | 43.8 | 44.7 | 51.8 | 50.3 | 50.6 |

163

## 2007–2008 FACULTY SURVEY WEIGHTED NATIONAL NORMS
### Full-time Undergraduate Faculty at Baccalaureate Institutions

| Male Respondents | All Resp | Full Prof | Assoc Prof | Asst Prof | Lect | Inst | No Resp |
|---|---|---|---|---|---|---|---|
| **IN YOUR INTERACTIONS WITH UNDERGRAD-UATES, HOW OFTEN DO YOU ENCOURAGE THEM TO: [2]** | | | | | | | |
| **Ask questions in class** | | | | | | | |
| Frequently | 92.9 | 93.3 | 92.2 | 94.5 | 91.2 | 88.7 | 87.8 |
| Occasionally | 6.9 | 6.6 | 7.7 | 5.1 | 8.8 | 11.3 | 12.2 |
| Not at all | 0.2 | 0.1 | 0.2 | 0.4 | 0.0 | 0.0 | 0.0 |
| **Support their opinions with a logical argument** | | | | | | | |
| Frequently | 80.4 | 80.0 | 80.2 | 82.1 | 80.3 | 78.0 | 75.2 |
| Occasionally | 18.5 | 18.9 | 18.8 | 16.9 | 19.3 | 21.0 | 24.8 |
| Not at all | 1.0 | 1.1 | 1.0 | 1.0 | 0.4 | 1.1 | 0.0 |
| **Seek solutions to problems and explain them to others** | | | | | | | |
| Frequently | 71.3 | 69.3 | 70.8 | 72.7 | 77.6 | 76.3 | 70.2 |
| Occasionally | 26.7 | 28.4 | 27.0 | 25.7 | 21.6 | 23.2 | 29.8 |
| Not at all | 1.9 | 2.3 | 2.3 | 1.6 | 0.8 | 0.5 | 0.0 |
| **Revise their papers to improve their writing** | | | | | | | |
| Frequently | 52.3 | 53.4 | 52.4 | 50.6 | 52.9 | 49.4 | 84.6 |
| Occasionally | 37.2 | 36.5 | 37.3 | 38.5 | 32.7 | 42.5 | 15.4 |
| Not at all | 10.5 | 10.1 | 10.3 | 10.9 | 14.3 | 8.1 | 0.0 |
| **Evaluate the quality or reliability of information they receive** | | | | | | | |
| Frequently | 69.0 | 69.1 | 69.8 | 66.3 | 78.0 | 66.6 | 60.4 |
| Occasionally | 28.6 | 28.1 | 28.3 | 31.3 | 19.7 | 31.9 | 39.6 |
| Not at all | 2.4 | 2.7 | 1.9 | 2.4 | 2.4 | 1.6 | 0.0 |
| **Take risks for potential gains** | | | | | | | |
| Frequently | 33.8 | 32.2 | 33.2 | 34.8 | 39.1 | 37.7 | 62.6 |
| Occasionally | 50.3 | 51.2 | 50.9 | 48.1 | 49.2 | 51.6 | 35.4 |
| Not at all | 15.9 | 16.6 | 15.9 | 17.1 | 11.7 | 10.6 | 2.0 |
| **Seek alternative solutions to a problem** | | | | | | | |
| Frequently | 60.9 | 59.4 | 58.6 | 62.4 | 70.6 | 65.7 | 90.8 |
| Occasionally | 36.8 | 38.1 | 38.6 | 35.9 | 28.3 | 32.9 | 9.2 |
| Not at all | 2.3 | 2.6 | 2.9 | 1.7 | 1.1 | 1.4 | 0.0 |
| **Look up scientific research articles and resources** | | | | | | | |
| Frequently | 52.4 | 54.7 | 50.9 | 52.1 | 51.1 | 44.4 | 56.7 |
| Occasionally | 36.4 | 35.0 | 37.1 | 36.3 | 40.6 | 41.1 | 0.0 |
| Not at all | 11.2 | 10.2 | 12.0 | 11.6 | 8.2 | 14.5 | 43.3 |
| **Explore topics on their own, even though it was not required for a class** | | | | | | | |
| Frequently | 48.8 | 49.8 | 48.0 | 48.4 | 45.1 | 50.8 | 69.3 |
| Occasionally | 46.8 | 46.3 | 47.4 | 47.2 | 49.1 | 44.0 | 23.5 |
| Not at all | 4.4 | 4.0 | 4.5 | 4.5 | 5.8 | 5.2 | 7.2 |
| **Acknowledge failure as a necessary part of the learning process** | | | | | | | |
| Frequently | 46.2 | 43.5 | 46.5 | 47.6 | 50.3 | 54.0 | 70.1 |
| Occasionally | 46.2 | 48.0 | 45.9 | 45.3 | 44.8 | 40.6 | 22.7 |
| Not at all | 7.6 | 8.5 | 7.6 | 7.1 | 4.9 | 5.4 | 7.2 |
| **Seek feedback on their academic work** | | | | | | | |
| Frequently | 66.9 | 66.2 | 66.7 | 66.5 | 71.1 | 69.4 | 77.3 |
| Occasionally | 31.1 | 31.8 | 31.4 | 30.8 | 27.5 | 28.9 | 22.7 |
| Not at all | 2.1 | 2.0 | 1.9 | 2.7 | 1.4 | 1.7 | 0.0 |

[2]  This question asked for the first time in the 2007–2008 Faculty Survey.

164

**2007–2008 FACULTY SURVEY WEIGHTED NATIONAL NORMS**
**Full-time Undergraduate Faculty at Baccalaureate Institutions**

| Male Respondents | All Resp | Full Prof | Assoc Prof | Asst Prof | Lect | Inst | No Resp |
|---|---|---|---|---|---|---|---|
| **Methods you use in "all" or "most" of the courses you teach:** | | | | | | | |
| Multiple-choice exams [2] | 32.0 | 27.7 | 32.2 | 35.8 | 35.1 | 44.0 | 10.5 |
| Essay exams [2] | 45.0 | 47.6 | 44.9 | 43.0 | 38.0 | 42.9 | 28.6 |
| Short-answer exams [2] | 46.4 | 44.9 | 48.4 | 48.6 | 37.7 | 48.0 | 21.1 |
| Quizzes | 38.9 | 35.8 | 38.8 | 42.4 | 40.8 | 44.9 | 39.2 |
| Weekly essay assignments | 19.5 | 19.2 | 16.7 | 19.5 | 30.0 | 23.0 | 50.2 |
| Student presentations | 40.6 | 38.8 | 40.6 | 42.6 | 39.9 | 46.1 | 62.7 |
| Term/research papers | 42.5 | 42.8 | 42.9 | 44.2 | 37.8 | 34.9 | 57.9 |
| Student evaluations of each others' work | 19.7 | 16.7 | 16.8 | 23.3 | 28.2 | 29.8 | 64.6 |
| Grading on a curve | 20.8 | 22.8 | 21.6 | 17.6 | 23.5 | 14.0 | 3.2 |
| Competency-based grading | 51.6 | 52.6 | 51.4 | 47.7 | 61.5 | 51.4 | 77.9 |
| Class discussions | 78.3 | 76.6 | 76.4 | 80.7 | 80.3 | 87.4 | 80.5 |
| Cooperative learning (small groups) | 50.0 | 43.8 | 48.8 | 56.9 | 59.5 | 60.9 | 67.2 |
| Experiential learning/Field studies | 25.5 | 24.1 | 24.1 | 28.2 | 24.6 | 32.3 | 41.4 |
| Teaching assistants | 13.3 | 16.4 | 11.0 | 12.0 | 14.2 | 5.6 | 0.7 |
| Recitals/Demonstrations | 20.9 | 20.3 | 18.9 | 20.7 | 32.8 | 22.8 | 17.4 |
| Group projects | 31.1 | 27.8 | 30.8 | 35.1 | 33.3 | 36.7 | 62.7 |
| Extensive lecturing | 54.8 | 58.4 | 54.6 | 49.8 | 55.2 | 51.7 | 12.2 |
| Multiple drafts of written work | 21.2 | 20.1 | 20.2 | 23.5 | 25.7 | 18.3 | 67.0 |
| Readings on racial and ethnic issues | 17.9 | 15.1 | 16.8 | 21.8 | 25.2 | 19.3 | 52.4 |
| Readings on women and gender issues | 15.5 | 13.1 | 15.9 | 18.2 | 19.6 | 14.2 | 37.3 |
| Student-developed activities (assignments, exams, etc.) | 26.2 | 25.3 | 24.3 | 26.4 | 32.0 | 33.4 | 55.3 |
| Student-selected topics for course content | 15.2 | 13.9 | 13.3 | 16.4 | 21.7 | 21.9 | 40.0 |
| Reflective writing/journaling | 16.3 | 13.6 | 14.9 | 18.5 | 23.5 | 25.3 | 66.0 |
| Community service as part of coursework | 5.3 | 4.5 | 5.4 | 5.6 | 7.6 | 7.1 | 5.2 |
| Electronic quizzes with immediate feedback in class [2] | 6.3 | 4.6 | 6.2 | 8.0 | 10.0 | 7.1 | 0.0 |
| Using real-life problems [2] | 53.8 | 49.7 | 50.3 | 60.7 | 59.1 | 65.5 | 55.4 |
| Using student inquiry to drive learning | 43.7 | 40.6 | 40.2 | 48.8 | 50.8 | 52.5 | 73.5 |

[2]  This question asked for the first time in the 2007–2008 Faculty Survey.

165

# 2007–2008 FACULTY SURVEY WEIGHTED NATIONAL NORMS
## Full-time Undergraduate Faculty at Baccalaureate Institutions

| Male Respondents | All Resp | Full Prof | Assoc Prof | Asst Prof | Lect | Inst | No Resp |
|---|---|---|---|---|---|---|---|
| **YOUR BASE INSTITUTIONAL SALARY** | | | | | | | |
| **9/10 month contract** | | | | | | | |
| Less than $20,000 | 1.9 | 2.3 | 1.8 | 1.1 | 2.6 | 2.3 | 0.0 |
| $20,000 to 29,999 | 0.4 | 0.1 | 0.0 | 0.0 | 2.4 | 5.2 | 0.0 |
| $30,000 to 39,999 | 3.5 | 0.3 | 0.8 | 2.6 | 27.1 | 30.7 | 0.0 |
| $40,000 to 49,999 | 11.8 | 1.0 | 6.4 | 27.8 | 27.2 | 37.1 | 53.8 |
| $50,000 to 59,999 | 18.4 | 4.5 | 23.9 | 35.8 | 17.5 | 15.3 | 14.9 |
| $60,000 to 69,999 | 15.8 | 10.2 | 27.7 | 15.0 | 8.0 | 6.3 | 0.0 |
| $70,000 to 79,999 | 13.8 | 17.5 | 17.1 | 7.9 | 6.7 | 0.8 | 0.0 |
| $80,000 to 89,999 | 10.7 | 16.7 | 11.9 | 3.3 | 1.4 | 0.6 | 0.0 |
| $90,000 to 99,999 | 8.4 | 15.4 | 4.8 | 3.5 | 1.9 | 1.4 | 31.4 |
| $100,000 to 124,999 | 11.2 | 22.7 | 4.9 | 2.4 | 5.3 | 0.3 | 0.0 |
| $125,000 to 149,999 | 2.3 | 5.4 | 0.4 | 0.4 | 0.0 | 0.0 | 0.0 |
| $150,000 or more | 1.7 | 4.0 | 0.3 | 0.2 | 0.0 | 0.0 | 0.0 |
| **11/12 month contract** | | | | | | | |
| Less than $20,000 | 2.4 | 2.2 | 2.5 | 1.6 | 1.4 | 6.8 | 0.0 |
| $20,000 to 29,999 | 0.6 | 0.3 | 0.4 | 0.0 | 1.8 | 3.5 | 0.0 |
| $30,000 to 39,999 | 2.9 | 0.4 | 0.2 | 2.3 | 7.3 | 19.7 | 4.1 |
| $40,000 to 49,999 | 12.0 | 0.9 | 4.1 | 22.7 | 32.6 | 35.1 | 46.1 |
| $50,000 to 59,999 | 15.0 | 2.2 | 14.6 | 33.5 | 25.8 | 14.4 | 34.6 |
| $60,000 to 69,999 | 12.3 | 6.3 | 20.8 | 16.5 | 8.5 | 9.6 | 9.0 |
| $70,000 to 79,999 | 9.4 | 9.4 | 14.3 | 7.3 | 4.5 | 5.7 | 6.3 |
| $80,000 to 89,999 | 13.1 | 16.3 | 17.5 | 8.8 | 7.6 | 3.5 | 0.0 |
| $90,000 to 99,999 | 8.8 | 13.8 | 8.5 | 3.5 | 8.8 | 0.3 | 0.0 |
| $100,000 to 124,999 | 14.3 | 26.1 | 15.4 | 3.0 | 1.6 | 0.9 | 0.0 |
| $125,000 to 149,999 | 4.5 | 11.1 | 1.1 | 0.5 | 0.0 | 0.0 | 0.0 |
| $150,000 or more | 4.4 | 11.1 | 0.9 | 0.2 | 0.0 | 0.4 | 0.0 |
| **Your base institutional salary is based on:** | | | | | | | |
| 9/10 months | 74.4 | 75.4 | 76.8 | 76.8 | 60.1 | 60.8 | 41.7 |
| 11/12 months | 25.6 | 24.6 | 23.2 | 23.2 | 39.9 | 39.2 | 58.3 |
| **WHAT PERCENTAGE OF YOUR CURRENT YEAR'S SALARY COMES FROM: [2]** | | | | | | | |
| **Income from this institution** | | | | | | | |
| All | 59.8 | 58.3 | 61.2 | 64.7 | 44.6 | 59.8 | 38.6 |
| 75 to 99 | 31.5 | 34.4 | 32.7 | 28.1 | 27.9 | 23.2 | 39.1 |
| 50 to 74 | 6.3 | 6.0 | 4.4 | 5.1 | 16.2 | 12.3 | 7.3 |
| 25 to 49 | 1.7 | 1.1 | 1.1 | 1.3 | 9.3 | 3.5 | 15.1 |
| 1 to 24 | 0.4 | 0.1 | 0.4 | 0.4 | 1.9 | 0.8 | 0.0 |
| None | 0.2 | 0.1 | 0.2 | 0.3 | 0.0 | 0.5 | 0.0 |
| **Other academic income** | | | | | | | |
| All | 0.1 | 0.0 | 0.0 | 0.0 | 0.0 | 0.5 | 0.0 |
| 75 to 99 | 0.1 | 0.0 | 0.0 | 0.1 | 0.0 | 0.0 | 0.0 |
| 50 to 74 | 0.6 | 0.3 | 0.4 | 0.7 | 3.1 | 0.5 | 0.0 |
| 25 to 49 | 2.2 | 2.6 | 2.0 | 1.3 | 4.7 | 1.0 | 0.0 |
| 1 to 24 | 17.0 | 18.7 | 16.8 | 15.2 | 18.3 | 11.8 | 8.3 |
| None | 80.1 | 78.4 | 80.7 | 82.6 | 73.8 | 86.2 | 91.7 |
| **Non-academic income** | | | | | | | |
| All | 0.1 | 0.0 | 0.2 | 0.3 | 0.0 | 0.3 | 0.0 |
| 75 to 99 | 0.5 | 0.2 | 0.5 | 0.3 | 2.0 | 1.8 | 0.0 |
| 50 to 74 | 2.0 | 1.3 | 1.4 | 1.5 | 9.4 | 5.4 | 15.2 |
| 25 to 49 | 5.4 | 5.1 | 3.8 | 4.8 | 10.6 | 11.4 | 19.6 |
| 1 to 24 | 22.7 | 25.4 | 23.2 | 19.4 | 22.6 | 15.0 | 26.4 |
| None | 69.2 | 68.0 | 70.9 | 73.6 | 55.4 | 66.1 | 38.8 |

[2] This question asked for the first time in the 2007–2008 Faculty Survey.

166

**2007–2008 FACULTY SURVEY WEIGHTED NATIONAL NORMS**
**Full-time Undergraduate Faculty at Baccalaureate Institutions**

| Male Respondents | All Resp | Full Prof | Assoc Prof | Asst Prof | Lect | Inst | No Resp |
|---|---|---|---|---|---|---|---|
| **What is your age as of 12/31/2007?** | | | | | | | |
| Less than 30 | 1.4 | 0.0 | 0.0 | 2.6 | 1.8 | 13.0 | 2.1 |
| 30 to 34 | 5.8 | 0.0 | 1.4 | 18.6 | 7.9 | 11.8 | 0.0 |
| 35 to 39 | 11.5 | 0.5 | 11.3 | 28.4 | 13.6 | 17.4 | 11.6 |
| 40 to 44 | 11.8 | 4.0 | 18.6 | 17.8 | 12.1 | 9.3 | 0.0 |
| 45 to 49 | 12.8 | 10.4 | 18.7 | 11.2 | 11.2 | 10.6 | 0.0 |
| 50 to 54 | 14.2 | 17.0 | 16.7 | 7.1 | 10.8 | 15.2 | 30.2 |
| 55 to 59 | 16.4 | 23.3 | 14.7 | 8.2 | 18.4 | 8.2 | 3.2 |
| 60 to 64 | 14.6 | 23.8 | 11.6 | 3.8 | 13.9 | 9.7 | 23.3 |
| 65 to 69 | 8.6 | 16.0 | 5.4 | 1.7 | 3.9 | 3.2 | 17.5 |
| 70 or more | 2.9 | 4.9 | 1.5 | 0.5 | 6.6 | 1.7 | 12.2 |
| **Year of highest degree now held** | | | | | | | |
| Before 1970 | 8.0 | 14.9 | 4.2 | 1.0 | 10.6 | 3.4 | 0.0 |
| 1971 to 1975 | 9.5 | 17.8 | 5.7 | 1.0 | 7.0 | 5.4 | 30.7 |
| 1976 to 1980 | 11.3 | 19.2 | 9.1 | 2.7 | 8.7 | 4.9 | 0.0 |
| 1981 to 1985 | 11.7 | 18.1 | 9.4 | 3.0 | 14.2 | 11.7 | 23.6 |
| 1986 to 1990 | 12.2 | 16.2 | 13.9 | 5.3 | 9.4 | 8.1 | 0.0 |
| 1991 to 1995 | 12.3 | 10.3 | 20.6 | 8.4 | 7.9 | 10.0 | 7.6 |
| 1996 to 2000 | 15.1 | 2.7 | 28.2 | 19.8 | 18.3 | 18.9 | 0.0 |
| 2001 to 2005 | 15.4 | 0.7 | 8.0 | 44.7 | 18.8 | 26.9 | 14.1 |
| 2006 to 2007 | 4.5 | 0.1 | 0.9 | 14.2 | 5.2 | 10.7 | 24.0 |
| **Year of appointment at current position** | | | | | | | |
| Before 1970 | 4.8 | 9.8 | 2.4 | 0.7 | 2.7 | 0.0 | 0.0 |
| 1971 to 1975 | 4.7 | 9.7 | 2.2 | 0.3 | 2.7 | 0.5 | 0.0 |
| 1976 to 1980 | 7.1 | 14.1 | 4.8 | 0.6 | 1.2 | 0.8 | 15.4 |
| 1981 to 1985 | 8.4 | 14.6 | 7.1 | 1.6 | 4.4 | 3.0 | 0.0 |
| 1986 to 1990 | 12.0 | 20.3 | 11.0 | 1.4 | 9.5 | 3.5 | 0.0 |
| 1991 to 1995 | 10.6 | 14.5 | 13.0 | 2.9 | 6.9 | 7.2 | 7.4 |
| 1996 to 2000 | 15.9 | 9.6 | 34.3 | 5.3 | 21.3 | 12.3 | 17.5 |
| 2001 to 2005 | 25.4 | 5.7 | 21.7 | 56.0 | 35.7 | 45.8 | 42.5 |
| 2006 to 2007 | 11.1 | 1.7 | 3.5 | 31.1 | 15.5 | 26.8 | 17.2 |
| **If tenured, year tenure was awarded** | | | | | | | |
| Before 1970 | 1.6 | 2.1 | 0.3 | 4.6 | 6.7 | 6.2 | 0.0 |
| 1971 to 1975 | 5.2 | 7.1 | 2.0 | 3.5 | 40.3 | 0.0 | 0.0 |
| 1976 to 1980 | 7.5 | 10.7 | 2.2 | 6.2 | 5.8 | 0.0 | 0.0 |
| 1981 to 1985 | 11.1 | 15.5 | 4.8 | 0.8 | 0.0 | 0.0 | 100.0 |
| 1986 to 1990 | 13.1 | 16.5 | 7.4 | 13.3 | 0.0 | 0.0 | 0.0 |
| 1991 to 1995 | 16.7 | 20.6 | 10.7 | 9.4 | 11.4 | 13.0 | 0.0 |
| 1996 to 2000 | 15.3 | 17.1 | 13.3 | 6.4 | 14.9 | 4.9 | 0.0 |
| 2001 to 2005 | 17.9 | 8.5 | 34.0 | 18.1 | 20.9 | 11.2 | 0.0 |
| 2006 to 2007 | 11.6 | 1.8 | 25.3 | 37.6 | 0.0 | 64.6 | 0.0 |

167

## 2007–2008 FACULTY SURVEY WEIGHTED NATIONAL NORMS
### Full-time Undergraduate Faculty at Baccalaureate Institutions

| Male Respondents | All Resp | Full Prof | Assoc Prof | Asst Prof | Lect | Inst | No Resp |
|---|---|---|---|---|---|---|---|
| **WHAT IS THE MAJOR OF THE HIGHEST DEGREE YOU HOLD?** | | | | | | | |
| **Biological Science** | | | | | | | |
| Agriculture | 1.2 | 1.7 | 1.2 | 0.6 | 1.5 | 0.6 | 0.0 |
| Forestry | 0.3 | 0.1 | 0.2 | 0.7 | 0.0 | 0.2 | 0.0 |
| Bacteriology, Molecular Biology | 0.9 | 1.2 | 1.0 | 0.9 | 0.1 | 0.3 | 0.0 |
| Biochemistry | 1.0 | 1.0 | 0.8 | 1.2 | 1.2 | 0.4 | 0.0 |
| Biophysics | 0.1 | 0.0 | 0.1 | 0.1 | 0.0 | 0.0 | 0.0 |
| Botany | 0.8 | 1.1 | 0.6 | 0.6 | 0.1 | 0.2 | 0.0 |
| Environmental Science | 0.6 | 0.6 | 0.5 | 0.7 | 0.6 | 0.6 | 0.0 |
| Marine (life) Sciences | 0.2 | 0.2 | 0.3 | 0.1 | 0.2 | 0.0 | 0.0 |
| Physiology, Anatomy | 0.9 | 1.1 | 1.0 | 0.6 | 0.2 | 0.5 | 0.0 |
| Zoology | 1.4 | 2.3 | 1.2 | 0.6 | 0.2 | 0.4 | 0.0 |
| General, Other Biological Sciences | 1.9 | 2.2 | 1.8 | 1.4 | 2.6 | 1.2 | 0.0 |
| **Business** | | | | | | | |
| Accounting | 1.1 | 1.2 | 1.1 | 0.8 | 1.5 | 0.9 | 0.0 |
| Finance | 0.8 | 0.5 | 0.9 | 1.0 | 0.6 | 2.3 | 0.0 |
| International Business | 0.1 | 0.1 | 0.1 | 0.1 | 0.1 | 0.4 | 0.0 |
| Management | 2.4 | 1.5 | 2.3 | 3.9 | 2.2 | 2.8 | 0.0 |
| Marketing | 1.0 | 1.0 | 0.7 | 1.4 | 0.0 | 1.7 | 0.0 |
| Secretarial Studies | 0.0 | 0.0 | 0.0 | 0.0 | 0.0 | 0.0 | 0.0 |
| General, Other Business | 1.4 | 0.8 | 1.3 | 1.6 | 2.0 | 3.7 | 0.0 |
| **Education** | | | | | | | |
| Business Education | 0.2 | 0.2 | 0.2 | 0.1 | 0.1 | 0.5 | 0.0 |
| Educational Administration | 1.0 | 0.4 | 0.8 | 1.3 | 2.8 | 2.4 | 0.0 |
| Educational Psychology/Counseling | 0.7 | 0.4 | 0.8 | 1.3 | 0.6 | 0.3 | 0.0 |
| Elementary Education | 0.4 | 0.5 | 0.7 | 0.3 | 0.0 | 0.0 | 0.0 |
| Higher Education | 0.9 | 0.8 | 0.7 | 1.2 | 1.0 | 1.0 | 0.0 |
| Music or Art Education | 0.2 | 0.1 | 0.3 | 0.4 | 0.0 | 0.3 | 0.0 |
| Physical or Health Education | 1.6 | 1.6 | 1.0 | 1.1 | 3.5 | 4.7 | 0.0 |
| Secondary Education | 0.8 | 0.6 | 0.8 | 1.2 | 0.3 | 0.8 | 0.0 |
| Special Education | 0.4 | 0.2 | 0.4 | 1.0 | 0.0 | 0.4 | 0.0 |
| General, Other Education Fields | 2.0 | 1.3 | 1.8 | 2.8 | 1.5 | 3.7 | 17.5 |
| **Engineering** | | | | | | | |
| Aero-/Astronautical Engineering | 0.3 | 0.5 | 0.4 | 0.1 | 0.0 | 0.2 | 0.0 |
| Chemical Engineering | 0.5 | 0.6 | 0.4 | 0.4 | 0.2 | 0.0 | 0.0 |
| Civil Engineering | 1.1 | 1.3 | 1.1 | 0.8 | 0.6 | 0.2 | 0.0 |
| Electrical Engineering | 1.3 | 1.3 | 1.4 | 1.5 | 0.9 | 1.2 | 0.0 |
| Industrial Engineering | 0.3 | 0.3 | 0.4 | 0.3 | 0.0 | 0.4 | 0.0 |
| Mechanical Engineering | 1.5 | 1.4 | 2.1 | 1.4 | 1.0 | 0.9 | 0.0 |
| General, Other Engineering Fields | 1.4 | 1.6 | 1.3 | 1.4 | 1.1 | 0.6 | 0.0 |
| **Health** | | | | | | | |
| Dentistry | 0.4 | 0.1 | 1.3 | 0.3 | 0.0 | 0.0 | 0.0 |
| Health Technology | 0.0 | 0.0 | 0.0 | 0.0 | 0.0 | 0.0 | 0.0 |
| Medicine or Surgery | 0.2 | 0.3 | 0.1 | 0.2 | 0.0 | 0.0 | 0.0 |
| Nursing | 0.3 | 0.0 | 0.4 | 0.2 | 0.2 | 2.2 | 0.0 |
| Pharmacy, Pharmacology | 0.7 | 0.4 | 1.6 | 0.6 | 0.0 | 0.2 | 0.0 |
| Therapy (speech, physical, occup.) | 0.2 | 0.1 | 0.4 | 0.2 | 0.0 | 0.3 | 0.0 |
| Veterinary Medicine | 0.1 | 0.0 | 0.2 | 0.1 | 0.0 | 0.0 | 0.0 |
| General, Other Health Fields | 0.6 | 0.3 | 0.7 | 0.6 | 0.6 | 1.7 | 0.0 |

| Male Respondents | All Resp | Full Prof | Assoc Prof | Asst Prof | Lect | Inst | No Resp |
|---|---|---|---|---|---|---|---|
| **WHAT IS THE MAJOR OF THE HIGHEST DEGREE YOU HOLD?** | | | | | | | |
| **Humanities** | | | | | | | |
| History | 4.5 | 4.8 | 5.5 | 4.0 | 3.3 | 1.5 | 3.1 |
| Political Science, Government | 2.9 | 3.3 | 3.2 | 2.9 | 1.3 | 1.1 | 0.0 |
| English Language & Literature | 5.6 | 5.4 | 5.3 | 5.1 | 9.1 | 6.1 | 23.3 |
| Foreign Languages & Literature | 0.8 | 0.7 | 0.6 | 1.0 | 0.8 | 1.4 | 0.0 |
| French | 0.4 | 0.5 | 0.3 | 0.4 | 0.0 | 0.1 | 0.0 |
| German | 0.3 | 0.4 | 0.3 | 0.3 | 0.4 | 0.0 | 0.0 |
| Spanish | 0.8 | 0.7 | 0.9 | 1.0 | 0.9 | 1.0 | 0.0 |
| Other Foreign Languages | 0.4 | 0.5 | 0.4 | 0.3 | 0.4 | 0.1 | 0.0 |
| Linguistics | 0.5 | 0.4 | 0.8 | 0.3 | 0.8 | 0.6 | 0.0 |
| Philosophy | 2.5 | 2.4 | 2.6 | 2.8 | 1.6 | 1.1 | 11.6 |
| Religion or Theology | 2.3 | 2.3 | 2.5 | 2.2 | 3.6 | 1.4 | 0.0 |
| General, Other Humanities Fields | 1.0 | 0.8 | 1.0 | 1.1 | 2.1 | 0.0 | 0.0 |
| **Fine Arts** | | | | | | | |
| Architecture/Urban Planning | 0.7 | 0.7 | 0.6 | 0.9 | 0.0 | 0.2 | 0.0 |
| Art | 1.8 | 1.7 | 2.0 | 1.3 | 3.6 | 2.4 | 0.0 |
| Dramatics or Speech | 1.6 | 1.6 | 1.7 | 1.3 | 1.8 | 1.8 | 0.0 |
| Music | 3.4 | 3.3 | 3.8 | 3.1 | 3.3 | 4.0 | 7.4 |
| Television or Film | 0.4 | 0.2 | 0.4 | 0.7 | 0.4 | 1.3 | 0.0 |
| Other Fine Arts | 0.9 | 0.6 | 0.7 | 0.8 | 1.6 | 2.8 | 0.0 |
| **Physical Science** | | | | | | | |
| Mathematics and/or Statistics | 6.1 | 6.8 | 5.6 | 4.9 | 6.3 | 8.3 | 0.0 |
| Astronomy | 0.3 | 0.4 | 0.4 | 0.2 | 0.2 | 0.1 | 0.0 |
| Atmospheric Sciences | 0.2 | 0.2 | 0.2 | 0.3 | 0.2 | 0.0 | 0.0 |
| Chemistry | 4.1 | 4.7 | 3.3 | 4.5 | 1.8 | 3.3 | 0.0 |
| Earth Sciences | 1.4 | 2.0 | 1.2 | 0.7 | 0.9 | 1.6 | 3.2 |
| Geography | 0.9 | 0.9 | 1.3 | 0.9 | 0.0 | 0.6 | 0.0 |
| Marine Sciences (incl. Oceanography) | 0.1 | 0.2 | 0.1 | 0.2 | 0.0 | 0.0 | 0.0 |
| Physics | 3.0 | 3.6 | 2.7 | 2.9 | 3.1 | 0.6 | 0.0 |
| General, Other Physical Sciences | 0.1 | 0.1 | 0.1 | 0.2 | 0.1 | 0.0 | 0.0 |
| **Social Science** | | | | | | | |
| Anthropology | 1.0 | 0.7 | 0.9 | 1.7 | 1.1 | 0.5 | 6.6 |
| Archaeology | 0.0 | 0.1 | 0.1 | 0.0 | 0.0 | 0.0 | 0.0 |
| Clinical Psychology | 1.1 | 0.7 | 0.9 | 1.3 | 4.2 | 0.2 | 0.0 |
| Counseling and Guidance | 0.4 | 0.3 | 0.5 | 0.1 | 1.0 | 0.6 | 0.0 |
| Experimental Psychology | 1.4 | 2.1 | 1.2 | 0.7 | 0.7 | 0.0 | 0.0 |
| Social Psychology | 0.8 | 1.0 | 0.8 | 0.5 | 1.3 | 0.1 | 0.0 |
| General, Other Psychology | 0.9 | 1.1 | 0.9 | 0.9 | 0.0 | 0.4 | 0.0 |
| Economics | 3.1 | 3.9 | 2.5 | 2.8 | 3.6 | 1.1 | 0.0 |
| Sociology | 2.2 | 2.5 | 1.4 | 2.8 | 2.5 | 0.6 | 0.0 |
| Social Work, Social Welfare | 0.6 | 0.4 | 0.5 | 1.0 | 0.0 | 0.8 | 0.0 |
| General, Other Social Sciences | 1.3 | 1.5 | 1.6 | 0.9 | 0.2 | 2.2 | 0.0 |

## 2007–2008 FACULTY SURVEY WEIGHTED NATIONAL NORMS
### Full-time Undergraduate Faculty at Baccalaureate Institutions

| Male Respondents | All Resp | Full Prof | Assoc Prof | Asst Prof | Lect | Inst | No Resp |
|---|---|---|---|---|---|---|---|
| **WHAT IS THE MAJOR OF THE HIGHEST DEGREE YOU HOLD?** | | | | | | | |
| **Technical** | | | | | | | |
| Computer Science | 2.2 | 1.3 | 2.9 | 2.5 | 3.1 | 2.6 | 12.2 |
| Data Processing, Computer Prog. | 0.0 | 0.1 | 0.0 | 0.0 | 0.0 | 0.0 | 0.0 |
| Drafting/Design | 0.0 | 0.0 | 0.0 | 0.0 | 0.0 | 0.0 | 0.0 |
| Electronics | 0.0 | 0.0 | 0.0 | 0.0 | 0.0 | 0.8 | 0.0 |
| Industrial Arts | 0.2 | 0.2 | 0.2 | 0.1 | 0.0 | 0.1 | 0.0 |
| Mechanics | 0.0 | 0.0 | 0.0 | 0.0 | 0.0 | 0.0 | 0.0 |
| Other Technical | 0.2 | 0.2 | 0.2 | 0.3 | 0.2 | 0.1 | 0.0 |
| **Other Fields** | | | | | | | |
| Building Trades | 0.0 | 0.0 | 0.0 | 0.0 | 0.0 | 0.2 | 0.0 |
| Communications | 2.0 | 1.5 | 1.5 | 2.3 | 2.0 | 5.5 | 15.2 |
| Ethnic Studies | 0.0 | 0.0 | 0.0 | 0.0 | 0.0 | 0.1 | 0.0 |
| Human Ecology/Family Science | 0.2 | 0.2 | 0.3 | 0.1 | 0.0 | 0.1 | 0.0 |
| Journalism | 0.5 | 0.3 | 0.5 | 0.4 | 2.6 | 0.4 | 0.0 |
| Law | 0.9 | 0.8 | 0.9 | 0.9 | 1.5 | 0.9 | 0.0 |
| Law Enforcement | 0.1 | 0.1 | 0.1 | 0.1 | 0.0 | 0.7 | 0.0 |
| Library Science | 0.3 | 0.1 | 0.2 | 0.4 | 0.1 | 1.9 | 0.0 |
| Women's Studies | 0.0 | 0.0 | 0.0 | 0.0 | 0.0 | 0.0 | 0.0 |
| Other Vocational | 0.0 | 0.1 | 0.0 | 0.0 | 0.0 | 0.0 | 0.0 |
| All Other Fields | 0.6 | 0.5 | 0.5 | 0.8 | 0.5 | 0.9 | 0.0 |

| Male Respondents | All Resp | Full Prof | Assoc Prof | Asst Prof | Lect | Inst | No Resp |
|---|---|---|---|---|---|---|---|
| **WHAT IS THE DEPARTMENT OF YOUR CURRENT FACULTY APPOINTMENT?** | | | | | | | |
| **Biological Science** | | | | | | | |
| Agriculture | 1.3 | 1.7 | 1.4 | 0.7 | 1.1 | 0.9 | 0.0 |
| Forestry | 0.1 | 0.1 | 0.2 | 0.1 | 0.0 | 0.0 | 0.0 |
| Bacteriology, Molecular Biology | 0.3 | 0.4 | 0.3 | 0.2 | 0.0 | 0.0 | 0.0 |
| Biochemistry | 0.3 | 0.4 | 0.3 | 0.2 | 1.0 | 0.0 | 0.0 |
| Biophysics | 0.0 | 0.0 | 0.0 | 0.0 | 0.0 | 0.0 | 0.0 |
| Botany | 0.3 | 0.3 | 0.4 | 0.4 | 0.0 | 0.7 | 0.0 |
| Environmental Science | 0.7 | 0.9 | 0.6 | 0.6 | 0.2 | 0.0 | 3.2 |
| Marine (life) Sciences | 0.1 | 0.1 | 0.0 | 0.2 | 0.0 | 0.0 | 0.0 |
| Physiology, Anatomy | 0.3 | 0.3 | 0.3 | 0.3 | 0.2 | 0.2 | 0.0 |
| Zoology | 0.5 | 1.0 | 0.3 | 0.3 | 0.0 | 0.0 | 0.0 |
| General, Other Biological Sciences | 4.7 | 5.9 | 4.2 | 3.9 | 4.0 | 2.4 | 0.0 |
| **Business** | | | | | | | |
| Accounting | 1.4 | 1.5 | 1.4 | 1.4 | 1.5 | 0.9 | 0.0 |
| Finance | 0.9 | 0.8 | 0.8 | 1.0 | 0.4 | 2.3 | 0.0 |
| International Business | 0.2 | 0.2 | 0.2 | 0.1 | 0.2 | 0.0 | 0.0 |
| Management | 2.6 | 1.9 | 2.5 | 3.5 | 3.3 | 3.2 | 0.0 |
| Marketing | 1.2 | 0.9 | 0.8 | 1.6 | 2.3 | 2.6 | 15.2 |
| Secretarial Studies | 0.0 | 0.0 | 0.0 | 0.0 | 0.0 | 0.0 | 0.0 |
| General, Other Business | 1.9 | 1.7 | 2.0 | 2.1 | 1.4 | 2.4 | 0.0 |
| **Education** | | | | | | | |
| Business Education | 0.0 | 0.1 | 0.0 | 0.0 | 0.0 | 0.1 | 0.0 |
| Educational Administration | 0.2 | 0.1 | 0.2 | 0.3 | 0.4 | 0.1 | 2.1 |
| Educational Psychology/Counseling | 0.3 | 0.4 | 0.1 | 0.4 | 0.0 | 0.0 | 0.0 |
| Elementary Education | 0.8 | 0.8 | 0.9 | 1.3 | 0.0 | 0.0 | 0.0 |
| Higher Education | 0.5 | 0.8 | 0.1 | 0.1 | 2.3 | 0.2 | 0.0 |
| Music or Art Education | 0.1 | 0.0 | 0.1 | 0.2 | 0.0 | 0.5 | 0.0 |
| Physical or Health Education | 2.2 | 1.9 | 1.8 | 1.7 | 3.8 | 6.6 | 0.0 |
| Secondary Education | 0.8 | 0.4 | 0.8 | 1.7 | 0.1 | 0.1 | 0.0 |
| Special Education | 0.3 | 0.1 | 0.3 | 0.5 | 0.0 | 0.4 | 0.0 |
| General, Other Education Fields | 1.3 | 0.9 | 0.9 | 1.6 | 0.2 | 5.7 | 0.0 |
| **Engineering** | | | | | | | |
| Aero-/Astronautical Engineering | 0.3 | 0.5 | 0.4 | 0.1 | 0.6 | 0.0 | 0.0 |
| Chemical Engineering | 0.5 | 0.6 | 0.5 | 0.4 | 0.0 | 0.0 | 0.0 |
| Civil Engineering | 1.0 | 1.5 | 0.9 | 0.8 | 0.5 | 0.0 | 0.0 |
| Electrical Engineering | 1.1 | 1.3 | 1.1 | 1.2 | 0.5 | 0.5 | 0.0 |
| Industrial Engineering | 0.2 | 0.2 | 0.3 | 0.0 | 0.4 | 0.0 | 0.0 |
| Mechanical Engineering | 1.6 | 1.5 | 2.2 | 1.3 | 1.0 | 0.5 | 0.0 |
| General, Other Engineering Fields | 1.4 | 1.4 | 1.4 | 1.8 | 1.3 | 0.4 | 0.0 |
| **Health** | | | | | | | |
| Dentistry | 0.4 | 0.1 | 1.3 | 0.3 | 0.0 | 0.0 | 0.0 |
| Health Technology | 0.0 | 0.0 | 0.0 | 0.1 | 0.0 | 0.0 | 0.0 |
| Medicine or Surgery | 0.4 | 0.3 | 0.1 | 0.9 | 0.0 | 0.0 | 0.0 |
| Nursing | 0.3 | 0.0 | 0.6 | 0.3 | 0.2 | 2.2 | 0.0 |
| Pharmacy, Pharmacology | 0.8 | 0.6 | 1.5 | 0.7 | 0.0 | 0.2 | 0.0 |
| Therapy (speech, physical, occup.) | 0.3 | 0.1 | 0.6 | 0.6 | 0.0 | 0.0 | 0.0 |
| Veterinary Medicine | 0.0 | 0.0 | 0.1 | 0.0 | 0.0 | 0.0 | 0.0 |
| General, Other Health Fields | 1.0 | 0.8 | 1.1 | 1.2 | 1.1 | 1.6 | 0.0 |

**2007–2008 FACULTY SURVEY WEIGHTED NATIONAL NORMS**
**Full-time Undergraduate Faculty at Baccalaureate Institutions**

| Male Respondents | All Resp | Full Prof | Assoc Prof | Asst Prof | Lect | Inst | No Resp |
|---|---|---|---|---|---|---|---|
| **WHAT IS THE DEPARTMENT OF YOUR CURRENT FACULTY APPOINTMENT?** | | | | | | | |
| **Humanities** | | | | | | | |
| History | 4.1 | 4.5 | 4.8 | 3.5 | 3.4 | 1.3 | 3.1 |
| Political Science, Government | 2.8 | 3.1 | 3.1 | 2.7 | 1.5 | 1.4 | 0.0 |
| English Language & Literature | 6.1 | 5.8 | 5.9 | 5.6 | 10.4 | 7.0 | 40.8 |
| Foreign Languages & Literature | 1.8 | 1.7 | 1.5 | 2.3 | 1.9 | 1.5 | 0.0 |
| French | 0.2 | 0.2 | 0.1 | 0.2 | 0.1 | 0.0 | 0.0 |
| German | 0.2 | 0.2 | 0.3 | 0.1 | 0.6 | 0.2 | 0.0 |
| Spanish | 0.5 | 0.5 | 0.4 | 0.4 | 1.2 | 0.9 | 0.0 |
| Other Foreign Languages | 0.3 | 0.4 | 0.3 | 0.1 | 0.2 | 0.5 | 0.0 |
| Linguistics | 0.2 | 0.0 | 0.3 | 0.3 | 0.0 | 0.2 | 0.0 |
| Philosophy | 2.3 | 2.4 | 2.3 | 2.6 | 1.6 | 0.8 | 0.0 |
| Religion or Theology | 2.2 | 2.4 | 2.7 | 2.2 | 0.6 | 1.2 | 4.5 |
| General, Other Humanities Fields | 1.3 | 1.2 | 1.3 | 1.1 | 1.1 | 2.7 | 11.6 |
| **Fine Arts** | | | | | | | |
| Architecture/Urban Planning | 0.8 | 0.9 | 1.0 | 0.7 | 0.4 | 0.2 | 0.0 |
| Art | 2.1 | 1.9 | 2.2 | 1.6 | 3.6 | 2.7 | 0.0 |
| Dramatics or Speech | 1.6 | 1.5 | 1.8 | 1.4 | 1.5 | 1.6 | 0.0 |
| Music | 3.6 | 3.4 | 3.9 | 3.4 | 3.3 | 3.9 | 7.4 |
| Television or Film | 0.3 | 0.2 | 0.4 | 0.4 | 0.5 | 0.6 | 0.0 |
| Other Fine Arts | 0.6 | 0.3 | 0.7 | 0.6 | 1.1 | 1.4 | 0.0 |
| **Physical Science** | | | | | | | |
| Mathematics and/or Statistics | 5.9 | 6.2 | 5.5 | 5.4 | 4.2 | 9.7 | 0.0 |
| Astronomy | 0.2 | 0.2 | 0.3 | 0.0 | 0.1 | 0.0 | 0.0 |
| Atmospheric Sciences | 0.1 | 0.1 | 0.1 | 0.0 | 0.0 | 0.0 | 0.0 |
| Chemistry | 4.1 | 4.8 | 3.3 | 4.5 | 1.8 | 3.4 | 0.0 |
| Earth Sciences | 1.4 | 1.8 | 1.3 | 0.8 | 0.7 | 1.3 | 0.0 |
| Geography | 0.9 | 1.0 | 0.9 | 1.0 | 0.0 | 0.4 | 0.0 |
| Marine Sciences (incl. Oceanography) | 0.1 | 0.1 | 0.1 | 0.0 | 0.0 | 0.0 | 0.0 |
| Physics | 2.9 | 3.3 | 2.3 | 3.2 | 3.1 | 1.2 | 0.0 |
| General, Other Physical Sciences | 0.4 | 0.3 | 0.7 | 0.4 | 0.1 | 0.4 | 0.0 |
| **Social Science** | | | | | | | |
| Anthropology | 0.7 | 0.6 | 0.6 | 1.0 | 0.6 | 0.0 | 0.0 |
| Archaeology | 0.0 | 0.0 | 0.0 | 0.0 | 0.0 | 0.0 | 0.0 |
| Clinical Psychology | 0.6 | 0.5 | 0.4 | 0.5 | 3.5 | 0.0 | 0.0 |
| Counseling and Guidance | 0.1 | 0.1 | 0.2 | 0.0 | 0.4 | 0.0 | 0.0 |
| Experimental Psychology | 0.7 | 1.1 | 0.6 | 0.5 | 0.2 | 0.0 | 0.0 |
| Social Psychology | 0.3 | 0.3 | 0.1 | 0.2 | 1.6 | 0.0 | 0.0 |
| General, Other Psychology | 2.1 | 2.5 | 2.3 | 1.9 | 1.5 | 0.4 | 0.0 |
| Economics | 2.5 | 3.3 | 2.0 | 2.2 | 3.1 | 0.6 | 0.0 |
| Sociology | 1.9 | 2.0 | 1.6 | 2.3 | 2.2 | 0.6 | 0.0 |
| Social Work, Social Welfare | 0.6 | 0.3 | 0.6 | 1.1 | 0.0 | 0.8 | 0.0 |
| General, Other Social Sciences | 2.1 | 2.2 | 2.2 | 2.0 | 1.5 | 2.0 | 0.0 |

172

**2007–2008 FACULTY SURVEY WEIGHTED NATIONAL NORMS**
**Full-time Undergraduate Faculty at Baccalaureate Institutions**

| Male Respondents | All Resp | Full Prof | Assoc Prof | Asst Prof | Lect | Inst | No Resp |
|---|---|---|---|---|---|---|---|
| **WHAT IS THE DEPARTMENT OF YOUR CURRENT FACULTY APPOINTMENT?** | | | | | | | |
| **Technical** | | | | | | | |
| Computer Science | 2.5 | 1.8 | 3.2 | 2.3 | 4.4 | 3.6 | 12.2 |
| Data Processing, Computer Prog. | 0.1 | 0.2 | 0.1 | 0.2 | 0.0 | 0.1 | 0.0 |
| Drafting/Design | 0.1 | 0.0 | 0.0 | 0.2 | 0.0 | 0.0 | 0.0 |
| Electronics | 0.1 | 0.1 | 0.1 | 0.2 | 0.0 | 0.0 | 0.0 |
| Industrial Arts | 0.1 | 0.1 | 0.2 | 0.1 | 0.0 | 0.1 | 0.0 |
| Mechanics | 0.0 | 0.0 | 0.1 | 0.0 | 0.0 | 0.0 | 0.0 |
| Other Technical | 0.7 | 0.5 | 0.8 | 0.7 | 1.0 | 2.1 | 0.0 |
| **Other Fields** | | | | | | | |
| Building Trades | 0.0 | 0.0 | 0.0 | 0.0 | 0.0 | 0.0 | 0.0 |
| Communications | 2.4 | 1.6 | 2.2 | 2.9 | 2.8 | 6.5 | 0.0 |
| Ethnic Studies | 0.2 | 0.1 | 0.0 | 0.3 | 1.9 | 0.0 | 0.0 |
| Human Ecology/Family Science | 0.1 | 0.1 | 0.3 | 0.1 | 0.0 | 0.0 | 0.0 |
| Journalism | 0.5 | 0.6 | 0.4 | 0.4 | 1.9 | 0.2 | 0.0 |
| Law | 0.1 | 0.1 | 0.1 | 0.2 | 0.0 | 0.3 | 0.0 |
| Law Enforcement | 0.2 | 0.2 | 0.1 | 0.3 | 0.0 | 0.7 | 0.0 |
| Library Science | 0.2 | 0.1 | 0.2 | 0.4 | 0.2 | 0.7 | 0.0 |
| Women's Studies | 0.0 | 0.0 | 0.0 | 0.0 | 0.0 | 0.0 | 0.0 |
| Other Vocational | 0.1 | 0.0 | 0.1 | 0.1 | 0.0 | 0.2 | 0.0 |
| All Other Fields | 1.2 | 0.8 | 1.4 | 1.4 | 1.9 | 1.4 | 0.0 |
| **HOW MANY CHILDREN DO YOU HAVE IN THE FOLLOWING AGE RANGES?** | | | | | | | |
| **Under 18 years old** | | | | | | | |
| None | 60.0 | 71.4 | 50.9 | 49.7 | 62.3 | 64.5 | 92.0 |
| One | 16.0 | 13.5 | 16.7 | 18.5 | 21.5 | 14.6 | 0.7 |
| Two | 16.3 | 10.8 | 21.9 | 21.5 | 9.3 | 14.0 | 7.3 |
| Three | 5.4 | 3.1 | 7.4 | 7.4 | 4.0 | 4.7 | 0.0 |
| Four or more | 2.2 | 1.2 | 3.0 | 2.9 | 2.9 | 2.1 | 0.0 |
| **18 years or older** | | | | | | | |
| None | 52.5 | 29.2 | 58.8 | 80.9 | 51.7 | 71.3 | 22.8 |
| One | 12.9 | 17.3 | 13.3 | 6.1 | 11.4 | 9.5 | 17.1 |
| Two | 19.7 | 30.1 | 15.5 | 8.6 | 22.5 | 8.8 | 45.0 |
| Three | 9.0 | 14.0 | 7.8 | 2.6 | 10.0 | 4.3 | 15.1 |
| Four or more | 5.9 | 9.5 | 4.6 | 1.8 | 4.4 | 6.0 | 0.0 |
| **How would you characterize your political views?** | | | | | | | |
| Far left | 8.0 | 6.9 | 8.5 | 9.7 | 9.3 | 6.1 | 5.7 |
| Liberal | 43.8 | 47.0 | 43.4 | 41.0 | 45.4 | 31.4 | 63.8 |
| Middle of the Road | 29.9 | 28.8 | 30.0 | 31.9 | 24.6 | 35.1 | 18.6 |
| Conservative | 17.3 | 16.6 | 16.9 | 16.7 | 18.8 | 26.5 | 11.9 |
| Far right | 0.9 | 0.8 | 1.2 | 0.7 | 1.9 | 1.0 | 0.0 |
| **Are you currently:** | | | | | | | |
| Single | 8.2 | 4.7 | 7.6 | 12.0 | 10.9 | 16.8 | 9.2 |
| Married | 82.9 | 87.7 | 83.8 | 77.8 | 76.2 | 72.6 | 71.6 |
| Unmarried, living with partner | 3.7 | 2.2 | 3.5 | 5.8 | 4.7 | 5.2 | 0.0 |
| Divorced | 3.9 | 3.6 | 4.1 | 3.4 | 6.6 | 4.8 | 19.2 |
| Widowed | 0.8 | 1.4 | 0.3 | 0.3 | 1.1 | 0.0 | 0.0 |
| Separated | 0.6 | 0.5 | 0.7 | 0.6 | 0.5 | 0.7 | 0.0 |

173

## 2007–2008 FACULTY SURVEY WEIGHTED NATIONAL NORMS
### Full-time Undergraduate Faculty at Baccalaureate Institutions

| Male Respondents | All Resp | Full Prof | Assoc Prof | Asst Prof | Lect | Inst | No Resp |
|---|---|---|---|---|---|---|---|
| **Is English your native language?** | | | | | | | |
| Yes | 89.0 | 90.8 | 89.6 | 84.1 | 89.9 | 94.3 | 100.0 |
| No | 11.0 | 9.2 | 10.4 | 15.9 | 10.1 | 5.7 | 0.0 |
| **Are you: [5]** | | | | | | | |
| White/Caucasian | 88.2 | 91.6 | 87.4 | 83.6 | 83.7 | 92.1 | 100.0 |
| African American/Black | 2.4 | 1.2 | 3.5 | 3.4 | 1.0 | 2.5 | 0.0 |
| American Indian/Alaska Native | 1.9 | 1.6 | 2.0 | 1.7 | 2.3 | 3.7 | 0.0 |
| Asian American/Asian | 5.3 | 3.9 | 4.4 | 8.8 | 8.2 | 0.7 | 0.0 |
| Native Hawaiian/Pacific Islander | 0.3 | 0.1 | 0.3 | 0.5 | 0.4 | 0.6 | 0.0 |
| Mexican American/Chicano | 1.2 | 0.8 | 0.9 | 1.1 | 4.9 | 1.4 | 0.0 |
| Puerto Rican | 0.3 | 0.1 | 0.4 | 0.5 | 0.7 | 0.1 | 0.0 |
| Other Latino | 1.7 | 1.0 | 1.7 | 2.2 | 3.7 | 1.3 | 0.0 |
| Other | 2.7 | 2.1 | 3.1 | 3.3 | 4.0 | 1.6 | 0.0 |
| **Do you give the Higher Education Research Institute (HERI) permission to retain your contact information (i.e., your email address and name) for possible follow-up research?** | | | | | | | |
| Yes | 71.2 | 72.5 | 73.3 | 64.6 | 79.5 | 73.3 | 29.8 |
| No | 28.8 | 27.5 | 26.7 | 35.4 | 20.5 | 26.7 | 70.2 |

[4] Percentages will sum to more than 100.0 if any respondent marked more than one category.

# Full-Time Undergraduate Faculty, Rank and Control for

# Women

# 2007–2008 FACULTY SURVEY WEIGHTED NATIONAL NORMS
## Full-time Undergraduate Faculty at Baccalaureate Institutions

| Female Respondents | All Resp | Full Prof | Assoc Prof | Asst Prof | Lect | Inst | No Resp |
|---|---|---|---|---|---|---|---|
| **Number of Respondents** | 9,879 | 2,208 | 3,035 | 3,341 | 504 | 775 | 16 |
| **What is your principal activity in your current position at this institution?** | | | | | | | |
| Administration | 5.5 | 9.7 | 6.4 | 2.5 | 5.9 | 4.7 | 34.5 |
| Teaching | 86.4 | 82.1 | 85.7 | 87.2 | 90.1 | 90.9 | 46.5 |
| Research | 6.2 | 7.0 | 6.9 | 8.6 | 0.5 | 0.3 | 0.0 |
| Services to clients and patients | 0.9 | 0.5 | 0.4 | 0.8 | 1.3 | 2.4 | 0.0 |
| Other | 1.0 | 0.7 | 0.5 | 0.9 | 2.2 | 1.8 | 18.9 |
| **What is your present academic rank?** | | | | | | | |
| Professor | 19.7 | 100.0 | 0.0 | 0.0 | 0.0 | 0.0 | 0.0 |
| Associate Professor | 26.3 | 0.0 | 100.0 | 0.0 | 0.0 | 0.0 | 0.0 |
| Assistant Professor | 33.2 | 0.0 | 0.0 | 100.0 | 0.0 | 0.0 | 0.0 |
| Lecturer | 9.5 | 0.0 | 0.0 | 0.0 | 100.0 | 0.0 | 0.0 |
| Instructor | 11.3 | 0.0 | 0.0 | 0.0 | 0.0 | 100.0 | 0.0 |
| **What is your tenure status at this institution?** | | | | | | | |
| Tenured | 43.5 | 93.5 | 85.5 | 7.2 | 0.4 | 1.5 | 24.3 |
| On tenure track, but not tenured | 26.0 | 0.6 | 5.7 | 69.5 | 0.9 | 10.8 | 0.0 |
| Not on tenure track, but institution has tenure system | 26.7 | 2.5 | 5.2 | 18.9 | 97.9 | 81.6 | 75.7 |
| Institution has no tenure system | 3.8 | 3.4 | 3.6 | 4.3 | 0.8 | 6.2 | 0.0 |
| **Are you currently serving in an administrative position as: [1]** | | | | | | | |
| Department Chair | 9.4 | 18.3 | 15.5 | 4.2 | 2.0 | 0.8 | 6.7 |
| Dean (Associate or Assistant) | 1.2 | 2.4 | 1.7 | 0.5 | 0.5 | 0.6 | 0.0 |
| President | 0.0 | 0.0 | 0.0 | 0.0 | 0.0 | 0.0 | 0.0 |
| Vice-President | 0.0 | 0.0 | 0.0 | 0.0 | 0.0 | 0.0 | 0.0 |
| Provost | 0.0 | 0.1 | 0.0 | 0.0 | 0.0 | 0.0 | 0.0 |
| Other | 16.3 | 20.3 | 17.6 | 11.7 | 24.8 | 11.9 | 42.5 |
| Not Applicable | 68.4 | 54.9 | 61.1 | 77.4 | 68.0 | 83.3 | 11.7 |
| **My primary place of employment in the last year was: [2]** | | | | | | | |
| In higher education: | | | | | | | |
|   at this institution | 94.0 | 98.5 | 98.2 | 89.3 | 92.7 | 91.7 | 100.0 |
|   at a different institution | 2.9 | 0.8 | 0.7 | 5.9 | 3.5 | 2.1 | 0.0 |
|   at more than one institution | 1.5 | 0.6 | 0.9 | 2.6 | 1.4 | 1.7 | 0.0 |
| Not in higher education | 1.1 | 0.1 | 0.2 | 1.5 | 1.5 | 3.9 | 0.0 |
| Not employed | 0.4 | 0.0 | 0.0 | 0.7 | 1.0 | 0.7 | 0.0 |
| **Noted as being personally "very important" or "essential": [2]** | | | | | | | |
| Research | 67.5 | 75.6 | 73.9 | 74.2 | 36.5 | 44.0 | 89.8 |
| Teaching | 97.7 | 98.7 | 96.5 | 97.4 | 99.6 | 98.1 | 90.2 |
| Service | 70.3 | 74.0 | 69.4 | 66.2 | 69.5 | 78.7 | 89.8 |

[1] Response options changed from earlier Faculty Surveys.
[2] This question asked for the first time in the 2007–2008 Faculty Survey.

**2007–2008 FACULTY SURVEY WEIGHTED NATIONAL NORMS**
**Full-time Undergraduate Faculty at Baccalaureate Institutions**

| Female Respondents | All Resp | Full Prof | Assoc Prof | Asst Prof | Lect | Inst | No Resp |
|---|---|---|---|---|---|---|---|
| **Highest degree earned** | | | | | | | |
| Bachelor's (B.A., B.S., etc.) | 0.8 | 0.3 | 0.2 | 0.4 | 1.5 | 3.4 | 0.0 |
| Master's (M.A., M.S., M.F.A., M.B.A., etc.) | 27.0 | 10.0 | 12.3 | 22.9 | 55.3 | 78.7 | 68.8 |
| LL.B., J.D. | 0.9 | 0.9 | 0.6 | 0.6 | 1.0 | 2.0 | 0.0 |
| M.D., D.D.S. (or equivalent) | 0.5 | 0.1 | 0.4 | 0.6 | 0.2 | 1.3 | 0.0 |
| Other first professional degree beyond B.A. (e.g., D.D., D.V.M.) | 0.6 | 0.7 | 0.5 | 0.9 | 0.0 | 0.3 | 0.0 |
| Ed.D. | 4.3 | 5.6 | 6.4 | 4.3 | 1.2 | 0.2 | 0.0 |
| Ph.D. | 63.2 | 79.0 | 76.5 | 68.6 | 38.6 | 10.1 | 31.2 |
| Other degree | 2.1 | 2.9 | 2.4 | 1.7 | 2.0 | 1.3 | 0.0 |
| None | 0.6 | 0.5 | 0.6 | 0.1 | 0.1 | 2.6 | 0.0 |
| **Degree currently working on** | | | | | | | |
| Bachelor's (B.A., B.S., etc.) | 0.1 | 0.2 | 0.2 | 0.1 | 0.0 | 0.0 | 0.0 |
| Master's (M.A., M.S., M.F.A., M.B.A., etc.) | 0.9 | 0.5 | 0.4 | 0.9 | 1.3 | 2.7 | 12.0 |
| LL.B., J.D. | 0.1 | 0.0 | 0.1 | 0.3 | 0.0 | 0.0 | 0.0 |
| M.D., D.D.S. (or equivalent) | 0.1 | 0.0 | 0.0 | 0.2 | 0.0 | 0.1 | 0.0 |
| Other first professional degree beyond B.A. (e.g., D.D., D.V.M.) | 0.0 | 0.0 | 0.1 | 0.0 | 0.0 | 0.0 | 0.0 |
| Ed.D. | 1.3 | 0.1 | 0.4 | 1.5 | 1.5 | 4.7 | 0.0 |
| Ph.D. | 6.7 | 1.2 | 1.2 | 7.6 | 10.2 | 23.6 | 61.4 |
| Other degree | 0.9 | 0.4 | 0.6 | 1.1 | 0.1 | 2.7 | 0.0 |
| None | 89.9 | 97.6 | 96.9 | 88.3 | 86.9 | 66.3 | 26.6 |
| **During the past two years, have you engaged in any of the following activities?** | | | | | | | |
| Taught an honors course | 18.3 | 23.7 | 20.6 | 16.6 | 16.7 | 9.7 | 22.1 |
| Taught an interdisciplinary course | 41.1 | 46.8 | 46.9 | 40.9 | 29.9 | 28.0 | 31.4 |
| Taught an ethnic studies course | 13.0 | 13.6 | 13.5 | 15.4 | 9.7 | 6.0 | 7.5 |
| Taught a women's studies course | 14.5 | 19.6 | 19.1 | 12.8 | 8.4 | 5.0 | 2.8 |
| Team-taught a course | 35.1 | 37.7 | 37.1 | 35.5 | 26.2 | 32.1 | 28.5 |
| Taught a service learning course | 24.8 | 24.6 | 26.9 | 22.9 | 26.6 | 24.3 | 16.1 |
| Placed or collected assignments on the Internet | 78.0 | 73.2 | 77.7 | 79.7 | 81.1 | 80.1 | 56.4 |
| Taught a course exclusively on the Internet | 16.1 | 13.8 | 17.0 | 16.5 | 16.5 | 16.3 | 9.0 |
| Participated in a teaching enhancement workshop | 66.5 | 58.1 | 66.1 | 71.9 | 65.9 | 66.5 | 59.6 |
| Advised student groups involved in service/volunteer work | 47.3 | 41.8 | 50.6 | 49.5 | 44.5 | 45.1 | 50.0 |
| Collaborated with the local community in research/teaching | 51.0 | 49.8 | 55.8 | 52.9 | 38.6 | 46.7 | 54.9 |
| Developed a new course | 68.2 | 68.5 | 73.3 | 72.7 | 58.5 | 50.5 | 69.7 |
| Conducted research/writing focused on: | | | | | | | |
| International/global issues | 26.5 | 33.6 | 30.0 | 26.7 | 14.6 | 15.6 | 0.0 |
| Racial or ethnic minorities | 25.4 | 26.7 | 27.9 | 28.6 | 17.5 | 14.5 | 33.1 |
| Women and gender issues | 29.9 | 35.7 | 33.4 | 32.4 | 15.2 | 16.6 | 9.5 |
| Taught a seminar for first-year students | 25.1 | 25.1 | 25.3 | 25.6 | 22.4 | 25.6 | 37.0 |
| Engaged undergraduates on <u>your</u> research project [2] | 36.2 | 42.4 | 43.0 | 39.9 | 15.4 | 15.9 | 57.4 |
| Worked with undergraduates on a research project | 52.5 | 60.1 | 60.7 | 53.3 | 37.4 | 30.2 | 47.8 |

[2]  This question asked for the first time in the 2007–2008 Faculty Survey.

178

| Female Respondents | All Resp | Full Prof | Assoc Prof | Asst Prof | Lect | Inst | No Resp |
|---|---|---|---|---|---|---|---|
| **DURING THE PRESENT TERM, HOW MANY HOURS PER WEEK ON AVERAGE DO YOU ACTUALLY SPEND ON:** | | | | | | | |
| **Scheduled teaching (actual, not credit hours)** | | | | | | | |
| None | 0.7 | 0.7 | 0.6 | 0.4 | 0.6 | 1.8 | 0.0 |
| 1 to 4 | 11.8 | 14.3 | 10.6 | 9.8 | 13.0 | 14.4 | 44.5 |
| 5 to 8 | 30.1 | 32.8 | 33.0 | 31.0 | 24.6 | 20.4 | 22.9 |
| 9 to 12 | 35.4 | 34.4 | 34.8 | 37.5 | 36.4 | 31.4 | 21.8 |
| 13 to 16 | 13.6 | 9.8 | 12.6 | 13.1 | 17.5 | 20.8 | 9.0 |
| 17 to 20 | 5.2 | 5.3 | 5.4 | 4.8 | 4.7 | 6.0 | 1.9 |
| 21 to 34 | 2.8 | 2.4 | 2.3 | 2.6 | 2.9 | 4.9 | 0.0 |
| 35 to 44 | 0.3 | 0.2 | 0.3 | 0.4 | 0.3 | 0.2 | 0.0 |
| 45 + | 0.2 | 0.2 | 0.4 | 0.2 | 0.1 | 0.2 | 0.0 |
| **Preparing for teaching (including reading student papers and grading)** | | | | | | | |
| None | 0.3 | 0.7 | 0.2 | 0.2 | 0.0 | 0.6 | 0.0 |
| 1 to 4 | 7.9 | 10.3 | 6.9 | 7.5 | 8.6 | 6.4 | 38.3 |
| 5 to 8 | 21.9 | 25.1 | 22.2 | 19.8 | 21.8 | 22.0 | 21.4 |
| 9 to 12 | 23.4 | 23.9 | 25.7 | 23.5 | 18.7 | 20.8 | 21.2 |
| 13 to 16 | 16.0 | 14.3 | 17.9 | 17.0 | 15.0 | 12.3 | 5.4 |
| 17 to 20 | 16.0 | 13.6 | 15.4 | 16.0 | 21.7 | 16.6 | 13.7 |
| 21 to 34 | 10.9 | 8.9 | 9.0 | 11.3 | 12.6 | 16.0 | 0.0 |
| 35 to 44 | 2.6 | 2.2 | 2.1 | 3.1 | 1.1 | 4.2 | 0.0 |
| 45 + | 1.0 | 0.9 | 0.7 | 1.5 | 0.4 | 1.2 | 0.0 |
| **Advising and counseling of students** | | | | | | | |
| None | 3.5 | 1.5 | 1.3 | 3.7 | 7.7 | 8.2 | 0.0 |
| 1 to 4 | 51.4 | 49.4 | 52.1 | 53.7 | 43.2 | 53.3 | 36.2 |
| 5 to 8 | 31.4 | 35.5 | 33.7 | 29.4 | 32.1 | 23.9 | 45.9 |
| 9 to 12 | 8.6 | 8.8 | 8.9 | 8.0 | 10.2 | 8.2 | 0.0 |
| 13 to 16 | 2.9 | 2.6 | 2.5 | 3.2 | 3.2 | 3.6 | 0.0 |
| 17 to 20 | 1.4 | 1.6 | 0.8 | 1.5 | 2.3 | 1.1 | 0.0 |
| 21 to 34 | 0.4 | 0.5 | 0.5 | 0.1 | 0.7 | 0.3 | 18.0 |
| 35 to 44 | 0.3 | 0.1 | 0.0 | 0.4 | 0.6 | 0.4 | 0.0 |
| 45 + | 0.2 | 0.0 | 0.2 | 0.0 | 0.0 | 1.1 | 0.0 |
| **Committee work and meetings** | | | | | | | |
| None | 4.1 | 1.2 | 0.7 | 3.1 | 13.9 | 11.4 | 9.5 |
| 1 to 4 | 55.2 | 47.5 | 47.8 | 60.1 | 65.8 | 62.2 | 50.7 |
| 5 to 8 | 28.2 | 33.4 | 34.4 | 26.9 | 15.0 | 19.9 | 17.4 |
| 9 to 12 | 8.3 | 11.1 | 11.5 | 6.7 | 4.1 | 4.2 | 5.8 |
| 13 to 16 | 2.6 | 4.8 | 3.4 | 1.9 | 0.6 | 1.0 | 7.8 |
| 17 to 20 | 1.1 | 1.5 | 1.5 | 0.9 | 0.5 | 0.6 | 8.9 |
| 21 to 34 | 0.4 | 0.7 | 0.5 | 0.3 | 0.2 | 0.2 | 0.0 |
| 35 to 44 | 0.1 | 0.0 | 0.0 | 0.0 | 0.0 | 0.3 | 0.0 |
| 45 + | 0.1 | 0.0 | 0.2 | 0.1 | 0.0 | 0.0 | 0.0 |
| **Other administration** | | | | | | | |
| None | 29.3 | 21.9 | 22.8 | 33.1 | 33.7 | 42.8 | 3.5 |
| 1 to 4 | 38.6 | 35.6 | 39.9 | 44.1 | 29.6 | 32.0 | 34.8 |
| 5 to 8 | 15.4 | 18.4 | 17.2 | 12.6 | 19.0 | 11.6 | 8.1 |
| 9 to 12 | 7.7 | 10.0 | 10.0 | 5.0 | 7.0 | 7.1 | 20.1 |
| 13 to 16 | 3.2 | 4.9 | 3.8 | 2.1 | 3.1 | 2.2 | 19.6 |
| 17 to 20 | 3.2 | 4.8 | 3.7 | 1.5 | 5.0 | 2.2 | 14.0 |
| 21 to 34 | 1.8 | 3.1 | 2.1 | 1.0 | 1.8 | 1.2 | 0.0 |
| 35 to 44 | 0.5 | 0.7 | 0.5 | 0.4 | 0.9 | 0.3 | 0.0 |
| 45 + | 0.3 | 0.5 | 0.2 | 0.2 | 0.0 | 0.6 | 0.0 |

## 2007–2008 FACULTY SURVEY WEIGHTED NATIONAL NORMS
### Full-time Undergraduate Faculty at Baccalaureate Institutions

| Female Respondents | All Resp | Full Prof | Assoc Prof | Asst Prof | Lect | Inst | No Resp |
|---|---|---|---|---|---|---|---|
| **DURING THE PRESENT TERM, HOW MANY HOURS PER WEEK ON AVERAGE DO YOU ACTUALLY SPEND ON:** | | | | | | | |
| **Research and scholarly writing** | | | | | | | |
| None | 19.1 | 12.7 | 11.5 | 13.0 | 44.4 | 43.8 | 24.5 |
| 1 to 4 | 36.9 | 37.4 | 42.4 | 36.5 | 28.7 | 31.2 | 37.3 |
| 5 to 8 | 19.1 | 22.2 | 21.8 | 20.6 | 9.0 | 11.6 | 35.3 |
| 9 to 12 | 11.1 | 11.6 | 11.3 | 12.1 | 12.4 | 6.3 | 2.8 |
| 13 to 16 | 5.1 | 5.7 | 4.8 | 6.5 | 3.0 | 2.9 | 0.0 |
| 17 to 20 | 4.4 | 5.0 | 4.7 | 5.6 | 1.6 | 1.2 | 0.0 |
| 21 to 34 | 2.6 | 2.9 | 2.7 | 3.0 | 0.6 | 2.2 | 0.0 |
| 35 to 44 | 1.1 | 1.5 | 0.6 | 1.9 | 0.1 | 0.4 | 0.0 |
| 45 + | 0.6 | 1.1 | 0.2 | 0.8 | 0.1 | 0.4 | 0.0 |
| **Other creative products/performances** | | | | | | | |
| None | 51.3 | 52.4 | 56.0 | 50.4 | 48.7 | 43.8 | 34.5 |
| 1 to 4 | 29.8 | 27.0 | 27.6 | 31.0 | 28.5 | 37.7 | 42.6 |
| 5 to 8 | 11.0 | 10.6 | 9.8 | 11.0 | 13.8 | 12.3 | 10.3 |
| 9 to 12 | 4.3 | 5.2 | 3.9 | 4.2 | 5.6 | 3.4 | 0.0 |
| 13 to 16 | 1.6 | 2.4 | 1.3 | 1.6 | 1.5 | 1.3 | 0.0 |
| 17 to 20 | 1.0 | 1.3 | 0.8 | 0.8 | 1.0 | 1.3 | 0.0 |
| 21 to 34 | 0.6 | 0.9 | 0.5 | 0.7 | 0.5 | 0.1 | 12.6 |
| 35 to 44 | 0.1 | 0.1 | 0.1 | 0.1 | 0.3 | 0.1 | 0.0 |
| 45 + | 0.1 | 0.1 | 0.1 | 0.2 | 0.1 | 0.0 | 0.0 |
| **Consultation with clients/patients** | | | | | | | |
| None | 79.4 | 81.9 | 82.9 | 79.5 | 73.6 | 71.7 | 76.1 |
| 1 to 4 | 12.2 | 12.1 | 10.0 | 11.8 | 15.8 | 15.3 | 9.5 |
| 5 to 8 | 4.5 | 3.3 | 4.4 | 4.3 | 6.7 | 5.5 | 14.4 |
| 9 to 12 | 1.8 | 1.4 | 1.1 | 2.4 | 0.2 | 3.8 | 0.0 |
| 13 to 16 | 0.8 | 0.4 | 0.7 | 1.1 | 1.4 | 0.4 | 0.0 |
| 17 to 20 | 0.6 | 0.5 | 0.6 | 0.3 | 0.8 | 1.6 | 0.0 |
| 21 to 34 | 0.4 | 0.2 | 0.3 | 0.4 | 1.5 | 0.5 | 0.0 |
| 35 to 44 | 0.0 | 0.0 | 0.0 | 0.1 | 0.0 | 0.0 | 0.0 |
| 45 + | 0.2 | 0.0 | 0.1 | 0.1 | 0.0 | 1.1 | 0.0 |
| **Community or public service** | | | | | | | |
| None | 33.1 | 30.2 | 31.3 | 36.3 | 39.7 | 27.0 | 27.8 |
| 1 to 4 | 52.3 | 53.7 | 52.8 | 50.6 | 47.7 | 57.1 | 49.8 |
| 5 to 8 | 11.1 | 11.5 | 12.7 | 9.4 | 9.3 | 13.2 | 22.1 |
| 9 to 12 | 2.7 | 3.2 | 2.7 | 2.8 | 2.6 | 1.7 | 0.0 |
| 13 to 16 | 0.6 | 0.9 | 0.3 | 0.7 | 0.5 | 0.5 | 0.0 |
| 17 to 20 | 0.2 | 0.4 | 0.0 | 0.2 | 0.1 | 0.4 | 0.0 |
| 21 to 34 | 0.1 | 0.0 | 0.1 | 0.0 | 0.1 | 0.0 | 0.4 |
| 35 to 44 | 0.0 | 0.0 | 0.1 | 0.0 | 0.0 | 0.0 | 0.0 |
| 45 + | 0.0 | 0.1 | 0.0 | 0.0 | 0.0 | 0.1 | 0.0 |
| **Outside consulting/freelance work** | | | | | | | |
| None | 70.3 | 67.6 | 72.3 | 73.3 | 61.3 | 69.6 | 65.4 |
| 1 to 4 | 22.5 | 24.3 | 21.2 | 20.9 | 28.2 | 22.7 | 13.6 |
| 5 to 8 | 4.8 | 6.1 | 4.5 | 3.8 | 5.4 | 5.2 | 21.0 |
| 9 to 12 | 1.7 | 1.5 | 1.3 | 1.3 | 4.3 | 1.6 | 0.0 |
| 13 to 16 | 0.3 | 0.3 | 0.4 | 0.3 | 0.3 | 0.1 | 0.0 |
| 17 to 20 | 0.3 | 0.2 | 0.1 | 0.4 | 0.1 | 0.6 | 0.0 |
| 21 to 34 | 0.1 | 0.0 | 0.1 | 0.1 | 0.2 | 0.1 | 0.0 |
| 35 to 44 | 0.0 | 0.0 | 0.0 | 0.0 | 0.2 | 0.0 | 0.0 |
| 45 + | 0.0 | 0.0 | 0.1 | 0.0 | 0.0 | 0.0 | 0.0 |

180

| Female Respondents | All Resp | Full Prof | Assoc Prof | Asst Prof | Lect | Inst | No Resp |
|---|---|---|---|---|---|---|---|
| **DURING THE PRESENT TERM, HOW MANY HOURS PER WEEK ON AVERAGE DO YOU ACTUALLY SPEND ON:** | | | | | | | |
| **Household/childcare duties** | | | | | | | |
| None | 5.4 | 6.0 | 4.3 | 5.7 | 5.4 | 6.1 | 0.0 |
| 1 to 4 | 16.1 | 19.7 | 14.2 | 16.9 | 13.5 | 14.1 | 18.8 |
| 5 to 8 | 25.2 | 29.2 | 24.6 | 24.6 | 24.9 | 21.4 | 29.2 |
| 9 to 12 | 17.2 | 18.0 | 17.6 | 14.6 | 21.9 | 18.5 | 28.4 |
| 13 to 16 | 8.8 | 10.2 | 9.4 | 7.6 | 7.9 | 9.1 | 6.9 |
| 17 to 20 | 9.0 | 6.3 | 10.7 | 8.8 | 7.8 | 11.1 | 16.6 |
| 21 to 34 | 7.7 | 5.0 | 7.7 | 9.0 | 8.8 | 7.3 | 0.0 |
| 35 to 44 | 4.7 | 2.6 | 5.4 | 5.2 | 4.0 | 6.2 | 0.0 |
| 45 + | 6.0 | 3.0 | 6.2 | 7.7 | 6.0 | 6.1 | 0.0 |
| **Communicating via email** | | | | | | | |
| None | 0.1 | 0.1 | 0.1 | 0.1 | 0.2 | 0.3 | 0.0 |
| 1 to 4 | 21.9 | 18.3 | 18.5 | 22.7 | 24.5 | 30.9 | 29.3 |
| 5 to 8 | 39.4 | 40.7 | 39.6 | 40.1 | 40.2 | 34.4 | 38.1 |
| 9 to 12 | 21.4 | 22.1 | 23.0 | 21.3 | 18.9 | 19.2 | 0.8 |
| 13 to 16 | 9.8 | 11.0 | 10.3 | 8.9 | 11.8 | 7.3 | 31.9 |
| 17 to 20 | 4.7 | 4.9 | 5.8 | 4.4 | 1.7 | 5.4 | 0.0 |
| 21 to 34 | 1.7 | 2.3 | 1.7 | 1.5 | 1.3 | 1.8 | 0.0 |
| 35 to 44 | 0.5 | 0.2 | 0.4 | 0.6 | 1.0 | 0.2 | 0.0 |
| 45 + | 0.5 | 0.3 | 0.5 | 0.5 | 0.4 | 0.5 | 0.0 |
| **Commuting to campus [2]** | | | | | | | |
| None | 5.4 | 5.5 | 5.7 | 5.7 | 2.5 | 5.9 | 0.0 |
| 1 to 4 | 57.9 | 64.6 | 57.1 | 56.1 | 59.4 | 51.7 | 70.6 |
| 5 to 8 | 25.1 | 21.5 | 26.1 | 25.4 | 27.8 | 25.8 | 29.4 |
| 9 to 12 | 9.6 | 6.7 | 9.5 | 10.3 | 9.2 | 13.7 | 0.0 |
| 13 to 16 | 1.3 | 1.4 | 1.1 | 1.6 | 0.5 | 1.6 | 0.0 |
| 17 to 20 | 0.5 | 0.2 | 0.3 | 0.5 | 0.5 | 1.3 | 0.0 |
| 21 to 34 | 0.1 | 0.0 | 0.1 | 0.3 | 0.0 | 0.0 | 0.0 |
| 35 to 44 | 0.0 | 0.0 | 0.0 | 0.1 | 0.0 | 0.0 | 0.0 |
| 45 + | 0.1 | 0.1 | 0.1 | 0.2 | 0.1 | 0.1 | 0.0 |
| **Other employment, outside of academia [2]** | | | | | | | |
| None | 86.7 | 89.2 | 90.3 | 87.5 | 80.7 | 76.9 | 86.2 |
| 1 to 4 | 6.7 | 6.7 | 5.7 | 6.7 | 5.5 | 10.3 | 0.0 |
| 5 to 8 | 3.6 | 3.1 | 2.3 | 2.7 | 8.3 | 6.1 | 13.8 |
| 9 to 12 | 1.5 | 0.5 | 1.0 | 1.7 | 2.4 | 3.1 | 0.0 |
| 13 to 16 | 0.7 | 0.3 | 0.3 | 0.9 | 1.8 | 0.5 | 0.0 |
| 17 to 20 | 0.3 | 0.1 | 0.2 | 0.1 | 0.3 | 1.7 | 0.0 |
| 21 to 34 | 0.3 | 0.0 | 0.1 | 0.2 | 0.8 | 1.0 | 0.0 |
| 35 to 44 | 0.1 | 0.0 | 0.0 | 0.1 | 0.2 | 0.2 | 0.0 |
| 45 + | 0.1 | 0.0 | 0.0 | 0.1 | 0.0 | 0.3 | 0.0 |

[2]  This question asked for the first time in the 2007–2008 Faculty Survey.

## 2007–2008 FACULTY SURVEY WEIGHTED NATIONAL NORMS
### Full-time Undergraduate Faculty at Baccalaureate Institutions

| Female Respondents | All Resp | Full Prof | Assoc Prof | Asst Prof | Lect | Inst | No Resp |
|---|---|---|---|---|---|---|---|
| **Including all institutions at which you teach, how many undergraduate courses are you teaching this term? [2]** | | | | | | | |
| None | 0.0 | 0.0 | 0.0 | 0.0 | 0.0 | 0.0 | 0.0 |
| One | 20.0 | 26.5 | 20.7 | 17.7 | 21.5 | 12.4 | 27.3 |
| Two | 27.7 | 29.3 | 31.6 | 27.5 | 22.8 | 20.0 | 41.6 |
| Three | 27.0 | 25.9 | 25.9 | 29.3 | 21.6 | 29.8 | 12.6 |
| Four | 16.7 | 11.8 | 15.2 | 16.7 | 22.4 | 24.3 | 18.5 |
| Five | 5.2 | 3.6 | 4.0 | 5.5 | 7.9 | 7.6 | 0.0 |
| Six or more | 3.3 | 2.9 | 2.5 | 3.2 | 3.9 | 5.8 | 0.0 |
| **FOR UP TO FOUR OF THE UNDERGRADUATE COURSES MENTIONED ABOVE, HOW MANY STUDENTS ARE ENROLLED IN: [2]** | | | | | | | |
| **Course #1** | | | | | | | |
| 10 or fewer | 11.5 | 13.7 | 12.4 | 10.8 | 5.9 | 12.8 | 11.4 |
| 11 to 20 | 29.2 | 30.6 | 28.2 | 29.5 | 27.7 | 29.2 | 42.1 |
| 21 to 30 | 27.2 | 26.9 | 29.2 | 26.4 | 26.8 | 26.0 | 20.1 |
| 31 to 50 | 19.9 | 17.8 | 17.9 | 20.3 | 26.7 | 20.8 | 26.3 |
| 51 to 100 | 8.6 | 7.7 | 8.2 | 9.7 | 7.7 | 8.8 | 0.0 |
| More than 100 | 3.6 | 3.3 | 4.0 | 3.4 | 5.2 | 2.3 | 0.0 |
| **Course #2** | | | | | | | |
| 10 or fewer | 16.6 | 19.1 | 18.7 | 15.9 | 14.0 | 12.2 | 33.2 |
| 11 to 20 | 33.1 | 37.0 | 35.3 | 31.8 | 22.1 | 35.0 | 37.5 |
| 21 to 30 | 26.9 | 22.1 | 26.5 | 28.9 | 29.5 | 27.6 | 17.0 |
| 31 to 50 | 17.3 | 16.8 | 15.5 | 17.2 | 24.3 | 16.8 | 12.4 |
| 51 to 100 | 4.7 | 3.6 | 2.9 | 4.9 | 7.4 | 7.2 | 0.0 |
| More than 100 | 1.4 | 1.4 | 1.1 | 1.3 | 2.6 | 1.2 | 0.0 |
| **Course #3** | | | | | | | |
| 10 or fewer | 24.8 | 31.3 | 30.2 | 24.2 | 13.5 | 17.9 | 75.5 |
| 11 to 20 | 33.3 | 33.3 | 31.6 | 35.9 | 34.8 | 28.7 | 0.0 |
| 21 to 30 | 25.2 | 22.9 | 23.0 | 23.2 | 30.9 | 32.1 | 24.5 |
| 31 to 50 | 13.4 | 9.9 | 13.1 | 12.8 | 17.7 | 16.7 | 0.0 |
| 51 to 100 | 2.6 | 1.7 | 1.8 | 2.8 | 2.5 | 4.4 | 0.0 |
| More than 100 | 0.7 | 0.9 | 0.3 | 1.1 | 0.7 | 0.2 | 0.0 |
| **Course #4** | | | | | | | |
| 10 or fewer | 29.6 | 35.3 | 39.3 | 31.3 | 11.4 | 22.1 | 58.8 |
| 11 to 20 | 32.6 | 36.5 | 27.9 | 34.2 | 30.8 | 33.8 | 25.9 |
| 21 to 30 | 25.2 | 22.7 | 22.5 | 23.2 | 34.9 | 27.4 | 15.3 |
| 31 to 50 | 10.9 | 5.2 | 9.5 | 9.9 | 18.2 | 14.2 | 0.0 |
| 51 to 100 | 1.6 | 0.1 | 0.7 | 1.3 | 4.3 | 2.5 | 0.0 |
| More than 100 | 0.2 | 0.2 | 0.2 | 0.1 | 0.4 | 0.0 | 0.0 |

[2]  This question asked for the first time in the 2007–2008 Faculty Survey.

182

| Female Respondents | All Resp | Full Prof | Assoc Prof | Asst Prof | Lect | Inst | No Resp |
|---|---|---|---|---|---|---|---|
| **HOW MANY OF THE FOLLOWING COURSES ARE YOU TEACHING THIS ACADEMIC YEAR?** | | | | | | | |
| **General education courses** | | | | | | | |
| None | 56.1 | 58.1 | 57.9 | 55.9 | 51.0 | 53.7 | 51.9 |
| One | 16.7 | 19.7 | 17.7 | 16.5 | 14.1 | 11.5 | 33.7 |
| Two | 11.7 | 11.8 | 12.7 | 11.9 | 9.9 | 10.5 | 8.8 |
| Three | 6.2 | 4.5 | 5.3 | 6.2 | 8.9 | 9.3 | 5.6 |
| Four | 4.4 | 3.4 | 3.3 | 4.7 | 6.3 | 6.5 | 0.0 |
| Five or more | 4.7 | 2.4 | 3.2 | 4.7 | 9.8 | 8.5 | 0.0 |
| **Developmental/remedial courses** | | | | | | | |
| None | 94.0 | 96.1 | 96.1 | 93.7 | 91.8 | 88.3 | 65.6 |
| One | 3.3 | 2.5 | 2.0 | 3.6 | 4.3 | 5.6 | 34.4 |
| Two | 1.1 | 0.5 | 0.7 | 1.3 | 1.4 | 2.3 | 0.0 |
| Three | 0.7 | 0.3 | 0.4 | 0.7 | 1.2 | 1.4 | 0.0 |
| Four | 0.5 | 0.4 | 0.5 | 0.3 | 1.0 | 1.2 | 0.0 |
| Five or more | 0.4 | 0.2 | 0.3 | 0.4 | 0.4 | 1.2 | 0.0 |
| **Other undergraduate credit courses** | | | | | | | |
| None | 18.8 | 15.2 | 13.5 | 17.5 | 28.7 | 32.8 | 25.3 |
| One | 19.3 | 21.6 | 20.9 | 18.5 | 16.5 | 15.8 | 28.3 |
| Two | 21.5 | 24.7 | 24.3 | 21.1 | 19.5 | 12.2 | 17.6 |
| Three | 15.8 | 15.7 | 17.9 | 17.8 | 8.9 | 11.4 | 0.0 |
| Four | 10.6 | 10.2 | 9.3 | 11.0 | 11.0 | 13.0 | 5.1 |
| Five or more | 14.0 | 12.6 | 14.0 | 14.1 | 15.4 | 14.9 | 23.6 |
| **Graduate courses** | | | | | | | |
| None | 65.7 | 57.1 | 58.6 | 65.0 | 77.7 | 89.5 | 72.4 |
| One | 19.9 | 24.6 | 23.0 | 20.6 | 16.7 | 5.0 | 5.0 |
| Two | 8.0 | 10.2 | 11.0 | 7.6 | 3.2 | 2.4 | 13.6 |
| Three | 3.5 | 4.8 | 4.2 | 3.5 | 1.3 | 1.6 | 0.0 |
| Four | 1.7 | 2.2 | 1.9 | 1.8 | 0.8 | 0.4 | 9.0 |
| Five or more | 1.2 | 1.0 | 1.4 | 1.4 | 0.2 | 1.1 | 0.0 |
| **Vocational or technical courses** | | | | | | | |
| None | 97.7 | 98.2 | 98.0 | 97.7 | 98.0 | 96.0 | 100.0 |
| One | 0.9 | 0.6 | 0.7 | 0.9 | 0.7 | 1.6 | 0.0 |
| Two | 0.5 | 0.3 | 0.5 | 0.8 | 0.2 | 0.4 | 0.0 |
| Three | 0.4 | 0.5 | 0.3 | 0.3 | 0.3 | 0.4 | 0.0 |
| Four | 0.3 | 0.2 | 0.2 | 0.1 | 0.1 | 1.3 | 0.0 |
| Five or more | 0.3 | 0.2 | 0.3 | 0.2 | 0.7 | 0.3 | 0.0 |
| **Non-credit courses (other than above)** | | | | | | | |
| None | 94.2 | 93.3 | 95.0 | 93.9 | 95.8 | 93.2 | 86.8 |
| One | 4.0 | 5.1 | 3.6 | 3.9 | 2.5 | 4.9 | 10.9 |
| Two | 1.2 | 0.9 | 1.0 | 1.7 | 0.9 | 0.8 | 0.0 |
| Three | 0.3 | 0.5 | 0.2 | 0.2 | 0.5 | 0.7 | 2.3 |
| Four | 0.1 | 0.2 | 0.1 | 0.2 | 0.1 | 0.1 | 0.0 |
| Five or more | 0.1 | 0.0 | 0.1 | 0.1 | 0.1 | 0.4 | 0.0 |
| **Do you teach remedial/developmental skills in any of the following areas?** | | | | | | | |
| Reading | 5.3 | 3.7 | 4.8 | 6.7 | 5.4 | 4.9 | 0.8 |
| Writing | 13.0 | 11.7 | 12.3 | 14.1 | 12.5 | 14.1 | 0.0 |
| Mathematics | 3.8 | 3.4 | 3.9 | 3.7 | 5.0 | 3.6 | 0.0 |
| ESL | 1.6 | 1.2 | 0.7 | 1.6 | 3.4 | 2.5 | 1.9 |
| General academic skills | 10.0 | 8.3 | 10.3 | 11.6 | 5.9 | 10.5 | 30.8 |
| Other subject areas | 6.4 | 5.7 | 5.0 | 7.7 | 5.3 | 8.0 | 0.4 |

| Female Respondents | All Resp | Full Prof | Assoc Prof | Asst Prof | Lect | Inst | No Resp |
|---|---|---|---|---|---|---|---|
| **HAVE YOU ENGAGED IN ANY OF THE FOLLOWING PROFESSIONAL DEVELOPMENT OPPORTUNITIES AT YOUR INSTITUTION? [2]** | | | | | | | |
| **Workshops focused on teaching in the classroom** | | | | | | | |
| Yes | 76.4 | 73.9 | 78.8 | 76.5 | 81.4 | 70.7 | 65.3 |
| No | 20.8 | 24.1 | 18.8 | 19.7 | 16.5 | 26.4 | 16.7 |
| Not eligible | 0.2 | 0.1 | 0.0 | 0.1 | 0.8 | 0.0 | 18.0 |
| Not available | 2.7 | 1.9 | 2.3 | 3.7 | 1.2 | 2.9 | 0.0 |
| **Paid workshops outside the institution focused on teaching** | | | | | | | |
| Yes | 32.6 | 30.6 | 32.8 | 31.9 | 33.5 | 36.6 | 39.8 |
| No | 61.7 | 64.1 | 61.9 | 61.7 | 60.2 | 58.3 | 60.2 |
| Not eligible | 0.8 | 0.3 | 0.2 | 0.7 | 2.3 | 2.5 | 0.0 |
| Not available | 4.9 | 4.9 | 5.1 | 5.7 | 4.0 | 2.7 | 0.0 |
| **Paid sabbatical leave** | | | | | | | |
| Yes | 23.6 | 54.5 | 36.9 | 7.5 | 5.4 | 1.4 | 13.4 |
| No | 54.0 | 39.7 | 53.5 | 61.2 | 49.6 | 62.2 | 45.3 |
| Not eligible | 19.3 | 3.3 | 7.0 | 28.0 | 38.3 | 34.2 | 41.3 |
| Not available | 3.1 | 2.6 | 2.6 | 3.3 | 6.8 | 2.1 | 0.0 |
| **Travel funds paid by the institution** | | | | | | | |
| Yes | 79.7 | 86.2 | 88.1 | 81.8 | 60.1 | 58.6 | 95.5 |
| No | 17.0 | 11.5 | 10.2 | 16.0 | 30.7 | 34.2 | 4.5 |
| Not eligible | 1.8 | 0.3 | 0.2 | 0.9 | 7.6 | 5.6 | 0.0 |
| Not available | 1.5 | 1.9 | 1.5 | 1.3 | 1.5 | 1.6 | 0.0 |
| **Association membership/dues paid by the institution** | | | | | | | |
| Yes | 28.6 | 28.7 | 29.5 | 31.1 | 23.8 | 23.1 | 57.2 |
| No | 51.0 | 55.5 | 49.0 | 47.4 | 52.9 | 57.0 | 20.6 |
| Not eligible | 3.5 | 0.8 | 1.5 | 2.8 | 10.7 | 8.7 | 0.0 |
| Not available | 16.9 | 15.0 | 20.0 | 18.7 | 12.6 | 11.3 | 22.2 |
| **Tuition remission** | | | | | | | |
| Yes | 14.8 | 16.9 | 14.5 | 12.2 | 12.6 | 21.1 | 18.8 |
| No | 75.9 | 73.1 | 78.7 | 77.4 | 76.2 | 69.8 | 67.5 |
| Not eligible | 4.1 | 5.2 | 2.3 | 4.3 | 5.5 | 4.1 | 13.7 |
| Not available | 5.2 | 4.8 | 4.5 | 6.0 | 5.7 | 4.9 | 0.0 |
| **Internal grants for research** | | | | | | | |
| Yes | 44.1 | 56.5 | 55.3 | 45.4 | 21.1 | 11.8 | 38.9 |
| No | 50.7 | 39.2 | 42.3 | 50.0 | 68.0 | 78.5 | 34.2 |
| Not eligible | 2.7 | 1.6 | 0.5 | 1.7 | 8.7 | 7.1 | 26.9 |
| Not available | 2.4 | 2.7 | 1.8 | 2.8 | 2.1 | 2.6 | 0.0 |
| **Training for administrative leadership** | | | | | | | |
| Yes | 12.8 | 19.8 | 16.5 | 8.0 | 8.5 | 9.4 | 21.7 |
| No | 74.0 | 68.7 | 71.0 | 78.6 | 75.4 | 75.3 | 65.2 |
| Not eligible | 3.8 | 1.9 | 1.6 | 3.7 | 8.6 | 8.3 | 0.0 |
| Not available | 9.5 | 9.5 | 10.8 | 9.7 | 7.6 | 7.0 | 13.2 |

[2]  This question asked for the first time in the 2007–2008 Faculty Survey.

| Female Respondents | All Resp | Full Prof | Assoc Prof | Asst Prof | Lect | Inst | No Resp |
|---|---|---|---|---|---|---|---|
| **Goals for undergraduates noted as "very important" or "essential"** | | | | | | | |
| Develop ability to think critically | 99.9 | 99.9 | 99.9 | 99.9 | 99.8 | 99.9 | 100.0 |
| Prepare students for employment after college | 85.2 | 81.9 | 82.7 | 86.3 | 86.0 | 92.6 | 96.6 |
| Prepare students for graduate or advanced education | 76.7 | 79.2 | 76.0 | 78.5 | 71.0 | 73.2 | 76.4 |
| Develop moral character | 74.1 | 73.4 | 70.7 | 73.6 | 77.0 | 82.5 | 74.1 |
| Provide for students' emotional development | 55.4 | 52.7 | 51.3 | 56.5 | 54.6 | 67.3 | 42.3 |
| Prepare students for family living | 23.0 | 22.6 | 20.9 | 21.8 | 20.3 | 34.1 | 10.8 |
| Teach students the classic works of Western civilization [2] | 32.1 | 37.0 | 31.9 | 29.0 | 35.8 | 30.5 | 48.7 |
| Help students develop personal values | 70.2 | 70.1 | 67.9 | 70.6 | 64.6 | 79.4 | 69.3 |
| Enhance students' self-understanding | 76.8 | 75.9 | 75.7 | 77.7 | 75.8 | 79.2 | 64.5 |
| Instill in students a commitment to community service | 64.5 | 62.6 | 61.9 | 64.5 | 64.8 | 73.5 | 66.9 |
| Enhance students' knowledge of and appreciation for other racial/ethnic groups | 87.2 | 88.0 | 86.2 | 87.8 | 85.7 | 87.3 | 86.8 |
| Study a foreign language [2] | 60.0 | 64.2 | 62.1 | 58.4 | 57.2 | 54.5 | 75.6 |
| Help master knowledge in a discipline | 95.6 | 95.7 | 96.1 | 96.2 | 92.0 | 95.9 | 100.0 |
| Develop creative capacities | 81.2 | 81.6 | 79.1 | 82.4 | 81.2 | 82.1 | 87.5 |
| Instill a basic appreciation of the liberal arts | 76.7 | 81.7 | 79.4 | 75.9 | 73.9 | 66.6 | 68.4 |
| Promote ability to write effectively | 98.1 | 99.2 | 98.8 | 97.4 | 98.2 | 96.4 | 100.0 |
| Help students evaluate the quality and reliability of information [2] | 98.6 | 99.2 | 99.1 | 98.0 | 98.4 | 98.1 | 100.0 |
| Engage students in civil discourse around controversial issues [2] | 79.7 | 83.7 | 82.1 | 79.4 | 75.8 | 71.2 | 91.6 |
| Teach students tolerance and respect for different beliefs [2] | 91.6 | 91.8 | 92.6 | 91.7 | 93.1 | 87.6 | 95.2 |
| Encourage students to become agents of social change [2] | 71.5 | 71.6 | 70.3 | 72.9 | 67.7 | 73.8 | 72.6 |

[2]  This question asked for the first time in the 2007–2008 Faculty Survey.

| Female Respondents | All Resp | Full Prof | Assoc Prof | Asst Prof | Lect | Inst | No Resp |
|---|---|---|---|---|---|---|---|
| **HOW MANY OF THE FOLLOWING HAVE YOU PUBLISHED?** | | | | | | | |
| **Articles in academic or professional journals** | | | | | | | |
| None | 24.5 | 11.0 | 11.7 | 23.7 | 49.0 | 59.5 | 34.3 |
| 1 to 2 | 23.0 | 11.7 | 17.7 | 33.1 | 22.9 | 25.0 | 29.0 |
| 3 to 4 | 16.8 | 12.2 | 20.2 | 20.2 | 14.9 | 8.9 | 9.5 |
| 5 to 10 | 17.8 | 20.5 | 27.5 | 15.9 | 8.0 | 4.7 | 14.0 |
| 11 to 20 | 9.4 | 17.8 | 14.0 | 5.2 | 4.5 | 0.4 | 4.8 |
| 21 to 50 | 6.2 | 17.0 | 8.3 | 1.7 | 0.2 | 0.7 | 8.4 |
| 51+ | 2.3 | 9.7 | 0.6 | 0.2 | 0.4 | 0.8 | 0.0 |
| **Chapters in edited volumes** | | | | | | | |
| None | 54.4 | 33.8 | 42.2 | 59.3 | 74.7 | 86.9 | 62.0 |
| 1 to 2 | 26.6 | 25.4 | 31.5 | 30.1 | 20.4 | 11.9 | 19.8 |
| 3 to 4 | 10.0 | 15.7 | 14.6 | 7.6 | 4.2 | 1.2 | 13.2 |
| 5 to 10 | 6.4 | 15.8 | 8.9 | 2.6 | 0.6 | 0.0 | 5.0 |
| 11 to 20 | 2.0 | 6.8 | 2.1 | 0.3 | 0.1 | 0.0 | 0.0 |
| 21 to 50 | 0.6 | 2.1 | 0.7 | 0.0 | 0.0 | 0.0 | 0.0 |
| 51+ | 0.1 | 0.5 | 0.0 | 0.0 | 0.0 | 0.0 | 0.0 |
| **Books, manuals, or monographs** | | | | | | | |
| None | 67.3 | 44.1 | 60.1 | 77.2 | 74.8 | 88.9 | 80.0 |
| 1 to 2 | 23.9 | 31.3 | 31.6 | 19.8 | 18.6 | 9.9 | 14.7 |
| 3 to 4 | 5.7 | 14.5 | 6.4 | 2.4 | 3.5 | 0.6 | 0.0 |
| 5 to 10 | 2.3 | 7.1 | 1.8 | 0.3 | 2.5 | 0.5 | 5.2 |
| 11 to 20 | 0.6 | 2.0 | 0.1 | 0.2 | 0.5 | 0.1 | 0.0 |
| 21 to 50 | 0.2 | 0.9 | 0.0 | 0.1 | 0.0 | 0.0 | 0.0 |
| 51+ | 0.0 | 0.0 | 0.0 | 0.0 | 0.0 | 0.0 | 0.0 |
| **Other, such as patents or computer software products** | | | | | | | |
| None | 89.8 | 85.7 | 89.6 | 91.0 | 89.7 | 93.6 | 100.0 |
| 1 to 2 | 6.6 | 7.6 | 6.2 | 6.6 | 9.0 | 3.8 | 0.0 |
| 3 to 4 | 1.9 | 3.2 | 2.6 | 1.4 | 0.6 | 1.2 | 0.0 |
| 5 to 10 | 1.0 | 2.5 | 1.0 | 0.5 | 0.5 | 0.4 | 0.0 |
| 11 to 20 | 0.3 | 0.5 | 0.3 | 0.1 | 0.0 | 0.7 | 0.0 |
| 21 to 50 | 0.1 | 0.4 | 0.2 | 0.0 | 0.0 | 0.0 | 0.0 |
| 51+ | 0.2 | 0.3 | 0.0 | 0.3 | 0.2 | 0.4 | 0.0 |
| **IN THE <u>LAST TWO</u> YEARS, HOW MANY:** | | | | | | | |
| **Exhibitions or performances in the fine or applied arts have you presented?** | | | | | | | |
| None | 80.8 | 78.3 | 83.2 | 80.7 | 79.9 | 80.8 | 69.4 |
| 1 to 2 | 6.6 | 5.6 | 5.4 | 6.2 | 7.7 | 10.8 | 18.0 |
| 3 to 4 | 5.1 | 6.0 | 4.4 | 5.3 | 6.4 | 4.1 | 0.0 |
| 5 to 10 | 4.1 | 5.5 | 3.5 | 4.2 | 4.0 | 3.1 | 0.0 |
| 11 to 20 | 1.7 | 1.9 | 1.7 | 2.1 | 1.0 | 0.7 | 12.6 |
| 21 to 50 | 1.0 | 1.7 | 0.7 | 1.3 | 0.3 | 0.1 | 0.0 |
| 51+ | 0.7 | 1.0 | 1.0 | 0.3 | 0.8 | 0.4 | 0.0 |
| **Of your professional writings have been published or accepted for publication?** | | | | | | | |
| None | 35.9 | 24.9 | 26.0 | 30.6 | 63.8 | 70.4 | 35.5 |
| 1 to 2 | 33.9 | 31.7 | 37.7 | 38.4 | 26.5 | 21.3 | 43.4 |
| 3 to 4 | 19.1 | 23.3 | 24.2 | 20.2 | 8.2 | 5.6 | 9.8 |
| 5 to 10 | 9.2 | 16.2 | 10.3 | 9.2 | 1.0 | 1.5 | 2.8 |
| 11 to 20 | 1.4 | 2.6 | 1.4 | 1.2 | 0.2 | 0.9 | 8.4 |
| 21 to 50 | 0.4 | 1.1 | 0.3 | 0.2 | 0.1 | 0.3 | 0.0 |
| 51+ | 0.1 | 0.2 | 0.0 | 0.2 | 0.2 | 0.0 | 0.0 |

## 2007–2008 FACULTY SURVEY WEIGHTED NATIONAL NORMS
### Full-time Undergraduate Faculty at Baccalaureate Institutions

| Female Respondents | All Resp | Full Prof | Assoc Prof | Asst Prof | Lect | Inst | No Resp |
|---|---|---|---|---|---|---|---|
| **General activities** | | | | | | | |
| Are you a member of a faculty union? | 23.8 | 26.5 | 26.5 | 24.6 | 21.9 | 12.2 | 24.9 |
| Are you a U.S. citizen? | 94.6 | 98.4 | 94.4 | 91.0 | 97.0 | 97.1 | 100.0 |
| Were you born in the U.S.A.? | 86.6 | 88.1 | 87.1 | 84.6 | 83.2 | 91.7 | 90.8 |
| Do you plan to retire within the next three years? | 11.1 | 20.3 | 9.5 | 4.4 | 17.5 | 12.7 | 18.2 |
| Do you use your scholarship to address local community needs? | 52.3 | 54.4 | 53.4 | 51.6 | 44.3 | 54.6 | 53.6 |
| Have you been sexually harassed at this institution? | 10.0 | 16.5 | 11.8 | 6.9 | 9.7 | 3.9 | 5.1 |
| Have you ever interrupted your professional career for more than one year for family reasons? [2] | 22.1 | 11.3 | 17.4 | 22.4 | 39.1 | 36.2 | 23.3 |
| Have you ever received an award for outstanding teaching? | 40.3 | 54.2 | 43.8 | 31.9 | 40.9 | 32.4 | 6.8 |
| Have you published op-ed pieces or editorials? | 18.1 | 27.3 | 19.5 | 14.6 | 16.0 | 10.6 | 17.6 |
| Is (or was) your: | | | | | | | |
|     Father an academic? | 14.0 | 13.7 | 13.4 | 15.9 | 12.9 | 11.9 | 0.0 |
|     Mother an academic? | 11.2 | 10.8 | 9.1 | 11.7 | 11.7 | 14.8 | 0.0 |
|     Spouse/partner an academic? | 34.4 | 41.8 | 36.1 | 29.7 | 39.2 | 27.9 | 35.5 |
| Are you currently teaching courses at more than one institution? | 4.6 | 5.2 | 2.8 | 4.4 | 7.6 | 5.5 | 0.0 |
| **During the past two years, have you:** | | | | | | | |
| Considered early retirement? | 22.6 | 37.0 | 26.2 | 12.6 | 20.7 | 19.6 | 36.6 |
| Considered leaving academe for another job? | 37.4 | 27.5 | 40.1 | 40.1 | 40.1 | 38.4 | 39.6 |
| Considered leaving this institution for another? | 48.7 | 43.8 | 53.1 | 53.4 | 42.8 | 38.4 | 52.2 |
| Changed academic institutions? | 12.0 | 6.3 | 6.3 | 19.5 | 11.6 | 13.9 | 0.0 |
| Engaged in paid consulting outside of your institution? | 32.8 | 39.2 | 34.3 | 29.0 | 36.3 | 26.5 | 42.4 |
| Engaged in public service/professional consulting without pay? | 60.7 | 68.9 | 65.2 | 56.6 | 54.0 | 53.0 | 83.6 |
| Received at least one firm job offer? | 26.3 | 18.7 | 18.4 | 35.6 | 24.5 | 32.8 | 8.4 |
| Received funding for your work from: | | | | | | | |
|     Foundations? | 18.0 | 24.5 | 20.8 | 18.4 | 6.8 | 8.2 | 19.4 |
|     State or federal government? | 22.2 | 32.4 | 26.5 | 19.8 | 10.6 | 11.1 | 16.9 |
|     Business or industry? | 8.4 | 14.0 | 8.7 | 6.2 | 7.1 | 5.6 | 0.0 |
| Requested/sought an early promotion? | 7.4 | 6.5 | 10.8 | 5.7 | 9.0 | 4.3 | 4.7 |
| **IF YOU WERE TO BEGIN YOUR CAREER AGAIN, WOULD YOU STILL WANT TO:** | | | | | | | |
| **Come to this institution? [2]** | | | | | | | |
| Definitely yes | 33.9 | 29.3 | 30.2 | 33.6 | 40.0 | 45.8 | 41.7 |
| Probably yes | 34.6 | 36.5 | 33.3 | 34.8 | 32.7 | 35.2 | 13.7 |
| Not sure | 17.4 | 18.4 | 19.1 | 19.9 | 10.2 | 11.2 | 6.9 |
| Probably no | 9.0 | 9.7 | 10.7 | 7.3 | 14.5 | 4.1 | 25.1 |
| Definitely no | 5.1 | 6.1 | 6.7 | 4.4 | 2.6 | 3.7 | 12.6 |
| **Be a college professor?** | | | | | | | |
| Definitely yes | 59.2 | 65.5 | 57.3 | 56.9 | 57.0 | 62.1 | 19.0 |
| Probably yes | 27.0 | 25.0 | 28.6 | 27.7 | 28.1 | 23.6 | 49.7 |
| Not sure | 10.0 | 6.7 | 9.9 | 11.6 | 11.1 | 9.7 | 22.9 |
| Probably no | 2.8 | 1.8 | 3.6 | 3.1 | 2.3 | 2.7 | 8.4 |
| Definitely no | 0.9 | 1.0 | 0.6 | 0.7 | 1.6 | 1.9 | 0.0 |

[2] This question asked for the first time in the 2007–2008 Faculty Survey.

**2007–2008 FACULTY SURVEY WEIGHTED NATIONAL NORMS**
**Full-time Undergraduate Faculty at Baccalaureate Institutions**

| Female Respondents | All Resp | Full Prof | Assoc Prof | Asst Prof | Lect | Inst | No Resp |
|---|---|---|---|---|---|---|---|
| **Attributes noted as being "very descriptive" of your institution** | | | | | | | |
| It is easy for students to see faculty outside of regular office hours | 61.2 | 60.3 | 63.2 | 63.5 | 52.5 | 58.9 | 79.1 |
| There is a great deal of conformity among the students | 28.6 | 28.5 | 29.2 | 30.1 | 23.5 | 27.2 | 43.4 |
| The faculty are typically at odds with campus administration | 19.8 | 24.5 | 22.7 | 19.1 | 11.8 | 13.2 | 24.6 |
| Faculty here respect each other | 48.0 | 46.8 | 45.4 | 52.2 | 40.1 | 50.7 | 22.0 |
| Most students are treated like "numbers in a book" | 3.0 | 2.0 | 3.1 | 3.4 | 2.7 | 3.2 | 0.0 |
| Social activities are overemphasized | 8.1 | 9.6 | 9.1 | 7.0 | 7.0 | 7.4 | 0.8 |
| Faculty are rewarded for being good teachers | 15.6 | 17.2 | 14.3 | 17.6 | 10.3 | 14.6 | 19.2 |
| There is respect for the expression of diverse values and beliefs | 35.3 | 33.4 | 31.1 | 35.6 | 41.6 | 42.3 | 49.5 |
| Faculty are rewarded for their efforts to use instructional technology | 23.3 | 23.4 | 21.2 | 25.3 | 25.3 | 21.0 | 13.9 |
| Faculty are rewarded for their efforts to work with underprepared students | 6.5 | 5.8 | 4.7 | 6.9 | 5.8 | 10.9 | 0.0 |
| Administrators consider faculty concerns when making policy [2] | 12.4 | 11.1 | 11.4 | 12.1 | 14.3 | 16.5 | 19.7 |
| The administration is open about its policies | 15.8 | 13.3 | 13.1 | 16.5 | 15.0 | 25.0 | 21.0 |
| **Do you, "to a great extent":** | | | | | | | |
| Engage in academic work that spans multiple disciplines | 36.7 | 43.0 | 39.6 | 37.6 | 29.1 | 23.5 | 11.6 |
| Feel that the training you received in graduate school prepared you well for your role as a faculty mentor | 37.1 | 35.1 | 37.5 | 39.8 | 32.6 | 35.1 | 39.2 |
| Achieve a healthy balance between your personal life and your professional life | 27.3 | 34.2 | 24.2 | 21.9 | 34.1 | 32.5 | 41.9 |
| Experience close alignment between your work and your personal values | 66.2 | 68.6 | 64.4 | 63.2 | 71.3 | 71.0 | 63.7 |
| Feel that you have to work harder than your colleagues to be perceived as a legitimate scholar | 32.9 | 28.1 | 32.3 | 32.9 | 42.5 | 34.2 | 50.1 |
| Mentor new faculty [2] | 26.2 | 44.5 | 34.9 | 15.5 | 15.2 | 14.7 | 0.8 |

[2] This question asked for the first time in the 2007–2008 Faculty Survey.

188

| Female Respondents | All Resp | Full Prof | Assoc Prof | Asst Prof | Lect | Inst | No Resp |
|---|---|---|---|---|---|---|---|
| **Aspects of your job with which you are "very satisfied" or "satisfied": [3]** | | | | | | | |
| Salary [2] | 41.9 | 52.3 | 40.6 | 41.4 | 32.9 | 35.4 | 65.0 |
| Health benefits [2] | 68.9 | 69.0 | 65.4 | 69.1 | 79.2 | 68.1 | 60.4 |
| Retirement benefits [2] | 67.4 | 63.9 | 63.6 | 69.7 | 76.0 | 68.3 | 73.2 |
| Opportunity for scholarly pursuits | 47.4 | 50.8 | 42.2 | 46.0 | 50.4 | 55.3 | 59.3 |
| Teaching load | 53.5 | 53.3 | 49.2 | 51.5 | 62.2 | 62.6 | 65.8 |
| Quality of students | 59.7 | 60.6 | 56.8 | 58.0 | 65.7 | 64.8 | 56.5 |
| Office/lab space | 66.3 | 68.6 | 68.1 | 64.5 | 64.9 | 64.7 | 36.6 |
| Autonomy and independence | 83.6 | 85.4 | 82.5 | 82.8 | 82.7 | 85.7 | 69.4 |
| Professional relationships with other faculty | 77.4 | 78.8 | 74.9 | 79.3 | 74.1 | 78.5 | 47.7 |
| Social relationships with other faculty | 70.1 | 70.9 | 68.2 | 72.3 | 63.6 | 72.0 | 56.8 |
| Competency of colleagues | 79.9 | 79.7 | 77.5 | 80.7 | 79.7 | 84.2 | 69.9 |
| Visibility for jobs at other institutions/organizations | 51.6 | 54.2 | 48.6 | 52.5 | 54.3 | 49.5 | 34.0 |
| Job security | 72.8 | 92.3 | 86.1 | 63.1 | 51.6 | 53.0 | 77.9 |
| Relationship with administration | 57.0 | 54.4 | 55.8 | 58.2 | 57.1 | 61.2 | 38.4 |
| Departmental leadership [2] | 65.7 | 67.3 | 61.8 | 65.6 | 65.6 | 72.5 | 58.7 |
| Course assignments [2] | 81.7 | 84.5 | 82.6 | 78.9 | 81.4 | 83.4 | 88.5 |
| Freedom to determine course content [2] | 91.2 | 92.4 | 93.8 | 90.5 | 91.5 | 84.9 | 100.0 |
| Availability of child care at this institution | 26.9 | 31.0 | 24.4 | 25.0 | 27.5 | 34.2 | 11.7 |
| Prospects for career advancement | 49.9 | 58.2 | 49.4 | 54.5 | 26.4 | 40.8 | 39.3 |
| Clerical/administrative support | 57.4 | 51.1 | 50.9 | 58.9 | 65.8 | 72.1 | 41.2 |
| Overall job satisfaction | 72.1 | 74.4 | 68.5 | 71.8 | 71.2 | 78.3 | 61.9 |

[2] This question asked for the first time in the 2007–2008 Faculty Survey.
[3] Respondents marking "Not Applicable" were not included in the computation of these results.

| Female Respondents | All Resp | Full Prof | Assoc Prof | Asst Prof | Lect | Inst | No Resp |
|---|---|---|---|---|---|---|---|
| **Do you agree "strongly" or "somewhat"?** | | | | | | | |
| Faculty are interested in students' personal problems | 85.1 | 83.7 | 84.5 | 86.6 | 78.0 | 90.4 | 67.3 |
| Racial and ethnic diversity should be more strongly reflected in the curriculum | 67.9 | 68.1 | 70.8 | 70.4 | 60.6 | 59.4 | 79.3 |
| Faculty feel that most students are well-prepared academically | 45.1 | 44.3 | 42.7 | 45.1 | 46.8 | 51.1 | 30.5 |
| This institution should hire more faculty of color | 79.4 | 83.8 | 84.0 | 80.7 | 69.5 | 65.7 | 76.3 |
| Student Affairs staff have the support and respect of faculty | 79.4 | 74.2 | 76.1 | 83.7 | 77.6 | 85.0 | 60.0 |
| Faculty are committed to the welfare of this institution | 90.9 | 89.1 | 90.6 | 91.9 | 89.0 | 93.6 | 74.2 |
| Faculty here are strongly interested in the academic problems of undergraduates | 87.8 | 87.1 | 88.0 | 88.9 | 82.9 | 89.6 | 74.3 |
| There is a lot of campus racial conflict here | 13.6 | 15.7 | 15.2 | 13.9 | 12.4 | 6.4 | 10.3 |
| Most students are strongly committed to community service | 53.6 | 53.3 | 53.3 | 56.1 | 46.2 | 53.5 | 28.4 |
| My research is valued by faculty in my department | 70.1 | 74.4 | 69.5 | 73.3 | 59.9 | 62.7 | 55.3 |
| My teaching is valued by faculty in my department | 88.6 | 89.7 | 88.1 | 89.3 | 87.3 | 87.3 | 64.0 |
| Many courses include feminist perspectives | 46.6 | 47.8 | 47.2 | 46.0 | 43.3 | 48.0 | 31.6 |
| Faculty of color are treated fairly here | 83.6 | 82.3 | 78.7 | 83.9 | 86.6 | 94.2 | 75.9 |
| Women faculty are treated fairly here | 76.4 | 74.2 | 70.5 | 77.0 | 85.0 | 85.1 | 59.5 |
| Many courses involve students in community service | 54.4 | 53.4 | 52.0 | 54.7 | 50.3 | 64.6 | 39.8 |
| This institution should hire more women faculty | 63.1 | 67.8 | 65.7 | 63.6 | 58.6 | 51.3 | 53.7 |
| Gay and lesbian faculty are treated fairly here | 77.6 | 76.8 | 73.0 | 76.5 | 87.3 | 85.4 | 77.4 |
| My department does a good job of mentoring new faculty | 64.7 | 72.5 | 64.8 | 60.2 | 65.1 | 64.2 | 42.4 |
| Faculty are sufficiently involved in campus decision making | 53.5 | 47.1 | 48.9 | 56.8 | 60.9 | 59.9 | 62.4 |
| My values are congruent with the dominant institutional values | 73.3 | 69.3 | 69.1 | 75.3 | 76.6 | 81.2 | 82.6 |
| There is adequate support for integrating technology in my teaching | 81.7 | 80.0 | 79.3 | 82.8 | 84.9 | 84.8 | 70.0 |
| This institution takes responsibility for educating underprepared students | 60.9 | 60.8 | 56.2 | 61.8 | 61.7 | 68.7 | 59.9 |
| The criteria for advancement and promotion decisions are clear | 68.6 | 80.0 | 67.9 | 65.9 | 60.0 | 65.6 | 61.8 |
| Most of the students I teach lack the basic skills for college level work | 37.9 | 36.9 | 37.3 | 39.8 | 39.3 | 34.3 | 45.4 |
| There is adequate support for faculty development | 65.0 | 62.0 | 59.2 | 66.6 | 74.6 | 71.1 | 43.9 |
| This institution should not offer remedial/developmental education | 23.4 | 26.9 | 25.1 | 21.1 | 18.6 | 24.0 | 27.4 |

| Female Respondents | All Resp | Full Prof | Assoc Prof | Asst Prof | Lect | Inst | No Resp |
|---|---|---|---|---|---|---|---|
| **Issues you believe to be of "high" or "highest" priority at your institution:** | | | | | | | |
| To promote the intellectual development of students | 86.1 | 86.2 | 85.1 | 85.6 | 86.8 | 89.2 | 68.4 |
| To help students examine and understand their personal values | 57.5 | 56.9 | 55.6 | 59.0 | 52.6 | 63.0 | 48.5 |
| To develop a sense of community among students and faculty | 57.5 | 52.6 | 54.3 | 60.0 | 56.4 | 67.4 | 44.8 |
| To facilitate student involvement in community service | 51.3 | 48.0 | 48.0 | 54.0 | 50.0 | 58.1 | 41.4 |
| To help students learn how to bring about change in American society | 39.3 | 35.8 | 35.6 | 41.7 | 38.9 | 47.6 | 27.7 |
| To increase or maintain institutional prestige | 64.4 | 62.6 | 61.4 | 65.5 | 67.7 | 68.9 | 60.3 |
| To hire faculty "stars" | 29.6 | 29.9 | 26.5 | 28.3 | 40.6 | 31.5 | 0.9 |
| To recruit more minority students | 52.8 | 54.3 | 50.4 | 51.1 | 59.6 | 55.5 | 49.2 |
| To enhance the institution's national image | 68.6 | 66.8 | 65.5 | 68.5 | 76.6 | 72.4 | 58.3 |
| To create a diverse multi-cultural campus environment | 57.0 | 57.3 | 52.7 | 55.9 | 66.2 | 62.2 | 41.5 |
| To promote gender equity among faculty | 44.3 | 47.1 | 39.5 | 43.5 | 51.0 | 47.8 | 62.2 |
| To provide resources for faculty to engage in community-based teaching or research | 38.1 | 31.6 | 31.3 | 40.6 | 45.1 | 51.9 | 41.4 |
| To create and sustain partnerships with surrounding communities | 51.8 | 42.1 | 46.7 | 56.1 | 52.5 | 66.8 | 82.5 |
| To pursue extramural funding | 61.1 | 60.8 | 59.8 | 59.6 | 65.1 | 65.5 | 48.8 |
| To increase the representation of minorities in the faculty and administration | 45.3 | 47.7 | 41.9 | 45.2 | 49.9 | 45.2 | 53.4 |
| To strengthen links with the for-profit, corporate sector [2] | 50.2 | 45.9 | 49.8 | 48.2 | 58.0 | 58.2 | 23.8 |
| To develop leadership ability among students | 61.3 | 57.3 | 55.2 | 64.8 | 61.6 | 72.2 | 41.3 |
| To increase the representation of women in the faculty and administration | 33.1 | 34.9 | 30.0 | 33.6 | 31.1 | 37.0 | 46.5 |
| To develop an appreciation for multiculturalism [2] | 56.8 | 55.2 | 53.2 | 55.2 | 67.3 | 64.2 | 64.2 |

[2] This question asked for the first time in the 2007–2008 Faculty Survey.

**2007–2008 FACULTY SURVEY WEIGHTED NATIONAL NORMS**
**Full-time Undergraduate Faculty at Baccalaureate Institutions**

| Female Respondents | All Resp | Full Prof | Assoc Prof | Asst Prof | Lect | Inst | No Resp |
|---|---|---|---|---|---|---|---|
| **Do you agree "strongly" or "somewhat"?** | | | | | | | |
| Western civilization and culture should be the foundation for the undergraduate curriculum | 49.3 | 51.0 | 48.0 | 46.9 | 51.5 | 54.3 | 57.5 |
| College officials have the right to ban persons with extreme views from speaking on campus | 24.0 | 22.8 | 20.6 | 23.9 | 26.1 | 32.2 | 13.0 |
| The chief benefit of a college education is that it increases one's earning power | 28.0 | 23.4 | 25.0 | 28.8 | 28.6 | 40.0 | 17.5 |
| Promoting diversity leads to the admission of too many underprepared students | 17.3 | 14.8 | 15.5 | 16.5 | 24.7 | 22.5 | 0.0 |
| Colleges should be actively involved in solving social problems | 75.5 | 74.2 | 77.8 | 76.4 | 70.8 | 74.0 | 76.5 |
| Tenure is an outmoded concept | 37.2 | 19.2 | 25.7 | 41.7 | 63.6 | 60.1 | 32.8 |
| Colleges should encourage students to be involved in community service activities | 92.0 | 90.9 | 90.8 | 91.9 | 95.8 | 94.2 | 91.6 |
| Community service should be given weight in college admissions decisions | 69.5 | 65.7 | 70.1 | 70.3 | 68.6 | 73.3 | 72.2 |
| A racially/ethnically diverse student body enhances the educational experience of all students | 96.8 | 96.3 | 97.4 | 97.1 | 96.6 | 95.8 | 86.8 |
| Realistically, an individual can do little to bring about changes in society | 12.2 | 13.2 | 11.9 | 12.5 | 10.7 | 11.9 | 4.7 |
| Colleges should be concerned with facilitating undergraduate students' spiritual development | 35.9 | 32.1 | 33.4 | 36.9 | 36.0 | 45.1 | 34.1 |
| Colleges have a responsibility to work with their surrounding communities to address local issues | 90.6 | 89.0 | 91.4 | 91.7 | 84.1 | 93.7 | 98.5 |
| Private funding sources often prevent researchers from being completely objective in the conduct of their work | 61.4 | 61.8 | 63.6 | 58.0 | 64.9 | 62.9 | 69.5 |

192

| Female Respondents | All Resp | Full Prof | Assoc Prof | Asst Prof | Lect | Inst | No Resp |
|---|---|---|---|---|---|---|---|
| **Factors noted as a source of stress for you during the <u>last two</u> years** | | | | | | | |
| Managing household responsibilities | 80.5 | 73.0 | 82.8 | 82.1 | 79.1 | 84.9 | 74.2 |
| Child care | 31.2 | 24.5 | 36.0 | 33.5 | 26.0 | 29.8 | 13.9 |
| Care of elderly parent | 37.6 | 40.1 | 40.9 | 31.4 | 40.5 | 41.1 | 51.5 |
| My physical health | 53.9 | 53.3 | 56.4 | 54.2 | 53.3 | 48.6 | 40.3 |
| Health of spouse/partner | 31.4 | 32.2 | 33.2 | 29.5 | 33.5 | 29.8 | 23.9 |
| Review/promotion process | 57.9 | 28.8 | 60.7 | 77.5 | 49.0 | 52.7 | 56.8 |
| Subtle discrimination (e.g., prejudice, racism, sexism) | 38.7 | 41.4 | 44.3 | 38.0 | 32.4 | 28.7 | 31.4 |
| Personal finances | 65.2 | 50.5 | 63.0 | 72.3 | 68.1 | 72.7 | 44.3 |
| Committee work | 64.8 | 72.0 | 77.8 | 62.3 | 45.7 | 45.6 | 55.5 |
| Faculty meetings | 56.2 | 63.2 | 66.0 | 54.4 | 41.3 | 39.6 | 39.0 |
| Colleagues | 68.7 | 74.3 | 75.6 | 65.0 | 63.0 | 58.1 | 77.0 |
| Students | 69.0 | 63.2 | 70.1 | 73.7 | 62.7 | 68.1 | 39.7 |
| Research or publishing demands | 65.0 | 59.1 | 75.6 | 79.2 | 31.2 | 38.4 | 21.3 |
| Institutional procedures and "red tape" | 71.5 | 76.1 | 76.4 | 72.0 | 63.8 | 57.2 | 78.1 |
| Teaching load | 69.1 | 64.0 | 70.8 | 75.5 | 61.0 | 62.4 | 50.9 |
| Children's problems | 30.9 | 29.9 | 34.9 | 27.5 | 29.5 | 34.6 | 44.3 |
| Friction with spouse/partner | 24.6 | 20.0 | 25.4 | 28.1 | 18.6 | 25.6 | 5.0 |
| Lack of personal time | 83.7 | 82.5 | 85.7 | 85.3 | 76.3 | 82.6 | 89.0 |
| Keeping up with information technology | 59.4 | 68.5 | 62.0 | 51.7 | 66.3 | 54.1 | 88.4 |
| Job security | 39.3 | 11.6 | 25.7 | 56.4 | 53.6 | 56.6 | 22.1 |
| Being part of a dual career couple | 47.8 | 39.8 | 49.2 | 53.3 | 45.0 | 45.1 | 58.3 |
| Working with underprepared students | 64.5 | 61.7 | 64.4 | 66.1 | 64.5 | 64.9 | 62.7 |
| Classroom conflict | 24.3 | 21.4 | 23.4 | 27.7 | 20.3 | 25.1 | 14.7 |
| Self-imposed high expectations | 84.8 | 82.1 | 86.4 | 87.9 | 78.3 | 82.2 | 59.0 |
| Change in work responsibilities | 55.3 | 51.0 | 54.1 | 58.6 | 52.1 | 58.2 | 81.4 |
| **Personal goals noted as "very important" or "essential":** | | | | | | | |
| Becoming an authority in my field | 57.5 | 60.5 | 54.3 | 62.6 | 46.2 | 54.4 | 62.3 |
| Influencing the political structure | 20.7 | 23.6 | 20.1 | 22.1 | 18.3 | 15.2 | 11.4 |
| Influencing social values | 46.7 | 46.6 | 45.9 | 48.1 | 42.0 | 49.4 | 19.1 |
| Raising a family | 64.2 | 59.5 | 62.4 | 67.0 | 60.3 | 72.2 | 45.7 |
| Becoming very well off financially | 30.0 | 28.4 | 25.7 | 31.7 | 35.0 | 33.9 | 26.0 |
| Helping others who are in difficulty | 71.3 | 68.8 | 68.4 | 72.4 | 68.9 | 81.6 | 75.9 |
| Becoming involved in programs to clean up the environment | 38.1 | 38.9 | 36.7 | 38.6 | 33.1 | 42.5 | 46.7 |
| Developing a meaningful philosophy of life | 75.2 | 73.5 | 74.3 | 76.3 | 74.5 | 77.3 | 76.1 |
| Helping to promote racial understanding | 62.1 | 62.5 | 62.3 | 63.0 | 59.8 | 60.5 | 71.0 |
| Obtaining recognition from my colleagues for contributions to my special field | 48.2 | 48.3 | 47.5 | 54.4 | 37.5 | 40.4 | 25.2 |
| Integrating spirituality into my life | 53.1 | 47.7 | 49.0 | 54.3 | 53.5 | 68.2 | 32.3 |

| Female Respondents | All Resp | Full Prof | Assoc Prof | Asst Prof | Lect | Inst | No Resp |
|---|---|---|---|---|---|---|---|
| **IN YOUR INTERACTIONS WITH UNDERGRAD-UATES, HOW OFTEN DO YOU ENCOURAGE THEM TO: [2]** | | | | | | | |
| **Ask questions in class** | | | | | | | |
| Frequently | 97.1 | 96.7 | 96.9 | 96.9 | 97.9 | 98.0 | 100.0 |
| Occasionally | 2.7 | 3.0 | 2.9 | 2.9 | 2.1 | 2.0 | 0.0 |
| Not at all | 0.2 | 0.3 | 0.2 | 0.2 | 0.0 | 0.0 | 0.0 |
| **Support their opinions with a logical argument** | | | | | | | |
| Frequently | 86.4 | 86.2 | 87.0 | 85.6 | 91.3 | 83.9 | 81.9 |
| Occasionally | 13.0 | 12.9 | 12.3 | 14.0 | 8.6 | 15.6 | 18.1 |
| Not at all | 0.6 | 0.9 | 0.8 | 0.5 | 0.0 | 0.5 | 0.0 |
| **Seek solutions to problems and explain them to others** | | | | | | | |
| Frequently | 79.9 | 78.2 | 79.3 | 79.5 | 82.3 | 83.5 | 67.2 |
| Occasionally | 18.8 | 20.1 | 19.6 | 19.0 | 17.3 | 15.3 | 32.8 |
| Not at all | 1.3 | 1.7 | 1.1 | 1.5 | 0.4 | 1.1 | 0.0 |
| **Revise their papers to improve their writing** | | | | | | | |
| Frequently | 68.9 | 71.5 | 69.0 | 68.1 | 67.6 | 67.0 | 69.5 |
| Occasionally | 25.8 | 22.9 | 26.7 | 27.0 | 25.7 | 25.0 | 17.9 |
| Not at all | 5.4 | 5.5 | 4.3 | 4.8 | 6.6 | 8.0 | 12.6 |
| **Evaluate the quality or reliability of information they receive** | | | | | | | |
| Frequently | 80.2 | 81.9 | 82.3 | 79.3 | 78.4 | 76.3 | 87.4 |
| Occasionally | 18.4 | 16.7 | 17.0 | 19.0 | 19.3 | 22.5 | 12.6 |
| Not at all | 1.4 | 1.4 | 0.7 | 1.7 | 2.3 | 1.3 | 0.0 |
| **Take risks for potential gains** | | | | | | | |
| Frequently | 42.8 | 45.6 | 43.9 | 40.2 | 48.3 | 38.7 | 33.9 |
| Occasionally | 45.6 | 43.7 | 44.0 | 47.7 | 40.3 | 50.4 | 66.1 |
| Not at all | 11.6 | 10.7 | 12.0 | 12.1 | 11.4 | 10.9 | 0.0 |
| **Seek alternative solutions to a problem** | | | | | | | |
| Frequently | 71.7 | 72.7 | 69.1 | 70.7 | 76.2 | 75.3 | 68.9 |
| Occasionally | 26.2 | 25.2 | 29.1 | 27.1 | 20.3 | 23.3 | 31.1 |
| Not at all | 2.1 | 2.1 | 1.8 | 2.3 | 3.5 | 1.4 | 0.0 |
| **Look up scientific research articles and resources** | | | | | | | |
| Frequently | 59.6 | 58.7 | 59.7 | 60.6 | 58.5 | 58.3 | 76.7 |
| Occasionally | 29.0 | 27.1 | 28.2 | 28.8 | 33.9 | 30.5 | 22.9 |
| Not at all | 11.5 | 14.2 | 12.0 | 10.6 | 7.6 | 11.3 | 0.4 |
| **Explore topics on their own, even though it was not required for a class** | | | | | | | |
| Frequently | 57.1 | 58.5 | 55.3 | 54.7 | 63.8 | 60.0 | 66.8 |
| Occasionally | 39.9 | 38.8 | 42.1 | 41.9 | 33.0 | 37.0 | 33.2 |
| Not at all | 3.0 | 2.7 | 2.6 | 3.3 | 3.2 | 3.0 | 0.0 |
| **Acknowledge failure as a necessary part of the learning process** | | | | | | | |
| Frequently | 54.5 | 50.9 | 50.6 | 55.2 | 63.4 | 60.2 | 64.5 |
| Occasionally | 39.9 | 42.8 | 43.4 | 39.1 | 32.5 | 35.4 | 30.5 |
| Not at all | 5.6 | 6.3 | 6.1 | 5.7 | 4.1 | 4.3 | 5.0 |
| **Seek feedback on their academic work** | | | | | | | |
| Frequently | 82.5 | 81.2 | 82.2 | 81.8 | 87.9 | 83.1 | 71.5 |
| Occasionally | 16.5 | 17.2 | 16.6 | 17.5 | 11.7 | 15.9 | 28.5 |
| Not at all | 1.0 | 1.6 | 1.2 | 0.8 | 0.4 | 1.0 | 0.0 |

[2] This question asked for the first time in the 2007–2008 Faculty Survey.

**2007–2008 FACULTY SURVEY WEIGHTED NATIONAL NORMS**
**Full-time Undergraduate Faculty at Baccalaureate Institutions**

| Female Respondents | All Resp | Full Prof | Assoc Prof | Asst Prof | Lect | Inst | No Resp |
|---|---|---|---|---|---|---|---|
| **Methods you use in "all" or "most" of the courses you teach:** | | | | | | | |
| Multiple-choice exams [2] | 34.7 | 25.9 | 31.2 | 38.2 | 36.1 | 46.9 | 41.6 |
| Essay exams [2] | 43.1 | 50.0 | 47.8 | 42.1 | 37.8 | 27.7 | 43.6 |
| Short-answer exams [2] | 44.0 | 42.6 | 45.2 | 45.7 | 46.3 | 36.8 | 48.7 |
| Quizzes | 41.3 | 35.4 | 37.8 | 42.8 | 48.0 | 49.4 | 29.2 |
| Weekly essay assignments | 25.0 | 24.3 | 24.0 | 25.2 | 26.3 | 27.3 | 31.6 |
| Student presentations | 56.1 | 58.3 | 57.1 | 56.9 | 52.0 | 51.4 | 38.1 |
| Term/research papers | 47.1 | 48.3 | 49.1 | 48.9 | 44.5 | 37.9 | 24.2 |
| Student evaluations of each others' work | 29.5 | 27.8 | 27.6 | 29.9 | 35.1 | 30.5 | 38.6 |
| Grading on a curve | 10.7 | 15.6 | 9.5 | 9.8 | 11.5 | 6.9 | 16.0 |
| Competency-based grading | 55.1 | 51.6 | 54.1 | 55.0 | 59.0 | 60.3 | 77.6 |
| Class discussions | 88.2 | 86.7 | 89.3 | 89.4 | 86.2 | 86.2 | 91.6 |
| Cooperative learning (small groups) | 73.2 | 67.4 | 72.0 | 76.7 | 74.3 | 75.0 | 65.3 |
| Experiential learning/Field studies | 36.9 | 35.1 | 35.5 | 39.4 | 34.3 | 38.3 | 16.1 |
| Teaching assistants | 9.5 | 10.1 | 7.9 | 9.3 | 12.9 | 9.2 | 29.1 |
| Recitals/Demonstrations | 23.4 | 26.0 | 22.5 | 23.2 | 21.7 | 23.4 | 26.6 |
| Group projects | 42.9 | 40.7 | 40.5 | 46.1 | 45.6 | 40.7 | 59.3 |
| Extensive lecturing | 33.4 | 31.3 | 30.9 | 36.0 | 34.7 | 34.6 | 35.2 |
| Multiple drafts of written work | 30.6 | 31.4 | 30.6 | 29.9 | 33.0 | 28.9 | 22.9 |
| Readings on racial and ethnic issues | 33.0 | 33.6 | 34.5 | 34.4 | 28.2 | 28.3 | 14.6 |
| Readings on women and gender issues | 29.8 | 31.8 | 32.5 | 30.0 | 24.2 | 24.6 | 14.2 |
| Student-developed activities (assignments, exams, etc.) | 27.5 | 25.7 | 24.1 | 28.8 | 28.4 | 34.1 | 26.9 |
| Student-selected topics for course content | 19.7 | 19.6 | 17.6 | 20.6 | 20.7 | 21.0 | 31.0 |
| Reflective writing/journaling | 29.9 | 26.6 | 26.3 | 32.7 | 29.9 | 35.0 | 57.4 |
| Community service as part of coursework | 12.4 | 10.8 | 11.6 | 13.6 | 11.0 | 14.6 | 4.7 |
| Electronic quizzes with immediate feedback in class [2] | 7.6 | 5.1 | 6.5 | 7.7 | 13.2 | 9.2 | 8.9 |
| Using real-life problems [2] | 58.6 | 49.1 | 58.2 | 61.4 | 61.4 | 66.1 | 47.0 |
| Using student inquiry to drive learning | 52.3 | 49.3 | 49.3 | 54.2 | 55.3 | 56.1 | 53.3 |

[2] This question asked for the first time in the 2007–2008 Faculty Survey.

195

## 2007–2008 FACULTY SURVEY WEIGHTED NATIONAL NORMS
### Full-time Undergraduate Faculty at Baccalaureate Institutions

| Female Respondents | All Resp | Full Prof | Assoc Prof | Asst Prof | Lect | Inst | No Resp |
|---|---|---|---|---|---|---|---|
| **YOUR BASE INSTITUTIONAL SALARY** | | | | | | | |
| **9/10 month contract** | | | | | | | |
| Less than $20,000 | 2.1 | 2.1 | 2.5 | 1.8 | 1.7 | 2.0 | 0.0 |
| $20,000 to 29,999 | 1.1 | 0.0 | 0.0 | 0.1 | 3.0 | 7.9 | 0.0 |
| $30,000 to 39,999 | 6.7 | 0.4 | 0.7 | 3.4 | 24.6 | 30.8 | 0.0 |
| $40,000 to 49,999 | 18.7 | 2.2 | 6.8 | 28.1 | 35.0 | 38.0 | 0.0 |
| $50,000 to 59,999 | 27.8 | 8.1 | 30.0 | 42.9 | 18.2 | 17.9 | 59.9 |
| $60,000 to 69,999 | 18.3 | 18.6 | 30.3 | 14.0 | 14.0 | 3.0 | 0.0 |
| $70,000 to 79,999 | 10.4 | 20.2 | 17.3 | 4.2 | 1.9 | 0.0 | 40.1 |
| $80,000 to 89,999 | 6.1 | 18.1 | 6.7 | 1.7 | 0.8 | 0.4 | 0.0 |
| $90,000 to 99,999 | 4.4 | 14.3 | 3.5 | 1.7 | 0.5 | 0.0 | 0.0 |
| $100,000 to 124,999 | 3.4 | 12.7 | 1.7 | 1.4 | 0.2 | 0.0 | 0.0 |
| $125,000 to 149,999 | 0.7 | 2.3 | 0.4 | 0.4 | 0.0 | 0.0 | 0.0 |
| $150,000 or more | 0.3 | 1.1 | 0.1 | 0.3 | 0.0 | 0.0 | 0.0 |
| **11/12 month contract** | | | | | | | |
| Less than $20,000 | 2.9 | 5.2 | 2.0 | 2.1 | 3.5 | 2.5 | 0.0 |
| $20,000 to 29,999 | 0.5 | 0.1 | 0.1 | 0.1 | 1.9 | 1.3 | 0.0 |
| $30,000 to 39,999 | 6.4 | 0.2 | 0.3 | 1.8 | 12.1 | 31.2 | 0.0 |
| $40,000 to 49,999 | 17.3 | 1.3 | 7.9 | 22.6 | 30.3 | 29.8 | 0.0 |
| $50,000 to 59,999 | 23.3 | 5.7 | 21.0 | 34.1 | 29.9 | 18.5 | 39.7 |
| $60,000 to 69,999 | 19.6 | 12.1 | 27.2 | 24.2 | 12.7 | 13.3 | 28.2 |
| $70,000 to 79,999 | 10.9 | 14.1 | 20.5 | 7.6 | 5.8 | 3.3 | 32.1 |
| $80,000 to 89,999 | 6.9 | 15.3 | 9.3 | 5.4 | 1.8 | 0.1 | 0.0 |
| $90,000 to 99,999 | 4.5 | 15.6 | 5.8 | 1.0 | 0.0 | 0.0 | 0.0 |
| $100,000 to 124,999 | 5.8 | 22.4 | 5.1 | 0.8 | 1.5 | 0.1 | 0.0 |
| $125,000 to 149,999 | 1.2 | 4.4 | 0.8 | 0.3 | 0.4 | 0.0 | 0.0 |
| $150,000 or more | 0.7 | 3.4 | 0.1 | 0.0 | 0.0 | 0.0 | 0.0 |
| **Your base institutional salary is based on:** | | | | | | | |
| 9/10 months | 73.8 | 74.7 | 78.3 | 74.3 | 64.7 | 68.9 | 36.2 |
| 11/12 months | 26.2 | 25.3 | 21.7 | 25.7 | 35.3 | 31.1 | 63.8 |
| **WHAT PERCENTAGE OF YOUR CURRENT YEAR'S SALARY COMES FROM: [2]** | | | | | | | |
| **Income from this institution** | | | | | | | |
| All | 69.3 | 65.0 | 72.1 | 71.9 | 65.6 | 65.9 | 71.3 |
| 75 to 99 | 26.1 | 30.4 | 25.1 | 24.1 | 26.1 | 27.2 | 28.7 |
| 50 to 74 | 3.1 | 3.4 | 2.3 | 3.1 | 4.9 | 3.6 | 0.0 |
| 25 to 49 | 0.9 | 0.6 | 0.3 | 0.6 | 3.0 | 1.9 | 0.0 |
| 1 to 24 | 0.3 | 0.5 | 0.1 | 0.2 | 0.2 | 0.4 | 0.0 |
| None | 0.2 | 0.1 | 0.1 | 0.1 | 0.2 | 1.0 | 0.0 |
| **Other academic income** | | | | | | | |
| All | 0.1 | 0.1 | 0.1 | 0.0 | 0.0 | 0.5 | 0.0 |
| 75 to 99 | 0.1 | 0.4 | 0.0 | 0.2 | 0.2 | 0.0 | 0.0 |
| 50 to 74 | 0.3 | 0.4 | 0.1 | 0.3 | 0.6 | 0.4 | 0.0 |
| 25 to 49 | 1.5 | 1.7 | 1.6 | 1.7 | 0.4 | 1.6 | 0.0 |
| 1 to 24 | 14.4 | 20.4 | 15.1 | 12.2 | 12.8 | 10.3 | 7.5 |
| None | 83.6 | 77.2 | 83.2 | 85.7 | 86.0 | 87.2 | 92.5 |
| **Non-academic income** | | | | | | | |
| All | 0.2 | 0.0 | 0.2 | 0.1 | 0.2 | 0.3 | 0.0 |
| 75 to 99 | 0.2 | 0.2 | 0.2 | 0.1 | 0.1 | 0.5 | 0.0 |
| 50 to 74 | 1.3 | 0.8 | 0.4 | 1.2 | 4.2 | 2.5 | 0.0 |
| 25 to 49 | 2.9 | 2.6 | 2.2 | 2.6 | 4.5 | 4.7 | 0.0 |
| 1 to 24 | 17.4 | 19.0 | 15.2 | 16.4 | 18.8 | 21.1 | 26.3 |
| None | 78.0 | 77.4 | 81.7 | 79.6 | 72.3 | 70.9 | 73.7 |

[2]  This question asked for the first time in the 2007–2008 Faculty Survey.

| Female Respondents | All Resp | Full Prof | Assoc Prof | Asst Prof | Lect | Inst | No Resp |
|---|---|---|---|---|---|---|---|
| **What is your age as of 12/31/2007?** | | | | | | | |
| Less than 30 | 1.9 | 0.1 | 0.1 | 3.0 | 1.4 | 6.3 | 0.0 |
| 30 to 34 | 7.9 | 0.1 | 1.2 | 17.8 | 7.9 | 7.7 | 0.0 |
| 35 to 39 | 13.0 | 1.6 | 11.3 | 21.9 | 11.0 | 12.6 | 0.0 |
| 40 to 44 | 13.1 | 4.7 | 18.4 | 15.0 | 7.1 | 14.8 | 8.8 |
| 45 to 49 | 13.6 | 13.8 | 17.5 | 11.4 | 11.9 | 12.6 | 9.6 |
| 50 to 54 | 16.6 | 19.2 | 18.9 | 12.5 | 15.9 | 18.9 | 44.9 |
| 55 to 59 | 18.3 | 29.6 | 18.0 | 12.2 | 22.9 | 13.4 | 16.5 |
| 60 to 64 | 10.0 | 18.6 | 10.5 | 4.1 | 12.1 | 9.8 | 6.3 |
| 65 to 69 | 4.3 | 9.9 | 3.7 | 1.8 | 5.9 | 1.8 | 13.9 |
| 70 or more | 1.3 | 2.4 | 0.4 | 0.3 | 3.9 | 2.2 | 0.0 |
| **Year of highest degree now held** | | | | | | | |
| Before 1970 | 2.2 | 5.2 | 1.2 | 0.4 | 4.8 | 2.4 | 7.6 |
| 1971 to 1975 | 3.9 | 8.7 | 2.5 | 1.2 | 8.6 | 2.8 | 0.0 |
| 1976 to 1980 | 7.5 | 17.5 | 5.8 | 2.8 | 6.0 | 8.4 | 30.9 |
| 1981 to 1985 | 9.0 | 18.6 | 8.2 | 3.8 | 11.8 | 7.2 | 6.6 |
| 1986 to 1990 | 12.9 | 24.0 | 14.7 | 4.9 | 10.3 | 14.7 | 14.9 |
| 1991 to 1995 | 16.2 | 18.2 | 24.5 | 8.6 | 16.5 | 15.1 | 0.0 |
| 1996 to 2000 | 18.9 | 5.5 | 31.9 | 18.0 | 15.9 | 16.5 | 40.1 |
| 2001 to 2005 | 22.0 | 1.6 | 10.1 | 43.4 | 21.8 | 23.1 | 0.0 |
| 2006 to 2007 | 7.5 | 0.7 | 1.0 | 16.9 | 4.2 | 9.8 | 0.0 |
| **Year of appointment at current position** | | | | | | | |
| Before 1970 | 0.9 | 3.0 | 0.9 | 0.2 | 0.0 | 0.1 | 0.0 |
| 1971 to 1975 | 2.0 | 6.1 | 1.3 | 0.4 | 3.1 | 0.0 | 5.4 |
| 1976 to 1980 | 4.3 | 13.4 | 3.0 | 1.2 | 3.7 | 0.7 | 3.9 |
| 1981 to 1985 | 6.3 | 13.8 | 6.5 | 1.4 | 9.8 | 3.6 | 0.9 |
| 1986 to 1990 | 9.9 | 23.8 | 11.2 | 3.0 | 7.3 | 4.4 | 14.4 |
| 1991 to 1995 | 12.7 | 21.6 | 16.9 | 3.9 | 13.2 | 11.9 | 15.4 |
| 1996 to 2000 | 18.2 | 11.2 | 34.6 | 8.2 | 21.2 | 18.7 | 20.4 |
| 2001 to 2005 | 30.7 | 5.6 | 22.4 | 51.6 | 28.5 | 35.1 | 28.8 |
| 2006 to 2007 | 15.1 | 1.4 | 3.2 | 30.0 | 13.2 | 25.4 | 10.8 |
| **If tenured, year tenure was awarded** | | | | | | | |
| Before 1970 | 0.2 | 0.3 | 0.1 | 0.1 | 8.3 | 0.0 | 0.0 |
| 1971 to 1975 | 1.2 | 2.0 | 0.6 | 0.1 | 0.0 | 5.7 | 0.0 |
| 1976 to 1980 | 3.4 | 6.4 | 1.2 | 2.1 | 0.0 | 4.2 | 0.0 |
| 1981 to 1985 | 5.9 | 10.7 | 2.4 | 3.3 | 0.0 | 0.0 | 0.0 |
| 1986 to 1990 | 10.1 | 16.8 | 5.2 | 5.2 | 0.0 | 8.1 | 0.0 |
| 1991 to 1995 | 14.7 | 24.0 | 7.9 | 9.7 | 10.2 | 0.0 | 28.9 |
| 1996 to 2000 | 20.9 | 25.4 | 17.9 | 11.6 | 38.5 | 57.3 | 0.0 |
| 2001 to 2005 | 24.6 | 12.5 | 35.0 | 21.8 | 43.1 | 0.0 | 51.9 |
| 2006 to 2007 | 19.1 | 2.1 | 29.8 | 46.0 | 0.0 | 24.8 | 19.2 |

| Female Respondents | All Resp | Full Prof | Assoc Prof | Asst Prof | Lect | Inst | No Resp |
|---|---|---|---|---|---|---|---|
| **WHAT IS THE MAJOR OF THE HIGHEST DEGREE YOU HOLD?** | | | | | | | |
| **Biological Science** | | | | | | | |
| Agriculture | 0.4 | 1.0 | 0.4 | 0.2 | 0.0 | 0.1 | 0.0 |
| Forestry | 0.1 | 0.0 | 0.1 | 0.0 | 0.0 | 0.0 | 0.0 |
| Bacteriology, Molecular Biology | 0.9 | 0.6 | 0.9 | 1.2 | 0.9 | 0.3 | 0.0 |
| Biochemistry | 0.7 | 0.4 | 1.0 | 0.7 | 0.2 | 0.4 | 0.0 |
| Biophysics | 0.0 | 0.0 | 0.0 | 0.1 | 0.1 | 0.0 | 0.0 |
| Botany | 0.4 | 0.8 | 0.5 | 0.2 | 0.1 | 0.5 | 0.0 |
| Environmental Science | 0.3 | 0.4 | 0.3 | 0.2 | 0.3 | 0.1 | 0.0 |
| Marine (life) Sciences | 0.2 | 0.3 | 0.1 | 0.1 | 0.0 | 0.4 | 0.0 |
| Physiology, Anatomy | 0.5 | 1.1 | 0.3 | 0.3 | 0.1 | 0.4 | 0.0 |
| Zoology | 0.6 | 0.7 | 0.7 | 0.5 | 0.4 | 0.7 | 0.0 |
| General, Other Biological Sciences | 1.9 | 2.2 | 2.0 | 1.6 | 2.3 | 1.5 | 0.0 |
| **Business** | | | | | | | |
| Accounting | 0.9 | 0.9 | 0.8 | 0.8 | 0.9 | 1.6 | 0.0 |
| Finance | 0.4 | 0.3 | 0.5 | 0.5 | 0.2 | 0.4 | 0.0 |
| International Business | 0.1 | 0.1 | 0.1 | 0.0 | 0.0 | 0.3 | 0.0 |
| Management | 2.0 | 0.7 | 1.6 | 1.7 | 5.3 | 2.9 | 0.0 |
| Marketing | 0.7 | 0.6 | 0.8 | 0.8 | 0.3 | 0.3 | 0.0 |
| Secretarial Studies | 0.0 | 0.0 | 0.0 | 0.0 | 0.0 | 0.0 | 0.0 |
| General, Other Business | 0.8 | 0.5 | 0.5 | 0.8 | 1.4 | 1.8 | 0.0 |
| **Education** | | | | | | | |
| Business Education | 0.3 | 0.3 | 0.4 | 0.1 | 0.4 | 0.6 | 0.0 |
| Educational Administration | 1.7 | 1.1 | 1.8 | 1.7 | 1.8 | 2.1 | 0.0 |
| Educational Psychology/Counseling | 1.4 | 1.4 | 1.1 | 1.3 | 2.8 | 0.8 | 31.2 |
| Elementary Education | 1.5 | 1.3 | 1.1 | 1.8 | 1.2 | 1.9 | 4.7 |
| Higher Education | 2.4 | 2.7 | 2.3 | 2.3 | 3.6 | 1.5 | 0.0 |
| Music or Art Education | 0.4 | 0.5 | 0.2 | 0.6 | 0.0 | 0.2 | 0.0 |
| Physical or Health Education | 1.3 | 0.8 | 1.5 | 0.9 | 0.8 | 2.8 | 0.0 |
| Secondary Education | 0.9 | 0.5 | 1.2 | 0.9 | 0.8 | 1.6 | 0.0 |
| Special Education | 1.7 | 1.3 | 1.6 | 2.2 | 0.1 | 2.1 | 0.0 |
| General, Other Education Fields | 4.3 | 4.1 | 4.8 | 5.4 | 2.4 | 2.4 | 0.9 |
| **Engineering** | | | | | | | |
| Aero-/Astronautical Engineering | 0.1 | 0.0 | 0.2 | 0.0 | 0.0 | 0.0 | 0.0 |
| Chemical Engineering | 0.1 | 0.1 | 0.1 | 0.1 | 0.1 | 0.0 | 0.0 |
| Civil Engineering | 0.2 | 0.1 | 0.4 | 0.3 | 0.0 | 0.0 | 0.0 |
| Electrical Engineering | 0.2 | 0.3 | 0.1 | 0.3 | 0.0 | 0.1 | 0.0 |
| Industrial Engineering | 0.1 | 0.2 | 0.1 | 0.1 | 0.0 | 0.1 | 0.0 |
| Mechanical Engineering | 0.2 | 0.2 | 0.2 | 0.4 | 0.0 | 0.0 | 0.0 |
| General, Other Engineering Fields | 0.3 | 0.7 | 0.3 | 0.1 | 0.1 | 0.6 | 0.0 |
| **Health** | | | | | | | |
| Dentistry | 0.1 | 0.3 | 0.0 | 0.1 | 0.0 | 0.2 | 0.0 |
| Health Technology | 0.1 | 0.0 | 0.0 | 0.2 | 0.0 | 0.3 | 0.0 |
| Medicine or Surgery | 0.2 | 0.2 | 0.2 | 0.2 | 0.0 | 0.2 | 0.0 |
| Nursing | 7.4 | 2.1 | 5.9 | 9.3 | 5.0 | 16.3 | 0.0 |
| Pharmacy, Pharmacology | 0.8 | 1.9 | 0.7 | 0.8 | 0.0 | 0.1 | 0.0 |
| Therapy (speech, physical, occup.) | 1.2 | 0.6 | 0.4 | 1.9 | 2.2 | 0.7 | 0.0 |
| Veterinary Medicine | 0.1 | 0.1 | 0.0 | 0.1 | 0.0 | 0.0 | 0.0 |
| General, Other Health Fields | 1.5 | 0.8 | 1.1 | 1.9 | 2.1 | 1.7 | 0.0 |

## 2007–2008 FACULTY SURVEY WEIGHTED NATIONAL NORMS
### Full-time Undergraduate Faculty at Baccalaureate Institutions

| Female Respondents | All Resp | Full Prof | Assoc Prof | Asst Prof | Lect | Inst | No Resp |
|---|---|---|---|---|---|---|---|
| **WHAT IS THE MAJOR OF THE HIGHEST DEGREE YOU HOLD?** | | | | | | | |
| **Humanities** | | | | | | | |
| History | 3.5 | 3.2 | 4.0 | 3.8 | 2.0 | 3.0 | 0.0 |
| Political Science, Government | 1.7 | 1.6 | 1.9 | 2.3 | 0.4 | 0.4 | 0.0 |
| English Language & Literature | 8.7 | 9.9 | 6.8 | 7.4 | 10.8 | 13.3 | 8.8 |
| Foreign Languages & Literature | 1.9 | 2.1 | 2.0 | 2.0 | 0.9 | 1.5 | 0.0 |
| French | 1.2 | 1.2 | 1.3 | 0.3 | 5.0 | 0.2 | 2.1 |
| German | 0.5 | 0.5 | 1.1 | 0.3 | 0.0 | 0.2 | 0.0 |
| Spanish | 1.6 | 1.1 | 1.5 | 1.7 | 0.9 | 2.8 | 0.0 |
| Other Foreign Languages | 0.5 | 0.9 | 0.3 | 0.2 | 1.3 | 0.2 | 0.0 |
| Linguistics | 1.2 | 1.5 | 1.4 | 0.5 | 2.2 | 1.2 | 0.0 |
| Philosophy | 1.2 | 1.4 | 1.5 | 0.8 | 1.3 | 0.8 | 0.0 |
| Religion or Theology | 1.3 | 1.4 | 1.6 | 1.2 | 1.3 | 0.8 | 0.0 |
| General, Other Humanities Fields | 1.7 | 1.5 | 1.8 | 2.2 | 1.4 | 0.6 | 0.0 |
| **Fine Arts** | | | | | | | |
| Architecture/Urban Planning | 0.4 | 0.1 | 0.6 | 0.5 | 0.7 | 0.1 | 0.0 |
| Art | 2.0 | 3.4 | 1.9 | 1.6 | 2.4 | 0.4 | 0.0 |
| Dramatics or Speech | 1.7 | 2.7 | 1.3 | 1.6 | 1.9 | 1.1 | 14.4 |
| Music | 2.5 | 4.1 | 3.0 | 2.2 | 0.9 | 0.8 | 0.0 |
| Television or Film | 0.4 | 0.0 | 0.7 | 0.4 | 0.1 | 0.2 | 0.0 |
| Other Fine Arts | 1.5 | 1.6 | 1.2 | 1.3 | 2.0 | 2.2 | 0.0 |
| **Physical Science** | | | | | | | |
| Mathematics and/or Statistics | 2.7 | 2.4 | 2.3 | 2.3 | 5.4 | 3.5 | 0.0 |
| Astronomy | 0.1 | 0.1 | 0.1 | 0.2 | 0.2 | 0.1 | 0.0 |
| Atmospheric Sciences | 0.1 | 0.0 | 0.1 | 0.1 | 0.2 | 0.0 | 0.0 |
| Chemistry | 2.2 | 2.6 | 1.7 | 2.2 | 4.0 | 1.2 | 0.0 |
| Earth Sciences | 0.5 | 0.2 | 0.7 | 0.5 | 0.3 | 0.3 | 0.0 |
| Geography | 0.4 | 0.6 | 0.3 | 0.3 | 0.5 | 0.1 | 0.0 |
| Marine Sciences (incl. Oceanography) | 0.1 | 0.2 | 0.1 | 0.1 | 0.0 | 0.1 | 0.0 |
| Physics | 0.6 | 1.1 | 0.6 | 0.5 | 0.5 | 0.1 | 0.0 |
| General, Other Physical Sciences | 0.1 | 0.0 | 0.0 | 0.1 | 0.0 | 0.2 | 0.0 |
| **Social Science** | | | | | | | |
| Anthropology | 1.3 | 1.2 | 1.6 | 1.4 | 1.0 | 0.4 | 5.3 |
| Archaeology | 0.2 | 0.2 | 0.2 | 0.1 | 0.1 | 0.1 | 0.0 |
| Clinical Psychology | 1.1 | 1.2 | 1.4 | 1.3 | 0.3 | 0.8 | 0.0 |
| Counseling and Guidance | 0.3 | 0.3 | 0.2 | 0.1 | 1.0 | 0.3 | 0.0 |
| Experimental Psychology | 1.1 | 1.4 | 1.6 | 1.1 | 0.8 | 0.1 | 0.0 |
| Social Psychology | 1.0 | 0.9 | 1.2 | 0.9 | 0.1 | 2.3 | 0.0 |
| General, Other Psychology | 2.0 | 2.5 | 2.7 | 1.8 | 1.6 | 0.2 | 9.6 |
| Economics | 1.2 | 1.3 | 1.4 | 1.3 | 1.4 | 0.5 | 0.0 |
| Sociology | 2.8 | 3.4 | 3.7 | 3.1 | 0.5 | 0.5 | 0.0 |
| Social Work, Social Welfare | 1.0 | 1.2 | 1.1 | 1.1 | 0.7 | 0.7 | 0.0 |
| General, Other Social Sciences | 1.5 | 1.0 | 1.8 | 1.7 | 1.2 | 1.0 | 5.4 |

199

| Female Respondents | All Resp | Full Prof | Assoc Prof | Asst Prof | Lect | Inst | No Resp |
|---|---|---|---|---|---|---|---|
| **WHAT IS THE MAJOR OF THE HIGHEST DEGREE YOU HOLD?** | | | | | | | |
| **Technical** | | | | | | | |
| Computer Science | 0.9 | 1.0 | 0.6 | 0.8 | 0.9 | 1.7 | 0.0 |
| Data Processing, Computer Prog. | 0.0 | 0.0 | 0.0 | 0.0 | 0.0 | 0.1 | 0.0 |
| Drafting/Design | 0.1 | 0.1 | 0.0 | 0.1 | 0.0 | 0.2 | 0.0 |
| Electronics | 0.0 | 0.0 | 0.0 | 0.0 | 0.0 | 0.0 | 0.0 |
| Industrial Arts | 0.0 | 0.0 | 0.0 | 0.0 | 0.0 | 0.1 | 0.0 |
| Mechanics | 0.0 | 0.0 | 0.0 | 0.0 | 0.0 | 0.0 | 0.0 |
| Other Technical | 0.3 | 0.1 | 0.2 | 0.3 | 0.7 | 0.3 | 0.0 |
| **Other Fields** | | | | | | | |
| Building Trades | 0.0 | 0.0 | 0.0 | 0.0 | 0.0 | 0.0 | 0.0 |
| Communications | 2.2 | 1.9 | 2.2 | 2.1 | 3.6 | 2.3 | 0.0 |
| Ethnic Studies | 0.0 | 0.0 | 0.1 | 0.0 | 0.0 | 0.0 | 0.0 |
| Human Ecology/Family Science | 0.8 | 1.0 | 1.4 | 0.6 | 0.0 | 0.2 | 0.0 |
| Journalism | 0.6 | 0.3 | 0.3 | 0.5 | 1.0 | 1.6 | 0.0 |
| Law | 0.7 | 1.3 | 0.6 | 0.5 | 0.5 | 0.4 | 0.0 |
| Law Enforcement | 0.1 | 0.1 | 0.0 | 0.0 | 0.5 | 0.0 | 0.0 |
| Library Science | 0.8 | 0.7 | 0.4 | 0.7 | 0.5 | 2.1 | 17.6 |
| Women's Studies | 0.0 | 0.1 | 0.0 | 0.0 | 0.0 | 0.0 | 0.0 |
| Other Vocational | 0.0 | 0.1 | 0.0 | 0.0 | 0.0 | 0.0 | 0.0 |
| All Other Fields | 1.0 | 1.4 | 1.1 | 0.9 | 0.5 | 0.8 | 0.0 |

| Female Respondents | All Resp | Full Prof | Assoc Prof | Asst Prof | Lect | Inst | No Resp |
|---|---|---|---|---|---|---|---|
| **WHAT IS THE DEPARTMENT OF YOUR CURRENT FACULTY APPOINTMENT?** | | | | | | | |
| **Biological Science** | | | | | | | |
| Agriculture | 0.5 | 1.1 | 0.5 | 0.3 | 0.0 | 0.1 | 0.0 |
| Forestry | 0.0 | 0.1 | 0.0 | 0.0 | 0.0 | 0.0 | 0.0 |
| Bacteriology, Molecular Biology | 0.3 | 0.2 | 0.0 | 0.6 | 0.1 | 0.1 | 0.0 |
| Biochemistry | 0.1 | 0.0 | 0.1 | 0.1 | 0.4 | 0.0 | 0.0 |
| Biophysics | 0.0 | 0.0 | 0.1 | 0.0 | 0.0 | 0.0 | 0.0 |
| Botany | 0.1 | 0.2 | 0.0 | 0.0 | 0.0 | 0.0 | 0.0 |
| Environmental Science | 0.4 | 0.5 | 0.7 | 0.2 | 0.1 | 0.3 | 0.0 |
| Marine (life) Sciences | 0.0 | 0.1 | 0.0 | 0.1 | 0.0 | 0.0 | 0.0 |
| Physiology, Anatomy | 0.2 | 0.1 | 0.2 | 0.2 | 0.3 | 0.1 | 0.0 |
| Zoology | 0.1 | 0.0 | 0.2 | 0.2 | 0.0 | 0.0 | 0.0 |
| General, Other Biological Sciences | 4.2 | 5.3 | 4.7 | 3.4 | 3.7 | 3.6 | 0.0 |
| **Business** | | | | | | | |
| Accounting | 1.2 | 1.2 | 0.9 | 1.1 | 1.4 | 2.0 | 0.0 |
| Finance | 0.5 | 0.4 | 0.4 | 0.6 | 0.4 | 0.6 | 0.0 |
| International Business | 0.1 | 0.0 | 0.0 | 0.1 | 0.0 | 0.1 | 0.0 |
| Management | 2.0 | 1.1 | 1.9 | 2.0 | 4.7 | 1.9 | 0.0 |
| Marketing | 0.9 | 0.9 | 0.8 | 0.9 | 1.3 | 0.9 | 0.0 |
| Secretarial Studies | 0.0 | 0.0 | 0.0 | 0.0 | 0.0 | 0.0 | 0.0 |
| General, Other Business | 1.3 | 1.3 | 1.4 | 1.1 | 1.5 | 1.6 | 0.0 |
| **Education** | | | | | | | |
| Business Education | 0.0 | 0.1 | 0.1 | 0.0 | 0.0 | 0.0 | 0.0 |
| Educational Administration | 0.2 | 0.4 | 0.1 | 0.2 | 0.1 | 0.3 | 0.0 |
| Educational Psychology/Counseling | 0.5 | 0.6 | 0.5 | 0.6 | 0.0 | 0.0 | 0.0 |
| Elementary Education | 3.0 | 2.1 | 3.2 | 3.6 | 2.6 | 2.5 | 4.7 |
| Higher Education | 0.4 | 0.3 | 0.4 | 0.6 | 0.2 | 0.4 | 8.8 |
| Music or Art Education | 0.1 | 0.1 | 0.1 | 0.2 | 0.0 | 0.0 | 0.0 |
| Physical or Health Education | 1.6 | 1.3 | 1.8 | 1.4 | 1.1 | 3.1 | 0.0 |
| Secondary Education | 0.8 | 0.3 | 0.9 | 0.9 | 0.4 | 0.9 | 0.0 |
| Special Education | 1.0 | 0.5 | 1.0 | 1.6 | 0.5 | 0.6 | 0.0 |
| General, Other Education Fields | 3.1 | 3.3 | 3.2 | 3.2 | 1.0 | 3.7 | 31.2 |
| **Engineering** | | | | | | | |
| Aero-/Astronautical Engineering | 0.0 | 0.0 | 0.0 | 0.0 | 0.0 | 0.0 | 0.0 |
| Chemical Engineering | 0.0 | 0.1 | 0.0 | 0.0 | 0.0 | 0.0 | 0.0 |
| Civil Engineering | 0.2 | 0.1 | 0.5 | 0.2 | 0.1 | 0.0 | 0.0 |
| Electrical Engineering | 0.2 | 0.3 | 0.2 | 0.2 | 0.0 | 0.0 | 0.0 |
| Industrial Engineering | 0.0 | 0.0 | 0.0 | 0.1 | 0.0 | 0.0 | 0.0 |
| Mechanical Engineering | 0.2 | 0.1 | 0.1 | 0.3 | 0.0 | 0.0 | 0.0 |
| General, Other Engineering Fields | 0.5 | 1.0 | 0.3 | 0.3 | 0.5 | 0.4 | 0.0 |
| **Health** | | | | | | | |
| Dentistry | 0.2 | 0.3 | 0.2 | 0.2 | 0.0 | 0.1 | 0.0 |
| Health Technology | 0.2 | 0.1 | 0.1 | 0.3 | 0.0 | 0.4 | 0.0 |
| Medicine or Surgery | 0.2 | 0.2 | 0.1 | 0.3 | 0.0 | 0.1 | 0.0 |
| Nursing | 8.7 | 3.9 | 7.6 | 10.7 | 5.1 | 17.3 | 0.0 |
| Pharmacy, Pharmacology | 0.8 | 1.5 | 0.7 | 0.9 | 0.0 | 0.1 | 0.0 |
| Therapy (speech, physical, occup.) | 1.5 | 0.9 | 0.8 | 2.5 | 1.6 | 1.3 | 0.0 |
| Veterinary Medicine | 0.0 | 0.1 | 0.0 | 0.0 | 0.0 | 0.0 | 0.0 |
| General, Other Health Fields | 1.7 | 1.1 | 1.3 | 1.9 | 2.7 | 2.0 | 0.0 |

| Female Respondents | All Resp | Full Prof | Assoc Prof | Asst Prof | Lect | Inst | No Resp |
|---|---|---|---|---|---|---|---|
| **WHAT IS THE DEPARTMENT OF YOUR CURRENT FACULTY APPOINTMENT?** | | | | | | | |
| **Humanities** | | | | | | | |
| History | 2.8 | 2.9 | 3.7 | 3.2 | 0.8 | 0.6 | 5.3 |
| Political Science, Government | 1.5 | 1.1 | 1.6 | 2.2 | 0.8 | 0.3 | 0.0 |
| English Language & Literature | 9.5 | 10.5 | 7.6 | 8.2 | 12.0 | 14.2 | 0.0 |
| Foreign Languages & Literature | 3.8 | 3.6 | 3.8 | 3.0 | 7.5 | 3.5 | 0.0 |
| French | 0.3 | 0.3 | 0.5 | 0.1 | 0.7 | 0.4 | 0.0 |
| German | 0.3 | 0.2 | 0.7 | 0.1 | 0.1 | 0.1 | 0.0 |
| Spanish | 1.1 | 0.6 | 1.0 | 1.3 | 0.9 | 1.7 | 0.0 |
| Other Foreign Languages | 0.7 | 0.6 | 0.3 | 0.2 | 3.5 | 0.6 | 0.0 |
| Linguistics | 0.2 | 0.1 | 0.4 | 0.2 | 0.0 | 0.2 | 0.0 |
| Philosophy | 1.0 | 1.4 | 1.3 | 0.8 | 0.3 | 0.6 | 0.0 |
| Religion or Theology | 1.4 | 1.6 | 1.8 | 1.3 | 1.2 | 0.6 | 0.0 |
| General, Other Humanities Fields | 2.0 | 2.2 | 2.1 | 2.0 | 1.9 | 1.7 | 0.0 |
| **Fine Arts** | | | | | | | |
| Architecture/Urban Planning | 0.5 | 0.1 | 0.6 | 0.8 | 0.0 | 0.1 | 0.0 |
| Art | 2.7 | 4.3 | 2.8 | 2.5 | 2.4 | 0.5 | 0.0 |
| Dramatics or Speech | 1.6 | 2.5 | 1.2 | 1.6 | 1.5 | 0.8 | 14.4 |
| Music | 2.5 | 4.5 | 2.9 | 2.2 | 1.1 | 0.7 | 0.0 |
| Television or Film | 0.4 | 0.7 | 0.5 | 0.3 | 0.2 | 0.1 | 0.0 |
| Other Fine Arts | 1.1 | 1.2 | 1.1 | 0.7 | 1.8 | 1.2 | 0.0 |
| **Physical Science** | | | | | | | |
| Mathematics and/or Statistics | 3.4 | 2.9 | 2.8 | 2.6 | 7.2 | 4.7 | 0.0 |
| Astronomy | 0.0 | 0.0 | 0.0 | 0.0 | 0.0 | 0.0 | 0.0 |
| Atmospheric Sciences | 0.0 | 0.0 | 0.0 | 0.1 | 0.0 | 0.0 | 0.0 |
| Chemistry | 2.5 | 2.7 | 1.7 | 2.7 | 4.8 | 1.4 | 0.0 |
| Earth Sciences | 0.5 | 0.3 | 0.8 | 0.4 | 0.3 | 0.2 | 0.0 |
| Geography | 0.4 | 0.5 | 0.3 | 0.3 | 0.7 | 0.0 | 0.0 |
| Marine Sciences (incl. Oceanography) | 0.1 | 0.1 | 0.0 | 0.1 | 0.0 | 0.0 | 0.0 |
| Physics | 0.7 | 1.2 | 0.7 | 0.6 | 0.2 | 0.8 | 0.0 |
| General, Other Physical Sciences | 0.2 | 0.1 | 0.3 | 0.3 | 0.2 | 0.3 | 0.0 |
| **Social Science** | | | | | | | |
| Anthropology | 1.1 | 1.0 | 1.7 | 1.0 | 0.7 | 0.4 | 0.0 |
| Archaeology | 0.0 | 0.1 | 0.0 | 0.0 | 0.0 | 0.0 | 0.0 |
| Clinical Psychology | 0.5 | 0.6 | 0.5 | 0.6 | 0.0 | 0.2 | 0.0 |
| Counseling and Guidance | 0.2 | 0.2 | 0.2 | 0.1 | 0.3 | 0.0 | 0.0 |
| Experimental Psychology | 0.9 | 0.9 | 0.8 | 0.6 | 0.4 | 2.4 | 0.0 |
| Social Psychology | 0.2 | 0.2 | 0.2 | 0.3 | 0.2 | 0.0 | 0.0 |
| General, Other Psychology | 3.1 | 3.5 | 4.2 | 3.2 | 2.2 | 0.6 | 9.6 |
| Economics | 1.0 | 1.2 | 0.9 | 1.0 | 1.3 | 0.4 | 0.0 |
| Sociology | 2.7 | 3.2 | 3.2 | 3.4 | 1.1 | 0.4 | 0.0 |
| Social Work, Social Welfare | 1.1 | 0.9 | 1.2 | 1.3 | 0.7 | 0.7 | 0.0 |
| General, Other Social Sciences | 2.0 | 1.5 | 2.3 | 2.0 | 1.4 | 2.9 | 0.0 |

| Female Respondents | All Resp | Full Prof | Assoc Prof | Asst Prof | Lect | Inst | No Resp |
|---|---|---|---|---|---|---|---|
| **WHAT IS THE DEPARTMENT OF YOUR CURRENT FACULTY APPOINTMENT?** | | | | | | | |
| **Technical** | | | | | | | |
| Computer Science | 1.0 | 0.9 | 0.9 | 1.0 | 0.6 | 1.6 | 0.0 |
| Data Processing, Computer Prog. | 0.0 | 0.0 | 0.0 | 0.0 | 0.0 | 0.2 | 0.0 |
| Drafting/Design | 0.1 | 0.0 | 0.1 | 0.1 | 0.0 | 0.3 | 0.0 |
| Electronics | 0.0 | 0.0 | 0.0 | 0.1 | 0.0 | 0.0 | 0.0 |
| Industrial Arts | 0.0 | 0.0 | 0.0 | 0.0 | 0.3 | 0.0 | 0.0 |
| Mechanics | 0.0 | 0.0 | 0.0 | 0.0 | 0.0 | 0.0 | 0.0 |
| Other Technical | 0.3 | 0.2 | 0.3 | 0.3 | 0.6 | 0.1 | 0.0 |
| **Other Fields** | | | | | | | |
| Building Trades | 0.0 | 0.0 | 0.0 | 0.0 | 0.0 | 0.2 | 0.0 |
| Communications | 2.6 | 2.0 | 2.4 | 2.2 | 5.4 | 2.6 | 5.4 |
| Ethnic Studies | 0.2 | 0.2 | 0.3 | 0.3 | 0.0 | 0.0 | 0.0 |
| Human Ecology/Family Science | 0.9 | 1.1 | 1.3 | 0.7 | 0.5 | 0.2 | 0.0 |
| Journalism | 0.7 | 0.5 | 0.4 | 0.8 | 0.8 | 1.0 | 0.0 |
| Law | 0.3 | 0.6 | 0.2 | 0.2 | 0.3 | 0.1 | 0.0 |
| Law Enforcement | 0.1 | 0.1 | 0.0 | 0.1 | 0.2 | 0.0 | 0.0 |
| Library Science | 0.8 | 0.8 | 0.5 | 0.7 | 0.5 | 2.1 | 17.6 |
| Women's Studies | 0.3 | 0.3 | 0.5 | 0.3 | 0.3 | 0.0 | 0.0 |
| Other Vocational | 0.2 | 0.2 | 0.0 | 0.1 | 0.0 | 1.1 | 0.0 |
| All Other Fields | 1.6 | 1.9 | 1.9 | 0.9 | 1.5 | 2.5 | 3.0 |
| **HOW MANY CHILDREN DO YOU HAVE IN THE FOLLOWING AGE RANGES?** | | | | | | | |
| **Under 18 years old** | | | | | | | |
| None | 66.3 | 76.4 | 62.7 | 62.4 | 73.1 | 63.4 | 66.1 |
| One | 16.9 | 12.8 | 18.9 | 19.1 | 12.7 | 15.8 | 25.1 |
| Two | 13.3 | 9.2 | 15.0 | 14.2 | 10.8 | 16.2 | 8.7 |
| Three | 2.6 | 1.0 | 2.6 | 3.6 | 1.9 | 3.2 | 0.0 |
| Four or more | 0.9 | 0.6 | 0.8 | 0.7 | 1.5 | 1.4 | 0.0 |
| **18 years or older** | | | | | | | |
| None | 59.6 | 46.6 | 62.7 | 72.0 | 46.7 | 49.3 | 58.5 |
| One | 13.0 | 19.5 | 12.6 | 8.3 | 14.0 | 15.6 | 19.5 |
| Two | 18.4 | 22.6 | 16.9 | 12.8 | 28.6 | 22.5 | 19.7 |
| Three | 5.9 | 8.5 | 4.8 | 4.4 | 7.3 | 7.7 | 2.2 |
| Four or more | 3.1 | 2.8 | 3.0 | 2.5 | 3.5 | 5.0 | 0.0 |
| **How would you characterize your political views?** | | | | | | | |
| Far left | 9.9 | 11.6 | 12.4 | 10.4 | 5.6 | 3.6 | 17.1 |
| Liberal | 51.9 | 59.7 | 56.1 | 50.2 | 49.0 | 35.4 | 59.7 |
| Middle of the Road | 26.0 | 19.1 | 21.6 | 28.3 | 30.9 | 37.3 | 14.6 |
| Conservative | 11.9 | 9.6 | 9.5 | 10.7 | 14.3 | 23.4 | 8.6 |
| Far right | 0.3 | 0.1 | 0.3 | 0.4 | 0.2 | 0.3 | 0.0 |
| **Are you currently:** | | | | | | | |
| Single | 14.8 | 13.9 | 15.2 | 18.0 | 11.6 | 9.1 | 14.3 |
| Married | 67.4 | 65.8 | 67.1 | 66.0 | 68.0 | 74.3 | 80.4 |
| Unmarried, living with partner | 5.7 | 5.7 | 6.2 | 6.3 | 5.1 | 3.4 | 0.0 |
| Divorced | 8.8 | 10.3 | 9.4 | 7.7 | 7.3 | 9.3 | 5.3 |
| Widowed | 2.4 | 3.6 | 1.4 | 1.2 | 7.0 | 2.7 | 0.0 |
| Separated | 0.8 | 0.7 | 0.8 | 0.8 | 1.0 | 1.2 | 0.0 |

## 2007–2008 FACULTY SURVEY WEIGHTED NATIONAL NORMS
### Full-time Undergraduate Faculty at Baccalaureate Institutions

| Female Respondents | All Resp | Full Prof | Assoc Prof | Asst Prof | Lect | Inst | No Resp |
|---|---|---|---|---|---|---|---|
| **Is English your native language?** | | | | | | | |
| Yes | 90.4 | 91.2 | 91.7 | 87.9 | 90.0 | 93.5 | 100.0 |
| No | 9.6 | 8.8 | 8.3 | 12.1 | 10.0 | 6.5 | 0.0 |
| **Are you: [5]** | | | | | | | |
| White/Caucasian | 89.2 | 91.5 | 88.8 | 86.6 | 92.5 | 90.9 | 100.0 |
| African American/Black | 3.4 | 2.9 | 3.2 | 3.8 | 3.6 | 3.3 | 0.0 |
| American Indian/Alaska Native | 1.5 | 1.6 | 1.2 | 1.6 | 1.3 | 1.5 | 0.0 |
| Asian American/Asian | 3.4 | 2.6 | 3.0 | 4.8 | 2.2 | 2.8 | 0.0 |
| Native Hawaiian/Pacific Islander | 0.2 | 0.1 | 0.3 | 0.1 | 0.5 | 0.3 | 0.0 |
| Mexican American/Chicano | 1.0 | 0.8 | 0.8 | 1.2 | 0.7 | 1.2 | 0.0 |
| Puerto Rican | 0.4 | 0.4 | 0.4 | 0.5 | 0.1 | 0.1 | 0.0 |
| Other Latino | 1.9 | 1.9 | 1.9 | 2.5 | 0.7 | 1.4 | 0.0 |
| Other | 2.4 | 1.9 | 3.0 | 2.4 | 2.6 | 1.4 | 0.0 |
| **Do you give the Higher Education Research Institute (HERI) permission to retain your contact information (i.e., your email address and name) for possible follow-up research?** | | | | | | | |
| Yes | 74.6 | 75.6 | 76.4 | 74.1 | 76.9 | 67.8 | 81.7 |
| No | 25.4 | 24.4 | 23.6 | 25.9 | 23.1 | 32.2 | 18.3 |

[4] Percentages will sum to more than 100.0 if any respondent marked more than one category.

# Appendix A

# Research Methodology

# Research Methodology

The procedures for administering the Faculty survey in 2007 were markedly different from those in preceding years, due to significant technological and logistical enhancements developed by HERI and its Scanning Center, operated by Data Recognition Corporation. To understand the scope of these changes, let us briefly review the administration procedure in place up until the 2004 Faculty Survey, and contrast it to the procedure used in 2007.

## 2004 and Previous

The survey was conducted using a paper form only. The logistics of creating and distributing survey packets[1] for large numbers of faculty and hundreds of institutions (over 187,000 faculty at 511 institutions in 2004) were formidable. The amount of staff time at HERI, the Scanning Center and the participating institutions, not to mention the expense of handling so much paper, were considerable—so much so that HERI was compelled to distribute the initial wave of survey packets and a single follow-up on the same dates for all institutions. Because the institutions were free to administer their first and second waves on their own schedules, a substantial number of institutions did not have their first wave in the field before the second-wave survey packets arrived.

Communications and transfers of necessary data (such as the names and addresses of faculty) between the individual institutions and the Processing Center were all mediated by HERI to ensure consistent procedures. The three-way communications, mainly by telephone, fax, and email, were slow and prone to delays when any one of the three parties was unavailable. Communication between individual faculty and the Processing Center—for example a faculty wishing to "opt out"[2] of the survey—were subject to similar delays.

Finally, the second wave of survey packets, complete with faculty name and addresses, went to each participating institution. This procedure identified individual faculty who had not responded to the first wave of surveys. This was a matter of concern to UCLA's Institutional Review Board as a potential violation of privacy.

---

[1] A survey packet consisted of the survey instrument itself, a separate cover letter from HERI, and a postage paid return envelope. The survey packets for each institution were shipped by the Processing Center unsealed, in the event an institution wanted to add its own cover letter on official stationery. The institution then mailed the survey packets to the individual faculty.

[2] By opting out, a faculty member indicates he/she does not want to participate in the survey, and directs that no more survey materials be sent to her/him.

**2007**

Unlike earlier administrations of the Faculty Survey, the 2007 survey was in electronic form only. Individual faculty were invited to participate via email, and filled out the survey by linking to the HERI Portal (see below) via their own web browsers. The immediate benefits of switching to a web-only version of the instrument included:

- Removing virtually all transfer of physical documents with their attendant costs in mailing and staff commitment.
- Freeing the survey from the restrictions of fitting within the boundaries defined by the paper on which the instrument is printed. The 2007 survey instrument, for example, contains almost 30% more items than the 2004 version.
- Notifying respondents which questions have been left unanswered and providing a second opportunity for the respondent to answer.
- In conjunction with the HERI Portal (see below), allowing a faculty member to opt out of the survey without having to contact his/her institution or HERI.
- Finally, since electronic delivery of the survey from the Processing Center to individual faculty is automated, individual institutions can customize the dates of initial administration of the survey (and up to two follow-up administrations) to meet their individual calendars, provided they administer within the 6-month data collection phase of the survey.

In the Fall of 2005, HERI and Data Recognition Corporation embarked on a collaborative effort to design and construct the HERI Portal. The Portal is a website that allows a robust variety of secure communications between institutions, the Processing Center, and HERI. Moreover, the communications are standardized for consistency, removing the need to route interactions between the institutions and the Processing Center through HERI.

In 2007, an institution's interaction with the Portal began with registration, at which time an institution designated the person overseeing the survey's administration. At that time, or at any time within 2 days of the initial distribution of surveys, the institutional contact used the Portal to specify the date of the initial administration, and (optionally) the dates of a second and third administration, as well as up to two reminder messages to be sent to non-respondents.

The Portal has default texts written by HERI for the initial invitation to participate, as well as reminder e-mails and invitations associated with the second (and third) distributions. The institutional contact could add, via the Portal, additional text to these invitations and reminders, including an institutional logo, in order to "personalize" the invitation to the institution.

Once the survey was launched for a particular institution, the process of issuing reminders and additional waves of administration were handled automatically by the Portal without further need of any action by the institutional contact. Not only did this insure that administration was executed according to the schedule established by the institutional contact, but it eliminated the possibility of an institution obtaining specific knowledge of which faculty had not responded to any wave of administration, thereby removing an important source of privacy concerns.

As with all HERI Surveys, the Faculty Survey data collected from an institution were made available to that institution for secondary analyses. In previous administrations the data were not available until all data from all institutions were collected, which for some institutions was months after the survey was administered. In 2007, however, the data from each completed survey were available within 24 hours of its collection. Thus, the institution could perform its secondary analyses as soon as, or even before, the administration process is complete.

## Supplemental Sample

In every administration of the Faculty Survey save one (1992–1993), HERI has created a supplemental sample to enhance the number of respondents from types of institutions that participated at a lower rate than others, for example large public colleges and universities. Until 2004, the lists of faculty to be surveyed in Supplemental Sample institutions were obtained from vendors specializing in mass mailings to colleges and universities. Survey packets were prepared with standardized invitation letters from HERI, and administered directly by the Processing Center.

This model proved inadequate for the 2007 Supplemental Sample, as the vendors we had relied on for faculty mailing addresses did not have available any faculty e-mail addresses, making it impossible to survey them under the current administration protocol.

Fortunately, a pair of decisions HERI made in the last Faculty Survey administration provided a serendipitous solution to our dilemma. First, when we requested lists of faculty names and addresses from participating institutions, we asked for e-mail addresses as well. Second, we included a question in the 2004 survey asking respondents if we could retain their contact information for follow-up research. An examination of the 2004 respondents found a pool of 15,127 faculty at 199 institutions not participating in the 2007 Faculty Survey who gave HERI permission for further contact and whose institutions provided e-mail addresses. This pool became the Supplemental Sample.

## Survey Response

Of the 104,924 questionnaires mailed out, usable surveys were eventually received from 34,479 respondents, constituting a 33 percent response rate, down from 38 percent in 2004, 43 percent in 1998, and 55 percent in 1989. These results are consistent with a general decline in response to remotely-administered HERI surveys over the years.

Unlike earlier administrations of the Faculty Survey, the response rate for the Supplemental Sample was slightly higher than the response rate of the participating institutions (34.5 percent vs. 32.6 percent respectively) and considerably higher than the 2004 Supplemental Sample response rate (21 percent). The higher response rate in 2007 is attributable to two factors: a) the e-mail addresses received from institutions were more likely to be accurate and up-to-date than addresses from external vendors, and; b) the current Supplemental Sample consisted of faculty who had already responded to a previous Faculty Survey.

Administering the Faculty Survey electronically through the HERI Portal allowed us to examine specific types of non-response. Records were kept on the Portal of potential respondents who: a) opted out; b) partially completed the survey and took advantage of the survey's ability to save responses already entered, and; c) accessed the survey but did not save entered responses. Overall, 2.4 percent of all members of the sample pool opted out, while 12.5 percent accessed the survey but did not complete it. Slightly more than half of the sample pool (52.2 percent) never accessed the survey. Table A1 shows the opt-out and partial response rates broken out by the sample type.

Table A1
*Response, Opt-out and Partial Response Rates by Sample Type*

| | Sample Type | | |
| --- | --- | --- | --- |
| | Participating | Supplemental | Overall |
| Responded | 32.6 | 34.5 | 32.9 |
| Opted out | 2.3 | 3.5 | 2.4 |
| Accessed survey | | | |
|    Saved partial responses | 4.9 | 3.4 | 4.7 |
|    Did not save partial responses | 8.0 | 7.5 | 7.8 |
| Did not access survey | 52.4 | 51.0 | 52.2 |

## The National Normative Sample

For a participating institution's data to be included in the normative sample, HERI required that a minimum percentage of all full-time undergraduate (FTUG) faculty at that institution be surveyed. Total full-time faculty counts were obtained from the 2006 IPEDS Faculty Salary and Tenure survey conducted by the U.S. Department of Education. Participating two- and four-year colleges were required to have surveyed at least 35 percent of their FTUG faculty. Participating universities were required to survey at least 25 percent.[3]

---

[3]Universities faced a less stringent requirement because the IPEDS survey does not distinguish between undergraduate and graduate faculty. Since the Faculty Survey focuses on undergraduate faculty, total faculty counts for universities are inflated.

Because the Supplemental Sample was based on individual respondents rather than all faculty from an institution, the standard method of inclusion in the normative sample did not apply. All faculty from the Supplemental Sample that responded to the survey were included in the sample, provided that: a) they were determined to be FTUG faculty in 2007, and; b) they were based at four-year colleges and universities (see below).

The number of two-year colleges (public and private) participating in the Faculty Survey has dropped off considerably over the years. In 2007, only 17 two-year colleges actively participated, while faculty from 24 additional two-year colleges were included in the Supplemental Sample. These 41 institutions represent less than four percent of all two-year colleges in the United States. HERI believes that it is not possible for such a small sample of institutions to adequately represent the national population. Accordingly, no National Norms are reported for two-year colleges, and the broadest group reported on in this publication is "all four-year colleges and universities."

As a result of these requirements, results from 77 out of 449 participating institutions were dropped from the normative sample, leaving a total of 372. Of these, 41 were dropped because they were two-year colleges, while the other 36 were dropped for not meeting participation requirements.

Inclusion in the normative sample should not be confused with response rate. An institution's response rate depends on the number of *sampled* faculty returned. If the institution sampled only a small proportion of its full-time undergraduate faculty, it might not meet the norms requirements even if it had a very high response rate.

Table 2 shows the total number of institutions and total number of institutional participants by institutional type, together with the total number of faculty members, faculty surveyed, and faculty respondents for each cell.

## Weighting Procedures

In order to approximate as closely as possible the results that would have been obtained if all college and university teaching faculty in all institutions had responded to the survey, a two-stage weighting procedure was employed following Astin, Korn, and Dey (1991).

It should be noted that the first stage of the weighting procedure is based on the assumption that the population of which the weights are an estimate is the total number of FTUG faculty at each institution. Because the 2007 Supplemental Sample was not based on institutions, a different method of producing the first-stage weight was required. Accordingly, the discussion below breaks out the procedure by sample type.

Table A2

*Institutional and Faculty Participation in the 2007–2008 HERI Faculty Survey*

| | Institutions | | | Faculty | | | |
|---|---|---|---|---|---|---|---|
| Institutional type | National Total | Partici-pating (1) | Used in Norms | National Total | Mailout Sample | Respon-dents (2) | Used in Norms (3) |
| All institutions | 2,686 | 449 | (4) | 521,383 | 104,924 | 34,479 | (4) |
| All universities/4-year colleges | 1,592 | 408 | 372 | 401,803 | 99,650 | 32,815 | 22,562 |
| All two-year colleges | 1,094 | 41 | (4) | 119,580 | 5,274 | 1,664 | (4) |
| | | | | | | | |
| Universities | | | | | | | |
|   Public | 131 | 34 | 31 | 128,725 | 21,207 | 4,913 | 2,967 |
|   Private | 71 | 29 | 25 | 51,318 | 14,552 | 4,907 | 3,002 |
| | | | | | | | |
| Four-year colleges | | | | | | | |
|   Public | 402 | 88 | 80 | 123,417 | 26,245 | 8,473 | 5,629 |
|   All Private | 988 | 257 | 236 | 98,343 | 37,646 | 14,522 | 10,964 |
|     Nonsectarian | 425 | 112 | 101 | 46,785 | 17,889 | 6,719 | 5,005 |
|     Catholic | 177 | 49 | 47 | 19,218 | 6,494 | 2,383 | 1,029 |
|     Other Religious | 386 | 96 | 88 | 32,340 | 13,263 | 5,420 | 4,030 |
| | | | | | | | |
| Two-year Colleges | | | | | | | |
|   Public | 950 | 38 | (4) | 113,645 | 5,148 | 1,602 | (4) |
|   Private | 144 | 3 | (4) | 5,935 | 126 | 62 | (4) |

(1) Includes 199 institutions from which the supplemental sample was taken.
(2) Includes respondents who were not classified as full-time undergraduate faculty.
(3) Full-time undergraduate faculty only.
(4) Two-year colleges were not included in the National Norms. See text.


**First Weight—Participating Institutions**

The first set of weights was designed to adjust for response bias <u>within</u> participating institutions. The entire faculty at each institution was sorted into eight categories representing all combinations of gender (male or female) and rank (professor, associate professor, assistant professor, and all other ranks). The ratio between the total number of faculty in the institution and the number of respondents in each category was used as the first weight. Thus, if there were 20 female full professors and 10 of those responded, each of these respondent's weights would be 2.0 (20 divided by 10). This within-institution weight, which is designed to correct for any response bias related to the gender or rank of the faculty member, adjusts the total number of respondents up to the total number of faculty at the institution.[4]

---

[4]In the event that an institution did not report the distribution of its faculty across different ranks, the within-institution weight was based on gender alone.

**First Weight—Supplemental Sample**

Creating a first weight for the Supplemental Sample presented a challenge and an opportunity. On the one hand, there was no formal unit of population as was the case for the participating institutions, since membership in the Supplemental Sample did not depend on where the faculty member taught, but rather on the fact that he/she participated in the 2004 Faculty Survey. Accordingly, we chose to use the mailout population of 15,127 as the population for the purposes of the first-weight calculation.

On the other hand, HERI did have considerable information about each of the 15,127 members of the Supplemental Sample, namely the data collected from their participation in 2004. Using these data, profiles could be developed for those in the sample pool that participated in 2007, and those that did not.

To create these profiles, we used a model developed to analyze response bias in HERI follow-up surveys where Freshman Survey data were available (see for example, the series of "American College Student" surveys which ran from 1982–1990). Using multiple stepwise regression, we developed a regression equation that would estimate the probability that every member of the Sample Pool would respond. The dependent variable of the regression was whether or not the faculty member responded, and the independent variables were every variable in the 2004 Faculty Survey. (Because our research has shown that men and women tend to respond to surveys for different reasons, we ran separate regressions for each gender.)

Having completed the regression, we then examined only those members of the Supplemental Sample who responded to the 2007 survey. Using the equation developed during the regression run, we computed how likely the respondent was to have responded based on his or her characteristics. The reciprocal of the computed probability was then used as the first weight. Thus, a respondent with an 80% probability of response would receive a weight of 1/0.8, or 1.25. A respondent with a 20% probability of response would receive a weight of 1/0.2, or 5.00.


**Second Weight—All Sample Types**

To develop the second set of weights, institutions were sorted into 23 stratification cells based upon type (four-year college, university), control (public, private-nonsectarian, Roman Catholic, other religious), and selectivity (defined as the average admissions test score of the entering freshman class). Within each of these stratification cells, faculty in all institutions in the population were sorted into the same 8 gender-by-rank categories described above. Data from all respondents within each institutional stratification cell were then combined, and the weighted number of respondents (using the first weight described above) was then determined separately for each of the gender-by-rank combinations. Thus, for each gender-by-rank combination within a stratification cell, we had two values: the total number of faculty in the higher education population, and the weighted number of respondents to our survey. The ratio between these two totals became the second weight, which was designed to correct for between-stratification cell differences in institutional participation. The final weight used for each respondent consisted of the product of the two weights (that is, the within-institution weight and the between-stratification weight).

## Defining Faculty Groups

As already noted, only those full-time employees who were engaged in teaching undergraduates were included in the normative data reported here. Full-time administrators, full-time researchers, or faculty members who teach <u>only</u> at the postgraduate level have been excluded. More specifically, a respondent was included in the normative data if one of the following conditions was met:

1) if he or she indicated full-time employment at an institution [question 2] **and** noted teaching as his/her principal activity [question 1] **and** either
   a) taught at least one undergraduate-level course [question 14 **or**
   b) taught no classes at all in the most recent term (this last condition is included for faculty on sabbatical leave or those currently engaged in research full-time).

2) if he or she indicated full-time employment at an institution [question 2] **and** taught at least two courses in the last term [question 14], at least one of which was at the undergraduate level.

3) if he or she indicated full-time employment at an institution [question 2] **and** indicated that he/she spent at least 9 hours per week in scheduled teaching [question 12], but did not indicate any specific types of courses being taught [question 14].

It should be noted that HERI has received some comment from participating institutions that had surveyed *only* full-time undergraduate faculty, yet some of their respondents were classified as being of another respondent type (primarily "other"). An investigation led us to the conclusion that respondents were misclassified because they had not responded to one or more of the key questions above. For the purposes of the results in this report, however, HERI felt it preferable to not include them, to assure that those in the normative sample were positively identified as meeting the requirements for inclusion.

## Reference

Astin, A. W., Korn, W. S., & Dey, E. L. (1991). *The American college teacher: National norms for the 1989–1990 HERI faculty survey.* Los Angeles, CA: Higher Education Research Institute, UCLA.

# Appendix B

# 2007–2008
HERI Faculty Survey Questions

1. What is your principal activity in your current position at this institution?
2. Are you considered a full-time employee of your institution for at least nine months of the current academic year?
3. If given the choice, I would prefer to work full-time at this institution.
4. Mark all institutional resources available to you in your last term as part-time faculty.

5. Please indicate your agreement with the following statements. Part-time instructors at this institution:
   a. Are given specific training before teaching
   b. Rarely get hired into full-time positions
   c. Receive respect from students
   d. Are primarily responsible for introductory classes
   e. Have no guarantee of employment security
   f. Have access to support services
   g. Are compensated for advising/counseling students
   h. Are required to attend meetings
   i. Have good working relationships with the administration
   j. Are respected by full-time faculty

6. What is your present academic rank?
7. What is your tenure status at this institution?

8. Are you currently serving in an administrative position as:
   a. Department Chair
   b. Dean (Assoc or Asst)
   c. President
   d. Vice-President
   e. Provost
   f. Other
   g. Not Applicable

9. My primary place of employment in the last year was:
10. Personally, how important to you is:
    a. Research
    b. Teaching
    c. Service

11. Highest degree earned:
12. Degree currently working on:

13. During the past two years, have you engaged in any of the following activities?
    a. Taught an honors course
    b. Taught an interdisciplinary course
    c. Taught an ethnic studies course
    d. Taught a women's studies course
    e. Team-taught a course
    f. Taught a service learning course
    g. Placed or collected assignments on the Internet
    h. Taught a course exclusively on the Internet
    i. Participated in a teaching enhancement workshop
    j. Advised student groups involved in service/volunteer work
    k. Collaborated with the local community in research/teaching
    l. Developed a new course
    m. Conducted research or writing focused on international/global issues
    n. Conducted research or writing focused on racial or ethnic minorities
    o. Conducted research or writing focused on women and gender issues
    p. Taught a seminar for first-year students
    q. Engaged undergraduates on your research project
    r. Worked with undergraduates on a research project

14. During the present term, how many hours per week on the average do you actually spend on each of the following activities?
    a. Scheduled teaching (give actual, not credit hours)
    b. Preparing for teaching (including reading student papers and grading)
    c. Advising and counseling of students
    d. Committee work and meetings
    e. Other administration
    f. Research and scholarly writing
    g. Other creative products/performances
    h. Consultation with clients/patients
    i. Community or public service
    j. Outside consulting/freelance work
    k. Household/childcare duties
    l. Communicating via email
    m. Commuting to campus
    n. Other employment, outside of academia

15. Including all institutions at which you teach, how many undergraduate courses are you teaching this term?
16. How many students are enrolled in Course #1 to Course #10?

17. How many of the following courses are you teaching this academic year?
    a. General education courses
    b. Developmental/remedial courses
    c. Other undergraduate credit courses
    d. Graduate courses
    e. Vocational or technical courses
    f. Non-credit courses (other than above)

---

18. Do you teach remedial/developmental skills in any of the following areas?
    a. Reading
    b. Writing
    c. Mathematics
    d. ESL
    e. General academic skills
    f. Other subject areas

---

19. Have you engaged in any of the following professional development opportunities at your institution?
    a. Workshops focused on teaching in the classroom
    b. Paid workshops outside the institution focused on teaching
    c. Paid sabbatical leave
    d. Travel funds paid by the institution
    e. Association membership/dues paid by the institution
    f. Tuition remission
    g. Internal grants for research
    h. Training for administrative leadership

---

20. Indicate the importance to you of each of the following education goals for undergraduate students:
    a. Develop ability to think critically
    b. Prepare students for employment after college
    c. Prepare students for graduate or advanced education
    d. Develop moral character
    e. Provide for students' emotional development
    f. Prepare students for family living
    g. Teach students the classic works of Western civilization
    h. Help students develop personal values
    i. Enhance students' self-understanding
    j. Instill in students a commitment to community service
    k. Enhance students' knowledge of and appreciation for other racial/ethnic groups
    l. Study a foreign language
    m. Help master knowledge in a discipline
    n. Develop creative capacities
    o. Instill a basic appreciation of the liberal arts
    p. Promote ability to write effectively
    q. Help students evaluate the quality and reliability of information
    r. Engage students in civil discourse around controversial issues
    s. Teach students tolerance and respect for different beliefs
    t. Encourage students to become agents of social change

---

21. How many of the following have you published?
    a. Articles in academic or professional journals
    b. Chapters in edited volumes
    c. Books, manuals, or monographs
    d. Other, such as patents or computer software products

---

22. How many exhibitions or performances in the fine or applied arts have you presented in the last two years?
23. How many of your professional writings have been published or accepted for publication in the last two years?

---

24. General activities:
    a. Are you a member of a faculty union?
    b. Are you a U.S. citizen?
    c. Were you born in the U.S.A.?
    d. Do you plan to retire within the next three years?
    e. Do you use your scholarship to address local community needs?
    f. Have you been sexually harassed at this institution?
    g. Have you ever interrupted your professional career for more than one year for family reasons?
    h. Have you ever received an award for outstanding teaching?
    i. Have you published op-ed pieces or editorials?
    j. Is (or was) your father an academic?
    k. Is (or was) your mother an academic?
    l. Is (or was) your spouse/partner an academic?
    m. Are you currently teaching courses at more than one institution?

---

25. General activities during the past two years:
    a. Considered early retirement
    b. Considered leaving academe for another job
    c. Considered leaving this institution for another
    d. Changed academic institutions
    e. Engaged in paid consulting outside of your institution
    f. Engaged in public service/professional consulting without pay
    g. Received at least one firm job offer
    h. Received funding for your work from foundations
    i. Received funding for your work from state or federal government
    j. Received funding for your work from business or industry
    k. Requested/sought an early promotion

---

26. If you were to begin your career again, would you:
    a. Still want to come to this institution
    b. Still want to be a college professor

27. Indicate how well each of the following describes your college or university:
    a. It is easy for students to see faculty outside of regular office hours
    b. There is a great deal of conformity among the students
    c. The faculty are typically at odds with campus administration
    d. Faculty here respect each other
    e. Most students are treated like "numbers in a book"
    f. Social activities are overemphasized
    g. Faculty are rewarded for being good teachers
    h. There is respect for the expression of diverse values and beliefs
    i. Faculty are rewarded for their efforts to use instructional technology
    j. Administrators consider faculty concerns when making policy
    k. The administration is open about its policies

28. Indicate the extent to which you:
    a. Engage in academic work that spans multiple disciplines
    b. Feel that the training you received in graduate school prepared you well for your role as a faculty mentor
    c. Achieve a healthy balance between your personal life and your professional life
    d. Experience close alignment between your work and your personal values
    e. Feel that you have to work harder than your colleagues to be perceived as a legitimate scholar
    f. Mentor new faculty

29. How satisfied are you with the following aspects of your job?
    a. Salary
    b. Health benefits
    c. Retirement benefits
    d. Opportunity for scholarly pursuits
    e. Teaching load
    f. Quality of students
    g. Office/lab space
    h. Autonomy and independence
    i. Professional relationships with other faculty
    j. Social relationships with other faculty
    k. Competency of colleagues
    l. Visibility for jobs at other institutions/organizations
    m. Job security
    n. Relationship with administration
    o. Departmental leadership
    p. Course assignments
    q. Freedom to determine course content
    r. Availability of child care at this institution
    s. Prospects for career advancement
    t. Clerical/administrative support
    u. Overall job satisfaction

30. Indicate the extent to which you agree or disagree with each of the following statements about your college or university:
    a. Faculty are interested in students' personal problems
    b. Racial and ethnic diversity should be more strongly reflected in the curriculum
    c. Faculty feel that most students are well-prepared academically
    d. This institution should hire more faculty of color
    e. Student Affairs staff have the support and respect of faculty
    f. Faculty are committed to the welfare of this institution
    g. Faculty here are strongly interested in the academic problems of undergraduates
    h. There is a lot of campus racial conflict here
    i. Most students are strongly committed to community service
    j. My research is valued by faculty in my department
    k. My teaching is valued by faculty in my department
    l. Many courses include feminist perspectives
    m. Faculty of color are treated fairly here
    n. Women faculty are treated fairly here
    o. Many courses involve students in community service
    p. This institution should hire more women faculty
    q. Gay and lesbian faculty are treated fairly here
    r. My department does a good job of mentoring new faculty
    s. Faculty are sufficiently involved in campus decision making
    t. My values are congruent with the dominant institutional values
    u. There is adequate support for integrating technology in my teaching
    v. This institution takes responsibility for educating underprepared students
    w. The criteria for advancement and promotion decisions are clear
    x. Most of the students I teach lack the basic skills for college level work
    y. There is adequate support for faculty development
    z. This institution should not offer remedial/developmental education

---

31. Indicate how important you believe each priority listed below is at your college or university:
    a. To promote the intellectual development of students
    b. To help students examine and understand their personal values
    c. To develop a sense of community among students and faculty
    d. To facilitate student involvement in community service
    e. To help students learn how to bring about change in American society
    f. To increase or maintain institutional prestige
    g. To hire faculty "stars"
    h. To recruit more minority students
    i. To enhance the institution's national image
    j. To create a diverse multi-cultural campus environment
    k. To promote gender equity among faculty
    l. To provide resources for faculty to engage in community-based teaching or research
    m. To create and sustain partnerships with surrounding communities
    n. To pursue extramural funding
    o. To increase the representation of minorities in the faculty and administration
    p. To strengthen links with the for-profit, corporate sector
    q. To develop leadership ability among students
    r. To increase the representation of women in the faculty and administration
    s. To develop an appreciation for multiculturalism

---

32. Indicate your agreement with each of the following statements:
    a. Western civilization and culture should be the foundation for the undergraduate curriculum
    b. College officials have the right to ban persons with extreme views from speaking on campus
    c. The chief benefit of a college education is that it increases one's earning power
    d. Promoting diversity leads to the admission of too many underprepared students
    e. Colleges should be actively involved in solving social problems
    f. Tenure is an outmoded concept
    g. Colleges should encourage students to be involved in community service activities
    h. Community service should be given weight in college admissions decisions
    i. A racially/ethnically diverse student body enhances the educational experience of all students
    j. Realistically, an individual can do little to bring about changes in society
    k. Colleges should be concerned with facilitating undergraduate students' spiritual development
    l. Colleges have a responsibility to work with their surrounding communities to address local issues
    m. Private funding sources often prevent researchers from being completely objective in the conduct of their work

---

33. Indicate the extent to which each of the following has been a source of stress for you during the last two years:
    a. Managing household responsibilities
    b. Child care
    c. Care of elderly parent
    d. My physical health
    e. Health of spouse/partner
    f. Review/promotion process
    g. Subtle discrimination (e.g., prejudice, racism, sexism)
    h. Personal finances
    i. Committee work
    j. Faculty meetings
    k. Colleagues
    l. Students
    m. Research or publishing demands
    n. Institutional procedures and "red tape"
    o. Teaching load
    p. Children's problems
    q. Friction with spouse/partner
    r. Lack of personal time
    s. Keeping up with information technology
    t. Job security
    u. Being part of a dual career couple
    v. Working with underprepared students
    w. Classroom conflict
    x. Self-imposed high expectations
    y. Change in work responsibilities

---

34. Indicate the importance to you personally of each of the following:
    a. Becoming an authority in my field
    b. Influencing the political structure
    c. Influencing social values
    d. Raising a family
    e. Becoming very well off financially
    f. Helping others who are in difficulty
    g. Becoming involved in programs to clean up the environment
    h. Developing a meaningful philosophy of life
    i. Helping to promote racial understanding
    j. Obtaining recognition from my colleagues for contributions to my special field
    k. Integrating spirituality into my life

35. In your interactions with undergraduates, how often do you encourage them to:
    a. Ask questions in class
    b. Support their opinions with a logical argument
    c. Seek solutions to problems and explain them to others
    d. Revise their papers to improve their writing
    e. Evaluate the quality or reliability of information they receive
    f. Take risks for potential gains
    g. Seek alternative solutions to a problem
    h. Look up scientific research articles and resources
    i. Explore topics on their own, even though it was not required for a class
    j. Acknowledge failure as a necessary part of the learning process
    k. Seek feedback on their academic work

36. In how many of the courses that you teach do you use each of the following:
    a. Multiple-choice exams
    b. Essay exams
    c. Short-answer exams
    d. Quizzes
    e. Weekly essay assignments
    f. Student presentations
    g. Term/research papers
    h. Student evaluations of each others' work
    i. Grading on a curve
    j. Competency-based grading

37. In how many of the courses that you teach do you use each of the following:
    a. Class discussions
    b. Cooperative learning (small groups)
    c. Experiential learning/Field studies
    d. Teaching assistants
    e. Recitals/Demonstrations
    f. Group projects
    g. Extensive lecturing
    h. Multiple drafts of written work
    i. Readings on racial and ethnic issues
    j. Readings on women and gender issues
    k. Student-developed activities (assignments, exams, etc.)
    l. Student-selected topics for course content
    m. Reflective writing/journaling
    n. Community service as part of coursework
    o. Electronic quizzes with immediate feedback in class
    p. Using real-life problems
    q. Using student inquiry to drive learning

38. Your base institutional salary, rounded to the nearest $1,000.
39. Your base institutional salary is based on 9/10 months or 11/12 months.

40. What percentage of your current year's salary comes from:
    a. Income from this institution
    b. Other academic income
    c. Non-academic income

41. Date of Birth.
42. Year of highest degree now held.
43. Year of appointment at present institution.
44. If tenured, year tenure was awarded.
45. Major of highest degree held.
46. Department of current faculty appointment.
47. How many children do you have in the following age ranges?
48. How would you characterize your political views?
49. Marital Status.
50. Gender.
51. Is English your native language?
52. Race/Ethnicity.

Optional questions and special questions for two-year colleges are not listed above.
For the copies of the web survey, go to www.heri.ucla.edu

# Appendix C

# Institutional Participation

# NOTES

**Table C1** lists the active participants in the 2007–2008 Faculty Survey, organized by institutional control and type. An active participant is an institution that formally registered for the Faculty Survey. Administration of the Survey was managed by an individual at the institution.

**Table C2** lists the institutions from which the 2007–2008 Supplemental Sample was taken, organized by institutional control and type. The number of respondents from individual institutions in the list ranged from 1 to 193, with a median of 19.

**Table C3** shows the participation history for all institutions that participated in the Faculty Survey from 1989–1990 through 2007–2008. Please note:
- A Supplemental Sample was not selected for the 1992–1993 administration.
- The Supplemental Sample in 2007–2008 was selected using different criteria than in all other Faculty Surveys. See Appendix A for details.

Table C1

*Active Participants in the 2007–2008 Faculty Survey*

**Public Universities**

| | |
|---|---|
| Miami University | OH |
| North Dakota State University | ND |
| South Dakota State University | SD |
| Texas A&M U-Corpus Christi | TX |
| U of Alabama | AL |
| U of California-Los Angeles | CA |
| U of Cincinnati | OH |
| U of Colorado-Colorado Springs | CO |
| U of Idaho | ID |
| U of North Carolina-Charlotte | NC |
| U of North Dakota | ND |
| Utah State University | UT |

**Private Universities**

| | |
|---|---|
| American University | DC |
| Biola University | CA |
| Brigham Young University | UT |
| Carnegie-Mellon University | PA |
| Catholic University of America | DC |
| Creighton University | NE |
| Drexel University | PA |
| Duquesne University | PA |
| Loyola University-New Orleans | LA |
| Northeastern University | MA |
| Saint John's University-Queens | NY |
| Santa Clara University | CA |
| Seton Hall University | NJ |
| Tufts University | MA |
| U of the Pacific | CA |
| Villanova University | PA |
| Wake Forest University | NC |
| Western U of Health Sciences | CA |

**Public Four-year Colleges**

| | |
|---|---|
| California State U-Northridge | CA |
| Central Washington University | WA |
| Christopher Newport University | VA |
| Dickinson State University | ND |
| Eastern Connecticut State U | CT |
| Eastern Michigan University | MI |
| Empire State College | NY |
| Florida Gulf Coast University | FL |
| Fort Hays State University | KS |
| Georgia College & State University | GA |
| Grand Valley State University | MI |
| Indiana University-Kokomo | IN |
| Indiana U-Purdue U-Fort Wayne | IN |
| Lander University | SC |
| Lock Haven U of Pennsylvania | PA |
| Mayville State University | ND |
| Metropolitan State U | MN |

**Public Four-year Colleges**

| | |
|---|---|
| Millersville U of Pennsylvania | PA |
| Minot State University | ND |
| Montclair State University | NJ |
| North Georgia College & State U | GA |
| Northeastern Illinois University | IL |
| Oakland University | MI |
| Penn State Erie-The Behrend College | PA |
| Radford University | VA |
| San Jose State University | CA |
| Southeast Missouri State U | MO |
| Southern Illinois U-Edwardsville | IL |
| Southern Utah University | UT |
| SUNY A & T College-Cobleskill | NY |
| SUNY College-Geneseo | NY |
| SUNY College-Old Westbury | NY |
| SUNY College-Purchase | NY |
| Truman State University | MO |
| U of Arkansas-Little Rock | AR |
| U of Central Missouri | MO |
| U of Central Oklahoma | OK |
| U of Montevallo | AL |
| U of Nebraska-Omaha | NE |
| U of North Carolina-Asheville | NC |
| U of North Carolina-Wilmington | NC |
| U of Northern Colorado | CO |
| U of Wisconsin-Green Bay | WI |
| U of Wisconsin-Stout | WI |
| Valley City State University | ND |
| West Texas A & M University | TX |

**Nonsectarian Four-year Colleges**

| | |
|---|---|
| Alaska Pacific University | AK |
| Alfred University | NY |
| Allegheny College | PA |
| Aurora University | IL |
| Brigham Young U-Hawaii Campus | HI |
| Bryan College | TN |
| Bryn Mawr College | PA |
| Bucknell University | PA |
| Carleton College | MN |
| Cazenovia College | NY |
| Cedar Crest College | PA |
| Chapman University | CA |
| Coe College | IA |
| Colgate University | NY |
| College of Wooster | OH |
| Colorado College | CO |
| Defiance College | OH |
| Denison University | OH |
| Dickinson College | PA |
| Furman University | SC |

**Nonsectarian Four-year Colleges**

| | |
|---|---|
| Gettysburg College | PA |
| Grand View College | IA |
| Hamilton College | NY |
| Harrisburg University of S & T | PA |
| Hartwick College | NY |
| Haverford College | PA |
| Hood College | MD |
| Hope College | MI |
| Illinois College | IL |
| Illinois Wesleyan University | IL |
| Judson University | IL |
| Juniata College | PA |
| Kenyon College | OH |
| Laboratory Inst of Merchandising | NY |
| Lawrence University | WI |
| Long Island U-Brooklyn | NY |
| Long Island U-CW Post | NY |
| Long Island U-Regional Campuses | NY |
| Metropolitan College of New York | NY |
| Mills College | CA |
| National-Louis University | IL |
| Nazareth College of Rochester | NY |
| Northwestern College | MN |
| Occidental College | CA |
| Pace University | NY |
| Pacific Northwest College of Art | OR |
| Philadelphia University | PA |
| Pomona College | CA |
| Rockford College | IL |
| Rollins College | FL |
| Saint Lawrence University | NY |
| Scripps College | CA |
| Smith College | MA |
| Swarthmore College | PA |
| Taylor University | IN |
| The University of Tampa | FL |
| Trinity College | CT |
| U of Puget Sound | WA |
| U of the Sciences in Philadelphia | PA |
| Union College | NY |
| Ursinus College | PA |
| Vassar College | NY |
| Vaughn Coll of Aeronautics & Tech | NY |
| Villa Julie College | MD |
| Washington and Lee University | VA |
| Wheaton College | MA |
| Widener University | PA |
| Williams College | MA |
| Wilson College | PA |

**Catholic Four-year Colleges**

| | |
|---|---|
| Canisius College | NY |
| College of Notre Dame of Maryland | MD |
| College of Saint Scholastica | MN |
| Fairfield University | CT |
| Fontbonne University | MO |
| Georgian Court University | NJ |
| Gwynedd-Mercy College | PA |
| Holy Family University | PA |
| Immaculata University | PA |
| King's College | PA |
| Lewis University | IL |
| Mount Saint Mary's University | MD |
| Neumann College | PA |
| Niagara University | NY |
| Ohio Dominican University | OH |
| Saint Anselm College | NH |
| Saint Mary's U of Minnesota | MN |
| Saint Norbert College | WI |
| Saint Peter's College | NJ |
| Saint Thomas University | FL |
| Saint Vincent College | PA |
| Spring Hill College | AL |
| U of Detroit Mercy | MI |
| U of Portland | OR |
| U of San Francisco | CA |
| Walsh University | OH |

**Other Religious Four-year Colleges**

| | |
|---|---|
| Abilene Christian University | TX |
| Agnes Scott College | GA |
| Albright College | PA |
| Anderson University | SC |
| Augustana College | IL |
| Barton College | NC |
| Benedict College | SC |
| Bethel College | IN |
| Bethel University | MN |
| Bridgewater College | VA |
| Calvin College | MI |
| Carroll College | WI |
| Columbia College | SC |
| Earlham College | IN |
| East Texas Baptist University | TX |
| Eastern Mennonite University | VA |
| Elon University | NC |
| Goshen College | IN |
| Greensboro College | NC |
| Greenville College | IL |
| Hampden-Sydney College | VA |
| Huntington University | IN |
| Iowa Wesleyan College | IA |

Table C1 (continued)

*Active Participants in the 2007–2008 Faculty Survey*

**Other Religious Four-year Colleges**

| | |
|---|---|
| Lakeland College | WI |
| Lebanon Valley College | PA |
| Lee University | TN |
| Lycoming College | PA |
| Lyon College | AR |
| Mercer University | GA |
| Moravian College | PA |
| Morningside College | IA |
| Nebraska Wesleyan University | NE |
| North Greenville University | SC |
| Northwest Christian College | OR |
| Ohio Northern University | OH |
| Oklahoma City University | OK |
| Palm Beach Atlantic University | FL |
| Park University | MO |
| Peace College | NC |
| Pepperdine University | CA |
| Point Loma Nazarene University | CA |
| Queens University of Charlotte | NC |
| Rhodes College | TN |
| Roberts Wesleyan College | NY |
| Saint Olaf College | MN |
| Seattle Pacific University | WA |
| Shenandoah University | VA |
| Simpson College | IA |
| Simpson University | CA |
| Southern Nazarene University | OK |
| Susquehanna University | PA |
| Texas Lutheran University | TX |
| Trinity University | TX |
| U of Dubuque | IA |
| U of Indianapolis | IN |
| U of the South | TN |
| Union University | TN |
| University of Mobile | AL |
| Valparaiso University | IN |
| Wartburg College | IA |
| Whitworth University | WA |
| William Jewell College | MO |

**Two-year Colleges**

| | |
|---|---|
| Bismarck State College | ND |
| Clinton Cmty College | NY |
| Gulf Coast Cmty College | FL |
| Hocking College | OH |
| Hudson County Cmty College | NJ |
| Illinois Valley Cmty College | IL |
| Kennebec Valley Community College | ME |
| Lake Region State College | ND |
| Minot State University-Bottineau | ND |
| New Mexico State U-Alamogordo | NM |
| North Dakota State Coll of Science | ND |
| Ocean County College | NJ |
| Paul Smith's College | NY |
| South Texas College | TX |
| SUNY Coll of Technology-Canton | NY |
| Utah Valley State College | UT |
| Williston State College | ND |

Table C2

*Supplemental Sample Institutions in the 2007–2008 Faculty Survey*

**Public Universities**

| | |
|---|---|
| Cleveland State University | OH |
| East Carolina University | NC |
| Florida State University | FL |
| Georgia Institute of Technology | GA |
| Iowa State University | IA |
| Northern Arizona University | AZ |
| Ohio State University | OH |
| Purdue University | IN |
| Southern Illinois U-Carbondale | IL |
| Texas A & M University | TX |
| U of California-Irvine | CA |
| U of Colorado-Denver | CO |
| U of Connecticut | CT |
| U of Michigan | MI |
| U of Missouri-Kansas City | MO |
| U of Montana | MT |
| U of North Carolina-Chapel Hill | NC |
| U of Oregon | OR |
| U of Pittsburgh | PA |
| U of Southern Indiana | IN |
| U of Virginia | VA |
| Wayne State University | MI |

**Private Universities**

| | |
|---|---|
| Adelphi University | NY |
| Boston College | MA |
| Drake University | IA |
| La Sierra University | CA |
| Loyola University of Chicago | IL |
| Marquette University | WI |
| Massachusetts Inst of Technology | MA |
| Rensselaer Polytechnic Institute | NY |
| Rice University | TX |
| Southern Methodist University | TX |
| Syracuse University | NY |

**Public Four-year Colleges**

| | |
|---|---|
| Bowie State University | MD |
| California State U-Bakersfield | CA |
| California State U-Fresno | CA |
| California State U-Los Angeles | CA |
| Clarion U of Pennsylvania | PA |
| Clayton State University | GA |
| College of Charleston | SC |
| Colorado State University-Pueblo | CO |
| Fort Lewis College | CO |
| Frostburg State University | MD |
| Georgia Southwestern State U | GA |
| Humboldt State University | CA |
| Longwood University | VA |
| Mansfield U of Pennsylvania | PA |

**Public Four-year Colleges**

| | |
|---|---|
| Minnesota State U-Moorhead | MN |
| New College of Florida | FL |
| Norfolk State University | VA |
| Northern Kentucky University | KY |
| Richard Stockton College of NJ | NJ |
| Saginaw Valley State University | MI |
| Saint Cloud State University | MN |
| Sonoma State University | CA |
| Southern Connecticut State U | CT |
| Southern Oregon University | OR |
| Southwest Minnesota State U | MN |
| State University of West Georgia | GA |
| Texas State University-San Marcos | TX |
| U of Louisiana at Lafayette | LA |
| U of Massachusetts-Dartmouth | MA |
| U of Michigan-Dearborn | MI |
| U of Minnesota-Morris | MN |
| U of Nebraska-Kearney | NE |
| U of Pittsburgh-Bradford | PA |
| U of South Carolina-Aiken | SC |
| U of South Carolina-Upstate | SC |
| U of Tennessee-Chattanooga | TN |
| U of the Virgin Islands | VI |
| U of Wisconsin-Stevens Point | WI |
| US Coast Guard Academy | CT |
| Washburn University | KS |
| Western Illinois University | IL |
| Worcester State College | MA |

**Nonsectarian Four-year Colleges**

| | |
|---|---|
| Antioch University | OH |
| Asbury College | KY |
| Bard College | NY |
| Bates College | ME |
| Beloit College | WI |
| Bentley College | MA |
| Berea College | KY |
| Berry College | GA |
| Bethune-Cookman University | FL |
| Centre College | KY |
| Clark University | MA |
| College of the Southwest | NM |
| Daniel Webster College | NH |
| Drury University | MO |
| Goucher College | MD |
| Grinnell College | IA |
| Kalamazoo College | MI |
| Lewis and Clark College | OR |
| Lincoln University | PA |
| Macalester College | MN |
| Marymount Manhattan College | NY |

Table C2 (continued)
*Supplemental Sample Institutions in the 2007–2008 Faculty Survey*

**Nonsectarian Four-year Colleges**

| | |
|---|---|
| Mass Col of Pharmacy & Hlth Sci | MA |
| Meredith College | NC |
| Minneapolis Coll of Art and Design | MN |
| Oberlin College | OH |
| Pine Manor College | MA |
| Regis College | MA |
| Rider University | NJ |
| Ripon College | WI |
| Saint John Fisher College | NY |
| Sarah Lawrence College | NY |
| Spelman College | GA |
| St Louis College of Pharmacy | MO |
| Stetson University | FL |
| Trinity Christian College | IL |
| Valley Forge Christian College | PA |
| Washington College | MD |
| Webb Institute | NY |
| Webster University | MO |
| Western New England College | MA |
| Westmont College | CA |
| Wheelock College | MA |
| Whitman College | WA |

**Catholic Four-year Colleges**

| | |
|---|---|
| Alvernia College | PA |
| Belmont Abbey College | NC |
| Benedictine College | KS |
| Benedictine University | IL |
| Cabrini College | PA |
| Christian Brothers University | TN |
| College of Saint Benedict | MN |
| College of Saint Mary | NE |
| Divine Word College | IA |
| Edgewood College | WI |
| Marymount University | VA |
| Mount Aloysius College | PA |
| Saint Joseph's University | PA |
| Saint Leo University | FL |
| Saint Mary-of-the-Woods College | IN |
| Saint Mary's College | IN |
| Saint Mary's University | TX |
| Saint Xavier University | IL |
| U of Saint Thomas | MN |
| U of Scranton | PA |
| University of Saint Francis | IL |
| Ursuline College | OH |
| Viterbo University | WI |

**Other Religious Four-year Colleges**

| | |
|---|---|
| Albion College | MI |
| Anderson University | IN |
| Augustana College | SD |
| Austin College | TX |
| Birmingham-Southern College | AL |
| Bluffton University | OH |
| California Baptist University | CA |
| Central College | IA |
| Concordia University | MN |
| Dakota Wesleyan University | SD |
| Dordt College | IA |
| Florida Southern College | FL |
| Geneva College | PA |
| George Fox University | OR |
| Hendrix College | AR |
| Manchester College | IN |
| Maryville College | TN |
| McPherson College | KS |
| MidAmerica Nazarene University | KS |
| Midway College | KY |
| Mount Union College | OH |
| Mount Vernon Nazarene University | OH |
| Northwest University | WA |
| Presbyterian College | SC |
| Regent University | VA |
| Roanoke College | VA |
| Saint Andrews Presbyterian College | NC |
| Southwestern University | TX |
| Tennessee Temple University | TN |
| U of Findlay | OH |
| U of Mary Hardin-Baylor | TX |
| Virginia Wesleyan College | VA |
| Wesleyan College | GA |
| Wittenberg University | OH |

230

Table C2 (continued)
*Supplemental Sample Institutions in the 2007–2008 Faculty Survey*

**Two-year Colleges**

| | |
|---|---|
| Brookhaven College | TX |
| Chemeketa Cmty College | OR |
| Cochise College | AZ |
| Cuesta College | CA |
| Cumberland County College | NJ |
| Highline Cmty College | WA |
| Iowa Western Cmty College | IA |
| Lake Michigan College | MI |
| Lake Superior College | MN |
| Lower Columbia College | WA |
| Manor College | PA |
| Navarro College | TX |
| Nazarene Bible College | CO |
| New Mexico Junior College | NM |
| North Arkansas College | AR |
| Northampton County Area Cmty Coll | PA |
| Northeast State Tech Cmty College | TN |
| Oxnard College | CA |
| Patrick Henry Cmty College | VA |
| Purdue University-North Central | IN |
| Roane State Cmty College | TN |
| San Joaquin Delta College | CA |
| University of Wisconsin Colleges | WI |
| Wilbur Wright College | IL |

Table C3
*Participation History*

| Institution | State | Strat | 1989 | 1992 | 1995 | 1998 | 2001 | 2004 | 2007 |
|---|---|---|---|---|---|---|---|---|---|
| Abilene Christian University | TX | 23 | P* | P | N | N | N | N | N |
| Adams State College | CO | 7 | N | – | – | – | – | – | – |
| Adelphi University | NY | 4 | – | – | – | – | N | N | N* |
| Adirondack Cmty College | NY | 28 | – | – | – | – | N | – | – |
| Agnes Scott College | GA | 23 | N | N | N | N | N | N | N |
| Alaska Pacific University | AK | 11 | – | – | N | – | N | N | N |
| Albion College | MI | 23 | N | – | – | N* | – | N | N* |
| Albright College | PA | 22 | N | – | – | – | N | N | N |
| Alexandria Technical College | MN | 28 | N | – | – | – | – | – | – |
| Alfred State College | NY | 7 | N* | P | N | – | N | P* | – |
| Alfred University | NY | 13 | N | – | N | – | N | – | N |
| Allan Hancock College | CA | 28 | – | – | – | – | N | – | – |
| Allegheny College | PA | 13 | P* | – | – | N* | – | N | N |
| Allen County Cmty College | KS | 26 | N | – | – | – | – | – | – |
| Alma College | MI | 23 | P* | N | – | – | – | – | – |
| Alvernia College | PA | 16 | – | – | – | – | – | N | N* |
| Amarillo College | TX | 26 | N | – | – | – | – | – | – |
| American Baptist College | TN | 24 | – | – | – | – | P | N | – |
| American Samoa Cmty College | AS | 28 | – | – | – | – | – | N | – |
| American University | DC | 5 | N* | N | N | N | – | – | N |
| American University of Beirut | | 5 | – | P | – | – | – | – | – |
| Anderson University | IN | 22 | – | – | N | N | – | N | N* |
| Anderson University | SC | 22 | N | N | – | N | – | N | N |
| Andrew College | GA | 31 | – | N | – | N | – | – | – |
| Antioch University | OH | 13 | N | N | N | N | – | P | N* |
| Antioch University-Seattle | WA | 15 | – | – | – | N | – | – | – |
| Arcadia University | PA | 22 | N | – | – | – | – | – | – |
| Arizona State University | AZ | 1 | – | – | – | N | – | – | – |
| Arkansas State University | AR | 8 | – | N | – | P | – | – | – |
| Art Center College of Design | CA | 12 | P | – | N | – | – | – | – |
| Asbury College | KY | 13 | – | – | N | N | – | N | N* |
| Ashland University | OH | 20 | – | – | – | – | N | – | – |
| Atlanta College of Art | GA | 12 | – | N | – | – | – | – | – |
| Atlantic Union College | MA | 21 | P* | P | – | – | – | – | – |
| Augsburg College | MN | 23 | – | N | – | – | – | – | – |
| Augustana College | IL | 23 | N* | N | N | N | N | N | N |
| Augustana College | SD | 23 | – | – | – | – | P | P | N* |
| Aurora University | IL | 11 | N | – | – | – | N | – | N |
| Austin College | TX | 23 | N | – | N | N* | – | N | N* |
| Austin Peay State University | TN | 8 | N | – | – | – | – | – | – |
| Azusa Pacific University | CA | 12 | – | – | N | N | N | N* | – |
| Babson College | MA | 14 | – | – | N | – | – | – | – |
| Bacone College | OK | 24 | – | – | – | – | N | – | – |
| Baker University | KS | 22 | N | – | – | – | – | – | – |
| Bard College | NY | 14 | P | – | – | N* | – | N | N* |
| Barnard College | NY | 14 | – | – | N | N | – | – | – |

P—Participated    N—Participated and included in National Norms    *—Supplemental Sample

232

Table C3 (continued)

*Participation History*

| Institution | State | Strat | 1989 | 1992 | 1995 | 1998 | 2001 | 2004 | 2007 |
|---|---|---|---|---|---|---|---|---|---|
| Barry University | FL | 16 | N | N | – | – | – | – | – |
| Barstow College | CA | 25 | N | – | – | – | – | P* | – |
| Barton College | NC | 20 | – | – | – | N | – | N | N |
| Barton County Cmty College | KS | 27 | – | N | – | – | – | – | – |
| Bates College | ME | 14 | – | N | – | – | – | N | N* |
| Baton Rouge Cmty College | LA | 28 | – | – | – | – | – | N | – |
| Baylor University | TX | 5 | N* | N | – | N* | N | N* | – |
| Becker College | MA | 33 | N | – | – | – | – | – | – |
| Bellarmine University | KY | 18 | – | N | – | – | – | – | – |
| Belmont Abbey College | NC | 16 | – | – | – | – | – | N | N* |
| Belmont University | TN | 23 | – | N | – | N | – | – | – |
| Beloit College | WI | 13 | N | N | – | N | N | N | N* |
| Bemidji State University | MN | 8 | N | – | – | – | – | – | – |
| Benedictine College | KS | 17 | – | – | – | – | – | N | N* |
| Benedictine University | IL | 18 | N* | – | – | N* | – | N | N* |
| Bentley College | MA | 13 | – | N | P* | – | N | N | N* |
| Berea College | KY | 12 | N | – | – | N* | – | N | N* |
| Berkeley College | NJ | 33 | P | N | – | – | – | – | – |
| Berklee College of Music | MA | 11 | P | – | – | – | – | – | – |
| Berry College | GA | 13 | – | – | – | – | N | N | N* |
| Bethany College | WV | 13 | N | – | N | N | – | – | – |
| Bethany Lutheran College | MN | 22 | – | – | – | – | – | P* | – |
| Bethel College | KS | 22 | N | – | N | – | – | – | – |
| Bethel College | IN | 22 | – | – | N | N | N | N | N |
| Bethel University | MN | 23 | – | N | N | N | N | – | N |
| Bethune-Cookman University | FL | 35 | N | – | – | N | – | N | N* |
| Big Bend Cmty College | WA | 27 | – | – | N | – | – | – | – |
| Binghamton University | NY | 3 | N | P | – | N | N | – | – |
| Biola University | CA | 4 | – | – | – | N | – | N | N |
| Birmingham-Southern College | AL | 23 | N | – | – | N | – | N | N* |
| Bismarck State College | ND | 28 | – | – | – | – | – | N | N | N |
| Black Hills State University | SD | 8 | N | N | P | – | – | – | – |
| Bloomfield College | NJ | 20 | – | – | – | N | – | – | – |
| Bloomsburg U of Pennsylvania | PA | 8 | P* | – | – | N* | – | – | – |
| Blue Mountain Cmty College | OR | 27 | N | – | – | – | – | – | – |
| Bluefield State College | WV | 7 | – | – | – | N | – | – | – |
| Bluffton University | OH | 22 | – | – | N | N | N | N | N* |
| Boston College | MA | 5 | – | – | – | – | – | N | N* |
| Boston University | MA | 5 | – | – | N* | – | – | – | – |
| Bowdoin College | ME | 14 | – | N | N | – | – | – | – |
| Bowie State University | MD | 34 | – | – | – | – | – | P | N* |
| Bowling Green State University | OH | 1 | N | – | N | N | N | – | – |
| Bradley University | IL | 4 | – | – | – | N | – | – | – |
| Brandeis University | MA | 6 | N | – | – | N* | – | N* | – |
| Brazosport College | TX | 27 | N | – | – | – | – | – | – |
| Brenau University | GA | 12 | N | – | – | – | – | – | – |

P—Participated   N—Participated and included in National Norms   *—Supplemental Sample

233

Table C3 (continued)
*Participation History*

| Institution | State | Strat | 1989 | 1992 | 1995 | 1998 | 2001 | 2004 | 2007 |
|---|---|---|---|---|---|---|---|---|---|
| Brevard Cmty College | FL | 29 | – | – | – | – | N | – | – |
| Bridgewater College | VA | 21 | N | – | * – | N | N | N | N |
| Brigham Young U-Hawaii Campus | HI | 12 | – | – | – | – | N | N | N |
| Brigham Young University | UT | 5 | – | N | – | N | N | N | N |
| Brookhaven College | TX | 27 | – | – | – | – | – | N | N* |
| Broome Cmty College | NY | 29 | – | N | – | – | – | – | – |
| Bryan College | TN | 12 | – | – | – | – | – | – | N |
| Bryn Athyn Coll of the New Church | PA | 23 | N | – | – | – | – | – | – |
| Bryn Mawr College | PA | 14 | P* | – | N | N | N | P | N |
| Bucknell University | PA | 14 | – | – | N | N | N | N | N |
| Buena Vista University | IA | 22 | N | – | N | N | – | – | – |
| Butler University | IN | 4 | – | N | N | – | N | N* | – |
| Cabrini College | PA | 16 | – | – | – | – | N | N | N* |
| Cal Poly State U-Pomona | CA | 8 | – | – | P | – | – | – | – |
| Caldwell College | NJ | 16 | – | N | – | – | – | – | – |
| California Baptist University | CA | 20 | – | N | N | N | – | N | N* |
| California Institute of Technology | CA | 6 | P* | – | – | P* | – | P* | – |
| California Lutheran University | CA | 22 | N | N | – | N | – | – | – |
| California Maritime Academy | CA | 8 | N | – | – | – | – | – | – |
| California State U-Bakersfield | CA | 7 | N | N | N | N | N | N | N* |
| California State U-Dominguez Hills | CA | 7 | – | – | – | N | – | – | – |
| California State U-Fresno | CA | 7 | – | – | – | P | – | N | N* |
| California State U-Fullerton | CA | 7 | – | – | – | N | N | – | – |
| California State U-Los Angeles | CA | 7 | N | P | P | P | – | P | N* |
| California State U-Northridge | CA | 7 | – | – | – | – | – | – | N |
| California State U-San Bernardino | CA | 7 | – | – | – | N | – | – | – |
| California State U-San Marcos | CA | 7 | – | – | – | – | N | – | – |
| California State U-Stanislaus | CA | 7 | – | – | – | N | – | – | – |
| Calvin College | MI | 23 | N* | P | N | N | N | N | N |
| Cameron University | OK | 8 | – | – | N | – | – | – | – |
| Canisius College | NY | 18 | N* | N | N | N | N | N | N |
| Cape Cod Cmty College | MA | 28 | – | N | – | – | – | – | – |
| Cardinal Stritch University | WI | 17 | – | – | N | – | – | – | – |
| Carl Albert State College | OK | 27 | – | – | – | – | – | N | – |
| Carleton College | MN | 14 | N* | N | N | N* | N | N | N |
| Carlow University | PA | 16 | P* | – | – | – | – | – | – |
| Carnegie-Mellon University | PA | 6 | P* | – | – | N* | – | N | P |
| Carroll College | WI | 22 | N | – | N | N | N | N | N |
| Carthage College | WI | 23 | – | N | – | – | – | – | – |
| Case Western Reserve University | OH | 6 | P* | – | N* | – | P* | N* | |
| Casper College | WY | 28 | – | – | – | – | N | – | – |
| Catawba College | NC | 21 | N | – | – | – | N | – | – |
| Catholic University of America | DC | 4 | P* | – | – | – | N | N | N |
| Cayuga County Cmty College | NY | 27 | – | N | – | – | N | – | – |
| Cazenovia College | NY | 11 | – | – | – | – | – | – | N |
| Cedar Crest College | PA | 12 | P* | – | N | N | P | N | N |

P—Participated    N—Participated and included in National Norms    *—Supplemental Sample

Table C3 (continued)
*Participation History*

| Institution | State | Strat | 1989 | 1992 | 1995 | 1998 | 2001 | 2004 | 2007 |
|---|---|---|---|---|---|---|---|---|---|
| Cedarville University | OH | 23 | – | – | N | N | – | – | – |
| Centenary College of Louisiana | LA | 23 | N | – | – | – | – | – | – |
| Central College | IA | 23 | – | – | N | – | N | N | N* |
| Central Connecticut State U | CT | 8 | – | – | P | P | – | N* | – |
| Central Methodist University | MO | 20 | – | – | – | – | – | N* | |
| Central Michigan University | MI | 8 | – | – | P | – | – | – | – |
| Central Washington University | WA | 7 | N | N | N | N | N | N | P |
| Centralia College | WA | 28 | N | – | – | – | – | – | – |
| Centre College | KY | 13 | – | – | – | N | – | N | N* |
| Cerritos College | CA | 28 | – | – | N | – | – | – | – |
| Chadron State College | NE | 8 | N | N | N | – | – | – | – |
| Chapman University | CA | 13 | N | – | – | N | N | N | N |
| Charleston Southern University | SC | 22 | N | – | – | – | – | – | – |
| Chatham University | PA | 12 | N | – | – | N* | – | N* | – |
| Chemeketa Cmty College | OR | 29 | – | – | – | – | – | N | N* |
| Chowan University | NC | 20 | – | – | – | – | N | N | – |
| Christian Brothers University | TN | 18 | – | – | – | – | – | N | N* |
| Christopher Newport University | VA | 9 | – | N | N | N | N | N | N |
| Cincinnati Bible College & Sem | OH | 22 | – | P | N | N | – | – | – |
| City College | NY | 9 | – | – | – | P | – | – | – |
| Claremont McKenna College | CA | 14 | N* | – | – | N | N | – | – |
| Clarion U of Pennsylvania | PA | 8 | – | – | – | – | – | N | N* |
| Clark State Cmty College | OH | 26 | N | – | – | – | – | – | – |
| Clark University | MA | 13 | N | – | N | N* | N | P | N* |
| Clarke College | IA | 18 | – | – | N | – | – | – | – |
| Clarkson College | NE | 12 | – | N | N | – | – | – | – |
| Clarkson University | NY | 5 | – | N | N | N | N | – | – |
| Clayton State University | GA | 7 | – | – | – | – | – | N | N* |
| Clearwater Christian College | FL | 11 | N | – | – | – | – | – | – |
| Cleary University | MI | 15 | N | – | – | – | – | – | – |
| Clemson University | SC | 3 | – | N | – | – | N | – | – |
| Cleveland Institute of Art | OH | 12 | – | N | N | – | – | – | – |
| Cleveland Institute of Music | OH | 14 | – | P | P | – | – | – | – |
| Cleveland State University | OH | 1 | N | – | P | N | – | N | N* |
| Clinton Cmty College | NY | 27 | – | – | – | – | N | – | N |
| Cloud County Cmty College | KS | 26 | N | N | N | – | N* | – | – |
| Cmty Colleges of Allegheney County | PA | 29 | – | – | P | – | – | – | – |
| Coastal Georgia Community College | GA | 27 | N | – | – | – | N | – | – |
| Coastline Cmty College | CA | 25 | – | – | – | N | – | – | – |
| Cochise College | AZ | 28 | – | – | – | – | – | N | N* |
| Coe College | IA | 13 | – | – | N | – | N | N | N |
| Coker College | SC | 11 | – | N | – | – | – | – | – |
| Colgate University | NY | 14 | N | – | – | N* | N | N | P |
| College Misericordia | PA | 16 | N* | – | – | – | – | – | – |
| College of Charleston | SC | 9 | – | N | – | – | N | N | N* |
| College of Eastern Utah | UT | 27 | N | – | N | – | P* | – | – |

P—Participated    N—Participated and included in National Norms    *—Supplemental Sample

Table C3 (continued)
*Participation History*

| Institution | State | Strat | 1989 | 1992 | 1995 | 1998 | 2001 | 2004 | 2007 |
|---|---|---|---|---|---|---|---|---|---|
| College of Idaho | ID | 13 | N | – | – | N | N | N* | – |
| College of Lake County | IL | 28 | N | – | – | – | P* | – | – |
| College of Marin | CA | 27 | P | – | – | – | – | – | – |
| College of Mount Saint Joseph | OH | 17 | – | N | – | – | – | – | – |
| College of Mount Saint Vincent | NY | 16 | P* | – | N | – | – | – | – |
| College of New Jersey | NJ | 9 | – | – | – | P | – | – | – |
| College of Notre Dame of Maryland | MD | 17 | – | – | – | – | N | – | N |
| College of Saint Benedict | MN | 18 | N | – | N | – | N | N | N* |
| College of Saint Mary | NE | 17 | N | N | – | – | – | N | N* |
| College of Saint Rose | NY | 17 | – | – | – | N | N | – | – |
| College of Saint Scholastica | MN | 18 | – | N | N | N | N | N | N |
| College of Santa Fe | NM | 18 | – | – | – | – | N | – | – |
| College of Southern Idaho | ID | 26 | – | N | – | N | – | – | – |
| College of Southern Nevada | NV | 25 | N | – | – | – | – | P* | – |
| College of the Canyons | CA | 27 | – | – | N | – | – | – | – |
| College of the Holy Cross | MA | 18 | – | – | N | – | – | – | – |
| College of the Sequoias | CA | 29 | – | – | – | – | – | P* | – |
| College of the Southwest | NM | 11 | – | – | – | – | – | P | P* |
| College of William and Mary | VA | 9 | – | – | – | – | P | N | – |
| College of Wooster | OH | 13 | – | – | – | N | N | – | N |
| Colorado College | CO | 14 | N* | N | N | N | N | N | N |
| Colorado State University | CO | 2 | – | – | – | – | – | N* | – |
| Colorado State University-Pueblo | CO | 7 | N | – | – | – | – | N | N* |
| Columbia College | SC | 21 | – | – | – | – | – | – | P |
| Columbia College | IL | 15 | – | – | N | – | – | – | – |
| Columbia International U | SC | 12 | – | – | P | – | – | – | – |
| Columbia Union College | MD | 20 | – | N | N | – | – | – | – |
| Columbia University | NY | 6 | – | – | P* | – | P* | – | – |
| Columbia-Greene Cmty College | NY | 26 | – | N | – | – | N | – | – |
| Columbus State University | GA | 7 | N | N | N | N | – | – | – |
| Conception Seminary College | MO | 17 | N | N | – | – | – | – | – |
| Concord College | WV | 7 | – | N | – | – | – | – | – |
| Concordia College | MN | 23 | – | N | – | – | – | – | – |
| Concordia College | NY | 21 | – | – | N | – | – | – | – |
| Concordia University | IL | 22 | – | – | N | – | – | – | – |
| Concordia University | MI | 21 | N | N | N | N | N | – | – |
| Concordia University | MN | 23 | – | – | – | – | N | N | N* |
| Concordia University | NE | 22 | N | N | – | – | – | – | – |
| Concordia University | OR | 21 | N | – | – | – | – | – | – |
| Concordia University Wisconsin | WI | 12 | – | – | – | – | N | – | – |
| Connecticut College | CT | 14 | – | – | P | – | – | – | – |
| Converse College | SC | 12 | N* | – | – | – | – | – | – |
| Copiah-Lincoln Cmty College | MS | 27 | P | – | – | – | – | – | – |
| Coppin State College | MD | 34 | P | P | – | – | – | – | – |
| Corban College | OR | 21 | – | – | N | N | – | – | – |
| Cornell College | IA | 23 | – | N | N | – | N | N | – |

P—Participated     N—Participated and included in National Norms     *—Supplemental Sample

Table C3 (continued)
*Participation History*

| Institution | State | Strat | 1989 | 1992 | 1995 | 1998 | 2001 | 2004 | 2007 |
|---|---|---|---|---|---|---|---|---|---|
| Cornell University | NY | 6 | N | – | N* | – | N* | N* | – |
| Cornerstone University | MI | 21 | N | – | – | N | – | – | – |
| Corning Cmty College | NY | 28 | – | N | – | N | N | – | – |
| Creighton University | NE | 5 | – | N | N | N | N | N | N |
| Crowder College | MO | 26 | – | – | – | – | N | – | – |
| Cuesta College | CA | 28 | P | – | – | – | – | N | N* |
| Culver-Stockton College | MO | 22 | – | – | N | – | – | – | – |
| Cumberland County College | NJ | 27 | N | – | – | – | – | N | N* |
| Cypress College | CA | 28 | N | – | N | – | N* | – | – |
| Dakota State University | SD | 7 | – | N | P | – | – | – | – |
| Dakota Wesleyan University | SD | 21 | – | – | – | – | – | N | N* |
| Dalton State College | GA | 28 | N | – | – | – | – | – | – |
| Daniel Webster College | NH | 12 | – | – | – | – | – | N | N* |
| Dartmouth College | NH | 14 | – | – | – | N | – | – | – |
| Davenport U-Eastern Region | MI | 15 | – | N | – | – | – | – | – |
| Davenport U-Western Region | MI | 33 | – | N | – | – | – | – | – |
| Davis and Elkins College | WV | 20 | N | N | – | – | – | – | – |
| Daytona Beach Cmty College | FL | 25 | – | – | – | – | N | – | – |
| Defiance College | OH | 12 | N | – | – | – | – | – | N |
| Del Mar College | TX | 27 | – | – | N | – | – | – | – |
| Delaware Tech & CC-Wilmington | DE | 28 | – | – | N | – | – | – | – |
| Denison University | OH | 13 | N | N | N | N | N | N | P |
| Denmark Technical College | SC | 27 | P | – | – | – | – | – | – |
| DePaul University | IL | 4 | N* | – | N | N | – | – | – |
| DePauw University | IN | 23 | N | N | N | N | N | – | – |
| DeSales University | PA | 17 | P* | – | – | N* | – | – | – |
| Detroit College of Business | MI | 15 | – | – | – | P | – | – | – |
| DeVry University-Chicago | IL | 15 | N | – | – | – | – | – | – |
| Dickinson College | PA | 13 | – | – | – | N | N | N | N |
| Dickinson State University | ND | 7 | – | – | – | – | N | N | N |
| Dine College | AZ | 27 | – | – | – | N | – | – | – |
| Divine Word College | IA | 16 | – | – | N | – | – | N | N* |
| Dominican College of Blauvelt | NY | 16 | – | N | – | N | N | – | – |
| Dominican University | IL | 17 | N* | – | – | N* | N | N | – |
| Dominican University of California | CA | 17 | – | N | N | N | – | – | – |
| Dordt College | IA | 23 | – | – | N | N | – | N | N* |
| D-Q University | CA | 30 | – | – | – | – | N* | – | – |
| Drake University | IA | 4 | P* | – | N | N* | N | N | N* |
| Drew University | NJ | 23 | N | – | – | – | – | – | – |
| Drexel University | PA | 5 | P | – | N | P | P | P | N |
| Drury University | MO | 13 | N* | N | N | N | N | N | N* |
| Duquesne University | PA | 4 | – | – | – | – | – | N | N |
| Dutchess Cmty College | NY | 28 | N | N | N | N | – | N* | – |
| Dyersburg State Cmty College | TN | 27 | N | – | – | N | – | – | – |
| Earlham College | IN | 23 | N | N | N | – | N | N | N |
| East Carolina University | NC | 1 | – | – | – | N | N | N | N* |

P—Participated   N—Participated and included in National Norms   *—Supplemental Sample

237

Table C3 (continued)
*Participation History*

| Institution | State | Strat | 1989 | 1992 | 1995 | 1998 | 2001 | 2004 | 2007 |
|---|---|---|---|---|---|---|---|---|---|
| East Central University | OK | 8 | N | – | – | – | – | – | – |
| East Texas Baptist University | TX | 21 | – | N | – | – | N | N | N |
| Eastern Connecticut State U | CT | 7 | – | – | N | – | – | N | N |
| Eastern Kentucky University | KY | 7 | – | – | – | P | – | – | – |
| Eastern Mennonite University | VA | 22 | P* | – | N | N | N | N | N |
| Eastern Michigan University | MI | 8 | – | – | – | P | – | – | N |
| Eastern Nazarene College | MA | 20 | – | – | N | N | – | – | – |
| Eastern New Mexico University | NM | 7 | – | – | N | – | – | N* | – |
| Eastern New Mexico U-Roswell | NM | 10 | – | – | – | P | – | – | – |
| Eastern Oregon University | OR | 7 | – | – | N | – | – | – | – |
| Eastern University | PA | 22 | N | – | – | N | – | – | – |
| Eastern Washington University | WA | 8 | N | N | – | N | P | – | – |
| Eckerd College | FL | 23 | N | N | N | – | N | N | – |
| Edgewood College | WI | 17 | N | N | N | N | N | N | N* |
| Edinboro U of Pennsylvania | PA | 8 | P | – | P | – | – | – | – |
| Edison State Cmty College | OH | 26 | – | N | – | – | – | – | – |
| El Paso Cmty College | TX | 29 | – | – | N | – | – | P* | – |
| Elizabeth City State University | NC | 34 | N* | – | – | P* | – | – | – |
| Elizabethtown College | PA | 23 | – | – | N | N | – | – | – |
| Elmhurst College | IL | 22 | – | – | – | N | – | – | – |
| Elon University | NC | 23 | – | – | – | N | N | N | N |
| Emmanuel College | GA | 31 | – | – | – | N | – | – | – |
| Emory and Henry College | VA | 22 | N | – | N | N | – | – | – |
| Emory University | GA | 6 | P* | – | – | N | – | – | – |
| Empire State College | NY | 10 | N | N | – | – | N | – | N |
| Emporia State University | KS | 8 | N | – | – | – | – | – | – |
| Erie Cmty College City Campus | NY | 28 | – | – | – | – | N | – | – |
| Erie Cmty College North (Amherst) | NY | 29 | – | N | – | – | P | – | – |
| Erie Cmty College South Campus | NY | 28 | – | – | – | – | N | – | – |
| Erskine College | SC | 23 | – | N | – | N | – | – | – |
| Eureka College | IL | 22 | N | – | – | – | – | – | – |
| Fairfield University | CT | 18 | – | – | – | – | – | N | N |
| Fairleigh Dickinson University | NJ | 12 | N | – | – | – | – | – | – |
| Fairmont State College | WV | 7 | – | – | – | N | – | – | – |
| Felician College | NJ | 16 | P | – | – | – | – | – | – |
| Finger Lakes Cmty College | NY | 28 | – | – | – | – | N | – | – |
| Fisk University | TN | 35 | – | – | – | – | P | – | – |
| Fitchburg State College | MA | 7 | – | P | – | – | – | – | – |
| Flagler College | FL | 12 | – | P | – | – | – | – | – |
| Florida Atlantic University | FL | 8 | – | – | – | P | – | – | – |
| Florida College | FL | 22 | – | – | – | – | – | N* | – |
| Florida Gulf Coast University | FL | 9 | – | – | – | P | – | – | N |
| Florida Memorial College | FL | 35 | – | – | – | – | P | – | – |
| Florida Southern College | FL | 22 | – | – | – | – | – | N | N* |
| Florida State University | FL | 3 | – | – | N | – | N | N | N* |
| Fontbonne University | MO | 17 | N | – | – | – | N | – | N |

P—Participated   N—Participated and included in National Norms   *—Supplemental Sample

238

Table C3 (continued)
*Participation History*

| Institution | State | Strat | 1989 | 1992 | 1995 | 1998 | 2001 | 2004 | 2007 |
|---|---|---|---|---|---|---|---|---|---|
| Foothill College | CA | 28 | N | – | P | – | N* | – | – |
| Fordham University | NY | 4 | – | P | – | N | N | N | – |
| Fort Hays State University | KS | 8 | P* | N | – | – | N | N | N |
| Fort Lewis College | CO | 7 | N | – | – | – | – | N | N* |
| Framingham State College | MA | 8 | N | N | N | – | – | – | – |
| Francis Marion University | SC | 7 | – | – | N | N | – | – | – |
| Franklin and Marshall College | PA | 14 | N | – | N | N | – | – | – |
| Franklin College of Indiana | IN | 12 | – | – | N | N | – | – | – |
| Franklin Pierce College | NH | 11 | – | – | N | – | N | – | – |
| Frederick Cmty College | MD | 27 | – | – | – | N | – | – | – |
| Free Will Baptist Bible College | TN | 20 | – | N | N | – | – | – | – |
| Freed-Hardeman University | TN | 22 | N* | – | N | N | – | – | – |
| Fresno Pacific University | CA | 21 | – | – | – | – | N | – | – |
| Frostburg State University | MD | 7 | – | – | N | – | – | N | N* |
| Fulton-Montgomery Cmty College | NY | 27 | – | N | – | – | N | – | – |
| Furman University | SC | 14 | N* | – | – | N | N | N | N |
| Gadsden State Cmty College | AL | 29 | N | – | – | – | – | – | – |
| Gainesville College | GA | 28 | N | – | N | – | P* | – | – |
| Gallaudet University | DC | 11 | N | – | – | – | – | – | – |
| Garden City Cmty College | KS | 27 | – | N | – | – | – | – | – |
| Garrett College | MD | 26 | N | – | – | – | – | – | – |
| Genesee Cmty College | NY | 28 | – | – | – | N | N | – | – |
| Geneva College | PA | 22 | N | – | N | N | N | N | N* |
| George C Wallace State Cmty Coll | AL | 27 | N | – | – | – | – | – | – |
| George Fox University | OR | 23 | – | – | N | N | N | N | N* |
| George Mason University | VA | 1 | – | – | P | – | – | – | – |
| George Washington University | DC | 5 | – | P | N | – | P | – | – |
| Georgetown College | KY | 22 | – | N | – | – | – | – | – |
| Georgetown University | DC | 6 | N | N | N | – | N* | – | – |
| Georgia College & State University | GA | 8 | – | – | – | – | – | – | N |
| Georgia Institute of Technology | GA | 3 | P* | P | – | P | – | P* | N* |
| Georgia Southern University | GA | 9 | – | – | N | – | N | P* | – |
| Georgia Southwestern State U | GA | 9 | – | – | – | – | N | N | N* |
| Georgian Court University | NJ | 16 | – | – | N | – | – | N | N |
| Gettysburg College | PA | 14 | – | – | N | P | N | N | N |
| Golden Gate University | CA | 12 | – | P | – | – | – | – | – |
| Gonzaga University | WA | 18 | N | – | N* | – | – | – | – |
| Gordon College | MA | 13 | N | – | N | N | – | N | – |
| Goshen College | IN | 22 | – | – | N | N | N | N | N |
| Goucher College | MD | 13 | – | – | N | N | – | N | N* |
| Grace College | IN | 21 | – | – | – | P | – | N | – |
| Grand Canyon University | AZ | 21 | – | – | N | N | – | – | – |
| Grand Valley State University | MI | 9 | N | N | N | N | N | N | P |
| Grand View College | IA | 11 | – | – | – | – | – | N | N |
| Great Basin College | NV | 25 | – | N | – | – | N | – | – |
| Greensboro College | NC | 20 | – | N | N | N | – | N | N |

P—Participated   N—Participated and included in National Norms   *—Supplemental Sample

Table C3 (continued)
*Participation History*

| Institution | State | Strat | 1989 | 1992 | 1995 | 1998 | 2001 | 2004 | 2007 |
|---|---|---|---|---|---|---|---|---|---|
| Greenville College | IL | 22 | – | – | N | N | N | N | N |
| Grinnell College | IA | 14 | N | – | – | N | – | N | N* |
| Guilford College | NC | 23 | N | N | N* | – | N | – | – |
| Guilford Technical Cmty College | NC | 29 | – | N | – | – | – | – | – |
| Gulf Coast Cmty College | FL | 27 | – | – | – | – | – | – | P |
| Gustavus Adolphus College | MN | 23 | – | N | – | – | – | N | – |
| Gwynedd-Mercy College | PA | 16 | – | – | – | – | – | N | P |
| Hagerstown Community College | MD | 28 | – | N | N | – | – | – | – |
| Hamilton College | NY | 14 | – | – | N | N | N | N | N |
| Hampden-Sydney College | VA | 23 | N | – | N | – | – | N | N |
| Hampshire College | MA | 13 | N | N | N | P | – | – | – |
| Hampton University | VA | 35 | N | – | – | – | – | – | – |
| Hannibal-LaGrange College | MO | 22 | – | – | N | – | N | – | – |
| Harcum College | PA | 32 | – | – | – | – | – | P* | – |
| Harold Washington College | IL | 36 | – | – | N | – | P | – | – |
| Harrisburg Area Cmty College | PA | 29 | – | N | – | – | – | – | – |
| Harrisburg University of S & T | PA | 15 | – | P | – | – | – | – | P |
| Harry S Truman College | IL | 28 | – | P | – | – | – | – | – |
| Hartwick College | NY | 13 | – | – | N | P | – | N | N |
| Harvard University | MA | 6 | – | – | P* | – | – | – | – |
| Harvey Mudd College | CA | 14 | N | N | N | – | – | – | – |
| Haskell Indian Nations University | KS | 27 | – | – | – | N | – | – | – |
| Haverford College | PA | 14 | – | – | N | – | N | N | N |
| Heidelberg College | OH | 21 | – | – | – | N | – | – | – |
| Henderson State University | AR | 8 | – | – | – | – | – | N | – |
| Hendrix College | AR | 23 | – | – | – | N | – | N | N* |
| Heritage Christian University | AL | 24 | – | – | – | N | – | – | – |
| Heritage College | WA | 16 | – | – | N | – | – | – | – |
| Highland Cmty College | IL | 27 | – | – | – | – | N | N* | – |
| Highline Cmty College | WA | 29 | – | – | – | N | – | N | N* |
| Hillsborough Cmty College | FL | 28 | N | – | – | – | – | – | – |
| Hiram College | OH | 13 | – | N | N | N | N | – | – |
| Hobart and William Smith Colleges | NY | 13 | N | – | N | – | – | – | – |
| Hocking College | OH | 29 | – | – | N | N | – | N | P |
| Hofstra University | NY | 4 | – | N | – | – | – | – | – |
| Holy Cross College | IN | 31 | – | – | N | – | P* | P* | – |
| Holy Family University | PA | 16 | – | – | – | N | N | N | N |
| Hood College | MD | 13 | N | – | – | N* | N | – | N |
| Hope College | MI | 13 | – | – | – | – | – | N | N |
| Hope International University | CA | 20 | N | – | N | N | – | – | – |
| Horry-Georgetown Technical College | SC | 27 | N | – | – | – | – | – | – |
| Houghton College | NY | 23 | P* | – | N | N | – | – | – |
| Howard Payne University | TX | 21 | – | – | N | N | – | – | – |
| Hudson County Cmty College | NJ | 28 | P | – | – | – | – | – | N |
| Hudson Valley Cmty College | NY | 29 | – | P | N | P | P | – | – |
| Humboldt State University | CA | 8 | – | – | – | – | – | N | N* |

P—Participated    N—Participated and included in National Norms    *—Supplemental Sample

Table C3 (continued)
*Participation History*

| Institution | State | Strat | 1989 | 1992 | 1995 | 1998 | 2001 | 2004 | 2007 |
|---|---|---|---|---|---|---|---|---|---|
| Hunter College | NY | 8 | – | – | P | P | – | – | – |
| Huntingdon College | AL | 23 | – | – | – | – | N | – | – |
| Huntington University | IN | 22 | N | N | – | N | – | N | N |
| IAU of Puerto Rico-Metropolitan | PR | 15 | – | P | – | – | – | – | – |
| Idaho State University | ID | 8 | – | – | – | – | N | – | – |
| Illinois Central College | IL | 29 | N | – | – | – | – | – | – |
| Illinois College | IL | 12 | – | N | – | N | N | N | N |
| Illinois Institute of Art | IL | 15 | – | – | – | – | – | N | – |
| Illinois State University | IL | 8 | N | – | N | – | – | – | – |
| Illinois Valley Cmty College | IL | 28 | – | – | – | – | – | N | N |
| Illinois Wesleyan University | IL | 14 | – | – | N | N | N | N | N |
| Immaculata University | PA | 16 | – | – | – | – | – | – | N |
| Imperial Valley College | CA | 25 | – | N | – | – | – | – | – |
| Indiana U of Pennsylvania | PA | 9 | N* | – | P* | – | N* | – | – |
| Indiana University Bloomington | IN | 2 | N | – | N* | – | – | – | – |
| Indiana University Northwest | IN | 1 | – | – | N | – | – | – | – |
| Indiana University Southeast | IN | 7 | N | N | N | N | – | – | – |
| Indiana University-Kokomo | IN | 7 | – | – | – | – | – | – | N |
| Indiana University-South Bend | IN | 7 | – | – | – | N | – | – | – |
| Indiana U-Purdue U-Fort Wayne | IN | 7 | – | – | – | – | N | – | N |
| Iona College | NY | 16 | – | – | N | – | – | – | – |
| Iowa State University | IA | 3 | N* | – | – | N* | – | P* | N* |
| Iowa Wesleyan College | IA | 21 | N | – | – | – | N | N | N |
| Iowa Western Cmty College | IA | 27 | – | – | N | – | N | N | N* |
| Itasca Cmty College | MN | 27 | N | – | – | – | – | – | – |
| Ithaca College | NY | 13 | N | – | – | – | – | – | – |
| Ivy Tech State College-Indianapolis | IN | 26 | – | – | – | – | – | N | – |
| Ivy Tech State College-Muncie | IN | 26 | – | N | – | – | – | – | – |
| Jackson Cmty College | MI | 27 | N | – | – | – | – | – | – |
| Jackson State Cmty College | TN | 27 | – | N | N | – | – | – | – |
| Jacksonville University | FL | 12 | – | – | – | – | N | – | – |
| James Madison University | VA | 9 | – | – | N | – | – | – | – |
| Jamestown Cmty College | NY | 28 | – | – | N | – | N | P* | – |
| Jefferson Cmty College | NY | 27 | – | N | – | – | N | – | – |
| Jefferson Community College | OH | 26 | – | – | N | – | – | – | – |
| Jewish Theological Sem of America | NY | 24 | – | P | – | – | – | – | – |
| John Brown University | AR | 13 | P* | N | – | N | N | N | – |
| Johns Hopkins University | MD | 6 | N | – | P* | N* | – | P* | – |
| Joliet Junior College | IL | 29 | – | P | N | – | – | – | – |
| Judson University | IL | 12 | – | – | – | – | – | N | N |
| Juniata College | PA | 13 | N | N | N | N | N | N | N |
| Kalamazoo College | MI | 14 | N | – | – | – | – | N | N* |
| Kankakee Cmty College | IL | 27 | N | – | – | – | – | – | – |
| Kansas City Kansas Cmty College | KS | 27 | N | N | – | – | – | – | – |
| Kauai Cmty College | HI | 26 | N | – | N | – | N* | – | – |
| Kean University | NJ | 8 | – | – | – | N | N | – | – |

P—Participated   N—Participated and included in National Norms   *—Supplemental Sample

Table C3 (continued)
*Participation History*

| Institution | State | Strat | 1989 | 1992 | 1995 | 1998 | 2001 | 2004 | 2007 |
|---|---|---|---|---|---|---|---|---|---|
| Keene State College | NH | 7 | – | – | – | N* | – | – | – |
| Keiser College | FL | 30 | – | N | – | – | – | – | – |
| Kendall College of Art and Design | MI | 11 | N | – | – | – | – | – | – |
| Kennebec Valley Community College | ME | 26 | – | – | – | – | – | – | N |
| Kennesaw State University | GA | 8 | – | – | – | – | – | N | – |
| Kent State U-Ashtabula | OH | 26 | N | – | – | – | – | – | – |
| Kentucky State University | KY | 8 | N | – | – | – | – | – | – |
| Kenyon College | OH | 14 | – | N | – | – | – | N | N |
| Kettering College of Medical Arts | OH | 31 | – | N | – | – | – | – | – |
| Keuka College | NY | 12 | N | – | N | – | – | – | – |
| Keystone College | PA | 11 | – | – | – | – | – | N | – |
| King College | TN | 23 | – | N | – | – | – | – | – |
| King's College | PA | 17 | N | N | – | N* | N | N | N |
| Kirtland Cmty College | MI | 26 | N | N | N | N | – | N* | – |
| Knox College | IL | 13 | N | N | N | N | – | – | – |
| Kutztown U of Pennsylvania | PA | 8 | – | – | – | – | – | P* | – |
| La Guardia Cmty College | NY | 29 | – | – | P | – | – | – | – |
| La Sierra University | CA | 4 | – | – | – | – | – | N | N* |
| Laboratory Inst of Merchandising | NY | 12 | – | – | – | – | – | – | N |
| Laboure College | MA | 30 | – | – | – | – | – | N | – |
| Lafayette College | PA | 14 | N | – | N* | – | – | N* | – |
| LaGrange College | GA | 20 | – | – | N | – | N | – | – |
| Lake Erie College | OH | 12 | N | – | – | – | – | – | – |
| Lake Forest College | IL | 13 | – | – | N | N | N | – | – |
| Lake Michigan College | MI | 27 | N | – | – | – | – | N | N* |
| Lake Region State College | ND | 26 | – | – | – | – | N | P | N |
| Lake Superior College | MN | 28 | – | – | – | – | – | N | N* |
| Lakeland College | WI | 21 | – | N | – | – | – | N | N |
| Lamar University | TX | 7 | – | – | – | – | – | N | – |
| Lander University | SC | 8 | – | – | – | – | – | – | N |
| Lane Cmty College | OR | 29 | – | – | – | N | – | – | – |
| Lawrence Technological University | MI | 12 | – | P | – | – | – | – | – |
| Lawrence University | WI | 14 | – | – | N | – | – | – | N |
| Lawson State Cmty College | AL | 36 | N | – | – | – | – | P* | – |
| Le Moyne College | NY | 18 | N* | – | – | N* | – | – | – |
| Lebanon Valley College | PA | 23 | N | N | N | – | N | N | N |
| Lee University | TN | 22 | N | – | N | N | – | N | N |
| Leeward Cmty College | HI | 28 | N | – | – | – | – | – | – |
| Lehigh Carbon Cmty College | PA | 27 | – | – | N | N | – | – | – |
| Lehigh University | PA | 5 | – | – | – | N | – | – | – |
| Lesley University | MA | 11 | – | – | P | N | – | – | – |
| LeTourneau University | TX | 13 | – | – | N | N | – | – | – |
| Lewis and Clark College | OR | 13 | – | P | P* | – | – | N | N* |
| Lewis College of Business | MI | 37 | – | – | N* | – | – | – | – |
| Lewis University | IL | 17 | – | – | N | N | – | N | N |
| Lewis-Clark State College | ID | 7 | N | – | – | – | – | – | – |

P—Participated    N—Participated and included in National Norms    *—Supplemental Sample

242

Table C3 (continued)
*Participation History*

| Institution | State | Strat | 1989 | 1992 | 1995 | 1998 | 2001 | 2004 | 2007 |
|---|---|---|---|---|---|---|---|---|---|
| LIFE University | GA | 15 | – | – | – | N | – | – | – |
| Lincoln Memorial University | TN | 12 | N | – | – | – | – | – | – |
| Lincoln University | MO | 7 | N* | N | – | – | – | P* | – |
| Lincoln University | PA | 35 | P | – | – | P* | – | N | N* |
| Lindsey Wilson College | KY | 11 | N | – | N | N | N | N | – |
| Linfield College | OR | 23 | N | – | N | N | – | – | – |
| Lipscomb University | TN | 22 | – | N | – | – | – | – | – |
| Lock Haven U of Pennsylvania | PA | 7 | – | N | P | – | – | N | P |
| Long Island U-Brooklyn | NY | 11 | – | – | – | – | – | – | P |
| Long Island U-CW Post | NY | 12 | – | – | – | – | – | – | P |
| Long Island U-Regional Campuses | NY | 12 | – | – | – | – | – | – | P |
| Longwood University | VA | 9 | N | N | N | N | N | N | N* |
| Lord Fairfax Cmty College | VA | 27 | – | N | – | – | – | – | – |
| Los Angeles Trade-Tech College | CA | 28 | N | – | – | – | – | – | – |
| Louisiana College | LA | 22 | N* | – | – | N | – | – | – |
| Louisiana State U and A&M Coll | LA | 2 | – | – | P | – | – | – | – |
| Louisiana State U-Eunice | LA | 26 | – | N | – | – | – | N* | – |
| Lower Columbia College | WA | 28 | – | – | – | – | – | N | N* |
| Loyola College in Maryland | MD | 18 | P* | – | – | – | – | – | – |
| Loyola Marymount University | CA | 4 | – | N | N | N | N | N* | – |
| Loyola University of Chicago | IL | 4 | P* | – | – | N* | – | N | N* |
| Loyola University-New Orleans | LA | 5 | – | – | – | N* | – | N | N |
| Luther College | IA | 23 | – | – | – | N | – | – | – |
| Lycoming College | PA | 22 | – | N | N | N | N | N | N |
| Lynchburg College | VA | 11 | – | – | – | – | N | N* | – |
| Lynn University | FL | 11 | N | – | – | – | – | – | – |
| Lyon College | AR | 23 | N | – | – | N* | N | N | P |
| Macalester College | MN | 14 | – | – | – | N | – | N | N* |
| MacMurray College | IL | 20 | N | – | – | – | – | P* | – |
| Madison Area Technical College | WI | 29 | N | – | – | – | – | – | – |
| Madonna University | MI | 16 | – | N | N | N | N | N | – |
| Malone College | OH | 22 | N | N | N | N | N | – | – |
| Manchester College | IN | 21 | – | – | – | N | N | N | N* |
| Manhattan College | NY | 18 | – | N | – | – | – | – | – |
| Manor College | PA | 31 | – | – | – | – | – | N | P* |
| Mansfield U of Pennsylvania | PA | 8 | – | – | – | N | – | N | N* |
| Marian College | IN | 16 | N | – | – | – | – | – | – |
| Marietta College | OH | 12 | P* | – | N | N | – | – | – |
| Marist College | NY | 13 | – | – | – | – | N | – | – |
| Marquette University | WI | 4 | N* | N | – | N* | – | N | N* |
| Marshalltown Cmty College | IA | 29 | – | – | N | – | – | – | – |
| Martin Luther College | MN | 24 | N | – | P | N | – | – | – |
| Mary Baldwin College | VA | 20 | – | – | – | – | – | N* | – |
| Marymount Manhattan College | NY | 12 | – | – | – | – | N | N | N* |
| Marymount University | VA | 16 | – | – | – | – | – | N | N* |
| Maryville College | TN | 23 | – | – | – | – | – | N | N* |

P—Participated   N—Participated and included in National Norms   *—Supplemental Sample

243

Table C3 (continued)
*Participation History*

| Institution | State | Strat | 1989 | 1992 | 1995 | 1998 | 2001 | 2004 | 2007 |
|---|---|---|---|---|---|---|---|---|---|
| Marywood University | PA | 17 | N | – | N | – | N | N | – |
| Mass Col of Pharmacy & Hlth Sci | MA | 11 | – | – | – | – | P | N | N* |
| Massachusetts Coll of Liberal Arts | MA | 9 | – | N | – | – | – | – | – |
| Massachusetts Inst of Technology | MA | 6 | – | – | P | P | P | P | N* |
| Master's College | CA | 23 | – | N | N | N | – | – | – |
| Mayville State University | ND | 7 | – | – | – | – | N | N | N |
| McHenry County College | IL | 26 | N | – | N | – | N* | – | – |
| McKendree College | IL | 23 | – | – | – | N | – | – | – |
| McPherson College | KS | 20 | – | – | N | N | N | N | N* |
| Medaille College | NY | 11 | – | – | – | – | – | N | – |
| Medgar Evers College | NY | 34 | – | – | – | – | P | – | – |
| Menlo College | CA | 13 | – | N | – | – | – | – | – |
| Merced College | CA | 28 | N | – | – | – | – | – | – |
| Mercer County Cmty College | NJ | 29 | – | – | N | N | – | P* | – |
| Mercer University | GA | 23 | – | – | – | – | – | – | N |
| Mercy College | NY | 12 | P | N | – | – | – | – | – |
| Mercyhurst College | PA | 18 | N* | – | – | N | N | – | – |
| Meredith College | NC | 12 | – | – | – | – | N | N | N* |
| Meridian Cmty College | MS | 27 | N | – | – | – | – | – | – |
| Merrimack College | MA | 17 | – | N | – | – | – | – | – |
| Messiah College | PA | 23 | N | – | N | N | – | – | – |
| Metropolitan Cmty College | NE | 27 | – | N | N | – | – | – | – |
| Metropolitan College of New York | NY | 15 | – | – | – | – | P | – | N |
| Metropolitan State U | MN | 10 | – | – | – | – | – | N | N |
| Miami University | OH | 3 | – | – | N | N | N | N | N |
| Miami University-Hamilton | OH | 27 | – | – | N | N | – | – | – |
| Michigan State University | MI | 2 | – | P | P | – | P | P | – |
| Michigan Technological University | MI | 9 | N | – | – | – | – | P* | – |
| Mid Michigan Cmty College | MI | 26 | N | – | N | – | N* | – | – |
| MidAmerica Nazarene University | KS | 21 | – | – | – | – | – | N | N* |
| Middle Tennessee State University | TN | 8 | – | – | – | N | N | – | – |
| Middlebury College | VT | 14 | – | – | – | P | – | P* | – |
| Middlesex County College | NJ | 29 | N | – | – | – | – | – | – |
| Middletown Campus | OH | 27 | – | – | – | N | – | – | – |
| Midway College | KY | 22 | – | – | – | – | – | P | N* |
| Millersville U of Pennsylvania | PA | 9 | N* | – | – | – | – | N | N |
| Milligan College | TN | 13 | P* | – | – | N* | – | – | – |
| Millikin University | IL | 23 | – | – | – | – | N | – | – |
| Mills College | CA | 13 | – | N | – | – | – | N | N |
| Minneapolis Coll of Art and Design | MN | 12 | – | N | – | – | – | N | N* |
| Minot State University | ND | 8 | – | – | – | – | N | N | P |
| Minot State University-Bottineau | ND | 26 | – | – | – | – | P | N | N |
| Mississippi College | MS | 23 | N* | – | N | N | – | – | – |
| Mississippi State University | MS | 2 | – | – | – | – | – | P* | – |
| Missouri S & T | MO | 9 | – | – | – | N | N | – | – |
| Missouri State U | MO | 9 | – | – | – | N | N | N | – |

P—Participated    N—Participated and included in National Norms    *—Supplemental Sample

Table C3 (continued)
*Participation History*

| Institution | State | Strat | 1989 | 1992 | 1995 | 1998 | 2001 | 2004 | 2007 |
|---|---|---|---|---|---|---|---|---|---|
| Missouri Western State College | MO | 7 | – | – | – | N | – | N | – |
| Mohave Cmty College | AZ | 27 | – | N | – | – | – | – | – |
| Molloy College | NY | 16 | – | – | – | – | N | N | – |
| Monmouth University | NJ | 12 | N* | N | – | – | – | – | – |
| Monroe Cmty College | NY | 29 | – | N | N | – | N | – | – |
| Montana State University | MT | 2 | P* | – | – | – | – | – | – |
| Montana Tech of the U of Montana | MT | 9 | N | – | – | – | – | – | – |
| Montay College | IL | 30 | N | – | – | – | – | – | – |
| Montclair State University | NJ | 8 | – | – | P | – | N | N | P |
| Montreat College | NC | 21 | – | N | N | N | – | – | – |
| Moorhead State University | MN | 8 | – | – | – | N | – | N | N* |
| Moorpark College | CA | 28 | N | – | N | – | N* | – | – |
| Moraine Valley Cmty College | IL | 29 | N | – | N | – | N* | – | – |
| Moravian College | PA | 23 | N | – | – | – | N | N | N |
| Morehead State University | KY | 7 | N | – | N | – | – | – | – |
| Morehouse College | GA | 35 | P* | P | – | P* | – | – | – |
| Morgan Cmty College | CO | 26 | N | – | – | – | – | – | – |
| Morgan State University | MD | 34 | – | – | – | – | P | – | – |
| Morningside College | IA | 22 | – | – | – | – | – | N | N |
| Mount Aloysius College | PA | 16 | – | N | – | N | N | N | N* |
| Mount Holyoke College | MA | 14 | – | N | – | – | – | N* | – |
| Mount Mary College | WI | 17 | N* | – | N | – | – | – | – |
| Mount Saint Mary College | NY | 12 | – | N | N | – | – | N* | – |
| Mount Saint Mary's College | CA | 17 | N | – | N* | N* | N | – | – |
| Mount Saint Mary's University | MD | 18 | – | – | – | N | N | N | N |
| Mount San Antonio College | CA | 29 | – | – | – | – | – | N* | – |
| Mount Union College | OH | 23 | – | – | – | – | N | N | N* |
| Mount Vernon Nazarene University | OH | 22 | – | N | – | N | – | N | N* |
| Mount Wachusetts Cmty College | MA | 27 | – | N | – | – | – | – | – |
| Muhlenberg College | PA | 23 | – | N | – | – | – | – | – |
| Napa Valley College | CA | 27 | – | – | – | – | N | – | – |
| Naropa University | CO | 15 | – | – | – | – | – | P* | – |
| Nassau Cmty College | NY | 29 | – | – | – | N | P | – | – |
| National American University | SD | 11 | N | – | – | – | – | – | – |
| National-Louis University | IL | 11 | – | – | – | – | N | – | P |
| Naugatuck Valley Cmty-Tech College | CT | 28 | N | – | – | – | – | – | – |
| Navarro College | TX | 27 | – | N | – | – | – | N | N* |
| Nazarene Bible College | CO | 30 | – | – | – | – | N | N | P* |
| Nazareth College of Rochester | NY | 13 | – | – | – | N | N | N | N |
| Nebraska Wesleyan University | NE | 23 | – | N | N | – | N | N | N |
| Neumann College | PA | 16 | – | N | N | N | – | N | N |
| New College of Florida | FL | 9 | – | – | – | – | – | N | N* |
| New Mexico Junior College | NM | 27 | N | – | – | – | – | N | N* |
| New Mexico State U-Alamogordo | NM | 26 | – | N | – | N | N* | P |
| New York University | NY | 6 | – | – | P* | – | – | – | – |
| Niagara County Cmty College | NY | 29 | – | N | – | – | N | – | – |

P—Participated    N—Participated and included in National Norms    *—Supplemental Sample

# Table C3 (continued)
## *Participation History*

| Institution | State | Strat | 1989 | 1992 | 1995 | 1998 | 2001 | 2004 | 2007 |
|---|---|---|---|---|---|---|---|---|---|
| Niagara University | NY | 17 | – | – | N | P | N | N | N |
| Nicolet Area Technical College | WI | 26 | – | – | N | – | – | – | – |
| Norfolk State University | VA | 34 | – | – | – | – | – | P | N* |
| North Arkansas College | AR | 27 | N | – | – | N | – | N | N* |
| North Carolina A & T State U | NC | 34 | N | – | – | P | – | – | – |
| North Carolina State University | NC | 3 | – | – | N | – | – | – | – |
| North Carolina Wesleyan College | NC | 20 | – | – | N | N | – | – | – |
| North Central Michigan College | MI | 26 | N | – | – | – | – | – | – |
| North Country Cmty College | NY | 26 | – | – | – | – | N | – | – |
| North Dakota State Coll of Science | ND | 28 | – | – | – | – | N | N | N |
| North Dakota State University | ND | 2 | N | – | – | – | N | N | P |
| North Georgia College & State U | GA | 9 | – | – | N | N | N | N | N |
| North Greenville University | SC | 21 | – | – | – | – | – | N | – | N |
| North Harris College | TX | 28 | N | – | – | – | – | – | – |
| North Park University | IL | 22 | N | – | – | N | – | N | – |
| North Seattle Cmty College | WA | 28 | – | N | – | – | – | – | – |
| Northampton County Area Cmty Coll | PA | 28 | N | N | N | P | – | N | N* |
| Northeast State Tech Cmty College | TN | 27 | – | – | – | – | N | N | N* |
| Northeast Texas Cmty College | TX | 26 | – | – | N | – | N | P* | – |
| Northeastern Illinois University | IL | 7 | – | – | – | – | N | – | P |
| Northeastern Oklahoma A&M College | OK | 27 | – | – | N | – | – | – | – |
| Northeastern State University | OK | 7 | P* | – | – | N* | – | N | – |
| Northeastern University | MA | 4 | N | N | N* | N | – | N | P |
| Northern Arizona University | AZ | 1 | N | – | – | – | N | N | N* |
| Northern Illinois University | IL | 1 | N* | N | N | N | N | P | – |
| Northern Kentucky University | KY | 7 | – | – | – | – | – | N | N* |
| Northern State University | SD | 8 | – | N | P | – | – | – | – |
| Northland College | WI | 13 | N | – | – | N | N | – | – |
| Northwest Christian College | OR | 21 | – | – | N | N | N | N | N |
| Northwest Mississippi Cmty College | MS | 29 | P | – | – | – | – | – | – |
| Northwest Missouri State U | MO | 8 | P* | – | – | N* | – | N* | – |
| Northwest Nazarene University | ID | 22 | – | – | N | N | – | – | – |
| Northwest University | WA | 21 | – | N | – | N | – | N | N* |
| Northwestern College | IA | 23 | N | N | – | – | – | – | – |
| Northwestern College | MN | 12 | – | – | N | N | – | N* | N |
| Northwestern University | IL | 6 | P* | P | P* | – | – | P* | – |
| Norwalk Cmty College | CT | 27 | N | – | – | – | – | – | – |
| Notre Dame College | NH | 16 | P* | – | – | – | – | – | – |
| Notre Dame de Namur University | CA | 16 | – | – | N | P | – | – | – |
| Nova Southeastern University | FL | 12 | – | – | N | – | – | – | – |
| Nyack College | NY | 21 | N | – | – | – | – | N | – |
| Oakland Cmty College-Orchard Ridge | MI | 28 | N | – | – | – | – | – | – |
| Oakland University | MI | 8 | P* | – | – | N* | – | – | N |
| Oakton Cmty College | IL | 28 | – | – | – | N | – | – | – |
| Oberlin College | OH | 14 | – | – | N | – | – | N | N* |
| Occidental College | CA | 13 | N | N | N | N | P | N | N |

P—Participated   N—Participated and included in National Norms   *—Supplemental Sample

Table C3 (continued)
*Participation History*

| Institution | State | Strat | 1989 | 1992 | 1995 | 1998 | 2001 | 2004 | 2007 |
|---|---|---|---|---|---|---|---|---|---|
| Ocean County College | NJ | 29 | – | N | – | – | N | – | N |
| Oglethorpe University | GA | 13 | – | – | – | N | – | – | – |
| Ohio Dominican University | OH | 16 | – | N | N | N | – | – | N |
| Ohio Northern University | OH | 23 | – | – | – | – | N | N | N |
| Ohio State University | OH | 2 | P* | – | P* | N | N | N | N* |
| Ohio State University-Marion | OH | 7 | N | – | – | – | – | – | – |
| Ohio University-Belmont | OH | 26 | N | – | – | – | – | – | – |
| Ohio Wesleyan University | OH | 23 | N | – | N* | – | – | – | – |
| Oklahoma Baptist University | OK | 23 | N | – | – | – | – | – | – |
| Oklahoma City University | OK | 22 | – | – | – | – | – | N | P |
| Oklahoma State U | OK | 3 | P | – | – | – | – | – | – |
| Oklahoma Wesleyan University | OK | 22 | – | – | – | N | – | – | – |
| Olivet College | MI | 11 | – | – | – | N | – | N* | – |
| Olivet Nazarene University | IL | 22 | – | – | – | N | – | – | – |
| Olympic College | WA | 29 | N | – | – | – | – | – | – |
| Onondaga Cmty College | NY | 29 | – | N | N | – | N | P* | – |
| Oral Roberts University | OK | 12 | – | – | – | N | N | – | – |
| Orange County Cmty College | NY | 28 | – | N | – | – | N | – | – |
| Oregon State University | OR | 2 | N | – | – | – | – | N* | – |
| Ottawa University | KS | 21 | – | – | N | – | – | – | – |
| Otterbein College | OH | 22 | P | N | – | – | – | – | – |
| Ouachita Baptist University | AR | 21 | – | – | N | – | – | – | – |
| Our Lady of the Holy Cross College | LA | 11 | P | – | – | – | N | – | – |
| Our Lady of the Lake College | LA | 19 | – | – | – | N | – | – | – |
| Our Lady of the Lake University | TX | 16 | N | – | N | N* | – | – | – |
| Owensboro Cmty College | KY | 27 | – | – | P | – | – | – | – |
| Oxnard College | CA | 27 | – | – | – | – | – | N | N* |
| Ozarks Technical Cmty College | MO | 29 | – | – | – | N | – | – | – |
| Pace University | NY | 12 | P | P | – | – | – | P | P |
| Pacific Lutheran University | WA | 23 | – | N | N | – | – | – | – |
| Pacific Northwest College of Art | OR | 15 | – | – | – | – | – | N | N |
| Pacific Union College | CA | 22 | N | – | – | N | – | – | – |
| Pacific University | OR | 13 | – | – | N | – | – | – | – |
| Palm Beach Atlantic University | FL | 22 | – | – | N | N | – | – | N |
| Panola College | TX | 27 | – | – | N | – | – | – | – |
| Park University | MO | 21 | – | – | – | – | – | – | N |
| Parkland College | IL | 29 | N | – | – | – | – | – | – |
| Patrick Henry Cmty College | VA | 26 | – | – | – | – | – | N | N* |
| Paul Smith's College | NY | 32 | – | – | – | – | – | N | P |
| Peace College | NC | 20 | – | N | – | – | – | – | N |
| Penn State Erie-The Behrend College | PA | 9 | – | – | N | – | – | N | N |
| Penn State U-Mont Alto | PA | 27 | N | – | – | – | – | – | – |
| Pensacola Junior College | FL | 29 | N | – | – | – | – | – | – |
| Pepperdine University | CA | 23 | N | – | N | N | N | N | P |
| Peru State College | NE | 7 | N | – | – | – | – | – | – |
| Phila College of Performing Arts | PA | 12 | N | – | – | – | – | – | – |

P—Participated   N—Participated and included in National Norms   *—Supplemental Sample

Table C3 (continued)

*Participation History*

| Institution | State | Strat | 1989 | 1992 | 1995 | 1998 | 2001 | 2004 | 2007 |
|---|---|---|---|---|---|---|---|---|---|
| Philadelphia Biblical University | PA | 12 | – | N | – | – | – | – | – |
| Philadelphia University | PA | 12 | – | P | – | – | – | – | N |
| Piedmont Cmty College | NC | 26 | N | – | – | – | – | – | – |
| Piedmont Virginia Cmty College | VA | 26 | – | – | N | – | – | – | – |
| Pikes Peak Cmty College | CO | 27 | – | – | P | – | – | – | – |
| Pima County Cmty College District | AZ | 29 | – | – | – | P | N | – | – |
| Pine Manor College | MA | 11 | – | – | – | – | – | N | N* |
| Pitzer College | CA | 13 | N | N | – | N | – | – | – |
| Point Loma Nazarene University | CA | 21 | N | N | N | N | N | N | N |
| Point Park University | PA | 11 | – | N | – | P | – | – | – |
| Polytechnic University | NY | 13 | – | – | P | N | – | – | – |
| Pomona College | CA | 14 | – | – | N | N | N | – | N |
| Portland State University | OR | 8 | – | – | – | – | N | P | – |
| Pratt Institute | NY | 4 | – | – | – | – | – | P* | – |
| Presbyterian College | SC | 23 | N | N | – | N | N | P | N* |
| Princeton University | NJ | 6 | P | – | – | N* | – | – | – |
| Pueblo Cmty College | CO | 27 | N | – | – | – | – | – | – |
| Purdue University | IN | 2 | – | – | – | – | – | P | N* |
| Purdue University-Calumet | IN | 7 | – | – | – | – | N | – | – |
| Purdue University-North Central | IN | 27 | N | – | N | – | N* | N | N* |
| Queens University of Charlotte | NC | 21 | – | – | – | – | – | – | N |
| Radford University | VA | 8 | – | – | – | – | – | N | N |
| Rainy River Cmty College | MN | 26 | N | – | – | – | – | – | – |
| Ramapo College of New Jersey | NJ | 9 | N | – | – | N | – | N | – |
| Randolph College | VA | 23 | – | – | N | N | N | – | – |
| Randolph-Macon College | VA | 22 | – | – | – | N | – | – | – |
| Red Rocks Cmty College | CO | 27 | N | – | – | – | – | – | – |
| Regent University | VA | 24 | – | – | – | – | – | P | N* |
| Regis College | MA | 11 | – | – | N | N | – | N | N* |
| Rend Lake College | IL | 28 | – | – | N | – | – | – | – |
| Rensselaer Polytechnic Institute | NY | 5 | – | – | – | – | – | P | N* |
| Rhode Island College | RI | 7 | N | – | N | – | – | N* | – |
| Rhode Island School of Design | RI | 13 | – | – | – | – | – | N | – |
| Rhodes College | TN | 23 | N | – | N | – | N | P | N |
| Rice University | TX | 6 | – | – | N | N | N | N | N* |
| Richard Stockton College of NJ | NJ | 9 | N | – | – | – | N | N | N* |
| Richland Cmty College | IL | 27 | – | N | – | – | – | – | – |
| Richland College | TX | 28 | N | – | – | – | – | – | – |
| Rider University | NJ | 12 | – | – | N | – | – | N | N* |
| Ridgewater College-Willmar | MN | 27 | – | N | – | – | – | – | – |
| Ripon College | WI | 13 | N | – | N | – | – | N | N* |
| Riverside Cmty College | CA | 27 | – | – | – | N | – | – | – |
| Roane State Cmty College | TN | 28 | – | – | – | – | – | N | N* |
| Roanoke College | VA | 23 | N | – | – | – | N | N | N* |
| Robert Morris College | IL | 15 | – | N | – | – | – | – | – |
| Roberts Wesleyan College | NY | 22 | – | – | N | N | – | – | N |

P—Participated   N—Participated and included in National Norms   *—Supplemental Sample

Table C3 (continued)
*Participation History*

| Institution | State | Strat | 1989 | 1992 | 1995 | 1998 | 2001 | 2004 | 2007 |
|---|---|---|---|---|---|---|---|---|---|
| Rochester Institute of Technology | NY | 13 | P* | N | N | P* | – | – | – |
| Rockford College | IL | 12 | N | N | – | – | – | N | N |
| Rockland Cmty College | NY | 29 | – | – | – | – | N | – | – |
| Rollins College | FL | 13 | N | N | N | – | N | P | P |
| Roosevelt University | IL | 11 | – | – | – | – | N | – | – |
| Rowan University | NJ | 9 | – | – | – | – | N | – | – |
| Rowan-Cabarrus Cmty College | NC | 27 | – | N | – | – | – | – | – |
| Roxbury Cmty College | MA | 36 | – | – | P | – | – | – | – |
| Russell Sage College | NY | 12 | – | – | – | – | – | P* | – |
| Rutgers University-New Brunswick | NJ | 3 | N | – | N* | – | P* | – | – |
| Sacred Heart University | CT | 17 | N | N | – | – | – | – | – |
| Saginaw Valley State University | MI | 8 | P | – | – | – | – | N | N* |
| Saint Ambrose University | IA | 17 | – | N | N | – | – | – | – |
| Saint Andrews Presbyterian College | NC | 21 | N | – | – | P* | – | N | N* |
| Saint Anselm College | NH | 18 | – | – | – | – | N | N | N |
| Saint Bonaventure University | NY | 17 | – | – | N | N | – | – | – |
| Saint Charles Community College | MO | 31 | – | – | – | N | N | N* | – |
| Saint Cloud State University | MN | 8 | – | – | – | – | – | P | N* |
| Saint Edward's University | TX | 18 | N | N | N* | – | – | – | – |
| Saint Francis College | NY | 16 | – | – | – | N | – | – | – |
| Saint John Fisher College | NY | 12 | N | N | N | N | N | N | N* |
| Saint John's University | MN | 18 | P* | – | – | N* | – | – | – |
| Saint John's University-Queens | NY | 4 | – | – | – | N | N | N | N |
| Saint Joseph's College | IN | 17 | N | – | – | N* | – | – | – |
| Saint Joseph's College of Maine | ME | 17 | – | – | N | – | – | – | – |
| Saint Joseph's University | PA | 18 | – | N | N* | – | – | N | N* |
| Saint Lawrence University | NY | 13 | P* | – | – | N | N | N | N |
| Saint Leo University | FL | 16 | N | – | – | – | – | N | N* |
| Saint Mary-of-the-Woods College | IN | 16 | N | N | – | – | – | N | N* |
| Saint Mary's College | IN | 18 | N* | – | P | N* | N | N | N* |
| Saint Mary's College | NC | 31 | – | – | P | – | – | – | – |
| Saint Mary's College of California | CA | 18 | – | – | N | P | P | P | – |
| Saint Mary's U of Minnesota | MN | 17 | N | – | N | N | – | N | N |
| Saint Mary's University | TX | 17 | N | – | – | N | – | N | N* |
| Saint Michael's College | VT | 18 | N | – | – | – | – | – | – |
| Saint Norbert College | WI | 18 | N | N | – | N | – | N | N |
| Saint Olaf College | MN | 23 | – | – | – | N | N | N | N |
| Saint Peter's College | NJ | 16 | – | N | N | N | – | N | N |
| Saint Philip's College | TX | 27 | N | – | – | – | – | – | – |
| Saint Thomas University | FL | 16 | – | – | – | N | – | N | N |
| Saint Vincent College | PA | 17 | – | – | – | – | – | N | N |
| Saint Xavier University | IL | 17 | – | – | – | – | N | N | N* |
| Salisbury University | MD | 9 | – | – | – | – | N | – | – |
| Salve Regina University | RI | 16 | – | – | – | – | N | – | – |
| Sam Houston State University | TX | 7 | – | N | – | – | – | – | – |
| San Joaquin Delta College | CA | 28 | – | – | – | – | – | P | N* |

P—Participated   N—Participated and included in National Norms   *—Supplemental Sample

249

Table C3 (continued)
*Participation History*

| Institution | State | Strat | 1989 | 1992 | 1995 | 1998 | 2001 | 2004 | 2007 |
|---|---|---|---|---|---|---|---|---|---|
| San Jose State University | CA | 7 | N | – | P | – | N | N | P |
| Santa Clara University | CA | 5 | P* | N | N | – | N | N | N |
| Sarah Lawrence College | NY | 13 | N | – | – | N | N | P | N* |
| Savannah State University | GA | 34 | – | – | N | – | – | – | – |
| Schenectady County Cmty College | NY | 27 | – | N | – | – | N | – | – |
| Schreiner University | TX | 21 | – | – | N | N | N | – | – |
| Scripps College | CA | 14 | – | – | N | N | N | N | N |
| Seattle Pacific University | WA | 23 | – | – | – | – | N | N | N |
| Seattle University | WA | 18 | N* | – | N | – | – | P | – |
| Seton Hall University | NJ | 4 | – | – | – | – | N | – | N |
| Seton Hill University | PA | 16 | N | P | – | – | – | – | – |
| Shawnee State University | OH | 27 | – | – | N | – | – | – | – |
| Shenandoah University | VA | 21 | – | – | – | – | – | – | P |
| Shepherd College | WV | 9 | – | N | – | – | – | – | – |
| Shimer College | IL | 13 | N | – | – | – | – | – | – |
| Shippensburg U of Pennsylvania | PA | 9 | N* | N | N | – | – | – | – |
| Shorter College | GA | 22 | – | N | N | N | N | – | – |
| Siena College | NY | 13 | N | – | N | – | – | – | – |
| Simmons College | MA | 12 | N | – | P | – | – | – | – |
| Simpson College | IA | 23 | – | – | – | – | – | – | N |
| Simpson University | CA | 21 | – | – | N | – | – | N | N |
| Sinclair Cmty College | OH | 29 | N | – | – | – | – | – | – |
| Skagit Valley College | WA | 28 | N | – | – | – | – | – | – |
| Skidmore College | NY | 13 | P* | N | N | N* | – | – | – |
| Skyline College | CA | 28 | – | – | – | N | – | – | – |
| Slippery Rock U of Pennsylvania | PA | 7 | – | N | N | – | N | – | – |
| Smith College | MA | 14 | N | N | N | N | N | N | N |
| Sonoma State University | CA | 8 | – | – | – | – | – | N | N* |
| South Dakota Schl of Mines & Tech | SD | 9 | – | N | P | – | – | – | – |
| South Dakota State University | SD | 1 | – | N | P | N | N | N | N |
| South Florida Cmty College | FL | 26 | N | N | – | – | – | N* | – |
| South Suburban Coll of Cook County | IL | 28 | P | – | – | – | – | – | – |
| South Texas College | TX | 29 | – | – | – | – | – | N | N |
| Southeast Missouri State U | MO | 8 | – | N | N | N | – | N | N |
| Southeastern Louisiana University | LA | 7 | – | N | – | – | – | – | – |
| Southeastern University | DC | 7 | – | – | – | – | N | – | – |
| Southern Arkansas U | AR | 7 | N | – | N | – | – | – | – |
| Southern Connecticut State U | CT | 7 | – | – | N | – | N* | N | N* |
| Southern Illinois U-Carbondale | IL | 1 | – | – | – | N | – | P | N* |
| Southern Illinois U-Edwardsville | IL | 8 | N* | N | N | N | N | N | N |
| Southern Methodist University | TX | 5 | – | – | N | – | – | N | N* |
| Southern Nazarene University | OK | 21 | – | – | N | N | – | – | N |
| Southern New Hampshire University | NH | 11 | – | – | – | – | – | P* | – |
| Southern Oregon University | OR | 8 | – | – | – | – | – | N | N* |
| Southern University-New Orleans | LA | 34 | – | N | – | – | – | – | – |
| Southern Utah University | UT | 8 | – | N | – | – | – | N | N |

P—Participated   N—Participated and included in National Norms   *—Supplemental Sample

250

Table C3 (continued)

Participation History

| Institution | State | Strat | 1989 | 1992 | 1995 | 1998 | 2001 | 2004 | 2007 |
|---|---|---|---|---|---|---|---|---|---|
| Southern Virginia University | VA | 31 | – | – | – | – | – | P* | – |
| Southern Wesleyan University | SC | 21 | – | – | N | N | – | – | – |
| Southwest Minnesota State U | MN | 8 | P | – | – | – | – | N | N* |
| Southwest Tennessee Cmty College | TN | 36 | – | – | N | – | – | – | – |
| Southwestern College | CA | 28 | N | – | – | – | – | – | – |
| Southwestern Oklahoma State U | OK | 8 | – | N | – | – | – | – | – |
| Southwestern University | TX | 23 | N | N | – | – | – | N | N* |
| Spartanburg Methodist College | SC | 32 | – | N | – | – | P* | – | – |
| Spelman College | GA | 35 | N | – | – | N* | P | P | N* |
| Spring Arbor University | MI | 21 | N* | – | N | N | N | – | – |
| Spring Hill College | AL | 18 | – | – | – | – | – | – | N |
| Springfield College | MA | 11 | – | – | N | – | – | – | – |
| Springfield Technical Cmty College | MA | 28 | N | – | – | N | – | – | – |
| St Louis College of Pharmacy | MO | 13 | N | N | – | – | – | N | N* |
| Stanford University | CA | 6 | P* | – | P* | N* | – | P* | – |
| State University of West Georgia | GA | 7 | N | – | – | N | – | P | N* |
| Stephen F Austin State University | TX | 8 | – | – | N | N | – | – | – |
| Stephens College | MO | 12 | N | – | – | N* | – | – | – |
| Sterling College | KS | 22 | – | – | N | N | N | – | – |
| Stetson University | FL | 13 | N* | N | – | N* | N | P | N* |
| Stevens Institute of Technology | NJ | 14 | – | – | P | – | – | – | – |
| Stonehill College | MA | 18 | – | – | – | – | N | – | – |
| Suffolk Cmty College-Ammerman | NY | 29 | – | – | – | – | P | – | – |
| Suffolk Cmty College-Western | NY | 27 | – | – | – | – | P | – | – |
| Suffolk County Cmty Coll-Eastern | NY | 27 | – | – | – | – | P | – | – |
| Suffolk University | MA | 11 | P* | – | – | – | – | – | – |
| Sullivan County Cmty College | NY | 28 | – | N | – | N | N | – | – |
| SUNY A & T College-Cobleskill | NY | 8 | N* | N | N | P | N | N | N |
| SUNY A & T College-Morrisville | NY | 29 | – | N | – | – | N | – | – |
| SUNY Coll of Technology-Canton | NY | 28 | N | N | – | – | N | – | N |
| SUNY Coll of Technology-Delhi | NY | 29 | – | N | – | – | N | – | – |
| SUNY Coll of Technology-Farmingdale | NY | 10 | P | – | P | P | N | – | – |
| SUNY College of Env Sci & Forestry | NY | 9 | – | – | – | – | N | P | – |
| SUNY College-Brockport | NY | 8 | P* | N | N | N | N | P | – |
| SUNY College-Buffalo | NY | 8 | – | – | – | – | N | – | – |
| SUNY College-Cortland | NY | 8 | – | N | – | N | N | – | – |
| SUNY College-Fredonia | NY | 9 | – | N | – | – | N | – | – |
| SUNY College-Geneseo | NY | 9 | P* | N | N | N | N | N | N |
| SUNY College-New Paltz | NY | 9 | – | N | P | – | P | – | – |
| SUNY College-Old Westbury | NY | 7 | – | N | – | N | P | – | N |
| SUNY College-Oneonta | NY | 9 | – | N | – | – | N | – | – |
| SUNY College-Oswego | NY | 9 | N | P | – | – | P | – | – |
| SUNY College-Plattsburgh | NY | 8 | – | – | – | – | N | – | – |
| SUNY College-Potsdam | NY | 8 | N* | N | N | N | N | – | – |
| SUNY College-Purchase | NY | 9 | – | N | – | – | N | – | N |
| SUNY Maritime College | NY | 7 | N | N | – | – | P | – | – |

P—Participated   N—Participated and included in National Norms   *—Supplemental Sample

| Institution | State | Strat | 1989 | 1992 | 1995 | 1998 | 2001 | 2004 | 2007 |
|---|---|---|---|---|---|---|---|---|---|
| SUNY-Albany | NY | 2 | – | P | – | – | N | – | – |
| SUNY-Stony Brook | NY | 3 | – | N | – | – | N | – | – |
| SUNY-University at Buffalo | NY | 3 | P | P | N | N* | N | – | – |
| Susquehanna University | PA | 23 | – | – | N | – | – | N | N |
| Swarthmore College | PA | 14 | N | – | – | – | – | N | N |
| Sweet Briar College | VA | 13 | – | – | N | N | N | – | – |
| Syracuse University | NY | 5 | – | – | N | – | N | N | N* |
| Tabor College | KS | 22 | – | – | N | N | – | – | – |
| Tacoma Cmty College | WA | 28 | N | – | – | – | – | – | – |
| Talladega College | AL | 35 | N | – | – | – | – | – | – |
| Tallahassee Cmty College | FL | 28 | – | – | – | P | – | – | – |
| Tarleton State University | TX | 8 | – | N | – | – | – | – | – |
| Taylor University | IN | 13 | N | N | N | N | N | N | N |
| Teikyo Post University | CT | 11 | – | – | – | – | N | – | – |
| Tennessee Temple University | TN | 24 | – | – | – | – | – | N | N* |
| Texas A & M University | TX | 3 | – | – | – | – | – | N* | N* |
| Texas A&M U-Commerce | TX | 8 | N | N | N | N | N | – | – |
| Texas A&M U-Corpus Christi | TX | 1 | – | – | – | – | – | N | N |
| Texas A&M University-Kingsville | TX | 7 | – | – | – | N | – | – | – |
| Texas Christian University | TX | 4 | – | – | – | N* | – | – | – |
| Texas Lutheran University | TX | 22 | N | – | – | N | – | N | N |
| Texas State University-San Marcos | TX | 9 | – | N | – | – | – | N | N* |
| Texas Tech University | TX | 2 | – | N | – | – | – | – | – |
| Texas Wesleyan University | TX | 21 | P* | – | N | – | – | – | – |
| Texas Woman's University | TX | 1 | N | – | N | – | – | – | – |
| The Evergreen State College | WA | 9 | N* | P | – | P | – | – | – |
| The University of Tampa | FL | 12 | P | – | – | N | – | – | N |
| Thiel College | PA | 20 | – | – | – | – | N | – | – |
| Thomas More College | KY | 16 | N* | N | – | – | – | – | – |
| Tiffin University | OH | 11 | – | – | – | P | – | – | – |
| Tompkins Cortland Cmty College | NY | 26 | – | N | N | N | N | N* | – |
| Touro College | NY | 11 | – | – | – | – | N | N | – |
| Towson University | MD | 9 | N* | – | – | N* | – | – | – |
| Treasure Valley Cmty College | OR | 26 | – | – | N | – | – | – | – |
| Trinity (Washington) University | DC | 16 | – | – | N | P | N | – | – |
| Trinity Christian College | IL | 12 | – | – | N | N | N | N | N* |
| Trinity College | CT | 14 | – | – | – | – | – | – | N |
| Trinity College of Vermont | VT | 16 | N | – | N | – | – | – | – |
| Trinity International University | IL | 22 | – | – | N | N | – | – | – |
| Trinity University | TX | 23 | – | – | – | – | – | N | N |
| Trinity Western University | BC | 24 | – | – | – | – | – | P | – |
| Troy U in Montgomery | AL | 10 | – | – | – | – | N | – | – |
| Truett McConnell College | GA | 32 | – | – | – | N | – | – | – |
| Truman State University | MO | 9 | N | N | N | N | N | N | N |
| Tufts University | MA | 6 | – | – | – | – | N* | N | N |
| Tulane University | LA | 5 | – | – | – | – | P* | – | – |

P—Participated    N—Participated and included in National Norms    *—Supplemental Sample

Table C3 (continued)

Participation History

| Institution | State | Strat | 1989 | 1992 | 1995 | 1998 | 2001 | 2004 | 2007 |
|---|---|---|---|---|---|---|---|---|---|
| Tunxis Cmty College | CT | 27 | N | – | – | – | – | – | – |
| Tusculum College | TN | 11 | N | – | – | – | – | – | – |
| Tuskegee University | AL | 35 | N | – | N | P* | – | P* | – |
| U of Akron | OH | 1 | N | – | – | – | – | – | – |
| U of Alabama | AL | 2 | – | – | – | – | N | P | P |
| U of Alabama-Birmingham | AL | 1 | – | – | N | – | – | – | – |
| U of Alabama-Huntsville | AL | 2 | P* | – | N | – | – | – | – |
| U of Alaska-Fairbanks | AK | 1 | – | – | – | – | – | N | – |
| U of Arizona | AZ | 2 | N | – | P* | N | N | – | – |
| U of Arkansas-Fayetteville | AR | 2 | – | N | – | – | – | N* | – |
| U of Arkansas-Little Rock | AR | 7 | – | – | N | – | P | P* | P |
| U of Arkansas-Pine Bluff | AR | 34 | – | – | – | N* | – | – | – |
| U of Bridgeport | CT | 11 | N* | – | – | – | – | – | – |
| U of California-Berkeley | CA | 3 | P* | – | N* | – | – | – | – |
| U of California-Davis | CA | 3 | N | – | N | – | – | – | – |
| U of California-Irvine | CA | 3 | P* | – | – | – | – | N* | N* |
| U of California-Los Angeles | CA | 3 | N | – | P | N | P* | P | P |
| U of California-Riverside | CA | 1 | N | – | – | – | – | – | – |
| U of California-Santa Cruz | CA | 3 | P* | – | – | – | – | – | – |
| U of Central Arkansas | AR | 9 | – | – | – | N | – | – | – |
| U of Central Missouri | MO | 9 | N | N | N | N | – | N | N |
| U of Central Oklahoma | OK | 8 | – | – | – | – | – | N | N |
| U of Charleston | WV | 11 | – | N | N | N | – | – | – |
| U of Chicago | IL | 6 | – | – | P* | – | P* | P* | – |
| U of Cincinnati | OH | 2 | – | – | – | – | – | – | N |
| U of Colorado-Colorado Springs | CO | 2 | – | – | N | N | N | – | N |
| U of Colorado-Denver | CO | 1 | – | – | – | – | – | P | N* |
| U of Connecticut | CT | 2 | – | – | – | N | – | N | N* |
| U of Connecticut-Waterbury | CT | 27 | P | – | – | – | – | – | – |
| U of Dayton | OH | 18 | – | – | N | – | – | – | – |
| U of Delaware | DE | 3 | P* | N | – | – | – | – | – |
| U of Detroit Mercy | MI | 17 | – | – | N | – | – | N | N |
| U of Dubuque | IA | 22 | – | – | – | – | – | – | N |
| U of Evansville | IN | 23 | – | – | N | – | – | – | – |
| U of Findlay | OH | 21 | N* | N | – | – | – | N | N* |
| U of Florida | FL | 3 | – | – | – | – | N* | – | – |
| U of Guam | GU | 10 | N | – | – | – | N | – | – |
| U of Hartford | CT | 12 | P* | – | – | – | – | – | – |
| U of Hawaii-Hilo | HI | 7 | – | – | – | – | N | – | – |
| U of Hawaii-Manoa | HI | 1 | N | – | – | – | – | – | – |
| U of Idaho | ID | 2 | N | – | – | N | N | N | N |
| U of Illinois-Chicago | IL | 9 | N | P | – | – | – | P* | – |
| U of Illinois-Urbana-Champaign | IL | 3 | – | – | – | – | P | – | – |
| U of Indianapolis | IN | 21 | N | – | – | N | – | – | N |
| U of Kentucky | KY | 1 | – | – | – | – | – | P* | – |
| U of La Verne | CA | 11 | – | N | – | – | – | N* | – |

P—Participated    N—Participated and included in National Norms    *—Supplemental Sample

Table C3 (continued)

*Participation History*

| Institution | State | Strat | 1989 | 1992 | 1995 | 1998 | 2001 | 2004 | 2007 |
|---|---|---|---|---|---|---|---|---|---|
| U of Louisiana at Lafayette | LA | 7 | – | – | – | – | – | N | N* |
| U of Louisville | KY | 2 | P* | – | – | N* | – | – | – |
| U of Maine-Farmington | ME | 8 | – | N | N | – | – | – | – |
| U of Maine-Fort Kent | ME | 7 | – | N | – | – | – | – | – |
| U of Maine-Presque Isle | ME | 7 | – | – | – | N | – | P* | – |
| U of Mary | ND | 17 | N | – | – | – | – | – | – |
| U of Mary Hardin-Baylor | TX | 21 | – | – | – | – | – | N | N* |
| U of Maryland College Park | MD | 3 | – | N | N* | – | – | – | – |
| U of Maryland Eastern Shore | MD | 34 | – | N | – | – | – | – | – |
| U of Massachusetts-Amherst | MA | 3 | N | – | – | N | – | – | – |
| U of Massachusetts-Boston | MA | 1 | N | – | – | – | – | – | – |
| U of Massachusetts-Dartmouth | MA | 8 | – | – | – | – | – | N | N* |
| U of Miami | FL | 5 | P* | – | N* | – | N* | – | – |
| U of Michigan | MI | 3 | – | – | P* | – | P* | P* | N* |
| U of Michigan-Dearborn | MI | 9 | P | N | – | – | N | N | N* |
| U of Minnesota-Crookston | MN | 27 | – | – | – | N | – | – | – |
| U of Minnesota-Duluth | MN | 1 | P | – | – | – | – | – | – |
| U of Minnesota-Morris | MN | 9 | – | – | – | – | – | N | N* |
| U of Minnesota-Twin Cities | MN | 3 | – | – | P* | – | – | – | – |
| U of Mississippi | MS | 1 | N | – | – | – | – | – | – |
| U of Missouri-Columbia | MO | 3 | – | – | N | N* | – | – | – |
| U of Missouri-Kansas City | MO | 3 | – | – | – | N | – | N | N* |
| U of Montana | MT | 1 | – | – | N | – | N | N | N* |
| U of Montevallo | AL | 8 | – | N | – | N | – | N | N |
| U of Nebraska-Kearney | NE | 8 | – | – | – | N | N | N | N* |
| U of Nebraska-Omaha | NE | 8 | N | – | – | – | N | N | N |
| U of Nevada-Las Vegas | NV | 8 | – | – | N | P | – | – | – |
| U of New England | ME | 17 | N | – | P | – | – | – | – |
| U of New Mexico | NM | 1 | N | – | N | – | N* | N* | – |
| U of North Carolina-Asheville | NC | 9 | – | N | – | N | N | N | N |
| U of North Carolina-Chapel Hill | NC | 3 | P* | – | N* | N | – | N* | N* |
| U of North Carolina-Charlotte | NC | 1 | – | – | – | N | P | N | N |
| U of North Carolina-Greensboro | NC | 8 | – | – | N | – | – | – | – |
| U of North Carolina-Wilmington | NC | 9 | – | – | – | N | – | – | N |
| U of North Dakota | ND | 1 | – | N | – | – | N | N | N |
| U of North Florida | FL | 9 | – | – | – | – | P | – | – |
| U of North Texas | TX | 1 | – | – | – | – | N | N | – |
| U of Northern Colorado | CO | 8 | – | – | N | – | – | – | N |
| U of Notre Dame | IN | 6 | P* | – | N* | N* | N | – | – |
| U of Oregon | OR | 2 | – | – | N | – | N* | N | N* |
| U of Pennsylvania | PA | 6 | – | – | P* | – | P* | P* | – |
| U of Pittsburgh | PA | 3 | – | – | P* | – | – | P* | N* |
| U of Pittsburgh-Bradford | PA | 7 | – | N | N | – | – | N | N* |
| U of Pittsburgh-Greensburg | PA | 8 | N | – | – | – | – | – | – |
| U of Pittsburgh-Johnstown | PA | 8 | – | – | – | N* | – | – | – |
| U of Portland | OR | 18 | – | – | N | – | N* | N | N |

P—Participated   N—Participated and included in National Norms   *—Supplemental Sample

254

| Institution | State | Strat | 1989 | 1992 | 1995 | 1998 | 2001 | 2004 | 2007 |
|---|---|---|---|---|---|---|---|---|---|
| U of Puerto Rico-Rio Piedras | PR | 1 | – | P | – | – | – | – | – |
| U of Puget Sound | WA | 13 | – | – | N | N | N | N | N |
| U of Redlands | CA | 13 | P* | – | – | – | N | – | – |
| U of Richmond | VA | 14 | N | N | – | N | N | P* | – |
| U of Rio Grande | OH | 12 | – | N | N | N | – | – | – |
| U of Rochester | NY | 6 | N | – | N* | – | – | – | – |
| U of Saint Mary | KS | 17 | N | N | – | – | – | – | – |
| U of Saint Thomas | MN | 18 | – | N | – | N | N | N | N* |
| U of San Diego | CA | 5 | N* | N | N | N | – | N | – |
| U of San Francisco | CA | 18 | – | N | – | P | – | N | P |
| U of Science and Arts of Oklahoma | OK | 8 | – | N | – | N | N | – | – |
| U of Scranton | PA | 18 | – | N | N | N | N | N | N* |
| U of Sioux Falls | SD | 22 | – | – | N | N | – | – | – |
| U of South Alabama | AL | 9 | – | N | N | N | – | – | – |
| U of South Carolina-Aiken | SC | 8 | – | – | – | – | – | N | N* |
| U of South Carolina-Beaufort | SC | 25 | – | – | – | – | – | N* | – |
| U of South Carolina-Columbia | SC | 2 | – | – | – | N* | – | – | – |
| U of South Carolina-Sumter | SC | 26 | N | – | – | – | – | – | – |
| U of South Carolina-Union | SC | 25 | N | – | – | – | – | P* | – |
| U of South Carolina-Upstate | SC | 7 | N | N | – | – | – | N | N* |
| U of South Dakota | SD | 1 | – | N | P | – | – | – | – |
| U of South Florida | FL | 9 | N | – | – | – | P | – | – |
| U of Southern California | CA | 6 | – | – | P* | – | P* | P* | – |
| U of Southern Indiana | IN | 1 | – | – | – | – | N | N | N* |
| U of Southern Mississippi | MS | 8 | – | N | – | – | N | – | – |
| U of Tennessee-Chattanooga | TN | 8 | – | N | N | – | – | N | N* |
| U of Tennessee-Knoxville | TN | 2 | N | – | – | N* | – | – | – |
| U of Texas-Arlington | TX | 8 | – | – | – | N | – | – | – |
| U of Texas-Austin | TX | 3 | – | – | N* | – | – | – | – |
| U of Texas-El Paso | TX | 1 | – | P | N | – | P | – | – |
| U of Texas-Pan American | TX | 8 | – | – | P | – | – | – | – |
| U of Texas-San Antonio | TX | 8 | – | P | – | – | – | – | – |
| U of the Ozarks | AR | 20 | – | N | N | – | – | – | – |
| U of the Pacific | CA | 4 | – | – | – | – | – | N | P |
| U of the Sciences in Philadelphia | PA | 13 | – | – | N | N | N | N | N |
| U of the South | TN | 23 | – | N | – | N | N | N | N |
| U of the Virgin Islands | VI | 34 | – | P | – | – | – | N | N* |
| U of Toledo | OH | 1 | N | – | – | – | – | N* | – |
| U of Utah | UT | 2 | N | – | – | – | – | – | – |
| U of Vermont | VT | 3 | – | – | – | N* | – | – | – |
| U of Virginia | VA | 3 | – | – | N* | N* | – | N* | N* |
| U of Virginia College at Wise | VA | 7 | N | – | N | – | N | – | – |
| U of West Alabama | AL | 7 | N | – | – | – | – | – | – |
| U of Wisconsin-Green Bay | WI | 9 | – | – | – | – | – | N | N |
| U of Wisconsin-Madison | WI | 3 | – | – | N* | – | N* | – | – |
| U of Wisconsin-Milwaukee | WI | 1 | P* | – | – | – | – | – | – |

P—Participated   N—Participated and included in National Norms   *—Supplemental Sample

Table C3 (continued)
*Participation History*

| Institution | State | Strat | 1989 | 1992 | 1995 | 1998 | 2001 | 2004 | 2007 |
|---|---|---|---|---|---|---|---|---|---|
| U of Wisconsin-Parkside | WI | 8 | N | – | – | N | – | – | – |
| U of Wisconsin-River Falls | WI | 9 | – | – | N | – | – | – | – |
| U of Wisconsin-Stevens Point | WI | 8 | N | – | – | – | – | N | N* |
| U of Wisconsin-Stout | WI | 8 | – | – | N | – | N | N | N |
| Ulster County Cmty College | NY | 28 | – | N | – | – | N | – | – |
| Umpqua Cmty College | OR | 28 | – | – | – | N | – | – | – |
| Union College | NY | 13 | – | – | N | – | N | P | N |
| Union University | TN | 23 | – | N | – | N | – | N | P |
| University of Mobile | AL | 22 | – | – | – | – | – | – | N |
| University of Saint Francis | IL | 17 | – | – | – | – | – | N | N* |
| University of the Incarnate Word | TX | 16 | P | – | N | N | – | – | – |
| University of Wisconsin Colleges | WI | 29 | N | – | – | – | N | N | N* |
| Ursinus College | PA | 13 | N | – | – | N | N | N | N |
| Ursuline College | OH | 17 | N | – | N | – | – | N | N* |
| US Air Force Academy | CO | 9 | P* | – | – | P* | P | – | – |
| US Coast Guard Academy | CT | 9 | – | – | N | – | – | N | N* |
| US Military Academy | NY | 9 | – | N | N | N* | P | – | – |
| US Naval Academy | MD | 9 | P* | – | – | N | N | N | – |
| Utah State University | UT | 2 | – | – | N | – | N | N | N |
| Utah Valley State College | UT | 29 | – | – | – | – | – | – | N |
| Utica College of Syracuse U | NY | 11 | – | – | – | – | N | – | – |
| Valley City State University | ND | 8 | N | – | – | – | N | N | N |
| Valley Forge Christian College | PA | 24 | – | – | – | – | – | N | N* |
| Valley Forge Military College | PA | 31 | – | – | N | N | – | P* | – |
| Valparaiso University | IN | 23 | N | – | – | – | N | N | P |
| Vanderbilt University | TN | 6 | P* | – | N* | – | N* | – | – |
| Vanguard U of Southern California | CA | 20 | N | – | N | N | – | – | – |
| Vassar College | NY | 14 | – | – | – | – | N | N | N |
| Vaughn Coll of Aeronautics & Tech | NY | 11 | – | – | – | – | P | P | P |
| Vermont Technical College | VT | 27 | – | – | N | – | – | – | – |
| Villa Julie College | MD | 12 | – | – | – | – | – | N | N |
| Villa Maria College of Buffalo | NY | 16 | – | – | – | – | – | N* | – |
| Villanova University | PA | 5 | P | – | – | – | – | N | N |
| Virginia Commonwealth University | VA | 1 | – | – | – | – | N | – | – |
| Virginia Polytechnic Inst and St U | VA | 3 | P* | – | N* | N* | – | – | – |
| Virginia State University | VA | 34 | N | – | – | – | – | – | – |
| Virginia Wesleyan College | VA | 23 | N | N | N | – | N | N | N* |
| Viterbo University | WI | 17 | – | – | – | – | – | N | N* |
| Wagner College | NY | 22 | – | – | – | – | – | P | – |
| Wake Forest University | NC | 5 | – | – | – | N | N | N | N |
| Waldorf College | IA | 32 | N | – | – | – | – | – | – |
| Walsh University | OH | 17 | N* | – | – | – | – | – | N |
| Warner Southern College | FL | 11 | – | – | N | N | – | – | – |
| Wartburg College | IA | 22 | – | – | – | – | N | N | N |
| Washburn University | KS | 8 | – | – | N | – | N | N | N* |
| Washington and Lee University | VA | 14 | – | – | – | N | – | N | N |

P—Participated    N—Participated and included in National Norms    *—Supplemental Sample

| Institution | State | Strat | 1989 | 1992 | 1995 | 1998 | 2001 | 2004 | 2007 |
|---|---|---|---|---|---|---|---|---|---|
| Washington College | MD | 13 | N | – | – | N | – | N | N* |
| Washington State Cmty College | OH | 26 | – | N | – | – | – | – | – |
| Washington State University | WA | 1 | – | – | N | – | – | – | – |
| Wayland Baptist University | TX | 20 | – | – | N | – | N | – | – |
| Wayne State College | NE | 8 | – | N | N | – | N | – | – |
| Wayne State University | MI | 1 | – | – | – | P | N | N | N* |
| Waynesburg University | PA | 21 | N | – | N | – | – | – | – |
| Webb Institute | NY | 14 | – | – | – | – | N | N | N* |
| Weber State University | UT | 8 | – | N | – | – | – | N | – |
| Webster University | MO | 13 | – | – | N | – | N | N | N* |
| Wellesley College | MA | 14 | – | – | – | N | – | P* | – |
| Wells College | NY | 13 | – | – | N | – | – | – | – |
| Wentworth Institute of Technology | MA | 11 | P | – | – | – | – | P* | – |
| Wesleyan College | GA | 23 | N* | – | – | – | – | N | N* |
| Wesleyan University | CT | 14 | N | N | – | N* | – | – | – |
| West Chester U of Pennsylvania | PA | 8 | N | N | P | – | – | – | – |
| West Liberty State College | WV | 7 | – | – | – | N | – | – | – |
| West Texas A & M University | TX | 9 | – | N | – | N | – | N | N |
| West Virginia University | WV | 1 | – | N | – | – | – | – | – |
| West Virginia U-Parkersburg | WV | 28 | N | – | N | – | N* | – | – |
| West Virginia Wesleyan College | WV | 21 | – | N | – | – | – | – | – |
| Westchester Cmty College | NY | 29 | N | N | P | N | N | – | – |
| Western Carolina University | NC | 8 | N | N | – | – | – | – | – |
| Western Connecticut State U | CT | 7 | – | N | – | P | – | P* | – |
| Western Illinois University | IL | 8 | – | – | – | – | – | N | N* |
| Western Kentucky University | KY | 8 | – | – | N | – | – | – | – |
| Western Nebraska Cmty College | NE | 26 | N | – | – | – | – | – | – |
| Western New England College | MA | 12 | N | – | – | P | P | N | N* |
| Western New Mexico University | NM | 7 | – | – | N | N | N | – | – |
| Western Oregon University | OR | 8 | – | – | N | – | – | – | – |
| Western State College of Colorado | CO | 7 | – | – | – | N | – | – | – |
| Westminster College | MO | 23 | N | – | N | – | N | – | – |
| Westminster College | PA | 22 | – | – | N | – | – | – | – |
| Westmont College | CA | 13 | N | N | – | N | N | N | N* |
| Westmoreland County Cmty College | PA | 28 | – | – | – | – | N | – | – |
| Wheaton College | IL | 14 | N | N | N | N | N | – | – |
| Wheaton College | MA | 13 | N | – | N | N | N | N | N |
| Wheeling Jesuit University | WV | 17 | P* | – | N | N | N | – | – |
| Wheelock College | MA | 12 | – | – | – | – | – | N | N* |
| Whitman College | WA | 14 | – | N | N | N | N | N | N* |
| Whitworth University | WA | 23 | – | – | N | N | N | N | N |
| Widener University | PA | 13 | – | – | – | – | – | – | N |
| Wilbur Wright College | IL | 28 | N | – | – | – | N | N | N* |
| Willamette University | OR | 13 | – | – | – | – | N | N | – |
| William Jewell College | MO | 23 | N | – | N | – | – | – | N |
| William Paterson U of New Jersey | NJ | 8 | – | – | N | N | N | – | – |

P—Participated   N—Participated and included in National Norms   *—Supplemental Sample

Table C3 (continued)

*Participation History*

| Institution | State | Strat | 1989 | 1992 | 1995 | 1998 | 2001 | 2004 | 2007 |
|---|---|---|---|---|---|---|---|---|---|
| William Rainey Harper College | IL | 27 | N | N | P | – | N | – | – |
| Williams Baptist College | AR | 21 | – | – | N | – | – | – | – |
| Williams College | MA | 14 | N | – | – | – | – | N | N |
| Williston State College | ND | 26 | – | – | – | – | N | N | N |
| Wilmington College | OH | 21 | – | N | N | – | N | – | – |
| Wilson College | PA | 12 | – | – | – | – | – | N | N |
| Wingate University | NC | 11 | – | – | N | – | – | – | – |
| Winston-Salem State University | NC | 34 | N | – | – | – | – | P* | – |
| Winthrop University | SC | 8 | – | – | N | – | – | – | – |
| Wisconsin Lutheran College | WI | 23 | – | – | N | – | – | – | – |
| Wittenberg University | OH | 23 | – | – | – | – | – | N | N* |
| Wofford College | SC | 23 | N | N | – | – | – | – | – |
| Woodbury University | CA | 11 | P* | N | N | N | – | – | – |
| Worcester Polytechnic Institute | MA | 14 | – | N | – | N | – | – | – |
| Worcester State College | MA | 7 | – | – | – | P | N | N | N* |
| WVU Institute of Technology | WV | 7 | – | N | N | – | – | – | – |
| Xavier University | OH | 18 | N* | – | – | N | – | – | – |
| Youngstown State University | OH | 8 | – | – | – | – | – | N | – |

P—Participated    N—Participated and included in National Norms    *—Supplemental Sample

# Appendix D

# The Precision of the
# Normative Data and Their Comparisons

# The Precision of the
# Normative Data and Their Comparisons

A common question asked about sample surveys relates to the precision of the data, which is typically reported as the accuracy of a percentage "plus or minus x percentage points." This figure, which is known as a confidence interval, can be estimated for items of interest if one knows the response percentage and its standard error.

Given the Faculty Survey's large normative sample, the calculated standard error associated with any particular response percentage will be small (as will its confidence interval). It is important to note, however, that traditional methods of calculating standard error assume conditions which, (as is the case with most real sample survey data), do not apply here. Moreover, there are other possible sources of error which should be considered in comparing data across normative groups, across related item categories, and over time. In reference to the precision of the Faculty Survey data, these concerns include:

1) Traditional methods of calculating standard error assume that the <u>individuals</u> were selected through simple random sampling. Given the complex stratified design of the Faculty Survey, where whole <u>institutions</u> participate, it is likely that the actual standard errors will be somewhat larger than the standard error estimates produced through traditional computational methods. In addition, while every effort has been made to maximize the comparability of the institutional sample from year to year (repeat participation runs about 90 percent), comparability is reduced by non-repeat participation and year-to-year variation in the quality of data collected by continuing institutional participants. While the Faculty Survey stratification and weighting procedures are designed to minimize this institutional form of "response bias," an unknown amount of non-random variation is introduced into the results.

2) The wording of some questions in the survey instrument, the text and number of response options, and their order of presentation have changed over the years. We have found that even small changes can produce large order and context effects. Given this, the *exact* wording and order of items on the survey instrument (which is produced as Appendix B) should be examined carefully prior to making comparisons across survey years.

3) Substantial changes in the institutional stratification scheme were made in 1968, 1971, 1975 and 2000. These changes resulted in a revision of the weights applied to individual institutions between 1966 and 2007. Stratification cell assignments of a few institutions may also change from time to time, but the scale of these changes and their effect on the national normative results are likely to be small in comparison to other sources of bias.

Since it is impractical to report statistical indicators for every percentage in every Faculty Survey norms group, it is important for those who are interested to be able to estimate the precision of the data. Toward this end, Table E1 provides estimates of standard errors for norms groups of various sizes and for different percentages[1] which can be used to derive confidence interval estimates.

For example, suppose the item we are interested in has a response percentage of 18.7 percent among faculty at all nonsectarian four-year colleges (a normative group that is 5,005 in size). First, we choose the <u>column</u> that is closest to the observed percentage 18.7—in this case "20%."[2] Next, we select the <u>row</u> closest to the unweighted sample size of 5,005—in this case "5,000." With a sample size of about 5,000 and a percentage that is close to 20, the estimated standard error would be .566.

To calculate the confidence interval at the 95% probability level, we multiply the estimated standard error by the critical value of $t$ for the unweighted sample size (which, for all Faculty Survey norms groups, will be equal to 1.96 at the .05 level of probability).[3] In this example, we would multiply the estimated standard error of .566 by 1.96, which yields 1.109. If we round this figure to a single decimal point we would then estimate our confidence interval to be 18.7 ± 1.1. In practical terms, this confidence interval means that if we were to repeatedly replicate this survey using the same sample size but a different random sample, we would expect that the resulting percentage would fall between 17.6 percent and 19.8 percent 95 times out of 100.

Table D1

*Estimated Standard Errors of Percentages for Norms Groups of Various Sizes*

| Unweighted size of norms groups | Percentage | | | | | | | | | | |
|---|---|---|---|---|---|---|---|---|---|---|---|
| | 1% | 5% | 10% | 15% | 20% | 25% | 30% | 35% | 40% | 45% | 50% |
| 250 | .629 | 1.378 | 1.897 | 2.258 | 2.530 | 2.739 | 2.898 | 3.017 | 3.098 | 3.146 | 3.162 |
| 500 | .445 | .975 | 1.342 | 1.597 | 1.789 | 1.936 | 2.049 | 2.133 | 2.191 | 2.225 | 2.236 |
| 1,000 | .315 | .689 | .949 | 1.129 | 1.265 | 1.369 | 1.449 | 1.508 | 1.549 | 1.573 | 1.581 |
| 3,000 | .183 | .398 | .548 | .652 | .730 | .791 | .837 | .871 | .894 | .908 | .913 |
| 4,000 | .157 | .345 | .440 | .565 | .632 | .685 | .725 | .754 | .775 | .787 | .791 |
| 5,000 | .141 | .308 | .424 | .505 | .566 | .612 | .648 | .675 | .693 | .704 | .707 |
| 10,000 | .099 | .218 | .300 | .357 | .400 | .433 | .458 | .477 | .490 | .497 | .500 |
| 12,500 | .089 | .195 | .268 | .319 | .358 | .387 | .410 | .427 | .438 | .445 | .447 |
| 22,500 | .066 | .145 | .200 | .238 | .267 | .289 | .306 | .318 | .327 | .332 | .333 |

Note: Assumes simple random sampling.

---

[1]Calculated by $\sqrt{\frac{x\%(100-x\%)}{N}}$, where x is the percentage of interest and N is the population count from Table A3, column 2.

[2]Since the distribution of the standard errors is symmetrical around the 50 percent mid-point, for percentages over 50 simply subtract the percentage from 100 and use the result to select the appropriate column. For example, if the percentage we were interested in was 59, 100 – 59 percent yields 41, so we would use the column labeled '40%.'

[3]To calculate the confidence interval at the 99% probability level the critical $t$ value is 2.56.

# Appendix E

# Sample Report Furnished to Campuses Participating in the 2007–2008 HERI Faculty Survey

# NOTES ON THE SAMPLE REPORT

The Standard Institutional Profile Report contains up to four subreports depending on the type of respondents received from an institution:

**FULL-TIME UNDERGRADUATE FACULTY.** Faculty determined to be full-time employees that teach undergraduate courses. This subreport also includes two sets of comparison results from the weighted national norms, determined by the institution's control and type.

**PART-TIME UNDERGRADUATE FACULTY.** Faculty determined to be part-time employees that teach undergraduate courses. This subreport also includes two sets of comparison results from the unweighted national aggregates of part-time undergraduate faculty, determined by the institution's control and type.

**FULL-TIME ACADEMIC ADMINISTRATORS.** Respondents determined to be full-time employees whose principal activity is administration. This subreport also includes two sets of comparison results from the unweighted national aggregates of full-time academic faculty, determined by the institution's control and type.

**ALL RESPONDENTS.** Compares the responses of the three respondent types listed above, as well as "Graduate-only faculty" (faculty who teach at the graduate level only), and "Others" (respondents who fit in no other group). The results in this subreport apply only to the institution.

| Whatsamatta University<br>Full-time Undergraduate Faculty | # Respon-dents | Your Institution | | | Nonsect 4-yr Colls | | | All Priv 4-yr Colls | | |
|---|---|---|---|---|---|---|---|---|---|---|
| | | Men | Women | Total | Men | Women | Total | Men | Women | Total |
| **Number of Respondents** | 648 | 59.1 | 40.9 | 100.0 | 58.1 | 41.9 | 100.0 | 57.1 | 42.9 | 100.0 |
| **What is your principal activity in your current position at this institution?** | 647 | | | | | | | | | |
|   Administration | | 7.6 | 10.6 | 8.8 | 4.7 | 4.6 | 4.6 | 4.8 | 4.8 | 4.8 |
|   Teaching | | 82.0 | 83.7 | 82.7 | 93.7 | 93.3 | 93.5 | 93.6 | 92.9 | 93.3 |
|   Research | | 8.4 | 3.8 | 6.5 | 0.8 | 0.6 | 0.7 | 0.5 | 0.4 | 0.4 |
|   Services to clients and patients | | 1.0 | 1.1 | 1.1 | 0.3 | 0.2 | 0.2 | 0.6 | 0.9 | 0.7 |
|   Other | | 1.0 | 0.8 | 0.9 | 0.6 | 1.4 | 0.9 | 0.6 | 1.0 | 0.8 |
| **What is your present academic rank?** | 645 | | | | | | | | | |
|   Professor | | 25.7 | 15.2 | 21.4 | 35.9 | 21.4 | 29.8 | 34.7 | 19.6 | 28.2 |
|   Associate Professor | | 40.4 | 33.7 | 37.7 | 26.4 | 27.0 | 26.7 | 28.1 | 27.8 | 28.0 |
|   Assistant Professor | | 28.3 | 37.5 | 32.1 | 25.3 | 35.1 | 29.4 | 27.0 | 37.4 | 31.5 |
|   Lecturer | | 1.6 | 3.8 | 2.5 | 5.7 | 4.6 | 5.2 | 3.4 | 3.5 | 3.4 |
|   Instructor | | 3.9 | 9.8 | 6.4 | 6.8 | 11.8 | 8.9 | 6.7 | 11.7 | 8.9 |
| **What is your tenure status at this institution?** | 648 | | | | | | | | | |
|   Tenured | | 59.3 | 42.6 | 52.5 | 49.0 | 41.6 | 45.9 | 50.4 | 39.8 | 45.8 |
|   On tenure track, but not tenured | | 28.5 | 32.5 | 30.1 | 20.7 | 26.3 | 23.0 | 22.1 | 27.3 | 24.3 |
|   Not on tenure track, but institution<br>    has tenure system | | 12.0 | 23.8 | 16.8 | 17.4 | 21.3 | 19.0 | 15.6 | 21.7 | 18.2 |
|   Institution has no tenure system | | 0.3 | 1.1 | 0.6 | 13.0 | 10.9 | 12.1 | 12.0 | 11.2 | 11.6 |
| **Are you currently serving in an administrative position as: [1]** | 648 | | | | | | | | | |
|   Department Chair | | 12.3 | 7.5 | 10.3 | 21.0 | 17.3 | 19.4 | 21.1 | 16.4 | 19.1 |
|   Dean (Associate or Assistant) | | 3.7 | 2.6 | 3.2 | 1.2 | 0.7 | 1.0 | 2.1 | 1.1 | 1.7 |
|   President | | 0.0 | 0.4 | 0.2 | 0.0 | 0.0 | 0.0 | 0.0 | 0.0 | 0.0 |
|   Vice-President | | 0.0 | 0.0 | 0.0 | 0.9 | 0.0 | 0.5 | 0.6 | 0.0 | 0.4 |
|   Provost | | 0.0 | 0.0 | 0.0 | 0.4 | 0.0 | 0.2 | 0.2 | 0.0 | 0.1 |
|   Other | | 14.4 | 21.9 | 17.4 | 14.2 | 14.5 | 14.3 | 13.7 | 16.0 | 14.7 |
|   Not Applicable | | 64.2 | 61.1 | 63.0 | 57.2 | 62.5 | 59.5 | 57.3 | 62.5 | 59.5 |
| **My primary place of employment in the last year was: [2]** | 647 | | | | | | | | | |
|   In higher education: | | | | | | | | | | |
|     at this institution | | 94.5 | 92.5 | 93.7 | 93.7 | 92.5 | 93.2 | 93.9 | 93.2 | 93.6 |
|     at a different institution | | 3.4 | 3.4 | 3.4 | 2.7 | 3.3 | 2.9 | 2.8 | 3.2 | 3.0 |
|     at more than one institution | | 1.0 | 1.9 | 1.4 | 1.1 | 2.5 | 1.7 | 1.3 | 1.7 | 1.5 |
|   Not in higher education | | 0.3 | 1.5 | 0.8 | 2.3 | 1.1 | 1.8 | 1.8 | 1.2 | 1.5 |
|   Not employed | | 0.8 | 0.8 | 0.8 | 0.3 | 0.7 | 0.5 | 0.2 | 0.6 | 0.4 |
| **Noted as being personally "very important" or "essential": [2]** | | | | | | | | | | |
|   Research | 647 | 83.3 | 78.0 | 81.1 | 69.3 | 62.7 | 66.5 | 64.1 | 60.1 | 62.4 |
|   Teaching | 647 | 97.9 | 97.7 | 97.8 | 98.7 | 98.8 | 98.7 | 98.9 | 99.0 | 98.9 |
|   Service | 647 | 67.1 | 72.0 | 69.1 | 63.9 | 73.2 | 67.8 | 65.2 | 75.0 | 69.4 |

[1] Response options changed from earlier Faculty Surveys.
[2] This question asked for the first time in the 2007–2008 Faculty Survey.

| Whatsamatta University<br>Full-time Undergraduate Faculty | # Respon-dents | Your Institution | | | Nonsect 4-yr Colls | | | All Priv 4-yr Colls | | |
|---|---|---|---|---|---|---|---|---|---|---|
| | | Men | Women | Total | Men | Women | Total | Men | Women | Total |
| **Highest degree earned** | 647 | | | | | | | | | |
| Bachelor's (B.A., B.S., etc.) | | 1.3 | 1.5 | 1.4 | 1.1 | 0.8 | 1.0 | 0.7 | 0.7 | 0.7 |
| Master's (M.A., M.S., M.F.A., M.B.A., etc.) | | 12.3 | 22.3 | 16.4 | 20.6 | 26.9 | 23.3 | 20.1 | 30.2 | 24.4 |
| LL.B., J.D. | | 1.6 | 3.8 | 2.5 | 0.6 | 1.5 | 1.0 | 0.8 | 1.2 | 1.0 |
| M.D., D.D.S. (or equivalent) | | 0.8 | 1.1 | 0.9 | 0.5 | 1.6 | 1.0 | 0.6 | 0.9 | 0.7 |
| Other first professional degree beyond B.A. (e.g., D.D., D.V.M.) | | 0.5 | 0.8 | 0.6 | 2.9 | 1.6 | 2.3 | 1.7 | 1.0 | 1.4 |
| Ed.D. | | 3.1 | 4.9 | 3.9 | 2.2 | 6.1 | 3.8 | 2.9 | 6.3 | 4.4 |
| Ph.D. | | 77.3 | 61.7 | 70.9 | 70.1 | 59.0 | 65.4 | 70.6 | 57.0 | 64.7 |
| Other degree | | 2.9 | 3.0 | 2.9 | 1.9 | 2.1 | 2.0 | 2.4 | 2.4 | 2.4 |
| None | | 0.3 | 0.8 | 0.5 | 0.1 | 0.4 | 0.2 | 0.2 | 0.4 | 0.2 |
| **Degree currently working on** | 525 | | | | | | | | | |
| Bachelor's (B.A., B.S., etc.) | | 0.3 | 0.0 | 0.2 | 0.0 | 0.0 | 0.0 | 0.0 | 0.1 | 0.1 |
| Master's (M.A., M.S., M.F.A., M.B.A., etc.) | | 1.6 | 1.8 | 1.7 | 0.7 | 0.7 | 0.7 | 0.7 | 1.0 | 0.8 |
| LL.B., J.D. | | 0.3 | 0.5 | 0.4 | 0.0 | 0.6 | 0.3 | 0.0 | 0.3 | 0.2 |
| M.D., D.D.S. (or equivalent) | | 0.0 | 0.0 | 0.0 | 0.0 | 0.0 | 0.0 | 0.0 | 0.0 | 0.0 |
| Other first professional degree beyond B.A. (e.g., D.D., D.V.M.) | | 0.0 | 0.0 | 0.0 | 0.0 | 0.0 | 0.0 | 0.0 | 0.0 | 0.0 |
| Ed.D. | | 0.3 | 4.1 | 1.9 | 1.9 | 1.8 | 1.9 | 1.4 | 1.9 | 1.6 |
| Ph.D. | | 4.9 | 6.0 | 5.3 | 4.2 | 7.8 | 5.7 | 5.4 | 8.6 | 6.8 |
| Other degree | | 1.0 | 3.2 | 1.9 | 0.5 | 0.9 | 0.6 | 0.8 | 1.4 | 1.0 |
| None | | 91.5 | 84.4 | 88.6 | 92.6 | 88.1 | 90.7 | 91.5 | 86.7 | 89.5 |
| **During the past two years, have you engaged in any of the following activities?** | | | | | | | | | | |
| Taught an honors course | 644 | 22.1 | 17.4 | 20.2 | 21.3 | 17.9 | 19.9 | 21.8 | 17.0 | 19.7 |
| Taught an interdisciplinary course | 644 | 35.1 | 31.7 | 33.7 | 50.0 | 52.7 | 51.2 | 46.4 | 46.2 | 46.3 |
| Taught an ethnic studies course | 643 | 5.5 | 8.7 | 6.8 | 11.0 | 15.6 | 12.9 | 11.3 | 14.7 | 12.7 |
| Taught a women's studies course | 642 | 3.2 | 12.9 | 7.2 | 3.3 | 18.6 | 9.7 | 3.5 | 17.1 | 9.3 |
| Team-taught a course | 644 | 29.0 | 37.4 | 32.5 | 32.0 | 33.1 | 32.4 | 31.3 | 35.0 | 32.9 |
| Taught a service learning course | 643 | 14.8 | 19.7 | 16.8 | 16.3 | 25.6 | 20.2 | 17.4 | 25.3 | 20.7 |
| Placed or collected assignments on the Internet | 646 | 69.6 | 81.4 | 74.5 | 73.1 | 74.5 | 73.7 | 72.0 | 75.1 | 73.4 |
| Taught a course exclusively on the Internet | 640 | 10.6 | 11.1 | 10.8 | 7.7 | 7.7 | 7.7 | 8.5 | 10.5 | 9.3 |
| Participated in a teaching enhancement workshop | 644 | 46.2 | 67.2 | 54.8 | 51.7 | 71.5 | 60.0 | 55.8 | 71.9 | 62.7 |
| Advised student groups involved in service/volunteer work | 645 | 38.1 | 43.6 | 40.3 | 41.5 | 52.8 | 46.2 | 43.8 | 52.5 | 47.5 |
| Collaborated with the local community in research/teaching | 643 | 35.7 | 47.3 | 40.4 | 40.3 | 46.6 | 43.0 | 42.9 | 49.5 | 45.7 |
| Developed a new course | 646 | 66.0 | 64.8 | 65.5 | 74.2 | 72.6 | 73.6 | 71.3 | 71.0 | 71.2 |
| Conducted research/writing focused on: | | | | | | | | | | |
| International/global issues | 642 | 27.4 | 28.5 | 27.9 | 30.4 | 31.1 | 30.7 | 29.5 | 25.6 | 27.8 |
| Racial or ethnic minorities | 640 | 17.5 | 28.6 | 22.0 | 20.8 | 26.5 | 23.2 | 19.0 | 23.1 | 20.7 |
| Women and gender issues | 641 | 10.1 | 30.0 | 18.3 | 12.8 | 32.7 | 21.1 | 11.7 | 28.8 | 19.0 |
| Taught a seminar for first-year students | 642 | 23.0 | 21.3 | 22.3 | 30.3 | 33.5 | 31.6 | 29.1 | 31.5 | 30.1 |
| Engaged undergraduates on _your_ research project [2] | 642 | 37.7 | 34.2 | 36.3 | 48.0 | 38.7 | 44.1 | 42.2 | 34.3 | 38.8 |
| Worked with undergraduates on a research project | 643 | 46.7 | 39.8 | 43.9 | 66.3 | 58.1 | 62.9 | 61.0 | 54.2 | 58.1 |

[2] This question asked for the first time in the 2007–2008 Faculty Survey.

| Whatsamatta University<br>Full-time Undergraduate Faculty | # Respon-<br>dents | Your Institution | | | Nonsect 4-yr Colls | | | All Priv 4-yr Colls | | |
|---|---|---|---|---|---|---|---|---|---|---|
| | | Men | Women | Total | Men | Women | Total | Men | Women | Total |
| **DURING THE PRESENT TERM, HOW MANY HOURS PER WEEK ON AVERAGE DO YOU ACTUALLY SPEND ON:** | | | | | | | | | | |
| **Scheduled teaching (actual, not credit hours)** | 648 | | | | | | | | | |
| None | | 0.3 | 0.4 | 0.3 | 0.6 | 0.1 | 0.4 | 0.4 | 0.3 | 0.4 |
| 1 to 4 | | 12.8 | 14.7 | 13.6 | 8.4 | 8.9 | 8.6 | 6.9 | 8.4 | 7.5 |
| 5 to 8 | | 35.5 | 37.4 | 36.3 | 25.0 | 28.3 | 26.4 | 21.8 | 24.3 | 22.9 |
| 9 to 12 | | 36.6 | 32.8 | 35.0 | 40.2 | 40.0 | 40.1 | 42.4 | 41.4 | 42.0 |
| 13 to 16 | | 9.9 | 8.3 | 9.3 | 18.1 | 15.2 | 16.9 | 19.4 | 17.2 | 18.5 |
| 17 to 20 | | 3.1 | 1.9 | 2.6 | 5.1 | 5.4 | 5.2 | 6.2 | 5.5 | 5.9 |
| 21 to 34 | | 1.0 | 2.6 | 1.7 | 2.2 | 1.7 | 2.0 | 2.5 | 2.2 | 2.4 |
| 35 to 44 | | 0.5 | 1.1 | 0.8 | 0.1 | 0.2 | 0.1 | 0.1 | 0.4 | 0.2 |
| 45 + | | 0.3 | 0.8 | 0.5 | 0.4 | 0.2 | 0.3 | 0.2 | 0.3 | 0.3 |
| **Preparing for teaching (including reading student papers and grading)** | 648 | | | | | | | | | |
| None | | 0.3 | 0.4 | 0.3 | 0.5 | 0.4 | 0.4 | 0.3 | 0.2 | 0.3 |
| 1 to 4 | | 12.0 | 6.8 | 9.9 | 8.9 | 4.8 | 7.2 | 7.8 | 5.3 | 6.7 |
| 5 to 8 | | 25.6 | 23.4 | 24.7 | 21.5 | 19.8 | 20.8 | 20.9 | 18.8 | 20.0 |
| 9 to 12 | | 26.4 | 24.2 | 25.5 | 21.2 | 24.1 | 22.4 | 24.1 | 23.4 | 23.8 |
| 13 to 16 | | 16.7 | 17.7 | 17.1 | 17.2 | 15.9 | 16.7 | 17.8 | 16.9 | 17.4 |
| 17 to 20 | | 11.2 | 14.7 | 12.7 | 16.1 | 16.7 | 16.4 | 15.5 | 17.7 | 16.4 |
| 21 to 34 | | 6.3 | 9.4 | 7.6 | 10.9 | 14.6 | 12.4 | 10.3 | 13.3 | 11.6 |
| 35 to 44 | | 0.8 | 2.3 | 1.4 | 2.8 | 2.7 | 2.7 | 2.5 | 3.1 | 2.8 |
| 45 + | | 0.8 | 1.1 | 0.9 | 1.0 | 1.0 | 1.0 | 0.8 | 1.4 | 1.1 |
| **Advising and counseling of students** | 648 | | | | | | | | | |
| None | | 3.1 | 3.4 | 3.2 | 4.4 | 2.1 | 3.5 | 3.7 | 2.4 | 3.1 |
| 1 to 4 | | 53.8 | 55.5 | 54.5 | 57.5 | 50.5 | 54.6 | 58.0 | 50.2 | 54.6 |
| 5 to 8 | | 28.2 | 29.4 | 28.7 | 27.6 | 33.1 | 29.9 | 27.5 | 33.0 | 29.9 |
| 9 to 12 | | 10.2 | 5.3 | 8.2 | 7.8 | 7.8 | 7.8 | 7.7 | 8.9 | 8.2 |
| 13 to 16 | | 2.9 | 4.2 | 3.4 | 2.0 | 4.2 | 2.9 | 1.8 | 3.2 | 2.4 |
| 17 to 20 | | 0.3 | 1.5 | 0.8 | 0.4 | 1.4 | 0.8 | 1.0 | 1.4 | 1.2 |
| 21 to 34 | | 0.5 | 0.8 | 0.6 | 0.2 | 0.1 | 0.1 | 0.3 | 0.3 | 0.3 |
| 35 to 44 | | 0.5 | 0.0 | 0.3 | 0.1 | 0.8 | 0.4 | 0.0 | 0.6 | 0.3 |
| 45 + | | 0.5 | 0.0 | 0.3 | 0.0 | 0.0 | 0.0 | 0.0 | 0.0 | 0.0 |
| **Committee work and meetings** | 648 | | | | | | | | | |
| None | | 5.0 | 4.2 | 4.6 | 7.4 | 2.6 | 5.4 | 6.4 | 2.8 | 4.9 |
| 1 to 4 | | 65.3 | 58.5 | 62.5 | 64.0 | 62.4 | 63.3 | 63.4 | 60.2 | 62.0 |
| 5 to 8 | | 21.4 | 24.9 | 22.8 | 20.7 | 26.4 | 23.1 | 22.6 | 27.4 | 24.6 |
| 9 to 12 | | 5.2 | 7.2 | 6.0 | 5.2 | 5.5 | 5.3 | 5.0 | 6.5 | 5.6 |
| 13 to 16 | | 2.1 | 3.8 | 2.8 | 1.6 | 1.2 | 1.4 | 1.6 | 1.7 | 1.6 |
| 17 to 20 | | 0.3 | 1.1 | 0.6 | 1.0 | 1.5 | 1.2 | 0.8 | 1.0 | 0.9 |
| 21 to 34 | | 0.5 | 0.4 | 0.5 | 0.0 | 0.3 | 0.1 | 0.2 | 0.4 | 0.3 |
| 35 to 44 | | 0.0 | 0.0 | 0.0 | 0.1 | 0.0 | 0.1 | 0.0 | 0.0 | 0.0 |
| 45 + | | 0.3 | 0.0 | 0.2 | 0.0 | 0.1 | 0.0 | 0.0 | 0.1 | 0.1 |
| **Other administration** | 645 | | | | | | | | | |
| None | | 32.1 | 22.3 | 28.1 | 31.1 | 23.3 | 27.8 | 29.5 | 24.8 | 27.5 |
| 1 to 4 | | 38.7 | 42.3 | 40.2 | 40.4 | 46.7 | 43.0 | 41.1 | 43.3 | 42.0 |
| 5 to 8 | | 12.9 | 15.8 | 14.1 | 14.2 | 14.7 | 14.4 | 14.6 | 15.1 | 14.8 |
| 9 to 12 | | 7.6 | 6.8 | 7.3 | 6.0 | 6.9 | 6.4 | 6.4 | 8.1 | 7.1 |
| 13 to 16 | | 2.4 | 4.2 | 3.1 | 4.0 | 3.6 | 3.8 | 3.7 | 3.5 | 3.6 |
| 17 to 20 | | 2.4 | 3.8 | 2.9 | 2.1 | 2.0 | 2.0 | 2.5 | 2.4 | 2.5 |
| 21 to 34 | | 2.6 | 3.4 | 2.9 | 1.7 | 1.7 | 1.7 | 1.6 | 1.8 | 1.7 |
| 35 to 44 | | 0.5 | 1.1 | 0.8 | 0.4 | 1.0 | 0.7 | 0.4 | 0.9 | 0.6 |
| 45 + | | 0.8 | 0.4 | 0.6 | 0.2 | 0.1 | 0.2 | 0.2 | 0.2 | 0.2 |

| Whatsamatta University<br>Full-time Undergraduate Faculty | # Respon-<br>dents | Your Institution | | | Nonsect 4-yr Colls | | | All Priv 4-yr Colls | | |
|---|---|---|---|---|---|---|---|---|---|---|
| | | Men | Women | Total | Men | Women | Total | Men | Women | Total |
| **DURING THE PRESENT TERM, HOW MANY HOURS PER WEEK ON AVERAGE DO YOU ACTUALLY SPEND ON:** | | | | | | | | | | |
| **Research and scholarly writing** | 648 | | | | | | | | | |
| None | | 8.4 | 12.1 | 9.9 | 19.7 | 21.8 | 20.6 | 19.2 | 23.8 | 21.1 |
| 1 to 4 | | 24.5 | 31.7 | 27.5 | 34.2 | 41.7 | 37.4 | 38.9 | 43.5 | 40.9 |
| 5 to 8 | | 18.0 | 24.2 | 20.5 | 24.4 | 21.1 | 23.0 | 22.8 | 18.3 | 20.8 |
| 9 to 12 | | 16.4 | 16.2 | 16.4 | 11.9 | 8.5 | 10.5 | 10.0 | 8.1 | 9.2 |
| 13 to 16 | | 9.4 | 6.4 | 8.2 | 4.1 | 2.9 | 3.6 | 3.9 | 2.6 | 3.4 |
| 17 to 20 | | 11.2 | 4.2 | 8.3 | 3.1 | 2.0 | 2.6 | 3.0 | 2.0 | 2.6 |
| 21 to 34 | | 7.0 | 3.0 | 5.4 | 1.6 | 1.8 | 1.7 | 1.3 | 1.3 | 1.3 |
| 35 to 44 | | 2.9 | 1.1 | 2.2 | 0.6 | 0.2 | 0.4 | 0.6 | 0.2 | 0.4 |
| 45 + | | 2.1 | 1.1 | 1.7 | 0.4 | 0.1 | 0.3 | 0.3 | 0.2 | 0.3 |
| **Other creative products/performances** | 641 | | | | | | | | | |
| None | | 52.0 | 43.6 | 48.5 | 51.7 | 52.3 | 52.0 | 49.9 | 51.7 | 50.7 |
| 1 to 4 | | 27.9 | 31.8 | 29.5 | 27.4 | 31.1 | 28.9 | 30.0 | 31.1 | 30.4 |
| 5 to 8 | | 10.6 | 14.8 | 12.3 | 9.9 | 10.9 | 10.3 | 10.4 | 10.3 | 10.3 |
| 9 to 12 | | 4.2 | 5.7 | 4.8 | 7.4 | 1.9 | 5.1 | 5.8 | 3.0 | 4.6 |
| 13 to 16 | | 1.6 | 2.3 | 1.9 | 1.2 | 1.6 | 1.4 | 1.7 | 1.6 | 1.7 |
| 17 to 20 | | 1.3 | 0.8 | 1.1 | 1.3 | 0.8 | 1.1 | 1.3 | 1.1 | 1.2 |
| 21 to 34 | | 1.1 | 0.8 | 0.9 | 0.9 | 1.3 | 1.0 | 0.7 | 0.8 | 0.7 |
| 35 to 44 | | 0.8 | 0.0 | 0.5 | 0.1 | 0.0 | 0.0 | 0.1 | 0.2 | 0.1 |
| 45 + | | 0.5 | 0.4 | 0.5 | 0.2 | 0.1 | 0.2 | 0.2 | 0.2 | 0.2 |
| **Consultation with clients/patients** | 642 | | | | | | | | | |
| None | | 82.1 | 75.7 | 79.4 | 83.4 | 82.6 | 83.1 | 82.7 | 80.0 | 81.5 |
| 1 to 4 | | 9.5 | 13.3 | 11.1 | 11.6 | 9.0 | 10.5 | 11.7 | 10.8 | 11.3 |
| 5 to 8 | | 5.0 | 4.6 | 4.8 | 3.3 | 3.1 | 3.2 | 3.5 | 4.5 | 3.9 |
| 9 to 12 | | 2.4 | 3.0 | 2.6 | 1.1 | 2.8 | 1.8 | 1.1 | 2.3 | 1.6 |
| 13 to 16 | | 0.0 | 0.8 | 0.3 | 0.1 | 0.8 | 0.4 | 0.2 | 1.1 | 0.6 |
| 17 to 20 | | 0.3 | 1.9 | 0.9 | 0.3 | 0.6 | 0.4 | 0.5 | 0.6 | 0.6 |
| 21 to 34 | | 0.8 | 0.4 | 0.6 | 0.1 | 0.9 | 0.4 | 0.1 | 0.6 | 0.3 |
| 35 to 44 | | 0.0 | 0.0 | 0.0 | 0.1 | 0.1 | 0.1 | 0.1 | 0.1 | 0.1 |
| 45 + | | 0.0 | 0.4 | 0.2 | 0.1 | 0.0 | 0.0 | 0.0 | 0.1 | 0.1 |
| **Community or public service** | 645 | | | | | | | | | |
| None | | 46.6 | 32.8 | 40.9 | 42.9 | 39.5 | 41.5 | 37.5 | 33.0 | 35.5 |
| 1 to 4 | | 40.5 | 48.7 | 43.9 | 46.3 | 48.3 | 47.1 | 50.1 | 54.2 | 51.9 |
| 5 to 8 | | 9.5 | 13.2 | 11.0 | 8.0 | 8.5 | 8.2 | 9.4 | 9.5 | 9.5 |
| 9 to 12 | | 2.9 | 2.6 | 2.8 | 2.1 | 2.9 | 2.4 | 2.2 | 2.5 | 2.4 |
| 13 to 16 | | 0.0 | 1.1 | 0.5 | 0.3 | 0.6 | 0.4 | 0.4 | 0.6 | 0.5 |
| 17 to 20 | | 0.5 | 1.5 | 0.9 | 0.3 | 0.1 | 0.2 | 0.2 | 0.1 | 0.2 |
| 21 to 34 | | 0.0 | 0.0 | 0.0 | 0.0 | 0.1 | 0.0 | 0.0 | 0.1 | 0.1 |
| 35 to 44 | | 0.0 | 0.0 | 0.0 | 0.0 | 0.0 | 0.0 | 0.0 | 0.0 | 0.0 |
| 45 + | | 0.0 | 0.0 | 0.0 | 0.1 | 0.0 | 0.0 | 0.0 | 0.0 | 0.0 |
| **Outside consulting/freelance work** | 645 | | | | | | | | | |
| None | | 64.7 | 64.9 | 64.8 | 68.9 | 75.5 | 71.6 | 68.0 | 74.7 | 70.8 |
| 1 to 4 | | 24.2 | 25.3 | 24.7 | 23.7 | 17.5 | 21.1 | 24.3 | 18.4 | 21.8 |
| 5 to 8 | | 8.2 | 6.4 | 7.4 | 5.0 | 4.2 | 4.7 | 5.4 | 4.5 | 5.0 |
| 9 to 12 | | 1.3 | 2.6 | 1.9 | 1.5 | 2.1 | 1.8 | 1.4 | 1.8 | 1.6 |
| 13 to 16 | | 0.5 | 0.4 | 0.5 | 0.3 | 0.3 | 0.3 | 0.4 | 0.3 | 0.3 |
| 17 to 20 | | 0.8 | 0.4 | 0.6 | 0.2 | 0.0 | 0.2 | 0.3 | 0.1 | 0.2 |
| 21 to 34 | | 0.0 | 0.0 | 0.0 | 0.4 | 0.2 | 0.3 | 0.3 | 0.1 | 0.2 |
| 35 to 44 | | 0.0 | 0.0 | 0.0 | 0.0 | 0.0 | 0.0 | 0.0 | 0.0 | 0.0 |
| 45 + | | 0.3 | 0.0 | 0.2 | 0.0 | 0.0 | 0.0 | 0.0 | 0.0 | 0.0 |

| Whatsamatta University<br>Full-time Undergraduate Faculty | # Respon-<br>dents | Your Institution | | | Nonsect 4-yr Colls | | | All Priv 4-yr Colls | | |
|---|---|---|---|---|---|---|---|---|---|---|
| | | Men | Women | Total | Men | Women | Total | Men | Women | Total |
| **DURING THE PRESENT TERM, HOW MANY HOURS PER WEEK ON AVERAGE DO YOU ACTUALLY SPEND ON:** | | | | | | | | | | |
| **Household/childcare duties** | 643 | | | | | | | | | |
| None | | 19.7 | 4.6 | 13.5 | 10.9 | 3.9 | 8.0 | 13.1 | 4.1 | 9.3 |
| 1 to 4 | | 18.9 | 19.8 | 19.3 | 21.9 | 18.7 | 20.6 | 20.6 | 17.8 | 19.4 |
| 5 to 8 | | 23.6 | 19.8 | 22.1 | 25.5 | 26.5 | 25.9 | 25.9 | 26.5 | 26.1 |
| 9 to 12 | | 15.7 | 13.4 | 14.8 | 16.7 | 15.2 | 16.1 | 16.0 | 15.8 | 15.9 |
| 13 to 16 | | 7.9 | 6.5 | 7.3 | 8.6 | 8.9 | 8.7 | 8.2 | 9.1 | 8.6 |
| 17 to 20 | | 7.9 | 14.5 | 10.6 | 7.2 | 8.1 | 7.6 | 7.4 | 7.7 | 7.5 |
| 21 to 34 | | 4.5 | 7.3 | 5.6 | 5.1 | 7.4 | 6.1 | 4.7 | 7.5 | 5.9 |
| 35 to 44 | | 0.8 | 6.1 | 3.0 | 1.8 | 5.4 | 3.3 | 1.8 | 4.9 | 3.1 |
| 45 + | | 1.0 | 8.0 | 3.9 | 2.3 | 5.9 | 3.8 | 2.4 | 6.6 | 4.2 |
| **Communicating via email** | 648 | | | | | | | | | |
| None | | 0.3 | 0.0 | 0.2 | 1.5 | 0.1 | 0.9 | 1.0 | 0.2 | 0.6 |
| 1 to 4 | | 33.9 | 17.0 | 27.0 | 35.9 | 24.8 | 31.3 | 37.0 | 26.6 | 32.5 |
| 5 to 8 | | 39.2 | 39.2 | 39.2 | 39.2 | 43.0 | 40.8 | 39.8 | 41.1 | 40.3 |
| 9 to 12 | | 17.2 | 22.6 | 19.4 | 14.3 | 17.2 | 15.5 | 14.2 | 18.1 | 15.9 |
| 13 to 16 | | 4.7 | 12.8 | 8.0 | 6.4 | 8.2 | 7.2 | 5.0 | 7.8 | 6.2 |
| 17 to 20 | | 2.1 | 4.2 | 2.9 | 1.8 | 4.1 | 2.8 | 2.1 | 3.8 | 2.8 |
| 21 to 34 | | 1.8 | 3.0 | 2.3 | 0.7 | 1.5 | 1.1 | 0.6 | 1.5 | 1.0 |
| 35 to 44 | | 0.3 | 0.8 | 0.5 | 0.2 | 0.2 | 0.2 | 0.2 | 0.3 | 0.2 |
| 45 + | | 0.5 | 0.4 | 0.5 | 0.1 | 0.8 | 0.4 | 0.1 | 0.6 | 0.3 |
| **Commuting to campus [2]** | 648 | | | | | | | | | |
| None | | 4.2 | 0.8 | 2.8 | 10.1 | 7.8 | 9.1 | 8.5 | 6.8 | 7.8 |
| 1 to 4 | | 43.3 | 36.2 | 40.4 | 58.1 | 58.0 | 58.1 | 59.7 | 55.5 | 57.9 |
| 5 to 8 | | 30.5 | 40.0 | 34.4 | 22.0 | 21.8 | 21.9 | 22.0 | 24.5 | 23.1 |
| 9 to 12 | | 18.0 | 18.1 | 18.1 | 8.8 | 9.5 | 9.1 | 8.4 | 10.5 | 9.3 |
| 13 to 16 | | 1.8 | 3.4 | 2.5 | 0.8 | 2.4 | 1.5 | 1.0 | 1.8 | 1.4 |
| 17 to 20 | | 1.8 | 0.8 | 1.4 | 0.1 | 0.3 | 0.2 | 0.2 | 0.5 | 0.3 |
| 21 to 34 | | 0.3 | 0.4 | 0.3 | 0.0 | 0.1 | 0.1 | 0.1 | 0.1 | 0.1 |
| 35 to 44 | | 0.0 | 0.0 | 0.0 | 0.0 | 0.0 | 0.0 | 0.0 | 0.0 | 0.0 |
| 45 + | | 0.0 | 0.4 | 0.2 | 0.0 | 0.1 | 0.1 | 0.0 | 0.2 | 0.1 |
| **Other employment, outside of academia [2]** | 641 | | | | | | | | | |
| None | | 85.2 | 78.7 | 82.5 | 84.7 | 84.6 | 84.7 | 84.3 | 85.5 | 84.8 |
| 1 to 4 | | 7.1 | 11.0 | 8.7 | 8.7 | 8.6 | 8.6 | 8.4 | 7.5 | 8.0 |
| 5 to 8 | | 2.4 | 3.4 | 2.8 | 2.1 | 3.3 | 2.6 | 3.0 | 3.8 | 3.4 |
| 9 to 12 | | 2.1 | 4.2 | 3.0 | 2.9 | 1.3 | 2.2 | 2.1 | 1.5 | 1.8 |
| 13 to 16 | | 0.8 | 1.1 | 0.9 | 0.4 | 1.6 | 0.9 | 0.7 | 1.1 | 0.9 |
| 17 to 20 | | 1.1 | 1.1 | 1.1 | 0.3 | 0.3 | 0.3 | 0.6 | 0.3 | 0.5 |
| 21 to 34 | | 0.5 | 0.0 | 0.3 | 0.4 | 0.2 | 0.3 | 0.3 | 0.1 | 0.2 |
| 35 to 44 | | 0.5 | 0.4 | 0.5 | 0.5 | 0.0 | 0.3 | 0.4 | 0.1 | 0.3 |
| 45 + | | 0.3 | 0.0 | 0.2 | 0.1 | 0.0 | 0.0 | 0.1 | 0.1 | 0.1 |

[2]  This question asked for the first time in the 2007–2008 Faculty Survey.

| Whatsamatta University<br>Full-time Undergraduate Faculty | # Respon-<br>dents | Your Institution | | | Nonsect 4-yr Colls | | | All Priv 4-yr Colls | | |
|---|---|---|---|---|---|---|---|---|---|---|
| | | Men | Women | Total | Men | Women | Total | Men | Women | Total |
| **Including all institutions at which you teach, how many undergraduate courses are you teaching this term? [2]** | 647 | | | | | | | | | |
| None | | 0.0 | 0.0 | 0.0 | 0.0 | 0.0 | 0.0 | 0.0 | 0.0 | 0.0 |
| One | | 30.9 | 33.6 | 32.0 | 11.2 | 12.8 | 11.9 | 9.9 | 12.3 | 10.9 |
| Two | | 29.1 | 24.9 | 27.4 | 27.5 | 25.9 | 26.8 | 22.1 | 22.4 | 22.2 |
| Three | | 23.8 | 25.3 | 24.4 | 28.1 | 37.1 | 31.9 | 29.9 | 33.9 | 31.6 |
| Four | | 11.5 | 12.1 | 11.7 | 19.1 | 15.7 | 17.7 | 22.5 | 20.4 | 21.6 |
| Five | | 2.9 | 3.8 | 3.2 | 8.5 | 6.4 | 7.6 | 10.2 | 7.6 | 9.1 |
| Six or more | | 1.8 | 0.4 | 1.2 | 5.6 | 2.1 | 4.1 | 5.4 | 3.4 | 4.5 |
| **FOR UP TO FOUR OF THE UNDERGRADUATE COURSES MENTIONED ABOVE, HOW MANY STUDENTS ARE ENROLLED IN: [2]** | | | | | | | | | | |
| **Course #1** | 641 | | | | | | | | | |
| 10 or fewer | | 12.2 | 9.1 | 10.9 | 19.3 | 16.6 | 18.2 | 16.9 | 16.8 | 16.8 |
| 11 to 20 | | 30.4 | 29.3 | 30.0 | 35.4 | 41.1 | 37.7 | 33.9 | 37.9 | 35.6 |
| 21 to 30 | | 22.5 | 26.6 | 24.2 | 25.9 | 25.5 | 25.7 | 27.9 | 27.6 | 27.8 |
| 31 to 50 | | 22.8 | 22.8 | 22.8 | 13.5 | 11.9 | 12.8 | 16.1 | 13.0 | 14.7 |
| 51 to 100 | | 7.4 | 6.8 | 7.2 | 3.8 | 3.1 | 3.5 | 3.8 | 3.5 | 3.7 |
| More than 100 | | 4.8 | 5.3 | 5.0 | 2.2 | 1.8 | 2.0 | 1.5 | 1.2 | 1.4 |
| **Course #2** | 433 | | | | | | | | | |
| 10 or fewer | | 15.4 | 14.9 | 15.2 | 20.3 | 21.9 | 21.0 | 20.0 | 21.3 | 20.6 |
| 11 to 20 | | 34.4 | 32.2 | 33.5 | 42.3 | 45.3 | 43.5 | 39.2 | 42.4 | 40.5 |
| 21 to 30 | | 21.6 | 26.4 | 23.6 | 24.7 | 22.1 | 23.6 | 27.1 | 24.8 | 26.1 |
| 31 to 50 | | 21.6 | 17.2 | 19.9 | 9.1 | 9.0 | 9.1 | 11.1 | 9.5 | 10.4 |
| 51 to 100 | | 4.2 | 6.9 | 5.3 | 2.3 | 1.1 | 1.8 | 1.9 | 1.5 | 1.7 |
| More than 100 | | 2.7 | 2.3 | 2.5 | 1.2 | 0.7 | 1.0 | 0.7 | 0.5 | 0.6 |
| **Course #3** | 255 | | | | | | | | | |
| 10 or fewer | | 21.6 | 17.8 | 20.0 | 27.9 | 30.2 | 28.8 | 28.8 | 31.0 | 29.7 |
| 11 to 20 | | 35.8 | 31.8 | 34.1 | 38.3 | 37.9 | 38.1 | 38.5 | 38.6 | 38.5 |
| 21 to 30 | | 23.0 | 28.0 | 25.1 | 23.5 | 23.2 | 23.4 | 23.2 | 22.2 | 22.8 |
| 31 to 50 | | 14.9 | 15.9 | 15.3 | 6.5 | 7.3 | 6.9 | 7.5 | 7.3 | 7.4 |
| 51 to 100 | | 2.0 | 5.6 | 3.5 | 2.4 | 0.4 | 1.5 | 1.3 | 0.3 | 0.9 |
| More than 100 | | 2.7 | 0.9 | 2.0 | 1.5 | 1.0 | 1.3 | 0.7 | 0.6 | 0.6 |
| **Course #4** | 101 | | | | | | | | | |
| 10 or fewer | | 28.3 | 22.0 | 25.7 | 32.6 | 33.0 | 32.7 | 37.9 | 38.0 | 38.0 |
| 11 to 20 | | 38.3 | 39.0 | 38.6 | 35.2 | 43.3 | 38.0 | 34.8 | 37.6 | 35.9 |
| 21 to 30 | | 18.3 | 24.4 | 20.8 | 18.3 | 18.0 | 18.2 | 17.9 | 19.6 | 18.5 |
| 31 to 50 | | 13.3 | 7.3 | 10.9 | 12.5 | 5.2 | 10.0 | 8.1 | 4.2 | 6.6 |
| 51 to 100 | | 0.0 | 4.9 | 2.0 | 0.2 | 0.4 | 0.2 | 0.7 | 0.4 | 0.6 |
| More than 100 | | 1.7 | 2.4 | 2.0 | 1.3 | 0.1 | 0.9 | 0.6 | 0.2 | 0.4 |

[2] This question asked for the first time in the 2007–2008 Faculty Survey.

| Whatsamatta University<br>Full-time Undergraduate Faculty | # Respon-<br>dents | Your Institution | | | Nonsect 4-yr Colls | | | All Priv 4-yr Colls | | |
|---|---|---|---|---|---|---|---|---|---|---|
| | | Men | Women | Total | Men | Women | Total | Men | Women | Total |
| **HOW MANY OF THE FOLLOWING COURSES<br>ARE YOU TEACHING THIS ACADEMIC YEAR?** | | | | | | | | | | |
| **General education courses** | 638 | | | | | | | | | |
| None | | 63.4 | 69.3 | 65.8 | 49.8 | 47.8 | 49.0 | 45.8 | 48.8 | 47.1 |
| One | | 12.2 | 14.2 | 13.0 | 19.8 | 21.1 | 20.3 | 19.9 | 19.3 | 19.7 |
| Two | | 12.5 | 6.5 | 10.0 | 13.4 | 12.5 | 13.0 | 15.2 | 12.8 | 14.1 |
| Three | | 6.4 | 3.1 | 5.0 | 8.2 | 7.8 | 8.1 | 9.1 | 8.1 | 8.7 |
| Four | | 3.2 | 3.8 | 3.4 | 3.9 | 4.9 | 4.3 | 4.5 | 5.2 | 4.8 |
| Five or more | | 2.4 | 3.1 | 2.7 | 4.9 | 5.8 | 5.3 | 5.5 | 5.7 | 5.6 |
| **Developmental/remedial courses** | 630 | | | | | | | | | |
| None | | 96.2 | 93.8 | 95.2 | 92.4 | 90.3 | 91.5 | 93.2 | 91.8 | 92.6 |
| One | | 1.9 | 3.9 | 2.7 | 3.9 | 4.9 | 4.3 | 3.8 | 4.4 | 4.0 |
| Two | | 0.8 | 1.2 | 1.0 | 2.6 | 1.9 | 2.3 | 1.7 | 1.3 | 1.5 |
| Three | | 0.3 | 0.8 | 0.5 | 0.7 | 1.4 | 1.0 | 0.5 | 1.2 | 0.8 |
| Four | | 0.5 | 0.4 | 0.5 | 0.2 | 0.9 | 0.5 | 0.3 | 0.9 | 0.5 |
| Five or more | | 0.3 | 0.0 | 0.2 | 0.2 | 0.6 | 0.4 | 0.6 | 0.5 | 0.6 |
| **Other undergraduate credit courses** | 632 | | | | | | | | | |
| None | | 24.9 | 21.2 | 23.4 | 15.4 | 18.1 | 16.5 | 15.1 | 17.6 | 16.1 |
| One | | 26.5 | 26.3 | 26.4 | 14.2 | 16.1 | 15.0 | 14.0 | 15.4 | 14.6 |
| Two | | 19.6 | 21.2 | 20.3 | 21.3 | 22.5 | 21.8 | 19.9 | 20.9 | 20.3 |
| Three | | 16.6 | 15.4 | 16.1 | 18.7 | 17.8 | 18.3 | 18.9 | 17.8 | 18.4 |
| Four | | 6.7 | 8.5 | 7.4 | 12.3 | 9.7 | 11.2 | 13.6 | 11.7 | 12.8 |
| Five or more | | 5.6 | 7.3 | 6.3 | 18.1 | 15.8 | 17.2 | 18.5 | 16.7 | 17.7 |
| **Graduate courses** | 638 | | | | | | | | | |
| None | | 46.2 | 50.6 | 48.0 | 84.9 | 87.2 | 85.9 | 82.9 | 83.0 | 82.9 |
| One | | 32.6 | 28.7 | 31.0 | 7.9 | 6.6 | 7.4 | 9.1 | 8.7 | 8.9 |
| Two | | 13.3 | 14.6 | 13.8 | 4.3 | 3.4 | 3.9 | 4.2 | 4.0 | 4.1 |
| Three | | 3.4 | 3.4 | 3.4 | 1.2 | 1.2 | 1.2 | 1.6 | 1.9 | 1.7 |
| Four | | 1.6 | 1.5 | 1.6 | 0.8 | 0.7 | 0.8 | 0.9 | 1.2 | 1.1 |
| Five or more | | 2.9 | 1.1 | 2.2 | 0.8 | 0.8 | 0.8 | 1.2 | 1.2 | 1.2 |
| **Vocational or technical courses** | 628 | | | | | | | | | |
| None | | 95.4 | 98.1 | 96.5 | 96.9 | 98.2 | 97.4 | 97.5 | 97.7 | 97.6 |
| One | | 2.4 | 1.2 | 1.9 | 1.5 | 0.7 | 1.2 | 1.1 | 0.9 | 1.0 |
| Two | | 0.8 | 0.0 | 0.5 | 0.7 | 0.7 | 0.7 | 0.6 | 0.6 | 0.6 |
| Three | | 0.8 | 0.4 | 0.6 | 0.7 | 0.3 | 0.5 | 0.5 | 0.4 | 0.5 |
| Four | | 0.3 | 0.0 | 0.2 | 0.1 | 0.0 | 0.1 | 0.1 | 0.1 | 0.1 |
| Five or more | | 0.3 | 0.4 | 0.3 | 0.1 | 0.1 | 0.1 | 0.2 | 0.2 | 0.2 |
| **Non-credit courses (other than above)** | 629 | | | | | | | | | |
| None | | 95.7 | 94.2 | 95.1 | 95.2 | 94.0 | 94.7 | 95.5 | 93.7 | 94.7 |
| One | | 3.5 | 5.0 | 4.1 | 3.4 | 3.9 | 3.6 | 3.2 | 4.6 | 3.8 |
| Two | | 0.5 | 0.8 | 0.6 | 0.7 | 1.7 | 1.1 | 0.8 | 1.4 | 1.0 |
| Three | | 0.0 | 0.0 | 0.0 | 0.0 | 0.4 | 0.2 | 0.1 | 0.2 | 0.1 |
| Four | | 0.0 | 0.0 | 0.0 | 0.2 | 0.0 | 0.1 | 0.2 | 0.1 | 0.1 |
| Five or more | | 0.3 | 0.0 | 0.2 | 0.6 | 0.0 | 0.3 | 0.3 | 0.1 | 0.2 |
| **Do you teach remedial/developmental<br>skills in any of the following areas?** | 648 | | | | | | | | | |
| Reading | | 4.4 | 5.3 | 4.8 | 4.4 | 6.7 | 5.4 | 4.5 | 5.9 | 5.1 |
| Writing | | 9.9 | 12.1 | 10.8 | 11.6 | 16.5 | 13.6 | 10.5 | 14.0 | 12.0 |
| Mathematics | | 3.7 | 1.1 | 2.6 | 5.5 | 3.6 | 4.7 | 4.8 | 3.9 | 4.4 |
| ESL | | 0.5 | 1.5 | 0.9 | 0.6 | 2.2 | 1.3 | 0.8 | 2.0 | 1.3 |
| General academic skills | | 7.8 | 8.7 | 8.2 | 9.7 | 13.5 | 11.3 | 8.7 | 11.4 | 9.8 |
| Other subject areas | | 5.7 | 7.9 | 6.6 | 7.3 | 7.7 | 7.5 | 5.8 | 7.5 | 6.5 |

| Whatsamatta University<br>Full-time Undergraduate Faculty | # Respon-dents | Your Institution | | | Nonsect 4-yr Colls | | | All Priv 4-yr Colls | | |
|---|---|---|---|---|---|---|---|---|---|---|
| | | Men | Women | Total | Men | Women | Total | Men | Women | Total |
| **HAVE YOU ENGAGED IN ANY OF THE FOLLOWING PROFESSIONAL DEVELOPMENT OPPORTUNITIES AT YOUR INSTITUTION? [2]** | | | | | | | | | | |
| **Workshops focused on teaching in the classroom** | 646 | | | | | | | | | |
| Yes | | 59.6 | 73.2 | 65.2 | 70.5 | 77.0 | 73.2 | 71.4 | 77.4 | 74.0 |
| No | | 34.1 | 22.6 | 29.4 | 26.7 | 17.4 | 22.8 | 25.0 | 17.2 | 21.7 |
| Not eligible | | 1.0 | 0.8 | 0.9 | 0.2 | 0.2 | 0.2 | 0.2 | 0.1 | 0.2 |
| Not available | | 5.2 | 3.4 | 4.5 | 2.6 | 5.4 | 3.8 | 3.4 | 5.2 | 4.2 |
| **Paid workshops outside the institution focused on teaching** | 643 | | | | | | | | | |
| Yes | | 12.6 | 25.5 | 17.9 | 24.6 | 36.4 | 29.6 | 27.1 | 39.5 | 32.4 |
| No | | 81.6 | 65.0 | 74.8 | 70.9 | 58.4 | 65.6 | 68.5 | 55.1 | 62.8 |
| Not eligible | | 1.8 | 1.1 | 1.6 | 0.2 | 0.6 | 0.4 | 0.3 | 0.5 | 0.4 |
| Not available | | 3.9 | 8.4 | 5.8 | 4.2 | 4.7 | 4.4 | 4.0 | 4.9 | 4.4 |
| **Paid sabbatical leave** | 642 | | | | | | | | | |
| Yes | | 33.8 | 22.8 | 29.3 | 39.1 | 31.6 | 36.0 | 34.0 | 26.1 | 30.6 |
| No | | 55.9 | 51.3 | 54.0 | 45.8 | 48.3 | 46.8 | 51.1 | 53.1 | 52.0 |
| Not eligible | | 9.5 | 22.4 | 14.8 | 13.3 | 18.1 | 15.3 | 12.6 | 18.6 | 15.2 |
| Not available | | 0.8 | 3.4 | 1.9 | 1.9 | 1.9 | 1.9 | 2.2 | 2.2 | 2.2 |
| **Travel funds paid by the institution** | 645 | | | | | | | | | |
| Yes | | 76.6 | 76.9 | 76.7 | 80.3 | 80.5 | 80.4 | 80.2 | 80.7 | 80.4 |
| No | | 21.5 | 21.2 | 21.4 | 15.9 | 15.5 | 15.8 | 17.2 | 16.1 | 16.7 |
| Not eligible | | 0.8 | 1.5 | 1.1 | 1.9 | 2.3 | 2.1 | 1.1 | 1.8 | 1.4 |
| Not available | | 1.0 | 0.4 | 0.8 | 1.8 | 1.7 | 1.8 | 1.6 | 1.5 | 1.5 |
| **Association membership/dues paid by the institution** | 644 | | | | | | | | | |
| Yes | | 23.7 | 26.1 | 24.7 | 41.5 | 42.9 | 42.1 | 46.1 | 45.2 | 45.7 |
| No | | 59.7 | 51.5 | 56.4 | 47.1 | 38.9 | 43.7 | 43.4 | 38.0 | 41.1 |
| Not eligible | | 2.9 | 3.8 | 3.3 | 2.7 | 3.9 | 3.2 | 1.7 | 2.9 | 2.2 |
| Not available | | 13.7 | 18.6 | 15.7 | 8.7 | 14.3 | 11.1 | 8.7 | 14.0 | 11.0 |
| **Tuition remission** | 643 | | | | | | | | | |
| Yes | | 15.3 | 22.8 | 18.4 | 19.1 | 19.4 | 19.2 | 20.4 | 18.4 | 19.5 |
| No | | 81.3 | 71.1 | 77.1 | 72.9 | 70.4 | 71.8 | 73.0 | 72.0 | 72.6 |
| Not eligible | | 2.4 | 3.8 | 3.0 | 4.9 | 4.7 | 4.8 | 4.2 | 4.7 | 4.4 |
| Not available | | 1.1 | 2.3 | 1.6 | 3.1 | 5.6 | 4.1 | 2.5 | 4.9 | 3.5 |
| **Internal grants for research** | 644 | | | | | | | | | |
| Yes | | 44.4 | 41.8 | 43.3 | 46.0 | 45.0 | 45.6 | 42.4 | 39.0 | 41.0 |
| No | | 52.8 | 52.1 | 52.5 | 49.0 | 47.4 | 48.3 | 52.7 | 54.3 | 53.4 |
| Not eligible | | 1.6 | 4.2 | 2.6 | 1.8 | 2.5 | 2.1 | 1.5 | 2.2 | 1.8 |
| Not available | | 1.3 | 1.9 | 1.6 | 3.2 | 5.1 | 4.0 | 3.3 | 4.4 | 3.8 |
| **Training for administrative leadership** | 642 | | | | | | | | | |
| Yes | | 11.6 | 14.8 | 12.9 | 12.5 | 12.9 | 12.7 | 12.4 | 12.3 | 12.3 |
| No | | 77.3 | 69.2 | 74.0 | 74.5 | 69.6 | 72.5 | 75.8 | 71.1 | 73.8 |
| Not eligible | | 2.6 | 3.4 | 3.0 | 2.8 | 3.9 | 3.2 | 2.4 | 3.3 | 2.8 |
| Not available | | 8.4 | 12.5 | 10.1 | 10.1 | 13.6 | 11.6 | 9.5 | 13.2 | 11.1 |

[2] This question asked for the first time in the 2007–2008 Faculty Survey.

| Whatsamatta University<br>Full-time Undergraduate Faculty | # Respon-<br>dents | Your Institution | | | Nonsect 4-yr Colls | | | All Priv 4-yr Colls | | |
|---|---|---|---|---|---|---|---|---|---|---|
| | | Men | Women | Total | Men | Women | Total | Men | Women | Total |
| **Goals for undergraduates noted as<br>"very important" or "essential"** | | | | | | | | | | |
| Develop ability to think critically | 646 | 99.2 | 99.6 | 99.4 | 99.0 | 100.0 | 99.4 | 99.3 | 99.9 | 99.6 |
| Prepare students for employment after<br>college | 646 | 78.7 | 85.7 | 81.6 | 76.5 | 82.3 | 78.9 | 78.3 | 84.8 | 81.1 |
| Prepare students for graduate or<br>advanced education | 644 | 75.3 | 82.6 | 78.3 | 75.6 | 80.0 | 77.5 | 77.1 | 80.9 | 78.7 |
| Develop moral character | 646 | 79.0 | 87.9 | 82.7 | 70.0 | 76.1 | 72.5 | 75.5 | 80.3 | 77.6 |
| Provide for students' emotional<br>development | 646 | 51.2 | 64.2 | 56.5 | 47.7 | 58.0 | 52.0 | 51.3 | 62.0 | 55.9 |
| Prepare students for family living | 645 | 27.4 | 24.9 | 26.4 | 22.1 | 21.6 | 21.9 | 25.1 | 27.6 | 26.1 |
| Teach students the classic works of<br>Western civilization [2] | 643 | 50.4 | 36.6 | 44.8 | 36.9 | 31.5 | 34.6 | 40.8 | 35.7 | 38.6 |
| Help students develop personal values | 645 | 71.6 | 79.6 | 74.9 | 69.0 | 73.8 | 71.0 | 72.7 | 77.8 | 74.9 |
| Enhance students' self-understanding | 645 | 71.9 | 79.9 | 75.2 | 74.5 | 77.4 | 75.7 | 76.1 | 80.7 | 78.1 |
| Instill in students a commitment to<br>community service | 646 | 50.9 | 66.8 | 57.4 | 50.9 | 65.6 | 57.1 | 55.5 | 69.9 | 61.7 |
| Enhance students' knowledge of and<br>appreciation for other racial/ethnic<br>groups | 646 | 69.6 | 89.8 | 77.9 | 70.9 | 88.7 | 78.3 | 71.9 | 89.4 | 79.5 |
| Study a foreign language [2] | 646 | 57.7 | 62.3 | 59.6 | 53.2 | 64.2 | 57.8 | 54.4 | 63.6 | 58.3 |
| Help master knowledge in a discipline | 646 | 94.5 | 97.0 | 95.5 | 95.1 | 95.5 | 95.3 | 95.5 | 96.3 | 95.9 |
| Develop creative capacities | 646 | 80.1 | 76.2 | 78.5 | 84.2 | 83.6 | 84.0 | 82.1 | 81.4 | 81.8 |
| Instill a basic appreciation of the<br>liberal arts | 645 | 75.8 | 74.0 | 75.0 | 80.2 | 83.8 | 81.7 | 80.2 | 83.3 | 81.5 |
| Promote ability to write effectively | 646 | 95.3 | 98.5 | 96.6 | 97.1 | 99.1 | 97.9 | 96.8 | 99.0 | 97.8 |
| Help students evaluate the quality and<br>reliability of information [2] | 646 | 97.1 | 98.1 | 97.5 | 97.1 | 99.3 | 98.0 | 96.9 | 99.0 | 97.8 |
| Engage students in civil discourse<br>around controversial issues [2] | 645 | 71.9 | 75.4 | 73.3 | 74.2 | 85.6 | 79.0 | 75.3 | 83.3 | 78.7 |
| Teach students tolerance and respect<br>for different beliefs [2] | 646 | 77.7 | 92.1 | 83.6 | 79.9 | 91.9 | 84.9 | 80.1 | 92.8 | 85.5 |
| Encourage students to become agents of<br>social change [2] | 645 | 54.9 | 72.0 | 61.9 | 55.5 | 73.8 | 63.2 | 56.6 | 75.4 | 64.6 |

[2]  This question asked for the first time in the 2007–2008 Faculty Survey.

| Whatsamatta University<br>Full-time Undergraduate Faculty | # Respon-<br>dents | Your Institution | | | Nonsect 4-yr Colls | | | All Priv 4-yr Colls | | |
|---|---|---|---|---|---|---|---|---|---|---|
| | | Men | Women | Total | Men | Women | Total | Men | Women | Total |
| **HOW MANY OF THE FOLLOWING HAVE YOU PUBLISHED?** | | | | | | | | | | |
| **Articles in academic or professional journals** | 645 | | | | | | | | | |
| None | | 13.2 | 22.6 | 17.1 | 24.6 | 29.4 | 26.6 | 24.9 | 32.5 | 28.2 |
| 1 to 2 | | 14.5 | 20.4 | 16.9 | 18.9 | 23.0 | 20.7 | 21.2 | 25.9 | 23.2 |
| 3 to 4 | | 10.8 | 15.1 | 12.6 | 13.8 | 17.9 | 15.5 | 15.1 | 17.1 | 15.9 |
| 5 to 10 | | 20.0 | 21.9 | 20.8 | 19.6 | 17.1 | 18.5 | 18.9 | 14.5 | 17.0 |
| 11 to 20 | | 19.5 | 10.2 | 15.7 | 12.3 | 7.6 | 10.3 | 10.8 | 6.0 | 8.8 |
| 21 to 50 | | 14.5 | 6.8 | 11.3 | 8.6 | 4.0 | 6.7 | 7.1 | 3.3 | 5.5 |
| 51+ | | 7.6 | 3.0 | 5.7 | 2.2 | 1.0 | 1.7 | 2.0 | 0.7 | 1.4 |
| **Chapters in edited volumes** | 646 | | | | | | | | | |
| None | | 36.2 | 47.5 | 40.9 | 55.7 | 57.0 | 56.3 | 58.8 | 63.2 | 60.7 |
| 1 to 2 | | 27.6 | 29.4 | 28.3 | 25.2 | 26.8 | 25.9 | 24.4 | 24.6 | 24.5 |
| 3 to 4 | | 17.3 | 11.7 | 15.0 | 11.2 | 9.0 | 10.3 | 9.7 | 7.4 | 8.7 |
| 5 to 10 | | 12.1 | 6.8 | 9.9 | 5.5 | 5.2 | 5.4 | 5.1 | 3.5 | 4.4 |
| 11 to 20 | | 5.2 | 4.2 | 4.8 | 2.0 | 1.0 | 1.6 | 1.6 | 0.7 | 1.2 |
| 21 to 50 | | 1.3 | 0.4 | 0.9 | 0.3 | 0.8 | 0.5 | 0.3 | 0.5 | 0.4 |
| 51+ | | 0.3 | 0.0 | 0.2 | 0.0 | 0.1 | 0.1 | 0.0 | 0.1 | 0.0 |
| **Books, manuals, or monographs** | 644 | | | | | | | | | |
| None | | 52.5 | 65.0 | 57.6 | 63.5 | 73.8 | 67.8 | 66.0 | 76.3 | 70.4 |
| 1 to 2 | | 29.7 | 26.6 | 28.4 | 24.8 | 20.4 | 22.9 | 23.3 | 18.4 | 21.2 |
| 3 to 4 | | 8.9 | 7.2 | 8.2 | 5.4 | 3.5 | 4.6 | 5.5 | 3.3 | 4.6 |
| 5 to 10 | | 6.0 | 1.1 | 4.0 | 5.4 | 1.9 | 3.9 | 4.1 | 1.6 | 3.0 |
| 11 to 20 | | 2.1 | 0.0 | 1.2 | 0.7 | 0.4 | 0.6 | 0.9 | 0.4 | 0.7 |
| 21 to 50 | | 0.5 | 0.0 | 0.3 | 0.1 | 0.0 | 0.1 | 0.2 | 0.0 | 0.1 |
| 51+ | | 0.3 | 0.0 | 0.2 | 0.0 | 0.0 | 0.0 | 0.0 | 0.0 | 0.0 |
| **Other, such as patents or computer software products** | 640 | | | | | | | | | |
| None | | 84.8 | 91.7 | 87.7 | 87.9 | 90.8 | 89.1 | 87.3 | 91.6 | 89.2 |
| 1 to 2 | | 10.9 | 3.8 | 8.0 | 7.0 | 5.9 | 6.6 | 7.2 | 5.4 | 6.4 |
| 3 to 4 | | 2.1 | 3.0 | 2.5 | 2.2 | 1.9 | 2.0 | 2.7 | 1.7 | 2.3 |
| 5 to 10 | | 0.8 | 1.1 | 0.9 | 1.6 | 0.6 | 1.2 | 1.4 | 0.6 | 1.1 |
| 11 to 20 | | 1.1 | 0.0 | 0.6 | 0.6 | 0.3 | 0.5 | 0.7 | 0.4 | 0.5 |
| 21 to 50 | | 0.0 | 0.0 | 0.0 | 0.5 | 0.1 | 0.3 | 0.3 | 0.1 | 0.2 |
| 51+ | | 0.3 | 0.4 | 0.3 | 0.3 | 0.4 | 0.3 | 0.3 | 0.2 | 0.3 |
| **IN THE LAST TWO YEARS, HOW MANY:** | | | | | | | | | | |
| **Exhibitions or performances in the fine or applied arts have you presented?** | 641 | | | | | | | | | |
| None | | 83.6 | 82.4 | 83.2 | 73.5 | 77.6 | 75.2 | 76.6 | 78.6 | 77.4 |
| 1 to 2 | | 5.8 | 6.1 | 5.9 | 10.4 | 8.5 | 9.6 | 8.0 | 7.9 | 8.0 |
| 3 to 4 | | 3.4 | 5.3 | 4.2 | 4.9 | 4.8 | 4.9 | 4.6 | 4.9 | 4.8 |
| 5 to 10 | | 4.0 | 2.7 | 3.4 | 6.4 | 5.7 | 6.1 | 5.6 | 5.0 | 5.4 |
| 11 to 20 | | 1.1 | 1.5 | 1.2 | 2.2 | 2.1 | 2.1 | 2.3 | 2.0 | 2.1 |
| 21 to 50 | | 1.1 | 1.1 | 1.1 | 0.9 | 0.8 | 0.8 | 1.2 | 0.9 | 1.1 |
| 51+ | | 1.1 | 0.8 | 0.9 | 1.8 | 0.6 | 1.3 | 1.7 | 0.6 | 1.3 |
| **Of your professional writings have been published or accepted for publication?** | 647 | | | | | | | | | |
| None | | 21.5 | 27.9 | 24.1 | 38.6 | 42.1 | 40.0 | 40.2 | 46.6 | 43.0 |
| 1 to 2 | | 29.3 | 35.1 | 31.7 | 36.1 | 33.6 | 35.0 | 35.2 | 33.3 | 34.4 |
| 3 to 4 | | 26.2 | 19.2 | 23.3 | 16.7 | 16.8 | 16.8 | 16.2 | 14.2 | 15.3 |
| 5 to 10 | | 18.8 | 15.1 | 17.3 | 7.2 | 6.3 | 6.8 | 6.8 | 4.8 | 6.0 |
| 11 to 20 | | 3.9 | 2.6 | 3.4 | 1.1 | 1.2 | 1.2 | 0.9 | 0.9 | 0.9 |
| 21 to 50 | | 0.0 | 0.0 | 0.0 | 0.2 | 0.1 | 0.2 | 0.4 | 0.1 | 0.3 |
| 51+ | | 0.3 | 0.0 | 0.2 | 0.0 | 0.0 | 0.0 | 0.2 | 0.1 | 0.1 |

| Whatsamatta University<br>Full-time Undergraduate Faculty | # Respon-<br>dents | Your Institution | | | Nonsect 4-yr Colls | | | All Priv 4-yr Colls | | |
|---|---|---|---|---|---|---|---|---|---|---|
| | | Men | Women | Total | Men | Women | Total | Men | Women | Total |
| **General activities** | | | | | | | | | | |
| Are you a member of a faculty union? | 646 | 19.4 | 23.8 | 21.2 | 8.3 | 9.1 | 8.6 | 9.1 | 10.2 | 9.5 |
| Are you a U.S. citizen? | 646 | 90.0 | 95.5 | 92.3 | 94.4 | 94.8 | 94.6 | 94.7 | 95.5 | 95.0 |
| Were you born in the U.S.A.? | 645 | 76.4 | 85.2 | 80.0 | 84.5 | 87.7 | 85.8 | 87.4 | 88.1 | 87.7 |
| Do you plan to retire within the next three years? | 645 | 5.8 | 7.2 | 6.4 | 10.6 | 9.4 | 10.1 | 10.6 | 8.6 | 9.8 |
| Do you use your scholarship to address local community needs? | 646 | 39.1 | 47.9 | 42.7 | 34.4 | 45.2 | 38.9 | 41.2 | 48.9 | 44.5 |
| Have you been sexually harassed at this institution? | 647 | 1.3 | 9.8 | 4.8 | 2.5 | 7.6 | 4.6 | 2.2 | 7.9 | 4.6 |
| Have you ever interrupted your professional career for more than one year for family reasons? [2] | 646 | 2.6 | 20.0 | 9.8 | 5.2 | 18.3 | 10.7 | 5.8 | 20.9 | 12.3 |
| Have you ever received an award for outstanding teaching? | 647 | 40.3 | 31.3 | 36.6 | 37.3 | 37.4 | 37.4 | 39.5 | 37.2 | 38.6 |
| Have you published op-ed pieces or editorials? | 646 | 20.5 | 17.4 | 19.2 | 26.9 | 16.2 | 22.4 | 26.8 | 16.4 | 22.3 |
| Is (or was) your: | | | | | | | | | | |
|    Father an academic? | 646 | 17.1 | 12.1 | 15.0 | 13.1 | 15.7 | 14.2 | 13.3 | 15.0 | 14.0 |
|    Mother an academic? | 645 | 7.6 | 7.5 | 7.6 | 7.5 | 12.6 | 9.7 | 8.7 | 12.2 | 10.2 |
|    Spouse/partner an academic? | 646 | 25.2 | 26.0 | 25.5 | 33.4 | 36.2 | 34.6 | 33.8 | 33.3 | 33.6 |
| Are you currently teaching courses at more than one institution? | 646 | 5.8 | 4.2 | 5.1 | 7.9 | 6.2 | 7.2 | 7.6 | 5.3 | 6.6 |
| **During the <u>past two</u> years, have you:** | | | | | | | | | | |
| Considered early retirement? | 645 | 13.9 | 17.0 | 15.2 | 16.0 | 18.8 | 17.2 | 17.2 | 18.6 | 17.8 |
| Considered leaving academe for another job? | 645 | 23.4 | 28.7 | 25.6 | 32.6 | 34.0 | 33.2 | 31.2 | 35.3 | 32.9 |
| Considered leaving this institution for another? | 645 | 41.7 | 42.0 | 41.9 | 45.2 | 44.4 | 44.8 | 45.0 | 43.6 | 44.4 |
| Changed academic institutions? | 645 | 11.5 | 13.6 | 12.4 | 10.1 | 14.7 | 12.0 | 11.1 | 13.3 | 12.0 |
| Engaged in paid consulting outside of your institution? | 645 | 36.2 | 29.2 | 33.3 | 36.0 | 27.5 | 32.4 | 35.2 | 27.7 | 32.0 |
| Engaged in public service/professional consulting without pay? | 646 | 48.0 | 52.8 | 50.0 | 54.4 | 53.6 | 54.1 | 55.1 | 55.6 | 55.3 |
| Received at least one firm job offer? | 646 | 25.2 | 31.7 | 27.9 | 25.0 | 24.7 | 24.9 | 24.4 | 26.3 | 25.2 |
| Received funding for your work from: | | | | | | | | | | |
|    Foundations? | 646 | 20.5 | 15.8 | 18.6 | 19.9 | 15.4 | 18.1 | 17.3 | 15.4 | 16.5 |
|    State or federal government? | 645 | 17.8 | 15.5 | 16.9 | 17.7 | 15.3 | 16.7 | 14.1 | 12.7 | 13.5 |
|    Business or industry? | 644 | 13.6 | 8.0 | 11.3 | 12.7 | 6.3 | 10.0 | 11.3 | 6.6 | 9.3 |
| Requested/sought an early promotion? | 645 | 7.3 | 8.0 | 7.6 | 7.6 | 6.5 | 7.1 | 6.4 | 6.0 | 6.2 |
| **IF YOU WERE TO BEGIN YOUR CAREER AGAIN, WOULD YOU STILL WANT TO:** | | | | | | | | | | |
| **Come to this institution? [2]** | 643 | | | | | | | | | |
|    Definitely yes | | 39.6 | 35.2 | 37.8 | 39.0 | 40.1 | 39.4 | 38.6 | 39.7 | 39.1 |
|    Probably yes | | 31.7 | 38.3 | 34.4 | 33.6 | 35.6 | 34.4 | 33.9 | 34.0 | 33.9 |
|    Not sure | | 16.1 | 17.0 | 16.5 | 15.8 | 16.3 | 16.0 | 15.3 | 16.6 | 15.9 |
|    Probably no | | 6.6 | 5.7 | 6.2 | 7.5 | 5.7 | 6.7 | 8.2 | 6.7 | 7.5 |
|    Definitely no | | 6.1 | 3.8 | 5.1 | 4.2 | 2.4 | 3.4 | 4.0 | 3.0 | 3.6 |
| **Be a college professor?** | 644 | | | | | | | | | |
|    Definitely yes | | 70.8 | 65.5 | 68.6 | 64.5 | 61.5 | 63.2 | 66.5 | 62.2 | 64.7 |
|    Probably yes | | 20.5 | 26.9 | 23.1 | 26.8 | 27.2 | 27.0 | 25.2 | 26.5 | 25.8 |
|    Not sure | | 6.1 | 5.7 | 5.9 | 6.7 | 9.4 | 7.8 | 6.2 | 9.4 | 7.6 |
|    Probably no | | 2.1 | 1.1 | 1.7 | 1.8 | 1.7 | 1.8 | 1.7 | 1.7 | 1.7 |
|    Definitely no | | 0.5 | 0.8 | 0.6 | 0.2 | 0.1 | 0.2 | 0.3 | 0.3 | 0.3 |

[2]  This question asked for the first time in the 2007–2008 Faculty Survey.

| Whatsamatta University<br>Full-time Undergraduate Faculty | # Respon-<br>dents | Your Institution | | | Nonsect 4-yr Colls | | | All Priv 4-yr Colls | | |
|---|---|---|---|---|---|---|---|---|---|---|
| | | Men | Women | Total | Men | Women | Total | Men | Women | Total |
| **Attributes noted as being "very descriptive" of your institution** | | | | | | | | | | |
| It is easy for students to see faculty outside of regular office hours | 647 | 55.2 | 57.7 | 56.3 | 75.8 | 77.9 | 76.7 | 77.7 | 77.3 | 77.6 |
| There is a great deal of conformity among the students | 646 | 28.3 | 30.7 | 29.3 | 27.1 | 26.9 | 27.0 | 32.9 | 31.6 | 32.3 |
| The faculty are typically at odds with campus administration | 645 | 13.9 | 14.8 | 14.3 | 16.9 | 17.8 | 17.3 | 17.3 | 18.2 | 17.7 |
| Faculty here respect each other | 645 | 52.1 | 49.0 | 50.9 | 50.8 | 51.3 | 51.0 | 53.9 | 53.8 | 53.9 |
| Most students are treated like "numbers in a book" | 646 | 2.6 | 4.9 | 3.6 | 2.4 | 1.4 | 2.0 | 2.0 | 1.2 | 1.6 |
| Social activities are overemphasized | 643 | 7.4 | 3.8 | 5.9 | 11.4 | 8.4 | 10.1 | 11.0 | 8.5 | 9.9 |
| Faculty are rewarded for being good teachers | 645 | 18.4 | 12.5 | 16.0 | 24.5 | 24.9 | 24.7 | 21.0 | 20.8 | 20.9 |
| There is respect for the expression of diverse values and beliefs | 647 | 33.0 | 33.6 | 33.2 | 43.2 | 40.1 | 41.9 | 38.6 | 36.5 | 37.7 |
| Faculty are rewarded for their efforts to use instructional technology | 647 | 28.5 | 29.8 | 29.1 | 16.5 | 19.2 | 17.6 | 14.4 | 18.2 | 16.1 |
| Faculty are rewarded for their efforts to work with underprepared students | 645 | 10.2 | 7.6 | 9.1 | 8.1 | 9.2 | 8.5 | 6.6 | 8.4 | 7.4 |
| Administrators consider faculty concerns when making policy [2] | 646 | 17.0 | 10.6 | 14.4 | 20.5 | 17.4 | 19.2 | 19.4 | 16.6 | 18.2 |
| The administration is open about its policies | 645 | 19.4 | 13.3 | 16.9 | 23.4 | 19.0 | 21.6 | 22.0 | 18.8 | 20.6 |
| **Do you, "to a great extent":** | | | | | | | | | | |
| Engage in academic work that spans multiple disciplines | 647 | 39.5 | 35.8 | 38.0 | 44.5 | 37.3 | 41.5 | 40.3 | 34.6 | 37.8 |
| Feel that the training you received in graduate school prepared you well for your role as a faculty mentor | 647 | 45.5 | 42.3 | 44.2 | 36.9 | 31.5 | 34.6 | 37.9 | 34.5 | 36.4 |
| Achieve a healthy balance between your personal life and your professional life | 647 | 42.9 | 30.6 | 37.9 | 36.7 | 24.7 | 31.7 | 37.0 | 25.2 | 32.0 |
| Experience close alignment between your work and your personal values | 647 | 73.3 | 72.8 | 73.1 | 64.7 | 69.7 | 66.8 | 68.1 | 70.1 | 68.9 |
| Feel that you have to work harder than your colleagues to be perceived as a legitimate scholar | 645 | 26.4 | 30.4 | 28.1 | 23.2 | 30.2 | 26.1 | 21.8 | 28.8 | 24.8 |
| Mentor new faculty [2] | 646 | 18.3 | 25.8 | 21.4 | 17.7 | 27.9 | 22.0 | 17.2 | 26.3 | 21.1 |

[2]  This question asked for the first time in the 2007–2008 Faculty Survey.

| Whatsamatta University<br>Full-time Undergraduate Faculty | # Respon-<br>dents | Your Institution | | | Nonsect 4-yr Colls | | | All Priv 4-yr Colls | | |
|---|---|---|---|---|---|---|---|---|---|---|
| | | Men | Women | Total | Men | Women | Total | Men | Women | Total |
| **Aspects of your job with which you are "very satisfied" or "satisfied": [3]** | | | | | | | | | | |
| Salary [2] | 647 | 46.1 | 43.0 | 44.8 | 48.5 | 47.8 | 48.2 | 47.9 | 44.5 | 46.4 |
| Health benefits [2] | 623 | 60.9 | 66.7 | 63.2 | 60.1 | 61.3 | 60.6 | 58.2 | 60.0 | 59.0 |
| Retirement benefits [2] | 625 | 66.7 | 66.8 | 66.7 | 64.2 | 63.7 | 64.0 | 63.3 | 63.2 | 63.3 |
| Opportunity for scholarly pursuits | 639 | 56.2 | 48.8 | 53.2 | 55.3 | 45.5 | 51.2 | 52.0 | 44.3 | 48.7 |
| Teaching load | 645 | 61.4 | 58.0 | 60.0 | 60.0 | 54.9 | 57.9 | 56.5 | 54.0 | 55.4 |
| Quality of students | 647 | 50.8 | 62.6 | 55.6 | 58.4 | 64.0 | 60.8 | 55.8 | 61.3 | 58.2 |
| Office/lab space | 635 | 56.1 | 62.8 | 58.9 | 70.9 | 71.6 | 71.2 | 70.4 | 70.2 | 70.3 |
| Autonomy and independence | 644 | 80.6 | 81.4 | 80.9 | 86.9 | 87.1 | 87.0 | 85.8 | 85.5 | 85.7 |
| Professional relationships with other faculty | 646 | 75.6 | 74.3 | 75.1 | 80.4 | 83.2 | 81.6 | 81.7 | 83.4 | 82.5 |
| Social relationships with other faculty | 616 | 64.4 | 72.5 | 67.7 | 68.8 | 76.1 | 71.8 | 70.7 | 76.4 | 73.2 |
| Competency of colleagues | 646 | 73.6 | 80.7 | 76.5 | 81.0 | 84.5 | 82.4 | 80.6 | 83.9 | 82.0 |
| Visibility for jobs at other institutions/organizations | 496 | 56.9 | 56.3 | 56.7 | 48.5 | 46.2 | 47.6 | 48.0 | 48.7 | 48.3 |
| Job security | 639 | 82.4 | 74.9 | 79.3 | 75.8 | 73.8 | 75.0 | 77.0 | 74.4 | 75.9 |
| Relationship with administration | 644 | 62.8 | 60.0 | 61.6 | 63.9 | 64.1 | 64.0 | 63.1 | 62.9 | 63.0 |
| Departmental leadership [2] | 639 | 70.6 | 66.7 | 69.0 | 76.0 | 74.4 | 75.3 | 77.1 | 71.8 | 74.8 |
| Course assignments [2] | 641 | 81.2 | 79.5 | 80.5 | 88.3 | 89.1 | 88.6 | 87.6 | 86.2 | 87.0 |
| Freedom to determine course content [2] | 640 | 91.5 | 91.3 | 91.4 | 94.5 | 93.4 | 94.1 | 93.8 | 92.3 | 93.1 |
| Availability of child care at this institution | 189 | 19.2 | 17.6 | 18.5 | 26.9 | 19.6 | 23.7 | 24.5 | 20.1 | 22.5 |
| Prospects for career advancement | 599 | 58.4 | 54.0 | 56.6 | 55.8 | 54.6 | 55.3 | 56.6 | 54.6 | 55.7 |
| Clerical/administrative support | 642 | 58.2 | 59.1 | 58.6 | 63.3 | 60.0 | 61.9 | 62.4 | 58.4 | 60.7 |
| Overall job satisfaction | 645 | 76.1 | 75.0 | 75.7 | 79.3 | 78.1 | 78.8 | 77.9 | 76.2 | 77.2 |

[2]  This question asked for the first time in the 2007–2008 Faculty Survey.
[3]  Respondents marking "Not Applicable" were not included in the computation of these results.

| Whatsamatta University<br>Full-time Undergraduate Faculty | # Respon-<br>dents | Your Institution | | | Nonsect 4-yr Colls | | | All Priv 4-yr Colls | | |
|---|---|---|---|---|---|---|---|---|---|---|
| | | Men | Women | Total | Men | Women | Total | Men | Women | Total |
| **Do you agree "strongly" or "somewhat"?** | | | | | | | | | | |
| Faculty are interested in students' personal problems | 645 | 82.9 | 85.2 | 83.9 | 91.6 | 92.6 | 92.0 | 93.6 | 94.4 | 93.9 |
| Racial and ethnic diversity should be more strongly reflected in the curriculum | 640 | 54.1 | 68.6 | 60.0 | 56.5 | 71.5 | 62.8 | 58.2 | 71.7 | 64.0 |
| Faculty feel that most students are well-prepared academically | 647 | 41.9 | 47.5 | 44.2 | 49.9 | 48.9 | 49.5 | 47.7 | 48.6 | 48.1 |
| This institution should hire more faculty of color | 638 | 66.9 | 80.4 | 72.4 | 70.9 | 83.6 | 76.2 | 72.8 | 84.4 | 77.7 |
| Student Affairs staff have the support and respect of faculty | 633 | 80.0 | 79.8 | 79.9 | 78.7 | 81.0 | 79.6 | 79.4 | 82.1 | 80.6 |
| Faculty are committed to the welfare of this institution | 645 | 90.5 | 90.9 | 90.7 | 94.0 | 95.9 | 94.8 | 94.8 | 95.8 | 95.2 |
| Faculty here are strongly interested in the academic problems of undergraduates | 644 | 88.7 | 88.2 | 88.5 | 94.3 | 96.3 | 95.2 | 94.9 | 95.5 | 95.2 |
| There is a lot of campus racial conflict here | 644 | 6.8 | 10.6 | 8.4 | 9.8 | 15.8 | 12.3 | 8.9 | 14.7 | 11.4 |
| Most students are strongly committed to community service | 642 | 71.7 | 73.9 | 72.6 | 56.1 | 59.6 | 57.6 | 61.6 | 66.6 | 63.8 |
| My research is valued by faculty in my department | 636 | 82.1 | 76.3 | 79.7 | 78.2 | 72.4 | 75.8 | 78.3 | 72.7 | 75.9 |
| My teaching is valued by faculty in my department | 646 | 91.4 | 89.8 | 90.7 | 91.2 | 95.0 | 92.8 | 93.3 | 93.2 | 93.2 |
| Many courses include feminist perspectives | 634 | 30.1 | 35.9 | 32.5 | 51.0 | 58.9 | 54.3 | 46.7 | 52.3 | 49.1 |
| Faculty of color are treated fairly here | 633 | 91.8 | 87.2 | 89.9 | 93.0 | 88.9 | 91.3 | 92.4 | 87.9 | 90.4 |
| Women faculty are treated fairly here | 640 | 93.1 | 78.2 | 87.0 | 94.7 | 82.6 | 89.7 | 93.5 | 81.4 | 88.3 |
| Many courses involve students in community service | 635 | 58.6 | 69.7 | 63.1 | 51.1 | 58.0 | 54.0 | 56.7 | 63.4 | 59.6 |
| This institution should hire more women faculty | 631 | 56.9 | 72.5 | 63.2 | 44.5 | 56.1 | 49.4 | 46.4 | 55.7 | 50.4 |
| Gay and lesbian faculty are treated fairly here | 601 | 62.3 | 48.3 | 56.7 | 86.6 | 84.1 | 85.6 | 77.5 | 74.5 | 76.2 |
| My department does a good job of mentoring new faculty | 644 | 71.4 | 63.1 | 68.0 | 76.4 | 70.4 | 73.9 | 76.7 | 71.7 | 74.6 |
| Faculty are sufficiently involved in campus decision making | 641 | 45.8 | 50.6 | 47.7 | 63.7 | 62.2 | 63.0 | 60.3 | 59.9 | 60.1 |
| My values are congruent with the dominant institutional values | 643 | 77.3 | 75.0 | 76.4 | 79.1 | 80.6 | 79.7 | 80.8 | 82.2 | 81.4 |
| There is adequate support for integrating technology in my teaching | 645 | 91.1 | 88.6 | 90.1 | 84.6 | 81.0 | 83.1 | 82.8 | 79.3 | 81.3 |
| This institution takes responsibility for educating underprepared students | 642 | 73.1 | 68.8 | 71.3 | 68.6 | 66.0 | 67.5 | 69.1 | 65.4 | 67.5 |
| The criteria for advancement and promotion decisions are clear | 645 | 79.8 | 72.7 | 76.9 | 70.3 | 72.5 | 71.2 | 71.8 | 71.7 | 71.8 |
| Most of the students I teach lack the basic skills for college level work | 645 | 34.2 | 35.1 | 34.6 | 32.5 | 35.3 | 33.7 | 34.6 | 36.7 | 35.5 |
| There is adequate support for faculty development | 644 | 65.4 | 70.7 | 67.5 | 72.2 | 68.1 | 70.5 | 69.5 | 68.2 | 69.0 |
| This institution should not offer remedial/developmental education | 632 | 23.7 | 23.7 | 23.7 | 29.9 | 25.2 | 28.0 | 28.9 | 22.9 | 26.3 |

| Whatsamatta University<br>Full-time Undergraduate Faculty | # Respon-<br>dents | Your Institution | | | Nonsect 4-yr Colls | | | All Priv 4-yr Colls | | |
|---|---|---|---|---|---|---|---|---|---|---|
| | | Men | Women | Total | Men | Women | Total | Men | Women | Total |
| **Issues you believe to be of "high" or** | | | | | | | | | | |
| **"highest" priority at your institution:** | | | | | | | | | | |
| To promote the intellectual development of students | 644 | 89.7 | 85.6 | 88.0 | 88.6 | 90.5 | 89.4 | 88.0 | 90.3 | 89.0 |
| To help students examine and understand their personal values | 644 | 79.7 | 78.8 | 79.3 | 67.2 | 66.9 | 67.1 | 73.2 | 75.4 | 74.1 |
| To develop a sense of community among students and faculty | 644 | 64.2 | 65.9 | 64.9 | 63.5 | 69.3 | 66.0 | 65.9 | 72.2 | 68.6 |
| To facilitate student involvement in community service | 643 | 62.8 | 76.5 | 68.4 | 47.2 | 56.7 | 51.2 | 55.3 | 64.2 | 59.1 |
| To help students learn how to bring about change in American society | 640 | 39.6 | 50.4 | 44.1 | 40.4 | 44.8 | 42.3 | 40.8 | 48.0 | 43.9 |
| To increase or maintain institutional prestige | 643 | 61.3 | 66.5 | 63.5 | 64.1 | 63.7 | 64.0 | 59.4 | 60.8 | 60.0 |
| To hire faculty "stars" | 643 | 21.3 | 25.1 | 22.9 | 16.9 | 18.3 | 17.5 | 14.6 | 18.3 | 16.2 |
| To recruit more minority students | 642 | 41.2 | 44.9 | 42.7 | 51.9 | 54.7 | 53.1 | 47.3 | 51.4 | 49.1 |
| To enhance the institution's national image | 643 | 68.7 | 74.1 | 70.9 | 68.9 | 66.9 | 68.1 | 62.0 | 61.2 | 61.6 |
| To create a diverse multi-cultural campus environment | 644 | 48.9 | 57.2 | 52.3 | 58.8 | 57.8 | 58.4 | 53.0 | 54.6 | 53.7 |
| To promote gender equity among faculty | 639 | 51.9 | 39.5 | 46.8 | 59.2 | 47.6 | 54.3 | 54.6 | 43.8 | 50.0 |
| To provide resources for faculty to engage in community-based teaching or research | 639 | 37.2 | 48.3 | 41.8 | 34.6 | 34.5 | 34.5 | 32.9 | 36.2 | 34.3 |
| To create and sustain partnerships with surrounding communities | 641 | 40.2 | 49.8 | 44.1 | 43.7 | 43.2 | 43.4 | 43.8 | 47.5 | 45.4 |
| To pursue extramural funding | 635 | 50.8 | 60.3 | 54.6 | 45.5 | 48.4 | 46.7 | 44.3 | 47.6 | 45.7 |
| To increase the representation of minorities in the faculty and administration | 636 | 39.6 | 43.8 | 41.4 | 45.5 | 45.8 | 45.6 | 40.2 | 42.7 | 41.3 |
| To strengthen links with the for-profit, corporate sector [2] | 630 | 38.1 | 44.7 | 40.8 | 33.8 | 36.3 | 34.8 | 34.4 | 37.2 | 35.6 |
| To develop leadership ability among students | 638 | 60.6 | 67.2 | 63.3 | 66.7 | 71.8 | 68.8 | 66.3 | 72.4 | 68.9 |
| To increase the representation of women in the faculty and administration | 635 | 36.2 | 37.5 | 36.7 | 41.0 | 30.9 | 36.7 | 35.9 | 30.3 | 33.5 |
| To develop an appreciation for multiculturalism [2] | 639 | 51.1 | 60.1 | 54.8 | 62.5 | 61.9 | 62.3 | 57.6 | 60.6 | 58.9 |

[2]  This question asked for the first time in the 2007–2008 Faculty Survey.

| Whatsamatta University<br>Full-time Undergraduate Faculty | # Respon-<br>dents | Your Institution | | | Nonsect 4-yr Colls | | | All Priv 4-yr Colls | | |
|---|---|---|---|---|---|---|---|---|---|---|
| | | Men | Women | Total | Men | Women | Total | Men | Women | Total |
| **Do you agree "strongly" or "somewhat"?** | | | | | | | | | | |
| Western civilization and culture should be the foundation for the undergraduate curriculum | 641 | 72.3 | 58.4 | 66.6 | 62.6 | 47.5 | 56.2 | 66.6 | 52.2 | 60.4 |
| College officials have the right to ban persons with extreme views from speaking on campus | 641 | 49.5 | 36.9 | 44.3 | 33.9 | 25.4 | 30.3 | 39.1 | 29.8 | 35.1 |
| The chief benefit of a college education is that it increases one's earning power | 642 | 28.2 | 25.6 | 27.1 | 24.7 | 23.2 | 24.1 | 24.1 | 24.3 | 24.2 |
| Promoting diversity leads to the admission of too many underprepared students | 640 | 30.1 | 17.6 | 25.0 | 23.0 | 15.3 | 19.8 | 24.8 | 16.2 | 21.1 |
| Colleges should be actively involved in solving social problems | 642 | 64.7 | 69.1 | 66.5 | 66.6 | 74.3 | 69.8 | 68.6 | 75.6 | 71.6 |
| Tenure is an outmoded concept | 639 | 24.2 | 39.4 | 30.4 | 31.5 | 30.6 | 31.2 | 31.3 | 35.1 | 32.9 |
| Colleges should encourage students to be involved in community service activities | 642 | 88.4 | 93.5 | 90.5 | 86.8 | 94.5 | 90.0 | 89.2 | 95.4 | 91.8 |
| Community service should be given weight in college admissions decisions | 642 | 67.1 | 70.2 | 68.4 | 68.3 | 72.6 | 70.1 | 68.7 | 73.4 | 70.7 |
| A racially/ethnically diverse student body enhances the educational experience of all students | 642 | 90.5 | 96.2 | 92.8 | 90.4 | 98.2 | 93.7 | 91.6 | 97.4 | 94.1 |
| Realistically, an individual can do little to bring about changes in society | 643 | 25.8 | 11.4 | 19.9 | 23.0 | 9.4 | 17.3 | 21.8 | 9.9 | 16.7 |
| Colleges should be concerned with facilitating undergraduate students' spiritual development | 644 | 73.2 | 71.5 | 72.5 | 42.3 | 38.2 | 40.5 | 58.1 | 56.0 | 57.2 |
| Colleges have a responsibility to work with their surrounding communities to address local issues | 643 | 87.4 | 87.8 | 87.6 | 83.9 | 91.8 | 87.2 | 86.7 | 92.6 | 89.2 |
| Private funding sources often prevent researchers from being completely objective in the conduct of their work | 633 | 50.4 | 58.3 | 53.6 | 56.6 | 61.1 | 58.5 | 57.3 | 59.0 | 58.0 |

| Whatsamatta University<br>Full-time Undergraduate Faculty | # Respon-<br>dents | Your Institution | | | Nonsect 4-yr Colls | | | All Priv 4-yr Colls | | |
|---|---|---|---|---|---|---|---|---|---|---|
| | | Men | Women | Total | Men | Women | Total | Men | Women | Total |
| **Factors noted as a source of stress for you during the <u>last two</u> years [4]** | | | | | | | | | | |
| Managing household responsibilities | 643 | 67.5 | 78.6 | 72.0 | 70.9 | 82.6 | 75.8 | 70.8 | 81.9 | 75.5 |
| Child care | 644 | 33.6 | 32.3 | 33.1 | 35.5 | 31.9 | 34.0 | 34.1 | 33.0 | 33.6 |
| Care of elderly parent | 643 | 29.2 | 39.9 | 33.6 | 35.3 | 33.4 | 34.5 | 33.4 | 35.8 | 34.4 |
| My physical health | 644 | 43.3 | 49.0 | 45.7 | 43.1 | 53.2 | 47.3 | 44.7 | 53.9 | 48.6 |
| Health of spouse/partner | 644 | 31.2 | 28.5 | 30.1 | 39.0 | 34.1 | 37.0 | 38.4 | 31.2 | 35.3 |
| Review/promotion process | 643 | 45.0 | 59.7 | 51.0 | 45.2 | 57.5 | 50.4 | 45.7 | 55.1 | 49.7 |
| Subtle discrimination (e.g., prejudice, racism, sexism) | 644 | 16.3 | 39.2 | 25.6 | 18.4 | 31.8 | 24.1 | 16.9 | 33.4 | 24.0 |
| Personal finances | 644 | 64.0 | 61.6 | 63.0 | 65.2 | 67.5 | 66.2 | 65.5 | 66.3 | 65.8 |
| Committee work | 644 | 51.7 | 58.9 | 54.7 | 59.4 | 63.8 | 61.2 | 60.3 | 63.3 | 61.6 |
| Faculty meetings | 645 | 39.8 | 53.2 | 45.3 | 51.6 | 53.5 | 52.4 | 52.5 | 54.6 | 53.4 |
| Colleagues | 645 | 55.8 | 63.9 | 59.1 | 60.0 | 69.5 | 64.0 | 59.5 | 66.7 | 62.6 |
| Students | 643 | 56.8 | 68.1 | 61.4 | 62.3 | 69.0 | 65.2 | 64.4 | 70.5 | 67.0 |
| Research or publishing demands | 644 | 65.4 | 72.6 | 68.3 | 50.9 | 60.5 | 54.9 | 51.2 | 56.9 | 53.6 |
| Institutional procedures and "red tape" | 644 | 65.9 | 65.8 | 65.8 | 63.9 | 62.2 | 63.2 | 66.4 | 64.1 | 65.4 |
| Teaching load | 644 | 60.9 | 63.1 | 61.8 | 62.6 | 69.7 | 65.6 | 64.2 | 70.2 | 66.7 |
| Children's problems | 644 | 29.7 | 28.1 | 29.0 | 31.8 | 30.3 | 31.2 | 32.0 | 30.6 | 31.4 |
| Friction with spouse/partner | 644 | 23.9 | 20.9 | 22.7 | 28.5 | 25.4 | 27.2 | 27.7 | 24.6 | 26.4 |
| Lack of personal time | 644 | 67.5 | 83.3 | 73.9 | 68.2 | 86.0 | 75.7 | 69.2 | 85.2 | 76.1 |
| Keeping up with information technology | 644 | 44.6 | 51.7 | 47.5 | 48.7 | 52.9 | 50.5 | 49.7 | 56.7 | 52.7 |
| Job security | 644 | 27.0 | 35.0 | 30.3 | 35.7 | 36.7 | 36.1 | 34.1 | 36.5 | 35.1 |
| Being part of a dual career couple | 644 | 34.1 | 46.0 | 39.0 | 45.8 | 51.5 | 48.2 | 44.9 | 50.1 | 47.1 |
| Working with underprepared students | 644 | 60.6 | 57.4 | 59.3 | 59.7 | 62.8 | 61.0 | 64.2 | 67.1 | 65.5 |
| Classroom conflict | 644 | 12.9 | 20.2 | 15.8 | 15.2 | 24.2 | 19.0 | 16.9 | 25.1 | 20.4 |
| Self-imposed high expectations | 645 | 72.8 | 85.2 | 77.8 | 77.1 | 85.8 | 80.8 | 77.7 | 85.5 | 81.1 |
| Change in work responsibilities | 643 | 36.7 | 54.2 | 43.9 | 43.4 | 55.0 | 48.3 | 43.0 | 55.9 | 48.5 |
| **Personal goals noted as "very important" or "essential":** | | | | | | | | | | |
| Becoming an authority in my field | 645 | 70.1 | 66.7 | 68.7 | 53.3 | 52.3 | 52.9 | 52.8 | 51.8 | 52.4 |
| Influencing the political structure | 644 | 20.3 | 18.9 | 19.7 | 15.6 | 16.5 | 16.0 | 16.5 | 17.6 | 17.0 |
| Influencing social values | 644 | 39.2 | 53.4 | 45.0 | 37.3 | 47.3 | 41.5 | 39.9 | 48.2 | 43.5 |
| Raising a family | 644 | 73.0 | 69.8 | 71.7 | 75.4 | 65.8 | 71.4 | 74.9 | 66.0 | 71.1 |
| Becoming very well off financially | 644 | 35.3 | 28.6 | 32.6 | 30.4 | 25.1 | 28.2 | 28.3 | 24.6 | 26.7 |
| Helping others who are in difficulty | 645 | 67.2 | 74.6 | 70.2 | 61.3 | 72.2 | 65.9 | 64.0 | 73.6 | 68.1 |
| Becoming involved in programs to clean up the environment | 645 | 26.0 | 33.7 | 29.1 | 34.0 | 39.3 | 36.2 | 33.0 | 38.9 | 35.5 |
| Developing a meaningful philosophy of life | 643 | 77.3 | 77.3 | 77.3 | 74.9 | 76.6 | 75.6 | 75.2 | 78.0 | 76.4 |
| Helping to promote racial understanding | 644 | 49.5 | 62.9 | 55.0 | 53.2 | 63.7 | 57.6 | 52.4 | 64.0 | 57.4 |
| Obtaining recognition from my colleagues for contributions to my special field | 644 | 56.4 | 54.8 | 55.7 | 40.6 | 42.6 | 41.4 | 38.3 | 41.4 | 39.6 |
| Integrating spirituality into my life | 642 | 62.1 | 69.5 | 65.1 | 45.7 | 46.4 | 46.0 | 54.5 | 58.7 | 56.3 |

[4] Percentage represents those reporting "somewhat" or "extensive" stress.

| Whatsamatta University<br>Full-time Undergraduate Faculty | # Respon-<br>dents | Your Institution | | | Nonsect 4-yr Colls | | | All Priv 4-yr Colls | | |
|---|---|---|---|---|---|---|---|---|---|---|
| | | Men | Women | Total | Men | Women | Total | Men | Women | Total |
| **IN YOUR INTERACTIONS WITH UNDERGRAD-UATES, HOW OFTEN DO YOU ENCOURAGE THEM TO: [2]** | | | | | | | | | | |
| **Ask questions in class** | 645 | | | | | | | | | |
| Frequently | | 90.6 | 95.8 | 92.7 | 93.5 | 97.4 | 95.2 | 93.5 | 96.9 | 95.0 |
| Occasionally | | 8.7 | 4.2 | 6.8 | 6.4 | 2.6 | 4.8 | 6.4 | 3.1 | 5.0 |
| Not at all | | 0.8 | 0.0 | 0.5 | 0.0 | 0.0 | 0.0 | 0.1 | 0.1 | 0.1 |
| **Support their opinions with a logical argument** | 644 | | | | | | | | | |
| Frequently | | 80.3 | 85.9 | 82.6 | 82.5 | 88.3 | 84.9 | 82.0 | 86.7 | 84.0 |
| Occasionally | | 18.9 | 13.7 | 16.8 | 17.0 | 11.2 | 14.6 | 17.2 | 12.8 | 15.3 |
| Not at all | | 0.8 | 0.4 | 0.6 | 0.6 | 0.5 | 0.6 | 0.8 | 0.5 | 0.7 |
| **Seek solutions to problems and explain them to others** | 644 | | | | | | | | | |
| Frequently | | 67.4 | 75.0 | 70.5 | 73.2 | 81.2 | 76.5 | 71.3 | 80.0 | 75.1 |
| Occasionally | | 29.7 | 22.3 | 26.7 | 25.0 | 17.7 | 21.9 | 26.9 | 18.9 | 23.5 |
| Not at all | | 2.9 | 2.7 | 2.8 | 1.8 | 1.2 | 1.6 | 1.7 | 1.1 | 1.5 |
| **Revise their papers to improve their writing** | 644 | | | | | | | | | |
| Frequently | | 48.3 | 65.8 | 55.4 | 60.5 | 73.8 | 66.1 | 57.2 | 69.8 | 62.6 |
| Occasionally | | 39.4 | 30.0 | 35.6 | 32.0 | 22.5 | 28.0 | 34.8 | 25.8 | 30.9 |
| Not at all | | 12.3 | 4.2 | 9.0 | 7.5 | 3.8 | 5.9 | 8.0 | 4.3 | 6.4 |
| **Evaluate the quality or reliability of information they receive** | 645 | | | | | | | | | |
| Frequently | | 66.4 | 80.3 | 72.1 | 71.3 | 80.7 | 75.2 | 69.4 | 79.3 | 73.6 |
| Occasionally | | 31.5 | 18.2 | 26.0 | 26.8 | 18.2 | 23.2 | 28.4 | 19.1 | 24.4 |
| Not at all | | 2.1 | 1.5 | 1.9 | 2.0 | 1.1 | 1.6 | 2.2 | 1.6 | 1.9 |
| **Take risks for potential gains** | 644 | | | | | | | | | |
| Frequently | | 29.9 | 39.2 | 33.7 | 37.4 | 45.3 | 40.7 | 35.8 | 42.3 | 38.6 |
| Occasionally | | 50.7 | 44.9 | 48.3 | 49.7 | 45.7 | 48.0 | 51.0 | 47.3 | 49.4 |
| Not at all | | 19.4 | 16.0 | 18.0 | 12.9 | 9.0 | 11.3 | 13.2 | 10.4 | 12.0 |
| **Seek alternative solutions to a problem** | 644 | | | | | | | | | |
| Frequently | | 55.5 | 67.4 | 60.4 | 63.2 | 71.4 | 66.6 | 61.1 | 69.4 | 64.7 |
| Occasionally | | 40.8 | 30.3 | 36.5 | 34.6 | 27.1 | 31.4 | 36.5 | 28.8 | 33.2 |
| Not at all | | 3.7 | 2.3 | 3.1 | 2.2 | 1.5 | 1.9 | 2.4 | 1.8 | 2.2 |
| **Look up scientific research articles and resources** | 643 | | | | | | | | | |
| Frequently | | 50.0 | 59.7 | 54.0 | 49.2 | 57.5 | 52.7 | 46.4 | 55.8 | 50.4 |
| Occasionally | | 37.1 | 27.8 | 33.3 | 37.0 | 26.9 | 32.8 | 38.9 | 29.7 | 35.0 |
| Not at all | | 12.9 | 12.5 | 12.8 | 13.8 | 15.6 | 14.5 | 14.6 | 14.5 | 14.6 |
| **Explore topics on their own, even though it was not required for a class** | 644 | | | | | | | | | |
| Frequently | | 50.0 | 52.7 | 51.1 | 49.0 | 57.5 | 52.5 | 46.6 | 54.2 | 49.9 |
| Occasionally | | 44.7 | 43.2 | 44.1 | 45.7 | 40.6 | 43.6 | 48.3 | 43.1 | 46.1 |
| Not at all | | 5.3 | 4.2 | 4.8 | 5.3 | 1.9 | 3.9 | 5.1 | 2.7 | 4.1 |
| **Acknowledge failure as a necessary part of the learning process** | 644 | | | | | | | | | |
| Frequently | | 41.7 | 52.1 | 46.0 | 49.0 | 56.7 | 52.2 | 47.2 | 53.4 | 49.8 |
| Occasionally | | 47.5 | 41.8 | 45.2 | 45.1 | 37.8 | 42.0 | 46.4 | 41.6 | 44.3 |
| Not at all | | 10.8 | 6.1 | 8.9 | 6.0 | 5.4 | 5.8 | 6.4 | 5.0 | 5.8 |
| **Seek feedback on their academic work** | 643 | | | | | | | | | |
| Frequently | | 64.7 | 82.9 | 72.2 | 72.0 | 83.4 | 76.7 | 69.8 | 82.8 | 75.4 |
| Occasionally | | 32.9 | 15.6 | 25.8 | 26.4 | 16.2 | 22.1 | 28.5 | 16.5 | 23.3 |
| Not at all | | 2.4 | 1.5 | 2.0 | 1.6 | 0.4 | 1.1 | 1.7 | 0.6 | 1.2 |

[2] This question asked for the first time in the 2007–2008 Faculty Survey.

| Whatsamatta University<br>Full-time Undergraduate Faculty | # Respon-<br>dents | Your Institution | | | Nonsect 4-yr Colls | | | All Priv 4-yr Colls | | |
|---|---|---|---|---|---|---|---|---|---|---|
| | | Men | Women | Total | Men | Women | Total | Men | Women | Total |
| **Methods you use in "all" or "most" of** | | | | | | | | | | |
| **the courses you teach:** | | | | | | | | | | |
| Multiple-choice exams [2] | 644 | 28.3 | 41.1 | 33.5 | 25.9 | 24.9 | 25.4 | 31.0 | 33.7 | 32.1 |
| Essay exams [2] | 644 | 48.6 | 47.9 | 48.3 | 51.7 | 43.9 | 48.4 | 52.3 | 45.3 | 49.3 |
| Short-answer exams [2] | 641 | 40.8 | 46.0 | 42.9 | 48.0 | 43.3 | 46.1 | 49.7 | 46.3 | 48.3 |
| Quizzes | 642 | 36.2 | 40.6 | 38.0 | 35.6 | 38.1 | 36.6 | 39.5 | 41.8 | 40.5 |
| Weekly essay assignments | 644 | 16.5 | 25.9 | 20.3 | 23.4 | 30.0 | 26.2 | 21.2 | 27.6 | 24.0 |
| Student presentations | 644 | 31.3 | 52.7 | 40.1 | 49.4 | 62.7 | 55.0 | 46.0 | 61.3 | 52.6 |
| Term/research papers | 642 | 43.4 | 48.1 | 45.3 | 46.0 | 52.4 | 48.7 | 45.0 | 47.8 | 46.2 |
| Student evaluations of each others' work | 644 | 12.6 | 25.1 | 17.7 | 23.6 | 31.7 | 27.0 | 20.9 | 31.2 | 25.3 |
| Grading on a curve | 644 | 22.0 | 11.0 | 17.5 | 17.5 | 9.0 | 14.0 | 16.7 | 8.4 | 13.2 |
| Competency-based grading | 638 | 47.7 | 52.5 | 49.7 | 53.9 | 50.4 | 52.5 | 51.3 | 52.7 | 51.9 |
| Class discussions | 645 | 76.9 | 90.5 | 82.5 | 80.6 | 89.9 | 84.5 | 81.4 | 88.3 | 84.3 |
| Cooperative learning (small groups) | 645 | 37.8 | 65.2 | 49.0 | 53.7 | 74.3 | 62.3 | 54.6 | 75.1 | 63.4 |
| Experiential learning/Field studies | 643 | 16.9 | 35.2 | 24.4 | 27.9 | 37.0 | 31.7 | 27.0 | 38.6 | 32.0 |
| Teaching assistants | 641 | 11.6 | 13.7 | 12.5 | 8.2 | 8.3 | 8.2 | 6.5 | 6.7 | 6.6 |
| Recitals/Demonstrations | 644 | 16.1 | 23.5 | 19.1 | 21.5 | 21.1 | 21.3 | 20.0 | 22.3 | 21.0 |
| Group projects | 643 | 20.0 | 36.9 | 26.9 | 31.8 | 40.8 | 35.6 | 32.5 | 42.4 | 36.7 |
| Extensive lecturing | 642 | 59.2 | 42.4 | 52.3 | 47.1 | 27.2 | 38.8 | 48.5 | 29.8 | 40.5 |
| Multiple drafts of written work | 641 | 16.6 | 28.2 | 21.4 | 27.8 | 36.0 | 31.2 | 23.6 | 31.7 | 27.1 |
| Readings on racial and ethnic issues | 642 | 14.5 | 27.9 | 19.9 | 22.6 | 35.4 | 28.0 | 19.9 | 32.8 | 25.5 |
| Readings on women and gender issues | 644 | 11.5 | 25.5 | 17.2 | 16.2 | 31.6 | 22.6 | 15.6 | 29.3 | 21.4 |
| Student-developed activities<br>   (assignments, exams, etc.) | 644 | 29.2 | 37.5 | 32.6 | 26.0 | 26.2 | 26.1 | 24.5 | 27.1 | 25.6 |
| Student-selected topics for course<br>   content | 644 | 12.9 | 20.8 | 16.1 | 15.2 | 20.4 | 17.4 | 14.8 | 20.2 | 17.1 |
| Reflective writing/journaling | 643 | 17.2 | 30.3 | 22.6 | 17.3 | 33.3 | 24.0 | 18.3 | 32.9 | 24.6 |
| Community service as part of coursework | 643 | 6.6 | 14.4 | 9.8 | 5.2 | 11.6 | 7.9 | 6.1 | 12.3 | 8.8 |
| Electronic quizzes with immediate<br>   feedback in class [2] | 641 | 6.6 | 8.8 | 7.5 | 4.7 | 3.6 | 4.2 | 5.0 | 5.5 | 5.2 |
| Using real-life problems [2] | 644 | 46.3 | 58.0 | 51.1 | 52.1 | 55.4 | 53.4 | 53.1 | 57.7 | 55.1 |
| Using student inquiry to drive learning | 641 | 42.9 | 51.3 | 46.3 | 47.4 | 56.8 | 51.3 | 45.4 | 54.5 | 49.3 |

[2]  This question asked for the first time in the 2007–2008 Faculty Survey.

| Whatsamatta University<br>Full-time Undergraduate Faculty | # Respon-<br>dents | Your Institution | | | Nonsect 4-yr Colls | | | All Priv 4-yr Colls | | |
|---|---|---|---|---|---|---|---|---|---|---|
| | | Men | Women | Total | Men | Women | Total | Men | Women | Total |
| **YOUR BASE INSTITUTIONAL SALARY** | | | | | | | | | | |
| **9/10 month contract** | 389 | | | | | | | | | |
| Less than $20,000 | | 1.3 | 2.0 | 1.5 | 2.8 | 1.7 | 2.4 | 2.2 | 2.0 | 2.1 |
| $20,000 to 29,999 | | 0.4 | 0.7 | 0.5 | 0.0 | 0.1 | 0.1 | 0.2 | 0.5 | 0.3 |
| $30,000 to 39,999 | | 1.3 | 1.3 | 1.3 | 3.8 | 6.0 | 4.7 | 4.2 | 6.1 | 5.0 |
| $40,000 to 49,999 | | 2.1 | 4.6 | 3.1 | 16.5 | 16.9 | 16.6 | 20.0 | 23.7 | 21.5 |
| $50,000 to 59,999 | | 16.5 | 32.0 | 22.6 | 21.1 | 29.3 | 24.3 | 23.8 | 30.9 | 26.8 |
| $60,000 to 69,999 | | 19.5 | 19.6 | 19.5 | 16.3 | 19.2 | 17.5 | 16.5 | 18.0 | 17.2 |
| $70,000 to 79,999 | | 17.4 | 19.0 | 18.0 | 11.7 | 10.9 | 11.4 | 12.6 | 8.3 | 10.8 |
| $80,000 to 89,999 | | 14.4 | 7.8 | 11.8 | 9.6 | 6.5 | 8.4 | 8.1 | 5.0 | 6.8 |
| $90,000 to 99,999 | | 13.1 | 5.2 | 10.0 | 6.7 | 3.4 | 5.4 | 5.5 | 2.3 | 4.2 |
| $100,000 to 124,999 | | 10.6 | 3.3 | 7.7 | 8.2 | 4.8 | 6.9 | 5.0 | 2.5 | 4.0 |
| $125,000 to 149,999 | | 2.1 | 3.3 | 2.6 | 1.9 | 0.6 | 1.4 | 1.0 | 0.3 | 0.7 |
| $150,000 or more | | 1.3 | 1.3 | 1.3 | 1.3 | 0.5 | 1.0 | 0.7 | 0.2 | 0.5 |
| **11/12 month contract** | 237 | | | | | | | | | |
| Less than $20,000 | | 0.7 | 5.0 | 2.5 | 2.8 | 1.7 | 2.3 | 2.4 | 2.2 | 2.3 |
| $20,000 to 29,999 | | 0.7 | 0.0 | 0.4 | 0.1 | 0.2 | 0.1 | 0.9 | 0.5 | 0.7 |
| $30,000 to 39,999 | | 0.7 | 2.0 | 1.3 | 1.3 | 5.8 | 3.4 | 2.7 | 5.8 | 4.1 |
| $40,000 to 49,999 | | 9.5 | 12.0 | 10.5 | 18.7 | 17.4 | 18.1 | 21.2 | 23.1 | 22.1 |
| $50,000 to 59,999 | | 19.0 | 19.0 | 19.0 | 17.5 | 22.2 | 19.7 | 20.1 | 24.2 | 22.0 |
| $60,000 to 69,999 | | 18.2 | 18.0 | 18.1 | 15.0 | 20.0 | 17.3 | 14.9 | 19.4 | 17.0 |
| $70,000 to 79,999 | | 13.9 | 14.0 | 13.9 | 11.3 | 13.4 | 12.3 | 11.0 | 11.1 | 11.1 |
| $80,000 to 89,999 | | 10.9 | 16.0 | 13.1 | 10.6 | 9.0 | 9.9 | 10.2 | 6.7 | 8.6 |
| $90,000 to 99,999 | | 10.9 | 9.0 | 10.1 | 8.8 | 5.4 | 7.2 | 6.6 | 3.5 | 5.2 |
| $100,000 to 124,999 | | 12.4 | 4.0 | 8.9 | 10.8 | 4.0 | 7.7 | 7.6 | 3.0 | 5.5 |
| $125,000 to 149,999 | | 2.9 | 1.0 | 2.1 | 1.9 | 0.7 | 1.3 | 1.2 | 0.4 | 0.9 |
| $150,000 or more | | 0.0 | 0.0 | 0.0 | 1.1 | 0.2 | 0.7 | 1.2 | 0.1 | 0.7 |
| **Your base institutional salary is based on:** | 632 | | | | | | | | | |
| 9/10 months | | 63.5 | 60.3 | 62.2 | 67.6 | 61.9 | 65.2 | 70.2 | 66.8 | 68.7 |
| 11/12 months | | 36.5 | 39.7 | 37.8 | 32.4 | 38.1 | 34.8 | 29.8 | 33.2 | 31.3 |
| **WHAT PERCENTAGE OF YOUR CURRENT YEAR'S SALARY COMES FROM: [2]** | | | | | | | | | | |
| **Income from this institution** | 635 | | | | | | | | | |
| All | | 55.6 | 64.1 | 59.1 | 59.8 | 69.4 | 63.8 | 59.6 | 70.4 | 64.2 |
| 75 to 99 | | 36.2 | 31.7 | 34.3 | 29.5 | 26.1 | 28.1 | 30.6 | 24.8 | 28.1 |
| 50 to 74 | | 5.1 | 3.9 | 4.6 | 6.5 | 3.1 | 5.1 | 6.5 | 3.2 | 5.1 |
| 25 to 49 | | 2.9 | 0.4 | 1.9 | 3.6 | 1.0 | 2.5 | 2.9 | 1.1 | 2.1 |
| 1 to 24 | | 0.3 | 0.0 | 0.2 | 0.5 | 0.4 | 0.5 | 0.4 | 0.4 | 0.4 |
| None | | 0.0 | 0.0 | 0.0 | 0.2 | 0.0 | 0.1 | 0.1 | 0.1 | 0.1 |
| **Other academic income** | 570 | | | | | | | | | |
| All | | 0.0 | 0.0 | 0.0 | 0.0 | 0.0 | 0.0 | 0.0 | 0.1 | 0.0 |
| 75 to 99 | | 0.0 | 0.0 | 0.0 | 0.1 | 0.1 | 0.1 | 0.1 | 0.2 | 0.1 |
| 50 to 74 | | 0.3 | 0.0 | 0.2 | 0.5 | 0.1 | 0.3 | 0.4 | 0.2 | 0.3 |
| 25 to 49 | | 0.6 | 3.0 | 1.6 | 2.7 | 1.7 | 2.3 | 1.8 | 1.6 | 1.7 |
| 1 to 24 | | 21.5 | 13.9 | 18.4 | 19.1 | 12.9 | 16.5 | 18.6 | 13.0 | 16.2 |
| None | | 77.6 | 83.1 | 79.8 | 77.6 | 85.2 | 80.8 | 79.1 | 85.0 | 81.6 |
| **Non-academic income** | 578 | | | | | | | | | |
| All | | 0.0 | 0.0 | 0.0 | 0.2 | 0.0 | 0.1 | 0.1 | 0.1 | 0.1 |
| 75 to 99 | | 0.3 | 0.0 | 0.2 | 0.8 | 0.2 | 0.6 | 0.6 | 0.4 | 0.5 |
| 50 to 74 | | 4.6 | 0.9 | 3.1 | 3.7 | 1.5 | 2.8 | 3.0 | 1.5 | 2.4 |
| 25 to 49 | | 4.6 | 2.6 | 3.8 | 5.8 | 3.9 | 5.0 | 6.6 | 3.1 | 5.1 |
| 1 to 24 | | 25.2 | 24.9 | 25.1 | 19.7 | 17.6 | 18.8 | 20.9 | 17.4 | 19.4 |
| None | | 65.2 | 71.7 | 67.8 | 69.8 | 76.9 | 72.7 | 68.7 | 77.6 | 72.5 |

[2]  This question asked for the first time in the 2007–2008 Faculty Survey.

| Whatsamatta University<br>Full-time Undergraduate Faculty | # Respon-dents | Your Institution | | | Nonsect 4-yr Colls | | | All Priv 4-yr Colls | | |
|---|---|---|---|---|---|---|---|---|---|---|
| | | Men | Women | Total | Men | Women | Total | Men | Women | Total |
| **What is your age as of 12/31/2007?** | 628 | | | | | | | | | |
| Less than 30 | | 1.9 | 2.7 | 2.2 | 2.3 | 2.3 | 2.3 | 1.9 | 2.5 | 2.2 |
| 30 to 34 | | 8.1 | 9.4 | 8.6 | 7.7 | 8.7 | 8.1 | 7.6 | 8.6 | 8.0 |
| 35 to 39 | | 12.1 | 12.5 | 12.3 | 13.4 | 15.5 | 14.3 | 12.9 | 14.0 | 13.4 |
| 40 to 44 | | 12.4 | 14.8 | 13.4 | 13.0 | 15.4 | 14.0 | 12.5 | 14.2 | 13.3 |
| 45 to 49 | | 13.7 | 14.5 | 14.0 | 13.6 | 13.4 | 13.5 | 13.8 | 14.3 | 14.0 |
| 50 to 54 | | 12.4 | 14.1 | 13.1 | 13.9 | 15.7 | 14.7 | 14.1 | 16.5 | 15.1 |
| 55 to 59 | | 16.1 | 17.2 | 16.6 | 14.4 | 13.0 | 13.8 | 15.0 | 14.3 | 14.7 |
| 60 to 64 | | 11.6 | 7.4 | 9.9 | 13.3 | 9.4 | 11.6 | 13.1 | 10.0 | 11.8 |
| 65 to 69 | | 8.3 | 5.1 | 7.0 | 5.9 | 5.3 | 5.7 | 6.4 | 4.5 | 5.6 |
| 70 or more | | 3.5 | 2.3 | 3.0 | 2.5 | 1.1 | 2.0 | 2.7 | 1.1 | 2.0 |
| **Year of highest degree now held** | 629 | | | | | | | | | |
| Before 1970 | | 5.9 | 2.4 | 4.5 | 6.2 | 2.0 | 4.4 | 5.3 | 1.7 | 3.7 |
| 1971 to 1975 | | 8.3 | 2.7 | 6.0 | 6.8 | 4.0 | 5.6 | 7.6 | 3.2 | 5.7 |
| 1976 to 1980 | | 12.0 | 7.5 | 10.2 | 9.3 | 7.3 | 8.5 | 9.3 | 6.5 | 8.1 |
| 1981 to 1985 | | 10.4 | 11.4 | 10.8 | 11.6 | 8.9 | 10.4 | 11.0 | 8.6 | 10.0 |
| 1986 to 1990 | | 13.4 | 9.8 | 11.9 | 11.3 | 13.2 | 12.1 | 11.9 | 13.7 | 12.7 |
| 1991 to 1995 | | 11.0 | 15.7 | 12.9 | 15.1 | 14.1 | 14.7 | 14.7 | 15.2 | 14.9 |
| 1996 to 2000 | | 16.0 | 17.6 | 16.7 | 15.2 | 20.4 | 17.4 | 15.5 | 20.1 | 17.5 |
| 2001 to 2005 | | 18.4 | 23.9 | 20.7 | 18.7 | 23.7 | 20.8 | 18.8 | 22.9 | 20.6 |
| 2006 to 2007 | | 4.5 | 9.0 | 6.4 | 5.8 | 6.6 | 6.1 | 5.9 | 8.1 | 6.8 |
| **Year of appointment at current position** | 626 | | | | | | | | | |
| Before 1970 | | 4.0 | 2.0 | 3.2 | 3.8 | 1.0 | 2.6 | 3.6 | 1.0 | 2.5 |
| 1971 to 1975 | | 5.6 | 2.0 | 4.2 | 3.1 | 1.9 | 2.6 | 3.3 | 1.7 | 2.6 |
| 1976 to 1980 | | 5.6 | 2.4 | 4.3 | 6.0 | 3.8 | 5.1 | 5.6 | 3.4 | 4.7 |
| 1981 to 1985 | | 8.1 | 7.5 | 7.8 | 7.6 | 7.9 | 7.7 | 7.7 | 6.3 | 7.1 |
| 1986 to 1990 | | 11.8 | 11.0 | 11.5 | 11.2 | 10.4 | 10.8 | 10.5 | 10.6 | 10.5 |
| 1991 to 1995 | | 9.1 | 9.8 | 9.4 | 11.9 | 10.0 | 11.1 | 11.5 | 10.6 | 11.1 |
| 1996 to 2000 | | 15.9 | 15.0 | 15.5 | 17.3 | 19.3 | 18.1 | 16.6 | 18.8 | 17.6 |
| 2001 to 2005 | | 26.3 | 30.7 | 28.1 | 28.0 | 30.2 | 28.9 | 28.7 | 31.2 | 29.8 |
| 2006 to 2007 | | 13.4 | 19.7 | 16.0 | 11.2 | 15.5 | 13.0 | 12.6 | 16.4 | 14.2 |
| **If tenured, year tenure was awarded** | 334 | | | | | | | | | |
| Before 1970 | | 1.3 | 0.9 | 1.2 | 1.7 | 0.8 | 1.3 | 1.6 | 0.6 | 1.2 |
| 1971 to 1975 | | 4.9 | 2.7 | 4.2 | 3.7 | 0.4 | 2.4 | 3.2 | 0.7 | 2.3 |
| 1976 to 1980 | | 8.1 | 4.5 | 6.9 | 6.8 | 3.1 | 5.4 | 6.5 | 2.5 | 5.0 |
| 1981 to 1985 | | 9.0 | 2.7 | 6.9 | 8.7 | 5.4 | 7.5 | 8.3 | 5.0 | 7.1 |
| 1986 to 1990 | | 12.1 | 13.5 | 12.6 | 13.1 | 13.1 | 13.1 | 12.2 | 10.4 | 11.5 |
| 1991 to 1995 | | 17.9 | 21.6 | 19.2 | 17.5 | 13.6 | 16.0 | 16.5 | 15.0 | 15.9 |
| 1996 to 2000 | | 15.7 | 18.0 | 16.5 | 16.5 | 18.5 | 17.3 | 16.3 | 18.6 | 17.2 |
| 2001 to 2005 | | 20.2 | 18.9 | 19.8 | 17.5 | 25.9 | 20.7 | 19.5 | 26.6 | 22.1 |
| 2006 to 2007 | | 10.8 | 17.1 | 12.9 | 14.6 | 19.2 | 16.3 | 16.0 | 20.6 | 17.7 |

| Whatsamatta University<br>Full-time Undergraduate Faculty | # Respon-<br>dents | Your Institution | | | Nonsect 4-yr Colls | | | All Priv 4-yr Colls | | |
|---|---|---|---|---|---|---|---|---|---|---|
| | | Men | Women | Total | Men | Women | Total | Men | Women | Total |
| **WHAT IS THE MAJOR OF THE HIGHEST DEGREE YOU HOLD?** | | | | | | | | | | |
| **Biological Science** | 643 | | | | | | | | | |
| Agriculture | | 0.0 | 0.0 | 0.0 | 0.1 | 0.1 | 0.1 | 0.2 | 0.1 | 0.2 |
| Forestry | | 0.0 | 0.0 | 0.0 | 0.1 | 0.1 | 0.1 | 0.1 | 0.0 | 0.1 |
| Bacteriology, Molecular Biology | | 1.1 | 0.8 | 0.9 | 0.7 | 1.0 | 0.8 | 0.8 | 0.9 | 0.9 |
| Biochemistry | | 1.6 | 2.3 | 1.9 | 0.8 | 0.8 | 0.8 | 0.9 | 0.8 | 0.8 |
| Biophysics | | 0.3 | 0.0 | 0.2 | 0.1 | 0.1 | 0.1 | 0.1 | 0.1 | 0.1 |
| Botany | | 0.3 | 0.0 | 0.2 | 0.7 | 0.2 | 0.5 | 0.7 | 0.2 | 0.5 |
| Environmental Science | | 0.0 | 0.4 | 0.2 | 0.5 | 0.3 | 0.4 | 0.5 | 0.2 | 0.4 |
| Marine (life) Sciences | | 0.0 | 0.0 | 0.0 | 0.3 | 0.2 | 0.3 | 0.3 | 0.1 | 0.2 |
| Physiology, Anatomy | | 0.8 | 0.0 | 0.5 | 1.2 | 0.9 | 1.1 | 1.0 | 0.8 | 0.9 |
| Zoology | | 0.3 | 0.0 | 0.2 | 1.0 | 1.0 | 1.0 | 1.3 | 0.8 | 1.1 |
| General, Other Biological Sciences | | 2.1 | 2.3 | 2.2 | 2.6 | 2.4 | 2.5 | 2.1 | 2.1 | 2.1 |
| **Business** | | | | | | | | | | |
| Accounting | | 1.1 | 0.4 | 0.8 | 0.6 | 0.6 | 0.6 | 0.8 | 0.9 | 0.8 |
| Finance | | 1.3 | 0.8 | 1.1 | 0.5 | 0.2 | 0.4 | 0.6 | 0.4 | 0.5 |
| International Business | | 0.0 | 0.0 | 0.0 | 0.1 | 0.0 | 0.0 | 0.2 | 0.1 | 0.1 |
| Management | | 1.3 | 2.3 | 1.7 | 2.2 | 1.8 | 2.1 | 2.7 | 1.9 | 2.3 |
| Marketing | | 0.5 | 0.0 | 0.3 | 0.7 | 0.3 | 0.5 | 1.1 | 0.5 | 0.8 |
| Secretarial Studies | | 0.0 | 0.0 | 0.0 | 0.0 | 0.0 | 0.0 | 0.0 | 0.0 | 0.0 |
| General, Other Business | | 0.5 | 1.1 | 0.8 | 1.9 | 0.3 | 1.2 | 1.8 | 0.8 | 1.3 |
| **Education** | | | | | | | | | | |
| Business Education | | 0.0 | 0.0 | 0.0 | 0.1 | 0.2 | 0.1 | 0.1 | 0.2 | 0.1 |
| Educational Administration | | 1.8 | 2.3 | 2.0 | 0.8 | 0.8 | 0.8 | 1.7 | 1.8 | 1.8 |
| Educational Psychology/Counseling | | 0.3 | 2.3 | 1.1 | 0.7 | 0.5 | 0.6 | 0.7 | 0.8 | 0.8 |
| Elementary Education | | 0.0 | 1.5 | 0.6 | 0.3 | 0.6 | 0.4 | 0.2 | 1.3 | 0.7 |
| Higher Education | | 1.3 | 3.4 | 2.2 | 0.8 | 3.9 | 2.1 | 1.1 | 2.9 | 1.9 |
| Music or Art Education | | 0.5 | 0.4 | 0.5 | 0.1 | 0.5 | 0.3 | 0.3 | 0.4 | 0.3 |
| Physical or Health Education | | 0.3 | 0.4 | 0.3 | 1.0 | 1.7 | 1.3 | 1.6 | 1.7 | 1.6 |
| Secondary Education | | 0.3 | 0.4 | 0.3 | 0.5 | 0.4 | 0.5 | 0.5 | 0.6 | 0.5 |
| Special Education | | 0.0 | 0.4 | 0.2 | 1.4 | 0.5 | 1.0 | 0.9 | 1.3 | 1.1 |
| General, Other Education Fields | | 2.9 | 3.0 | 3.0 | 1.7 | 3.5 | 2.4 | 1.9 | 4.5 | 3.0 |
| **Engineering** | | | | | | | | | | |
| Aero-/Astronautical Engineering | | 0.0 | 0.0 | 0.0 | 0.0 | 0.0 | 0.0 | 0.1 | 0.0 | 0.1 |
| Chemical Engineering | | 0.0 | 0.0 | 0.0 | 0.1 | 0.0 | 0.1 | 0.1 | 0.1 | 0.1 |
| Civil Engineering | | 1.1 | 0.0 | 0.6 | 0.2 | 0.1 | 0.2 | 0.2 | 0.0 | 0.2 |
| Electrical Engineering | | 0.0 | 0.0 | 0.0 | 0.4 | 0.2 | 0.3 | 0.5 | 0.1 | 0.3 |
| Industrial Engineering | | 0.3 | 0.0 | 0.2 | 0.1 | 0.1 | 0.1 | 0.2 | 0.1 | 0.1 |
| Mechanical Engineering | | 0.5 | 0.0 | 0.3 | 0.5 | 0.1 | 0.3 | 0.5 | 0.1 | 0.3 |
| General, Other Engineering Fields | | 0.5 | 0.0 | 0.3 | 0.8 | 0.1 | 0.5 | 0.6 | 0.1 | 0.3 |
| **Health** | | | | | | | | | | |
| Dentistry | | 0.0 | 0.0 | 0.0 | 0.0 | 0.0 | 0.0 | 0.1 | 0.1 | 0.1 |
| Health Technology | | 0.0 | 0.0 | 0.0 | 0.0 | 0.0 | 0.0 | 0.0 | 0.0 | 0.0 |
| Medicine or Surgery | | 0.3 | 0.8 | 0.5 | 0.0 | 0.2 | 0.1 | 0.1 | 0.1 | 0.1 |
| Nursing | | 0.5 | 6.8 | 3.1 | 0.1 | 4.2 | 1.8 | 0.2 | 7.4 | 3.3 |
| Pharmacy, Pharmacology | | 3.7 | 4.6 | 4.0 | 1.7 | 2.1 | 1.9 | 1.0 | 1.1 | 1.0 |
| Therapy (speech, physical, occup.) | | 0.5 | 1.5 | 0.9 | 0.0 | 0.3 | 0.2 | 0.1 | 0.7 | 0.3 |
| Veterinary Medicine | | 0.0 | 0.0 | 0.0 | 0.0 | 0.3 | 0.2 | 0.0 | 0.1 | 0.1 |
| General, Other Health Fields | | 0.3 | 1.5 | 0.8 | 0.3 | 1.5 | 0.8 | 0.5 | 1.3 | 0.8 |

| Whatsamatta University<br>Full-time Undergraduate Faculty | # Respon-<br>dents | Your Institution | | | Nonsect 4-yr Colls | | | All Priv 4-yr Colls | | |
|---|---|---|---|---|---|---|---|---|---|---|
| | | Men | Women | Total | Men | Women | Total | Men | Women | Total |
| **WHAT IS THE MAJOR OF THE HIGHEST DEGREE YOU HOLD?** | | | | | | | | | | |
| **Humanities** | | | | | | | | | | |
| History | | 4.7 | 4.9 | 4.8 | 5.2 | 3.8 | 4.6 | 5.2 | 3.2 | 4.4 |
| Political Science, Government | | 3.7 | 0.4 | 2.3 | 3.2 | 2.2 | 2.8 | 2.8 | 1.8 | 2.4 |
| English Language & Literature | | 4.7 | 8.4 | 6.2 | 7.5 | 10.6 | 8.8 | 6.9 | 9.0 | 7.8 |
| Foreign Languages & Literature | | 1.3 | 3.4 | 2.2 | 1.0 | 3.5 | 2.0 | 0.9 | 2.6 | 1.7 |
| French | | 0.3 | 0.8 | 0.5 | 0.6 | 1.1 | 0.8 | 0.4 | 1.0 | 0.6 |
| German | | 0.3 | 0.4 | 0.3 | 0.5 | 0.8 | 0.6 | 0.4 | 0.5 | 0.4 |
| Spanish | | 0.0 | 0.8 | 0.3 | 0.9 | 1.7 | 1.2 | 1.0 | 1.9 | 1.4 |
| Other Foreign Languages | | 0.8 | 0.4 | 0.6 | 0.5 | 0.6 | 0.5 | 0.4 | 0.3 | 0.4 |
| Linguistics | | 0.5 | 0.0 | 0.3 | 0.3 | 2.6 | 1.2 | 0.3 | 1.3 | 0.7 |
| Philosophy | | 7.1 | 2.3 | 5.1 | 2.3 | 0.9 | 1.7 | 3.1 | 1.1 | 2.3 |
| Religion or Theology | | 10.3 | 5.3 | 8.2 | 5.1 | 1.4 | 3.5 | 6.0 | 2.6 | 4.6 |
| General, Other Humanities Fields | | 0.8 | 0.8 | 0.8 | 0.8 | 2.0 | 1.3 | 0.9 | 1.6 | 1.2 |
| **Fine Arts** | | | | | | | | | | |
| Architecture/Urban Planning | | 1.1 | 0.0 | 0.6 | 0.2 | 0.1 | 0.2 | 0.2 | 0.1 | 0.1 |
| Art | | 0.8 | 0.8 | 0.8 | 3.2 | 3.5 | 3.3 | 2.4 | 2.6 | 2.5 |
| Dramatics or Speech | | 1.3 | 1.5 | 1.4 | 2.0 | 2.4 | 2.2 | 2.0 | 2.0 | 2.0 |
| Music | | 2.4 | 2.3 | 2.3 | 4.1 | 2.4 | 3.4 | 4.5 | 3.2 | 3.9 |
| Television or Film | | 0.5 | 0.0 | 0.3 | 0.8 | 0.3 | 0.6 | 0.5 | 0.3 | 0.4 |
| Other Fine Arts | | 1.3 | 0.8 | 1.1 | 0.9 | 1.8 | 1.3 | 0.7 | 1.4 | 1.0 |
| **Physical Science** | | | | | | | | | | |
| Mathematics and/or Statistics | | 3.4 | 1.1 | 2.5 | 5.6 | 3.1 | 4.6 | 5.6 | 3.0 | 4.5 |
| Astronomy | | 0.5 | 0.0 | 0.3 | 0.4 | 0.2 | 0.3 | 0.3 | 0.1 | 0.2 |
| Atmospheric Sciences | | 0.3 | 0.0 | 0.2 | 0.0 | 0.0 | 0.0 | 0.0 | 0.0 | 0.0 |
| Chemistry | | 5.3 | 2.3 | 4.0 | 3.8 | 2.0 | 3.1 | 4.0 | 2.5 | 3.3 |
| Earth Sciences | | 0.3 | 0.0 | 0.2 | 1.4 | 0.5 | 1.0 | 0.9 | 0.3 | 0.6 |
| Geography | | 0.0 | 0.0 | 0.0 | 0.3 | 0.2 | 0.2 | 0.2 | 0.2 | 0.2 |
| Marine Sciences (incl. Oceanography) | | 0.0 | 0.0 | 0.0 | 0.1 | 0.1 | 0.1 | 0.1 | 0.0 | 0.0 |
| Physics | | 1.8 | 0.8 | 1.4 | 3.5 | 0.8 | 2.4 | 2.9 | 0.6 | 1.9 |
| General, Other Physical Sciences | | 0.0 | 0.0 | 0.0 | 0.1 | 0.1 | 0.1 | 0.1 | 0.1 | 0.1 |
| **Social Science** | | | | | | | | | | |
| Anthropology | | 1.3 | 2.3 | 1.7 | 1.1 | 1.0 | 1.1 | 0.8 | 0.5 | 0.7 |
| Archaeology | | 0.0 | 0.0 | 0.0 | 0.0 | 0.1 | 0.1 | 0.1 | 0.1 | 0.1 |
| Clinical Psychology | | 1.1 | 3.0 | 1.9 | 0.9 | 0.8 | 0.9 | 1.0 | 1.3 | 1.1 |
| Counseling and Guidance | | 0.3 | 0.4 | 0.3 | 0.4 | 0.0 | 0.2 | 0.4 | 0.5 | 0.5 |
| Experimental Psychology | | 1.6 | 2.3 | 1.9 | 1.6 | 1.0 | 1.3 | 1.3 | 1.2 | 1.2 |
| Social Psychology | | 0.3 | 0.4 | 0.3 | 0.7 | 1.0 | 0.8 | 0.7 | 1.0 | 0.8 |
| General, Other Psychology | | 1.3 | 1.1 | 1.2 | 0.5 | 4.3 | 2.1 | 0.8 | 2.9 | 1.7 |
| Economics | | 3.4 | 0.4 | 2.2 | 3.4 | 1.4 | 2.6 | 3.2 | 1.0 | 2.3 |
| Sociology | | 2.9 | 2.7 | 2.8 | 1.6 | 1.7 | 1.6 | 1.7 | 1.8 | 1.8 |
| Social Work, Social Welfare | | 0.5 | 1.5 | 0.9 | 1.1 | 0.9 | 1.0 | 0.9 | 1.0 | 0.9 |
| General, Other Social Sciences | | 0.8 | 1.5 | 1.1 | 1.2 | 1.8 | 1.5 | 0.9 | 1.3 | 1.0 |

| Whatsamatta University<br>Full-time Undergraduate Faculty | # Respon-<br>dents | Your Institution | | | Nonsect 4-yr Colls | | | All Priv 4-yr Colls | | |
|---|---|---|---|---|---|---|---|---|---|---|
| | | Men | Women | Total | Men | Women | Total | Men | Women | Total |
| **WHAT IS THE MAJOR OF THE HIGHEST DEGREE YOU HOLD?** | | | | | | | | | | |
| **Technical** | | | | | | | | | | |
| Computer Science | | 1.8 | 0.8 | 1.4 | 2.3 | 1.0 | 1.8 | 2.0 | 1.2 | 1.7 |
| Data Processing, Computer Prog. | | 0.0 | 0.0 | 0.0 | 0.1 | 0.0 | 0.0 | 0.1 | 0.1 | 0.1 |
| Drafting/Design | | 0.0 | 0.0 | 0.0 | 0.0 | 0.0 | 0.0 | 0.0 | 0.0 | 0.0 |
| Electronics | | 0.0 | 0.0 | 0.0 | 0.0 | 0.0 | 0.0 | 0.0 | 0.0 | 0.0 |
| Industrial Arts | | 0.0 | 0.0 | 0.0 | 0.0 | 0.0 | 0.0 | 0.0 | 0.0 | 0.0 |
| Mechanics | | 0.0 | 0.0 | 0.0 | 0.0 | 0.0 | 0.0 | 0.0 | 0.0 | 0.0 |
| Other Technical | | 0.3 | 0.0 | 0.2 | 0.1 | 0.0 | 0.1 | 0.1 | 0.1 | 0.1 |
| **Other Fields** | | | | | | | | | | |
| Building Trades | | 0.0 | 0.0 | 0.0 | 0.0 | 0.0 | 0.0 | 0.0 | 0.0 | 0.0 |
| Communications | | 1.8 | 1.5 | 1.7 | 2.5 | 1.7 | 2.1 | 2.6 | 2.0 | 2.3 |
| Ethnic Studies | | 0.0 | 0.0 | 0.0 | 0.0 | 0.0 | 0.0 | 0.0 | 0.0 | 0.0 |
| Human Ecology/Family Science | | 0.0 | 0.0 | 0.0 | 0.2 | 0.2 | 0.2 | 0.2 | 0.3 | 0.2 |
| Journalism | | 0.0 | 0.4 | 0.2 | 0.1 | 0.3 | 0.2 | 0.3 | 0.3 | 0.3 |
| Law | | 1.6 | 2.7 | 2.0 | 0.9 | 0.5 | 0.7 | 1.0 | 0.6 | 0.8 |
| Law Enforcement | | 0.3 | 0.4 | 0.3 | 0.0 | 0.1 | 0.1 | 0.1 | 0.0 | 0.0 |
| Library Science | | 1.1 | 1.5 | 1.2 | 0.7 | 0.4 | 0.6 | 0.5 | 1.0 | 0.7 |
| Women's Studies | | 0.0 | 0.0 | 0.0 | 0.0 | 0.0 | 0.0 | 0.0 | 0.1 | 0.0 |
| Other Vocational | | 0.0 | 0.0 | 0.0 | 0.0 | 0.0 | 0.0 | 0.0 | 0.0 | 0.0 |
| All Other Fields | | 0.3 | 0.4 | 0.3 | 0.6 | 0.8 | 0.7 | 0.6 | 0.8 | 0.7 |

| Whatsamatta University<br>Full-time Undergraduate Faculty | # Respon-<br>dents | Your Institution | | | Nonsect 4-yr Colls | | | All Priv 4-yr Colls | | |
|---|---|---|---|---|---|---|---|---|---|---|
| | | Men | Women | Total | Men | Women | Total | Men | Women | Total |
| **WHAT IS THE DEPARTMENT OF YOUR CURRENT FACULTY APPOINTMENT?** | | | | | | | | | | |
| **Biological Science** | 641 | | | | | | | | | |
| Agriculture | | 0.0 | 0.0 | 0.0 | 0.1 | 0.1 | 0.1 | 0.1 | 0.1 | 0.1 |
| Forestry | | 0.0 | 0.0 | 0.0 | 0.0 | 0.0 | 0.0 | 0.0 | 0.0 | 0.0 |
| Bacteriology, Molecular Biology | | 0.3 | 0.0 | 0.2 | 0.2 | 0.1 | 0.2 | 0.2 | 0.1 | 0.1 |
| Biochemistry | | 0.3 | 0.0 | 0.2 | 0.2 | 0.1 | 0.2 | 0.2 | 0.1 | 0.1 |
| Biophysics | | 0.0 | 0.0 | 0.0 | 0.0 | 0.0 | 0.0 | 0.0 | 0.0 | 0.0 |
| Botany | | 0.3 | 0.0 | 0.2 | 0.0 | 0.0 | 0.0 | 0.0 | 0.0 | 0.0 |
| Environmental Science | | 0.3 | 0.0 | 0.2 | 0.9 | 0.7 | 0.8 | 0.7 | 0.4 | 0.6 |
| Marine (life) Sciences | | 0.0 | 0.0 | 0.0 | 0.0 | 0.0 | 0.0 | 0.0 | 0.0 | 0.0 |
| Physiology, Anatomy | | 0.0 | 0.0 | 0.0 | 0.0 | 0.4 | 0.2 | 0.2 | 0.3 | 0.3 |
| Zoology | | 0.0 | 0.0 | 0.0 | 0.1 | 0.0 | 0.1 | 0.1 | 0.0 | 0.1 |
| General, Other Biological Sciences | | 4.7 | 4.2 | 4.5 | 6.2 | 5.6 | 6.0 | 6.0 | 5.0 | 5.5 |
| **Business** | | | | | | | | | | |
| Accounting | | 1.3 | 0.4 | 0.9 | 0.9 | 0.8 | 0.9 | 1.3 | 1.3 | 1.3 |
| Finance | | 2.1 | 1.1 | 1.7 | 0.5 | 0.1 | 0.4 | 0.6 | 0.2 | 0.4 |
| International Business | | 0.0 | 0.0 | 0.0 | 0.5 | 0.1 | 0.3 | 0.6 | 0.1 | 0.4 |
| Management | | 1.8 | 1.9 | 1.9 | 2.1 | 1.2 | 1.7 | 2.9 | 1.5 | 2.3 |
| Marketing | | 0.5 | 0.0 | 0.3 | 1.0 | 0.4 | 0.8 | 1.1 | 0.5 | 0.9 |
| Secretarial Studies | | 0.0 | 0.0 | 0.0 | 0.0 | 0.0 | 0.0 | 0.0 | 0.0 | 0.0 |
| General, Other Business | | 1.8 | 1.9 | 1.9 | 2.4 | 1.3 | 1.9 | 3.0 | 1.9 | 2.5 |
| **Education** | | | | | | | | | | |
| Business Education | | 0.0 | 0.0 | 0.0 | 0.1 | 0.0 | 0.0 | 0.1 | 0.0 | 0.1 |
| Educational Administration | | 0.3 | 0.4 | 0.3 | 0.2 | 0.0 | 0.1 | 0.3 | 0.3 | 0.3 |
| Educational Psychology/Counseling | | 0.3 | 0.0 | 0.2 | 0.0 | 0.0 | 0.0 | 0.1 | 0.1 | 0.1 |
| Elementary Education | | 0.0 | 2.7 | 1.1 | 2.3 | 2.4 | 2.4 | 1.5 | 3.4 | 2.3 |
| Higher Education | | 0.3 | 1.1 | 0.6 | 1.3 | 0.5 | 1.0 | 0.8 | 0.7 | 0.8 |
| Music or Art Education | | 0.5 | 0.0 | 0.3 | 0.0 | 0.1 | 0.0 | 0.1 | 0.1 | 0.1 |
| Physical or Health Education | | 0.3 | 0.0 | 0.2 | 1.7 | 2.3 | 1.9 | 2.1 | 2.2 | 2.1 |
| Secondary Education | | 0.3 | 0.0 | 0.2 | 0.2 | 0.9 | 0.5 | 0.5 | 0.8 | 0.6 |
| Special Education | | 0.3 | 0.8 | 0.5 | 0.0 | 0.4 | 0.2 | 0.2 | 0.8 | 0.4 |
| General, Other Education Fields | | 0.8 | 3.1 | 1.7 | 1.6 | 2.7 | 2.0 | 1.9 | 3.2 | 2.5 |
| **Engineering** | | | | | | | | | | |
| Aero-/Astronautical Engineering | | 0.0 | 0.0 | 0.0 | 0.0 | 0.0 | 0.0 | 0.0 | 0.0 | 0.0 |
| Chemical Engineering | | 0.0 | 0.0 | 0.0 | 0.1 | 0.0 | 0.1 | 0.1 | 0.0 | 0.1 |
| Civil Engineering | | 1.1 | 0.0 | 0.6 | 0.1 | 0.1 | 0.1 | 0.1 | 0.0 | 0.1 |
| Electrical Engineering | | 0.3 | 0.0 | 0.2 | 0.3 | 0.0 | 0.2 | 0.4 | 0.0 | 0.2 |
| Industrial Engineering | | 0.0 | 0.0 | 0.0 | 0.1 | 0.0 | 0.1 | 0.1 | 0.0 | 0.0 |
| Mechanical Engineering | | 0.5 | 0.0 | 0.3 | 0.4 | 0.0 | 0.3 | 0.4 | 0.1 | 0.2 |
| General, Other Engineering Fields | | 0.3 | 0.0 | 0.2 | 0.7 | 0.1 | 0.5 | 0.6 | 0.1 | 0.4 |
| **Health** | | | | | | | | | | |
| Dentistry | | 0.0 | 0.0 | 0.0 | 0.0 | 0.4 | 0.2 | 0.1 | 0.4 | 0.2 |
| Health Technology | | 0.0 | 0.4 | 0.2 | 0.0 | 0.0 | 0.0 | 0.0 | 0.1 | 0.0 |
| Medicine or Surgery | | 0.0 | 1.1 | 0.5 | 0.0 | 0.1 | 0.1 | 0.0 | 0.1 | 0.1 |
| Nursing | | 0.5 | 8.8 | 3.9 | 0.1 | 7.2 | 3.1 | 0.2 | 9.7 | 4.3 |
| Pharmacy, Pharmacology | | 4.7 | 5.3 | 5.0 | 1.7 | 2.0 | 1.8 | 0.9 | 1.1 | 1.0 |
| Therapy (speech, physical, occup.) | | 1.1 | 3.4 | 2.0 | 0.1 | 0.3 | 0.2 | 0.1 | 0.9 | 0.5 |
| Veterinary Medicine | | 0.0 | 0.0 | 0.0 | 0.0 | 0.0 | 0.0 | 0.0 | 0.0 | 0.0 |
| General, Other Health Fields | | 0.0 | 0.4 | 0.2 | 0.4 | 0.4 | 0.4 | 0.6 | 0.7 | 0.6 |

| Whatsamatta University<br>Full-time Undergraduate Faculty | # Respon-<br>dents | Your Institution | | | Nonsect 4-yr Colls | | | All Priv 4-yr Colls | | |
|---|---|---|---|---|---|---|---|---|---|---|
| | | Men | Women | Total | Men | Women | Total | Men | Women | Total |
| **WHAT IS THE DEPARTMENT OF YOUR CURRENT FACULTY APPOINTMENT?** | | | | | | | | | | |
| **Humanities** | | | | | | | | | | |
| History | | 4.2 | 5.3 | 4.7 | 4.4 | 2.4 | 3.6 | 4.8 | 2.5 | 3.8 |
| Political Science, Government | | 3.4 | 0.4 | 2.2 | 2.6 | 2.0 | 2.3 | 2.6 | 1.7 | 2.2 |
| English Language & Literature | | 6.6 | 8.0 | 7.2 | 5.6 | 12.0 | 8.3 | 6.4 | 10.3 | 8.1 |
| Foreign Languages & Literature | | 1.8 | 5.0 | 3.1 | 1.8 | 3.4 | 2.5 | 1.8 | 3.5 | 2.6 |
| French | | 0.0 | 0.0 | 0.0 | 0.4 | 0.7 | 0.5 | 0.2 | 0.5 | 0.3 |
| German | | 0.0 | 0.0 | 0.0 | 0.3 | 0.4 | 0.4 | 0.2 | 0.2 | 0.2 |
| Spanish | | 0.3 | 0.4 | 0.3 | 0.7 | 2.0 | 1.3 | 0.7 | 1.6 | 1.1 |
| Other Foreign Languages | | 0.8 | 0.4 | 0.6 | 0.3 | 0.5 | 0.4 | 0.3 | 0.4 | 0.3 |
| Linguistics | | 0.5 | 0.0 | 0.3 | 0.1 | 0.1 | 0.1 | 0.1 | 0.1 | 0.1 |
| Philosophy | | 6.3 | 1.9 | 4.5 | 1.9 | 0.7 | 1.4 | 2.9 | 1.0 | 2.1 |
| Religion or Theology | | 11.1 | 4.2 | 8.3 | 4.1 | 1.3 | 2.9 | 5.6 | 2.6 | 4.3 |
| General, Other Humanities Fields | | 1.3 | 2.7 | 1.9 | 3.9 | 3.5 | 3.7 | 2.3 | 2.2 | 2.2 |
| **Fine Arts** | | | | | | | | | | |
| Architecture/Urban Planning | | 1.1 | 0.0 | 0.6 | 0.4 | 0.4 | 0.4 | 0.2 | 0.2 | 0.2 |
| Art | | 1.1 | 1.5 | 1.2 | 3.6 | 4.1 | 3.8 | 2.8 | 3.1 | 2.9 |
| Dramatics or Speech | | 0.5 | 0.4 | 0.5 | 2.4 | 2.3 | 2.3 | 2.2 | 1.8 | 2.0 |
| Music | | 2.1 | 3.1 | 2.5 | 4.2 | 2.5 | 3.5 | 4.6 | 3.2 | 4.0 |
| Television or Film | | 0.8 | 0.4 | 0.6 | 0.5 | 0.3 | 0.4 | 0.3 | 0.2 | 0.2 |
| Other Fine Arts | | 0.8 | 0.0 | 0.5 | 0.8 | 0.8 | 0.8 | 0.5 | 0.7 | 0.6 |
| **Physical Science** | | | | | | | | | | |
| Mathematics and/or Statistics | | 4.0 | 1.1 | 2.8 | 5.4 | 3.1 | 4.5 | 6.0 | 3.1 | 4.8 |
| Astronomy | | 0.0 | 0.0 | 0.0 | 0.2 | 0.0 | 0.1 | 0.2 | 0.0 | 0.1 |
| Atmospheric Sciences | | 0.0 | 0.0 | 0.0 | 0.0 | 0.0 | 0.0 | 0.0 | 0.0 | 0.0 |
| Chemistry | | 4.7 | 2.7 | 3.9 | 4.3 | 2.6 | 3.6 | 4.3 | 2.9 | 3.7 |
| Earth Sciences | | 0.0 | 0.0 | 0.0 | 1.2 | 0.5 | 0.9 | 0.7 | 0.3 | 0.6 |
| Geography | | 0.0 | 0.0 | 0.0 | 0.1 | 0.1 | 0.1 | 0.1 | 0.0 | 0.1 |
| Marine Sciences (incl. Oceanography) | | 0.0 | 0.0 | 0.0 | 0.0 | 0.0 | 0.0 | 0.0 | 0.0 | 0.0 |
| Physics | | 1.8 | 0.4 | 1.2 | 2.9 | 1.0 | 2.1 | 2.6 | 0.7 | 1.8 |
| General, Other Physical Sciences | | 0.5 | 0.0 | 0.3 | 0.9 | 0.3 | 0.6 | 0.6 | 0.4 | 0.5 |
| **Social Science** | | | | | | | | | | |
| Anthropology | | 1.3 | 1.1 | 1.2 | 0.7 | 0.8 | 0.7 | 0.5 | 0.4 | 0.5 |
| Archaeology | | 0.0 | 0.0 | 0.0 | 0.0 | 0.0 | 0.0 | 0.0 | 0.0 | 0.0 |
| Clinical Psychology | | 1.3 | 1.5 | 1.4 | 0.1 | 0.1 | 0.1 | 0.2 | 0.3 | 0.2 |
| Counseling and Guidance | | 0.3 | 0.0 | 0.2 | 0.0 | 0.3 | 0.1 | 0.2 | 0.2 | 0.2 |
| Experimental Psychology | | 0.5 | 0.8 | 0.6 | 1.0 | 0.7 | 0.8 | 0.7 | 0.6 | 0.6 |
| Social Psychology | | 0.0 | 0.4 | 0.2 | 0.1 | 0.1 | 0.1 | 0.1 | 0.2 | 0.2 |
| General, Other Psychology | | 1.8 | 3.4 | 2.5 | 3.2 | 5.5 | 4.2 | 3.2 | 4.8 | 3.9 |
| Economics | | 2.1 | 0.4 | 1.4 | 3.1 | 1.6 | 2.5 | 2.5 | 0.9 | 1.8 |
| Sociology | | 2.4 | 3.4 | 2.8 | 1.8 | 2.2 | 2.0 | 1.8 | 2.2 | 2.0 |
| Social Work, Social Welfare | | 0.5 | 0.8 | 0.6 | 1.0 | 0.5 | 0.8 | 0.9 | 0.8 | 0.8 |
| General, Other Social Sciences | | 1.3 | 1.5 | 1.4 | 2.2 | 3.5 | 2.8 | 1.6 | 2.4 | 1.9 |

| Whatsamatta University<br>Full-time Undergraduate Faculty | # Respon-<br>dents | Your Institution | | | Nonsect 4-yr Colls | | | All Priv 4-yr Colls | | |
|---|---|---|---|---|---|---|---|---|---|---|
| | | Men | Women | Total | Men | Women | Total | Men | Women | Total |
| **WHAT IS THE DEPARTMENT OF YOUR CURRENT FACULTY APPOINTMENT?** | | | | | | | | | | |
| **Technical** | | | | | | | | | | |
| Computer Science | | 1.8 | 0.8 | 1.4 | 2.3 | 1.3 | 1.9 | 2.3 | 1.4 | 1.9 |
| Data Processing, Computer Prog. | | 0.0 | 0.0 | 0.0 | 0.2 | 0.0 | 0.1 | 0.1 | 0.1 | 0.1 |
| Drafting/Design | | 0.0 | 0.0 | 0.0 | 0.0 | 0.0 | 0.0 | 0.0 | 0.0 | 0.0 |
| Electronics | | 0.0 | 0.0 | 0.0 | 0.0 | 0.0 | 0.0 | 0.0 | 0.0 | 0.0 |
| Industrial Arts | | 0.0 | 0.0 | 0.0 | 0.0 | 0.0 | 0.0 | 0.0 | 0.0 | 0.0 |
| Mechanics | | 0.0 | 0.0 | 0.0 | 0.0 | 0.0 | 0.0 | 0.0 | 0.0 | 0.0 |
| Other Technical | | 0.0 | 0.0 | 0.0 | 0.2 | 0.0 | 0.1 | 0.2 | 0.1 | 0.2 |
| **Other Fields** | | | | | | | | | | |
| Building Trades | | 0.0 | 0.0 | 0.0 | 0.0 | 0.0 | 0.0 | 0.0 | 0.0 | 0.0 |
| Communications | | 2.9 | 3.8 | 3.3 | 2.4 | 1.8 | 2.1 | 3.1 | 2.6 | 2.9 |
| Ethnic Studies | | 0.0 | 0.0 | 0.0 | 0.1 | 0.2 | 0.1 | 0.0 | 0.1 | 0.1 |
| Human Ecology/Family Science | | 0.0 | 0.0 | 0.0 | 0.0 | 0.2 | 0.1 | 0.0 | 0.4 | 0.2 |
| Journalism | | 0.8 | 0.8 | 0.8 | 0.1 | 0.2 | 0.1 | 0.1 | 0.1 | 0.1 |
| Law | | 1.3 | 2.3 | 1.7 | 0.2 | 0.1 | 0.1 | 0.1 | 0.2 | 0.2 |
| Law Enforcement | | 0.3 | 0.0 | 0.2 | 0.0 | 0.0 | 0.0 | 0.1 | 0.0 | 0.1 |
| Library Science | | 1.1 | 1.9 | 1.4 | 0.2 | 0.4 | 0.3 | 0.2 | 1.0 | 0.6 |
| Women's Studies | | 0.0 | 0.0 | 0.0 | 0.0 | 0.4 | 0.2 | 0.0 | 0.2 | 0.1 |
| Other Vocational | | 0.5 | 0.0 | 0.3 | 0.1 | 0.1 | 0.1 | 0.1 | 0.1 | 0.1 |
| All Other Fields | | 1.1 | 2.3 | 1.6 | 1.3 | 1.7 | 1.5 | 0.9 | 1.2 | 1.1 |
| **HOW MANY CHILDREN DO YOU HAVE IN THE FOLLOWING AGE RANGES?** | | | | | | | | | | |
| **Under 18 years old** | 633 | | | | | | | | | |
| None | | 58.2 | 61.5 | 59.6 | 56.5 | 65.2 | 60.2 | 56.7 | 64.4 | 60.0 |
| One | | 14.2 | 17.3 | 15.5 | 18.8 | 16.2 | 17.7 | 17.9 | 17.3 | 17.6 |
| Two | | 18.0 | 16.2 | 17.2 | 17.7 | 15.6 | 16.8 | 17.8 | 14.2 | 16.2 |
| Three | | 6.7 | 3.8 | 5.5 | 5.8 | 2.6 | 4.5 | 6.1 | 3.3 | 4.9 |
| Four or more | | 2.9 | 1.2 | 2.2 | 1.2 | 0.4 | 0.9 | 1.5 | 0.8 | 1.2 |
| **18 years or older** | 637 | | | | | | | | | |
| None | | 65.3 | 66.0 | 65.6 | 58.9 | 64.6 | 61.3 | 56.9 | 61.3 | 58.8 |
| One | | 13.2 | 13.9 | 13.5 | 12.1 | 13.8 | 12.8 | 11.9 | 13.8 | 12.7 |
| Two | | 12.7 | 13.1 | 12.9 | 16.9 | 14.7 | 16.0 | 17.8 | 16.6 | 17.3 |
| Three | | 5.0 | 5.0 | 5.0 | 7.6 | 4.3 | 6.2 | 8.4 | 5.8 | 7.3 |
| Four or more | | 3.7 | 1.9 | 3.0 | 4.5 | 2.6 | 3.7 | 5.0 | 2.6 | 4.0 |
| **How would you characterize your political views?** | 635 | | | | | | | | | |
| Far left | | 4.0 | 6.1 | 4.9 | 9.8 | 12.4 | 10.9 | 8.4 | 9.6 | 8.9 |
| Liberal | | 32.6 | 41.8 | 36.4 | 46.3 | 57.2 | 50.8 | 41.8 | 50.6 | 45.6 |
| Middle of the Road | | 35.3 | 32.2 | 34.0 | 24.8 | 21.5 | 23.4 | 27.7 | 25.3 | 26.7 |
| Conservative | | 25.9 | 18.8 | 23.0 | 18.1 | 8.7 | 14.2 | 21.2 | 14.0 | 18.1 |
| Far right | | 2.1 | 1.1 | 1.7 | 1.1 | 0.2 | 0.7 | 0.9 | 0.5 | 0.7 |
| **Are you currently:** | 641 | | | | | | | | | |
| Single | | 16.3 | 21.2 | 18.3 | 7.3 | 14.7 | 10.4 | 8.5 | 15.3 | 11.4 |
| Married | | 75.9 | 66.5 | 72.1 | 83.1 | 68.3 | 76.9 | 83.0 | 69.0 | 77.0 |
| Unmarried, living with partner | | 2.9 | 2.3 | 2.7 | 4.4 | 5.8 | 5.0 | 3.4 | 5.0 | 4.0 |
| Divorced | | 4.2 | 6.2 | 5.0 | 3.9 | 8.9 | 6.0 | 3.8 | 8.4 | 5.7 |
| Widowed | | 0.3 | 2.7 | 1.2 | 0.4 | 1.2 | 0.8 | 0.6 | 1.6 | 1.0 |
| Separated | | 0.5 | 1.2 | 0.8 | 0.9 | 1.0 | 1.0 | 0.9 | 0.8 | 0.8 |

| Whatsamatta University<br>Full-time Undergraduate Faculty | # Respon-<br>dents | Your Institution | | | Nonsect 4-yr Colls | | | All Priv 4-yr Colls | | |
|---|---|---|---|---|---|---|---|---|---|---|
| | | Men | Women | Total | Men | Women | Total | Men | Women | Total |
| **Is English your native language?** | 644 | | | | | | | | | |
| Yes | | 82.9 | 85.9 | 84.2 | 88.9 | 92.1 | 90.2 | 91.1 | 91.8 | 91.4 |
| No | | 17.1 | 14.1 | 15.8 | 11.1 | 7.9 | 9.8 | 8.9 | 8.2 | 8.6 |
| **Are you: [5]** | 628 | | | | | | | | | |
| White/Caucasian | | 85.9 | 86.5 | 86.1 | 88.1 | 89.9 | 88.8 | 89.9 | 90.6 | 90.2 |
| African American/Black | | 1.6 | 4.2 | 2.7 | 3.1 | 4.0 | 3.5 | 2.4 | 2.8 | 2.6 |
| American Indian/Alaska Native | | 0.5 | 0.0 | 0.3 | 1.8 | 1.2 | 1.5 | 1.6 | 1.1 | 1.4 |
| Asian American/Asian | | 7.6 | 5.8 | 6.8 | 4.4 | 3.1 | 3.8 | 3.5 | 3.1 | 3.3 |
| Native Hawaiian/Pacific Islander | | 0.3 | 0.0 | 0.2 | 0.3 | 0.1 | 0.2 | 0.4 | 0.1 | 0.3 |
| Mexican American/Chicano | | 0.5 | 0.8 | 0.6 | 1.4 | 0.7 | 1.1 | 1.1 | 0.5 | 0.8 |
| Puerto Rican | | 0.8 | 1.2 | 1.0 | 0.2 | 0.5 | 0.3 | 0.4 | 0.5 | 0.4 |
| Other Latino | | 1.9 | 2.7 | 2.2 | 2.0 | 2.0 | 2.0 | 1.8 | 2.3 | 2.0 |
| Other | | 3.3 | 1.5 | 2.5 | 2.6 | 1.9 | 2.3 | 2.8 | 1.7 | 2.3 |
| **Do you give the Higher Education Research Institute (HERI) permission to retain your contact information (i.e., your email address and name) for possible follow-up research?** | 648 | | | | | | | | | |
| Yes | | 56.9 | 61.9 | 59.0 | 70.4 | 74.2 | 72.0 | 71.1 | 73.3 | 72.0 |
| No | | 43.1 | 38.1 | 41.0 | 29.6 | 25.8 | 28.0 | 28.9 | 26.7 | 28.0 |

[5] Percentages will sum to more than 100.0 if any respondent marked more than one category.

# Higher Education Research Institute
3005 Moore Hall • Box 951521 • Los Angeles, California 90095-1521

## Publications List

### The American Freshman:
### National Norms for Fall 2008*
*December, 2008/189 pages    $25.00*

Provides national normative data on the characteristics
of students attending American colleges and universities
as first-time, full-time freshmen. In 2008, data from
240,580 freshmen students are statistically adjusted to
reflect the responses of 1.4 million students entering
college. The annual report covers: political engagement;
college choice and financial issues; students' personal
objectives and skills for a diverse workplace.

*Note: Publications from earlier years are also available: each year
dating back to 1999 for $25.00; earlier years dating back to 1966 for
$5.00 each.

### The American Freshman: Forty Year Trends
*March, 2006/261 pages    $30.00*

Summarizes trends data in the Cooperative Institutional
Research Program (CIRP) Freshman Survey between 1966
and 2006. The report examines changes in the diversity of
students entering college; parental income and students'
financial concerns, issues of access and affordability in
college. Trends in students' political and social attitudes
are also covered.

### Degree Attainment Rates at
### American Colleges and Universities
*January, 2005/74 pages    $15.00*

Provides latest information on four- and six-year degree
attainment rates collected longitudinally from 262
baccalaureate-granting institutions. Differences by race,
gender, and institutional type are examined. The study
highlights main predictors of degree completion and
provides several formulas for calculating expected
institutional completion rates.

### The American College Teacher: National Norms
### for the 2007–08 HERI Faculty Survey*
*February, 2009/298 pages    $25.00*

Provides an informative profile of teaching faculty at
American colleges and universities. The 2007–08
Norms covers two areas: Activities and Beliefs about
Undergraduate Education and Faculty Work-Life. Within
these two areas the following topics are covered: goals for
undergraduate education, working with underprepared
students, teaching and research practice and perspectives,
engaged scholarship and academic citizenship, attitudes
and beliefs about diversity, institutional values and
priorities as faculty perceive them, career satisfaction and
perspectives, technology use, and health and wellness.
Results are reported for all faculty, male and female
faculty, and faculty by academic rank and institutional
type.

*Note: Publications from earlier years are also available: 2004–05,
2001–02 for $25.00; 1998–99, 1995–96 for $22.00 each; 1992–93 for
$20.00

### Advancing in Higher Education:
### A Portrait of Latina/o College Freshmen
### at Four-Year Institutions, 1975–2006
*October, 2008/90 pages    $15.00*

The purpose of this report is to provide a portrait of
Latina/o students entering four-year colleges and
universities from 1975–2006. It is intended as a data
resource for higher education in understanding the unique
characteristics of the increasing numbers of Latina/o first-
time, full-time freshmen. The national data come from the
Cooperative Institutional Research Program (CIRP)
Freshman Survey. For the first time, CIRP trends are
disaggregated by specific Latina/o ethnic origin group and
by gender, to highlight the heterogeneity in the population
unavailable in other national reports on Hispanic college
students.

### Beyond Myths: The Growth and Diversity of
### Asian American College Freshmen: 1971–2005
*September, 2007/63 pages    $15.00*

The first-year student trends examined in this report help
to address some common characterizations of Asian
American students, particularly with respect to their
educational success, that are often overstated and taken out
of context. The findings suggest that Asian Americans still
have to overcome a number of obstacles, such as levels
of family income and financial aid, to earn a coveted spot
in higher education. This report features data collected
from Cooperative Institutional Research Program (CIRP)
Freshman Survey. It is based on the 361,271 Asian/Asian
American first-time full-time college students from 1971–
2005, representing the largest compilation and analysis of
data on Asian American college students ever undertaken.

### First in My Family:
### A Profile of First-Generation College Students
### at Four-Year Institutions Since 1971
*February, 2007/62 pages    $15.00*

First-generation college students are receiving increasing
attention from researchers, practitioners, and policymakers
with the aim of better understanding their college decision-
making process and supporting their progress in higher
education. This report explores the changing dynamic
between first-generation college students and their non
first-generation peers by utilizing longitudinal trends data
collected through the CIRP Freshman Survey (1971–2005).

### Black Undergraduates From *Bakke* to *Grutter*
*November, 2005/41 pages    $15.00*

Summarizes the status, trends and prospects of Black
college freshmen using data collected from 1971 to
2004 through the Cooperative Institutional Research
Program (CIRP). Based on more than half a million
Black freshman students, the report examines gender
differences; socioeconomic status; academic preparation
and aspirations; and civic engagement.

HERI accepts Visa, MasterCard & Discover. To order call 310-825-1925 or visit the HERI publications webpage:
**www.gseis.ucla.edu/heri/research-publications.php**